KU-588-836

FIELD GUIDE TO THE

BUTTERFLIES

AND OTHER INSECTS

OF BRITAIN

BUTTERFLIES AND OTHER INSECTS OF BRITAIN

was edited and designed by
The Reader's Digest Association Limited, London

Printed in Great Britain

The typeface used for text in this book
is 8 point Bembo roman

The picture of the peacock and common blue butterflies on the cover was painted by Colin Emberson

READER'S DIGEST
NATURE LOVER'S LIBRARY

FIELD GUIDE TO THE BUTTERFLIES AND OTHER INSECTS OF BRITAIN

PUBLISHED BY THE READER'S DIGEST ASSOCIATION LIMITED

LONDON · NEW YORK · MONTREAL · SYDNEY · CAPE TOWN

Contributors

The publishers wish to express their gratitude to the following people for their major contributions to this Field Guide to the Butterflies and Other Insects of Britain

PRINCIPAL
CONSULTANT AND AUTHOR

Dr John Feltwell, F.R.E.S., F.L.S., M.I.Biol.

OTHER CONSULTANTS

Dr Keith Porter
Anthony Wootton

PHOTOGRAPHERS

For a full list of acknowledgments to the photographers whose work appears in this book, see page 352

CARTOGRAPHY

The distribution maps of butterflies are based on information supplied by The Biological Records Centre of The Institute of Terrestrial Ecology, and were prepared by Clyde Surveys Ltd.

ARTISTS

Stephen Adams
David Baird
Rachel Birkett, M.A.
Dick Bonson
Leonora Box
Wendy Bramall
Josiane Campan
Jeane Colville, B.A.
Kevin Dean
Colin Emberson
Pat Flavel
Brenda Katte
Norman Lacey, M.I.S.T.C.
Richard Lewington
Line Mailhé
Guy Michel
Tricia Newell
Liz Pepperell
Sandra Pond, L.S.I.A.D.-E.A.C.
Elizabeth Rice, S.W.L.A.
Jim Russell
Ann Savage
Helen Senior
Sally Smith
Barbara Walker
Adrian Williams

A full list of the paintings contributed by each artist appears on page 352

Contents

Understanding insects

Not all 'creepy-crawlies' are insects. To qualify as an insect a creature must have six legs and a body divided into three parts – a head, a thorax and an abdomen. The head usually has a pair of antennae (feelers) which are used as noses to locate mates and food plants by smell, and as 'feelers' to probe their surroundings. 'Mouths' vary from the curled proboscis of butterflies to the chopping mandibles of beetles.

An insect's legs and wings arise from the thorax. Most insects have wings, except for fleas and lice which are parasites of animals and birds and have no need to fly. Ants and aphids have wings only at one time of the year when they colonise new areas.

The abdomen is made up of 11 segments, which are not always very obvious. In the case of the bumble-bee, for example, the body is covered with hairs. Most segments have a pair of air tubes, called spiracles, which the insect uses, instead of lungs, for breathing. On some insects, such as grasshoppers, the spiracles are sometimes very obvious.

Other insects, such as mayflies and wood wasps, have 'tails' which are used either for feeling their surroundings or for laying eggs. A male butterfly has a pair of claspers on the tip of its abdomen for clasping the female while they mate.

Insects are the most successful class of animals on earth, in terms of the number of species and the number of individuals of each species. As they are small, they can exploit almost every nook and cranny on the earth's surface, and many can be blown from place to place by the wind. They are fast breeders, and some have even dispensed with the sexes, reproducing by virgin birth, or parthenogenesis. They can live in all conditions – in the soil, on the land, in water or in the air. They are found in most habitats in Britain, sometimes – like aphids – by the million.

As well as insects, this book describes other creatures of a similar size which are found in similar conditions. Spiders, centipedes, millipedes, earthworms, snails and slugs are all well-known members of that wider, unofficial classification of the animal kingdom known, even to some biologists, as 'creepy-crawlies'.

Insect classification

Insects are the most numerous type of animal in Britain. There are 22,450 species known so far – ten for each of the 2,080 native British plants on which they are dependent. There are also 3,130 species of other British invertebrates (animals with no backbone), including spiders, earthworms and snails.

Most British insects have no common name. They are known only by their scientific name which, as Alice in Wonderland said to her friend the Gnat, is 'no use to *them*, but it's useful to the people that name them'.

The name of each insect consists of two words. The second word indicates the species, a group of identical insects that can interbreed. The first name indicates the genus, a group of closely related insects, usually with obvious similarities. The small blue butterfly, for example, is called *Cupido minimus*, from the Roman god of love and the butterfly's small size. *Cupido* is the genus, and *minimus* the species within the genus.

When one genus closely resembles another, they are grouped together into a family. Blue butterflies share similar characteristics of wing shape and metallic colour with hairstreaks and coppers, and so all belong to the family Lycaenidae.

The eight families of butterflies are all grouped into the insect order Lepidoptera (meaning 'scaly wings') which also includes moths. And all the orders of insects together make up the zoological class Insecta.

The butterflies of Britain

Britain has 62 species of butterfly, 54 of them residents which breed here and eight either regular or irregular immigrants. The large blue, which became extinct in 1979, is included in this book since it is likely to be re-introduced to Britain from French stock.

Most migrant insects, including larger moths and ladybirds as well as butterflies, fly westwards and northwards from central and southern Europe and North Africa in early summer, reaching Britain within a few weeks. Some continue as far north as Scotland and even Iceland. There is rarely a return migration in the autumn as the adult insects have a life of only about six weeks, and the eggs, caterpillars or chrysalises that they leave behind them die when winter arrives. The monarch butterfly is the only migrant which reaches Britain from across the Atlantic, accidentally blown across by autumn gales.

Many butterflies and moths have declined in numbers because of subtle climatic changes and modern farming techniques. But there are gains to the lists as well, as foreign moths exploit newly introduced garden plants and ornamental trees.

All the British butterflies and almost all the dragonflies, wasps and bumble-bees are described in the book, but there has been space to include only a selection of moths, beetles, flies and spiders, as the number of species is so great.

How to use this book

The creatures illustrated in this book are arranged in their zoological orders. Most of the common orders of insects are described, and large sections deal with butterflies and moths, dragonflies and damselflies, ants, bees, wasps, true bugs and beetles. Non-insects such as spiders, centipedes, millipedes, slugs and snails are also illustrated.

In 'How to identify insects' (pp. 18–25) all the major groups are listed, and one or more examples are illustrated. These are the first pages to turn to when you see an unfamiliar insect. Check through the descriptions and illustrations to establish the group to which the creature belongs. Then turn to the relevant pages in the main part of the book to complete the identification.

For beginners to insect study, the following pages (8–17) give information about the four stages of life through which insects pass – egg, caterpillar (larva), chrysalis (pupa) and adult. By looking at these pages you can train your eye to spot essential characteristics of different types of insect. For further information on how to study insects and where to find them, turn to pages 336–345.

Marked variations in colours and patterns of insects can occur according to where and when they are found, and also according to individual development. The most normal forms have been illustrated throughout the book. Sizes of insects given in the captions are average for the species, but sizes can vary greatly between individuals.

How to read the maps

Distribution maps for butterflies in the main part of the book show whether each species is a resident or a migrant, and where it is likely to be seen. The area of Britain where you see a butterfly and the time of year can be useful clues to its identity.

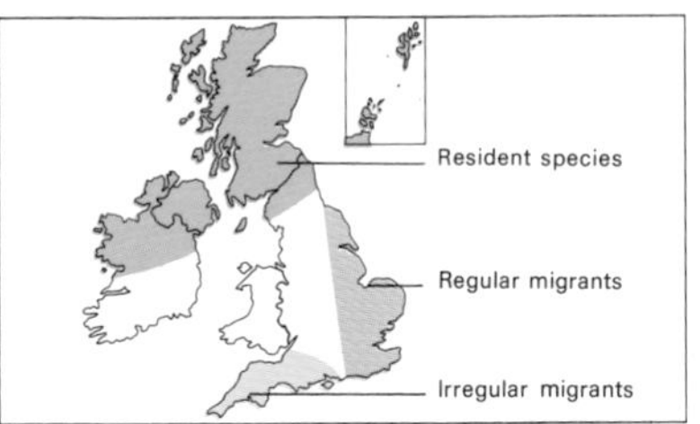

Green tints show the areas where resident species breed in Britain.

Red tints show the areas where regular migrants are likely to be seen.

Pink tints show the areas where irregular migrants are likely to be seen.

The summer range of migrant butterflies is less precise than the breeding range of residents. The range for migrants given in the maps indicates the areas where they are most likely to be seen, depending on whether they arrive from the south, south-east, south-west, east or west. Of course, some migrants and some home-reared and released butterflies may occasionally be found outside the usual range for the species.

The many-shaped life of the insect

Most insects begin life as an egg. After a period of time that can range from days to months, the egg hatches into a caterpillar (also known as a larva) which spends most of its time eating. When the caterpillar has absorbed the necessary amount of nutrients, it changes into the chrysalis or pupa. Inside the chrysalis, the insect turns into an organised 'soup' in which the cells rearrange themselves into the adult. The whole process is known as a complete metamorphosis. Some insects, including dragonflies and aphids, bypass the chrysalis stage, and turn directly from an adult-like nymph (larva) to the adult – an incomplete metamorphosis. The adult insect spends its short life – only about a day for the mayfly – mating and laying eggs to produce the next generation.

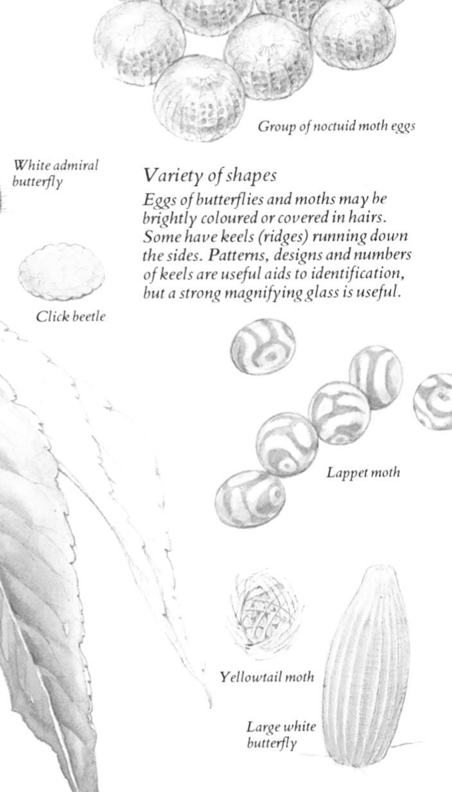

Variety of shapes

Eggs of butterflies and moths may be brightly coloured or covered in hairs. Some have keels (ridges) running down the sides. Patterns, designs and numbers of keels are useful aids to identification, but a strong magnifying glass is useful.

Ladybird beetle

Small tortoiseshell butterfly

Eggs in groups

Eggs may be laid in groups of ordered rows, as by the ladybird, or in a pile, like those of the small tortoiseshell butterfly. Wingless females of some species, such as the vapourer moth, lay their eggs on their cocoons which they never leave.

Vapourer moth

Lesser swallow prominent moth

Single eggs

Moths' eggs are often laid singly on leaves – usually on the underside, away from the harmful effects of the sun and from predators. Others are laid on bark or buds.

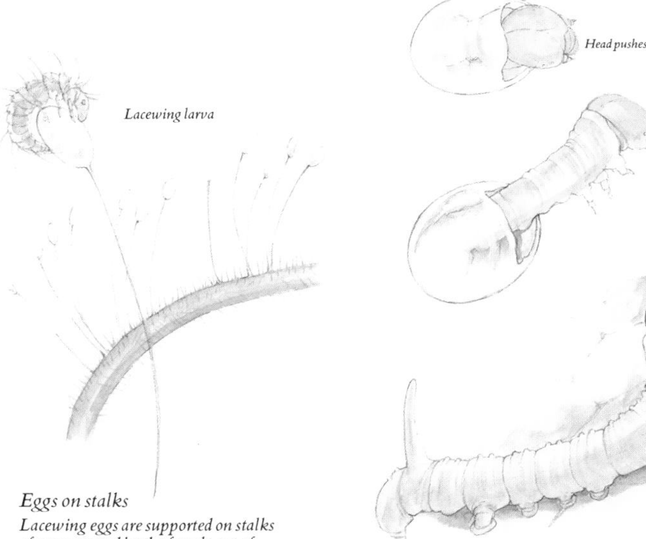

Eggs on stalks
Lacewing eggs are supported on stalks of gum secreted by the female out of reach of some predators. A few spiders also do this.

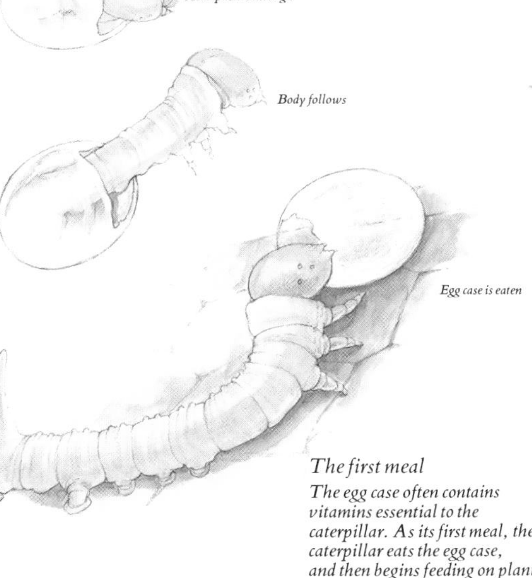

The first meal
The egg case often contains vitamins essential to the caterpillar. As its first meal, the caterpillar eats the egg case, and then begins feeding on plants. This sequence of drawings shows a death's-head hawk-moth caterpillar hatching.

Caring parent
Earwigs are among the few insects that show good parental care by guarding their eggs, and also the larvae once they have hatched.

Egg sacs
Spiders are more caring parents than most insects. Their eggs are laid in sacs of silk which are guarded by the female, which also guards the young when they have hatched.

Insect eggs: unique in shape and pattern

The colours and designs of eggs are unique to each type of insect and – like pollen grains – the eggs can be used to identify the species. Some insects lay one or two large masses of eggs, but most lay small groups or single eggs, spaced over a few days. A total of 1,000 eggs may be laid by a small tortoiseshell butterfly and about 200 by a ladybird. A queen honey-bee, however, lays 2,000 eggs every day in early spring. Most insect eggs develop in seven to ten days, but some lie dormant through autumn, winter and spring before hatching.

Butterflies and moths usually spend a lot of time finding the right food plant to lay their eggs on, so that the caterpillars will have a supply of food when they hatch. However, as many as 99 per cent of eggs may be killed by birds, mites, true bugs and ichneumon flies, or by disease.

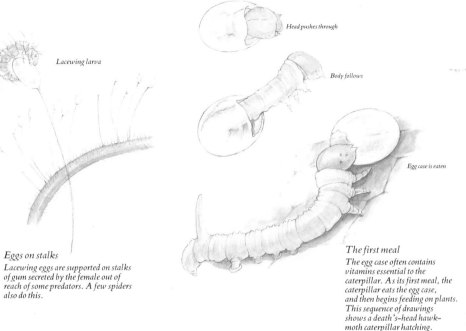

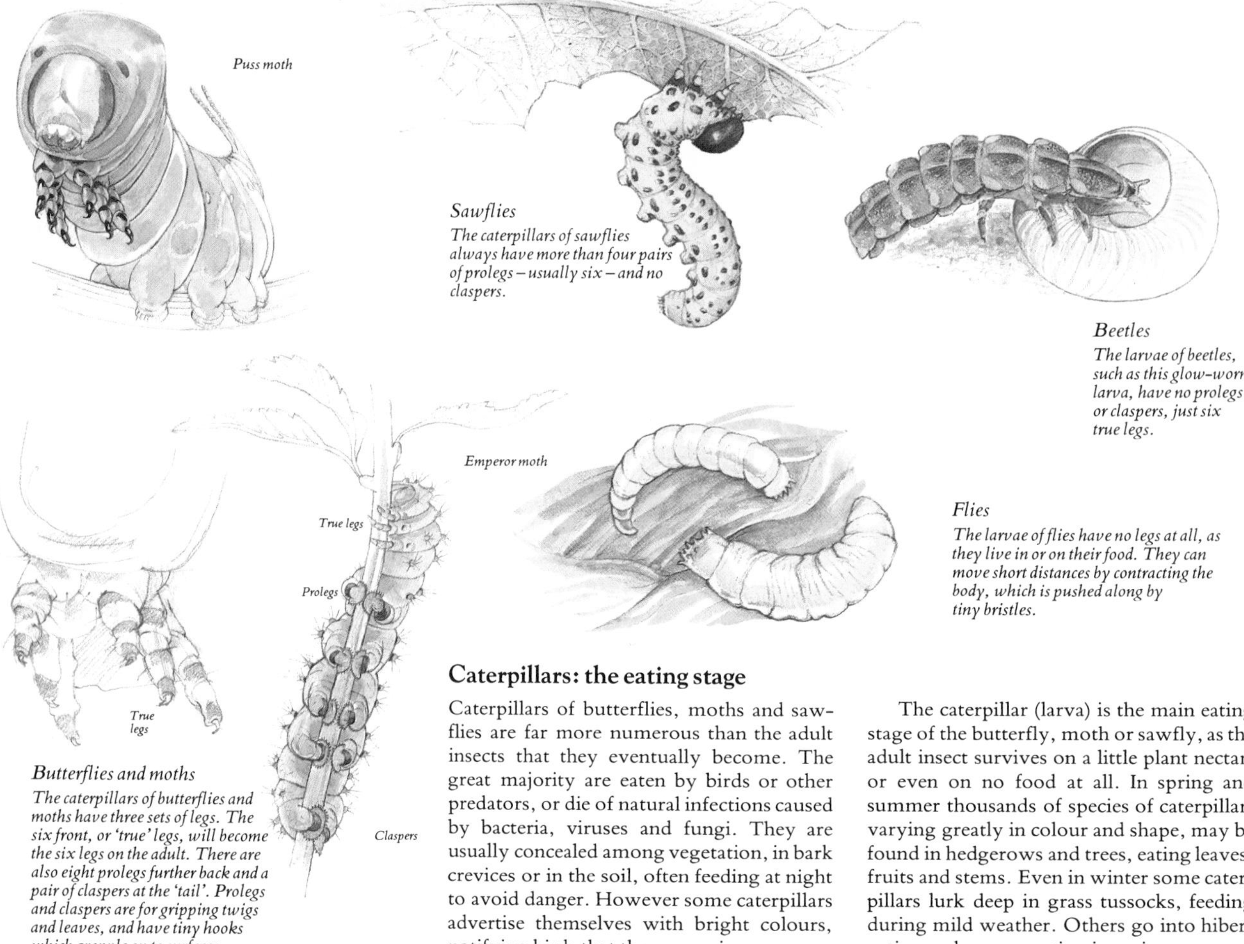

Sawflies

The caterpillars of sawflies always have more than four pairs of prolegs – usually six – and no claspers.

Beetles

The larvae of beetles, such as this glow-worm larva, have no prolegs or claspers, just six true legs.

Flies

The larvae of flies have no legs at all, as they live in or on their food. They can move short distances by contracting the body, which is pushed along by tiny bristles.

Butterflies and moths

The caterpillars of butterflies and moths have three sets of legs. The six front, or 'true' legs, will become the six legs on the adult. There are also eight prolegs further back and a pair of claspers at the 'tail'. Prolegs and claspers are for gripping twigs and leaves, and have tiny hooks which grapple on to surfaces.

Caterpillars: the eating stage

Caterpillars of butterflies, moths and sawflies are far more numerous than the adult insects that they eventually become. The great majority are eaten by birds or other predators, or die of natural infections caused by bacteria, viruses and fungi. They are usually concealed among vegetation, in bark crevices or in the soil, often feeding at night to avoid danger. However some caterpillars advertise themselves with bright colours, notifying birds that they are poisonous.

The caterpillar (larva) is the main eating stage of the butterfly, moth or sawfly, as the adult insect survives on a little plant nectar, or even on no food at all. In spring and summer thousands of species of caterpillar, varying greatly in colour and shape, may be found in hedgerows and trees, eating leaves, fruits and stems. Even in winter some caterpillars lurk deep in grass tussocks, feeding during mild weather. Others go into hibernation and resume eating in spring.

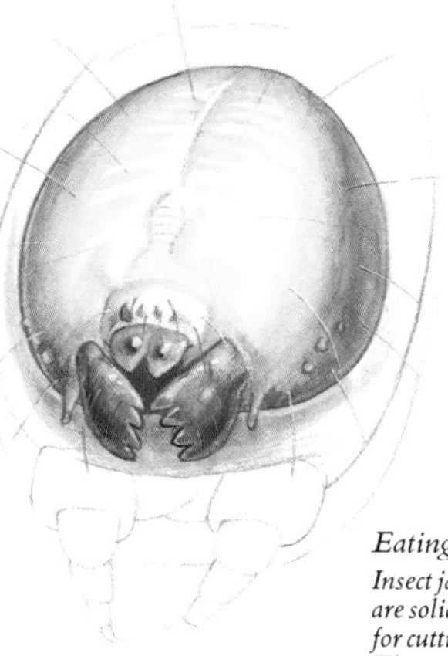

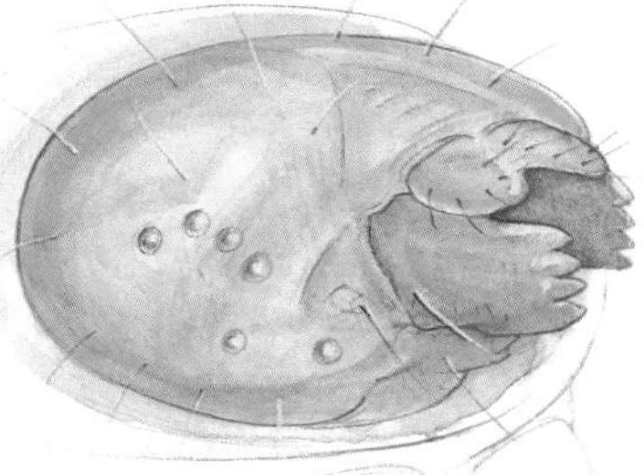

Eating

Insect jaws move sideways. They are solidly built and are toothed for cutting through leaves or bark. The correct food plant is recognised by chemical receptors in the cells of hairs around the caterpillar's face.

Camouflage

Many caterpillars, like this brown hairstreak, disguise themselves on leaves, using both shape and colour as forms of camouflage.

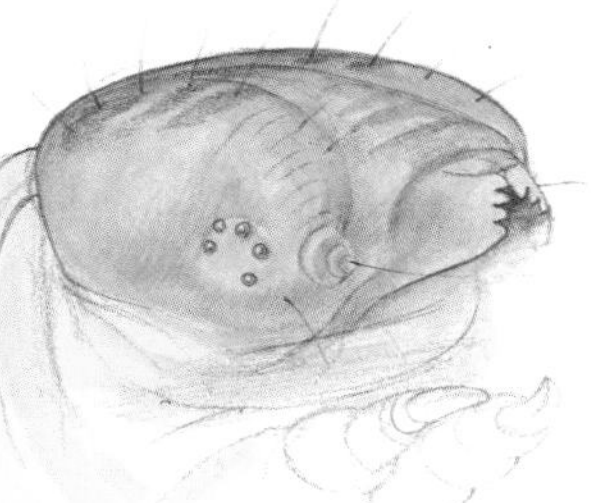

Sight

Caterpillars have only simple eyes at the side of the face, which cannot see detail but can detect light and dark. The simple eyes help the caterpillar to find its way around a plant, as light means up and dark means down.

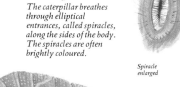

Breathing

The caterpillar breathes through elliptical entrances, called spiracles, along the sides of the body. The spiracles are often brightly coloured.

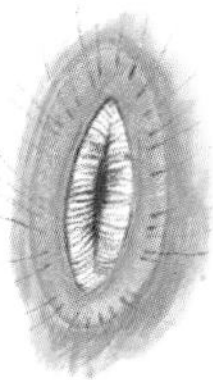

Spiracle enlarged

Poplar hawk-moth

Moulting

To increase in size, caterpillars must shed their tough old skins four times. Each new skin is soft and allows the caterpillar to grow before it dries as a hard external skeleton.

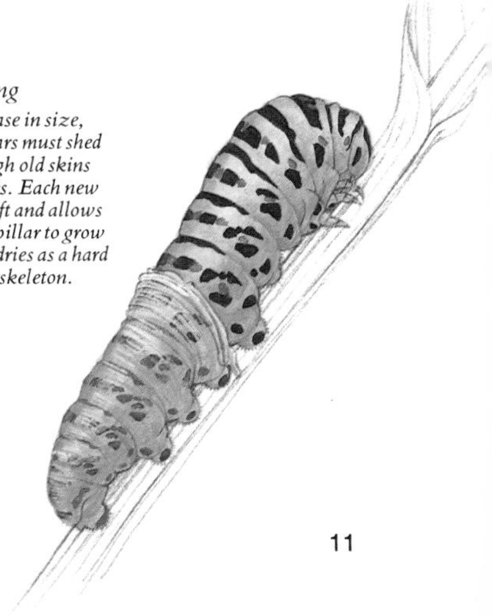

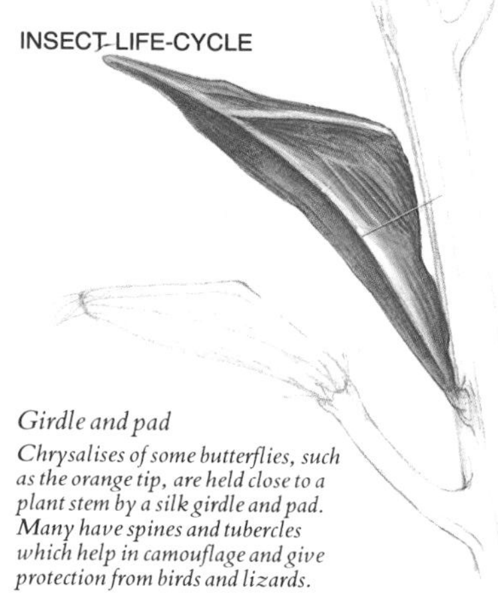

Girdle and pad
Chrysalises of some butterflies, such as the orange tip, are held close to a plant stem by a silk girdle and pad. Many have spines and tubercles which help in camouflage and give protection from birds and lizards.

The chrysalis: transformation stage

The chrysalis is the stage during which an insect is transformed from a caterpillar into an adult of a totally different shape. Chrysalises are formed only by insects which have a complete, four-stage metamorphosis – egg, caterpillar (also called larva), chrysalis (also called pupa) and adult. Examples are butterflies, moths, two-winged flies and beetles. Some other insects, including true bugs, grasshoppers and dragonflies, have an incomplete metamorphosis in which the larva (known as a nymph) turns directly into an adult. Chrysalises are difficult to identify because many species look the same. Those in the soil, for example, are usually a uniform brown.

The use of silk for protection and support varies from almost none in some species, through girdles and pads, to tough cocoons.

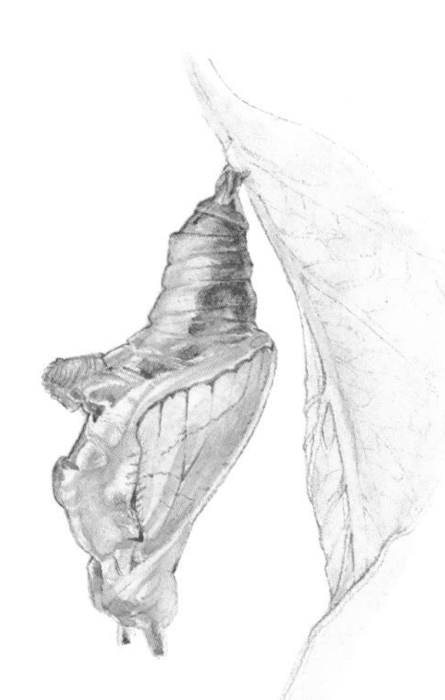

Hanging chrysalis
Chrysalises of some butterflies, such as the white admiral, and also of ladybirds have no silk girdle but hang from a silk pad.

Fly pupa
The pupa stage of the blowfly is barrel-shaped, segmented and brown.

Bumble-bee
Wax cells are used by bumble-bees to rear their larvae and protect the pupae.

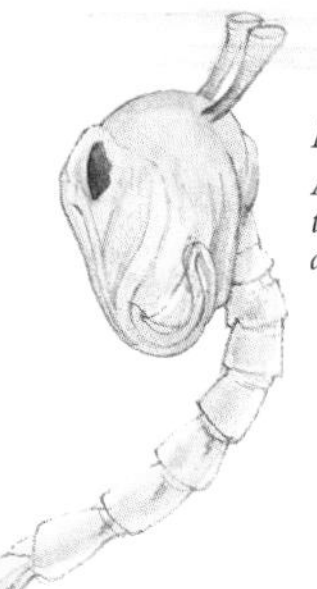

Mosquito
Aquatic mosquito chrysalises breathe through a siphon to the water surface. If disturbed, they wriggle up and down.

Noctuid chrysalis
Most noctuid moth chrysalises are about the same colour and size – about $\frac{3}{4}$ in. (20 mm). They are often found while digging in the garden, but individual species are difficult to identify.

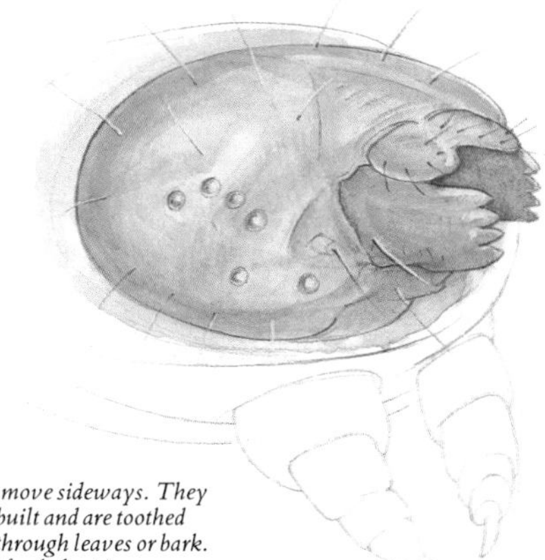

Eating

Insect jaws move sideways. They are solidly built and are toothed for cutting through leaves or bark. The correct food plant is recognised by chemical receptors in the cells of hairs around the caterpillar's face.

Camouflage

Many caterpillars, like this brown hairstreak, disguise themselves on leaves, using both shape and colour as forms of camouflage.

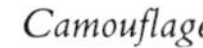

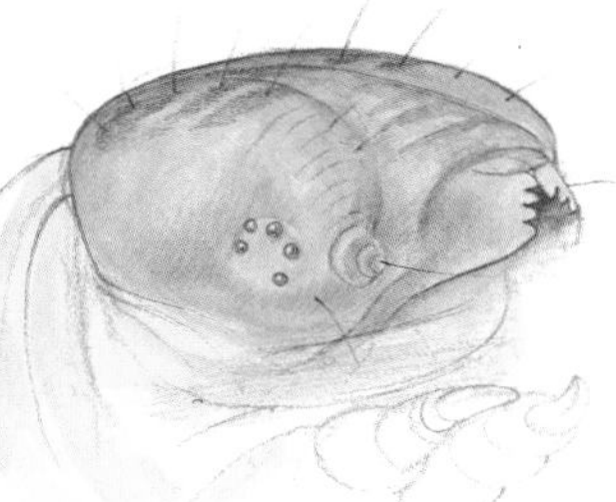

Sight

Caterpillars have only simple eyes at the side of the face, which cannot see detail but can detect light and dark. The simple eyes help the caterpillar to find its way around a plant, as light means up and dark means down.

Breathing

The caterpillar breathes through elliptical entrances, called spiracles, along the sides of the body. The spiracles are often brightly coloured.

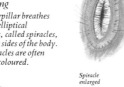

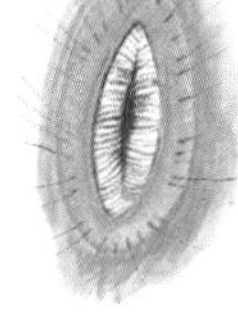

Spiracle enlarged

Poplar hawk-moth

Moulting

To increase in size, caterpillars must shed their tough old skins four times. Each new skin is soft and allows the caterpillar to grow before it dries as a hard external skeleton.

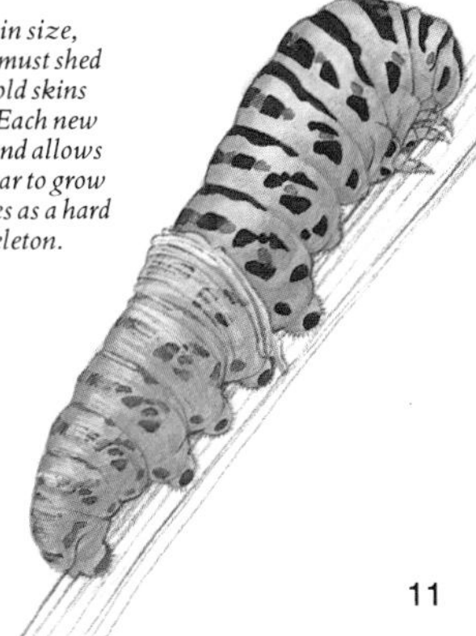

Girdle and pad
Chrysalises of some butterflies, such as the orange tip, are held close to a plant stem by a silk girdle and pad. Many have spines and tubercles which help in camouflage and give protection from birds and lizards.

The chrysalis: transformation stage

The chrysalis is the stage during which an insect is transformed from a caterpillar into an adult of a totally different shape. Chrysalises are formed only by insects which have a complete, four-stage metamorphosis – egg, caterpillar (also called larva), chrysalis (also called pupa) and adult. Examples are butterflies, moths, two-winged flies and beetles. Some other insects, including true bugs, grasshoppers and dragonflies, have an incomplete metamorphosis in which the larva (known as a nymph) turns directly into an adult. Chrysalises are difficult to identify because many species look the same. Those in the soil, for example, are usually a uniform brown.

The use of silk for protection and support varies from almost none in some species, through girdles and pads, to tough cocoons.

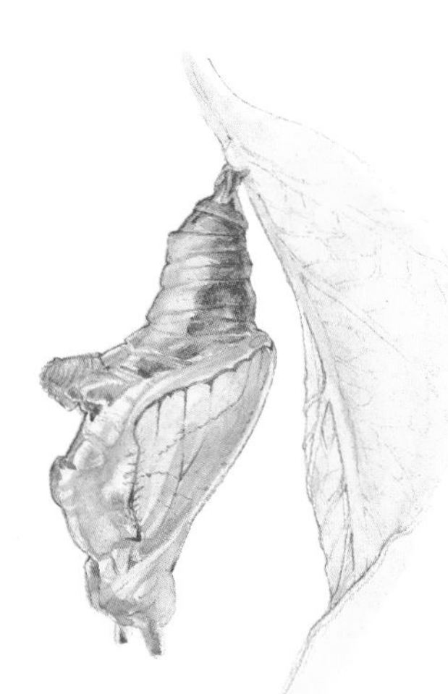

Hanging chrysalis
Chrysalises of some butterflies, such as the white admiral, and also of ladybirds have no silk girdle but hang from a silk pad.

Fly pupa
The pupa stage of the blowfly is barrel-shaped, segmented and brown.

Bumble-bee
Wax cells are used by bumble-bees to rear their larvae and protect the pupae.

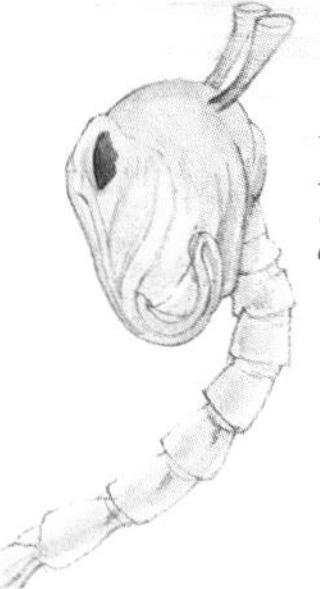

Mosquito
Aquatic mosquito chrysalises breathe through a siphon to the water surface. If disturbed, they wriggle up and down.

Noctuid chrysalis
Most noctuid moth chrysalises are about the same colour and size – about ¾ in. (20 mm). They are often found while digging in the garden, but individual species are difficult to identify.

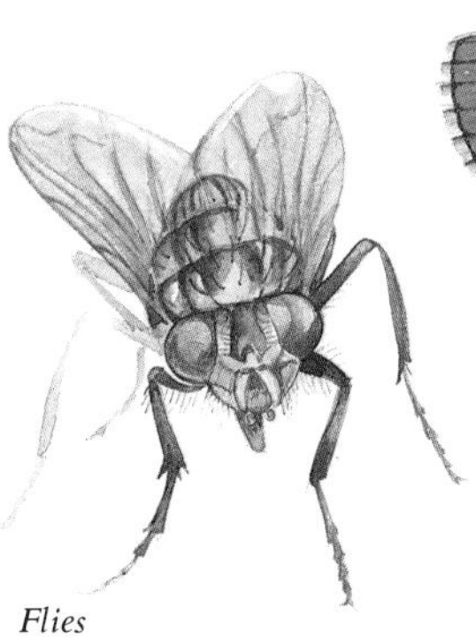

Flies

True flies such as houseflies and hover-flies have only a single pair of small transparent wings which beat at least 200 times a second. Their hind-wings are modified into tiny gyroscopic organs which alter pitch and roll.

Iridescence

The wings of blue butterflies have iridescent colours caused by the sun diffracting off minute corrugations on the surface of the scales, which absorb all the colours of the spectrum except blue.

Dark colouring

The brown colour of some insects, such as caddisflies, is caused by their external case, which is abnormally tough, giving protection against predators.

Transparent wings

Many insects, including lace-wings, dragonflies, aphids and ants, have transparent wings, because the wings have no scales. The network pattern of veins, or the subtle suffusions of colour, help in identifying different species.

Wings and colours of adult insects

Most insects have wings in the adult stage of their life-cycles, but the number and shape of the wings and the speed of wing-beat vary greatly from one type of insect to another. Less advanced insects – springtails, silverfish and bristletails – have no wings at all. Ants and aphids have winged and wingless forms at different times of the year. Most butter-flies have wings many times their body size.

The colours of insects have evolved to deter predators, find mates and compete with rivals of the same sex. Vivid colours are best seen in butterflies, day-flying moths, flies and some beetles.

Yellow and black

Wasps, some bumble-bees and some ladybirds have yellow and black colours, warning predators that they may sting or may be poisonous.

Whiteness

The white colouring in the wings of butterflies and moths is caused by excretory pigments, similar to the white in birds' droppings, which are pumped into the wings. As butterflies eat very little, they do not excrete in the usual way.

Red and black

Warning colours of red and black are found on several moth species, including the cinnabar and burnet moths, which are poisonous to birds.

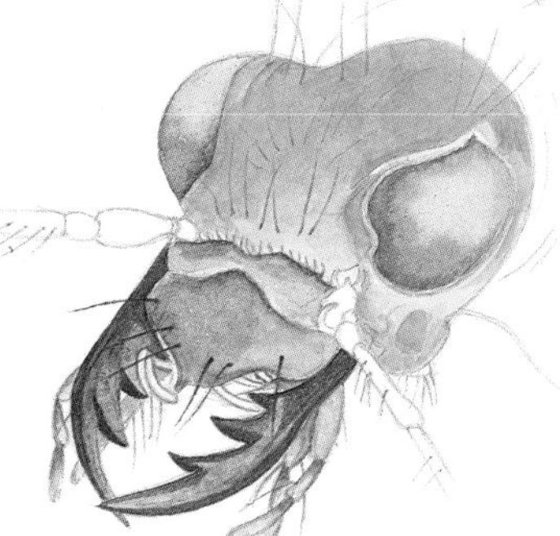

Chewing jaws
Beetles, dragonflies, cockroaches and crickets have jaws that move from side to side, whether they eat plants or animals.

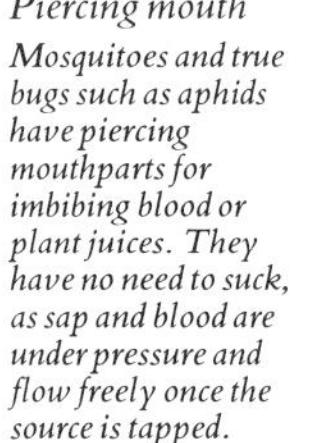

Piercing mouth
Mosquitoes and true bugs such as aphids have piercing mouthparts for imbibing blood or plant juices. They have no need to suck, as sap and blood are under pressure and flow freely once the source is tapped.

Proboscis
Most butterflies and moths have a long tongue or proboscis for drinking the nectar of flowers. It is curled up like a watch spring when not in use.

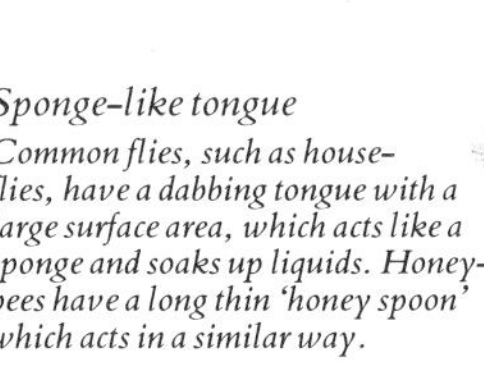

Sponge-like tongue
Common flies, such as house-flies, have a dabbing tongue with a large surface area, which acts like a sponge and soaks up liquids. Honey-bees have a long thin 'honey spoon' which acts in a similar way.

Simple eyes
Adult insects and caterpillars also possess three simple eyes, called ocelli, either on the top or side of the head to detect light or dark. They help the insect to tell which way is up (light) or down (dark).

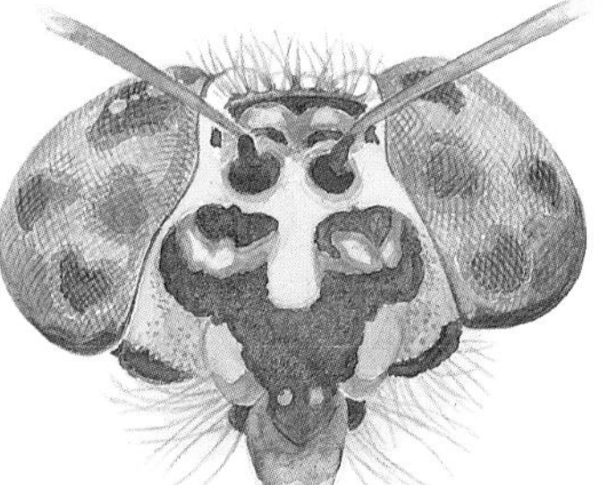

Compound eyes
Fast-flying dragonflies and hoverflies have large compound eyes made up of thousands of photo-receptors which respond to movement in the immediate vicinity. Slower insects, such as butterflies and moths, have fewer photo-receptors.

The 'noses' and mouths of insects

The most certain way of distinguishing a moth from a butterfly is by the shape of the antennae, the organs of smell. All butterflies have antennae with knobs at the ends. Moths have antennae of various shapes, but never with a definite knob.

Mouthparts vary greatly between insects that eat different types of food. The coiled tongue of a butterfly or moth is quite different from the dabbing mouthparts of house-flies, which are used for mopping up liquids. Beetles, grasshoppers and crickets have biting mouthparts for chewing mouthfuls of plant or animal food. True bugs have mouthparts that pierce a plant or other insect for drinking sap or body juices.

Green hairstreak butterfly

Silk moth

Butterfly and moth antennae

Antennae are insects' noses, and the more feathery the antennae the greater the sense of smell. Butterflies always have knobs at the end of their antennae, distinguishing them from moths.

Skipper butterfly

The antennae of the skipper butterfly are slightly hooked at the tip.

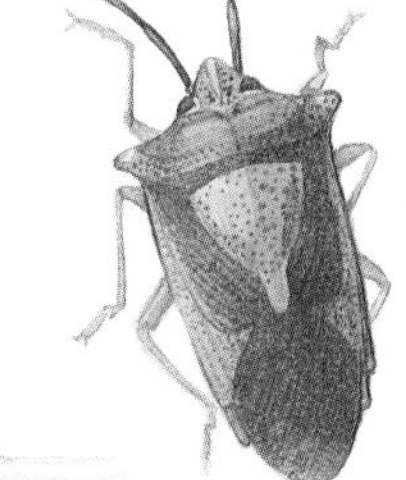

True bugs and wasps

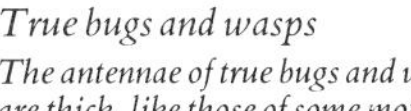

The antennae of true bugs and wasps are thick, like those of some moths.

Thread-like

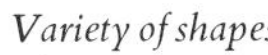

Variety of shapes

The antennae of moths vary widely in shape. They can be thread-like, toothed or feathery. Some are straight, others curled; some short, others long.

Slightly feathered

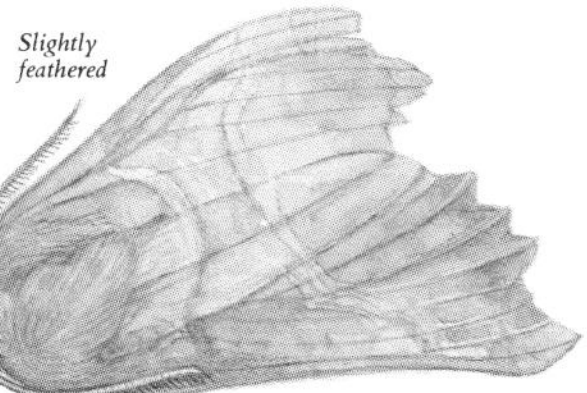

Toothed

Cricket

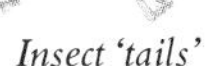

Insect 'tails'

Many insects have tails which are usually part of their reproductive organs. Female crickets and some parasitic wasps have very long egg-laying organs which protrude from the body and may be enclosed in protective sheaths. The three tails of the mayfly, however, are probably used for balancing in flight, and the tails of the bristletail are probably used for feeling.

Bristletail

Mayfly

How to identify insects

In this identification key, all the major groups of British insects, spiders and soil animals are described, with one or more species from each group illustrated. To identify an insect or other creature first compare it to the illustrations on these eight pages. Then turn to the appropriate section where the most common species are illustrated. More detailed keys for butterflies will be found at the beginning of the section on each family; for example, skippers and aristocrats. Although caterpillars are illustrated with the adult butterfly or moth, they have also been grouped together in a special section as an extra aid to identification.

Butterflies Pages 28–127

Order Lepidoptera

Insects with large, often colourful wings, and antennae with well-defined knobs. They fly by day, particularly in sunshine, and are seen mostly in summer.

Skippers Pages 28–37

Family Hesperiidae

Small, compact butterflies with wings the same length as the body, and swift, darting flight. Found on grassland.

Swallowtail Pages 38–39

Family Papilionidae

Largest butterfly resident in Britain. Found mostly in the Norfolk Broads.

Whites and yellows Pages 40–53

Family Pieridae

White or yellow butterflies found in gardens and waysides. Some may be common.

Monarch Pages 54–55

Family Danaidae

A rare autumn visitor from North America. Largest wingspan of any butterfly found in Britain.

Aristocrats Pages 56–71

Family Nymphalidae

Large colourful butterflies, attracted to garden flowers. Two pairs of functional legs.

Dark green fritillary

Fritillaries Pages 72–85

Family Nymphalidae

Brown speckled butterflies, mostly found in woodland glades and along sunny tracks.

Duke of Burgundy fritillary Page 83

Family Riodinidae

Common blue

Green hairstreak

Small copper

Blue, hairstreaks and copper Pages 86–107

Family Lycaenidae

Small and swift-flying, with iridescent colours in the males. Blues and coppers are found in flowery meadows, hairstreaks usually in woods and scrubby areas.

Meadow brown

Browns Pages 108–27

Family Satyridae

A widespread family, recognisable by the false eyes on the wings. Can be abundant in grassy areas.

What caterpillar is it? Pages 128–143

A chart of 130 caterpillars, grouped according to colour and shape. It includes caterpillars of butterflies, moths and sawflies, as well as the larvae of some beetles and flies.

Garden tiger moth

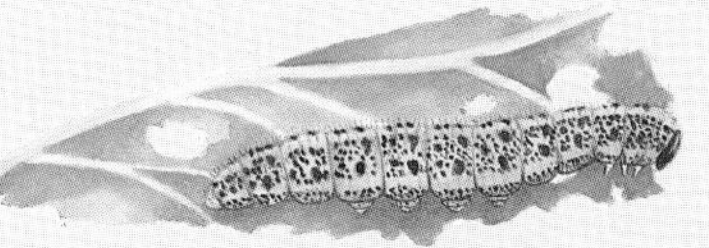
Large white butterfly

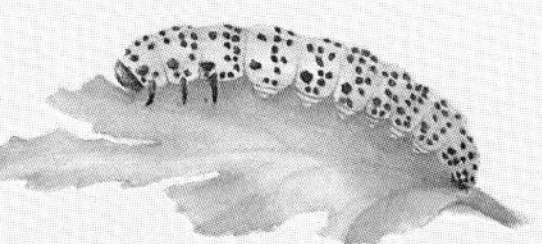
Gooseberry sawfly

Moths Pages 144–219

Order Lepidoptera

Most moths fly at night or at dusk, and are drab in colour. Day-flying moths often have bright butterfly colours. Antennae are not knobbed at the tips. Wings are similar in appearance to butterflies when in flight, but when at rest they are mostly held down over the body rather than vertically in the butterfly manner.

Hawk-moths Pages 144–55

Family Sphingidae

Britain's largest moths. Long narrow wings and fat bodies; usually with long tongues. Some fly at dusk.

Prominents Pages 156–61

Family Notodontidae

Large moths, many with a tuft of hairs on the thorax.

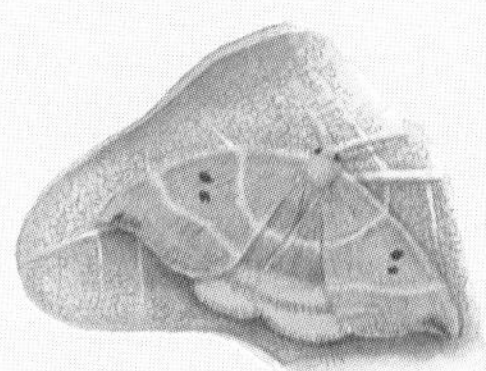

Hook-tips Page 162

Family Drepanidae

Fairly small moths, with hooked wingtips.

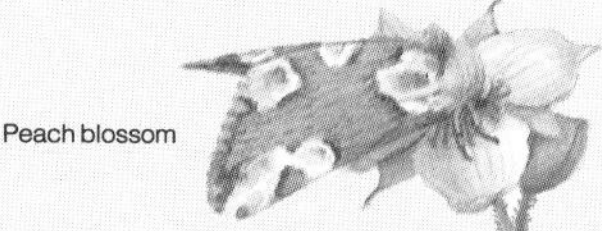

Thyatirids Page 163

Family Thyatiridae

Fairly small moths with distinctive wing patterns.

Tussocks Pages 164–7

Family Lymantriidae

Moderate sized moths with hairy thorax and abdomen.

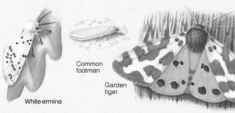

Noctuids Pages 170–5

Family Noctuidae

Fairly small, mostly night-flying moths. Often dull brown.

Eggars and lappets Pages 176–7

Family Lasiocampidae

Heavy-bodied, fairly large moths. Usually brown with feathered antennae.

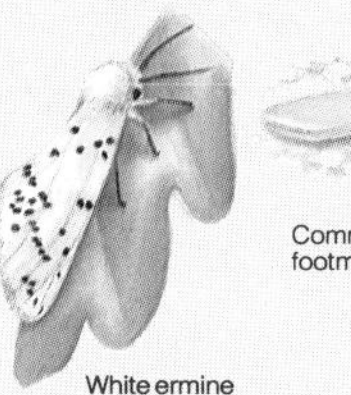

Tigers, ermines and footmen Pages 178–85

Family Arctiidae

Tigers and ermines are brightly coloured; footmen are small and drab.

Geometers Pages 188–93

Family Geometridae

Delicate moths, with slim bodies and large wings. Often attracted to lights in urban and woody areas. Mottled and wavy patterns on wings.

Carpets, waves and pugs Pages 194–5

Delicate moths with large wings, small bodies and intricate patterns over their wings.

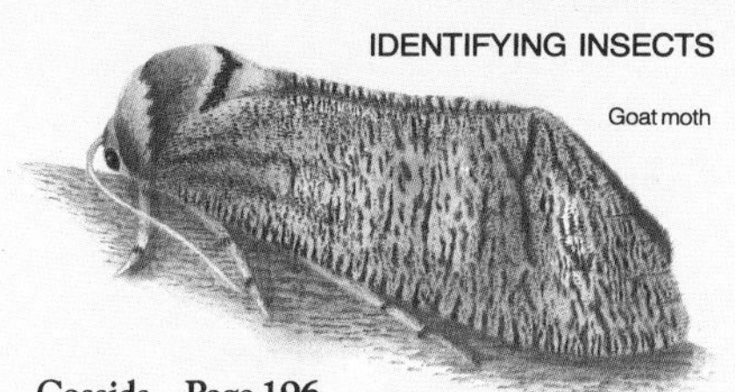

Cossids Page 196

Family Cossidae

Large, heavy-bodied moths often attracted to lights. Seen in gardens and orchards.

Clearwings Page 197

Family Sessiidae

Day-flying moths with narrow transparent wings. They are mimics of bees and wasps.

Burnets Pages 198–9

Family Zygaenidae

Brightly coloured moths that fly during the day, often on downland.

Swifts Pages 200–1

Family Hepialidae

Strong-flying evening moths with tufts of hair over the thorax.

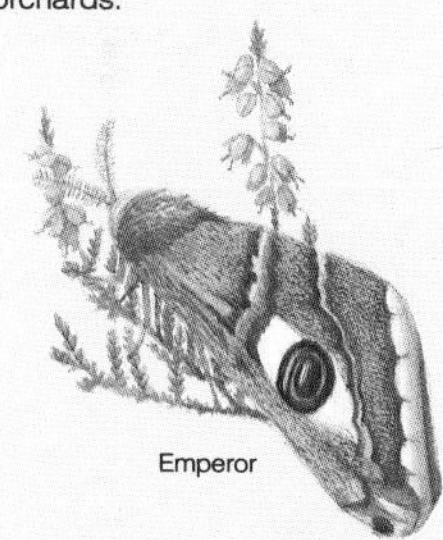

Saturnids Page 202

Family Saturniidae

Large moths, some with prominent false eyes on the wings. Males usually with feathery antennae.

Endromids Page 203

Family Endromidae

A small family with only one species in Britain, found in northern Scotland.

Silk moth Pages 204–5

Family Saturniidae

White moths found only in captivity.

Tortrix moths Pages 206–7

Family Tortricidae

Fairly small moths with a characteristic bell shape when at rest.

Other British moths Pages 212–17

A selection of other interesting or common moths to be found in Britain.

Dragonflies and damselflies Pages 220–31
Order Odonata

Large colourful insects with two pairs of long transparent wings that are found near water. Damselflies are smaller and thinner-bodied than dragonflies.

Emperor dragonfly

Banded demoiselle damselfly

Mayflies Page 232
Order Ephemeroptera

Large transparent fore-wings, small hind-wings; three tail filaments. Found beside streams and lakes.

Ephemera danica

Stoneflies Page 233
Order Plecoptera

Two pairs of wings; long antennae and tail filaments. Found among stones beside upland streams.

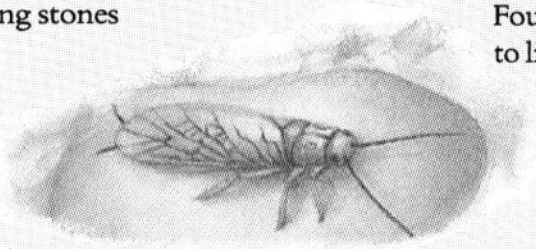

Perla bipunctata

Caddisflies Page 234
Order Trichoptera

Moth-like insects with long antennae. Found near water. Often attracted to lights at night.

Phryganea grandis

Scorpionflies Page 235
Order Mecoptera

Four-winged insect with a beak-like head. Male's abdomen curled like a scorpion's tail.

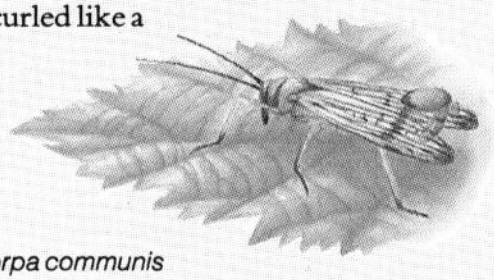

Panorpa communis

Alderflies Page 236
Order Megaloptera

Two pairs of transparent wings, strongly veined. Found on vegetation near water.

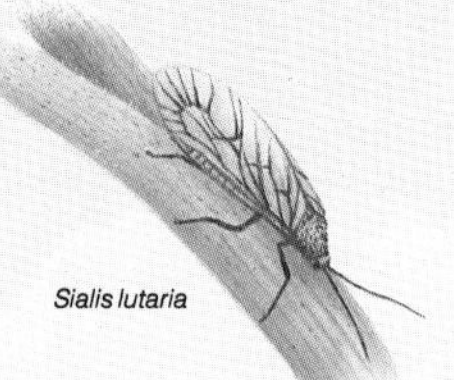

Sialis lutaria

Snakeflies Page 237
Order Raphidioptera

Two pairs of large, delicate wings; the head projecting from the thorax. Found in light woodland or near water.

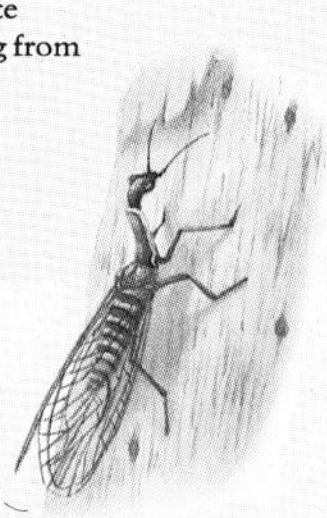

Raphidia maculicollis

Lacewings Pages 238–9
Order Neuroptera

Two pairs of translucent wings covered by a lacework of veins; long antennae. Found on plants in gardens.

Chrysopa carnea

Wasps Pages 240–5

Order Hymenoptera

Two pairs of wings, the front pair larger; usually with black-and-yellow stripes.

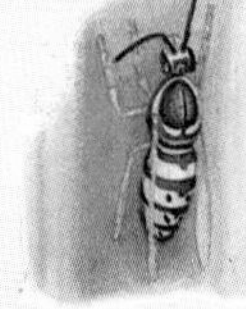

Common wasp

Bees Pages 246–53

Order Hymenoptera

Two pairs of wings, the front pair larger; large bodies, usually black or brown.

Honey-bee

Ants Pages 254–9

Order Hymenoptera

Usually wingless; body clearly divided into three parts. Found on the ground or on trees and bushes in daylight.

Black garden ant

True bugs Pages 260–5

Order Hemiptera

Small insects with stabbing mouthparts, usually seen on plants.

Hawthorn shield bug

Aphid

Two-winged flies Pages 266–75

Order Diptera

Insects with only one pair of wings are the true flies. In place of the hind-wings flies have a pair of small knobs which help them to balance in flight.

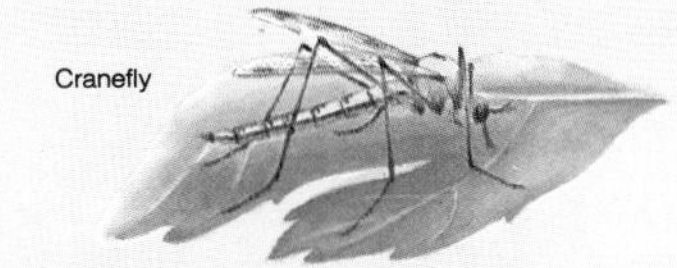

Cranefly

Biting midge

Long-legged flies Pages 266–7

Two-winged flies with long legs; bodies may be slender or stout. Non-biting.

Predatory and biting flies Pages 268–9

Two-winged flies which live on the blood or body juices of animals or other insects. Some bite humans.

Hoverfly

Bee and wasp mimics Pages 270–1

Two-winged flies that mimic the appearance of bees and wasps as a form of defence.

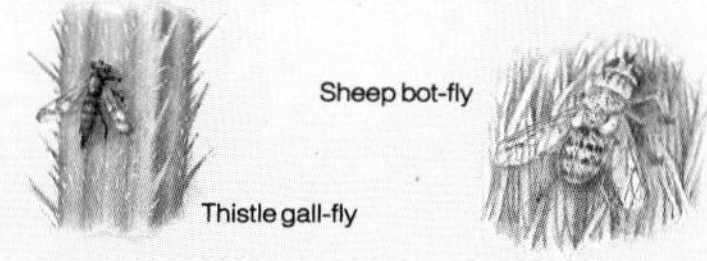

Thistle gall-fly

Sheep bot-fly

Plant-feeders and parasites Pages 272–3

Two-winged flies whose larvae develop inside plants or inside the bodies of animals or other insects.

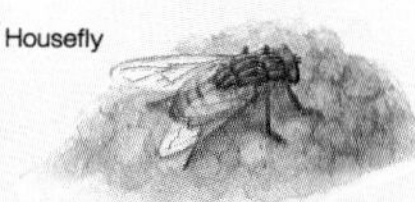

Housefly

Houseflies and other pests Pages 274–5

Two-winged flies that enter houses and create potential health hazards by transmitting disease organisms to food.

Plant galls Pages 276–9

Abnormal growths on plants can be caused by small insects laying their eggs inside the plant tissue, or by viruses, fungi, bacteria or mites.

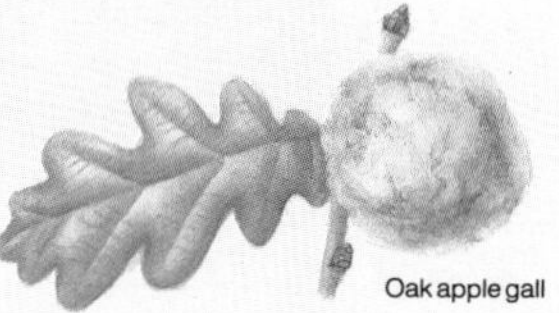

Oak apple gall

Beetles Pages 280–307

Order Coleoptera

Insects with hard fore-wings that cover the abdomen and protect the delicate hind-wings.

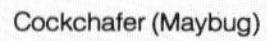

Cockchafer (Maybug)

Stag beetle

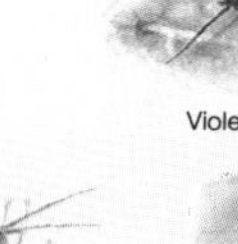

Soldier beetle

Violet ground beetle

Ladybird

Grasshoppers and crickets Pages 308–13

Order Orthoptera

Heavy-bodied insects with large back legs used for jumping and 'singing'.

Common field grasshopper

Dark bush cricket

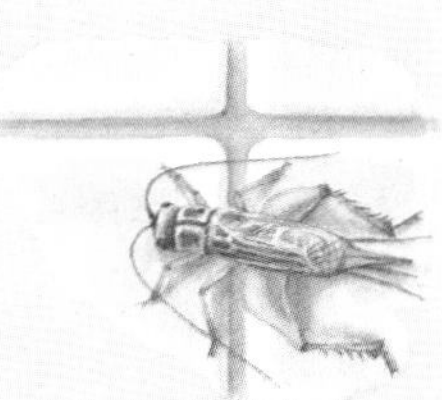

House cricket

Grasshoppers Pages 308–9

The antennae are much shorter than those of crickets. The two pairs of wings are used for gliding. Found among grass.

Bush crickets Pages 310–11

Very long antennae and long, thin hind legs. Live in hedgerows, scrub and gardens. Great songsters, particularly in the evening.

Crickets Pages 312–13

Broad, flat bodies with long antennae and long pair of 'tails' (cerci). Rapid runners.

Cockroaches Page 314

Order Dictyoptera

Brown, beetle-like insects that are seen in buildings at night.

Common cockroach

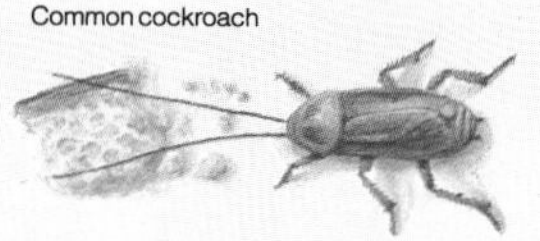

Earwigs Page 315

Order Dermaptera

Beetle-like insects with prominent pincers at the rear end of the body; short wings.

Common earwig

'Minibeasts' Pages 316–17

Primitive insects and tiny spiders found in great numbers in leaf litter, and some in the house or garden. Very small and often overlooked.

Silverfish

Spiders and harvestmen Pages 318–23

The most obvious difference between spiders and insects is that spiders have eight legs, insects only six. Spiders are in the class Arachnida; all insects are in the class Insecta.

Garden spider

Wolf spider

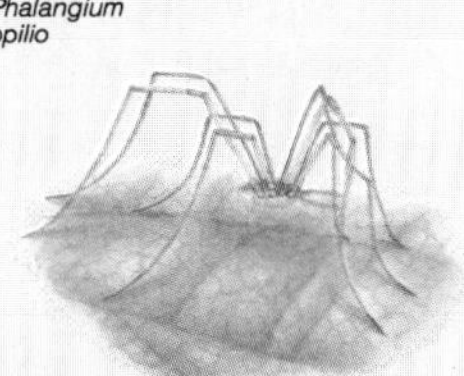
Phalangium opilio

Web-making spiders Pages 318–19

Order Araneae

Some species of spiders spin webs of different types to trap insects, which they then eat.

Webless spiders Pages 320–1

Order Araneae

Spiders that do not make webs capture their prey by speed or camouflage.

Harvestmen Pages 322–3

Order Opiliones

Arachnids with one-piece bodies and a very long second pair of legs.

Soil animals Pages 324–33

Some of the most common creatures that inhabit gardens and the woodland floor are neither insects nor arachnids.

Common centipede

Centipedes Pages 324–5

Orange-coloured creatures that shelter under logs and stones during the day. They have one pair of legs on each segment and can run fast.

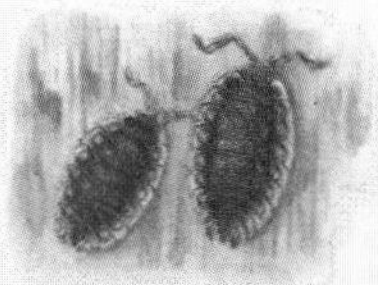
Common woodlice

Woodlice Page 327

Common creatures in damp, dark places. Land-living relatives of crabs and lobsters.

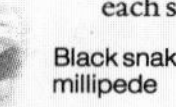
Black snake millipede

Millipedes Page 326

Many-legged black creatures that shelter in the dark by day. Two pairs of legs on each segment.

Common earthworm

Earthworms Pages 328–9

Familiar, soft-bodied creatures that live in great numbers in the soil.

Garden snail

Snails Pages 330–1

Slow-moving, shelled creatures found in damp, dark places. Common in areas where the soil contains lime.

Great black slug

Slugs Pages 332–3

Slimy, soft-bodied creatures that leave a silvery trail of dried mucus wherever they go.

BUTTERFLIES AND OTHER INSECTS OF BRITAIN

THE SKIPPER FAMILY

A lively habit of flitting from flower to flower and darting off to chase away other insects has led to the family name of 'skipper'. These are small, compact butterflies which fly with great speed and manoeuvrability. The ratio of the wings to the rest of the body is quite different from that of other butterflies. The wings and the body are the same length, whereas other families have wings proportionately much longer. The skipper's head is also unusual in being the same width as the thorax, with large compound eyes for all-round vision at high speed. The fore-wings are highly flexible; they can not only be raised and lowered during flight but can be drawn backwards, like a swing-wing aircraft. When resting, the butterfly may hold the fore-wings partially raised and the hind-wings horizontal – a typical skipper attitude. This may help it to absorb the sun's warmth, heating the butterfly's naturally cold blood and giving it energy.

Skippers are often aggressive in defence of a patch of grass or wild flowers. Using tall plants or grass stems as look-out posts they will make sudden sorties to intercept passing insects, including other skippers, flies and bumble-bees.

The skipper caterpillars all feed inside a curled leaf or in a protective tent of several leaves drawn together with silk. This structure may also serve the caterpillar as a safe place, or hibernaculum, during the winter. One adaptation to this sheltered way of life is that the caterpillar has a comb-like flap which propels its droppings away from the feeding area, sometimes by as much as 3 ft.

Some of the skippers, including the small, large and Essex, hold their wings in this characteristic manner while resting – the fore-wing partially raised and the hind-wing horizontal. The dingy skipper, however, rests like a moth with the wings flat on the abdomen.

Male *Female* *Underside*

Small skipper
Thymelicus sylvestris
Page 30

Male *Female* *Underside*

Essex skipper
Thymelicus lineola
Page 31

Male *Female* *Underside*

Lulworth skipper
Thymelicus acteon
Page 33

Male

Female

Underside

Large skipper
Ochlodes venata
Page 32

Chequered skipper
Carterocephalus palaemon
Page 35

Underside

Male

Female

Underside

Silver-spotted skipper
Hesperia comma
Page 34

Grizzled skipper
Pyrgus malvae
Page 37

Underside

Male

Female

Underside

Dingy skipper
Erynnis tages
Page 36

Black edge

Female

The whitish eggs are laid in groups down the centre of curled leaves, where they are protected from predators. They hatch in about three weeks. [× 5]

The chrysalis is protected by a loose cocoon, spun around a few leaves and drawn together.

Male

Dark scent marks

Widespread in England and Wales, but absent entirely from Scotland and Ireland.

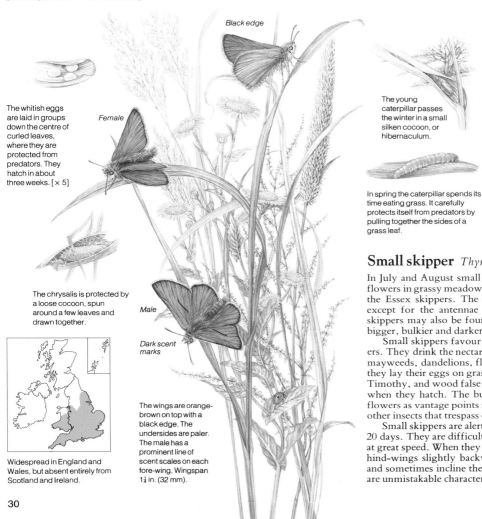

The wings are orange-brown on top with a black edge. The undersides are paler. The male has a prominent line of scent scales on each fore-wing. Wingspan 1¼ in. (32 mm).

The young caterpillar passes the winter in a small silken cocoon, or hibernaculum.

In spring the caterpillar spends its time eating grass. It carefully protects itself from predators by pulling together the sides of a grass leaf.

Delicately poised on slender blades of grass, a male and female small skipper mate after their courting ritual.

Small skipper *Thymelicus sylvestris*

In July and August small skippers will be seen darting among flowers in grassy meadows in company with their close relatives the Essex skippers. The two butterflies are almost identical, except for the antennae (see Essex skipper opposite). Large skippers may also be found in the same meadow but they are bigger, bulkier and darker than the other two species.

Small skippers favour long grass with plenty of wild flowers. They drink the nectar of the flowers, particularly scabious, mayweeds, dandelions, fleabane, thistles and knapweeds. And they lay their eggs on grasses such as Yorkshire fog, soft grass, Timothy, and wood false brome, which the caterpillars will eat when they hatch. The butterflies also use the tall grasses and flowers as vantage points from which to conduct sorties against other insects that trespass on their territory.

Small skippers are alert little butterflies which live for about 20 days. They are difficult to follow in flight as they dart about at great speed. When they are resting they sometimes hold their hind-wings slightly backwards – like a swing-wing aircraft – and sometimes incline their fore-wings upwards. The attitudes are unmistakable characteristics of the skippers.

The feature which distinguishes the Essex skipper from the small skipper is the underside of the tips of the antennae, which are black on the Essex skipper only. [× 5]

The eggs are laid in a row in a curled blade of grass. Unlike the small skipper's eggs they do not hatch until the next spring. [× 5]

The Essex skipper visits many meadow wild flowers, including thistles, to collect their sugary nectar.

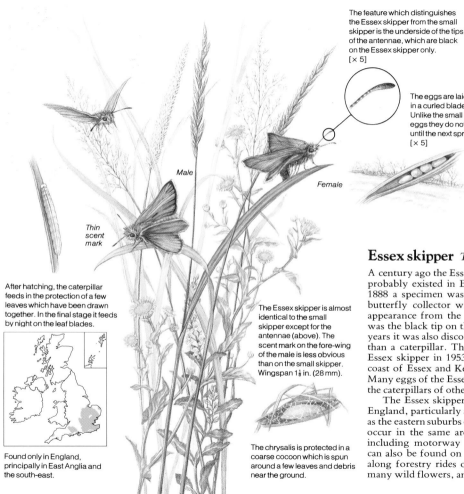

Male

Female

Thin scent mark

After hatching, the caterpillar feeds in the protection of a few leaves which have been drawn together. In the final stage it feeds by night on the leaf blades.

Found only in England, principally in East Anglia and the south-east.

The Essex skipper is almost identical to the small skipper except for the antennae (above). The scent mark on the fore-wing of the male is less obvious than on the small skipper. Wingspan $1\frac{1}{8}$ in. (28 mm).

The chrysalis is protected in a coarse cocoon which is spun around a few leaves and debris near the ground.

Essex skipper *Thymelicus lineola*

A century ago the Essex skipper was unknown, although it had probably existed in Britain throughout history. Then in July 1888 a specimen was recognised in Essex by a Mr Hawes, a butterfly collector who saw that it was slightly different in appearance from the small skipper. Its main visual difference was the black tip on the underside of each antenna, but in later years it was also discovered that it overwinters as an egg, rather than a caterpillar. This feature had vital consequences for the Essex skipper in 1953 when winter floods devastated the east coast of Essex and Kent where its population is at its densest. Many eggs of the Essex skipper survived the flood waters while the caterpillars of other butterflies died in great numbers.

The Essex skipper is found over a wide area of south-east England, particularly along the Thames estuary as far upstream as the eastern suburbs of London. These quick-flying butterflies occur in the same areas of long grass as the small skippers, including motorway verges and coastal embankments. They can also be found on grassy areas of heath and downland, and along forestry rides or on farms. They feed on the nectar of many wild flowers, and the caterpillars live on grass.

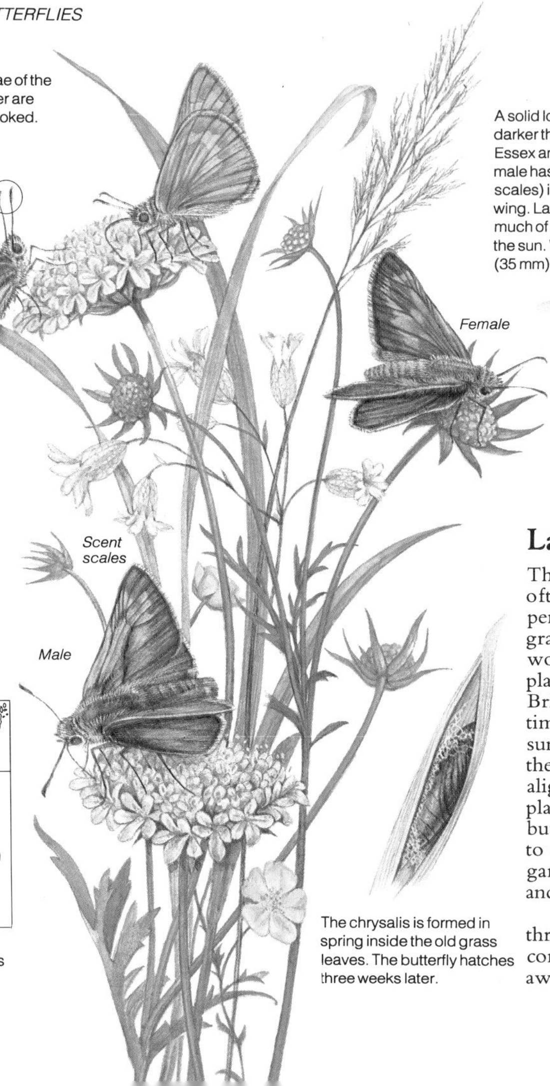

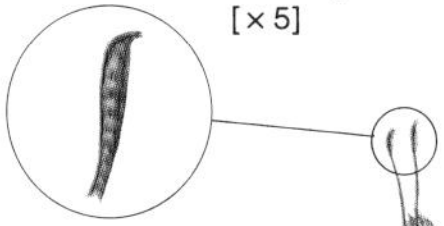

The antennae of the large skipper are distinctly hooked. [× 5]

A solid looking body, much darker than the Lulworth, Essex and small skippers. The male has a dark bar (the scent scales) in the centre of the forewing. Large skippers spend much of their time basking in the sun. Wingspan 1$\frac{3}{8}$ in. (35 mm).

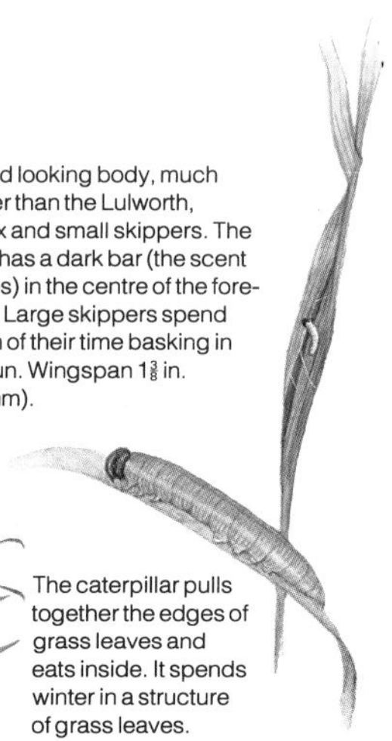

Female

The caterpillar pulls together the edges of grass leaves and eats inside. It spends winter in a structure of grass leaves.

The completion of a summer courtship: a pair of large skipper butterflies mate on a thistle flower.

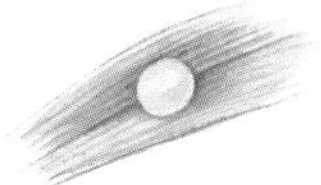

The eggs are laid singly on the underside of grass leaves. Just before they hatch, the dark head of the caterpillar can be seen through the egg case. [× 4]

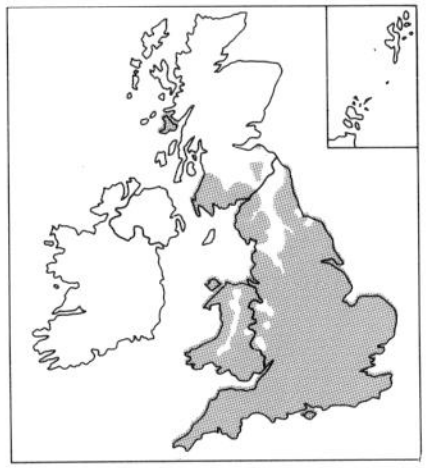

Scent scales

Male

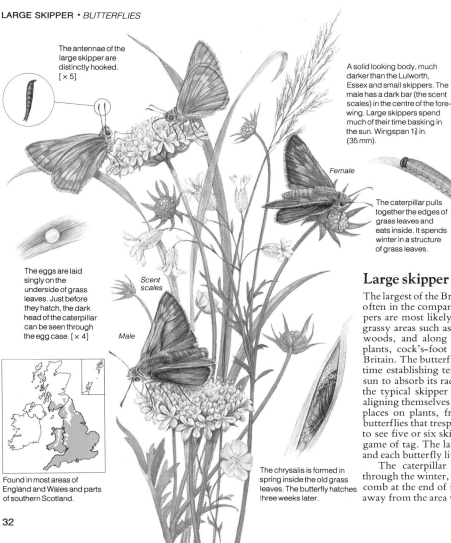

Found in most areas of England and Wales and parts of southern Scotland.

The chrysalis is formed in spring inside the old grass leaves. The butterfly hatches three weeks later.

Large skipper *Ochlodes venata*

The largest of the British skippers is found throughout England, often in the company of small and Essex skippers. Large skippers are most likely to be seen from early June to mid-July in grassy areas such as meadows, hillsides, paths and clearings in woods, and along coastal cliffs. The caterpillar's two food plants, cock's-foot and false brome grass, are widespread in Britain. The butterflies feed on flowers, but spend most of their time establishing territories, finding mates and basking in the sun to absorb its radiant energy. They rest with their wings in the typical skipper manner (see p. 28) and fidget about as if aligning themselves to the sun's rays. They have favourite perch places on plants, from which they sally out to engage rival butterflies that trespass on their territories. It is a common sight to see five or six skippers in hot pursuit of each other as if in a game of tag. The large skipper produces one generation a year, and each butterfly lives for about three weeks.

The caterpillar lives for about 11 months, hibernating through the winter, and has one unusual feature – an 18-toothed comb at the end of its abdomen which flicks its droppings well away from the area where it is feeding.

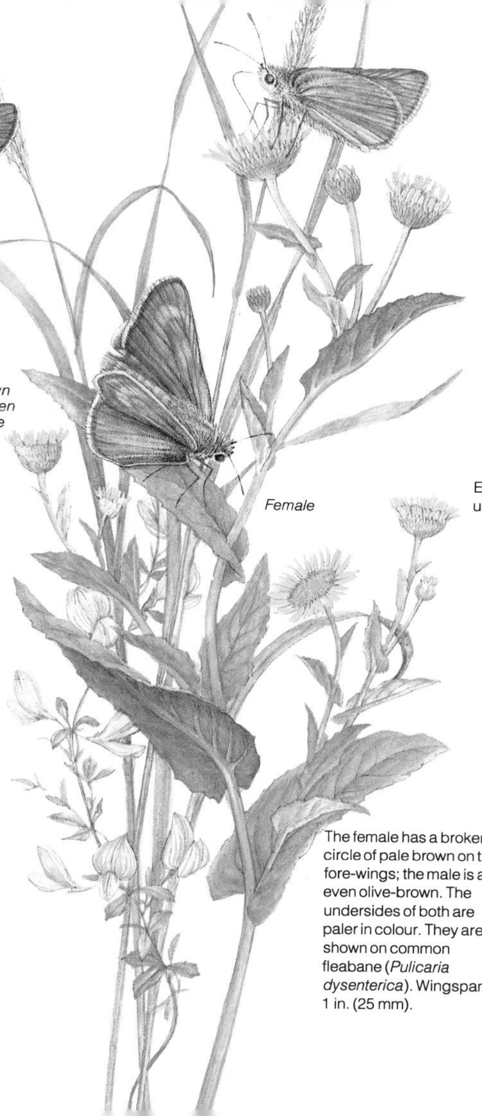

Male

Pale brown broken circle

Female

The chrysalis is formed in a loose cocoon of leaf fragments, and lasts for about 14 days.

The Lulworth skipper occurs only along the Dorset coast from Swanage to Bridport.

The female has a broken circle of pale brown on the fore-wings; the male is an even olive-brown. The undersides of both are paler in colour. They are shown on common fleabane (*Pulicaria dysenterica*). Wingspan 1 in. (25 mm).

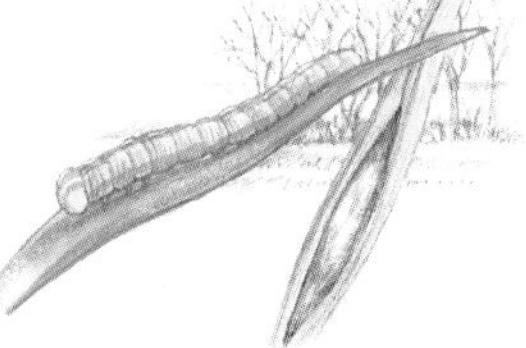

When it emerges, the caterpillar eats the nutritious egg case and then hibernates until the following spring when it begins feeding on grass.

Eggs are laid in rows along the curled-up underside of a grass leaf. [× 4]

When feeding, the butterfly bends its long proboscis almost at right-angles to penetrate the flower.

Lulworth skipper *Thymelicus acteon*

The butterfly is named after Lulworth Cove in Dorset where it was discovered in 1832. It has never been recorded in any numbers out of the coastal area between Swanage and Bridport. But where this small butterfly does occur it can be very numerous. An entomologist who studied Lulworth skippers in the Purbeck Hills before the First World War wrote of them 'swarming up the precipitous slopes of Corfe Castle'.

The Lulworth skipper prefers warm, south-facing slopes on the coastal cliffs. The caterpillar feeds on two species of grass – chalk false brome and couch grass. Some of the Lulworth Cove area is owned by the Ministry of Defence, so the butterfly is probably prospering better than if its breeding grounds were crowded with holiday-makers in summer.

The Lulworth skipper is a little dull to look at and could be confused with the small skipper. It rests in the typical skipper attitude (see p. 28) and is fond of wild flowers such as restharrow, cow parsley, ragwort, marjoram and thistles. Like other skippers, it is a powerful flyer. There is one generation a year – between July and August – and each butterfly lives for about three weeks.

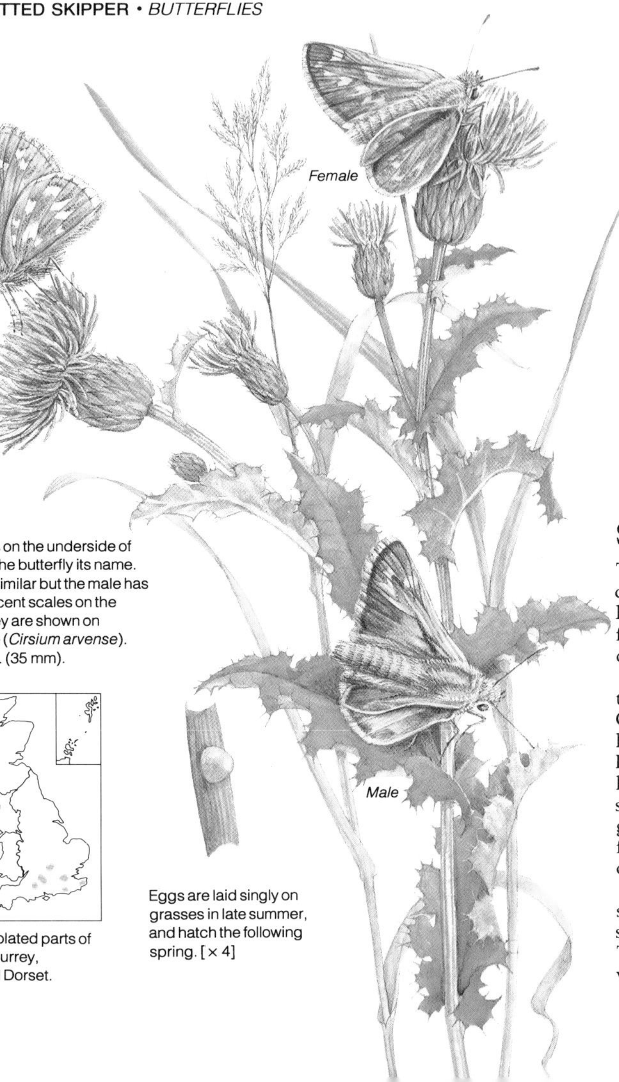

Female

Silver spots

The silver spots on the underside of the wings give the butterfly its name. The sexes are similar but the male has a black bar of scent scales on the fore-wings. They are shown on creeping thistle (*Cirsium arvense*). Wingspan 1$\frac{3}{8}$ in. (35 mm).

Male

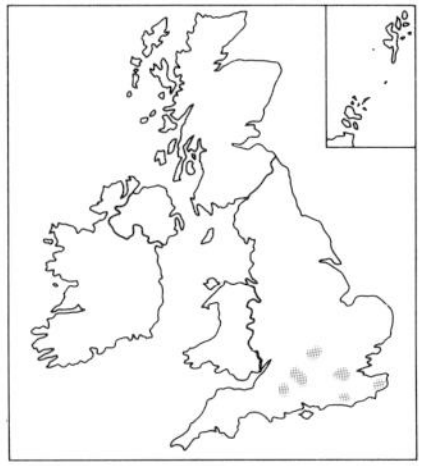

Restricted to isolated parts of Kent, Sussex, Surrey, Hampshire and Dorset.

Eggs are laid singly on grasses in late summer, and hatch the following spring. [× 4]

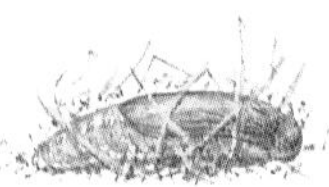

The chrysalis is formed in a substantial cocoon of pieces of grass and soil at ground level. The butterfly hatches in August.

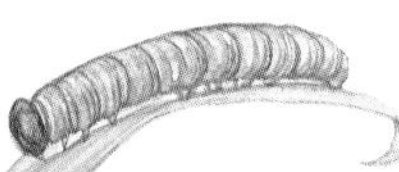

When freshly hatched the caterpillar is bright yellow, but later becomes dark with a distinctive black head.

Silver-spotted skippers have a life-span of two weeks as butterflies, and are on the wing during August.

Silver-spotted skipper *Hesperia comma*

These active little butterflies are found on open chalk grassland containing a mixture of wild flowers and grasses. The caterpillars eat sheep's-fescue grass and tufted hair-grass. The butterflies feed on flowers growing low down, such as stemless and carline thistles, hawkbits and clovers.

Distribution maps of the silver-spotted skipper published at the end of the Second World War showed a clear outline of the Chilterns and the South and North Downs. Today the butterfly has contracted to isolated pockets along these chalky corridors. Its decline has been brought about by the loss of suitable habitats. Old chalk pastures have been ploughed up, new crops such as oil-seed rape have replaced fields of clover, and areas of grassland have been given over to forestry. The loss of rabbits from myxomatosis may have resulted in other areas becoming overgrown with scrub.

Silver-spotted skippers are easily confused with the large and small skippers which may be flying in the same area. The silver spots on the undersides are the main distinguishing features. They are alert insects, and often rest with wings slanted backwards and antennae forwards, ready to chase off other insects.

The caterpillar lives in a leaf 'tent', made by pulling together the edges of a blade of grass. It spends the winter in a shelter made of several pieces of grass.

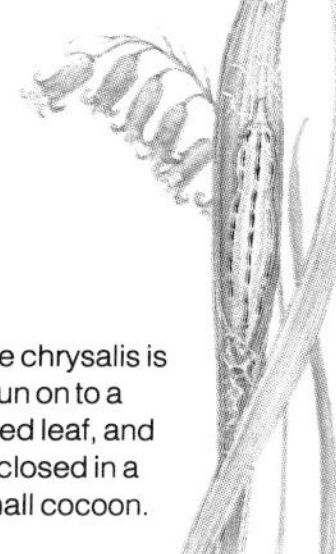

The chrysalis is spun on to a dried leaf, and enclosed in a small cocoon.

Chequered skippers are seen from late May to early July, flying close to the ground. They live for two or three weeks.

Spherical white eggs are laid singly on grass leaves. [× 4]

Now extinct in England; survives only near the Great Glen in western Scotland.

The most strongly patterned of the brown skippers. The upper side of the wings has large yellow spots on a dark brown background. The underside has a much paler background. The butterflies are shown on bugle (*Ajuga reptans*). Wingspan $1\frac{1}{4}$ in. (32 mm).

Chequered skipper *Carterocephalus palaemon*

The chequered skipper became extinct in England in 1975, 177 years after it was discovered in Bedfordshire. It now survives in Britain only in small populations in the western Scottish highlands, and is protected by the 1981 Wildlife and Countryside Act. Before it disappeared from England, the butterfly lived in a diagonal strip of limestone countryside from Devon to Lincolnshire – the same area as the large blue (which became extinct at about the same time) and the black hairstreak. Fifty-four colonies were recorded in the east Midlands before they declined in the 1960s. One of the main English localities was Rockingham Forest, around Corby in Northamptonshire. The chequered skipper lived in clearings and rides in ancient coppice woodlands or old grasslands on chalky soils. The caterpillars' food plants are upright brome grass and tor grass.

Several factors were responsible for the loss of the chequered skipper from England. Coppices have been neglected and become overgrown. Other woodlands have been removed or turned over to pine forests. Grazing, even by rabbits, is necessary to maintain a suitable grassy habitat, and the rabbit population has been severely reduced by myxomatosis.

The caterpillar spends much of its time out of view in a tent of leaves, where it also hibernates through the winter.

A dull brown butterfly with a grey fringe to the hind-wings. The underside of the wings is light brown with white spots, and the antennae are ringed with black and white. The only food plant, bird's-foot-trefoil (*Lotus corniculatus*), is known in coastal areas as 'bacon-and-eggs'. Wingspan 1 in. (25 mm).

Grey fringe

White spots

The chrysalis is formed in spring, inside the caterpillar's winter quarters. The butterfly hatches a month later.

A dingy skipper basks in the sun on a bugle flower, a plant that is commonly found in meadows and waysides.

Single eggs, each with 12 or 13 'keels' down the side, are laid on the leaves of the food plant. [× 4]

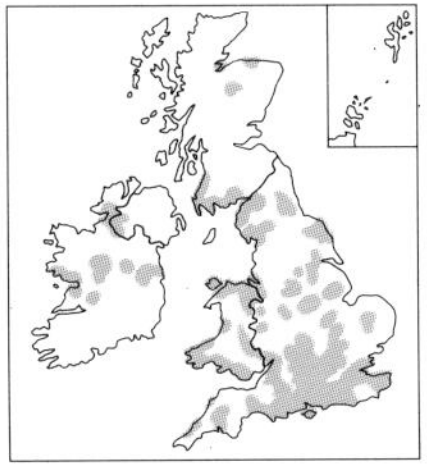

Mostly found in southern and central Britain. The only skipper in Ireland.

Dingy skipper *Erynnis tages*

Despite the name, which reflects its dull colours, the dingy skipper has attractive mottled patterns on the wings, especially the border of grey hairs around the hind-wing. It is unique among British skippers for two reasons: it is the only skipper that is also found in Ireland, and it rests at night like a moth with its wings flat over the abdomen. In sunshine it does not assume the typical skipper stance (see p. 28), but basks with the wings spread out flat. Its distribution in Britain is rather patchy, mostly in southern and central England, parts of Wales and a few places in Scotland. In Ireland it is found in limestone areas such as Counties Clare, Mayo and Galway.

The caterpillars have only one food plant, bird's-foot-trefoil, which is found throughout the British Isles but grows best on chalk and limestone soils. Dingy skippers are most likely to be seen on chalk downlands and in flowery woodland clearings in limestone districts. Like some other skippers, they overwinter as caterpillars which turn into chrysalises in April or May. The butterflies are on the wing in May and June, each one living for about 20 days. There is normally only one generation a year, with occasionally a second in favourable years.

A brown-and-white speckled butterfly, with evenly spaced dark patches around the edges of the wings. It can be seen in spring, often on the flowers of the lesser celandine (*Ranunculus ficaria*). Wingspan $1\frac{1}{8}$ in. (28 mm).

At first, the caterpillar protects itself under a silk web but later feeds in a leaf 'tent' in the typical skipper manner.

Eggs are laid singly on the upper side of wild strawberry leaves. They are delicately sculptured with 20 'keels'. [× 6]

The butterfly is so tiny that it fits neatly on to one of its favourite flowers, lesser celandine, as it drinks the nectar.

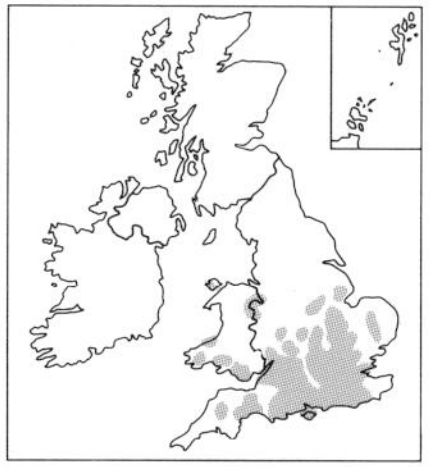

Mainly in southern England and Wales. Rarely north of the Humber.

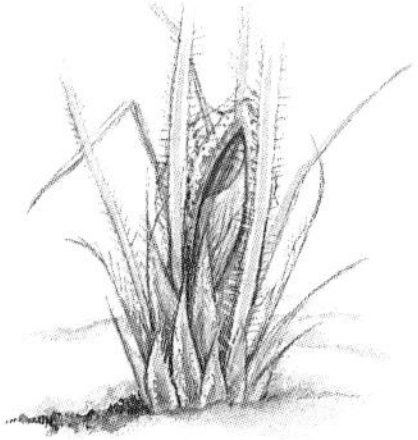

The grizzled skipper is the only British skipper that overwinters as a chrysalis. It hatches as a butterfly about May.

Grizzled skipper *Pyrgus malvae*

This conspicuous and attractive little butterfly is easy to identify with its brown-and-white markings and grey (or 'grizzled') hairs. It basks in the sun with its wings spread out flat, but in dull weather the wings are firmly closed together over its back. In flight it is so swift and darting that it may be quite difficult to follow.

The grizzled skipper is found in central and southern England in flowery meadows and on chalk downland, especially in hollows and on sheltered slopes. The caterpillar's main food plants are wild potentillas such as barren strawberry, creeping cinquefoil and silverweed. Other plants that are sometimes used for food by the caterpillars are wild strawberry and raspberry, which grow in many parts of the North and South Downs, and also brambles in scrubby lowland areas.

The butterflies are never seen in great numbers like the blues, but they can usually be found in suitable localities. There is usually only one generation a year, with the butterfly in flight during May and June. In warm years a second generation may occur, and they appear again in August. Each butterfly lives for about two weeks.

The claspers on the male's abdomen are well developed in the swallowtail. All male butterflies and moths have them for gripping the female's abdomen while mating.

Eggs are laid singly on the fenland plant milk parsley (*Peucedanum palustre*), and hatch after about two weeks.

The 'tails' and false eyes on the hind-wing mimic the head and antennae of the butterfly. This is a defensive device, evolved to confuse birds as to the true head of their prey, and giving the butterfly a 50 per cent chance of surviving an attack.

The caterpillars at first look like bird droppings, but when fully grown become an attractive green, black and orange.

The chrysalis can be either green or brown according to the colour of the background, and is attached by a silk pad and silk girdle. It usually overwinters in this state.

To frighten away predators the caterpillars display a pair of orange 'horns' and produce a smell like ripe pineapple.

A swallowtail butterfly displays its 'eyes' and 'tails' while drinking nectar from the flat-topped flower-head of a milk parsley plant.

Prominent 'tail'

Swallowtail *Papilio machaon*

These lovely butterflies survive in Britain as fragile populations in a man-made habitat, the Norfolk Broads, which were excavated for peat in the Middle Ages. They are entirely dependent on the caterpillar's food plant, milk parsley, which varies in its numbers each year. The swallowtail was much more widespread in the past, occurring throughout the fens of East Anglia and probably in the marshes of the Thames and Lea rivers. It became extinct in the Wicken Sedge Fen in Cambridgeshire in the early 1950s, and an attempt was made in 1975 to reintroduce it. Conservationists planted 3,500 milk parsley plants and released 228 butterflies, but the drought of 1976 followed and the attempt failed. The butterfly is now protected by the Wildlife and Countryside Act of 1981.

Visitors to the Broads may see swallowtails from late May to mid-July. Each butterfly lives a month, but its chance of reaching the butterfly stage is small because of high losses of caterpillars and chrysalises to spiders, birds and small mammals. Land drainage was responsible for the swallowtail's disappearance in the past. Maintenance of high water levels and preservation of milk parsley are necessary for its survival in the future.

This bright black-and-yellow butterfly with its red-and-blue false eyes is unmistakable. It is the largest butterfly resident in Britain, and its name refers to the extensions on the hind-wings which give the appearance of a swallow's tail. It is shown feeding on thistle flowers. Wingspan 3¾ in. (95 mm).

Swallowtail butterflies are now restricted entirely to the Norfolk Broads.

THE WHITES AND YELLOWS

The British Pieridae family contains two major sub-families – the whites (Pierinae) and the yellows (Coliadinae) – and a third sub-family (Dismorphiinae) of which the wood white is the only British member. All species in the family contain white or yellow pigments. Their eggs are tall and ribbed, and the caterpillars are without spines. The caterpillars' food plants are mostly in the cabbage and pea families, but the brimstone caterpillar feeds solely on buckthorn. The brimstone is the only one of the British whites and yellows to hibernate as a butterfly; most of the others hibernate as chrysalises.

The white and yellow colours of the white sub-family are caused by waste products stored in the wings. The black marks are chemically similar to the pigments that tan human skin. Seasonal colour variation is evident; butterflies of the spring generation tend to be weakly marked with grey while those of summer generations tend to have heavy black marks. The black-and-white marking serves as a warning to predators. Birds soon learn that the butterflies contain poisons; they are mustard oil glycosides, which the butterflies obtain from cabbage leaves.

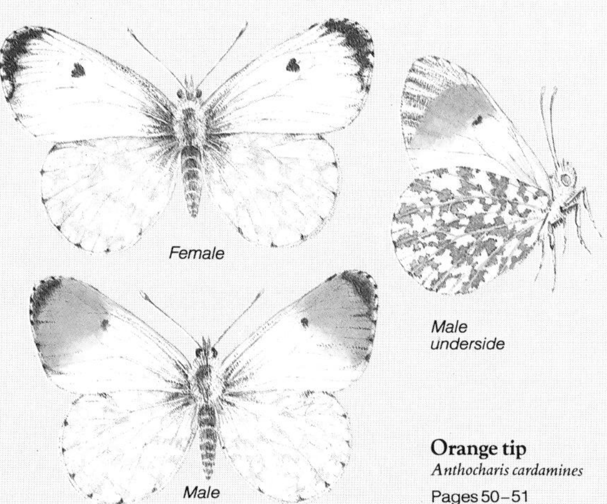

Female

Male

Male underside

Orange tip
Anthocharis cardamines
Pages 50–51

Female

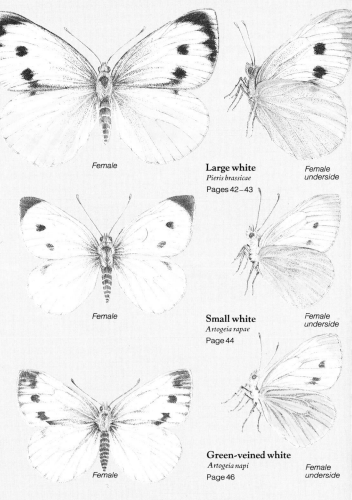

Large white
Pieris brassicae
Pages 42–43

Female underside

Female

Small white
Artogeia rapae
Page 44

Female underside

Female

Green-veined white
Artogeia napi
Page 46

Female underside

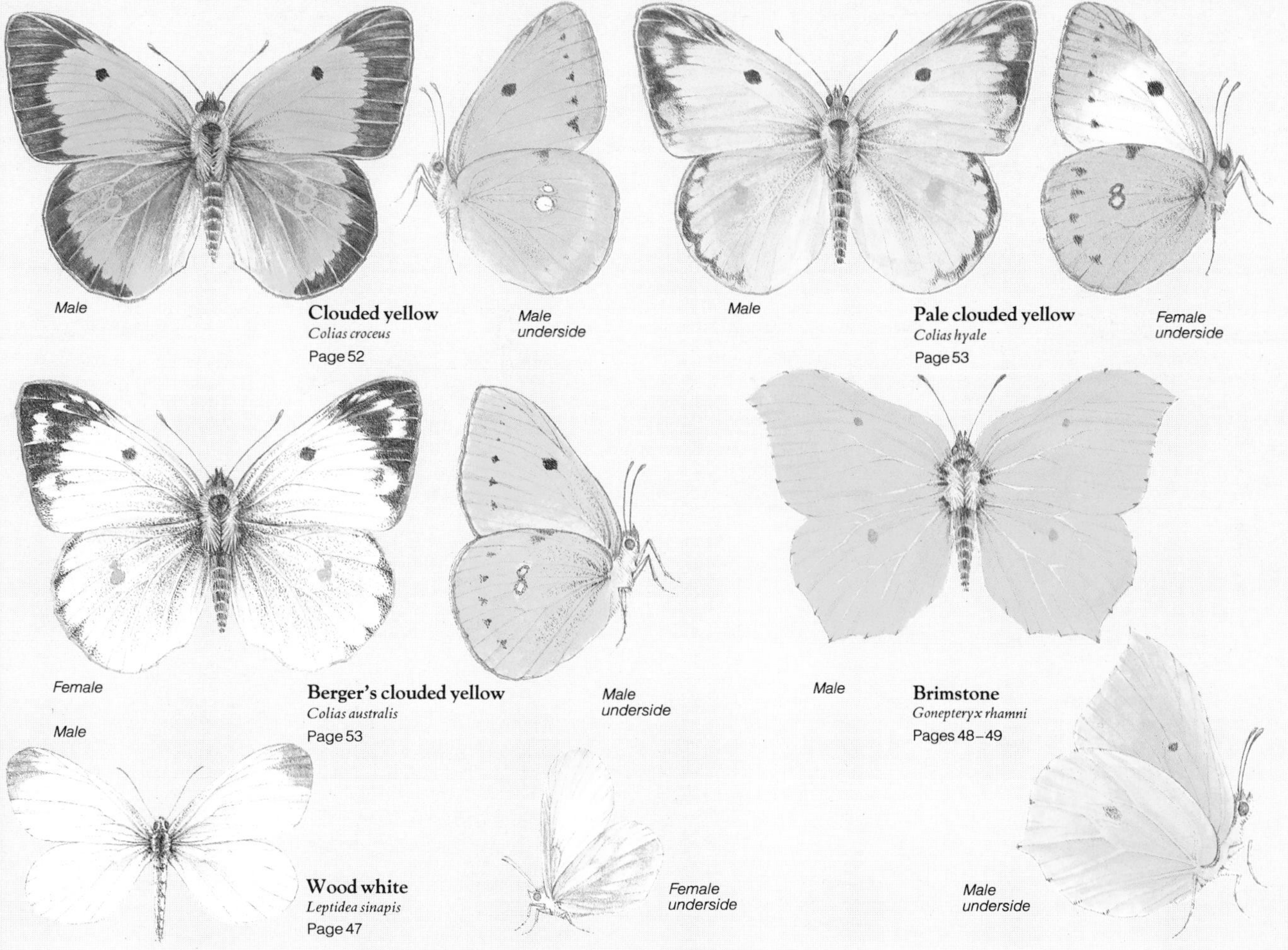

Clouded yellow
Colias croceus
Page 52

Pale clouded yellow
Colias hyale
Page 53

Berger's clouded yellow
Colias australis
Page 53

Brimstone
Gonepteryx rhamni
Pages 48–49

Wood white
Leptidea sinapis
Page 47

Courting butterflies respond to colour and size, chasing and spiralling with each other over meadows. As many as a dozen whites may be seen together.

Scent and sight are both necessary for a butterfly to recognise another of the correct species and sex. If a female has already mated she may raise her abdomen, refusing the male's advance.

Sensitive cells in the tips of the legs and antennae help the female to recognise the correct food plant for her caterpillars. She often lays her eggs on the underside of the leaf.

Eggs are laid in orderly groups of about 60, on leaves of the cabbage family, near the margin. As they get older, the yellow colour becomes more pronounced.

During bad weather, butterflies rest in vegetation, usually under leaves or flowers, or on grass stems. They may have to remain inactive for several days.

After a satisfactory courtship, a male and female may remain in the mating position for several hours. If disturbed, they will fly off, still joined together, with one sex carrying the passive partner below.

Male

[× 5]

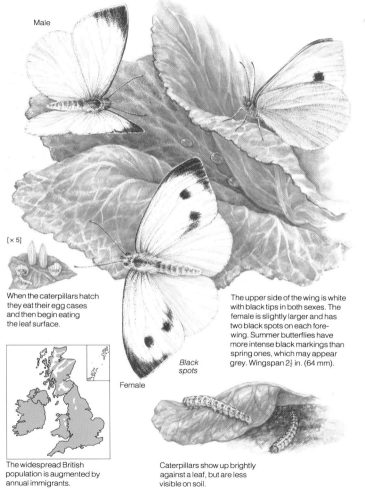

When the caterpillars hatch they eat their egg cases and then begin eating the leaf surface.

The widespread British population is augmented by annual immigrants.

Female

Black spots

The upper side of the wing is white with black tips in both sexes. The female is slightly larger and has two black spots on each forewing. Summer butterflies have more intense black markings than spring ones, which may appear grey. Wingspan $2\frac{1}{2}$ in. (64 mm).

Caterpillars show up brightly against a leaf, but are less visible on soil.

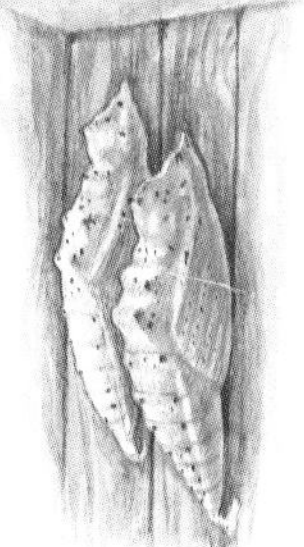

The chrysalis is found in a sheltered spot such as the eaves of a shed, and may be either green or brown. Hibernating chrysalises begin to hatch in April.

This female of the summer generation, with her strong black markings, visits a thistle to imbibe nectar from the flowers.

Large white *Pieris brassicae*

Before the 1940s, cabbage fields in Britain were often covered by a fluttering haze of large white butterflies. The caterpillars were major pests, destroying great numbers of cabbages. However, the widespread use of organic insecticides since the end of the Second World War has caused severe losses to the large whites (as well as other butterflies), and in 1955 they were stricken by a butterfly virus. They have never regained their previous numbers, despite regular migration of large whites from the Continent each year.

The popular name 'cabbage white' refers to both the small and large white butterflies. Both lay their eggs on cabbages, but the caterpillars of the large white are conspicuous and feed exposed on the outer leaves, while the small white caterpillars feed unseen in the heart of the cabbage. Sixty wild members of the cabbage family are recorded as food plants, though the caterpillars of the large white also eat garden nasturtiums and mignonettes.

There are normally two generations of the butterfly in Britain each year – from April to June and from July to September. The second generation have darker markings.

Male

Female

Dark wingtips

The fore-wings have black tips, with one black spot on the males and two on the females. The markings on the spring generation (shown here) are paler than those on the summer generation. Wingspan up to $1\frac{7}{8}$ in. (48 mm).

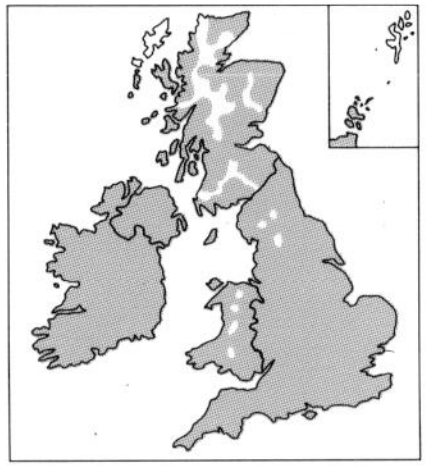

Small whites are found all over the British Isles, including Orkney.

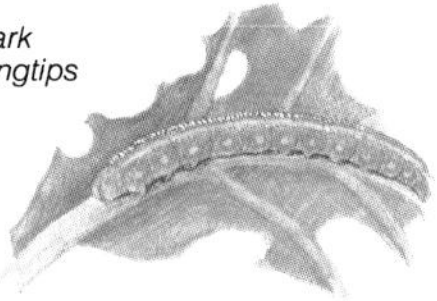

The caterpillar at first feeds in the heart of the cabbage, then later on the outer leaves.

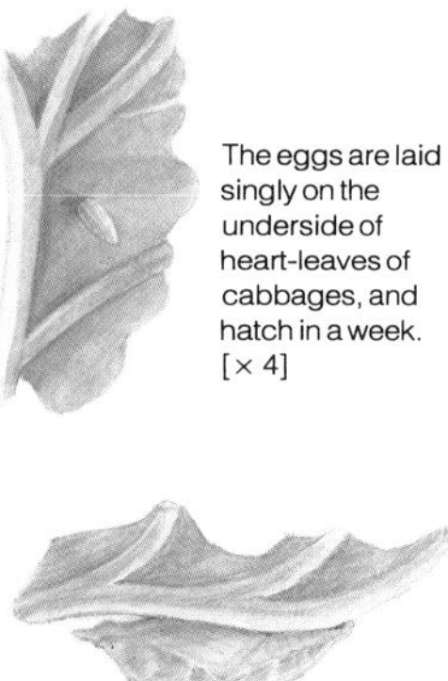

The eggs are laid singly on the underside of heart-leaves of cabbages, and hatch in a week. [× 4]

Summer chrysalises hatch in about three weeks; autumn chrysalises live through winter to produce the following year's spring generation of butterflies.

A common wayside sight, a female small white feeds on one of the many species of wild flowers that attract it.

Small white *Artogeia rapae*

Only the meadow brown (pp. 110–11) is more common in Britain than the small white butterfly. The first generation of small whites can be seen on the wing from March to May, while the second generation flies from June to September. Their caterpillars' food plants, wild and cultivated members of the cabbage family, grow almost everywhere, so small whites are seen throughout Britain.

Although the caterpillars do less damage to the cabbage crop than large white caterpillars, they can be a more serious pest, as they are very difficult to detect. They are small and, unlike large white caterpillars, are solitary and well camouflaged by their leaf-green colouring. In addition, they start by eating the heart of a cabbage and progress gradually to the outer leaves, so that by the time they can be seen, most of the damage is done.

As the name suggests, the small white butterfly is a smaller version of the large white butterfly and, because they share a food plant and fly in the same places at similar times, they are frequently confused with each other. Apart from the difference in size, the large white has broader wings, on which the markings are usually more clearly pronounced.

IDENTIFYING WHITE BUTTERFLIES

Six different types of white butterfly look almost identical at a glance, but recognition can be greatly helped by the location in which they are seen and the time of year. White butterflies in gardens, especially where cabbages are growing, are likely to be either small or large whites. The first of the season will be small whites, as large whites do not appear until late April. Waysides where wild flowers grow – particularly cuckoo flower and garlic mustard – are likely haunts for orange tips. Damp fields and ditches attract the green-veined white. And the smallest species, the wood white, is likely to be seen only in open areas of conifer plantations.

Small white
Artogeia rapae
Page 44

Wood white
Leptidea sinapis
Page 47

Large white
Pieris brassicae
Pages 42–43

Female brimstone
Gonepteryx rhamni
Pages 48–49

Green-veined white
Artogeia napi
Page 46

Female orange tip
Anthocharis cardamines
Pages 50–51

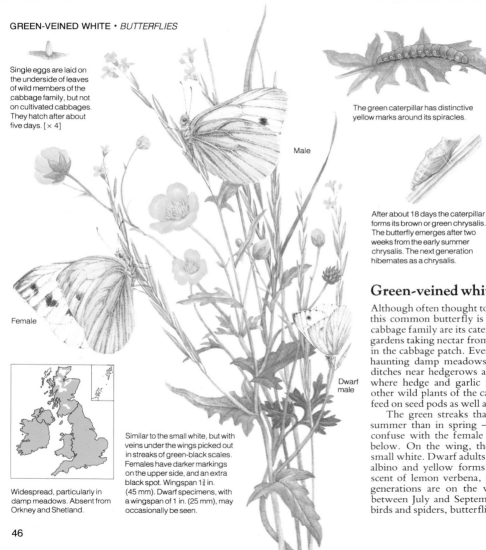

Single eggs are laid on the underside of leaves of wild members of the cabbage family, but not on cultivated cabbages. They hatch after about five days. [× 4]

The green caterpillar has distinctive yellow marks around its spiracles.

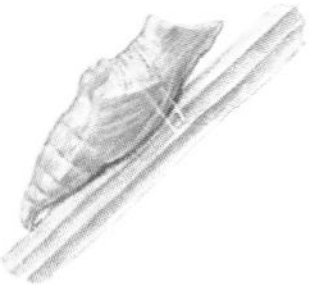

After about 18 days the caterpillar forms its brown or green chrysalis. The butterfly emerges after two weeks from the early summer chrysalis. The next generation hibernates as a chrysalis.

The first brood flies at bluebell time in May and June. One of the butterfly's haunts is moist woodland margins.

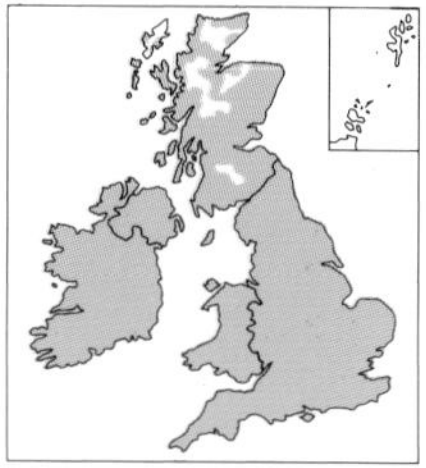

Male

Female

Dwarf male

Green-veined white *Artogeia napi*

Although often thought to be a garden pest that ruins cabbages, this common butterfly is blameless; only wild relatives in the cabbage family are its caterpillars' food plants. It may be seen in gardens taking nectar from radish flowers, but it does not breed in the cabbage patch. Even on dull days the butterfly is active, haunting damp meadows, wet fields, marshy land, wayside ditches near hedgerows and woodland edges. It may be seen where hedge and garlic mustard, charlock, mignonette and other wild plants of the cabbage family grow. The caterpillars feed on seed pods as well as leaves.

The green streaks that trace the veins – more heavily in summer than in spring – make the resting butterfly easy to confuse with the female orange tip, which is green-mottled below. On the wing, the green-veined white resembles the small white. Dwarf adults are sometimes seen, and there are rare albino and yellow forms. Males exude a strong but pleasant scent of lemon verbena, probably used in courting. The two generations are on the wing between April and June, and between July and September. If they escape the attentions of birds and spiders, butterflies may live for about a month.

Widespread, particularly in damp meadows. Absent from Orkney and Shetland.

Similar to the small white, but with veins under the wings picked out in streaks of green-black scales. Females have darker markings on the upper side, and an extra black spot. Wingspan 1¾ in. (45 mm). Dwarf specimens, with a wingspan of 1 in. (25 mm), may occasionally be seen.

The wood white is found in woodland glades and rides where it often stops to drink the nectar of flowers.

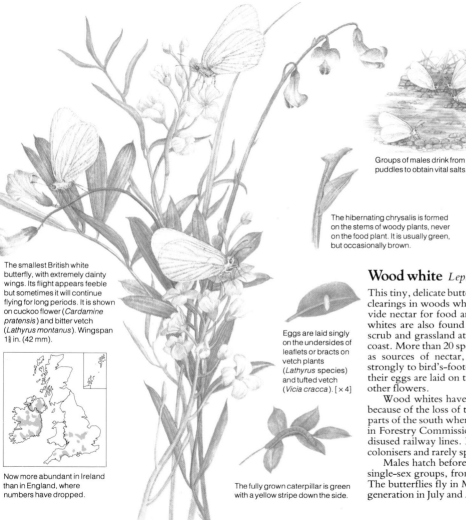

Groups of males drink from puddles to obtain vital salts.

The hibernating chrysalis is formed on the stems of woody plants, never on the food plant. It is usually green, but occasionally brown.

The smallest British white butterfly, with extremely dainty wings. Its flight appears feeble but sometimes it will continue flying for long periods. It is shown on cuckoo flower (*Cardamine pratensis*) and bitter vetch (*Lathyrus montanus*). Wingspan 1⅝ in. (42 mm).

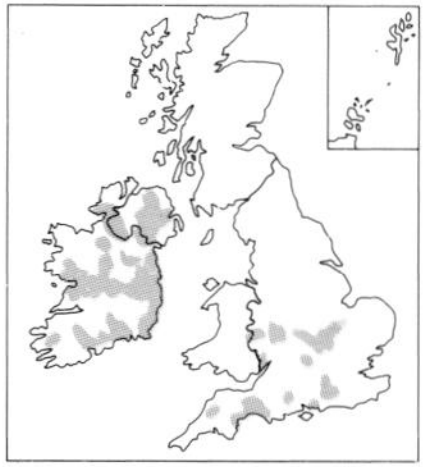

Now more abundant in Ireland than in England, where numbers have dropped.

Eggs are laid singly on the undersides of leaflets or bracts on vetch plants (*Lathyrus* species) and tufted vetch (*Vicia cracca*). [× 4]

The fully grown caterpillar is green with a yellow stripe down the side.

Wood white *Leptidea sinapis*

This tiny, delicate butterfly lives mainly along shady rides and in clearings in woods where profusely growing wild flowers provide nectar for food and suitable places for egg-laying. Wood whites are also found in sheltered meadows in Sussex and in scrub and grassland at the base of cliffs along the south Devon coast. More than 20 species of wild flowers have been identified as sources of nectar, but the butterflies are attracted most strongly to bird's-foot-trefoil, bugle and ragged robin. Most of their eggs are laid on tall food plants which stand up above the other flowers.

Wood whites have become extinct in the north of England because of the loss of their habitats. But they have prospered in parts of the south where many populations now live along rides in Forestry Commission plantations. They have also exploited disused railway lines. Because of their slow flight they are poor colonisers and rarely spread beyond limited localities.

Males hatch before females and have been seen drinking, as single-sex groups, from woodland puddles to obtain vital salts. The butterflies fly in May and June, and there may be a second generation in July and August in southern areas.

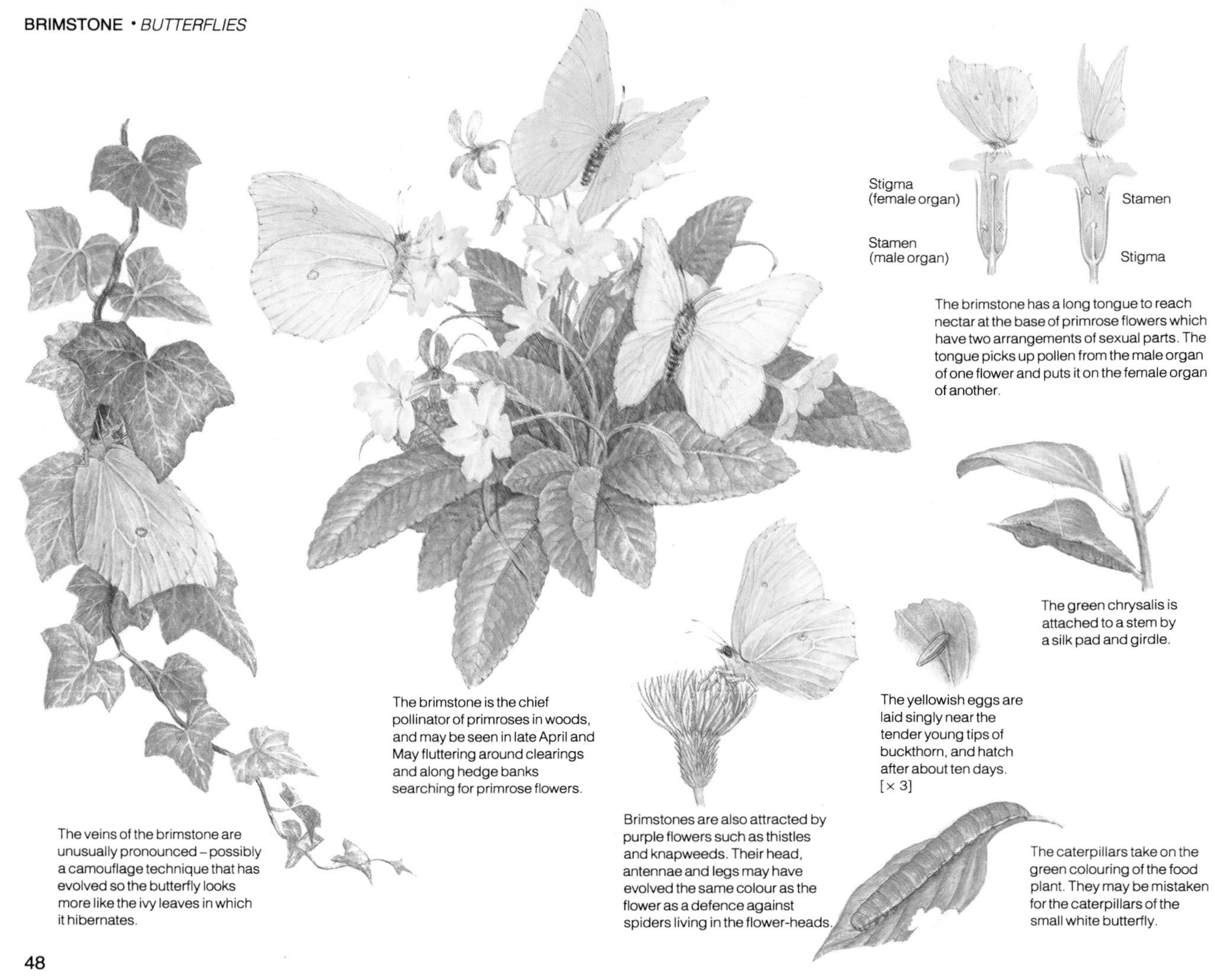

The brimstone has a long tongue to reach nectar at the base of primrose flowers which have two arrangements of sexual parts. The tongue picks up pollen from the male organ of one flower and puts it on the female organ of another.

The green chrysalis is attached to a stem by a silk pad and girdle.

The brimstone is the chief pollinator of primroses in woods, and may be seen in late April and May fluttering around clearings and along hedge banks searching for primrose flowers.

The yellowish eggs are laid singly near the tender young tips of buckthorn, and hatch after about ten days. [× 3]

The veins of the brimstone are unusually pronounced – possibly a camouflage technique that has evolved so the butterfly looks more like the ivy leaves in which it hibernates.

Brimstones are also attracted by purple flowers such as thistles and knapweeds. Their head, antennae and legs may have evolved the same colour as the flower as a defence against spiders living in the flower-heads.

The caterpillars take on the green colouring of the food plant. They may be mistaken for the caterpillars of the small white butterfly.

Female

Male

Orange spots

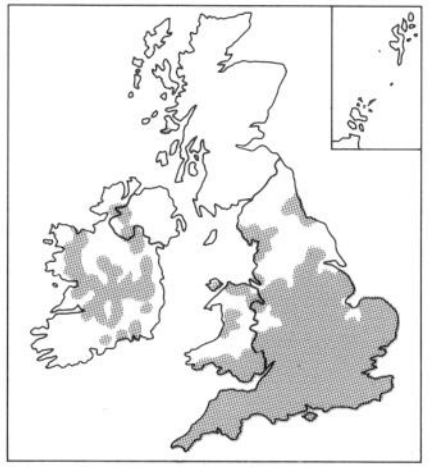

A male brimstone wakes up to the morning sun with hundreds of dew drops coating its wings. This autumn brimstone has spent the night on a thistle head.

Brimstone *Gonepteryx rhamni*

The word butterfly was probably first used to describe this butter-coloured insect. It is a common species and is probably the first and last butterfly seen each year, as it can be in flight from February to November. 'Butterfly' eventually came to include all species and the brimstone acquired its present name which relates to the colour of sulphur.

The distribution of the brimstone mirrors the distribution of its two food plants, buckthorn (*Rhamnus catharticus*) and alder buckthorn (*Frangula alnus*), on which its caterpillars are entirely dependent for their food. The butterflies are powerful flyers and males are sometimes seen miles away from their food plants, possibly migrating to fresh territories. Brimstones are usually found on the margins of woodland, along hedgerows, in scrubby areas and thickets. They are strongly attracted to wild flowers for nectar and often stay for long periods at one flower, always with their wings shut.

The underside colours and shape allow brimstones to blend in with vegetation, and they successfully hibernate through winter as adult butterflies. There is one generation a year, and individual butterflies live for up to a year.

The brimstone is widespread in England, Wales and parts of Ireland.

The male's upper side is a strong sulphur-yellow. The female's upper side is much paler in colour, but both sexes have an orange spot on each wing. The undersides of both sexes are pale yellow. They are shown on buckthorn. Wingspan 2¼ in. (57 mm).

Male butterflies emerge from the chrysalis before the females, and it is not unusual to see a group of males around a patch of their food plant.

Females prefer bluish pink and white flowers, and will occasionally visit lilac blossom in the garden.

The dappled green coloration of the underside provides perfect camouflage when the butterfly settles on a plant. When at rest, it moves its fore-wings backwards and inside the hind-wings.

Eggs are laid singly in the tight buds and flowers of a food plant. As the eggs grow older they change from greenish-white to orange.

The caterpillars are bluish-green, and are camouflaged on the long seed pods of their food plants.

More than 30 plants in the cabbage family have been recorded bearing eggs of the orange tip, but the caterpillars will not necessarily be successful on all of them.

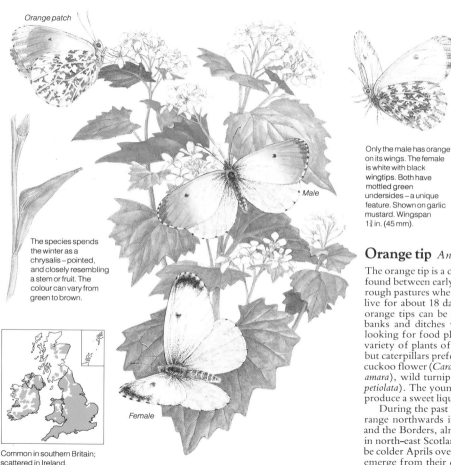

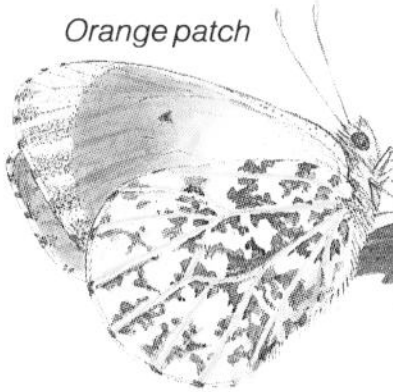

Orange patch

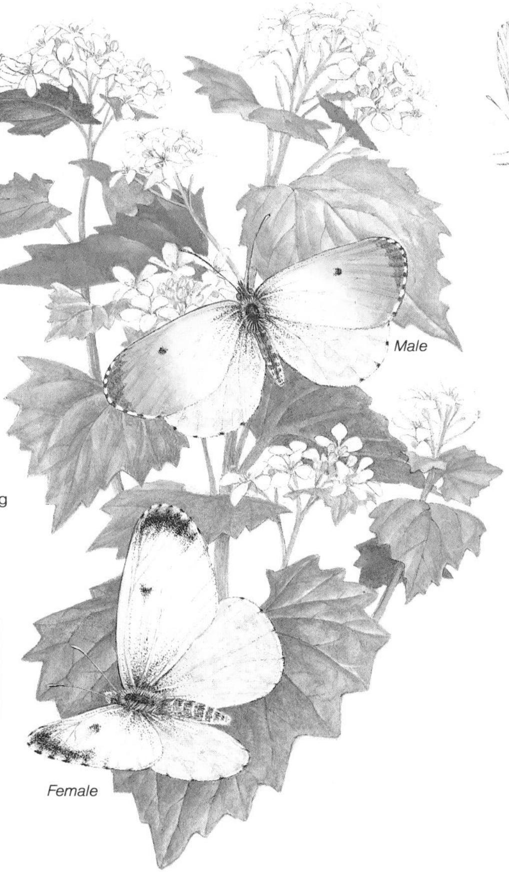

The species spends the winter as a chrysalis – pointed, and closely resembling a stem or fruit. The colour can vary from green to brown.

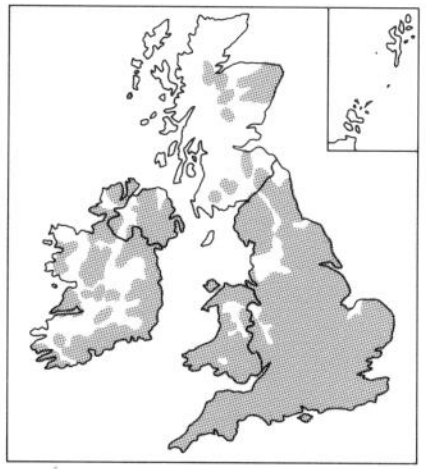

Common in southern Britain; scattered in Ireland. Spreading into Scotland.

Male

Female

Only the male has orange on its wings. The female is white with black wingtips. Both have mottled green undersides – a unique feature. Shown on garlic mustard. Wingspan 1¾ in. (45 mm).

A male orange tip butterfly, with its unmistakable orange wingtips showing through its mottled green underside, rests on a spring flower.

Orange tip *Anthocharis cardamines*

The orange tip is a colourful symbol of spring time. It is usually found between early May and June along roadsides, ditches and rough pastures where its food plants grow. The butterflies each live for about 18 days, with only one generation a year. Male orange tips can be seen patrolling their territories along river banks and ditches while females tend to move farther afield looking for food plants where they can lay their eggs. A wide variety of plants of the cabbage family may be used for food, but caterpillars prefer creeping yellow-cress (*Rorippa sylvestris*), cuckoo flower (*Cardamine pratensis*), large bittercress (*Cardamine amara*), wild turnip (*Brassica rapa*) and garlic mustard (*Alliaria petiolata*). The young caterpillars have long forked hairs which produce a sweet liquid on which ants feed.

During the past few decades the orange tip has extended its range northwards into Yorkshire, Durham, Northumberland and the Borders, almost linking up with an isolated population in north-east Scotland. The reason for the revival is thought to be colder Aprils over the past 20 years, causing the butterflies to emerge from their chrysalises later, when more flowers are in bloom in the countryside.

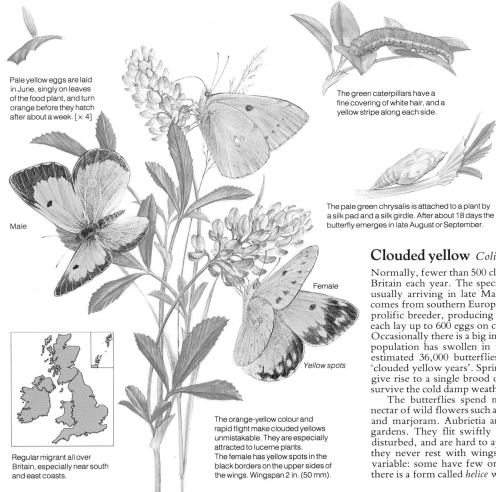

Pale yellow eggs are laid in June, singly on leaves of the food plant, and turn orange before they hatch after about a week. [× 4]

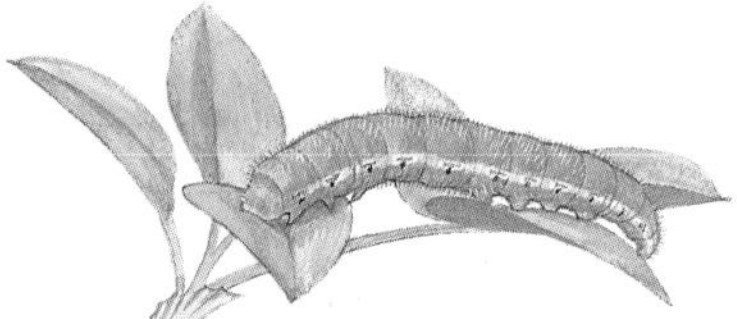

The green caterpillars have a fine covering of white hair, and a yellow stripe along each side.

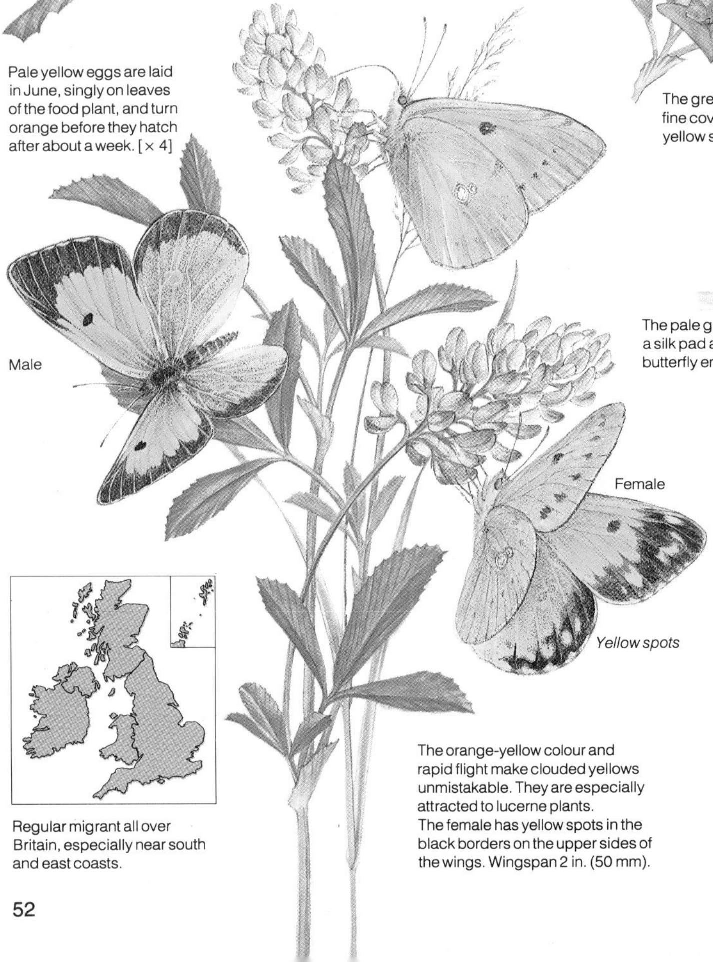

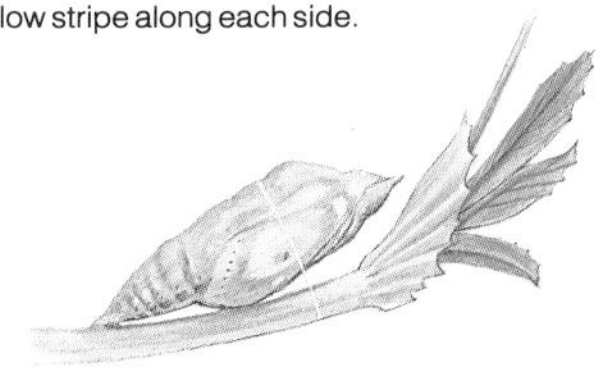

Male

The pale green chrysalis is attached to a plant by a silk pad and a silk girdle. After about 18 days the butterfly emerges in late August or September.

When feeding on lucerne or clover, the butterfly probes individual flowers with its bent tongue.

Female

Yellow spots

Regular migrant all over Britain, especially near south and east coasts.

The orange-yellow colour and rapid flight make clouded yellows unmistakable. They are especially attracted to lucerne plants.
The female has yellow spots in the black borders on the upper sides of the wings. Wingspan 2 in. (50 mm).

Clouded yellow *Colias croceus*

Normally, fewer than 500 clouded yellow butterflies are seen in Britain each year. The species is a regular migrant to Britain, usually arriving in late May. It is a strong, fast flyer which comes from southern Europe. In its warm native countries it is a prolific breeder, producing up to four broods a year. Females each lay up to 600 eggs on clover, lucerne, trefoils and melilot. Occasionally there is a big influx into Britain after the European population has swollen in favourable conditions. In 1947 an estimated 36,000 butterflies came; 1955 and 1983 were also 'clouded yellow years'. Spring migrants to Britain lay eggs that give rise to a single brood of autumn butterflies but none can survive the cold damp weather beyond November.

The butterflies spend most of their time feeding on the nectar of wild flowers such as lucerne, clover, thistle, knapweed and marjoram. Aubrietia and marigolds may attract them to gardens. They flit swiftly from flower to flower, are easily disturbed, and are hard to approach. Always poised for flight, they never rest with wings open. The females' colouring is variable: some have few or no spots in the black margin and there is a form called *helice* which has a whitish background.

Pearly-white eggs are laid in June by immigrants on lucerne and clover leaves. They change to a purple colour after about ten days, just before hatching. [× 3]

Male

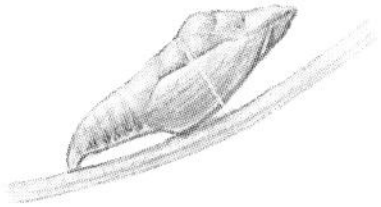

The chrysalis is yellowish-green, similar to the clouded yellow's. The butterfly emerges after 18 days.

The butterfly moves quickly from flower to flower, and is attracted to scabious, marjoram, clovers and thistles.

Berger's clouded yellow

Spots on black border

The male's wings lack the orange of the clouded yellow. The female is white. Both have light spots on the black border on the fore-wings. They feed on lucerne and clover. Wingspan 1⅞ in. (48 mm).

Female

Berger's clouded yellow
Colias australis

Similar to the pale clouded yellow but the male is a deeper lemon shade. The female is white. Often found on downland, feeding on horseshoe vetch (*Hippocrepis comosa*). Wingspan 2 in. (50 mm). The caterpillar has yellow and black markings.

Mostly seen in southern England, rarely in Ireland, not at all in Scotland.

The caterpillar is clover-green and velvety with a yellowish stripe along its sides. In a very mild winter it may hibernate.

Pale clouded yellow *Colias hyale*

The butterfly has been known in Britain since 1775. Sometimes it arrives in May with the clouded yellow but it is a much rarer migrant and there are long gaps between the years when it is common here. In 1947 it was comparatively common but its numbers here have never exceeded the 2,203 recorded in 1900. It is very similar to the clouded yellow but apart from its lighter background colour, the pale clouded yellow has narrower and more broken black margins to the wings. The two like the same flowery meadows but the pale clouded yellow, although a swift, strong flyer, never travels as far north as its relative.

In some years the early migrants reach Britain in time to produce a generation that is on the wing by August or September. These may lay eggs but the larvae have only a slight chance of surviving the winter unless they are artificially reared. It is the damp weather here that is their enemy.

In 1947 the Belgian lepidopterist L. A. Berger described the butterfly that is now called Berger's clouded yellow, but was previously regarded as a form of the pale clouded yellow. Because of its different caterpillars and food plants, the butterfly was designated a separate species.

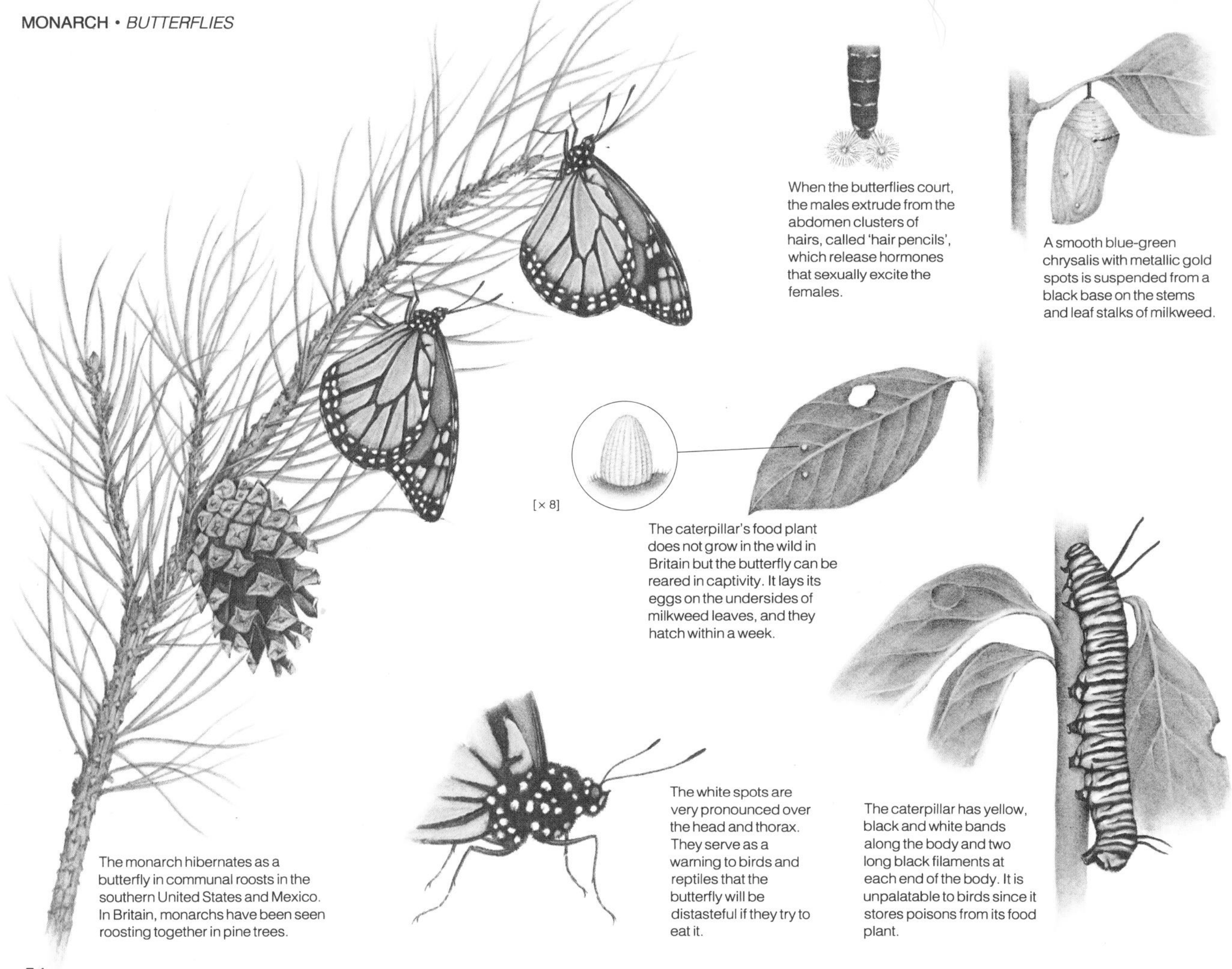

When the butterflies court, the males extrude from the abdomen clusters of hairs, called 'hair pencils', which release hormones that sexually excite the females.

A smooth blue-green chrysalis with metallic gold spots is suspended from a black base on the stems and leaf stalks of milkweed.

The caterpillar's food plant does not grow in the wild in Britain but the butterfly can be reared in captivity. It lays its eggs on the undersides of milkweed leaves, and they hatch within a week.

The white spots are very pronounced over the head and thorax. They serve as a warning to birds and reptiles that the butterfly will be distasteful if they try to eat it.

The caterpillar has yellow, black and white bands along the body and two long black filaments at each end of the body. It is unpalatable to birds since it stores poisons from its food plant.

The monarch hibernates as a butterfly in communal roosts in the southern United States and Mexico. In Britain, monarchs have been seen roosting together in pine trees.

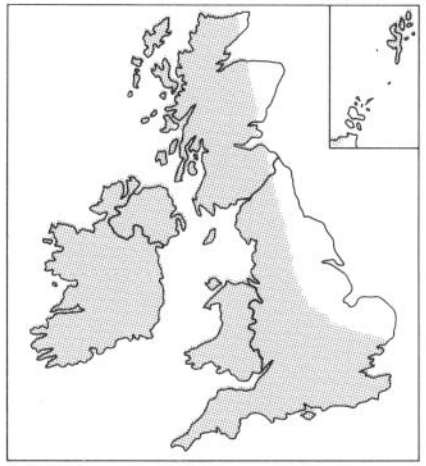

At the end of their long journey across the Atlantic Ocean, monarch butterflies feed on garden flowers and rest on trees.

Black veins

A rare migrant to the west of the British Isles, mostly south-west England.

This large black-and-orange butterfly with white spots is quite unmistakable. Sightings, which are rare, occur in the autumn, between August and November. Its wingspan of 4 in. (10 cm) is the largest of any butterfly found in Britain.

Monarch *Danaus plexippus*

The monarch is an American species of butterfly which, by chance, travels the vast distance of 3,500 miles across the Atlantic Ocean to Britain. It is also called the milkweed after the plant its caterpillars eat. Milkweed exists in Britain only as a very rare garden or greenhouse plant, and there is virtually no chance of the monarch breeding in this country. However monarchs have been known in Britain since 1876. They appear to be blown across the Atlantic by very strong winds, and may fly in company with the even rarer American painted lady and some North American birds. Occasionally butterflies may also arrive from the Canary Islands and Madeira.

The main migration of monarchs occurs every autumn from the northern United States and Canada to as far south as Mexico – about 1,400 miles. Those recorded in Britain are also seen in autumn – between August and October, very occasionally November. After their long sea passage they immediately feed on garden flowers, including buddleia and Michaelmas daisies. Several years may elapse between significant transatlantic crossings. A recent good year was 1981 when 140 were reported, mostly in the Isles of Scilly, Cornwall and Devon.

THE ARISTOCRAT BUTTERFLIES

Early entomologists devised the term aristocrats for the largest and most colourful butterflies in the British countryside, to which they gave noble-sounding names such as purple emperor, red admiral and painted lady.

The aristocrats, together with the fritillaries, make up the large family of British butterflies known as nymphalids. The nymphalids are also called brush-footed butterflies as their short, non-functional front legs are held forward, close to the head, and are covered with long hairs. Consequently they all appear to have only four legs instead of six.

Most of the aristocrats live through the winter as hibernating butterflies. But the red admiral, painted lady and Camberwell beauty are not normally able to survive a British winter, and they migrate to the British Isles from the Continent or North Africa each year.

The stinging nettle has been adopted by several aristocrats as their food plant. One of Britain's best known butterflies, the small tortoiseshell, lays its eggs on stinging nettles, and its dark, spiny caterpillars can be seen eating the leaves in spring and summer. However the large tortoiseshell, which lays its eggs on elm and other trees, is now rare, partly because of the loss of 25 million elm trees from Dutch elm disease since 1970.

The sexes of the aristocrats are not easy to tell apart by colour alone, except for the female purple emperor which lacks the purple in the wings. The females of the peacock and the white admiral are slightly larger than the males.

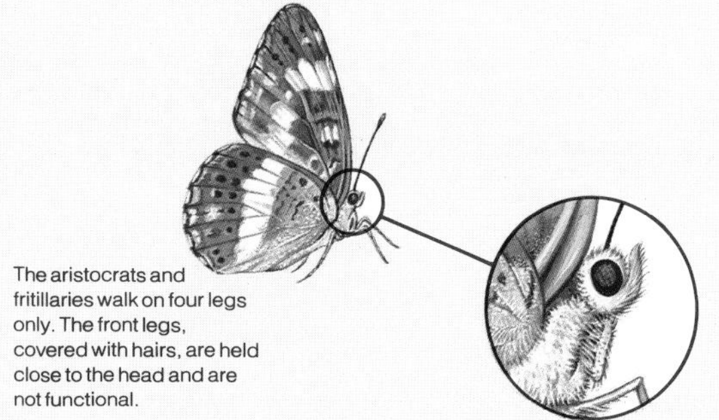

The aristocrats and fritillaries walk on four legs only. The front legs, covered with hairs, are held close to the head and are not functional.

White admiral
Ladoga camilla
Pages 70–71

Peacock
Inachis io
Page 64

Painted lady
Cynthia cardui
Page 65

Comma
Polygonia c-album
Page 67

Camberwell beauty
Nymphalis antiopa
Page 66

Large tortoiseshell
Nymphalis polychloros
Page 59

Purple emperor
Apatura iris
Pages 62–63
(Male above, female below.)

Red admiral
Vanessa atalanta
Pages 68–69

Small tortoiseshell
Aglais urticae
Page 58

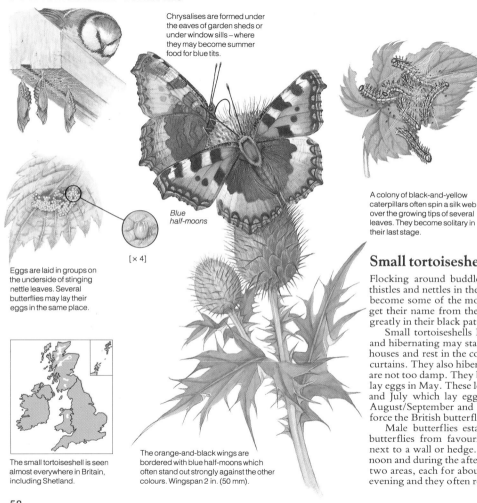

Chrysalises are formed under the eaves of garden sheds or under window sills – where they may become summer food for blue tits.

Blue half-moons

[× 4]

Eggs are laid in groups on the underside of stinging nettle leaves. Several butterflies may lay their eggs in the same place.

The small tortoiseshell is seen almost everywhere in Britain, including Shetland.

The orange-and-black wings are bordered with blue half-moons which often stand out strongly against the other colours. Wingspan 2 in. (50 mm).

A colony of black-and-yellow caterpillars often spin a silk web over the growing tips of several leaves. They become solitary in their last stage.

A group of small tortoiseshells, with their wings fully open, drink the nectar of ice-plant flowers.

Small tortoiseshell *Aglais urticae*

Flocking around buddleias and ice-plants in gardens and on thistles and nettles in the countryside, small tortoiseshells have become some of the most familiar of British butterflies. They get their name from their brightly speckled wings which vary greatly in their black pattern from one to another.

Small tortoiseshells live through the winter as butterflies, and hibernating may start as early as August. They often enter houses and rest in the corners of ceilings or under pelmets and curtains. They also hibernate in garages and garden sheds which are not too damp. They become active again in mid-March, and lay eggs in May. These lead to a generation of butterflies in June and July which lay eggs to produce butterflies that hatch in August/September and live through winter. Immigrants reinforce the British butterflies in July/August.

Male butterflies establish territories by driving off other butterflies from favourite patches in sunny situations, often next to a wall or hedge. Each day they set up a territory about noon and during the afternoon each male will hold, on average, two areas, each for about 90 minutes. Mating takes place in the evening and they often roost for the night under nettle leaves.

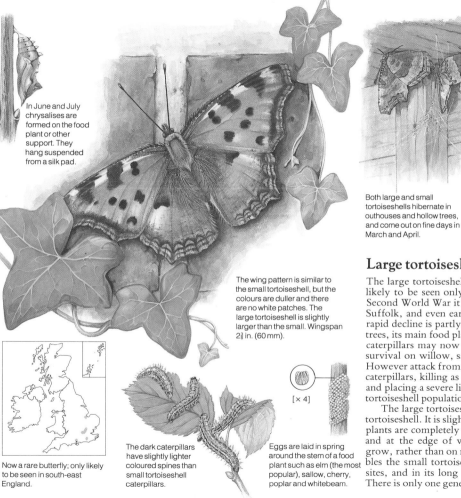

In June and July chrysalises are formed on the food plant or other support. They hang suspended from a silk pad.

The wing pattern is similar to the small tortoiseshell, but the colours are duller and there are no white patches. The large tortoiseshell is slightly larger than the small. Wingspan 2⅜ in. (60 mm).

Both large and small tortoiseshells hibernate in outhouses and hollow trees, and come out on fine days in March and April.

Large tortoiseshells are most likely to be seen resting on trees and walls in April and May.

Now a rare butterfly; only likely to be seen in south-east England.

The dark caterpillars have slightly lighter coloured spines than small tortoiseshell caterpillars.

[× 4]

Eggs are laid in spring around the stem of a food plant such as elm (the most popular), sallow, cherry, poplar and whitebeam.

Large tortoiseshell *Nymphalis polychloros*

The large tortoiseshell is now extremely rare in Britain, and is likely to be seen only in the south-east of England. Until the Second World War it was well established in parts of Essex and Suffolk, and even earlier it lived as far north as Yorkshire. Its rapid decline is partly due to the widespread destruction of elm trees, its main food plant, by Dutch elm disease since 1970. The caterpillars may now become increasingly dependent for their survival on willow, sallow, aspen, whitebeam and birch trees. However attack from ichneumon wasps takes a heavy toll of the caterpillars, killing as many as 99 per cent of colonies each year and placing a severe limitation on any increase in Britain's large tortoiseshell population.

The large tortoiseshell differs in many ways from the small tortoiseshell. It is slightly larger, its colours are dull, and its food plants are completely different. It is found beside country lanes and at the edge of woodlands, particularly where elm trees grow, rather than on nettles and in gardens. However it resembles the small tortoiseshell in its wing design, its hibernation sites, and in its long life of about ten months as a butterfly. There is only one generation each year.

Most nettle-feeding caterpillars leave the nettle-patch to form their chrysalises. They often wander many yards to find a suitable place, such as fence rails, tree bark or garden sheds.

Red admiral caterpillars live alone, taking shelter in leaf-tents.

The nettle feeders

Nettle patches – found in fields, farmyards, orchards and gardens throughout the British Isles – are breeding grounds for aristocrat butterflies. Small tortoiseshells, red admirals, peacocks and commas breed regularly on nettles, and painted ladies breed on them very occasionally. Butterflies bask on the plants and lay their eggs on the tender young leaves. The stinging hairs have no effect on their hard, light bodies. However they do not feed from the drab flowers, which are a poor source of nectar.

When the young caterpillars of small tortoiseshells and peacocks hatch, they live together in a mass of spun silk, eating the nettle tops. Red admiral caterpillars are solitary and live in a secluded leaf-tent.

The advantage of feeding on nettles is that most grazing animals leave the nettles alone because they are tough and will sting. In fact, more than 40 species of insect, including aphids, bugs and beetles, are either completely or partially dependent on nettles for food and shelter.

Small tortoiseshell caterpillars make jerking movements with their heads whenever the nettles are disturbed by a predatory bird. The sudden movement often startles the bird and drives it away.

A female red admiral lays a single egg on a nettle leaf. She will move on to other plants to lay more eggs – all singly.

As they develop, peacock caterpillars look distinctly black with orange feet. They are covered in spines.

The chrysalis is formed on a sallow leaf in June or July and hatches about 18 days later.

When they hatch, the tiny caterpillars have a round, black head, but as they shed their first skins they get two distinctive 'horns' which remain with them as they develop.

Purple emperors can be seen in July and August, flying along paths in deciduous woodland. In the morning they will feed on the nectar of flowers growing along the path. By noon they fly high up into the tops of the trees where they establish territories.

Older caterpillars can be recognised by the 'horns' on the head. They hibernate when small on the exposed twigs of sallow.

Purple emperors may sometimes be seen drinking moisture from animal dung or from dead mammals such as rabbits and field mice.

The female lays her eggs singly on the upper surface of the leaves of sallow in late summer. They hatch after two weeks. [× 2]

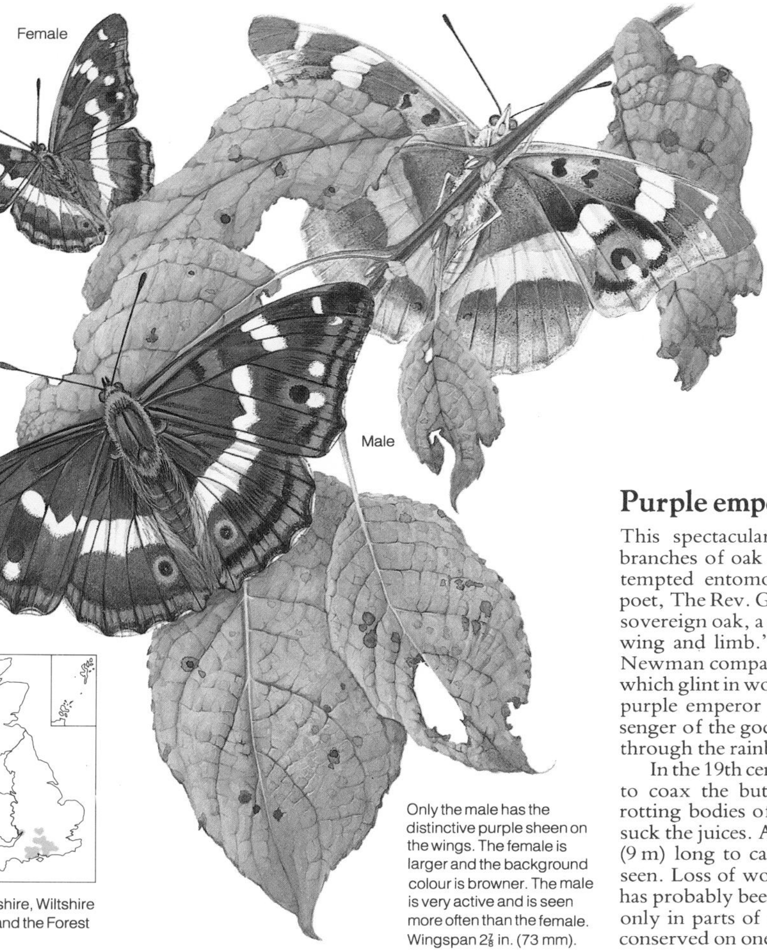

Female

Male

Purple sheen

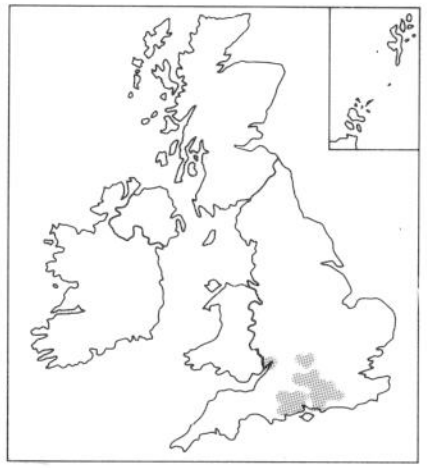

Found in Hampshire, Wiltshire and Berkshire, and the Forest of Dean.

Only the male has the distinctive purple sheen on the wings. The female is larger and the background colour is browner. The male is very active and is seen more often than the female. Wingspan $2\frac{7}{8}$ in. (73 mm).

A male purple emperor perches on an oak leaf, displaying the iridescent wings that have evolved through natural selection.

Purple emperor *Apatura iris*

This spectacular butterfly, which flies around the highest branches of oak trees, has attracted the attention of poets and tempted entomologists into lyrical description. The country poet, The Rev. George Crabbe, wrote 200 years ago: 'Above the sovereign oak, a sovereign skims, the Purple Emp'ror, strong in wing and limb.' And the 19th-century entomologist Edward Newman compared the iridescent colours of the male butterfly, which glint in woodland glades, to 'robes of Tyrian purple'. The purple emperor was given its species name *iris* after the messenger of the gods in Greek mythology who talked to mankind through the rainbow.

In the 19th century, naturalists went to extraordinary lengths to coax the butterflies from the tree-tops. They placed the rotting bodies of animals on the ground to lure them down to suck the juices. And they used nets mounted on poles up to 30 ft (9 m) long to catch them. Now the purple emperor is rarely seen. Loss of woodland, rather than the activities of collectors, has probably been the major reason for its decline. It now occurs only in parts of the New Forest and the Forest of Dean and is conserved on one Ministry of Defence site.

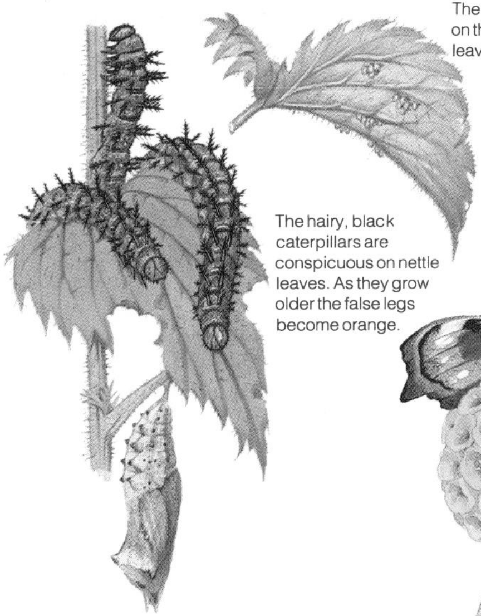

The eggs are laid in groups on the underside of nettle leaves.

The hairy, black caterpillars are conspicuous on nettle leaves. As they grow older the false legs become orange.

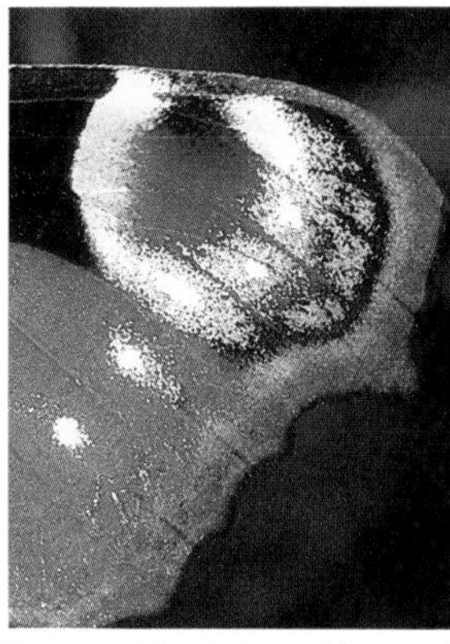

The peacock has the largest false eyes of any British butterfly. They evolved to deter birds and lizards.

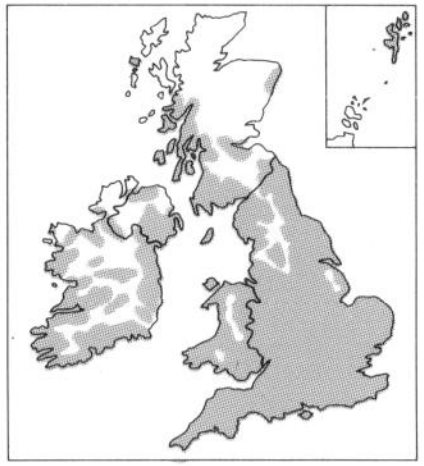

False eyes

The chrysalis is formed in a variety of places, including nettle stems and tree trunks. It always hangs from its silk pad, and may have gold marks.

The four false eyes on the peacock's wings make it unmistakable. At rest, only two are visible, as the fore-wings cover the hind-wings. The underside of the wings is almost black. Peacocks often feed on garden flowers, such as *Buddleia globosa*. Wingspan $2\frac{3}{8}$ in. (60 mm).

Widely distributed in Britain, except the north of Scotland and Orkney.

Peacock *Inachis io*

For butterfly lovers, the peacock is a particular favourite because of its rich colours and its ability to live and breed in patches of stinging nettles in corners of the garden. In June the black, hairy caterpillars are easily found on the nettle leaves. In late summer and autumn the butterflies visit buddleia, ice-plants and rotten fruit, jostling for position with other butterflies. Peacocks can become numerous in orchards when the fruit ripens. Their colours make them an almost startling sight as they bask in full sunshine.

The peacock can also be found along woodland rides, beside country roads and in waste areas. It patrols its territory, making frequent sorties to investigate intruding flies and other insects. It uses sound as well as its coloured false eyes to frighten away a predator such as a bird. As the predator approaches, the butterfly will open and close its wings rapidly, making a scraping noise as the wings rub together.

In winter peacocks hibernate on the ceiling or in the corners of sheds and outhouses, and may even come into houses and conservatories looking for suitable sites. They can live for almost a year – from July until the following May.

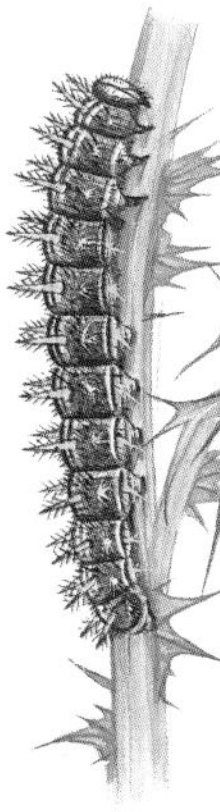

The chrysalis which is suspended from the food plant hatches after about two weeks.

The fully grown caterpillar has yellow or black spines and a yellow stripe down each side.

White markings

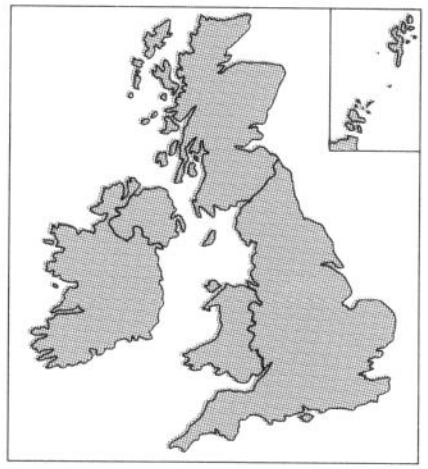

A regular migrant which has been seen over most parts of the British Isles.

The white marks on the black tips of the fore-wings distinguish the painted lady from the tortoiseshells. It is a large butterfly, with slightly pointed wings, seen on garden flowers and wayside thistles. It is shown here on tree mallow (*Malva arborea*). Wingspan 2¼ in. (57 mm).

Eggs are laid singly on the upper surface of plants including thistles, mallows, burdocks and stinging nettles.

Painted ladies are easily attracted to the nectar of many flowers in the garden, particularly buddleia.

Painted lady *Cynthia cardui*

Each May and June painted ladies migrate to Britain from south-west Europe and North Africa, a distance of more than 600 miles (1,000 km). In some years they are scarce, in others common. Britain was inundated with painted ladies in 1980, so many that the numbers were impossible to estimate, but there were certainly more than the 30,000 recorded in 1948. Other notable years have been 1952, 1966 and 1969.

The painted lady is a very powerful flyer. When migrating it flies at about 8 or 10 mph (13–15 kph), skimming over meadows and hedgerows. Some painted ladies reach the Shetlands and Iceland, but there is no evidence that they return in any numbers. The painted lady cannot survive the cold and humid British winter in any of its stages – egg, caterpillar, chrysalis or butterfly – but early migrants lay eggs on a wide variety of British wild flowers, giving rise to a second generation of butterflies in September and October. These die when the cold weather arrives.

When not migrating, the painted lady will settle down wherever there are flowers – perhaps on a good stand of thistles or in a garden – and devote themselves to seeking out the nectar.

Blue spots

Cream fringe

The dark colour of the wings, with their contrasting cream border lined with blue spots, makes the Camberwell beauty different from all other British butterflies. The undersides of the wings are similar, without the blue markings. Sexes are almost identical. Wingspan $2\frac{1}{2}$ in. (64 mm).

A Camberwell beauty feeds on ripe blackberries, characteristically keeping its wings fully outspread.

Camberwell beauty *Nymphalis antiopa*

This exquisite butterfly, with wings like maroon velvet, was first discovered in Britain in August 1748, at the village of Camberwell, just 2 miles south of London Bridge. It was attracted to the willow trees that grew abundantly there, and took its name from the village, which later became absorbed into London. It was given various names by early entomologists, including 'white petticoat' and 'mourning cloak' after the pale hem-like fringe.

The Camberwell beauty is rarely seen, as it migrates each year from Scandinavia and has never been known to breed in this country. Hibernating butterflies probably arrive at east-coast ports on imported timber, and fly off as the weather grows warmer in the spring. Others may fly across the North Sea from Scandinavia. Camberwell beauties may be seen any time between March and August, majestically gliding around the tops of willow trees or along the streams where willows grow. They are also seen in orchards feeding on ripe fruit. They spend hours basking in the sun but, when disturbed, will dart off at great speed. They have been recorded flying over short distances at about 17 mph (26 kph).

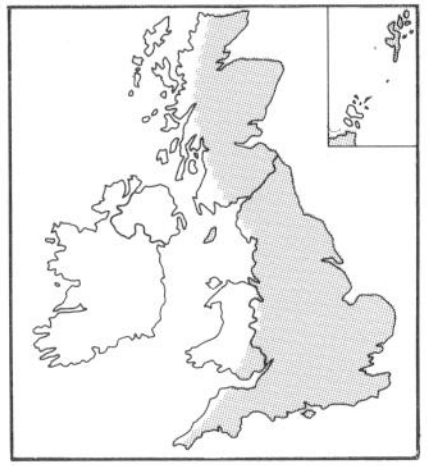

An irregular and rare visitor, most likely to be met along the eastern side of Britain.

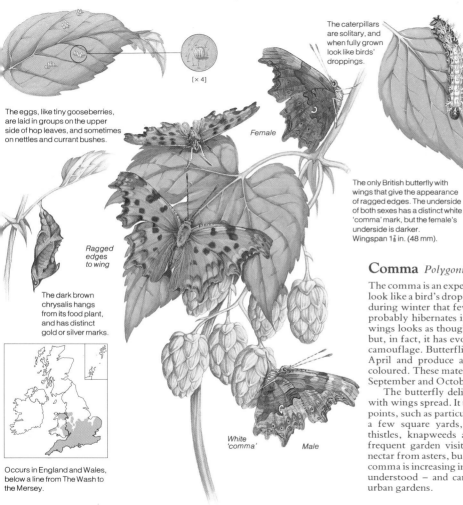

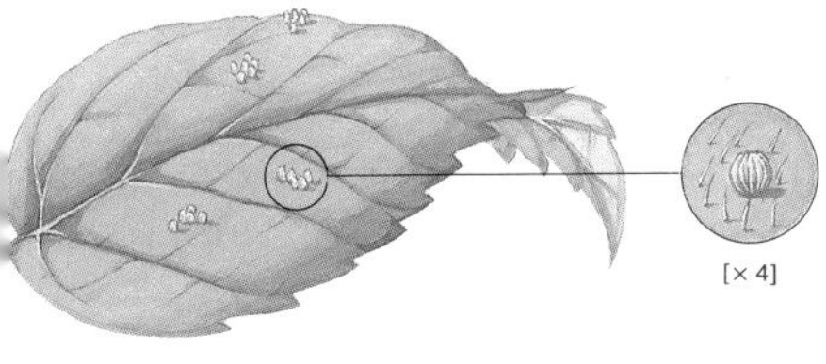

[× 4]

The eggs, like tiny gooseberries, are laid in groups on the upper side of hop leaves, and sometimes on nettles and currant bushes.

The caterpillars are solitary, and when fully grown look like birds' droppings.

Female

Ragged edges to wing

The dark brown chrysalis hangs from its food plant, and has distinct gold or silver marks.

The only British butterfly with wings that give the appearance of ragged edges. The underside of both sexes has a distinct white 'comma' mark, but the female's underside is darker. Wingspan $1\frac{7}{8}$ in. (48 mm).

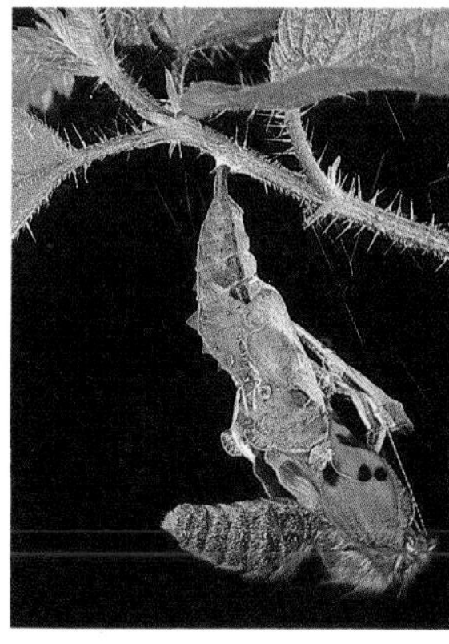

A comma butterfly works its way out of the chrysalis, suspended from a silk pad on a nettle stem.

White 'comma'

Male

Occurs in England and Wales, below a line from The Wash to the Mersey.

Comma *Polygonia c-album*

The comma is an expert at disguise. Not only does the caterpillar look like a bird's dropping but the butterfly hides so successfully during winter that few naturalists have seen its resting place. It probably hibernates in hollow trees. The ragged outline of the wings looks as though the butterfly has been torn on brambles but, in fact, it has evolved through natural selection to provide camouflage. Butterflies that have hibernated mate in March and April and produce a first generation in July which is light-coloured. These mate and produce a darker second generation in September and October.

The butterfly delights in sunshine, and will bask for hours with wings spread. It tends to be solitary and has favourite perch points, such as particular leaves. It may live in an area as small as a few square yards, sipping nectar from bramble flowers, thistles, knapweeds and hemp agrimony. Commas are also frequent garden visitors, and can spend all day drinking the nectar from asters, buddleias and Michaelmas daisies. Today the comma is increasing in population – for reasons that are not fully understood – and can be abundant in the countryside and in urban gardens.

The caterpillars rest in a characteristic bent shape inside their tents. There are both green and brown forms.

Single eggs are laid by spring migrants on the upper surface of nettle leaves, and occasionally on the leaves of hops and pellitory-of-the-wall.

Butterflies are on the wing from May to October. Those seen before July are migrants from the Continent.

The red admiral enjoys the juice of rotting fruit, and will compete on autumn windfalls with wasps and other butterflies, such as peacocks and commas, constantly opening and closing its wings.

The solitary caterpillars feed inside protective tents of leaves which they draw together with silk threads.

The chrysalis, which has attractive gold spots, is formed in summer and autumn, and may be seen suspended from the food plant.

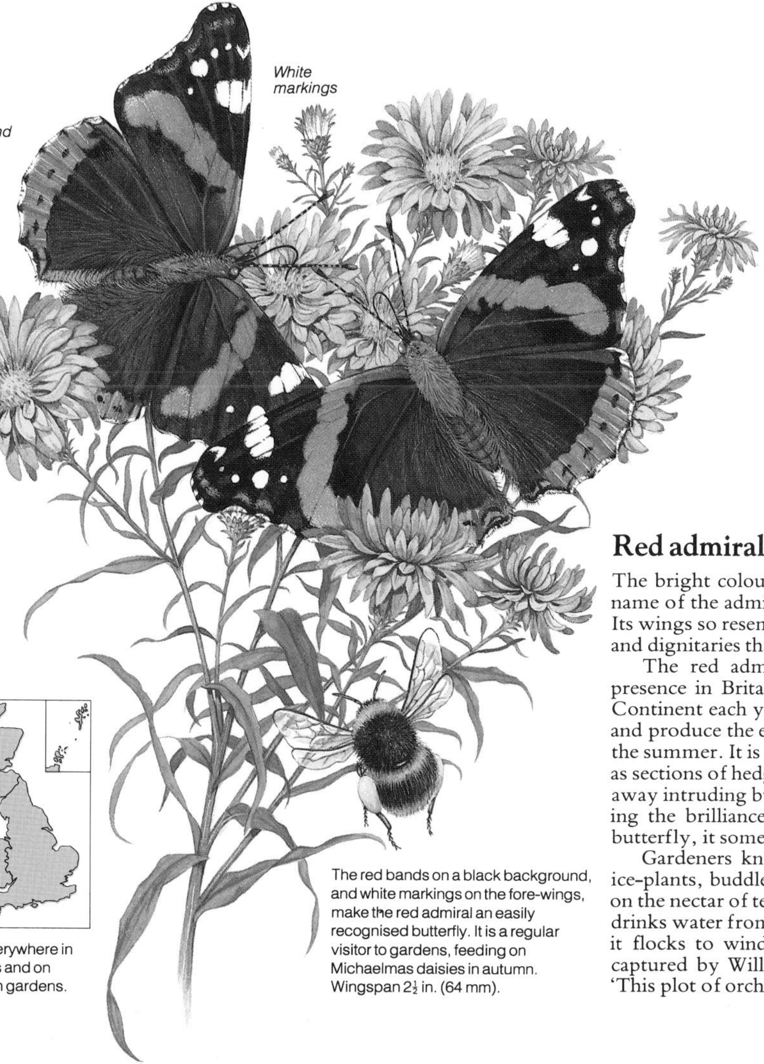

Red band

White markings

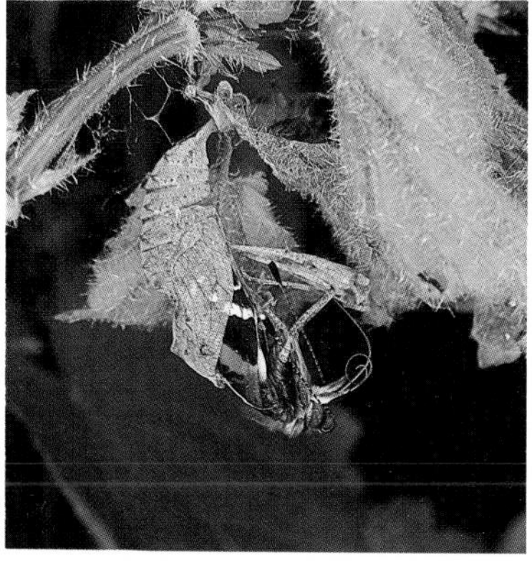

After spending 17 days transforming from a caterpillar to a butterfly, a red admiral emerges from its chrysalis which hangs from a nettle leaf.

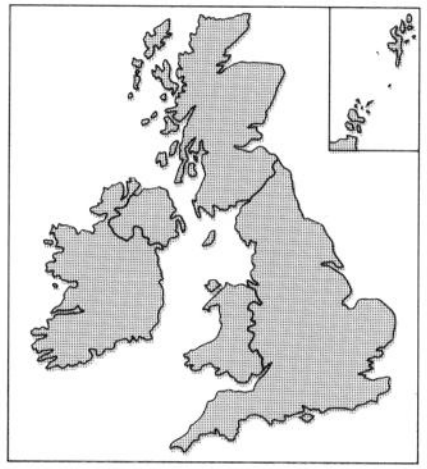

Red admiral *Vanessa atalanta*

The bright colours of the butterfly earned it the 18th-century name of the admirable, from which its modern name evolved. Its wings so resembled the robes and livery colours of noblemen and dignitaries that it was also called the alderman.

The red admiral is a familiar butterfly even though its presence in Britain depends on influxes of migrants from the Continent each year. The first butterflies start arriving in May and produce the eggs which give rise to a resident generation in the summer. It is a fast flyer which patrols small territories such as sections of hedgerows, lanes and woodland clearings, driving away intruding butterflies. It often rests and suns itself, displaying the brilliance of its outstretched wings. Unusually for a butterfly, it sometimes flies at night.

Gardeners know the red admiral as an autumn visitor to ice-plants, buddleia and Michaelmas daisies. In the wild it feeds on the nectar of teasel, scabious, clover and the flowers of ivy. It drinks water from puddles and the sap exuding from trees. And it flocks to windfall apples rotting on the ground – a scene captured by William Wordsworth in his poem *To a butterfly*: 'This plot of orchard-ground is ours.'

Found almost everywhere in Britain – in valleys and on mountains, and in gardens.

The red bands on a black background, and white markings on the fore-wings, make the red admiral an easily recognised butterfly. It is a regular visitor to gardens, feeding on Michaelmas daisies in autumn. Wingspan $2\frac{1}{2}$ in. (64 mm).

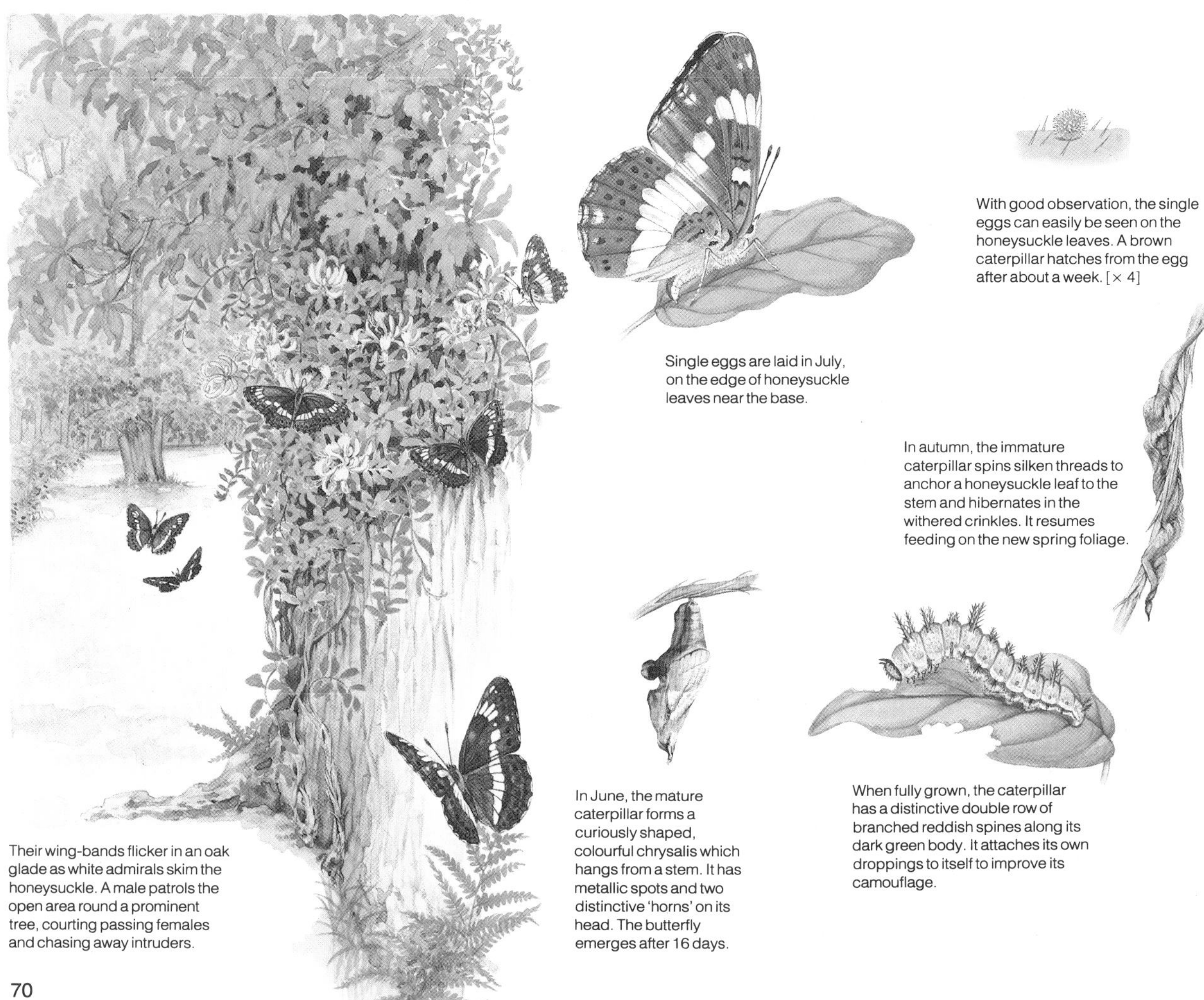

Single eggs are laid in July, on the edge of honeysuckle leaves near the base.

With good observation, the single eggs can easily be seen on the honeysuckle leaves. A brown caterpillar hatches from the egg after about a week. [× 4]

In autumn, the immature caterpillar spins silken threads to anchor a honeysuckle leaf to the stem and hibernates in the withered crinkles. It resumes feeding on the new spring foliage.

Their wing-bands flicker in an oak glade as white admirals skim the honeysuckle. A male patrols the open area round a prominent tree, courting passing females and chasing away intruders.

In June, the mature caterpillar forms a curiously shaped, colourful chrysalis which hangs from a stem. It has metallic spots and two distinctive 'horns' on its head. The butterfly emerges after 16 days.

When fully grown, the caterpillar has a distinctive double row of branched reddish spines along its dark green body. It attaches its own droppings to itself to improve its camouflage.

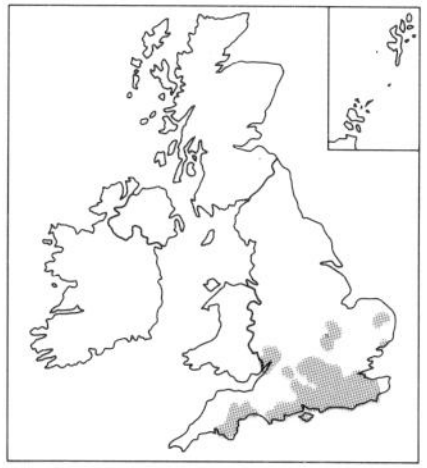

Newly emerged from its chrysalis, a white admiral butterfly dries its wings. It flies mostly in July but may appear earlier, in late June.

White band

Limited to southern England; mostly in Wiltshire, Dorset, Hampshire and Sussex.

A large, dark, woodland butterfly with a distinctive white band running across fore and hind-wings. The underside is attractively patterned. In some individuals the white band is darkened and the underside stained with black. The butterflies are shown feeding on the flowers of bramble, their favourite nectar source. Wingspan 2⅜ in. (60 mm).

White admiral *Ladoga camilla*

When this butterfly was called the white admiral in the 18th century it was an uncommon sight in the well-managed woods of England. However the mid-20th century has seen a population explosion, and the white admiral has spread out from the central counties of southern England into the West Country and Midlands. This expansion followed a series of warm summers in the 1930s and the neglect of coppice woodland where trees were once regularly trimmed and the undergrowth kept tidy. Neglect has allowed rampant growth of honeysuckle, the sole food plant of the white admiral's caterpillars.

The butterflies gather in sunny, secluded pockets of woodland throughout July. The males establish territories by making repeated powerful flights around their patch, one moment swooping low over the vegetation, the next soaring up to perch high in the trees. Solitary females flutter around honeysuckle, looking for suitable egg-laying sites. The butterflies may live for four weeks, frequently visiting clumps of brambles to drink nectar. By the end of the month their wings become torn and battered by thorns and a butterfly may end its life no longer able to take evading action from a predatory bird or dragonfly.

THE FRITILLARIES

The word fritillary is the name of both a spotted plant – the snake's-head fritillary – and of a group of spotted butterflies in the Nymphalidae family (see also Aristocrats, pp. 56–57). Both the snake's-head fritillary and the heath fritillary butterfly are now endangered species in Britain.

Fritillaries vary greatly in the spotted pattern on their wings and in the background colour. This can create difficulty in distinguishing one species from another; however, males and females are fairly easy to recognise in most species as the females are larger and lighter coloured, with rounded wingtips.

Most of the British fritillaries live in open sections of woodland – glades, rides, clearings and woodland margins. Five species are dependent for their caterpillars' food on woodland violets. Populations of fritillaries in Britain have suffered dramatically since the early 1960s, as woods and scrubland have been cleared for farming, and deciduous woods have been replaced by conifer plantations. The sight of large orange-brown fritillaries flying through woodland clearings in south-east England is now only a memory in many places.

Male

Dark green fritillary
Argynnis aglaja
Page 78

Male underside

Male

Marsh fritillary
Euphydryas aurinia
Page 75

Male underside

The snake's-head fritillary is a rare wild flower of meadows. The word fritillary comes from the Latin *fritillus*, meaning dice box. It may originally have been used to describe the chequer pattern on the flower in the mistaken belief that *fritillus* also meant chess-board.

Male

Female underside

Duke of Burgundy fritillary
Hamearis lucina

This species shares the fritillaries' colours and name, but is not one of the Nymphalidae family. It is the only British member of the Riodinidae family.

Page 83

Male

Small pearl-bordered fritillary
Boloria selene
Page 77

Male underside

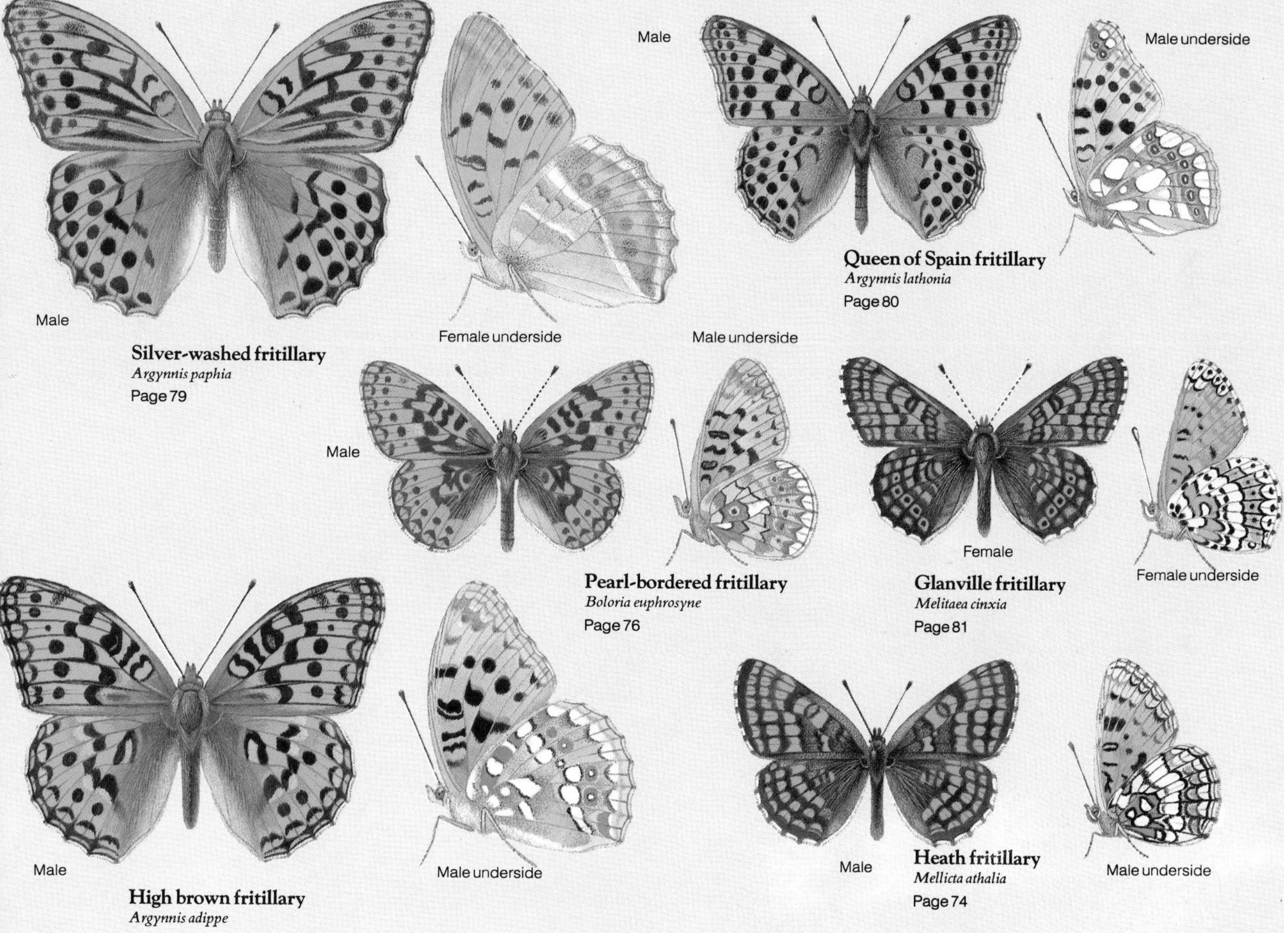

Silver-washed fritillary
Argynnis paphia
Page 79

Queen of Spain fritillary
Argynnis lathonia
Page 80

Pearl-bordered fritillary
Boloria euphrosyne
Page 76

Glanville fritillary
Melitaea cinxia
Page 81

High brown fritillary
Argynnis adippe
Page 82

Heath fritillary
Mellicta athalia
Page 74

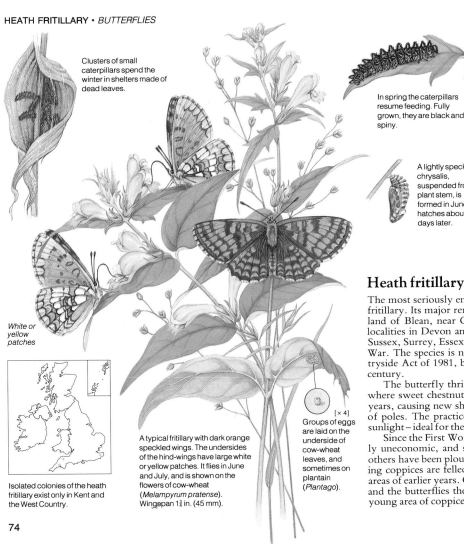

Clusters of small caterpillars spend the winter in shelters made of dead leaves.

In spring the caterpillars resume feeding. Fully grown, they are black and spiny.

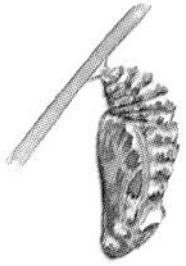

A lightly speckled chrysalis, suspended from a plant stem, is formed in June. It hatches about 25 days later.

A heath fritillary feeds on the nectar of groundsel in the sunlight of an open coppiced woodland.

White or yellow patches

A typical fritillary with dark orange speckled wings. The undersides of the hind-wings have large white or yellow patches. It flies in June and July, and is shown on the flowers of cow-wheat (*Melampyrum pratense*). Wingspan 1¾ in. (45 mm).

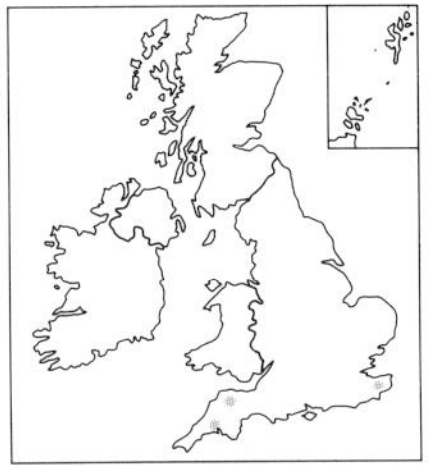

[× 4]
Groups of eggs are laid on the underside of cow-wheat leaves, and sometimes on plantain (*Plantago*).

Isolated colonies of the heath fritillary exist only in Kent and the West Country.

Heath fritillary *Mellicta athalia*

The most seriously endangered butterfly in Britain is the heath fritillary. Its major remaining stronghold is the Kentish woodland of Blean, near Canterbury. It also survives in two other localities in Devon and Cornwall, but it has become extinct in Sussex, Surrey, Essex and Gloucestershire since the First World War. The species is now protected by the Wildlife and Countryside Act of 1981, but it could become extinct in Britain this century.

The butterfly thrived well in traditional coppice woodland where sweet chestnut trees were cut back to a stump every 15 years, causing new shoots to grow and providing regular crops of poles. The practice created open woodland with plenty of sunlight – ideal for the caterpillar's main food plant, cow-wheat.

Since the First World War coppicing has become increasingly uneconomic, and some areas have become overgrown and others have been ploughed up or planted with conifers. Surviving coppices are felled in very large plots, instead of the small areas of earlier years. Consequently the seeds of the food plants, and the butterflies themselves, are less able to move from one young area of coppice to another.

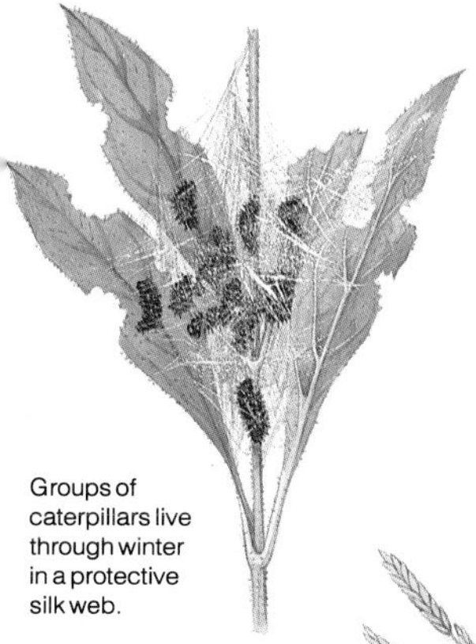

Groups of caterpillars live through winter in a protective silk web.

When fully grown the black caterpillars leave the web and can be found singly on food plants in spring.

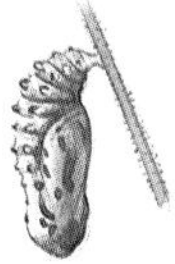

The chrysalis, which hangs from a stem in late spring, has black-and-orange specks.

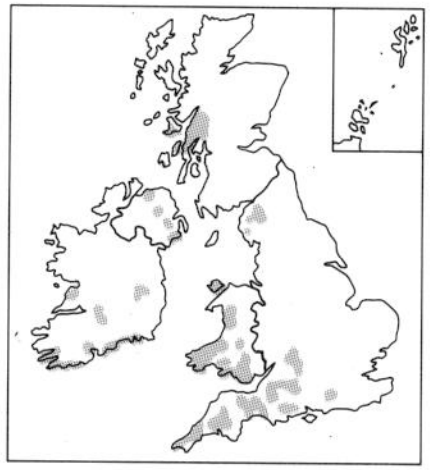

Found in western Scotland, Wales and England, and in Ireland.

The upper sides have orange-red and yellowish markings on a black background. The undersides are lighter. The butterfly is mostly found in wet meadows. Wingspan 1¾ in. (45 mm).

[× 3]

Piles of eggs are laid on the underside of the leaves of scabious and plantain.

The marsh fritillary is a slow flyer which may never leave the secluded meadow where it feeds on flower nectar.

Marsh fritillary *Euphydryas aurinia*

Until the beginning of this century, the marsh fritillary was called the greasy fritillary, because of the shiny undersides of the fore-wings. Another curious name was the dishclout, which likened the butterfly to a dirty dishcloth. The marsh fritillary can be locally abundant in late May and early June in places where devil's-bit scabious grows. The plant is eaten by the caterpillars, and thrives in damp meadows and wet hollows on chalk downs. At the end of the last century there were reports from Ireland of fields black with the caterpillars, which also eat plantain, foxglove, wood sage and honeysuckle. Both the butterflies and the caterpillars live and feed in groups.

The marsh fritillary is a vulnerable butterfly. The Nature Conservancy Council announced in 1981 that there had been a 60–70 per cent loss of populations of the species, which has now almost vanished from eastern England and the Midlands. The decline was due to drainage of wet meadows and the ploughing up of downland. The butterflies are not active flyers like other fritillaries, but the male flies more often than the female, often settling on yellow flowers such as dandelion, bird's-foot-trefoil and hawkbit. Each butterfly lives for about a month.

Seven 'pearls' border the margins of the underside of the hind-wings. The butterfly can be distinguished from the small pearl-bordered fritillary (opposite) in having only two silver patches on the central area of the underside. It is seen in May and June. Wingspan 1¾ in. (45 mm).

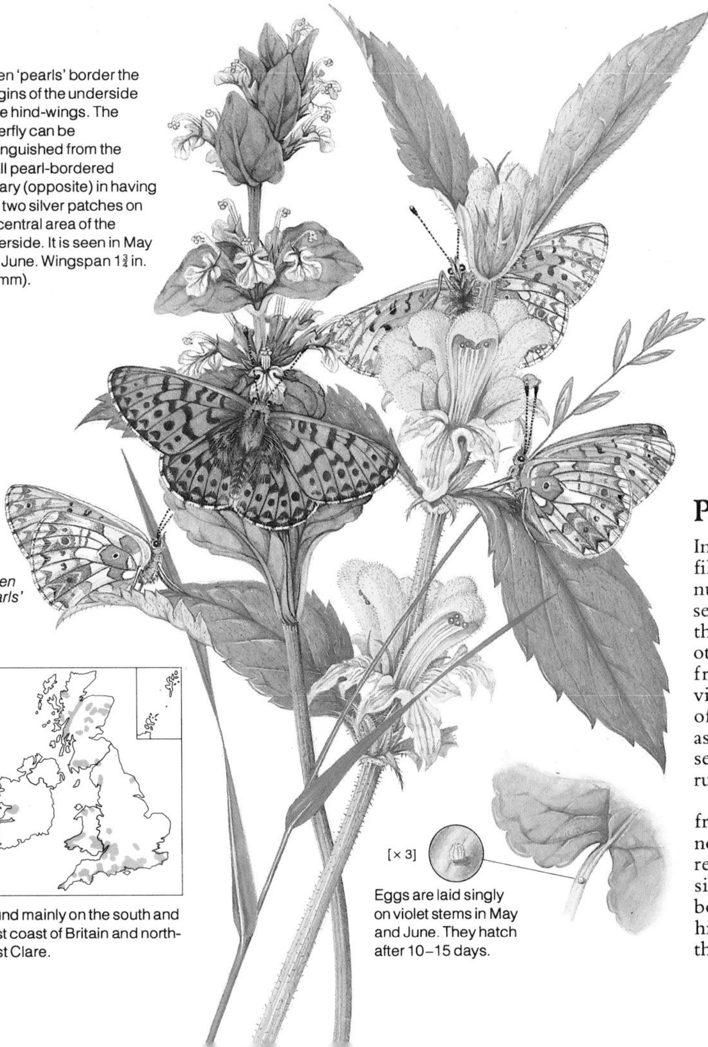

Seven 'pearls'

Found mainly on the south and west coast of Britain and north-west Clare.

[× 3]

Eggs are laid singly on violet stems in May and June. They hatch after 10–15 days.

The full-grown caterpillar, recognisable by the yellow spines, feeds on violets in spring after spending the winter in curled-up leaves.

The chrysalis, looking like a dead leaf, is formed in May. The butterfly hatches in about ten days.

The scientific term for the butterfly refers to Euphrosyne (meaning Joyfulness), one of the Graces of Greek mythology.

Pearl-bordered fritillary *Boloria euphrosyne*

In past centuries, spring meadows and woodland glades were filled with violets which attracted fritillary butterflies in great numbers to lay their eggs on the leaves. But the 20th century has seen meadows and glades ploughed up to grow crops. And in the meadows that remain herbicides are used to destroy plants other than grass, to give more efficient farming. Pearl-bordered fritillaries are restricted mostly to woods and coppices where violets still grow in clearings and along paths. They spend much of their time patrolling territories and visiting wild flowers such as bugles to drink the nectar. In the evenings they will bask in the setting sun, and at night they rest under the heads of grasses and rushes.

The pearl-bordered fritillary was once known as the April fritillary, but the calendar was put back by 11 days in 1752 and now it is not normally seen until May. It is very similar to its relative the small pearl-bordered fritillary (opposite). The upper sides of the wings are almost identical in the two species, and both have a 'string of pearls' decorating the underside of the hind-wings, but the pearl-bordered has fewer silver patches on the underside other than the 'pearls'.

The young caterpillars hibernate in a curled leaf. The full-grown caterpillar has orange spines – the first two protruding as 'horns'.

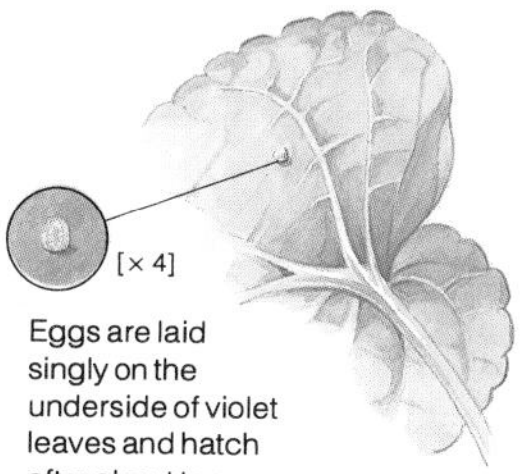

[× 4]

Eggs are laid singly on the underside of violet leaves and hatch after about ten days.

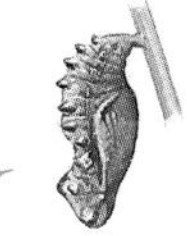

The dark chrysalis is formed in May or June on the stem of a violet or nearby plant.

A small pearl-bordered fritillary, with its wings outstretched, drinks the nectar from a bugle flower.

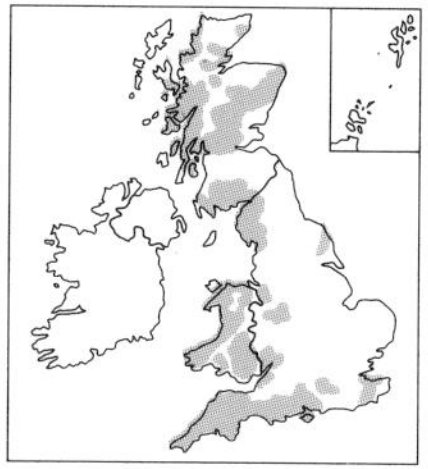

A wider distribution than the pearl-bordered, but absent from Ireland.

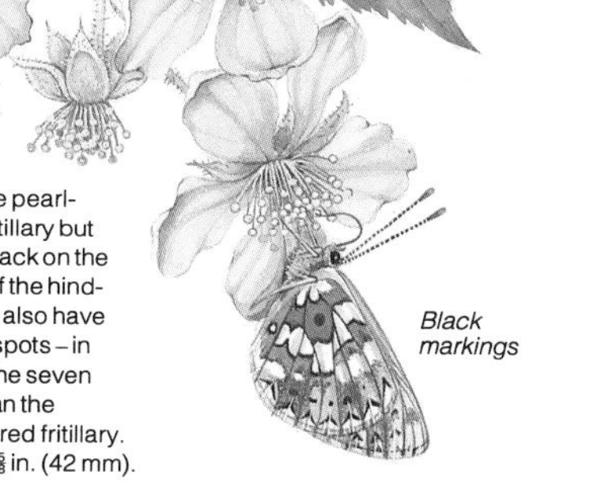

Similar to the pearl-bordered fritillary but with more black on the underside of the hind-wings. They also have more silver spots – in addition to the seven 'pearls' – than the pearl-bordered fritillary. Wingspan 1⅝ in. (42 mm).

Black markings

Small pearl-bordered fritillary *Boloria selene*

Time and place help to distinguish the small pearl-bordered fritillary from the very similar pearl-bordered fritillary. The small pearl-bordered flies in June and July – a little later than the pearl-bordered which is seen in May and June. And the small pearl-bordered is found in more open areas, such as grassy mountain slopes in Wales and Scotland, together with the moorlands and moist sea-cliffs of Cornwall. However both species may be encountered in woodland clearings in June, and there the most certain means of identification is the pattern on the underside of the hind-wings. The small pearl-bordered fritillary has more pronounced silver spots – in addition to the 'string of pearls' – than the pearl-bordered.

Both species are very active, flying to and fro in glades and clearings. The small pearl-bordered flies swiftly close to the ground in search of nectar-rich flowers such as bugle. There is normally one generation a year, but in hot summers there may be a second in late August and September.

Both species have become rare in eastern Britain since the Second World War because of loss of woodlands, coppices and grassy heathlands which have become farmland or pine forests.

Green underside and silver spots

A large fritillary which can be identified by the green markings and silver spots on the underside of the hind-wings. It may be found drinking the nectar of thistles. Wingspan 2¼ in. (57 mm).

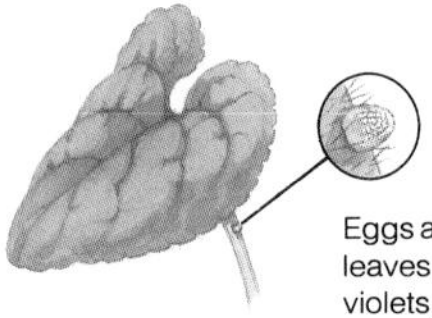

[× 4]

Eggs are laid on leaves and stems of violets, and hatch after about 17 days.

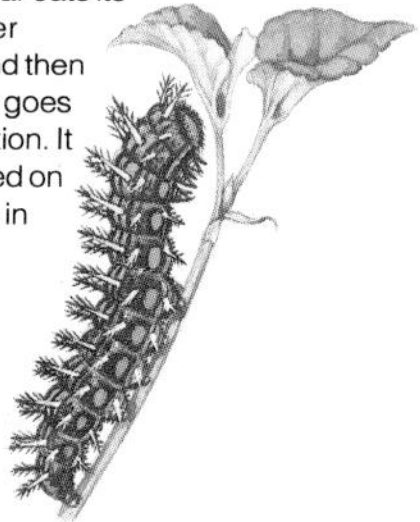

The caterpillar eats its eggshell after hatching, and then immediately goes into hibernation. It begins to feed on violet leaves in March.

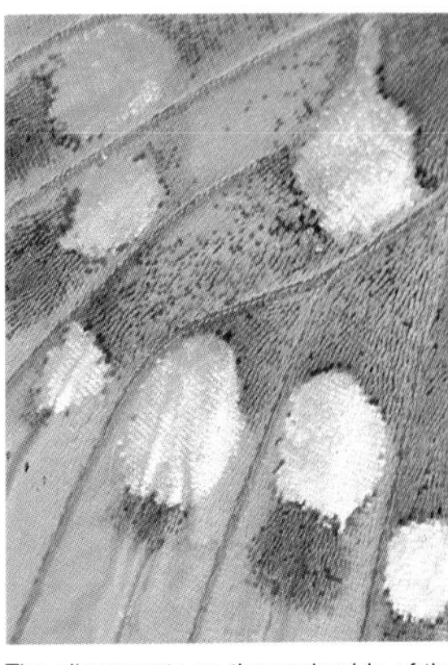

The silver spots on the underside of the hind-wings are typical of the larger fritillary butterflies.

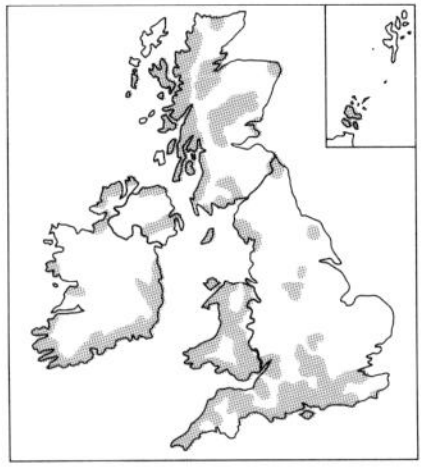

A predominantly western distribution in Britain; commonest near the coast.

The chrysalis is formed in June at the base of the violet plant, among a few leaves drawn together. The butterfly hatches a month later.

Dark green fritillary *Argynnis aglaja*

The butterfly gets its name from the olive-green colour suffused between the silver spots on the underside of the wings. The spots at the base of the wing can be fused together in a form of the butterfly called *charlotta*, which was once named the Queen of England fritillary. The dark green is one of Britain's three large fritillaries and has a similar colour and pattern on the upper side of the wings as the other two – the silver-washed and high brown fritillaries. However each species has its own characteristic markings on the underside of the wings. The dark green fritillary also differs from the other two species in being found outside woods. It is more often found in open meadows and downland, woodland margins, sea-cliffs and moorlands. All three species have decreased in Britain over the past 50 years, probably because large areas of their habitats have been turned over to agriculture.

The dark green fritillary is a very fast flyer which skims and soars between flowers and between its perch-points on trees. It often visits thistles for nectar and can also be seen basking on the ground and on ferns. Each butterfly lives about six weeks during July and August.

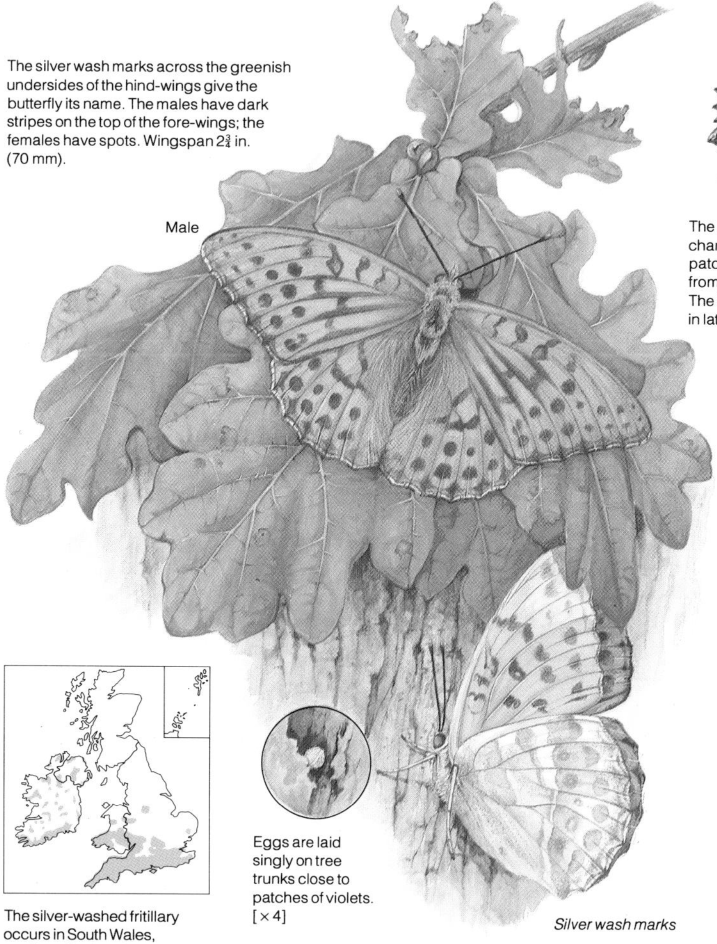

The silver wash marks across the greenish undersides of the hind-wings give the butterfly its name. The males have dark stripes on the top of the fore-wings; the females have spots. Wingspan 2¾ in. (70 mm).

Male

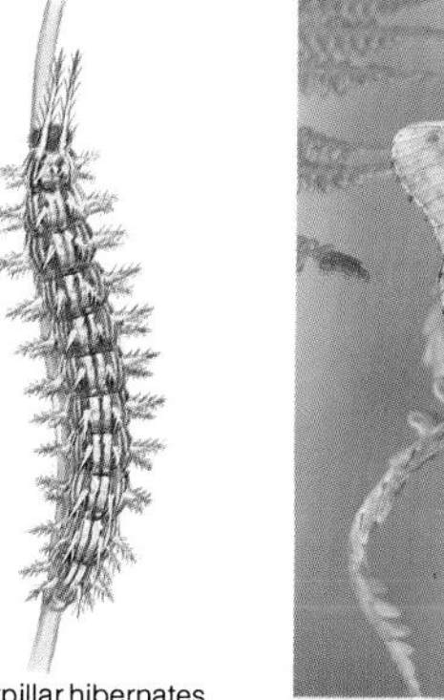

The chrysalis, with characteristic gold patches, hangs from the food plant. The butterfly hatches in late June or July.

The caterpillar hibernates on the tree trunk until spring, when it descends to feed on violet leaves.

A silver-washed fritillary rests on woodland bracken. It will also visit garden flowers such as marigolds and petunias.

The silver-washed fritillary occurs in South Wales, southern England and Ireland.

Eggs are laid singly on tree trunks close to patches of violets. [×4]

Silver wash marks

Silver-washed fritillary *Argynnis paphia*

This big-winged, colourful butterfly is the largest British fritillary. The sexes are easy to tell apart as the male has distinctive black bars on the fore-wings from which he produces scent to attract females. A dull green form of the female occasionally occurs, and is called the greenish silver-washed fritillary. The butterfly is a true woodland species, found in clearings, rides and wood margins and along foresters' tracks. In the New Forest they were described by the naturalist William Hudson at the turn of the century as 'playing about the bracken in some sunlit space in the oak woods . . . opening their orange-red spotted wings on the broad vivid fronds . . . like a mosaic of minute green tesserae'. They roost at the top of the trees at night and in dull weather, but when the sun shines they 'fall like leaves' to the bramble patches and thistles to which they are strongly attracted by the nectar in the flowers.

Each butterfly lives for about five weeks in July and August. They may be found warming themselves in the shafts of sunlight that pour into oak woods. There is one generation a year, and the butterfly is unique in Britain in laying its eggs on tree trunks.

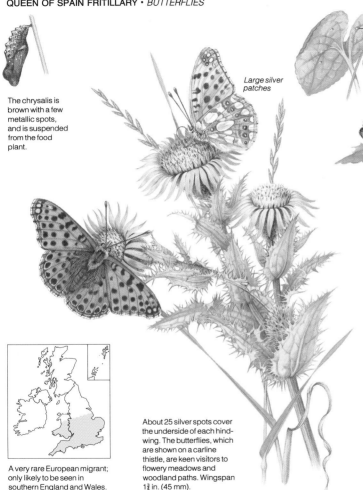

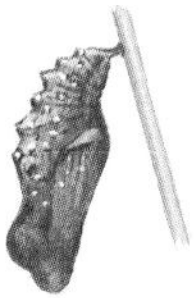

The chrysalis is brown with a few metallic spots, and is suspended from the food plant.

Large silver patches

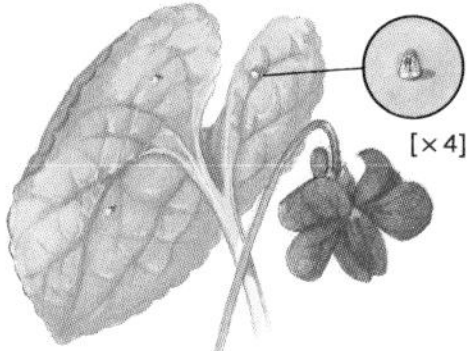

[×4]

Up to 100 eggs are laid separately on the flowers and leaves of violets. Borage and sainfoin are also recorded as food plants.

The black caterpillar has six rows of spines along its body and a yellow stripe along its sides. There is little chance of it surviving a British winter.

The large mirrors of silver on the underside of the wings glisten as a Queen of Spain rests on a wild flower.

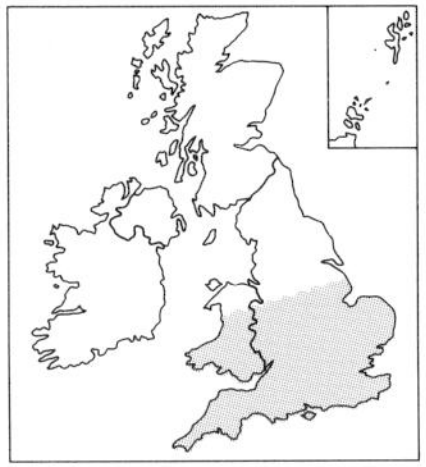

A very rare European migrant; only likely to be seen in southern England and Wales.

About 25 silver spots cover the underside of each hindwing. The butterflies, which are shown on a carline thistle, are keen visitors to flowery meadows and woodland paths. Wingspan 1¾ in. (45 mm).

Queen of Spain fritillary *Argynnis lathonia*

This is the grandest and rarest of the British fritillaries, with large pools of liquid silver on its wings that can glitter in the sunlight of a woodland clearing. The British lepidopterist W. Furneaux wrote in the 1890s: 'This royal personage is not easily mistaken for any of the meaner fritillaries.' It was given its regal name by another British butterfly enthusiast, Moses Harris, in 1775, but had been known as early as 1710 when it was called the lesser-spotted or Riga fritillary. In calling it the Queen of Spain, Harris was relating its silver spots to the riches of the Spanish monarchy.

The butterfly is a rare migrant from the Continent, and only two or three are recorded in Britain in most years. A chance encounter with one is most likely in the south-east and south-west of England between May and September. It is found in sunny woodland glades and along paths, and in meadows studded with wild flowers. It is a swift flyer that flits from flower to flower, especially scabious, knapweeds and thistles. The wings are usually held wide open, rarely revealing the spectacular silver spots on the undersides. Like most British fritillaries, it lays its eggs on hedgerow and woodland violets.

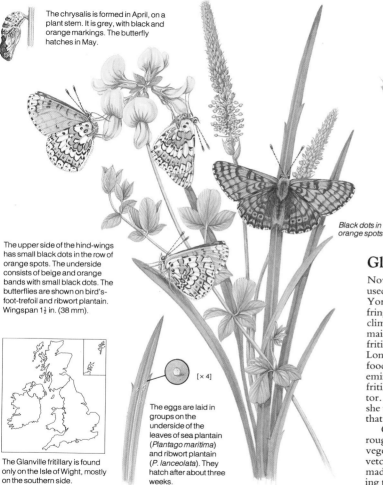

The chrysalis is formed in April, on a plant stem. It is grey, with black and orange markings. The butterfly hatches in May.

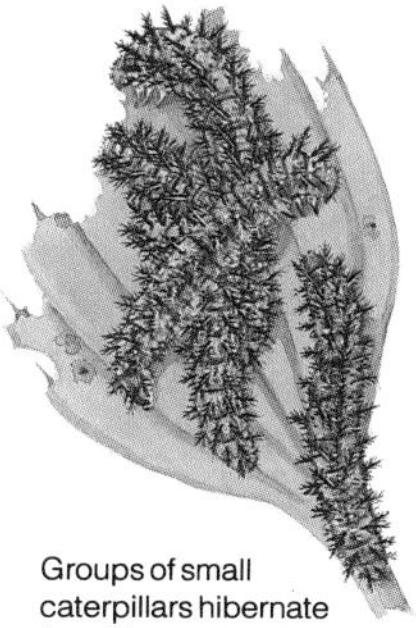

Groups of small caterpillars hibernate in a silken web until the spring. The fully grown caterpillar is black and spiny, with a distinctive reddish head.

With wings outspread, a butterfly feeds on the nectar of a buttercup, one of the yellow flowers that attract it.

Black dots in orange spots

The upper side of the hind-wings has small black dots in the row of orange spots. The underside consists of beige and orange bands with small black dots. The butterflies are shown on bird's-foot-trefoil and ribwort plantain. Wingspan 1½ in. (38 mm).

The Glanville fritillary is found only on the Isle of Wight, mostly on the southern side.

[× 4]

The eggs are laid in groups on the underside of the leaves of sea plantain (*Plantago maritima*) and ribwort plantain (*P. lanceolata*). They hatch after about three weeks.

Glanville fritillary *Melitaea cinxia*

Now found only on the Isle of Wight, the Glanville fritillary used to be common in parts of the English mainland from Yorkshire to Wiltshire. However Britain is on the northern fringe of its range in Europe, and a barely perceptible change in climate may have been the cause of its disappearance from the mainland. The butterfly was originally called the Dullidge fritillary as it occurred in Dulwich, now a suburb of south London. Another name, the plantain fritillary, referred to the food plant of its caterpillars. Then, in the early 18th century, the eminent entomologist James Petiver named it the Glanville fritillary after Eleanor Glanville, an enthusiastic amateur collector. Mrs Glanville's will was later contested on the grounds that she was not of sound mind, her unusual hobby being regarded at that time as evidence of eccentricity.

Glanville fritillaries are sun-loving butterflies that fly on rough grassy slopes near the sea. They glide low over the vegetation, visiting yellow flowers that grow on chalk, such as vetches and trefoils, to drink their nectar. Attempts have been made in recent years to introduce them to mainland sites including the New Forest and the Wirral, so far without success.

Eggs are laid singly in late July on the stems and leaves of dog violet (*Viola riviniana*) and sweet violet (*Viola odorata*), where they spend the winter.

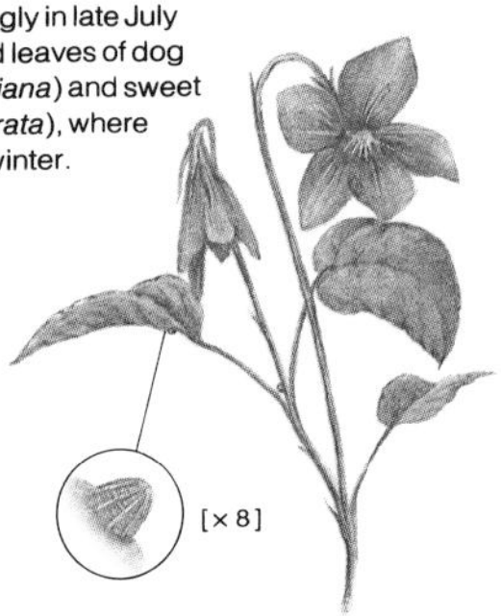

[× 8]

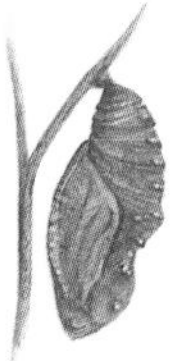

The chrysalis, formed in late May, is attached to a violet stem by a silk pad.

The caterpillars, which hatch in March or April, may be either dark or light reddish-brown. Both have a white stripe.

Between June and August, adults of the one annual generation are on the wing, often seen feeding on thistles.

Silver spots in red marks

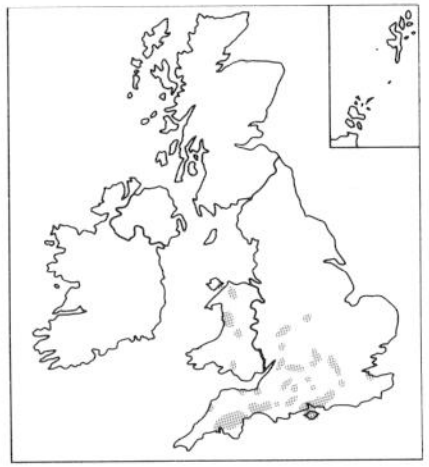

Now remaining only in isolated colonies in southern England and Wales.

The high brown can be distinguished from the dark green fritillary by the silver spots inside the red markings on the underside of the hind-wings. The butterflies are shown on a bramble (*Rubus fruticosus*). Wingspan $2\frac{3}{8}$ in. (60 mm).

High brown fritillary *Argynnis adippe*

In its deciduous woodland and forest haunts, this large butterfly is easily confused with the other two large fritillaries, the dark green and the silver-washed. They all flutter through glades, rides and bramble patches, and share the same food plants. The caterpillars feed on dog violet and sweet violet, which often grow on woodland floors, mossy banks, and along shady waysides. The high brown fritillary is always active in sunshine and spends hours flitting among the flower-heads of brambles and thistles, feeding there with other butterflies. It is a strong flyer and, as its name implies, reaches a good height among the trees, where it roosts at night or on dull days.

The butterfly has always had a restricted distribution in Britain. It has never been found in Ireland or Scotland, and the furthest north it has been recorded is Cumberland. Now it is becoming even less widespread; it has become extinct in south-east England and many other of its former localities since 1970. The major cause is loss of its habitat. Woods are being left unmanaged and their rides and glades become overgrown and dark, while at woodland margins the old rampant bramble thickets are frequently cut back.

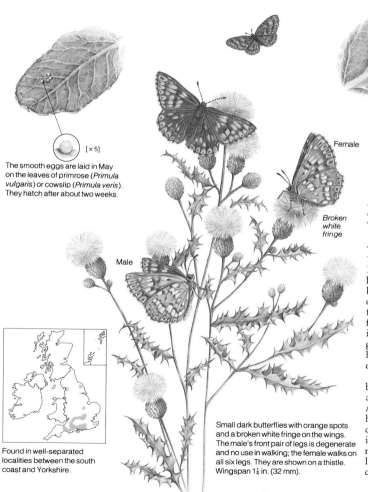

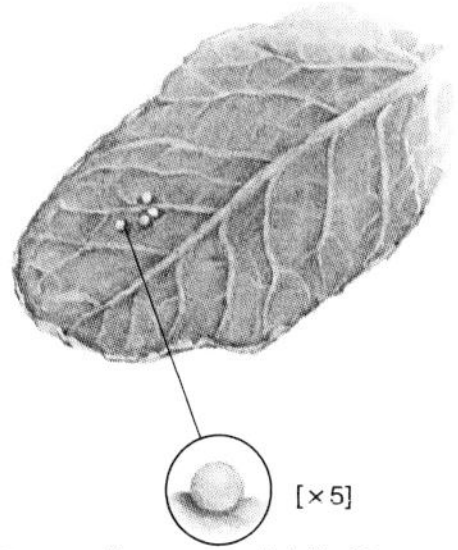

The smooth eggs are laid in May on the leaves of primrose (*Primula vulgaris*) or cowslip (*Primula veris*). They hatch after about two weeks.

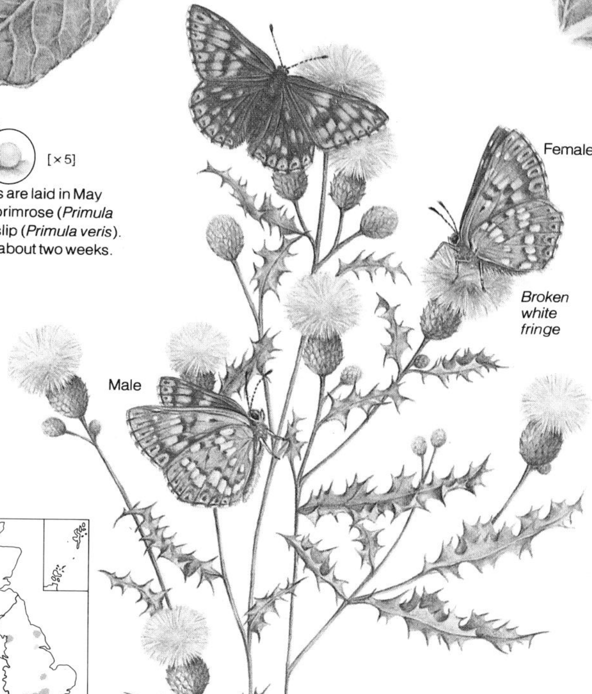

[×5]

Female

Broken white fringe

Male

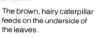

The brown, hairy caterpillar feeds on the underside of the leaves.

In September a light-coloured chrysalis forms on the underside of the leaf, where it spends the winter.

This small fritillary is seen in sunny woodland glades, resting on a low leaf and then flying to another leaf near by.

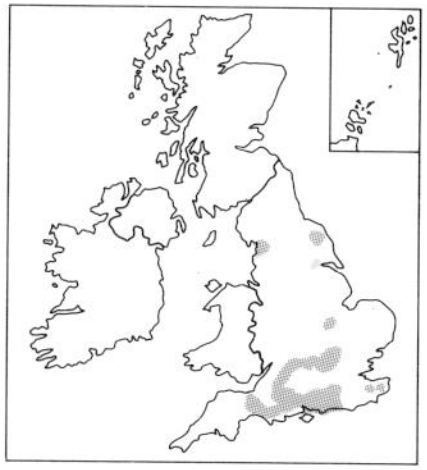

Found in well-separated localities between the south coast and Yorkshire.

Small dark butterflies with orange spots and a broken white fringe on the wings. The male's front pair of legs is degenerate and no use in walking; the female walks on all six legs. They are shown on a thistle. Wingspan $1\frac{1}{4}$ in. (32 mm).

Duke of Burgundy fritillary *Hamearis lucina*

Basking in the sun low down on vegetation or on bare earth is how this woodland butterfly spends most of its time. It seems to be attracted to wood spurge and blue flowers, but rarely visits other flowers for nectar. This very active flyer makes short flights between basking and often flutters over the caterpillar's food plants – primroses and cowslips. The caterpillar can be seen in the translucent greyish egg before it emerges. When fully grown, it forms a sturdy chrysalis that does not dangle but is held closely beneath a leaf by a silken girdle. The butterfly emerges in late May or June and lives about 20 days.

Although the butterfly is called a fritillary, from its resemblance to the fritillaries in pattern, it belongs to a different family and is the only species of the family – which is chiefly South American – found in Britain. Its caterpillars do not have the honey gland, which exudes sweet fluid, as fritillary caterpillars do. It has been known as a fritillary since the 18th century when it was called Mr Vernon's small fritillary. The butterfly has never been common in Britain but it lives in many scattered localities in woodland clearings, on scrubby hillsides, and on downlands – if primroses or cowslips grow there.

Fritillaries that depend on violets

Violets are as vital to many fritillaries as honeysuckle is to the white admiral. Six British fritillaries depend exclusively on violet plants as food for their caterpillars. The common dog violet, early dog violet, heath dog violet and wild pansy grow in woodland glades, on mossy banks and under hedgerows. Woodland fritillaries are usually seen around bramble thickets drinking nectar from the flowers. But the females also flutter close to the ground, inspecting each plant with their legs and antennae, and eventually laying eggs on violet leaves.

The caterpillars are easy to recognise, resting on the violet plants, with their distinctive black and brown spines. The silver-washed fritillary is the only species that does not lay its eggs directly on the violets. They are laid on the bark of trees, close to violet patches.

Dark green fritillaries are fast flyers, skimming over flowers and between perch points on trees.

Queen of Spain fritillaries, extremely rare immigrants from southern Europe, lay their eggs on violets, but the caterpillars are unlikely to survive the winter.

A silver-washed fritillary lays her eggs on the bark of an oak tree where they will spend the winter.
High brown fritillaries seek out violets on the woodland floor to lay their eggs.
Pearl-bordered and small pearl-bordered fritillaries are highly active butterflies, flying to and fro in glades.

Blues, hairstreaks and copper

The Lycaenidae family of butterflies includes the blues, the hairstreaks and Britain's only copper. They are all small butterflies, mostly swift flyers. The blues and the copper have bright metallic colours, while the hairstreaks have more modest colours, usually with a fine white line known as a 'hairstreak' on the underside of the wings. The blues and small copper are found only in open grassy areas rich in wild flowers. The hairstreaks, particularly the purple, black and brown hairstreaks, occur in woodlands and glades.

Caterpillars of the white-letter hairstreak, the green hairstreak, the silver-studded blue and the chalk-hill blue all have a 'honey-gland' on their bodies which secretes a fluid that ants like to drink. In return for the caterpillars' secretion, the ants probably help to keep predatory bugs, flies and wasps away from them. Ants are known to 'farm' caterpillars, moving them to suitable food plants in return for the secretion – an example of symbiosis (see also p. 97).

Male

Female

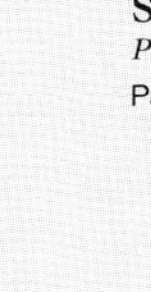

Female underside

Silver-studded blue
Plebejus argus
Page 91

Male

Female

Female underside

Common blue
Polyommatus icarus
Page 90

Male

Female

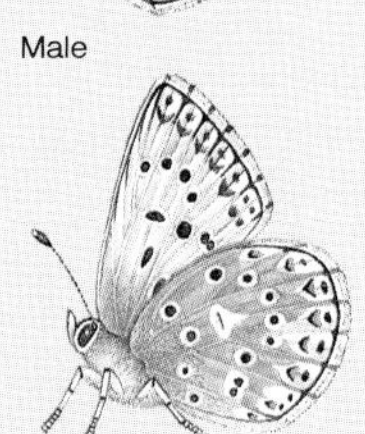

Male underside

Chalk-hill blue
Lysandra coridon
Page 92

Male

Female

Male underside

Small blue
Cupido minimus
Page 96

Male

Female

Male underside

Large blue
Maculinea arion
Page 97

Male

Female

Female underside

Adonis blue
Lysandra bellargus
Page 93

Male

Female

Male underside

Short-tailed blue
Everes argiades
Page 94

Mazarine blue
Cyaniris semiargus
Page 94

Long-tailed blue
Lampides boeticus
Page 95

Holly blue
Celastrina argiolus
Page 100

Brown argus
Aricia agestis
Page 98

Northern brown argus
Aricia artaxerxes
Page 99

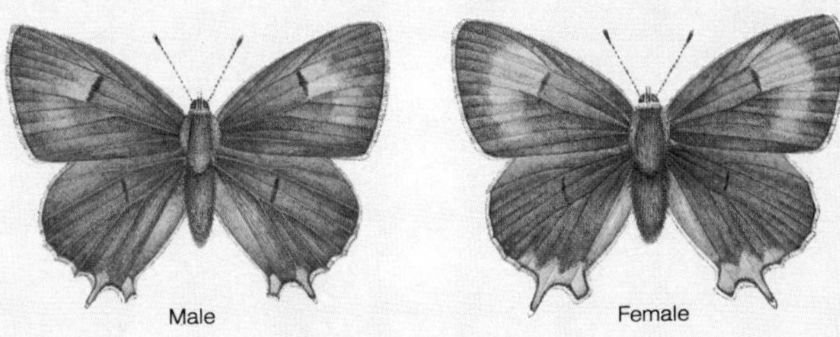

Brown hairstreak
Thecla betulae
Page 102

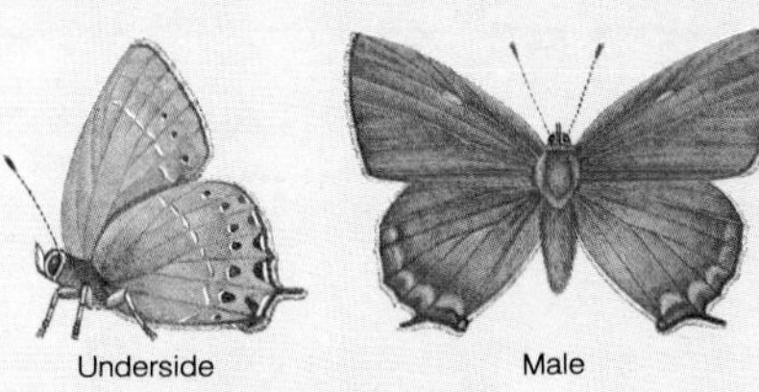

Black hairstreak
Strymonidia spini
Page 101

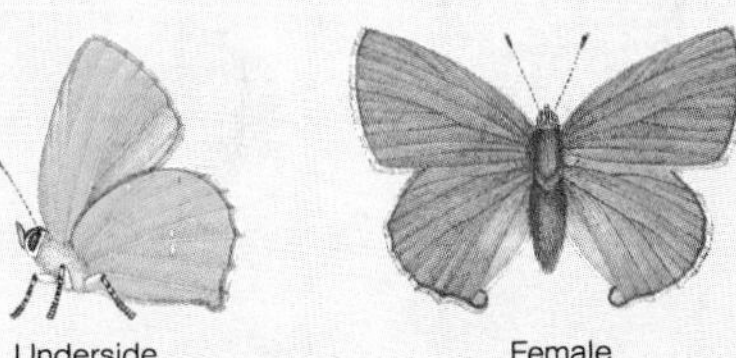

Green hairstreak
Callophrys rubi
Page 103

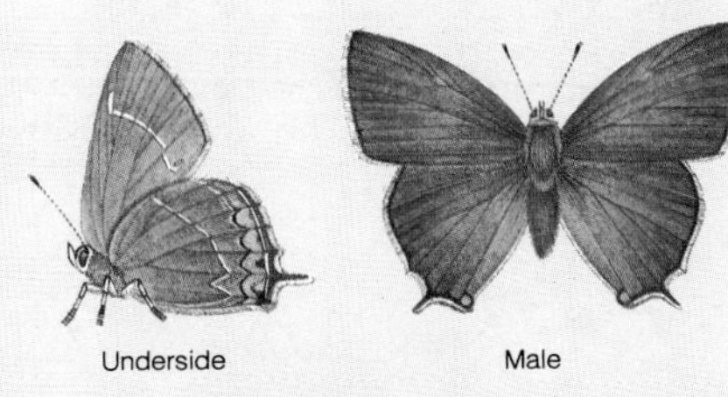

White-letter hairstreak
Strymonidia w-album
Page 105

Purple hairstreak
Quercusia quercus
Page 104

Small copper
Lycaena phlaeus
Page 106

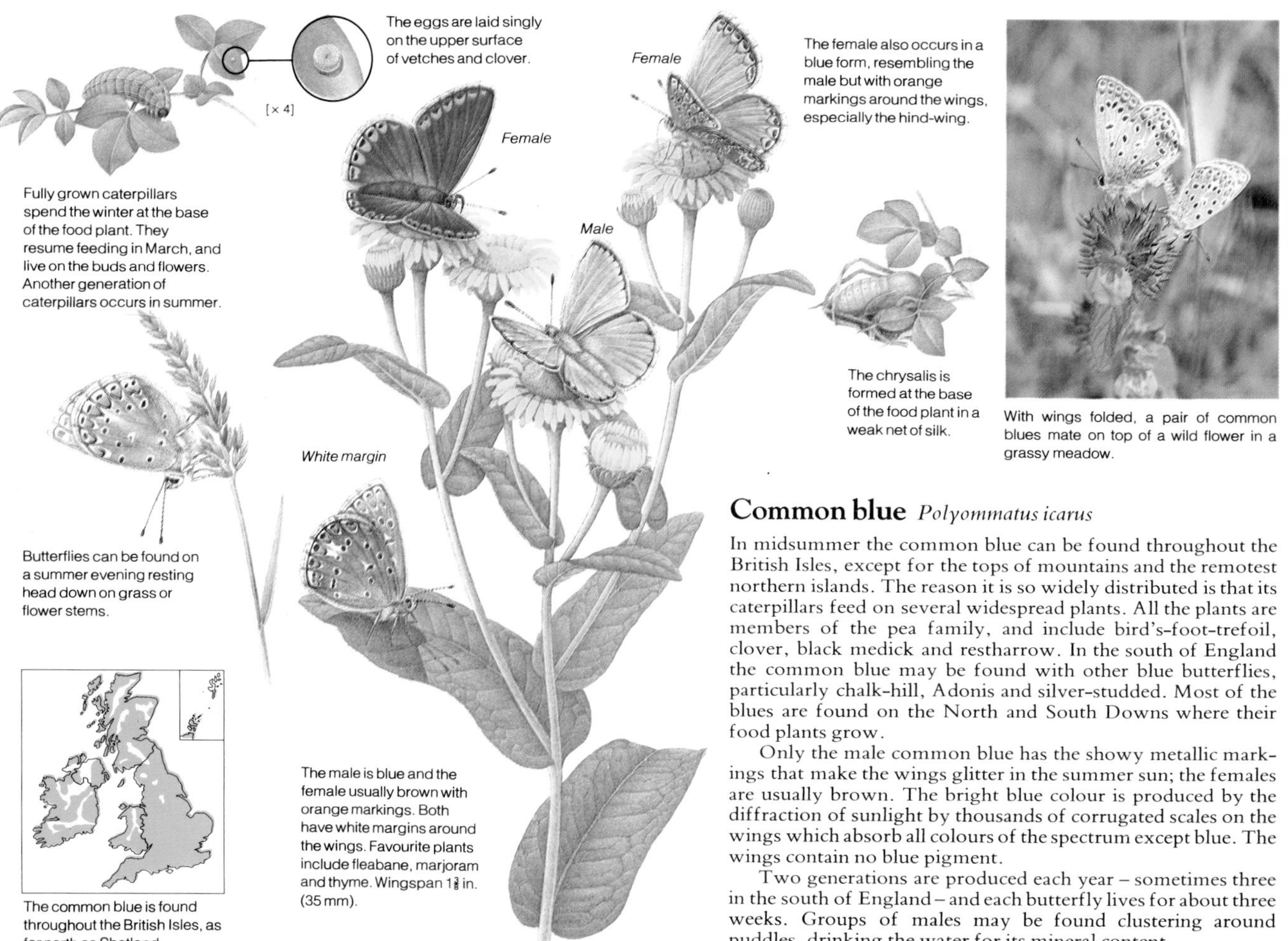

The eggs are laid singly on the upper surface of vetches and clover.

Fully grown caterpillars spend the winter at the base of the food plant. They resume feeding in March, and live on the buds and flowers. Another generation of caterpillars occurs in summer.

Butterflies can be found on a summer evening resting head down on grass or flower stems.

The common blue is found throughout the British Isles, as far north as Shetland.

The male is blue and the female usually brown with orange markings. Both have white margins around the wings. Favourite plants include fleabane, marjoram and thyme. Wingspan 1⅜ in. (35 mm).

The female also occurs in a blue form, resembling the male but with orange markings around the wings, especially the hind-wing.

The chrysalis is formed at the base of the food plant in a weak net of silk.

With wings folded, a pair of common blues mate on top of a wild flower in a grassy meadow.

Common blue *Polyommatus icarus*

In midsummer the common blue can be found throughout the British Isles, except for the tops of mountains and the remotest northern islands. The reason it is so widely distributed is that its caterpillars feed on several widespread plants. All the plants are members of the pea family, and include bird's-foot-trefoil, clover, black medick and restharrow. In the south of England the common blue may be found with other blue butterflies, particularly chalk-hill, Adonis and silver-studded. Most of the blues are found on the North and South Downs where their food plants grow.

Only the male common blue has the showy metallic markings that make the wings glitter in the summer sun; the females are usually brown. The bright blue colour is produced by the diffraction of sunlight by thousands of corrugated scales on the wings which absorb all colours of the spectrum except blue. The wings contain no blue pigment.

Two generations are produced each year – sometimes three in the south of England – and each butterfly lives for about three weeks. Groups of males may be found clustering around puddles, drinking the water for its mineral content.

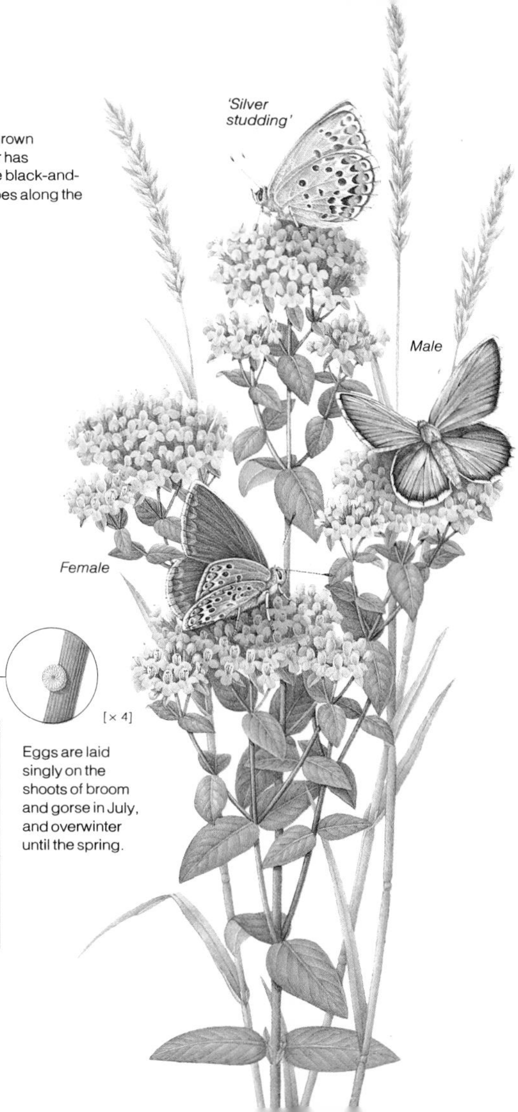

The fully grown caterpillar has distinctive black-and-white stripes along the side.

'Silver studding'

Male

Female

[× 4]

Eggs are laid singly on the shoots of broom and gorse in July, and overwinter until the spring.

Mostly the south and west of England; colonies in north Wales and Norfolk.

The pale chrysalis is formed at the base of the food plant on a loosely made silk net.

The male is silvery blue, with a white edge outside a black strip. The female is brown, with orange markings. The undersides are spotted with black, blue and orange – the blue spots giving the impression of 'silver studding'. Wingspan 1$\frac{3}{8}$ in. (35 mm).

A mostly male colony of silver-studded blues spread their wings on brambles, taking in the heat of the sun.

Silver-studded blue *Plebejus argus*

This attractive butterfly with its unique row of silver spots is typical of the diminishing heathland of Britain. Since the Second World War large areas of heath have been turned into farm land, removing food plants such as gorse, broom and heather. As a result, the butterfly has become extinct in Kent and probably in mid-Wales, central Norfolk and Dartmoor.

Where its food plants remain, as in parts of north Wales, the Ashdown Forest in Sussex, and the New Forest, the silver-studded blue can be common. The butterfly expert E. B. Ford wrote in 1945: 'The entomologist who in mid-July steps from his car in one of the great tracts of heather in the New Forest will find himself surrounded by immense numbers of this butterfly.' The numbers now, however, even in favourite spots, are probably smaller because of an indirect threat to the food plants – myxomatosis. The disease has reduced the rabbit population, allowing grass to grow and swamp the plants.

The caterpillars of the silver-studded blue are attractive to ants which milk them of a sweet secretion produced by their bodies. The ants even carry them to food plants in return for the free food supply.

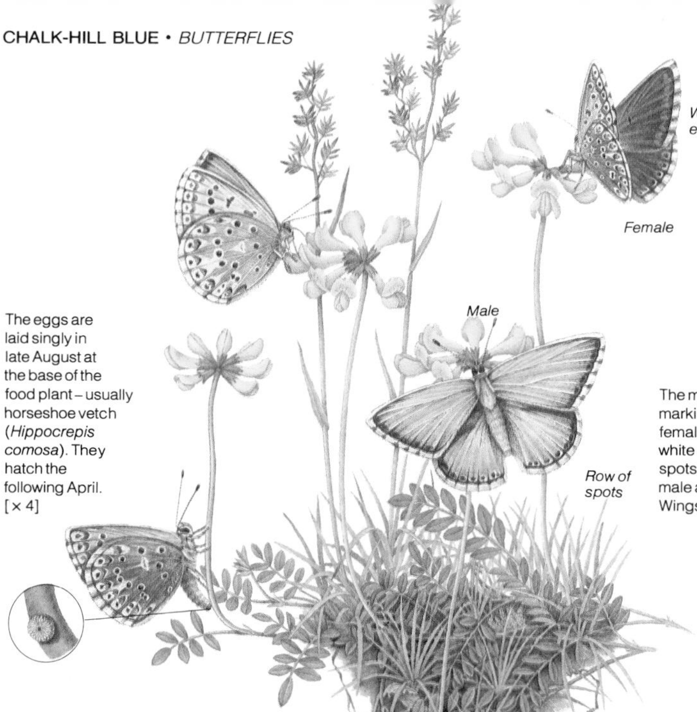

White edge

Female

Male

Row of spots

The eggs are laid singly in late August at the base of the food plant – usually horseshoe vetch (*Hippocrepis comosa*). They hatch the following April. [× 4]

The chrysalis forms in June or July on the ground beneath the food plant and hatches in about a month.

The male is silvery-blue with dark markings around the fore-wings; the female is brown. Both sexes have a white edge to the wings and a row of spots on the hind-wing – black in the male and orange in the female. Wingspan $1\frac{3}{8}$ in. (35 mm).

The chalk-hill blue feeds with its wings outstretched. The pale blue males are sometimes seen in groups.

Chalk-hill blue *Lysandra coridon*

Like many blues, the chalk-hill blue has males that are brightly coloured to attract females, and females that are drab to conceal them from predators. Both have spots on the underside of the wings but the spotting can be very variable. The males spend much time basking in the sun with wings open. They used to be seen in great numbers in their preferred localities – on chalky slopes, as their name suggests. The butterflies take nectar from many wild flowers and, like the Adonis blue, are also attracted to dung. There is only one generation a year, in July and August. The butterflies live up to 20 days.

The caterpillars are usually found on horseshoe vetch, but they also eat bird's-foot-trefoil and kidney vetch. Like the Adonis and silver-studded blues, the caterpillars are protected by ants, which keep away predators. The ants gain by 'milking' the caterpillars of a sweet fluid which they secrete.

The chalk-hill blue's decline – and even extinction in Lincolnshire, for example – has been attributed to myxomatosis, which seriously reduced the rabbit population. Where rabbits have ceased to graze, scrub has grown up and killed off the food plants. Ploughing of old pastures also destroys the food plants.

Found on the southern uplands, especially the Downs and the Chilterns.

The pale green, hairy caterpillar has delicate pale yellow lines along its body. Ants 'milk' the caterpillars and even carry them to leaves conveniently near the ants' nest.

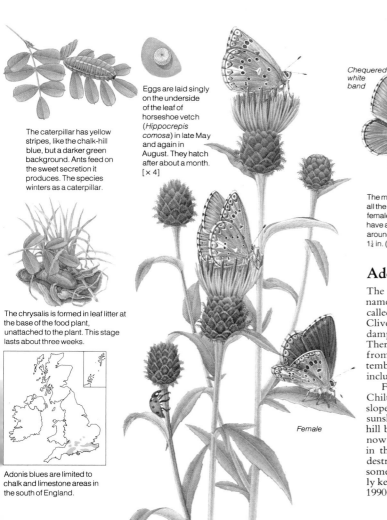

The caterpillar has yellow stripes, like the chalk-hill blue, but a darker green background. Ants feed on the sweet secretion it produces. The species winters as a caterpillar.

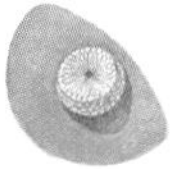

Eggs are laid singly on the underside of the leaf of horseshoe vetch (*Hippocrepis comosa*) in late May and again in August. They hatch after about a month. [× 4]

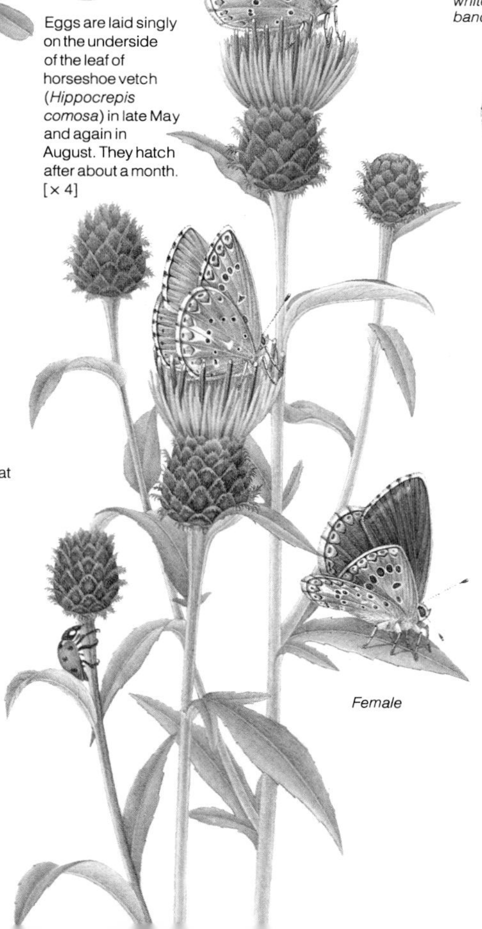

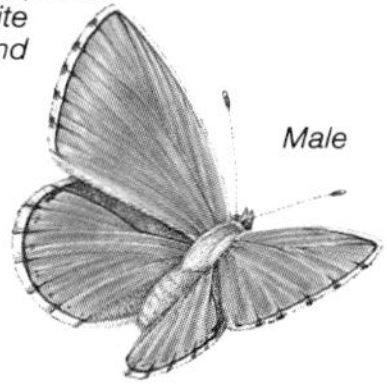

Chequered white band

Male

The male is the brightest blue of all the British butterflies; the female is brown. Both sexes have a chequered white band around all the wings. Wingspan 1¼ in. (32 mm).

Male Adonis blues are partial to the juices found in dung, which provide them with essential nutrients.

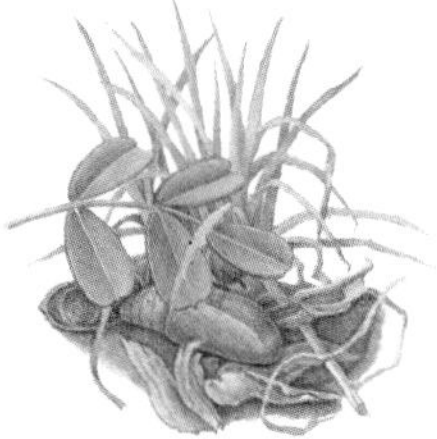

The chrysalis is formed in leaf litter at the base of the food plant, unattached to the plant. This stage lasts about three weeks.

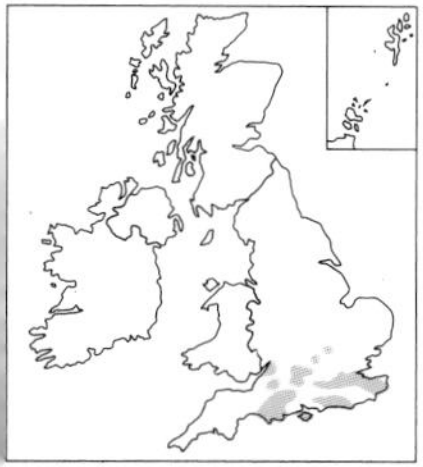

Adonis blues are limited to chalk and limestone areas in the south of England.

Female

Adonis blue *Lysandra bellargus*

The vivid blue of the males is so striking that the species is named after Adonis, the god of masculine beauty. It used to be called the Clifden Blue after one of its first known localities at Cliveden in Buckinghamshire. Males will congregate to drink at damp sand or dung, where they obtain salts essential to them. There are two generations a year and butterflies are on the wing from mid-May to mid-June and again in August and September. They feed on the nectar of a variety of wild flowers including vetches, trefoils, clovers and marjoram.

Flower-rich grassy slopes and hollows on the Downs and Chilterns are the places where Adonis blues might be seen. The slopes they prefer face south or west and receive plenty of sunshine. The Adonis blue may be seen flying with the chalk-hill blue but is much more local in its distribution. Indeed it is now declining rapidly in Britain and has recently become extinct in three-quarters of its former localities. The loss is due to destruction of its food plants, sometimes through ploughing, sometimes through the invasion of scrub which rabbits formerly kept down. It is likely to become extinct in Britain during the 1990s unless conservation measures are undertaken.

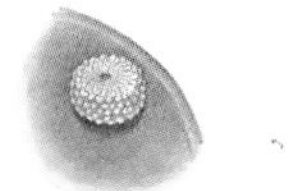

The eggs are laid singly at the base of leaves of bird's-foot-trefoil. [× 4]

Female

The caterpillars eat the buds, flowers and pods of the food plant. They hibernate on the plant.

A male short-tailed blue basks in the sun, highlighting its banded antennae and the black-and-white margins to the wings.

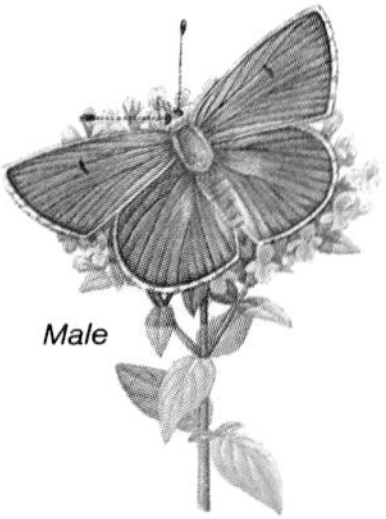

Male

The chrysalis is attached to a trefoil leaf by a silk girdle and pad.

Mazarine blue

Cyaniris semiargus

This former British resident became extinct early in the 1900s. Mazarine blues from Europe occasionally visit the south coast in summer. Wingspan $1\frac{1}{4}$ in. (32 mm).

Short 'tail'

A rare and irregular migrant that may be seen south of a line from London to Bristol.

The male has violet wings; the female has brown wings with faint blue colouring at the base. Both sexes have tiny 'tails' on the hind-wings. They are shown on bird's-foot-trefoil (*Lotus corniculatus*). Wingspan 1 in. (25 mm).

Short-tailed blue *Everes argiades*

This exceedingly rare migrant to England flies across the English Channel from northern France where it breeds successfully. It lays its eggs on bird's-foot-trefoil and medick and is most likely to be found on heathlands, rough pastures and flowery hillsides. The butterfly was first recorded in Britain in 1885, and was called Bloxworth blue after Bloxworth Heath in Dorset where it was captured. Shortly afterwards other specimens were discovered in old collections, including one in a collection made 25 years earlier; it had been captured at Blackpool.

The tiny 'tails' are not easy to see and are covered in large scales, appearing hairy. The upper side of the male is similar to the silver-studded blue or common blue and the underside to the holly blue. As a migrant from France, the butterfly is most likely to be found in southern England. It has never been recorded breeding here, but there is a chance that highly localised colonies might exist in Devon, Cornwall, Dorset and Avon where it has been recorded mostly in the past.

The mazarine blue is another very rare migrant to England which may sometimes be found around red clover, thrift, kidney vetch or melilot plants in summer.

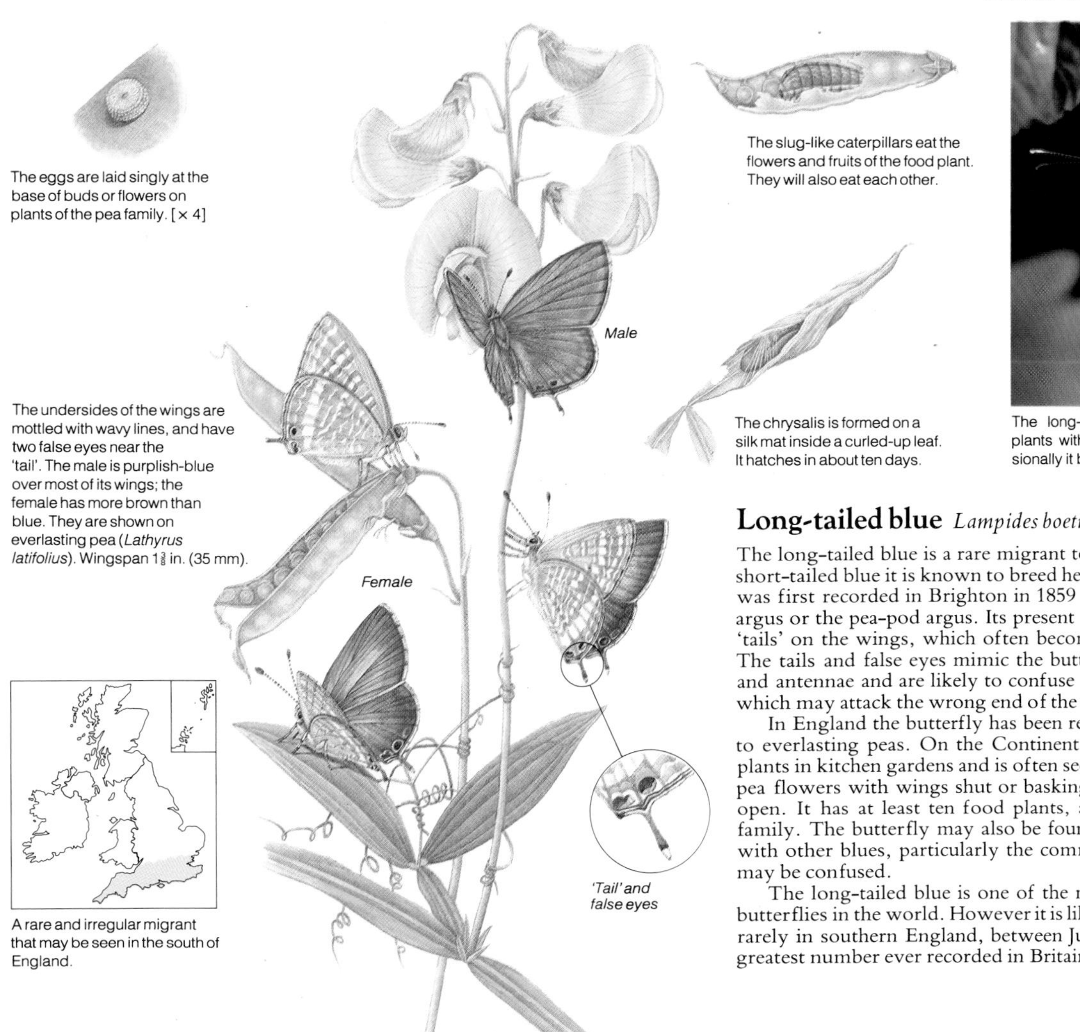

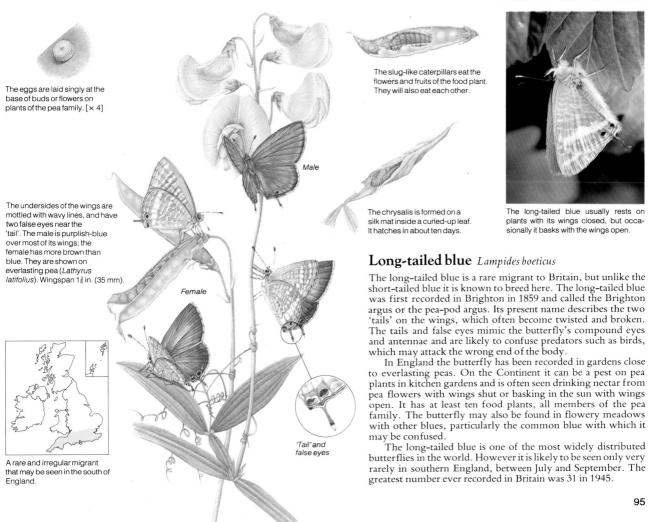

The eggs are laid singly at the base of buds or flowers on plants of the pea family. [× 4]

The slug-like caterpillars eat the flowers and fruits of the food plant. They will also eat each other.

The chrysalis is formed on a silk mat inside a curled-up leaf. It hatches in about ten days.

The long-tailed blue usually rests on plants with its wings closed, but occasionally it basks with the wings open.

The undersides of the wings are mottled with wavy lines, and have two false eyes near the 'tail'. The male is purplish-blue over most of its wings; the female has more brown than blue. They are shown on everlasting pea (*Lathyrus latifolius*). Wingspan $1\frac{3}{8}$ in. (35 mm).

A rare and irregular migrant that may be seen in the south of England.

Long-tailed blue *Lampides boeticus*

The long-tailed blue is a rare migrant to Britain, but unlike the short-tailed blue it is known to breed here. The long-tailed blue was first recorded in Brighton in 1859 and called the Brighton argus or the pea-pod argus. Its present name describes the two 'tails' on the wings, which often become twisted and broken. The tails and false eyes mimic the butterfly's compound eyes and antennae and are likely to confuse predators such as birds, which may attack the wrong end of the body.

In England the butterfly has been recorded in gardens close to everlasting peas. On the Continent it can be a pest on pea plants in kitchen gardens and is often seen drinking nectar from pea flowers with wings shut or basking in the sun with wings open. It has at least ten food plants, all members of the pea family. The butterfly may also be found in flowery meadows with other blues, particularly the common blue with which it may be confused.

The long-tailed blue is one of the most widely distributed butterflies in the world. However it is likely to be seen only very rarely in southern England, between July and September. The greatest number ever recorded in Britain was 31 in 1945.

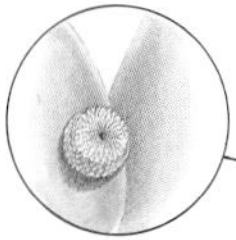

The eggs are laid singly in the flower-heads of kidney vetch (*Anthyllis vulneraria*), the caterpillar's only food plant. [x 4]

Blue base of wings

The chrysalis is formed on the plant in May. It has black spots and is covered in hairs.

Female

Male

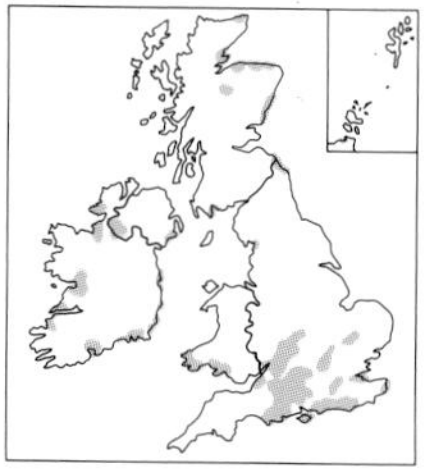

Found mainly in southern England; also parts of Wales, Ireland and Scotland.

Both sexes are sooty-brown in colour. The male usually has a tinge of blue on its upper wings, but very occasionally none at all. In both sexes the pale undersides have blue at the base of the wings. Wingspan $\frac{7}{8}$ in. (22 mm).

The caterpillar feeds on the flowers of the kidney vetch. In July, when fully grown, it hibernates until the following spring.

A small blue butterfly bears the marks of a bird's beak on its wings – souvenir of a narrow escape from death.

Small blue *Cupido minimus*

These frail little butterflies – the smallest in Britain – are vigorous flyers as they flit from flower to flower drinking the nectar. They can be quite numerous in sheltered localities, skimming low to the vegetation and even flying through thickets where they are well camouflaged by their colouring. The constant movement through plants gradually wears the scales off their wings, and the butterflies lose their colour, develop ragged edges, and become rather pathetic flyers. By the end of their two-week life they flutter ineffectually to the ground where they are likely to be eaten by ants or birds.

The small blue is found mostly in southern and central England in chalk and limestone country where its food plant, kidney vetch, grows well. But it is not exclusively associated with chalk and limestone. It is also found in coastal areas of South Wales, Scotland and parts of Ireland. The butterfly lives on downland slopes and in hollows, inside old sheltered chalk quarries, along disused railway cuttings, on sandhills and on coastal cliffs. Recently it has declined in Yorkshire, but a new breeding area has been discovered on the Cumbrian coast. The butterfly is on the wing from late May to the end of June.

Largest of the British blues, and the only one with black spots on the upper side of the fore-wing. The females have larger spots on the fore-wing. Wingspan $1\frac{1}{2}$ in. (38 mm).

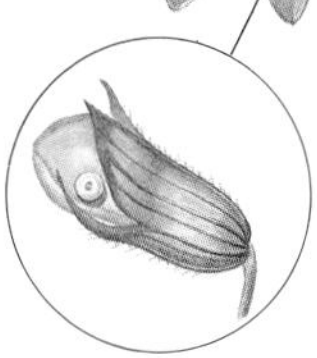

Female

Black spots

Male

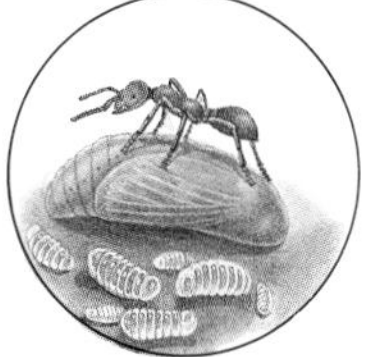

A pale chrysalis, unprotected by any cocoon, is formed in the ants' nest. The butterfly hatches three weeks later.

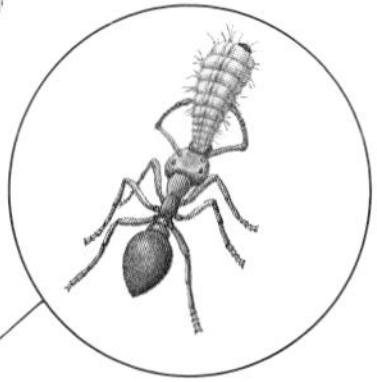

The caterpillar is carried off to the ants' nest where it feeds on ant grubs in return for providing more 'milk'. It hibernates in the nest through winter.

Large blues were found in old meadows where thyme often grows on ant hills. The last colony was near Bude, in Cornwall.

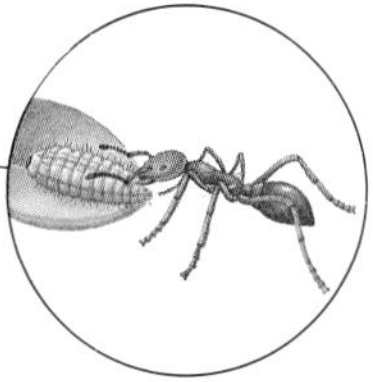

An ant stimulates the caterpillar with its antennae to produce a liquid called 'milk', on which the ant feeds.

Eggs are laid singly on the buds of thyme, the exclusive food plant of the large blue caterpillar. [× 4]

The well-camouflaged caterpillar feeds on the buds and flowers of the thyme plant.

Large blue *Maculinea arion*

The large blue was discovered in 1795 and became extinct in Britain 184 years later in 1979. However, the butterfly may fly again in Britain if French forms are liberated in suitable areas of the West Country. The extinction of the large blue followed changes in agricultural practice that disrupted its complex life-cycle. The butterfly had evolved an intimate association with wild thyme and with a species of ant, *Myrmica sabuleti*. The female butterflies laid their eggs on thyme plants, and after the caterpillars hatched they were carried off by the ants. In the ants' nest the caterpillars ate ant grubs in return for allowing the ants to 'milk' them of a sweet bodily secretion.

Large blues died out in areas where grazing land was ploughed up, destroying the thyme. But they also died out in areas where no ploughing was done. During the 1970s it was discovered that the butterflies thrived only where grass was grazed short by cattle, sheep or rabbits. Where farm grazing had been reduced, or rabbits had been eliminated by myxomatosis, the grass grew long and the butterflies were unable to find the thyme. The drought of 1976 reduced the last colony to 16 butterflies, and in 1979 no eggs were produced at all.

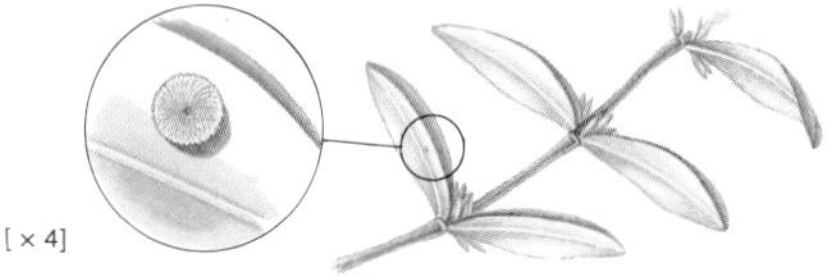

[× 4]

Single eggs are laid on the underside of the leaves of rock-rose (*Helianthemum*) or storksbill (*Erodium*).

The caterpillar feeds on the underside of rock-rose leaves and hibernates on the plant. Caterpillars are often found with ants.

Found in the south of England and the north and south coasts of Wales.

Orange half-moons

The chrysalis is formed at the base of the plant, among plant debris.

Dark brown with orange half-moons around the edge of the wings. Both sexes have a black spot in the centre of the fore-wings. The female is slightly larger and lighter coloured than the male. Wingspan 1$\frac{1}{8}$ in. (28 mm).

The butterflies are often seen sunning themselves, or feeding on flowers, with their wings spread wide open.

Brown argus *Aricia agestis*

The brown argus is a gregarious butterfly, usually seen in the sunshine with a group of others flitting among bramble flowers, bird's-foot-trefoil or the other wild flowers on which it feeds. At dusk, or on dull days, groups can be found roosting together head down on long grass stems, often in the company of common blues. There are two generations each year, with butterflies on the wing in May and June and again in July and August. Each butterfly lives for about three weeks. Courting males are said to smell strongly of chocolate. The caterpillars are often found with ants, which 'milk' them of secretions. The ants may be beneficial to the caterpillars in deterring predators.

The brown argus is not a typical 'blue' because it lacks the bright blue colours. It is easily confused with females of the common, chalk-hill, Adonis, and silver-studded blues. The species was first described in 1717 and was then thought to include the northern brown argus. The dividing line between the two seems to run through South Yorkshire. Distribution of the brown argus repeats the pattern of the chalk and limestone areas in south and central England. It can also be found on sandy coastal slopes where common storksbill grows.

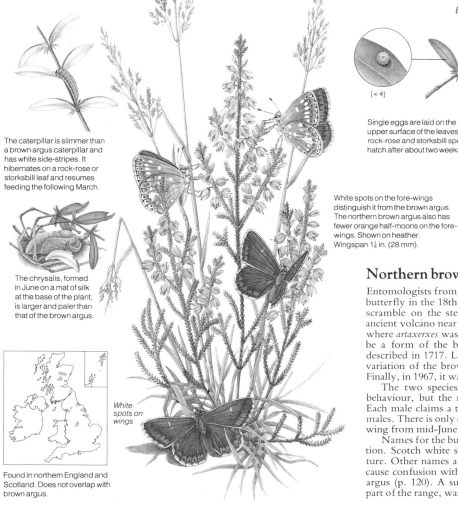

The caterpillar is slimmer than a brown argus caterpillar and has white side-stripes. It hibernates on a rock-rose or storksbill leaf and resumes feeding the following March.

The chrysalis, formed in June on a mat of silk at the base of the plant, is larger and paler than that of the brown argus.

Found in northern England and Scotland. Does not overlap with brown argus.

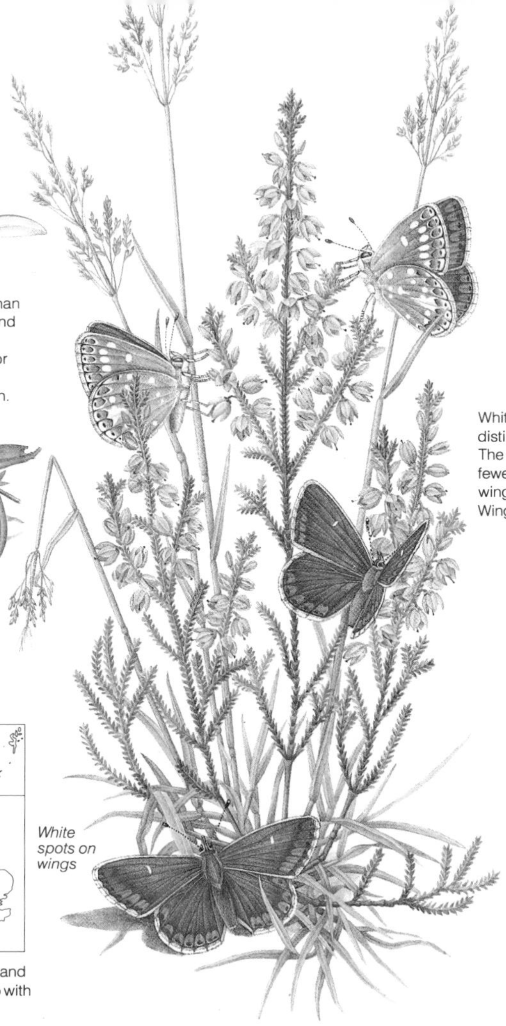

White spots on wings

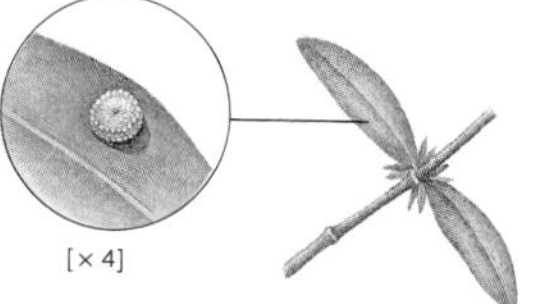

Single eggs are laid on the upper surface of the leaves of various rock-rose and storksbill species. They hatch after about two weeks.

White spots on the fore-wings distinguish it from the brown argus. The northern brown argus also has fewer orange half-moons on the fore-wings. Shown on heather. Wingspan $1\frac{1}{8}$ in. (28 mm).

The northern brown argus lives in flowery meadows, grassy hollows or wherever the caterpillar's food plants grow.

Northern brown argus *Aricia artaxerxes*

Entomologists from any part of Britain who wanted to see this butterfly in the 18th century had to journey to Edinburgh and scramble on the steep, tussocky slopes of Arthur's Seat, an ancient volcáno near the city centre. That was the only locality where *artaxerxes* was then known to live. It was then thought to be a form of the brown argus when that species was first described in 1717. Later it was classified as a species, then as a variation of the brown argus, and later still as a sub-species. Finally, in 1967, it was again given separate species status.

The two species are similar in their food plants and in behaviour, but the northern brown argus is not gregarious. Each male claims a territory as its own and drives away other males. There is only one generation a year. The adults are on the wing from mid-June into August.

Names for the butterfly have been as diverse as its classification. Scotch white spot aptly describes its distinguishing feature. Other names are mountain and Scotch argus, which can cause confusion with the other more commonly called Scotch argus (p. 120). A sub-species, *salmacis*, found in the southern part of the range, was called Durham or Castle Eden argus.

Eggs are laid singly on holly in May and on ivy in August. [× 5]

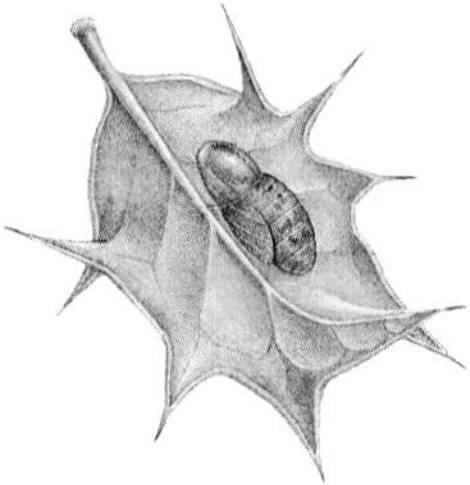

A chrysalis that is formed on holly in spring turns into a butterfly in July.

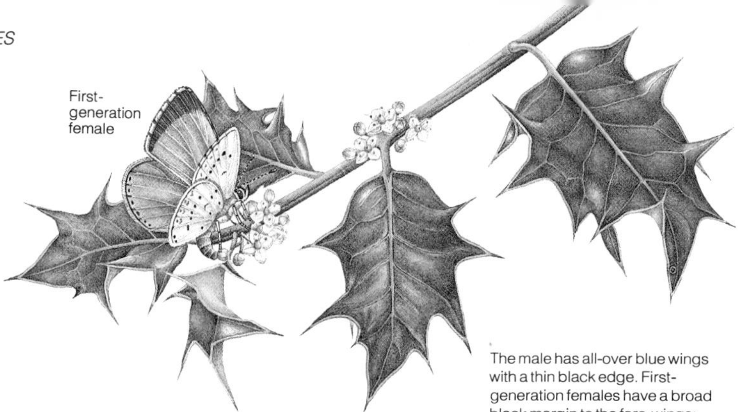

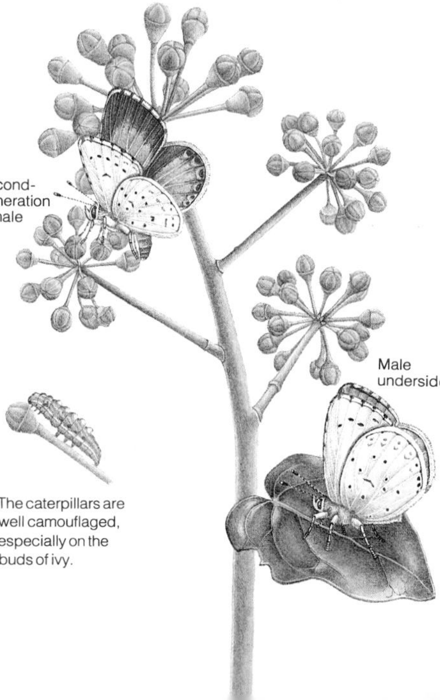

Mostly in southern England; also parts of Wales, Ireland and Scotland.

First-generation female

Second-generation female

Male underside

The caterpillars are well camouflaged, especially on the buds of ivy.

The male has all-over blue wings with a thin black edge. First-generation females have a broad black margin to the fore-wings; second-generation females have much more black. The undersides of both sexes is a delicate blue which cannot be confused with other species. Wingspan $1\frac{1}{4}$ in. (32 mm).

A second-generation female rests on a bramble bud, displaying its distinctive black-and-white antennae and legs.

Holly blue *Celastrina argiolus*

The holly blue is unique among British butterflies as its caterpillars have different food plants at different times of the year – holly in spring and ivy in autumn. There are two generations of the butterfly each year, and the caterpillars prefer the flower buds of their food plants to the leaves. The buds of the holly develop in spring in time for one generation, and the buds of the ivy develop in autumn for the other. In the absence of holly or ivy the caterpillars will feed on the flowers of dogwood, spindle, gorse and bramble.

In flight the holly blue can be confused with the common blue but at rest it usually holds its wings closed, showing the underside which is quite different from that of the common blue. It is pale blue with small black spots; the underside of the common blue is much more colourful (p. 90).

The butterflies are usually seen, from late March to mid-October, fluttering around bushes and trees looking for places to rest or lay their eggs. Holly trees in spring and ivy-bound hedgerows, trees and walls in summer particularly attract it. The holly blue is typically a hedgerow butterfly but it is also found on scrubby hillsides and in woodland clearings.

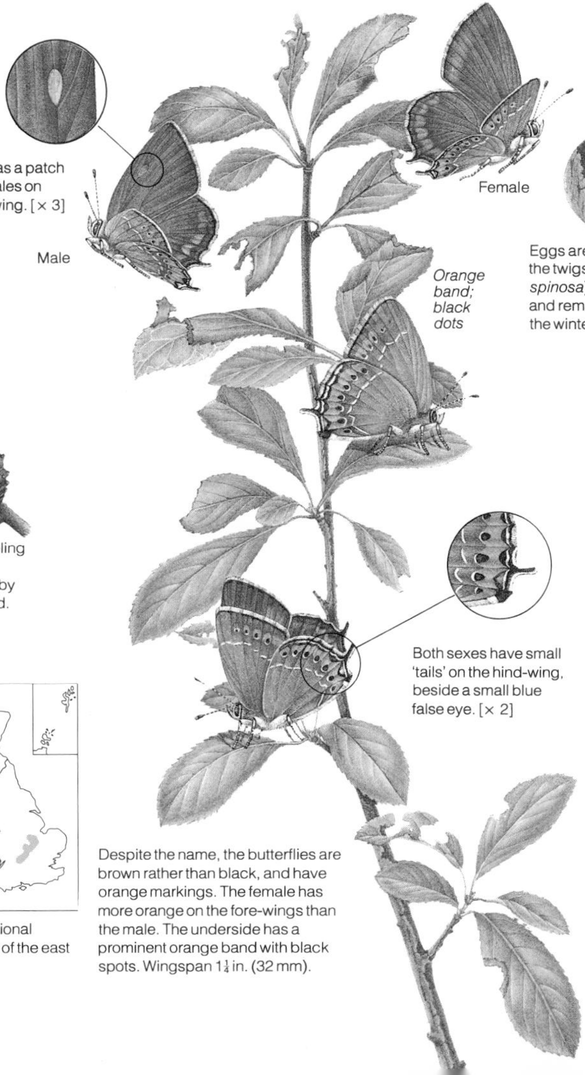

The male has a patch of scent scales on each fore-wing. [× 3]

Male

Female

Orange band; black dots

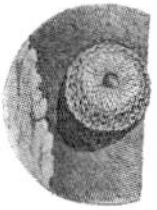

Eggs are laid singly on the twigs of sloe (*Prunus spinosa*) in late summer and remain there through the winter. [× 4]

In spring, the caterpillars feed on the flowers and buds of sloe.

Black hairstreaks usually rest with their wings closed, the orange band contrasting with the white hairstreak marks.

A chrysalis resembling a bird dropping is attached to a stem by a silk girdle and pad.

Both sexes have small 'tails' on the hind-wing, beside a small blue false eye. [× 2]

Found only in traditional coppice woodland of the east Midlands.

Despite the name, the butterflies are brown rather than black, and have orange markings. The female has more orange on the fore-wings than the male. The underside has a prominent orange band with black spots. Wingspan 1¼ in. (32 mm).

Black hairstreak *Strymonidia pruni*

Tiny black spots on the undersides of the wings give the black hairstreak its name. It is an extremely rare butterfly and is found only in old oak woodlands, especially coppice woodlands where the trees are regularly cut. The butterfly lays its eggs among old sloe thickets in shady glades and rides. It has been recorded in only four counties – Huntingdonshire (now part of Cambridgeshire), Oxfordshire, Northamptonshire and Buckinghamshire. Why it does not have a wider distribution is a mystery as the caterpillars will eat the leaves of bird cherry and birch as well as the leaves of sloe. The single generation of black hairstreaks are on the wing in June and July.

Half of the known colonies of the black hairstreak have become extinct in the last few decades. There are now fewer than 30 colonies left in England, and extinction from the British Isles is a real possibility. Some colonies have disappeared because of loss of deciduous woodlands and the creation of arable farmland. The butterflies spend a lot of time resting high up on the leaves of oak trees where they drink the sugary honey-dew left on the leaves by aphids. They also visit privet, wayfaring trees and brambles to take nectar from the flowers.

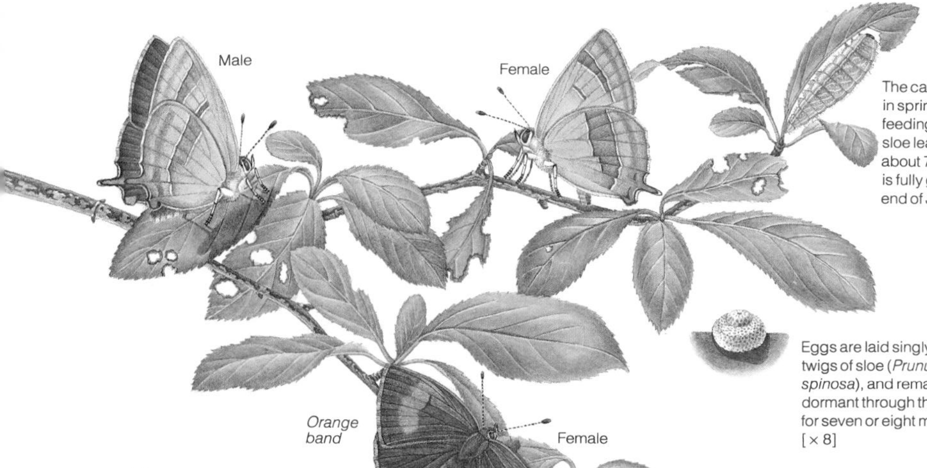

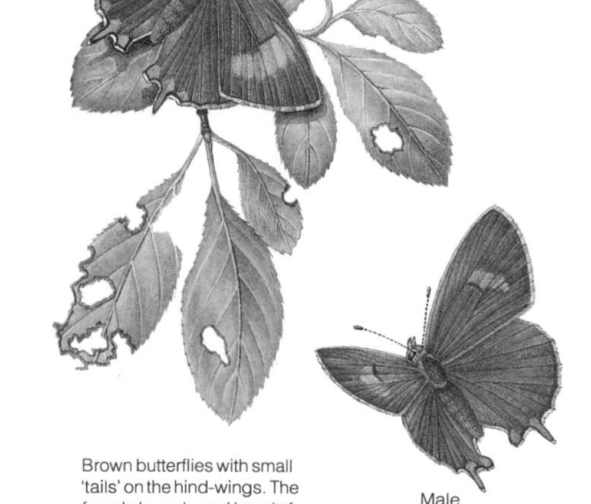

Male

Female

The caterpillar hatches in spring and begins feeding on the young sloe leaves. It lives for about 75 days and is fully grown by the end of June.

The largest British hairstreak, with a richly coloured underside to the wings containing two white 'hair'-streaks.

Eggs are laid singly on the twigs of sloe (*Prunus spinosa*), and remain dormant through the winter – for seven or eight months. [× 8]

Orange band

Female

The chrysalis is formed on a silk pad in leaf debris at the base of the food plant.

Found in the West Country and Wales, with isolated pockets elsewhere.

Brown butterflies with small 'tails' on the hind-wings. The female has a broad band of orange across the fore-wings. Wingspan 1⅜ in. (35 mm).

Male

Brown hairstreak *Thecla betulae*

In the 18th century butterflies whose sexes looked different were often thought to be two separate species. The colourful female of this butterfly was then called the golden hairstreak.

The brown hairstreak is an autumn species and flies between August and October, each butterfly living about three weeks. It is intimately associated with woodlands and hedgerows. The butterflies congregate around trees in woodland glades to conduct their courtship. They feed on the prolific honeydew exuded on leaves by aphids. And they perch high in the trees with their relatives the purple hairstreaks. Thickets of bramble and sloe – so typical of English woods and old hedgerows – attract the egg-laying females, which drink the nectar of the bramble flowers and lay their eggs on the leaves of sloe. By the time the chrysalis stage is reached, however, 90 per cent of the caterpillars and chrysalises have been eaten by predators – the caterpillars by birds, the chrysalises by small mammals.

The brown hairstreak has now become extinct in East Anglia and the south-east of England. The process has probably been hastened by hedge-cutting which can kill about half the eggs laid on the young growth of sloe each year.

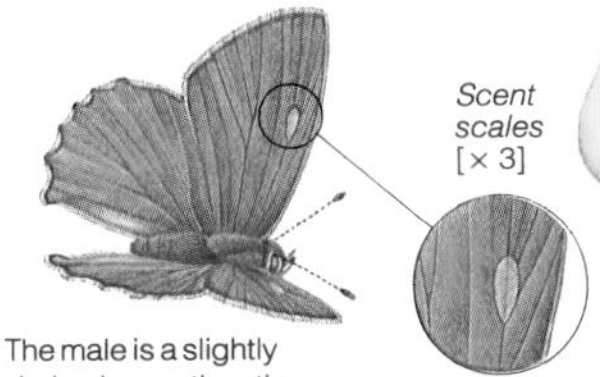

Scent scales [× 3]

The male is a slightly darker brown than the female and has a patch of scent scales on the fore-wing.

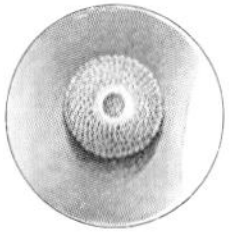

Eggs are laid in early summer, on a wide variety of scrub plants including broom, gorse and bramble. They hatch after about a week. [× 10]

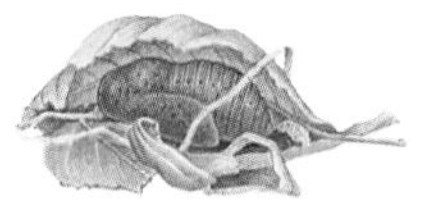

The chrysalis is formed in debris at the base of the plant, and there spends winter. It makes a creaking or scratching sound, presumably to deter predators.

A green hairstreak rests at right-angles to the sun, warming up against a rock in spring. It often drives off other insects.

The upper surface of the wings is brown, but as the butterfly always rests with its wings closed the vivid green of the undersides is often seen. The 'hairstreak' is a curved line of white spots against the green. These butterflies are shown resting on broom. Wingspan $1\frac{1}{8}$ in. (28 mm).

White spots

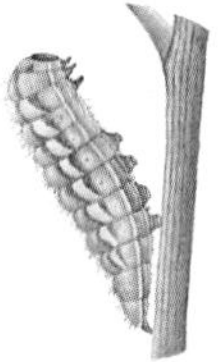

The full-grown caterpillar is green with yellow markings.

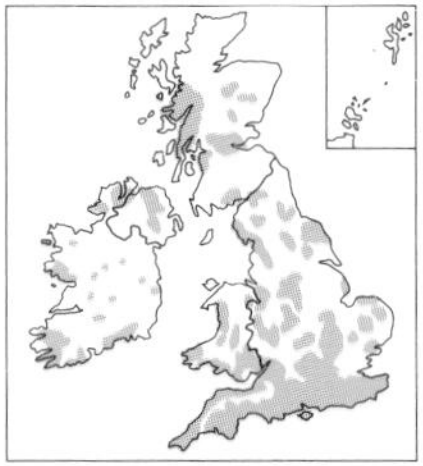

The legs and antennae are banded in black and white. [× 3]

Well distributed throughout the British Isles, particularly in the south of England.

Green hairstreak *Callophrys rubi*

The green metallic colour of the underside is unique among British butterflies. It is produced by the effects of light on the microscopic scales which cover the wings, resulting in only the green colour of the spectrum reaching the viewer's eye. The green hairstreak is unusual in other ways, too. Hairstreak butterflies get their name from the hair-like line across the underside of the wings, but on the green hairstreak this is reduced to a row of white dots. The species is the only British hairstreak which does not have small 'tails' on the hind-wings. And it hibernates as a chrysalis, while all other hairstreaks spend the winter as eggs.

The green hairstreak is a familiar butterfly in spring and early summer. It is also Britain's most common hairstreak as its caterpillars have at least ten food plants. Its favourite haunts include scrubby areas on downland, heathland and wasteland, together with woodland clearings and tracks. The butterflies are hardly ever seen feeding on the nectar of flowers. Instead they congregate in secluded corners, establishing territories, perching on vantage points and chasing each other in short bursts of swift flight around scrub bushes.

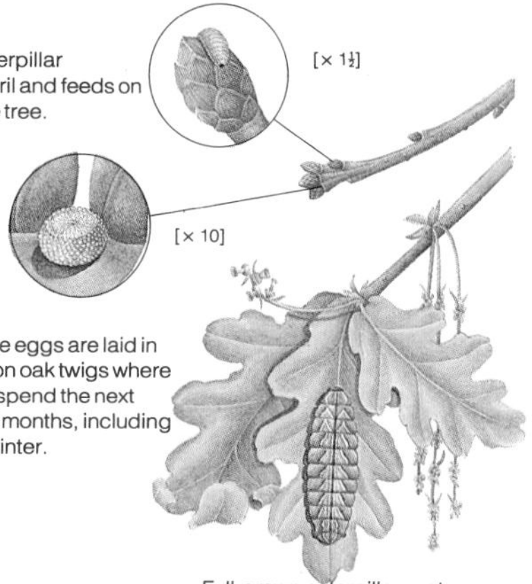

The young caterpillar emerges in April and feeds on the buds of the tree.

[× 1½]

Female

[× 10]

Orange spot and 'tail'

Single eggs are laid in July on oak twigs where they spend the next eight months, including the winter.

Full-grown caterpillars eat the young tender leaves. They are slug-like in shape and easily drop off if disturbed.

The purple hairstreak occasionally rests on the lower leaves of oak trees in woodland glades during high summer.

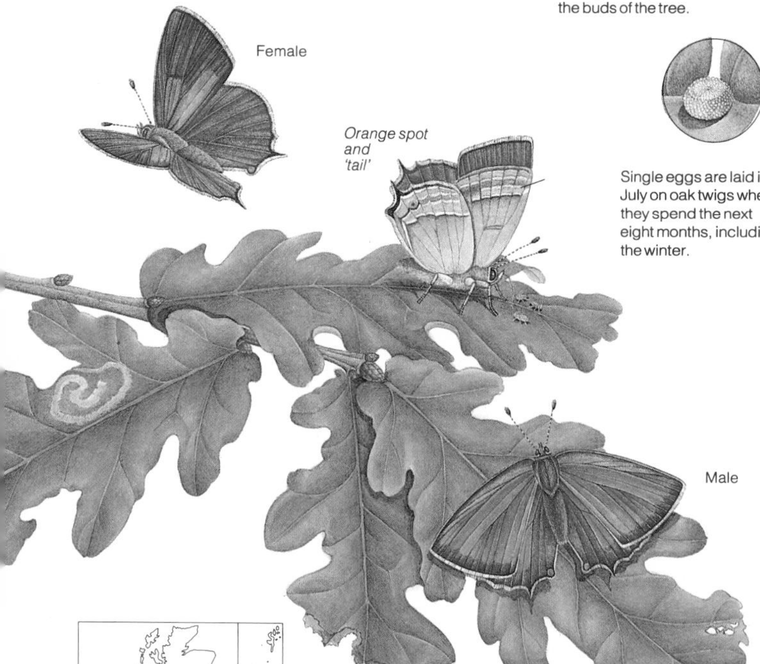

Male

Purple hairstreak *Quercusia quercus*

The purple colouring on the wings of this butterfly varies in strength as the light falls from different angles. It is the commonest of the British hairstreaks, but is seldom seen, as it lives in the canopy of oak trees and only rarely descends to paths and clearings. On sunny days in July and August, the movement of dark butterflies high up in oak woods may reveal groups of purple hairstreaks fluttering through the branches. The females, with their much smaller purple patches, are seen more often than the males, as they descend to lower branches to bask in the sun. Purple hairstreaks are pugnacious butterflies, and will attack other insects which stray into their territory, and even have squabbles with wasps. They feed on the sugar-rich honeydew deposited by aphids on ash and aspen leaves. Flowers are rarely visited for nectar, but the butterflies are occasionally seen feeding from the flowers of sweet chestnut and brambles.

The purple hairstreak is a true woodland butterfly, and its close association with oak trees is reflected in its scientific name which twice uses the Latin word *quercus*, meaning 'oak'. The caterpillars have been found on sweet chestnut and sallow, as well as oak, but they are probably only secondary food plants.

Mostly in southern England and Wales. Now extremely local in Ireland.

The chrysalis is formed on the tree or at the base, at the end of May or in June.

The males have a purple iridescence over all the wings. The females have a V-like area of purple on the fore-wings only. The undersides of both sexes are identical, with a white 'hairstreak', an orange spot and a tiny 'tail'. Wingspan $1\frac{5}{16}$ in. (34 mm).

Female

Scent scales

Male

[× 10]

Elms are the main food plants, and the eggs are laid singly on twigs where they spend the winter.

Caterpillars emerge in March and at first feed on the developing buds. Later they eat leaves and seeds, and are fully grown in May or June.

The orange tips of the antennae stand out against the green of woodland glades in July and August.

White letter W

The light brown chrysalis is attached to a leaf by a silk girdle and pad. It hatches after a month, in July.

White-tipped 'tail'

Wide distribution in England and Wales, as far as north Yorkshire.

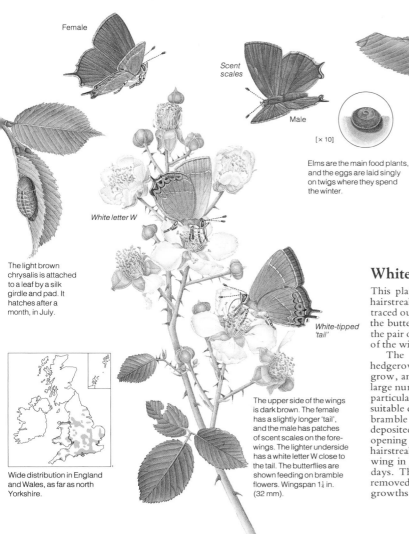

The upper side of the wings is dark brown. The female has a slightly longer 'tail', and the male has patches of scent scales on the fore-wings. The lighter underside has a white letter W close to the tail. The butterflies are shown feeding on bramble flowers. Wingspan 1¼ in. (32 mm).

White-letter hairstreak *Strymonidia w-album*

This plain brown butterfly is often confused with the black hairstreak, but it can be identified by the distinctive W mark traced out by the hairstreak line on its underside. This mark gave the butterfly its old name of W-hairstreak. Another feature is the pair of prominent black 'tails', tipped with white, at the rear of the wings.

The white-letter hairstreak is found in woods and hedgerows, especially where wych elms and common elms grow, and in favourable localities it can be plentiful. Each year large numbers of the butterfly and its caterpillars are found on particularly big elm trees, which seem to provide the most suitable conditions. They also spend a lot of their time visiting bramble and privet blossom for the nectar and the honeydew deposited on the leaves by aphids. They walk over leaves, opening and closing their wings, like their relatives the green hairstreaks and small coppers. White-letter hairstreaks are on the wing in July and August, and each butterfly lives for about 20 days. The loss of elms from Dutch elm disease in the 1970s removed many food plants, but the butterfly may be exploiting growths of scrub elm – suckers that grow up around dead trees.

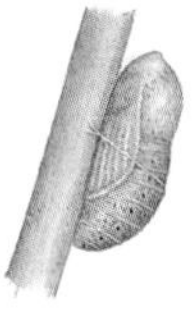

The chrysalis is attached to a stem or leaf by a silk girdle and pad. It hatches after three or four weeks.

[× 2]

Small coppers will occasionally be seen with a row of blue spots across the hind-wings.

The eggs are laid on the upper surface of the leaves of sorrel and dock (*Rumex* species), and occasionally knotgrass (*Polygonum*). They hatch after a week. [× 10]

A small copper butterfly basks on a heather flower, alert to chase off any insects that intrude into its territory.

The wings are copper-coloured with black markings on the fore-wings. These butterflies are shown on fleabane (*Pulicaria dysenterica*), a favourite nectar source. Wingspan 1⅛ in. (28 mm).

The hairy caterpillar is well camouflaged for its life on sorrel leaves. There are two colour forms – green and green-pink. There may be three generations a year and the caterpillars of the last generation hibernate.

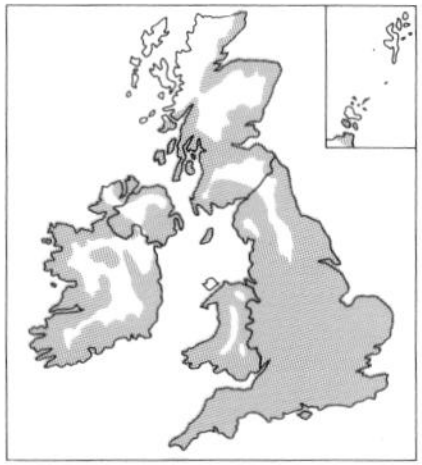

The small copper is widely distributed throughout most of the British Isles.

Small copper *Lycaena phlaeus*

The Yorkshire lepidopterist Adrian Haworth called this butterfly the common copper in 1803. True to its old name, it is still common in suitable places between April and October. It is the sole remaining member of the British coppers, as its relative the large copper became extinct in the fenland in 1865. The key to its abundance is that the caterpillar eats a variety of common dock and sorrel species which are widely distributed in Britain. The small copper frequents urban gardens and the verges of railway lines, roads and motorways, as well as heaths, downland and meadows. It is often in the company of blue butterflies, and is always found near flowers. It is a bright butterfly which is easy to spot as it basks, with wings open, on flowers or darts off to intercept rival blues, small heaths and hairstreaks that fly into its territory.

Variations in the size of the spots on the fore-wings and the width of the copper band on the hind-wing occur often, and albino specimens are known. There is a distinct sub-species in Ireland in which the band on the underside of the hind-wing is broader than on small coppers in Britain. Each butterfly lives for about a month.

Butterflies of sunny downlands

The gently rolling downlands of southern England provide a warm and bountiful home for a multicoloured population of butterflies. On sunny days in summer the grassy hills come alive with bright patches of colour as groups of butterflies flutter around their favourite plants. Clusters of blue butterflies, coppers, green hairstreaks and marbled whites sparkle like jewels in the sunshine.

The chalk soil of the downs favours chalk-loving wild flowers such as marjoram, thyme, vetches, knapweeds, scabious and yellow carline thistles. And the butterflies reap a harvest of nectar, particularly in warm hollows and on slopes facing south. A butterfly's life in the sun is spent establishing territories and fighting off rivals, having minor tussles with bumble-bees and hoverflies, courting and mating, feeding from flowers, basking and 'playing'. One active common blue might set off half a dozen other butterflies in a lightning chase over the grasses.

Hawthorn, whitebeam, dogwood and spindle bushes provide vantage points for butterflies, such as green hairstreaks, that seek out territories.

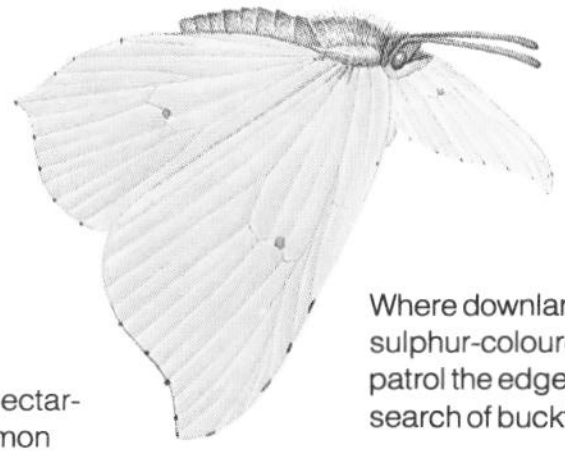

Where downland meets woodland, sulphur-coloured brimstones patrol the edge of the trees in search of buckthorn and ivy.

Fleabane, with its yellow nectar-rich flowers, attracts common blues, small coppers, small heaths and small skippers, especially where the chalk soil is overlaid with clay and flint.

THE BROWNS

The brown butterflies, or Satyridae family, all have false eyes either on the upper or lower surface of the wings. These marks confuse predatory birds or lizards about the position of the body, giving the butterfly a greater chance of surviving an attack. All but one of the brown family are in fact coloured brown; the odd one out is the marbled white which is black with white markings. The browns, like the aristocrats and the fritillaries, have only four walking legs.

The caterpillars of browns all eat grass, and all species spend the winter as caterpillars, feeding during mild weather. The speckled wood may also live through the winter as a chrysalis. Members of the brown family can be found all over Britain. Three of the 11 species – the large heath, the mountain ringlet and the Scotch argus – occur almost exclusively in the north. The gatekeeper and the marbled white are predominantly southern.

Female · Female underside

Meadow brown
Maniola jurtina
Pages 110–11

Male · Female

Small heath
Coenonympha pamphilus
Page 116

Large heath
Coenonympha tullia
Page 117

Male · Male underside

Ringlet
Aphantopus hyperantus
Page 118

Female underside · Female · Male

Gatekeeper
Pyronia tithonus
Pages 114–15

Male · Male underside

Small mountain ringlet
Erebia epiphron
Page 121

Marbled white
Melanargia galathea
Page 126

Grayling
Hipparchia semele
Page 127

Scotch argus
Erebia aethiops
Page 120

Speckled wood
Pararge aegeria
Pages 124–5

Wall
Lasiommata megera
Page 119

The caterpillars have a prolonged development period of eight to nine months. They feed at night during mild spells throughout winter.

A pale green chrysalis with black stripes is formed at the base of the food plant in May or June.

The eggs are laid singly in summer on several types of grass including cocksfoot and *Poa* species. [× 2]

The male is smaller than the female, and much darker, with less prominent false eyes.

The false eyes sometimes have a subsidiary pupil as well as the major one.

The female has a single prominent false eye on each fore-wing. It stands out strongly against the large orange patch.

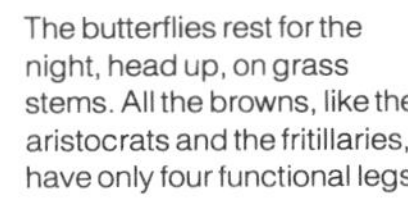

The butterflies rest for the night, head up, on grass stems. All the browns, like the aristocrats and the fritillaries, have only four functional legs.

Female

Single false eye

Light band

Male

These are the big brown butterflies that rise up from long grass in midsummer. The female's underside is paler than the male's and has a light band across the hind-wing. Both sexes have a single large false eye on the underside of the fore-wing. Wingspan up to 2 in. (50 mm).

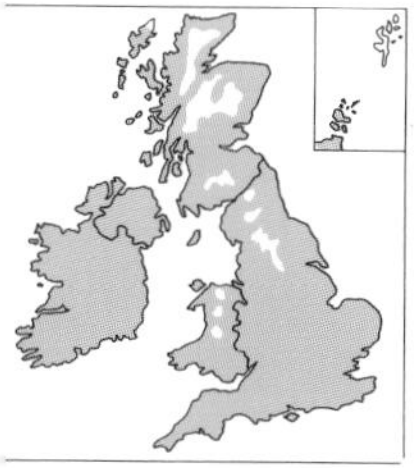

Found all over the British Isles, except the Shetlands and the highest mountains.

A female meadow brown butterfly perches on the tip of a grass flower spike, her prominent false eye shining in the light.

Meadow brown *Maniola jurtina*

Britain's commonest butterfly is the meadow brown. The pattern on its wings varies greatly, and the species has been classified into four sub-species in this country. However the butterflies seen throughout England, Wales and eastern Scotland are all the same type – the one illustrated on these pages. The female meadow brown is brighter than the male – an unusual feature as male butterflies are normally the more colourful. So marked are the differences that the 18th-century Swedish naturalist Linnaeus described the two sexes as separate species. Females are larger than males. They also have bigger false eyes on the fore-wings, which serve to frighten off predators. Nevertheless they are often caught and eaten by birds.

Meadow browns hatch between June and August, and the Suffolk poet John Clare seemed to describe them in his *Shepherd's Calendar* for June: 'Where their old visitors in russet brown, the haytime butterflies dance up and down.' Meadow browns are plentiful on roadside verges and rough areas, and in meadows in lowland and upland. They live about a month, and are always on the wing on sunny days. Unlike many other butterflies they will fly on dull days, and even in drizzle.

The butterflies of summer grasslands

Caterpillars that eat grass give rise to some of the most common butterflies. As their food is widespread and green throughout the year, the caterpillars – and hence the butterflies – have a relatively secure future. All Britain's grass-feeding caterpillars belong to the brown or skipper families. The butterflies are on the wing between June and September and can be seen in the corners of fields, beside country roads and anywhere else with long grass – waste ground, churchyards, old railway tracks.

Three of the skippers that can be common among long grass, forever chasing each other, are the small, the large and the Essex skippers. They are found in open areas, like some of the brown butterflies – the small heath, the marbled white and meadow brown. Other browns live in places sheltered from the wind. Gatekeepers and speckled woods, for example, keep to hedgerows, tracks or grassy woodland glades where they bask in the summer sun.

Rough open grasslands can become very hot and exposed to winds. Skippers fly fast over the grasses, and are still active on windy days. Marbled whites, which belong to the brown family, are sometimes plentiful on chalk grassland.

Woodland edges and corners of fields warm up into sun traps. Brown butterflies stake out their territories there, basking in the heat. Ringlets are recluses among butterflies, and prefer wet grassy hollows in or beside shady woodland.

Both sexes have three or four small white spots on the underside of the hind-wing, and a large false eye above, on the fore-wing.

The butterflies are often found basking with wings spread in warm corners of fields or woodland paths, and along hedgerows.

The chrysalis is similar to the meadow brown's and has a mottled black appearance. It is formed in June, suspended from grass by a silk pad.

Gatekeepers are named from their custom of taking up territories around corners of fields, sometimes near gates and stiles, particularly where nectar-rich brambles grow.

The caterpillar has white stripes along a brown body. It feeds at night during August and September, and rests at the base of the plant during the day. It hibernates from October to early spring, when it resumes feeding.

Two white pupils

Male

Female

Most common in southern England and Wales, and the south of Ireland.

Orange-brown butterflies that are usually found along hedgerows in July and August. The males are smaller and richer orange in colour than the females, with a distinct dark band of scent scales across the fore-wing. The false eye on the fore-wing of both sexes often has two white pupils. Wingspan of female $1\frac{1}{2}$ in. (38 mm).

The eggs are laid singly at the base of a leaf of grass. Several species of grass are suitable, including meadow grass (*Poa annua*) and couch grass (*Agropyron repens*). [× 3]

A pair of gatekeepers mate while perched on adjoining leaves in the warmth of the sun, revealing the white spots on the undersides of their wings.

Gatekeeper *Pyronia tithonus*

On sunny days in high summer, orange-brown butterflies flutter and settle along hedgerows and woodland paths. They are likely to be gatekeepers – also known as hedge browns because they are so often seen near country hedgerows. But the gatekeeper is easily mistaken for three other types of brown butterfly – the meadow brown, the speckled wood and the wall, which are also on the wing in July and August. They all have false eyes on their wings and are often found in the corners of fields near bramble thickets. However the wall is more likely to be seen basking on bare ground, while the gatekeeper visits hedgerows and the speckled wood enters woodland glades.

Male gatekeepers set up territories along hedgerows, and patrol them to keep out other insects. In search of sources of nectar, they are attracted to the flowers of marjoram, mint, wood sage and valerian, as well as bramble. And they are sometimes abundant in orchards. Each butterfly lives for about three weeks.

The caterpillars of the gatekeeper live from August until the following June, hibernating through the winter months low down among the grass.

Caterpillars that hatch from eggs laid in May produce butterflies by August. Other caterpillars live through the winter, feeding on grass during mild weather, and produce butterflies the following May.

Faint dark spot

False eyes on underside

The eggs are laid singly near the bottom of grass leaves. They hatch after about two weeks. [× 5]

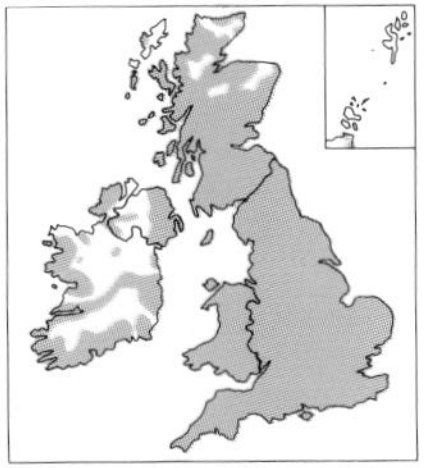

The small heath is found throughout Britain, with patchy distribution in Ireland.

A small, light brown butterfly with a faint dark spot at the tips of the fore-wings on the upper side. The underside has a prominent false eye on the fore-wing; the hind-wing is darker near the base and has a row of faint circles. Wingspan $1\frac{1}{8}$ in. (28 mm).

The chrysalis, suspended from a leaf, is similar but much smaller than the chrysalis of the meadow brown. It hatches after a month.

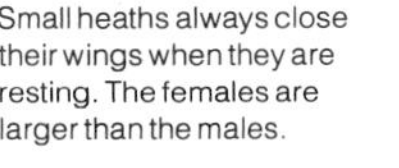

Small heaths always close their wings when they are resting. The females are larger than the males.

The small heath visits wayside flowers including daisies, yarrow, knapweed and scabious, right through summer.

Small heath *Coenonympha pamphilus*

This small tawny butterfly is very common throughout Britain during the summer wherever long grass grows. It is highly successful in this country because its caterpillars eat grass in both the uplands and the lowlands. Despite its name the small heath is not restricted to heathlands but can be numerous in areas ranging from urban wasteland to moorland, from meadows to railway embankments. It can be very common along roadside verges and ditches in September, often in the company of small coppers and common blues.

The butterflies live for about a month and are more often seen resting on grass than feeding from flowers. The warmer weather in the south of England allows for two generations a year. Butterflies may emerge from the chrysalis at any time between May and September since the caterpillar stage can develop as quickly as a month or as slowly as 11 months including hibernation through the winter.

Despite the similarity between female and male, early butterfly enthusiasts had separate names for each sex – the selvedged heath brown for the male and the golden heath eye for the female.

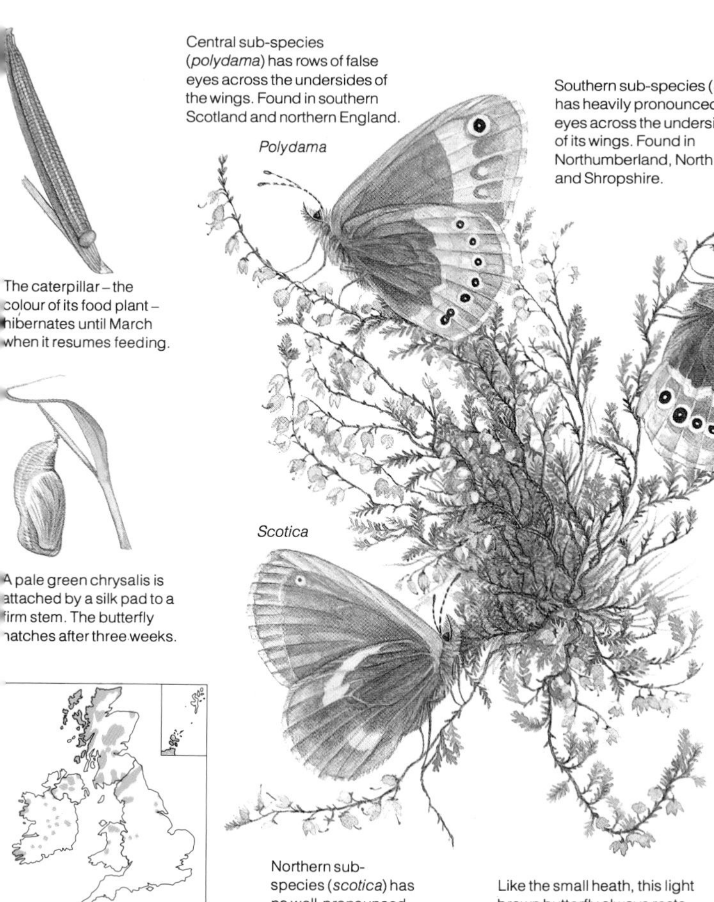

The caterpillar – the colour of its food plant – hibernates until March when it resumes feeding.

A pale green chrysalis is attached by a silk pad to a firm stem. The butterfly hatches after three weeks.

A northern butterfly, not found at all in southern counties of England.

Central sub-species (*polydama*) has rows of false eyes across the undersides of the wings. Found in southern Scotland and northern England.

Southern sub-species (*davus*) has heavily pronounced false eyes across the underside of its wings. Found in Northumberland, North Wales and Shropshire.

Eggs are laid singly on the leaves of white beak-sedge (*Rhynchospora alba*), the main food plant. They hatch after about two weeks. [× 7]

Northern sub-species (*scotica*) has no well-pronounced false eyes on the underside of its wings. Found in northern Scotland.

Like the small heath, this light brown butterfly always rests with its wings folded. All three sub-species are shown on heather (*Calluna vulgaris*). Wingspan 1⅜ in. (35 mm).

The light and dark colours on the wings help the large heath to blend with grass when it rests during the day.

Large heath *Coenonympha tullia*

This is a butterfly of the British uplands, typical of the Cairngorms, the Cheviots and Snowdonia. In Ireland it flies in boggy areas and is at its southernmost point in the British Isles in south-west Ireland. It used to occur as far south as Lincolnshire and Staffordshire, and was called the Manchester Argus or Manchester Ringlet when discovered in 1795. The large heath is found on marshes, bogs and moors up to 2,000 ft (610 m). These wet areas support rich growths of sedges, fescues and cottongrass – all food plants for the caterpillars.

The large heath is unusual in having three distinct geographical sub-species which vary in colour and pattern, becoming darker to the south. There is one generation a year, but in the extreme north of Scotland and in the Orkneys the caterpillars may take two years to develop in the grass. The butterflies are on the wing in June and July and live for two or three weeks. They rarely visit flowers and are frequently seen resting on grass stems or turf. They fly very close to the ground in windy weather and rest low down in the grass on wet, dull days. In suitable areas the butterflies may be very numerous, and they can be seen 'dancing' about in the long grass of summer.

The chrysalis is attached to a grass stem by a silk base near the ground. It hatches after about two weeks.

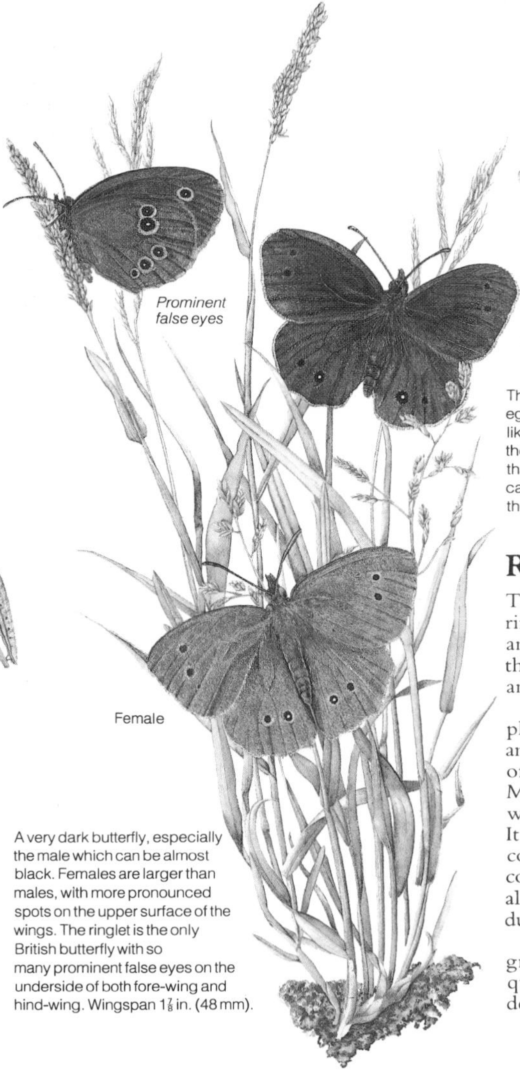

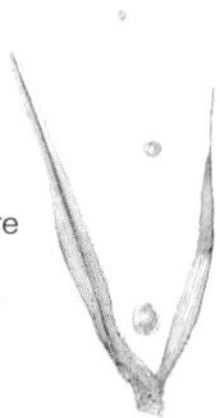

Prominent false eyes

Male

The female lays her eggs in flight. They are likely to fall on one of the common grasses that the young caterpillars will eat in the autumn.

Ringlets can be seen in long grass in June, July and August, or feeding on bramble flower nectar.

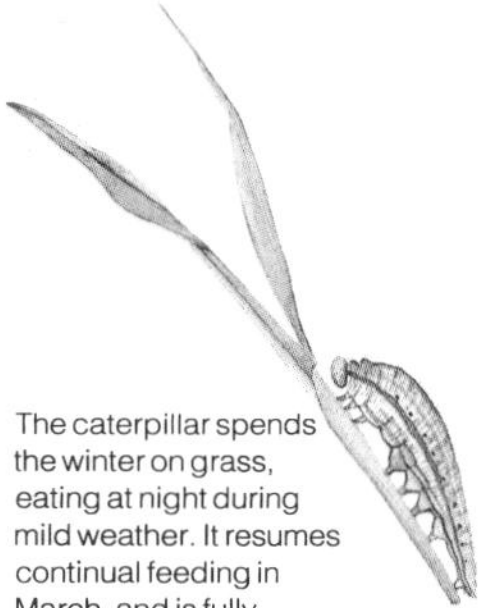

The caterpillar spends the winter on grass, eating at night during mild weather. It resumes continual feeding in March, and is fully grown in June.

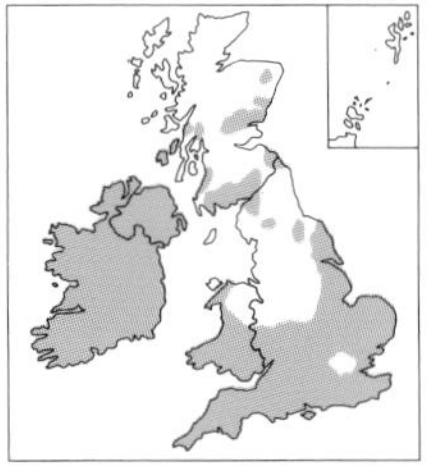

Female

Fairly widespread in Britain, particularly the south. Common in Ireland.

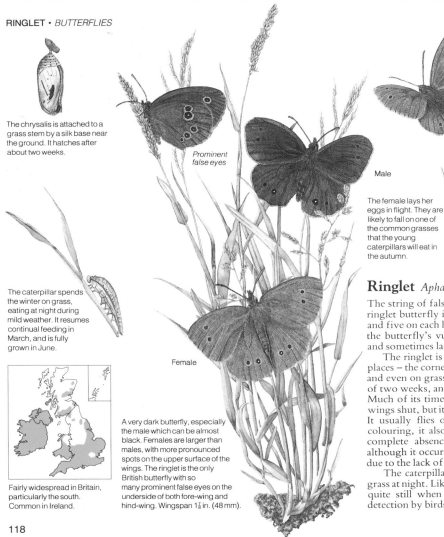

A very dark butterfly, especially the male which can be almost black. Females are larger than males, with more pronounced spots on the upper surface of the wings. The ringlet is the only British butterfly with so many prominent false eyes on the underside of both fore-wing and hind-wing. Wingspan 1⅞ in. (48 mm).

Ringlet *Aphantopus hyperantus*

The string of false eyes on the underside of the wings gives the ringlet butterfly its name. The spots – three on each fore-wing and five on each hind-wing – confuse birds as to the position of the butterfly's vulnerable body. They vary in size and colour and sometimes lack the white centre.

The ringlet is found from late June to August in wet grassy places – the corners of fields, along ditches, in woodland glades and even on grassy motorway embankments. It has a life-span of two weeks, and can occur in great numbers in secluded spots. Much of its time is spent in the grass, usually resting with its wings shut, but it also visits bramble flowers to drink the nectar. It usually flies on sunny days but, in keeping with its dull colouring, it also flies on dull days and even in the rain. The complete absence of the species from the London area – although it occurs in the surrounding counties – is presumably due to the lack of suitably wet grassy areas.

The caterpillars, which live for 11 months, usually feed on grass at night. Like many beetles, they drop to the ground and lie quite still when they are disturbed, in an attempt to evade detection by birds.

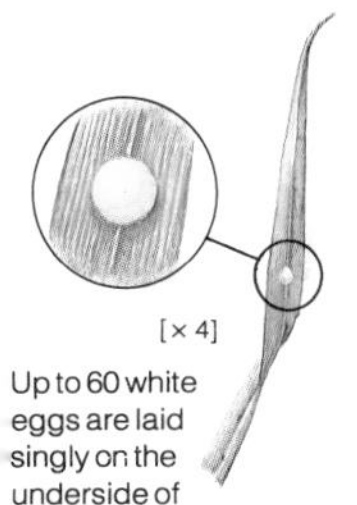

Up to 60 white eggs are laid singly on the underside of many types of grass.

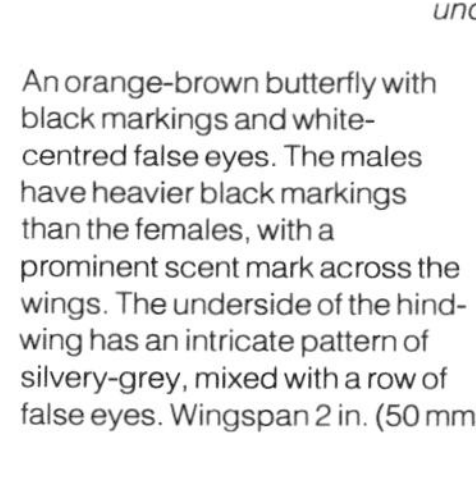

An orange-brown butterfly with black markings and white-centred false eyes. The males have heavier black markings than the females, with a prominent scent mark across the wings. The underside of the hind-wing has an intricate pattern of silvery-grey, mixed with a row of false eyes. Wingspan 2 in. (50 mm).

Early summer caterpillars develop in a month. Late summer caterpillars hibernate, eating intermittently, until April.

The wall spends much of its time basking in sunny places – on plants, embankments or walls – but it is easily disturbed.

The chrysalis is attached to a stem, and may vary in colour from green to black. It hatches after two weeks.

Common in England and Wales; also found in southern Scotland and Ireland.

The wall *Lasiommata megera*

The wall, or wall brown, is an energetic and brightly coloured butterfly which basks in the sunshine, often on warm rocks or walls, hence its name. Its rich orange colour may be seen glowing in the setting sun, as this is a butterfly that rises early and retires late. Males have strong territorial behaviour, and will perch on prominent places, making sorties to drive away intruding insects. They also patrol paths, hedgerows and fences looking for females, and visit wayside flowers to drink nectar. The wall is a restless butterfly and is easily disturbed when being photographed. It will accompany walkers in the countryside, rising up, flying further on and resting on the bare earth.

There are two broods of butterflies each year – the first on the wing in May and June, and the second in July and August. In very favourable seasons the first brood can appear as early as late April, giving rise to a second brood in June and July, and a third in September. The life-span of each butterfly is about three weeks. The wall could be confused with the speckled wood (p. 125) which might share the same lane. However the speckled wood prefers shady areas, while the wall is found in the open, obtaining as much sunshine as it can find.

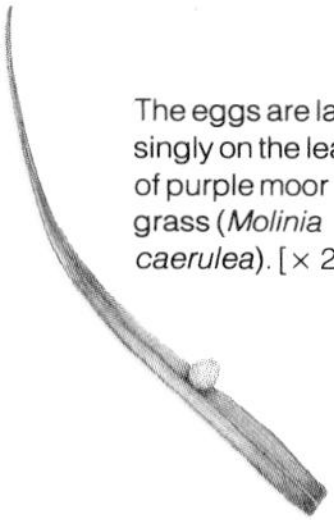

The eggs are laid singly on the leaves of purple moor grass (*Molinia caerulea*). [× 2]

White-centred spots

Male

Female

The pale bands across each wing contain black spots with white centres. Females are lighter in colour, with larger white spots. The underside of the hind-wing has a light-coloured band, more prominent on the female. Wingspan 1¾ in. (45 mm).

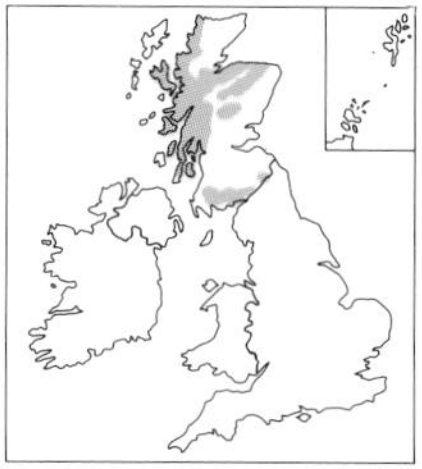

Female

Now exclusively a Scottish butterfly, found mostly in the west of the country.

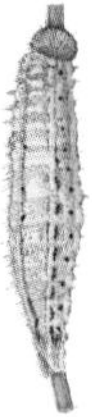

The brown caterpillar feeds by night and rests on the base of the plant by day. It hibernates from September until April.

The chrysalis is formed in leaf litter at the base of the food plant, and hatches after about 16 days. [× 2]

The Scotch argus is seen on sunny days in July and August. In dull weather it usually rests in the grass.

Scotch argus *Erebia aethiops*

The rows of false eyes on the wings of this Scottish butterfly are the source of its name – from the hundred-eyed hero of Greek mythology who was constantly on the alert for enemies. The false eyes on the female are particularly well pronounced. As the butterflies shelter in the grass in rainy weather, the eyes on the underside peep out from above the hind-wings. At rest, the Scotch argus looks remarkably like a withered leaf, and males have been seen making approaches to dead leaves in the grass.

The butterfly delights in sunshine, especially in places which receive the warming rays of early morning. Edges of woodlands, grassy hillsides, sheltered valleys and moors dance with the insects when the sun shines, but immediately it goes behind a cloud they all disappear. They will only be tempted to fly in dull weather if the air is very warm.

The slug-like caterpillars feed on grass by night, and readily fall from the stems and 'play dead' if disturbed. They live about ten months compared to about three weeks for the butterfly. The Scotch argus, which was once known as the northern brown, used to occur in several upland counties of northern England, but is now extinct there.

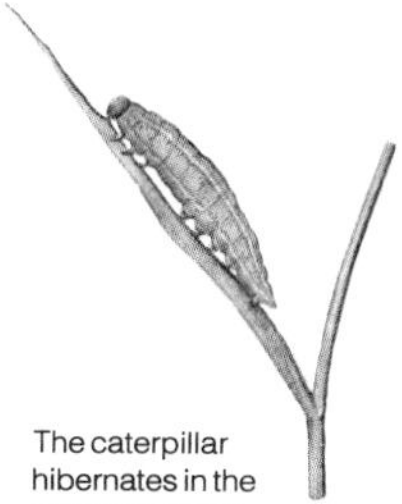

The caterpillar hibernates in the mat-grass from September to March. In spring it eats the tender young leaf tips of the mat-grass.

The pale bands on the wings contain black spots without white centres. Otherwise this species is similar to but smaller than the Scotch argus. The female is lighter coloured, with more pronounced spots than the male. Shown feeding on thyme. Wingspan $1\frac{1}{2}$ in. (38 mm).

Solid black spots

Female

Male

A green chrysalis with brown markings is formed in debris at the base of the mat-grass. [× 2]

The butterfly is found mainly in western Scotland and the Lake District.

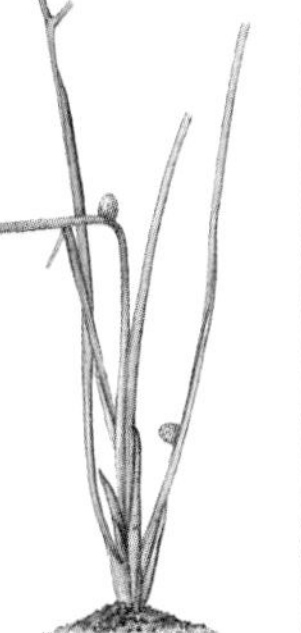

The eggs are laid singly in late summer on mat-grass (*Nardus stricta*). [× 2]

The small mountain ringlet shelters in the grass in dull weather, but when the sun shines it visits wild flowers.

Small mountain ringlet *Erebia epiphron*

One of Britain's true alpine butterflies, the small mountain ringlet is a legacy from the last Ice Age, with its origins dating back to 10,000 BC. It is a smaller relative of the Scotch argus which is also an alpine relic. (See overleaf.) Both butterflies belong to the *Erebia* genus, and have many other relatives in the Alps and the Pyrenees. The small mountain ringlet prefers northern latitudes and high altitudes in Britain, and is not found below 700 ft. It lives in boggy areas which support its principal food plant, clumps of mat-grass.

Small mountain ringlets are dark butterflies, easily seen against the light colours of moorland grasses in late June and July. They occasionally visit flowers and spend a lot of time resting in grass during dull weather. There is one generation a year, and each butterfly lives for about 20 days. The caterpillars hibernate for about ten months.

There are two sub-species – the Scottish (illustrated), which has an unbroken tawny band across the fore-wings, and the English, which has a broken band. The butterflies are abundant on the slopes of Ben Nevis in central Scotland. They are also found in the Lake District.

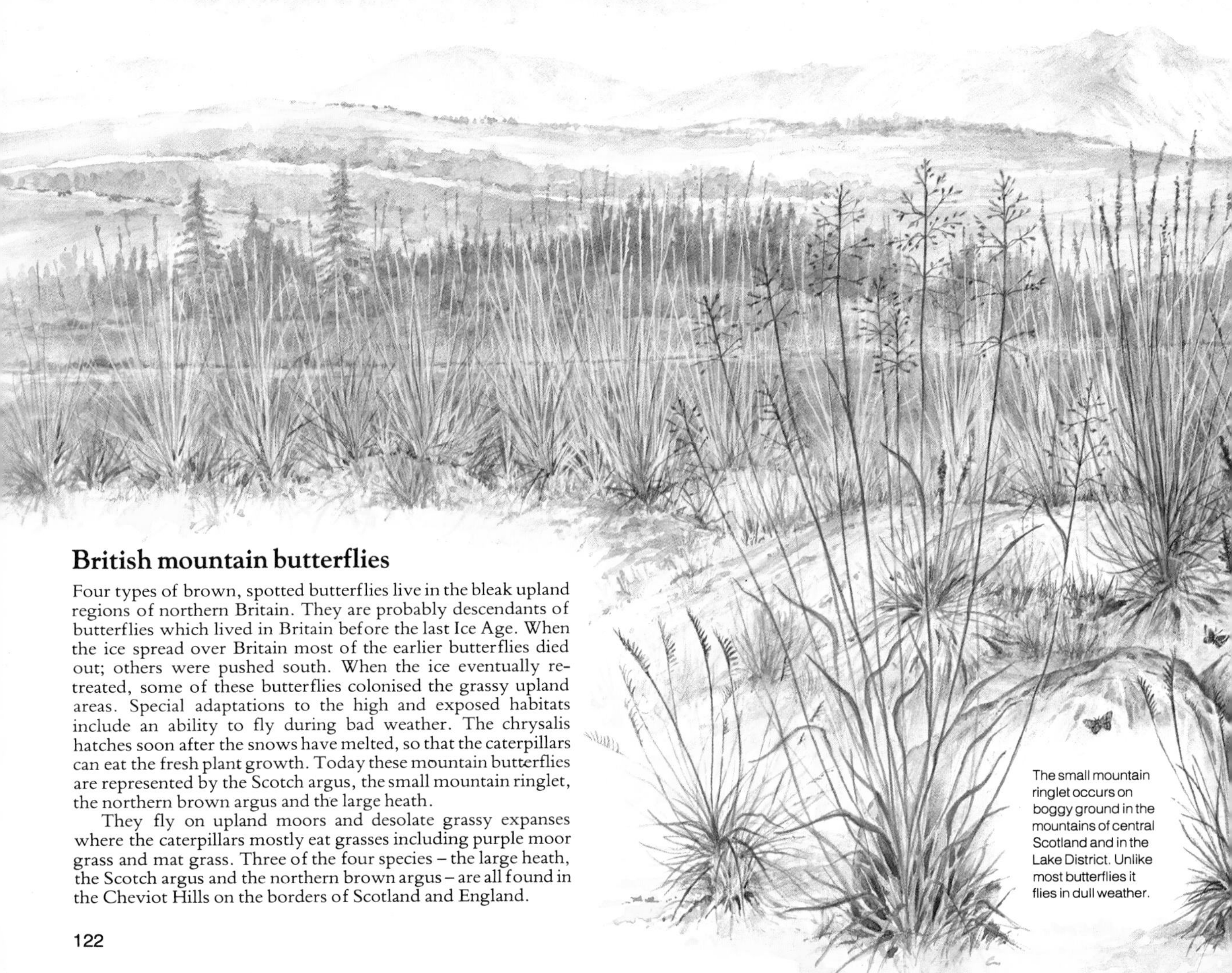

British mountain butterflies

Four types of brown, spotted butterflies live in the bleak upland regions of northern Britain. They are probably descendants of butterflies which lived in Britain before the last Ice Age. When the ice spread over Britain most of the earlier butterflies died out; others were pushed south. When the ice eventually retreated, some of these butterflies colonised the grassy upland areas. Special adaptations to the high and exposed habitats include an ability to fly during bad weather. The chrysalis hatches soon after the snows have melted, so that the caterpillars can eat the fresh plant growth. Today these mountain butterflies are represented by the Scotch argus, the small mountain ringlet, the northern brown argus and the large heath.

They fly on upland moors and desolate grassy expanses where the caterpillars mostly eat grasses including purple moor grass and mat grass. Three of the four species – the large heath, the Scotch argus and the northern brown argus – are all found in the Cheviot Hills on the borders of Scotland and England.

The small mountain ringlet occurs on boggy ground in the mountains of central Scotland and in the Lake District. Unlike most butterflies it flies in dull weather.

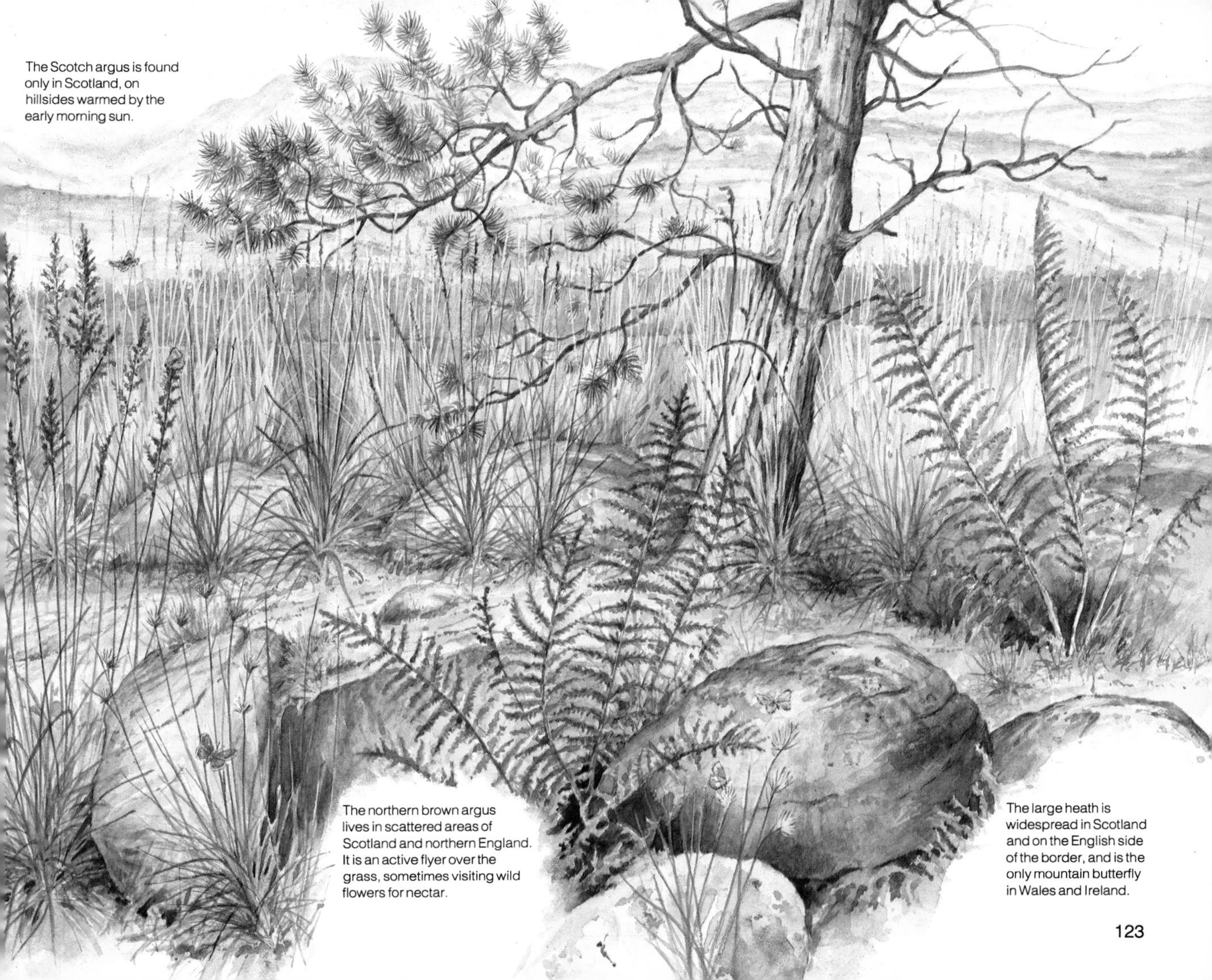

The Scotch argus is found only in Scotland, on hillsides warmed by the early morning sun.

The northern brown argus lives in scattered areas of Scotland and northern England. It is an active flyer over the grass, sometimes visiting wild flowers for nectar.

The large heath is widespread in Scotland and on the English side of the border, and is the only mountain butterfly in Wales and Ireland.

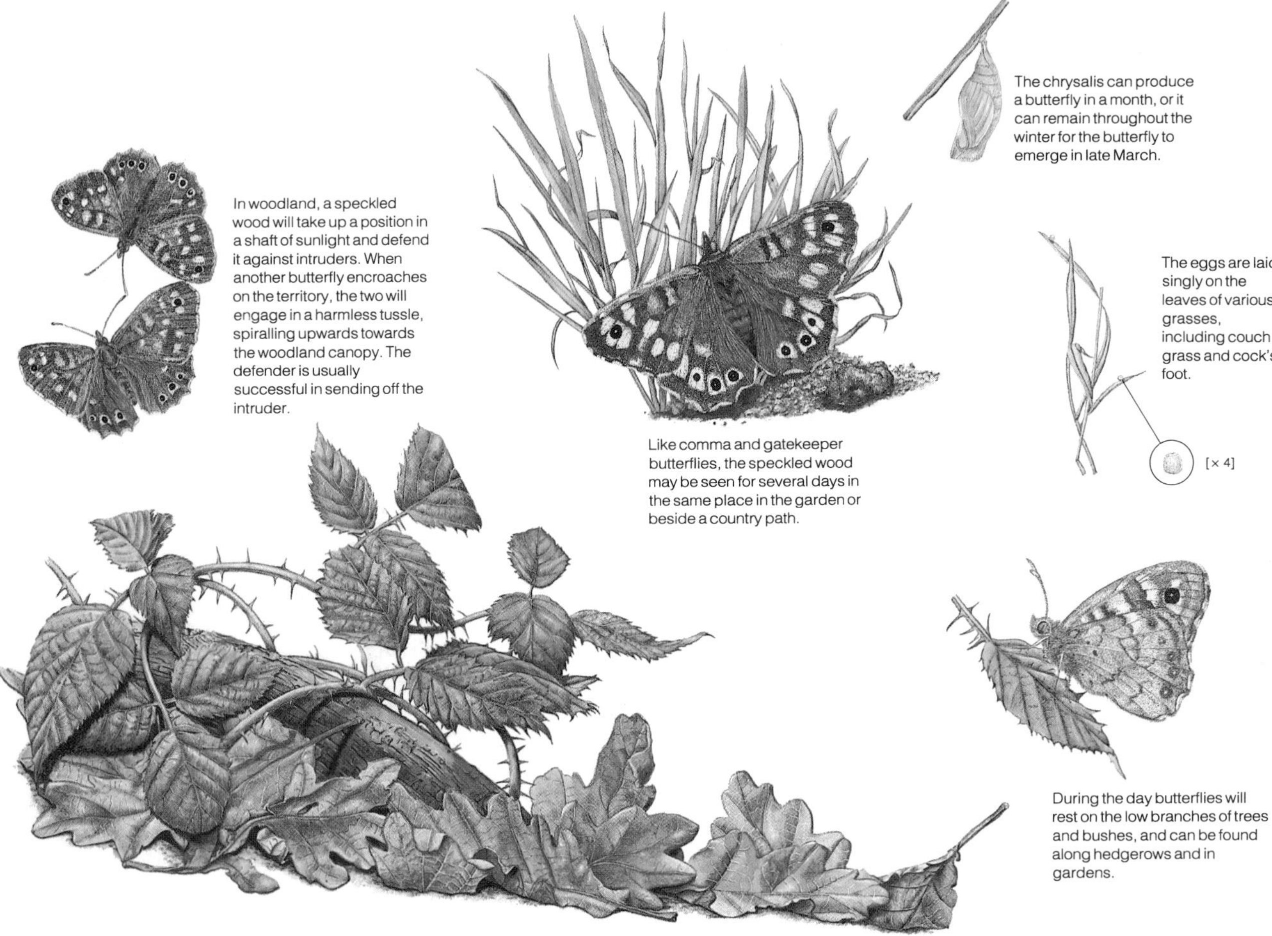

The chrysalis can produce a butterfly in a month, or it can remain throughout the winter for the butterfly to emerge in late March.

In woodland, a speckled wood will take up a position in a shaft of sunlight and defend it against intruders. When another butterfly encroaches on the territory, the two will engage in a harmless tussle, spiralling upwards towards the woodland canopy. The defender is usually successful in sending off the intruder.

The eggs are laid singly on the leaves of various grasses, including couch grass and cock's-foot.

Like comma and gatekeeper butterflies, the speckled wood may be seen for several days in the same place in the garden or beside a country path.

During the day butterflies will rest on the low branches of trees and bushes, and can be found along hedgerows and in gardens.

A dark brown butterfly with buff patches. Each fore-wing has a false eye with a white centre, and each hind-wing has three false eyes. The female has larger buff spots than the male, with slightly rounded wingtips. Wingspan $1\frac{3}{4}$ in. (45 mm).

There are two to four generations a year. Caterpillars of the early summer become fully grown in about a month. Autumn caterpillars live through the winter, feeding during warm spells, and take eight or nine months to become fully grown.

The speckled wood butterfly can live for about 20 days, but this one ends its life prematurely in the web of a garden spider.

Male

Female

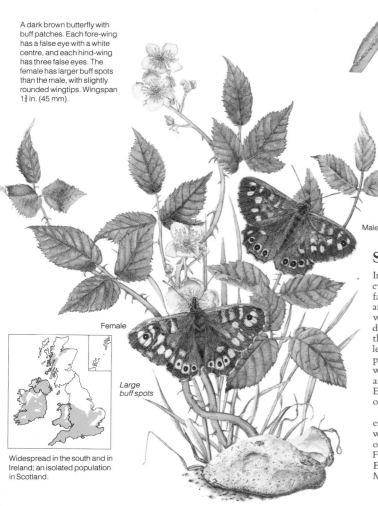

Large buff spots

Widespread in the south and in Ireland; an isolated population in Scotland.

Speckled wood *Pararge aegeria*

In the 18th century this butterfly became known as the Enfield eye when it was identified in rural Middlesex. Today it is a familiar butterfly of suburban parks, commons and the rough areas of golf courses. It is also a resident of southern English woodlands. Its speckled wings give it ideal camouflage in the dappled world of light and dark where sunlight percolates through the canopy and scatters over brambles and honeysuckle. It can be seen, as well, around woodland margins, along paths and hedgerows, and in clearings. Its spots and connection with woods gave it another 18th-century name, wood argus, after the many-eyed hero of Greek mythology. In the west of England and Wales the speckled wood can be found in more open habitats of hillsides and cliffs.

The butterflies exhibit a high degree of territorial behaviour, establishing themselves in sunny glades which they defend and where they conduct their courtship. The amount of speckling on the wings varies from region to region and season to season. Four sub-species occur – in Scotland, the Isles of Scilly, southern England and Snowdonia, each one with different wing patterns. Males that hatch in autumn are darker than those in spring.

The young caterpillar hibernates in the grass from autumn until February, when it resumes feeding. It rests close to the ground during the day and feeds on the stems at night.

The only British butterfly with this distinctive black-and-white pattern. The undersides of the wings are not so brightly marked. The females are larger than the males, with slightly broader fore-wings. Shown on the flowers of knapweed (*Centaurea scabiosa*). Wingspan $2\frac{1}{8}$ in. (54 mm).

Male

Female

In June or July the chrysalis is formed in the soil beneath the grass. The butterfly hatches in July after 20–30 days.

Found mostly in the south of Britain, but can occur as far north as York.

[× 4]

Like the ringlet, the marbled white lays its eggs while flying. There is a good chance that they will fall on one of the grasses that the caterpillars will eat, such as cock's-foot and sheep's-fescue.

Marbled whites are susceptible to attack from brightly coloured parasitic mites, which feed on their blood.

Marbled white *Melanargia galathea*

In the early 19th century the marbled white butterfly was known as the half-mourner. The term came from the black-and-white dresses that women wore during half-mourning, the period that followed full mourning for a dead relative when only black was worn. The name then changed to the marmoris and the marmoress, from the word marmoreal, meaning like marble. Later in the 19th century the butterfly finally came to be known as the marbled white.

This member of the brown family is actually a black butterfly with white spots, rather than a white butterfly with black spots. However the black-and-white wing patterns sometimes vary, and it may occasionally look as though it belongs to the white-butterfly family. Its most common breeding grounds are chalky downland slopes, but it also exploits Forestry Commission paths on chalk soil, open grassy wastelands, moors and damp meadows. In its favourite locations the butterfly can be extremely abundant in July and August. It feeds on flowers with the wings open, showing off the bright contrasting colours which are probably a visual deterrent to predatory birds. Knapweeds and scabious are favourite nectar sources.

The white eggs are laid singly on various species of grass and hatch after about 17 days. [× 4]

White-centred spots

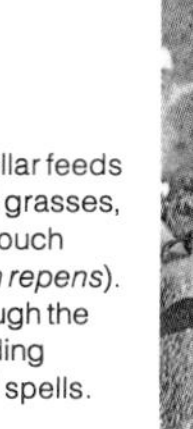

The caterpillar feeds on different grasses, including couch (*Agropyron repens*). It lives through the winter, feeding during mild spells.

At rest, the grayling retracts its fore-wings between the hind-wings, casting less shadow and becoming hard to see.

A powerful flyer that will not stay still to be examined closely. When it comes to rest on flowers it always closes its wings, showing two black spots with white centres. Wingspan up to 2 in. (50 mm).

The chrysalis is formed in a shallow chamber in the soil, and the butterfly hatches in June or July.

Found along the coast of Britain, particularly in the south and the west.

Grayling *Hipparchia semele*

Britain's largest brown butterfly, with its silver-grey underside, shares its common name of grayling with a freshwater fish of a similar colour. It is mostly a coastal butterfly, living on the grassy slopes and hollows at the top of cliffs. It is also found on the chalky downs, the heathlands of the New Forest and the grasslands of Salisbury Plain. But it is not at all common. The old name of the Tunbridge grayling refers to a time when it flew in the Weald of Kent near Tunbridge Wells, where it no longer exists.

The butterfly is an expert in concealment. When landing after swift, but very short flights, it tilts over sideways to the sun so as not to cast an obvious shadow. It often settles on stony or earthy ground where – after it retracts its fore-wings between the hind-wings – its underside coloration blends into the background. The false eyes on both sides of the wings are found throughout the brown family, and are used to confuse predatory birds as to the position of the head. Graylings rarely visit wild flowers for nectar, but they are believed to drink sap from oak and pine trees. There are six sub-species, including a small one on Great Orme Head in North Wales.

What caterpillar is it?

When attempting to name a caterpillar, try also to identify the plant it is eating. Some caterpillars have only one food plant, others have several; but the plant is always a good guide. The number of legs is another crucial point of identification. The caterpillars of butterflies and moths usually have four pairs of prolegs, the sucker-like false legs in the centre of the body. If there are more than four pairs, it is a sawfly larva. Some larvae of beetles and flies are also included in this chart as they, too, look rather like caterpillars.

Some caterpillars are brightly coloured – warning birds that they are unpalatable. Others defend themselves by blending in with the colours of their food plant. In the chart they have been grouped according to the colours and shapes that make them most distinctive. As caterpillars vary in colour and size according to age, all have been drawn life-size when fully grown.

Green caterpillars on plants other than grass

Green is a common colour for caterpillars, giving them camouflage on foliage or stems. Several of these species have only one food plant, or a few closely related ones.

Brown hairstreak butterfly
On sloe (blackthorn) bushes from April to June. Southern England, Wales and Co. Clare. Page 102

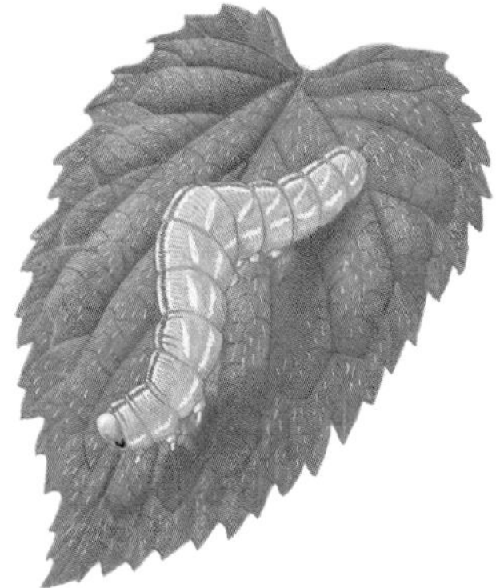

Burnished brass moth
On stinging nettles in April and May, and later in August and September. Throughout Britain. Page 174

Brimstone butterfly
On buckthorn and alder-buckthorn in June and July. England, Wales and Ireland; not in Scotland. Pages 48–49

Large birch sawfly
Feeds on birch leaves in May and June. Found in birch woods on sandy soils and heathlands. Page 241

Green oak tortrix moth
On oak, beech, sycamore and some other deciduous trees from April to June. Throughout Britain. Page 207

Eyed hawk-moth
On the undersides of willow, apple and poplar leaves between June and September. England, Wales and Ireland. Page 148

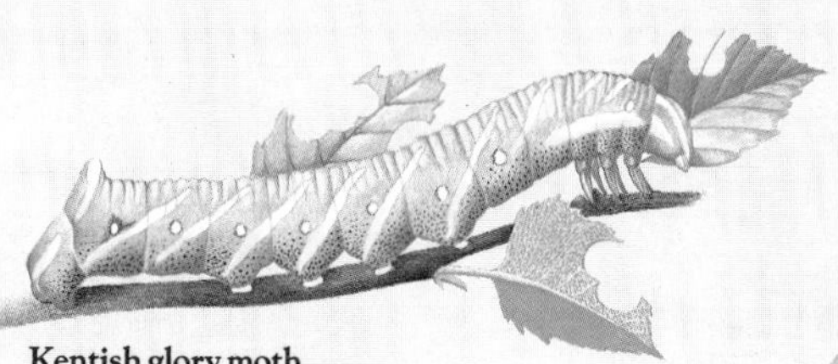

Kentish glory moth
On birch and alder trees from May to July. Scotland. Page 203

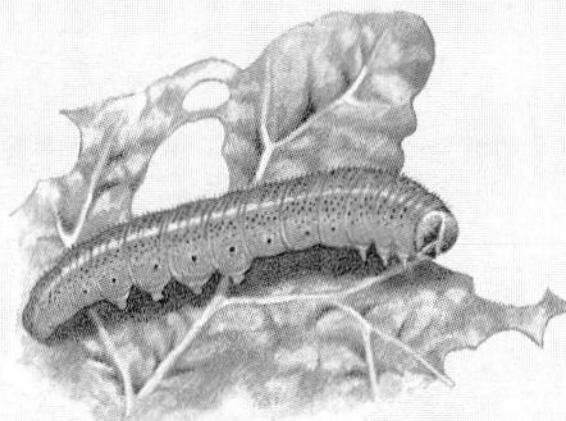

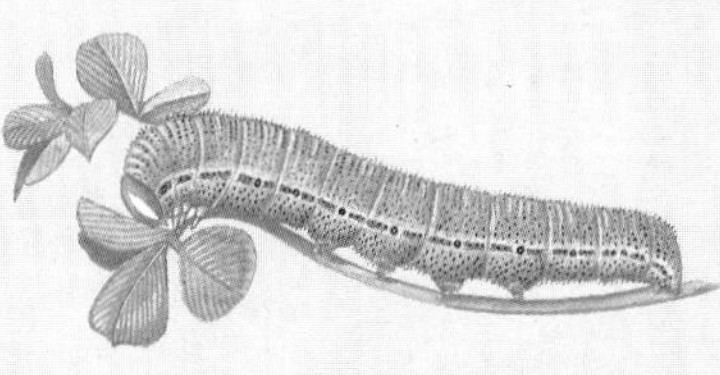

Pale clouded yellow butterfly
On clover and lucerne leaves in June and July. In southern England. Page 53

Small white butterfly
On plants of the cabbage family from June to September. Conceals itself in the heart of cabbage. Throughout Britain. Page 44

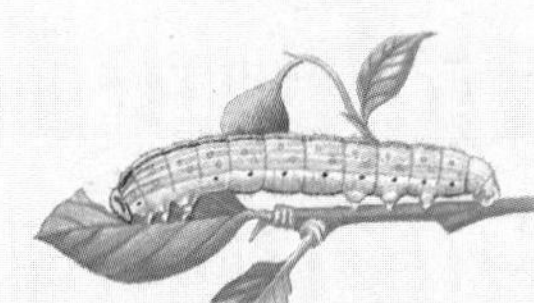

Silver Y moth
On almost any type of low-growing plant from May to September. Throughout Britain. Page 175

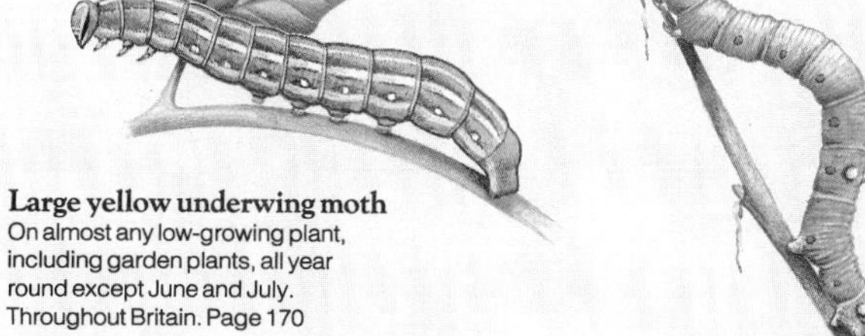

Large yellow underwing moth
On almost any low-growing plant, including garden plants, all year round except June and July. Throughout Britain. Page 170

Peppered moth
On most deciduous trees and shrubs in town or country from July to September. Throughout Britain. Page 192

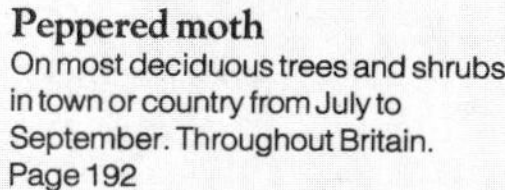

Winter moth
On almost any deciduous tree in town or country in spring. Throughout Britain. Page 189

Emperor moth
Colourful caterpillars that blend in well on heather. Also found on bramble and sallow in July. Throughout Britain. Page 202

Berger's clouded yellow butterfly
On horseshoe vetch or crown vetch from July until April. In southern England. Page 53

Golden plusia moth
On monkshood and larkspur in gardens in May and June. Another generation in July and August. Spreading through Britain. Page 174

Pine sawfly
A serious forestry pest which feeds in the summer on needles of Scots pine. Throughout Britain. Page 241

Black hairstreak butterfly
On sloe (blackthorn) bushes in April and May. Central England only. Page 101

Blair's shoulder-knot moth
On cypress trees in spring. Southern England, spreading northwards. Page 172

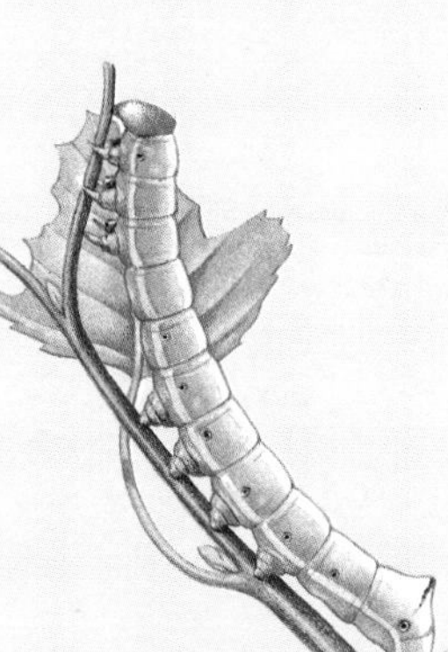

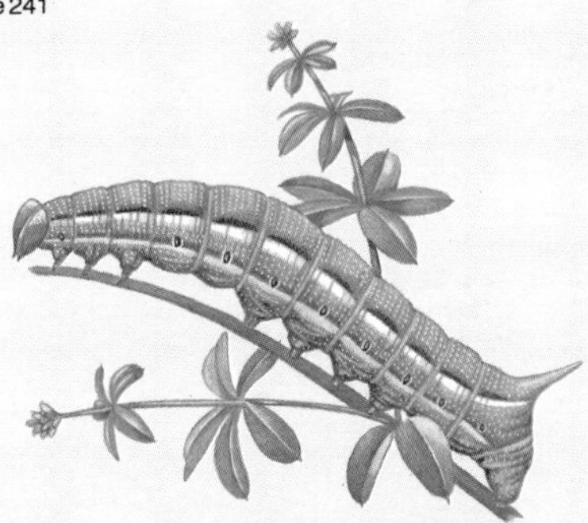

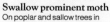

Humming-bird hawk-moth
On bedstraw during July and August. Throughout Britain. Page 147

Green-veined white butterfly
On garlic mustard, watercress and other members of the cabbage family (but not cultivated cabbages) from June to September. Throughout Britain. Page 46

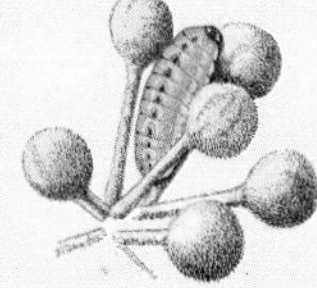

Holly blue butterfly
On holly in spring and on ivy in autumn. Mostly in England, Wales and Ireland. Page 100

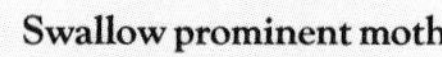

Swallow prominent moth
On poplar and sallow trees in June/July and September/ October. England and Wales; patchily in Scotland and Ireland. Page 158

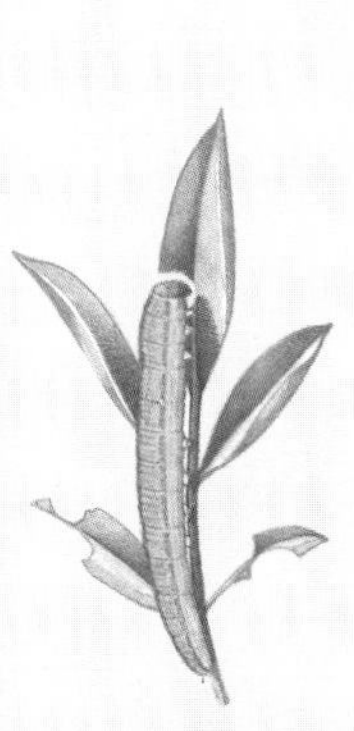

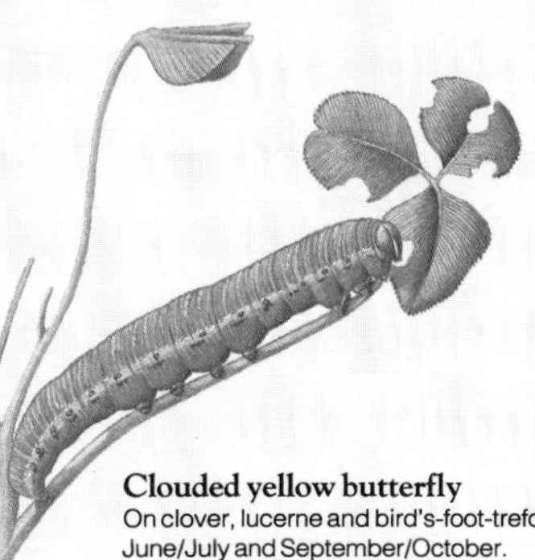

Green hairstreak butterfly
On gorse, broom, bramble and other shrubs in June and July. Many scattered localities throughout Britain.
Page 103

Clouded yellow butterfly
On clover, lucerne and bird's-foot-trefoil in June/July and September/October. Throughout Britain. Page 52

Wood white butterfly
On bitter vetch, bird's-foot-trefoil and other members of the pea family in summer. Southern England and Ireland. Page 47

Rose-leaf sawfly
Blennocampa pusilla
On rose bushes, concealed in a curled edge of the leaflet it is feeding on. Common in Britain.
See also pages 240–1

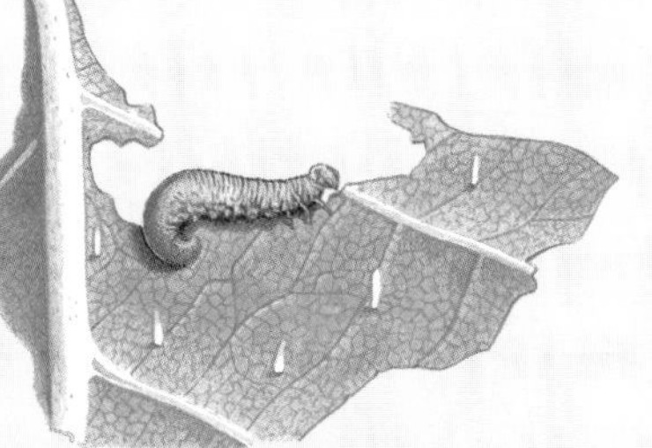

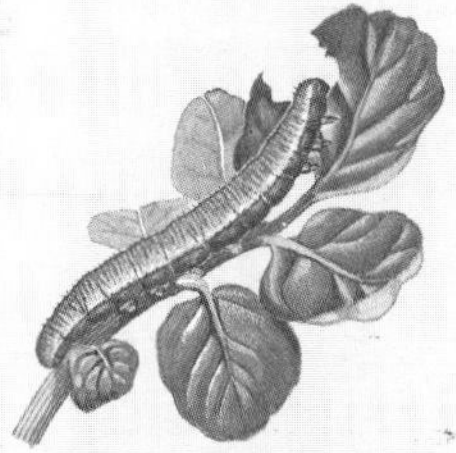

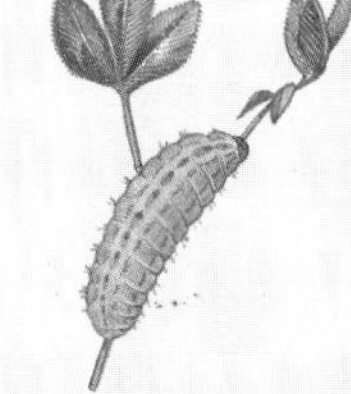

Palisade sawfly
Nematus compressicornis
Feeding on the edges of poplar leaves, dotting their surroundings with little white blobs resembling palisades.
See also pages 240–1

Northern brown argus butterfly
On rock rose from August to June the following year. Northern England and Scotland. Page 99

Common blue butterfly
On bird's-foot-trefoil, restharrow and clover from June to August and from September to April. Throughout Britain.
Page 90

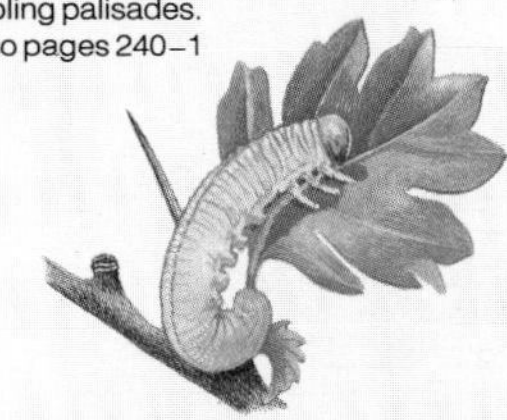

Large hawthorn sawfly
On hawthorn bushes from July to September, perhaps in groups. Throughout Britain. Page 241

Orange tip butterfly
On garlic mustard and cuckoo flower in June and July and occasionally in August and September. England, Wales and eastern Scotland.
Pages 50–51

Rose sawfly
On leaves of roses in spring and summer. Generally distributed in Britain. Page 241

Apple sawfly
Only on apple trees – eating apples rather than cookers – from May to June. In gardens and orchards throughout Britain. Page 241

Adonis blue butterfly
On horseshoe vetch in June and July and from October to April. Southern England only. Page 93

Gooseberry sawfly
On gooseberry and currant bushes from April to August. May be a pest in gardens. Page 241

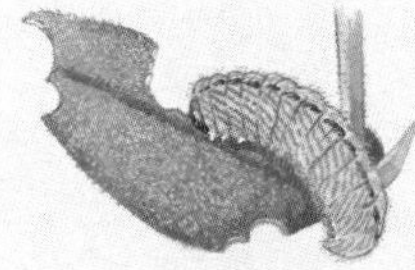

Brown argus butterfly
On rock rose and common storksbill in June and again from August to April the following year. Southern England and Wales. Page 98

Dingy skipper butterfly
On bird's-foot-trefoil only, as a hibernating caterpillar between July and April. Mostly southern England, but can occur elsewhere. Page 36

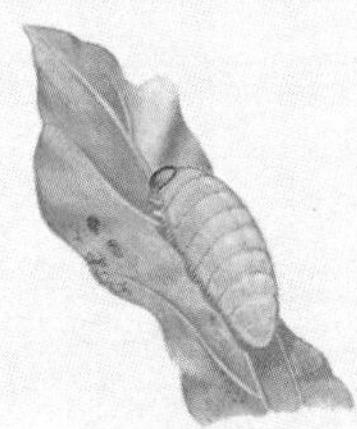

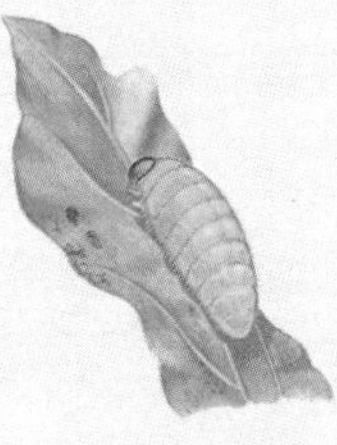

Small copper butterfly
On sorrel and dock from May to October. Throughout Britain. Page 106

Five-spot burnet moth
On bird's-foot-trefoil throughout the year except in June. Southern England, Wales and Isle of Man. Page 199

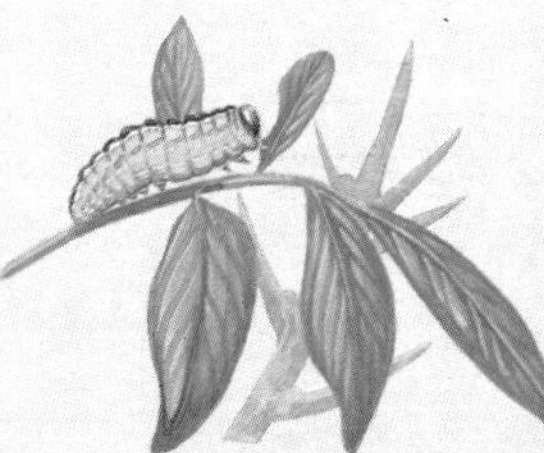

Silver-studded blue butterfly
On gorse, bird's-foot-trefoil and heather in spring. Southern England and Wales. Page 91

Green caterpillars found on grass

All these grass-feeding caterpillars eventually become butterflies. Most rest by day at the base of grass clumps, and may be discovered when clearing weeds in a garden.

Wall butterfly
Found in June and July and again from September to April in grassy areas. Throughout England, Wales and Ireland. Page 119

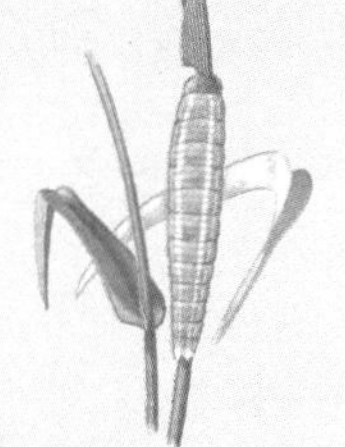

Small mountain ringlet butterfly
Found all year round, except in July, in woodland clearings and along hedgerows. Central Scotland and Lake District. Page 121

Large heath butterfly
Found all year round, except in June, on wet hillsides and marshland. Only in northern England, Wales, Scotland, Ireland. Page 117

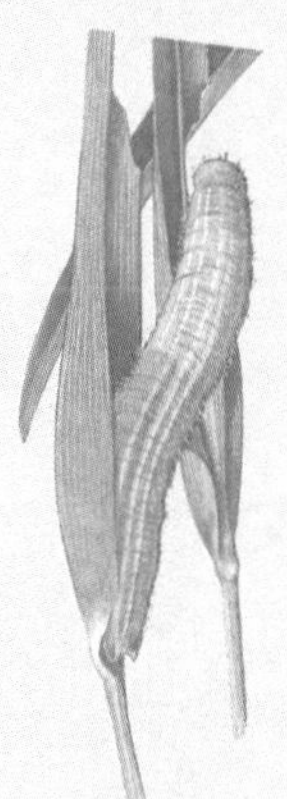

Speckled wood butterfly
Found throughout the year along waysides and by hedgerows. Southern England, Wales, northern Scotland, Ireland. Pages 124–5

Chequered skipper butterfly
Found all year round, except in May, in woodland clearings. Western Scotland only. Page 35

Large skipper butterfly
On cock's-foot grass and false brome grass from July to May. In England, Wales and southern Scotland. Page 32

Meadow brown butterfly
Found all year round, except in June, in most grassy areas, including roadside verges and waste ground. Throughout Britain. Pages 110–11

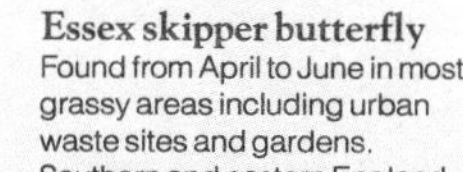

Essex skipper butterfly
Found from April to June in most grassy areas including urban waste sites and gardens. Southern and eastern England. Page 31

Yellow and orange caterpillars

Caterpillar colours often change with age, but these species are usually yellow-orange or yellow-green. The colour helps to camouflage the caterpillar.

Small skipper butterfly
Found all year round, except July, in most grassy areas including urban waste sites and gardens. Most of England and Wales. Page 30

Marbled white butterfly
Found all year round, except in July, on downland, hillsides and rough grassland. Southern England and Wales. Page 126

Small heath butterfly
Found all year round, except in May, along roadside verges and in grassy meadows, pastures and hayfields. Throughout Britain. Page 116

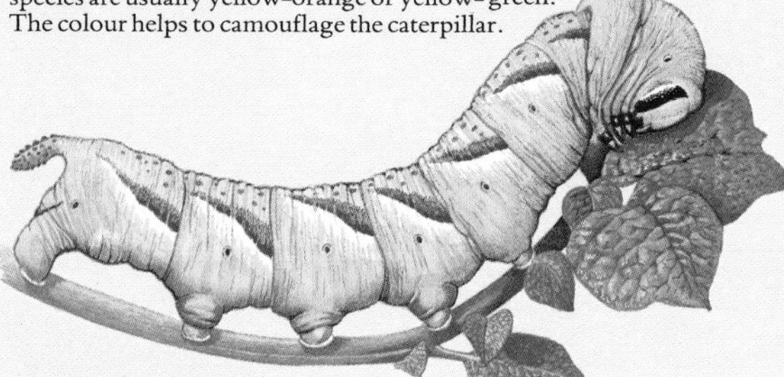

Death's head hawk-moth
On potato or Duke of Argyll's teaplant in September and October. Throughout Britain. Page 144

Hornet moth
In the lower trunks of poplar trees throughout the year. Mostly in eastern England. Page 197

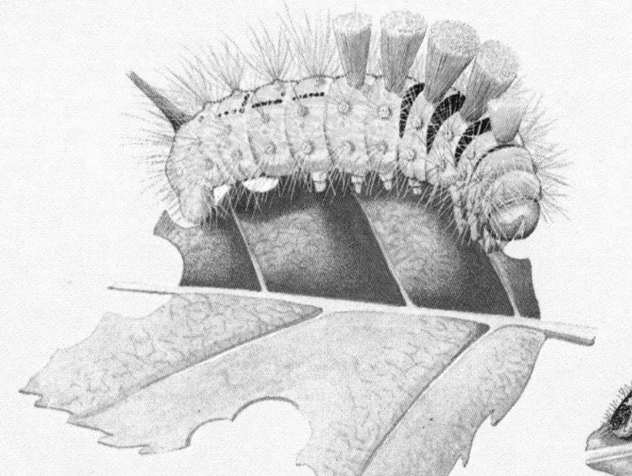

Pale tussock moth
On many deciduous trees and shrubs, including oak, birch, hazel and hops, from July to September. Throughout England and Wales. Page 166

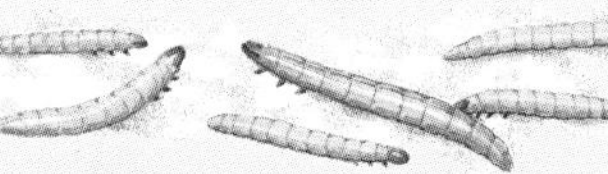

Mealworm beetle
In farmyard litter and granaries all year round. Sold in pet shops as food for birds and lizards. Throughout Britain. Page 306

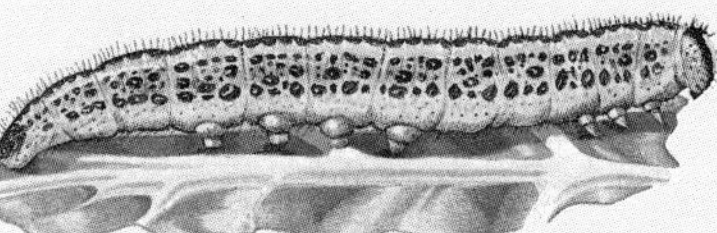

Large white butterfly
On wild or cultivated plants of the cabbage family from June to October. Feeds in groups. Throughout Britain. Pages 42–43

Mullein moth
On mullein, figwort and buddleia in June and July. England and Wales. The caterpillars are fairly common but the moths are seldom seen.

Swallowtail butterfly
On milk parsley in June and July in the Norfolk Broads. Protected by law.
Pages 38–39

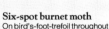

Six-spot burnet moth
On bird's-foot-trefoil throughout the year except June and July. Throughout Britain. Page 198

Buff tip moth
Found in groups on most deciduous trees in August and September. Throughout Britain. Page 160

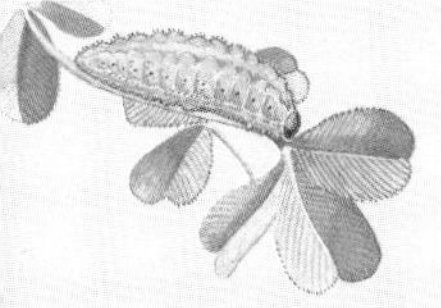

Chalk-hill blue butterfly
On horseshoe vetch and related plants on downland from April to June. Southern England.
Page 92

Cinnabar moth
On ragwort, groundsel and coltsfoot in summer in wayside and waste areas. Throughout Britain. Page 181

Small blue butterfly
On kidney vetch from June to May the following year. Many parts of Britain, especially coastal areas.
Page 96

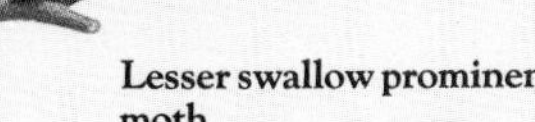

Lesser swallow prominent moth
On birch trees in June/July and again in September/October. Throughout Britain. Page 158

Magpie moth
On sloe (blackthorn), hawthorn, currant and gooseberry bushes, and *Euonymus* all year except July. Throughout Britain. Page 190

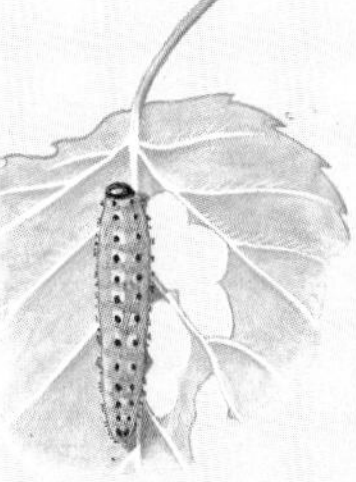

Poplar sawfly
Trichiocampus viminalis
On poplar trees in summer. Feeds in groups at first, but becomes solitary when older. Southern Britain.
See also pages 240–1

White or cream caterpillars

Caterpillars which spend their lives underground need no dark pigments to protect them against the harmful effects of the sun. They are often white or cream with dark heads.

Blowfly (bluebottle) larva
Found in decomposing flesh of dead animals. Widespread in Britain all year round. Page 275

Rat-tailed maggot
The larvae of various flies found in decomposing organic waste, usually on farms. Uses telescopic spiracle to breathe when below water. Common in Britain. Pages 270–1

Silk moth
Widely grown in schools on mulberry in May and July. Introduced to Britain. Pages 204–5

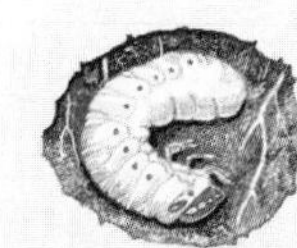

Cockchafer (maybug) larva
Lives in the soil, eating the roots of grass and crops and sometimes potato tubers. Common in Britain throughout the year. Pages 290–1

Codling moth
On apple, pear, quince and walnut trees all year round except June. Widespread in apple-growing areas. Page 206

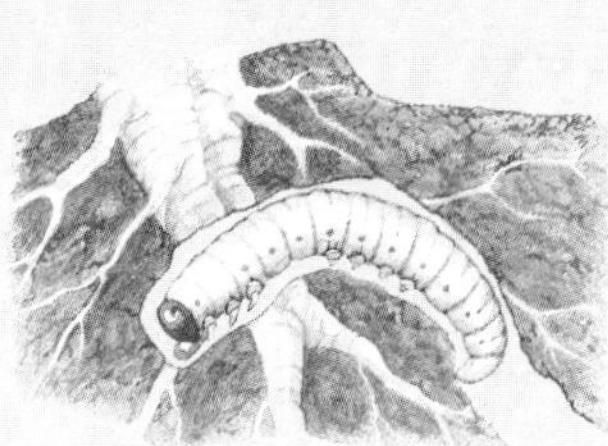

Common swift moth
On grass and most soft-stemmed plants all year round except May and June. Throughout Britain. Page 200

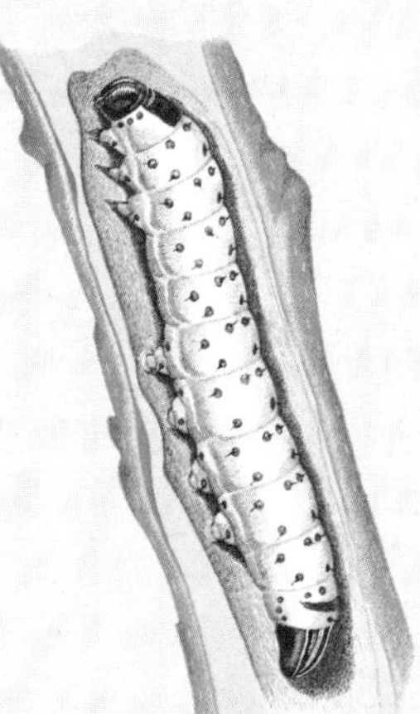

Leopard moth
On many deciduous trees all year round. In southern England and south Wales. Page 196

Grey or brown caterpillars

Dull coloured caterpillars are often found on twigs and bark where they are well camouflaged. Some may be twig-shaped and will keep still if disturbed by a predator.

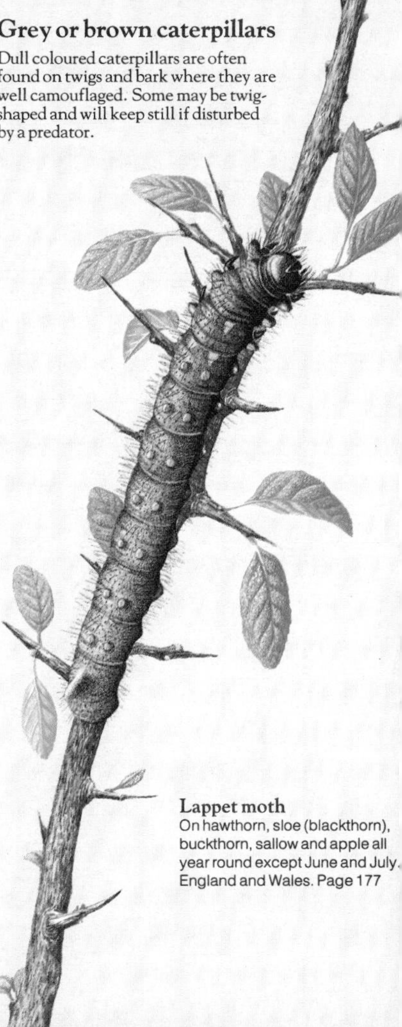

Lappet moth
On hawthorn, sloe (blackthorn), buckthorn, sallow and apple all year round except June and July. England and Wales. Page 177

Elephant hawk-moth
On willowherb and bedstraw in July and August. In England, Wales, Ireland and southern Scotland. Page 154

Grizzled skipper butterfly
On wild strawberry, brambles, creeping cinquefoil and wild raspberry in May, June and July. Southern England and Wales. Page 37

Slug worm
(Sawfly larva). On birch, oak and willow in gardens in June and July. See also pages 240–1

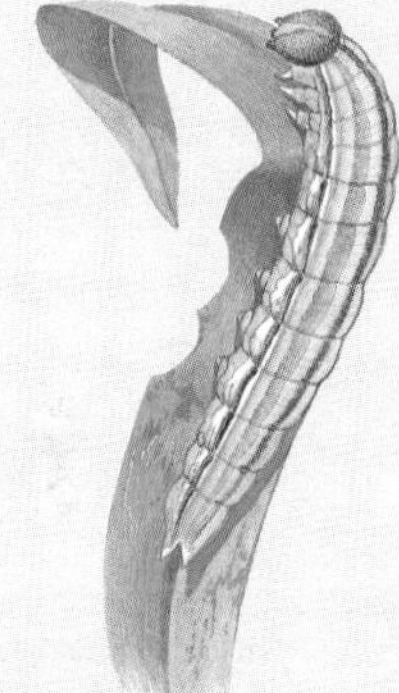

Grayling butterfly
On grass all year round except July. Throughout Britain. Page 127

Glow-worm larva
On chalk grassland in summer. Local in southern England only. Page 293

Ringlet butterfly
On grass all year round except July. South and east England, Wales, Ireland and parts of Scotland. Page 118

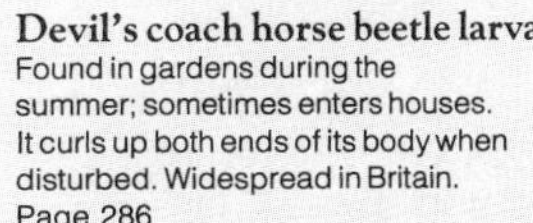

Devil's coach horse beetle larva
Found in gardens during the summer; sometimes enters houses. It curls up both ends of its body when disturbed. Widespread in Britain. Page 286

Silver-spotted skipper butterfly
On grass from May to July. Southern England. Page 34

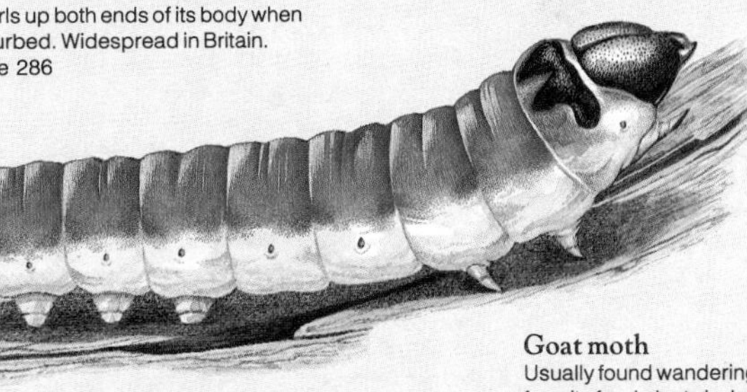

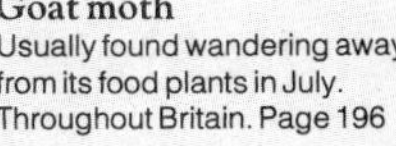

Goat moth
Usually found wandering away from its food plants in July. Throughout Britain. Page 196

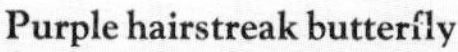

Purple hairstreak butterfly
On oak, sallow and sweet chestnut in April and May. England, Wales and west Scotland. Page 104

Turnip sawfly
Athalia colibri
Once a destructive pest of turnips in gardens, when it was called the black jack, but now quite rare. Found in East Anglia.
See also pages 240–1

Large emerald moth
On birch, hazel and beech all year round. Throughout Britain except northern Scotland. Page 188

Oak beauty moth
On oak, elm, birch and plum trees and on sloe (blackthorn) and rose bushes from May to June. England and Wales. Page 191

White-letter hairstreak butterfly
On wych elm and common elm from March to June. England and Wales.
Page 105

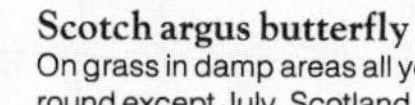

Scotch argus butterfly
On grass in damp areas all year round except July. Scotland, particularly the west. Page 120

Red underwing moth
On willow and poplar trees from April to July. South and east England and north Wales.
Page 171

Gatekeeper butterfly
On grass all year round except July England, Wales and southern Ireland. Pages 114–15

piny caterpillars

he spiny hairs are characteristic of the ristocrat and fritillary butterflies. ost of these caterpillars feed as a group.

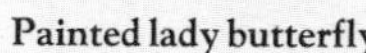

Painted lady butterfly
On thistles, burdocks, mallows and stinging nettles from June to September. Throughout Britain. Page 65

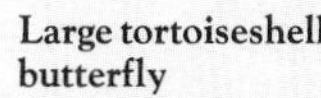

Large tortoiseshell butterfly
On elm, sallow, willow and cherry in May and June. Small areas of southern England and Wales. Rare. Page 59

High brown fritillary butterfly
On dog violets and sweet violets in April and May. Southern England and Wales. Page 82

Red admiral butterfly
Singly on stinging nettles, pellitory and hops in June, July and August. Throughout Britain. Pages 68–69

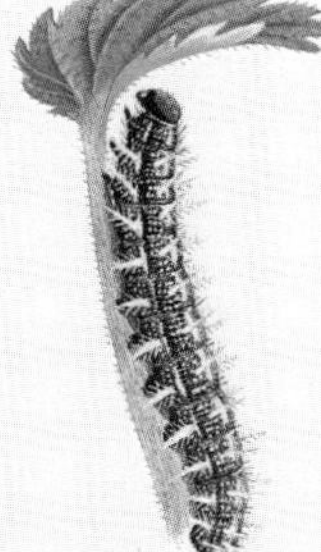

Small tortoiseshell butterfly
On stinging nettles in groups in May and June and again in July and August. Throughout Britain. Page 58

Marsh fritillary butterfly
On devil's-bit scabious throughout the year except May and June. Western England, Wales, western Scotland and Ireland. Page 75

ilver-washed fritillary butterfly
n dog violets all year round xcept July. Southern England, idlands and Wales. Page 79

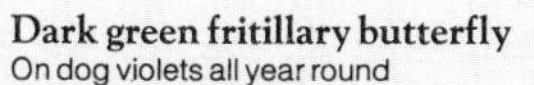

Dark green fritillary butterfly
On dog violets all year round except June and July. Mostly coastal areas of south and west England, Wales and Scotland. Page 78

Caterpillars with long hairs

Long detachable hairs give protection against birds. The hairs come off if the caterpillar is handled and may cause a skin rash.

Small pearl-bordered fritillary butterfly
On dog violets all year round except June. A westerly distribution in England, Wales and Scotland. Page 77

Peacock butterfly
On stinging nettles in June and July. Throughout Britain, except northern Scotland. Page 64

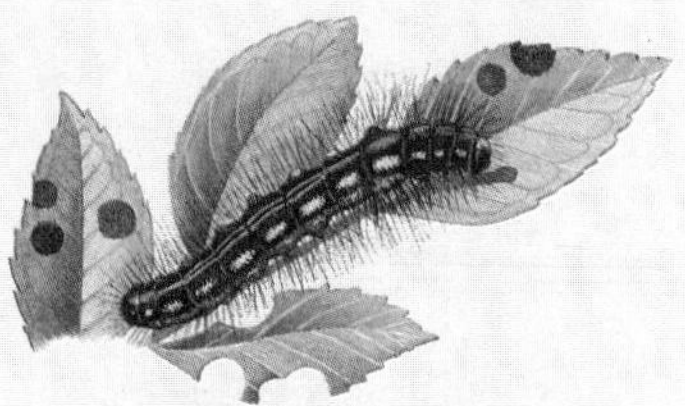

Yellow-tail tussock moth
Usually on hawthorn but also on deciduous trees and roses all year round except July. England and Wales. Page 165

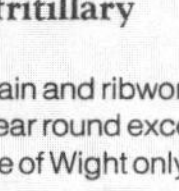

Glanville fritillary butterfly
On sea plantain and ribwort plantain all year round except May and June. Isle of Wight only. Page 81

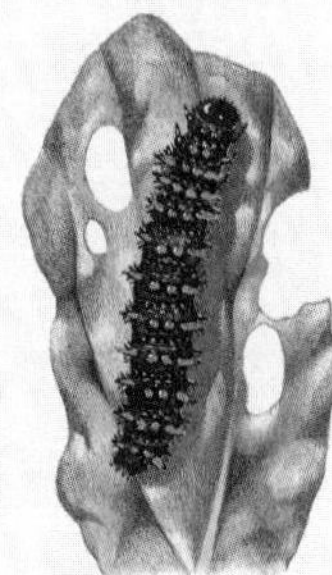

Heath fritillary butterfly
On cow-wheat all year round except June. Kent, Devon and Cornwall only. Rare and protected by law. Page 74

Pearl-bordered fritillary butterfly
On woodland violets all year round. South and west England, Wales and Scotland. Page 76

Buff ermine moth
On many low-growing plants, as well as birch and virginia creeper, from August to October. England, Wales, Ireland and north-west Scotland. Page 183

)ak eggar moth
)n heather and bramble, as well as
ome other plants, all year round as
ı hibernating caterpillar. Throughout
ritain. Page 176

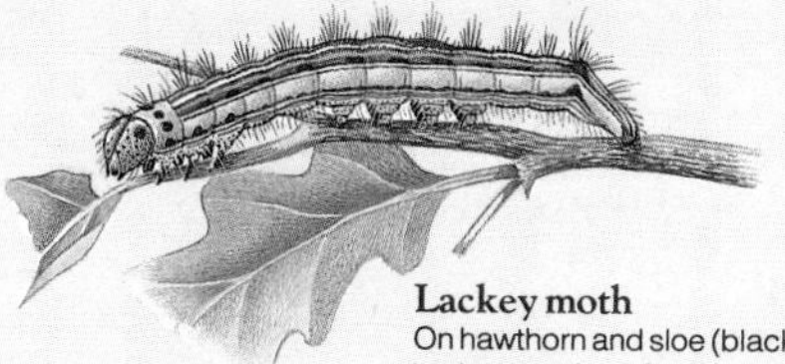

Lackey moth
On hawthorn and sloe (blackthorn) in hedgerows from April to June. Mostly in England and coastal regions of Wales, plus a few localities in Ireland. The caterpillars are seen most often as the moths fly at night only.

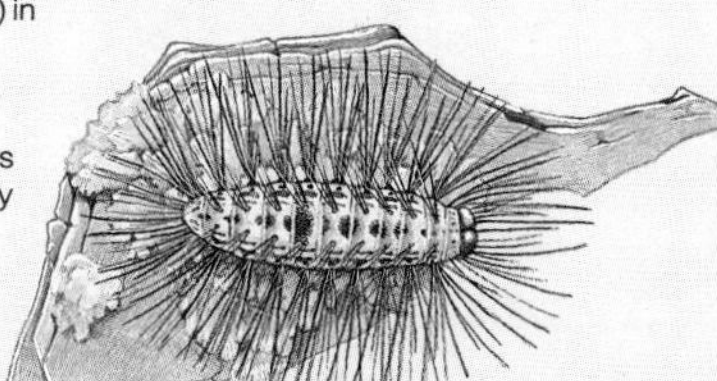

Muslin footman moth
On lichens and algae on walls in July and August. Throughout Britain. Page 185

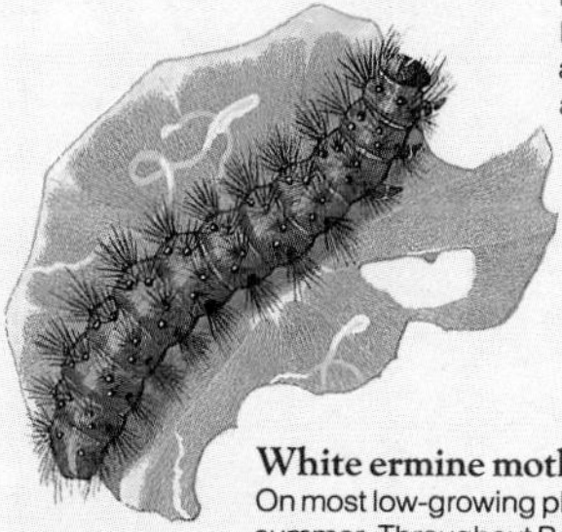

White ermine moth
On most low-growing plants in late summer. Throughout Britain. Page 182

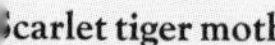

;carlet tiger moth
)n stinging nettles, dock and
omfrey in July and August and
gain from April to late May.
outh-west England and Wales.
age 180

Common footman moth
On oak, sallow and apple trees, also sloe (blackthorn) and buckthorn bushes all year round except July. Throughout Britain. Page 184

;mall eggar moth
/ebs of caterpillars in hedgerows in
Iay, June and July. Found in only a
w areas of England and Wales.
ee also oak eggar, page 176

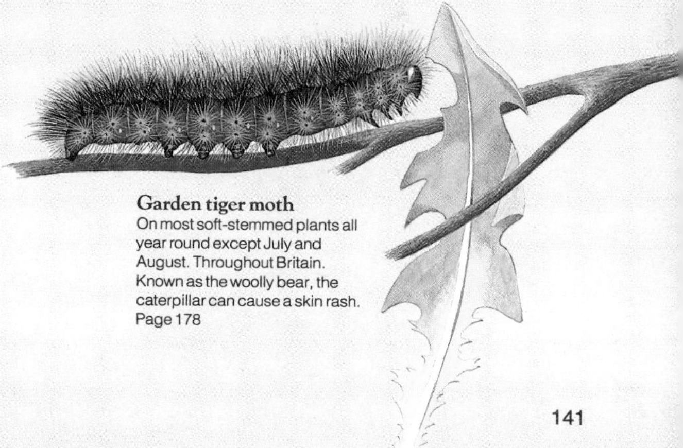

Garden tiger moth
On most soft-stemmed plants all year round except July and August. Throughout Britain. Known as the woolly bear, the caterpillar can cause a skin rash. Page 178

Brown-tail tussock moth
On roses and fruit trees and on hawthorn, sloe (blackthorn) and sea buckthorn all year round except July. Page 164

Ruby tiger moth
On dandelions, docks, plantains, golden rod and other low-growing plants in summer. Throughout Britain. Page 179

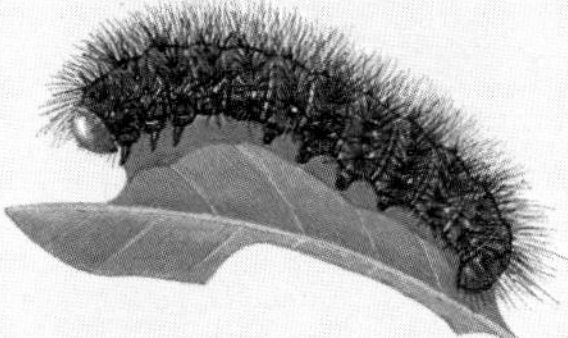

Cream-spot tiger moth
On most low-growing plants all year round except May and June. Southern England and south Wales. Page 179

Curiously shaped caterpillars

Natural selection has evolved these bizarre shapes so that the caterpillar is not easily recognised by predators.

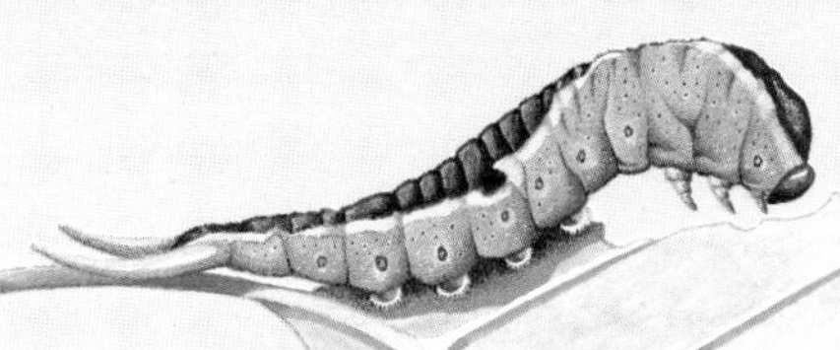

Poplar kitten moth
On poplar trees from July to September. Southern England. Page 157

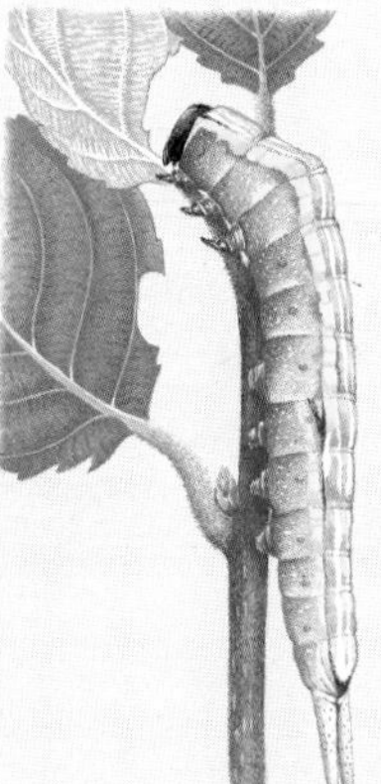

Sallow kitten moth
On sallow and willow from July to September. England, Wales and Scotland. Page 157

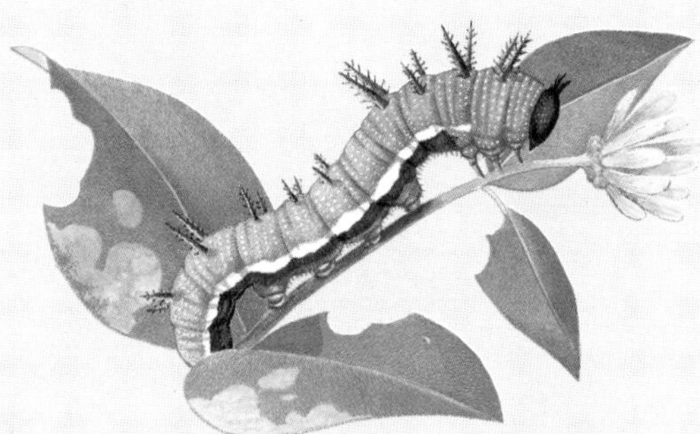

White admiral butterfly
On honeysuckle all year round. Southern England. Pages 70–71

Peach blossom moth
On brambles from July to September. Throughout Britain. Page 163

Ladybird larva
On garden plants and low vegetation during the summer throughout Britain. Pages 294–5

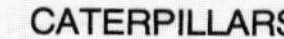

ebble hook-tip moth
1 oak leaves in July and August.
uthern and central England.
e also oak hook-tip, page 162

Vapourer moth
On most deciduous trees and shrubs from May to August. Throughout Britain. Page 167

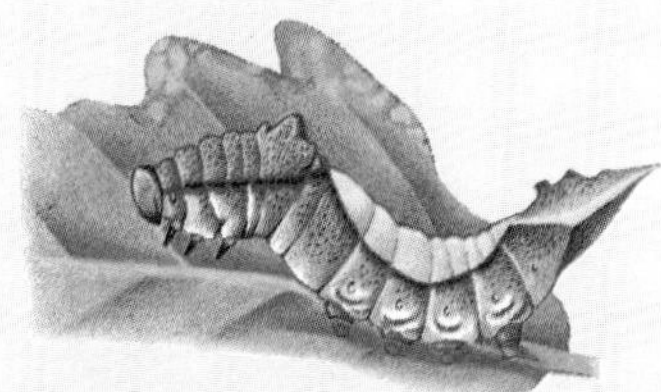

Oak hook-tip moth
On oak leaves in woods and hedgerows throughout England and Wales in June and July. Page 162

Coxcomb prominent moth
On birch, oak, hazel, sallow and beech in June/July and September/October. Throughout Britain. Page 159

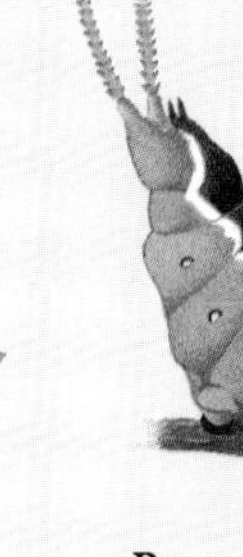

Lobster moth
On beech, birch, oak, hazel and apple trees all year round except August. Southern England and parts of Wales and south-west Ireland. Page 161

Puss moth
On sallow, willow and poplar from July to September. Throughout Britain. Spits formic acid and protrudes flagellae. Page 156

Swallow-tailed moth
On many trees and shrubs, including privet, holly and ivy, all year round except July. England, Wales and Ireland. Page 217

Single eggs are often laid on the upper surface of potato leaves.

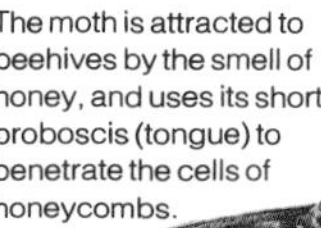

The moth is attracted to beehives by the smell of honey, and uses its short proboscis (tongue) to penetrate the cells of honeycombs.

The heaviest British moth, and – with the convolvulus hawk-moth – one of the largest. It holds its long wings on top of the body, drawing attention to the death's-head pattern on the thorax. Wingspan 4½ in. (11.5 cm).

The skull pattern includes eye socket and jaw. When the wings are open th yellow bands on the body look like ribs.

The caterpillar, shown half size, makes a clicking sound if it is disturbed. It feeds on potato plants, tomato leaves or the Duke of Argyll's Teaplant (*Lycium barbarum*).

Death's head pattern

The chrysalis is formed after the caterpillar has burrowed beneath the soil and made a frail cocoon.

Death's head hawk-moth *Acherontia atropos*

This huge moth with its fat body, visible claws and death's hea pattern can be a frightening sight to someone who encounters i for the first time. To add to the effect it can utter a high-pitche squeak if it is touched. The caterpillars too are alarming crea tures. They reach 5 in. (12.5 cm) in length when fully grow and have a 'horn' at the rear end. They used to frighten potat pickers before mechanical harvesting and insecticides were ex tensively used. The scientific name of the moth is taken from th Greek goddess Atropos who determined life or death, bu neither the moth nor the caterpillar is harmful.

The moths are regular migrants to Britain and may be foun anywhere in the country between May and October. They hav even been attracted to the lights on oil platforms in the Nort Sea, east of the Shetlands. Early migrants may give rise t another generation in the autumn.

The moths eat sweet sap exuded by some trees and will ro the hives of honey-bees, drinking the honey stored in th honeycomb. Their squeaking sound imitates the 'piping' of th queen bee and apparently deters the bees from harming them But bees will sometimes attack and kill a marauding moth.

The smooth, bright green eggs are laid singly on bindweed (*Convolvulus arvensis*), and sometimes on garden forms of convolvulus.

The fully grown caterpillar makes a loose chamber in the soil and changes into a brown chrysalis.

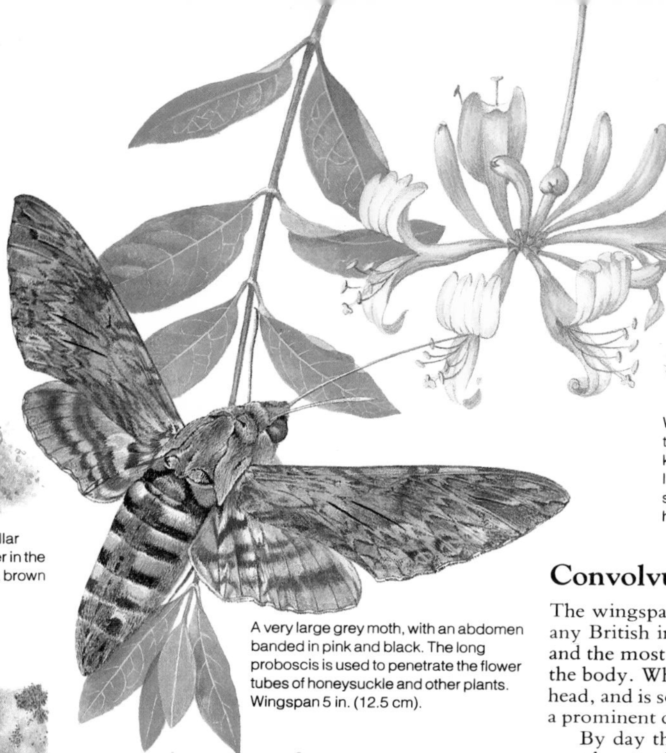

The colour of the moth makes it difficult to see as it rests on a rock or tree.

A very large grey moth, with an abdomen banded in pink and black. The long proboscis is used to penetrate the flower tubes of honeysuckle and other plants. Wingspan 5 in. (12.5 cm).

When not in use the proboscis is kept wound up like a watch spring below the head, barely visible.

A convolvulus hawk-moth in profile, resting on a twig. The large black compound eye stands out from the grey hairy head.

The caterpillars live on wild convolvulus (bindweed), and occasionally on morning glory. As the moth is a migrant only a few caterpillars have been recorded in Britain. There is also a brown form. [× ½]

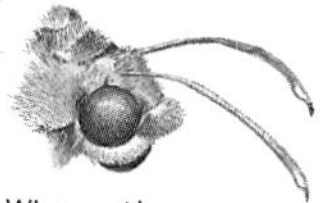

Convolvulus hawk-moth *Agrius convolvuli*

The wingspan of the convolvulus hawk-moth is the largest of any British insect. Its proboscis (or tongue) is also the longest and the most impressive; at 3½ in. (90 mm) it is twice as long as the body. When not in use the proboscis is curled up under the head, and is so big in the developing chrysalis that it is housed in a prominent case.

By day the moth rests on tree trunks, palings and posts. It may be seen from July to November flying at dusk and visiting wild flowers such as honeysuckle, evening primrose and soapwort. In the garden it feeds on clematis, petunias, tobacco plants and geraniums. It jabs its tongue into the tubular flowers while hovering in front of the plant.

The convolvulus hawk-moth is one of the most powerful flying insects to come to Britain. From the Mediterranean it travels as far north as Scotland and Iceland. The muscles in the thorax (the size of a small finger nail) are capable of sustained flight over 1,000 miles in just a few days. The moth is found mostly in south-east England. It is strongly attracted to light and may be seen around street lamps. Some early migrants breed in Britain, but the caterpillar is not often found.

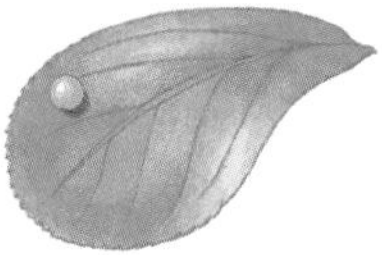

Eggs are laid singly or in small groups on the leaves of spurges (*Euphorbia* species). [× 2]

The caterpillar is safe from predators because a substance it stores from its food plants is poisonous to them.

Light brown moth with a pink band on the hind-wings. It is well camouflaged on bark, but when disturbed it moves the fore-wings forward, revealing the bright, pink patches. Wingspan 3 in. (76 mm).

The brightly coloured caterpillars are highly conspicuous on their food plants.

The chrysalis is formed just below the surface of the soil in a fragile cocoon.

Spurge hawk-moth *Hyles euphorbiae*

This very rare moth had never been seen in Britain before the beginning of the century, although its brilliantly coloured caterpillars had been recorded in Kent and Devon. The spurge hawk-moth is very common in Mediterranean countries, and a handful make the 1,000 mile flight to Britain each year.

Coastal areas along the south and east of England are the most likely places to find the moth – or more probably its caterpillars as they feed on sea spurge. The caterpillars may be seen from June to August, and the moths which derive from them are on the wing in September and October. The chrysalises normally hatch after 16 days, but they have been known to lie dormant in captivity for five years.

The striking caterpillar is highly poisonous to predators, and its vivid colours of red, white, black and orange serve as a warning to them, although seagulls have been recorded eating them without any ill effects. The moths have a characteristic way of defending themselves against attack by birds. They bob up and down quickly with the wings and antennae straight out, showing off the pink hind-wings and stabbing the ground with their curved bodies.

A grey moth that flies on warm summer days. It hovers in front of flowers, drinking the nectar with its long proboscis, and moving from one bloom to the next with a characteristic darting action. The wings make an audible sound as the moth hovers. Wingspan 2¼ in. (57 mm).

The moth often rests on walls with its wings swept back.

The chrysalis is formed in a loose cocoon on the ground near the food plant.

The moth holds its body perfectly still while hovering, only its tongue moving in and out of the flowers.

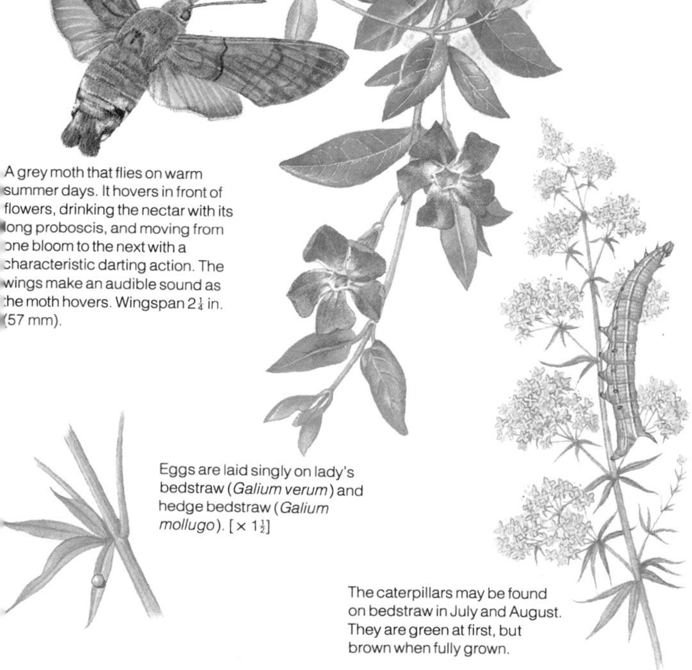

Eggs are laid singly on lady's bedstraw (*Galium verum*) and hedge bedstraw (*Galium mollugo*). [× 1½]

The caterpillars may be found on bedstraw in July and August. They are green at first, but brown when fully grown.

Humming-bird hawk-moth *Macroglossum stellatarum*

This hawk-moth is a summer visitor which migrates regularly each year from the south of France where it is extremely common. It is a day-flying moth, and feeds on flowers such as geraniums, honeysuckles, petunias, periwinkles and verbenas. Like a humming-bird, it hovers in front of the flower and inserts its long tongue deep into the petals. While hovering, it beats its wings at such high speed that they are barely visible. The accompanying high-pitched humming sound is said to be more audible to women than to men. The moth can suddenly disappear, only to return probing the same flower seconds later.

About 50 humming-bird hawk-moths are reported in Britain each year, although a record number of 4,250 were recorded in 1947. They are most likely to be seen along the south coast of England between May and September, but they can occur anywhere in the British Isles including northern Scotland and Ireland. Migrants lay eggs on bedstraw and wild madder plants between June and September. Some moths probably hibernate in the warm south and west of England, as individuals are regularly seen as early as February and March, before the migrants arrive.

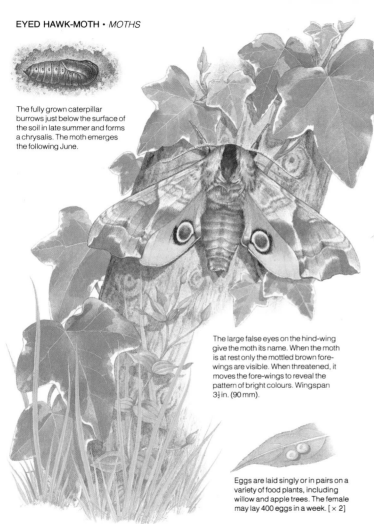

The fully grown caterpillar burrows just below the surface of the soil in late summer and forms a chrysalis. The moth emerges the following June.

The caterpillars are yellowish-green with white stripes and reddish rings on the sides. They may be seen from June to September.

A pair of moths at the moment of mating. Eyed hawk-moths can breed with other hawk-moths but with limited success.

The large false eyes on the hind-wing give the moth its name. When the moth is at rest only the mottled brown fore-wings are visible. When threatened, it moves the fore-wings to reveal the pattern of bright colours. Wingspan 3½ in. (90 mm).

Eggs are laid singly or in pairs on a variety of food plants, including willow and apple trees. The female may lay 400 eggs in a week. [× 2]

Eyed hawk-moth *Smerinthus ocellata*

Like the peacock butterfly, this hawk-moth has false eyes to startle predators. When confronted by a bird or small mammal seeking food, the moth will suddenly expose the 'eyes' on the hind-wings by moving the fore-wings forwards. The sudden flash of colour may frighten off the predator or surprise it sufficiently to give the moth time to escape.

The caterpillars eat the leaves of a wide variety of British native trees. They can be found on scrubby young willows, sallows, aspens and poplars which grow in damp places. They will also feed on fruit trees, including apple, crab apple, pear and plum. The caterpillar, which is more often seen than the moth, is very distinctive, with reddish rings along its sides and a blue 'horn'. The blueness of the horn distinguishes the mature caterpillar from the poplar hawk-moth caterpillar. It feeds at night, and during the day sometimes 'sunbathes' on the food plant. The moth also feeds at night, on the nectar of flowers, and rests by day on tree trunks. There is usually one generation a year, in June, with occasionally a second in July if the spring is early and warm. The moth is widely distributed in England and Wales, up to the Scottish border, and also occurs in Ireland.

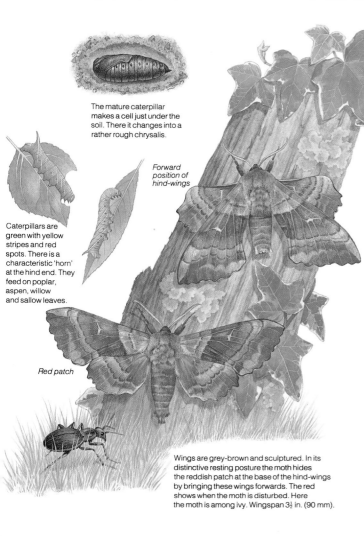

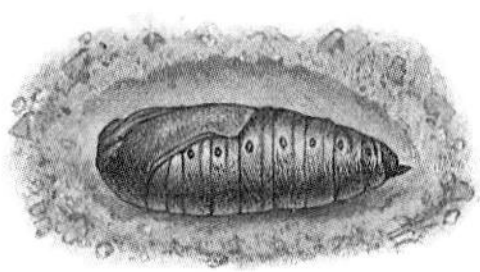

The mature caterpillar makes a cell just under the soil. There it changes into a rather rough chrysalis.

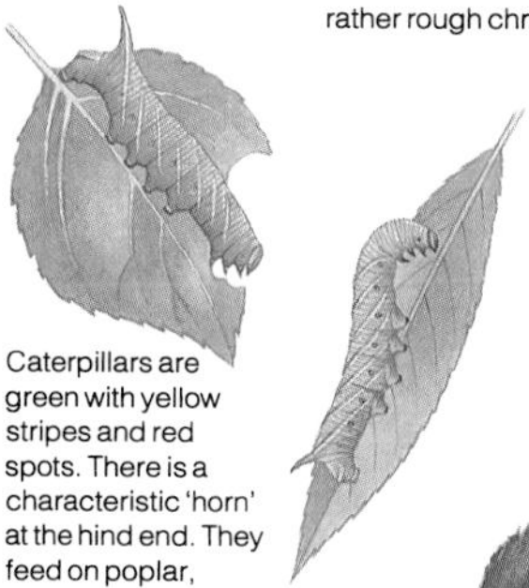

Caterpillars are green with yellow stripes and red spots. There is a characteristic 'horn' at the hind end. They feed on poplar, aspen, willow and sallow leaves.

Forward position of hind-wings

Red patch

Wings are grey-brown and sculptured. In its distinctive resting posture the moth hides the reddish patch at the base of the hind-wings by bringing these wings forwards. The red shows when the moth is disturbed. Here the moth is among ivy. Wingspan 3½ in. (90 mm).

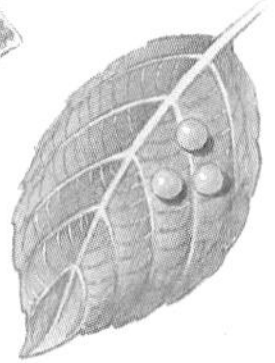

Shiny eggs are laid in small groups on the underside of leaves of the food plants. Those laid early in May become moths by late July.

The large compound eyes of a poplar hawk-moth nestle in its hairy thorax and are surmounted by comb-like antennae.

Poplar hawk-moth *Laothoe populi*

The sudden appearance of this large moth in a room at night can be alarming, but the poplar hawk-moth – like most moths – is quite harmless. It is active at night and is attracted to light from windows.

During the day its brown-sculptured wings help to camouflage it against tree trunks. When disturbed, it raises its fore-wings to reveal the red patch on the hind-wing. The flash of colour may be enough to frighten off the predator. The poplar hawk-moth is common in towns. It is also likely to be found in the damp areas where its food plants grow – along river banks and in water meadows, in coppiced woodland and in mixed oak woodland typical of the English lowlands. Poplar, after which it is named, is only one of the caterpillars' food plants. They will also eat the leaves of aspen, sallow and willow.

There are usually two generations of moths each year. Moths hatch from the chrysalis in May and June and produce another generation in late July. These lay eggs which become hibernating chrysalises by September. This hawk-moth is found throughout England and Wales, with a patchy distribution in southern Scotland, and in only a few localities in Ireland.

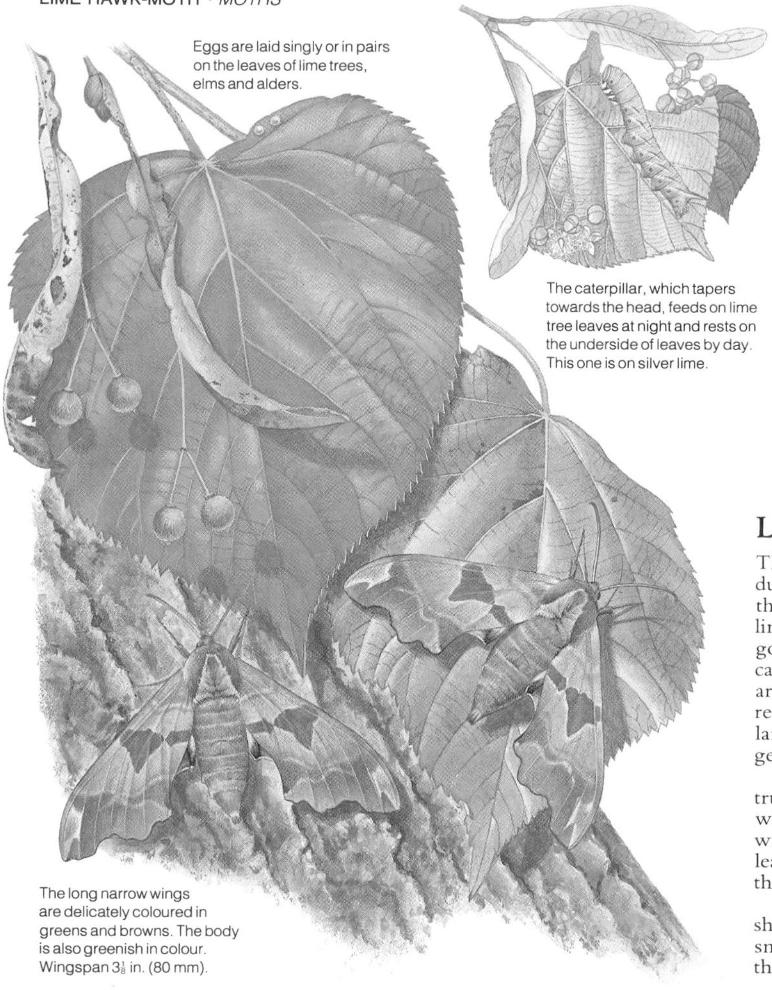

Eggs are laid singly or in pairs on the leaves of lime trees, elms and alders.

The caterpillar, which tapers towards the head, feeds on lime tree leaves at night and rests on the underside of leaves by day. This one is on silver lime.

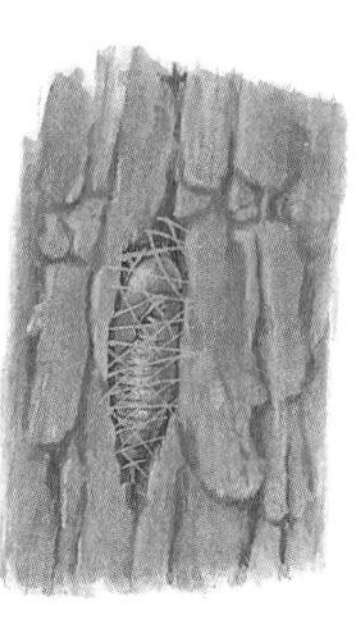

The chrysalis spends the winter in a cocoon – sometimes in a crevice in the bark but more often in the soil.

A pair of lime hawk-moths mate in early summer. Their eggs will produce caterpillars between July and September.

The long narrow wings are delicately coloured in greens and browns. The body is also greenish in colour. Wingspan $3\frac{1}{8}$ in. (80 mm).

Lime hawk-moth *Mimas tiliae*

This attractive hawk-moth with slim wings is frequently found during May and June in urban areas, especially in London and the south-east of England. Wherever there are groups of mature lime trees in parks, gardens, squares and city streets there is a good chance that they will support lime hawk-moths. The caterpillars are found from July until September. At first they are very small with a black 'horn'; later the horn becomes reddish and side stripes appear. When fully grown the caterpillars are ideally camouflaged on their plants. There is only one generation a year. They are not found north of the Humber.

The moths can be seen during the day resting on walls, tree trunks and fences close to lime trees, or to elm and alder trees which the caterpillar will also feed on. The moths always rest with their wings in a characteristic manner resembling young leaves, so that they are well camouflaged against trees. At night they are attracted to light.

The dark patches in the centre of the fore-wings vary in shape. Usually there are two, but sometimes the lower one is small, and occasionally they are united as a complete band. Or they might be completely absent.

Pink abdomen

The green caterpillars have seven white-and-pink stripes down the sides. Before forming a chrysalis they turn brown and slightly pink.

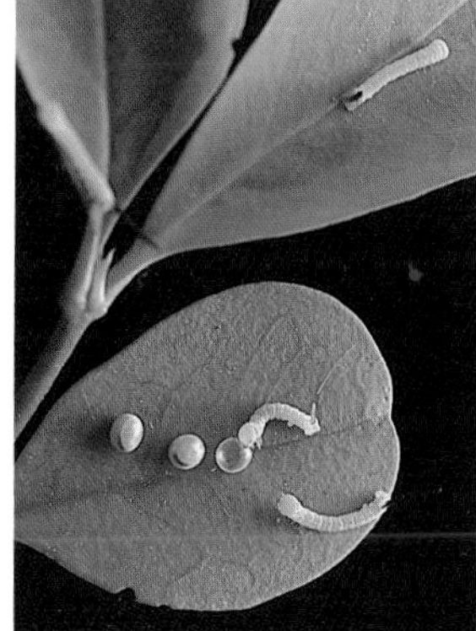

A caterpillar of the privet hawk-moth, which has just emerged from its egg, eats the transparent egg case as its first meal.

Privet hawk-moth *Sphinx ligustri*

The privet hawk-moth bears the scientific name *Sphinx* after the way it rests with the wings closed over its body, like the winged monster of Greek mythology. The moth has evolved on wild privet which grows abundantly on chalky slopes, and its survival has been helped by the numerous privet hedges planted in towns and gardens. The moth's species name *ligustri* comes from the scientific name of the privet, *Ligustrum*. Other food plants are the lilac, ash, elder and snowberry.

The large caterpillar, which can be found in July and August, is more often seen than the moth. When fully grown it is an obvious sight on privet bushes as its droppings and the chewed leaves near by give its position away. It changes to a dull brown before it burrows into the ground to form a chrysalis nearly 6 in. (15 cm) deep in the soil – probably the deepest of all British moths. It may remain dormant there for up to two years.

The moth is distinguished from the convolvulus hawk-moth, which looks similar, by the suffusion of pink over its wings and body. It is confined to southern England, and may be seen in June and July, but the species is becoming a less familiar sight in parks, gardens, downland and scrubby places.

A large moth with long pointed wings and a pink suffusion over the abdomen and base of the hind-wings. Wingspan 4½ in. (11.5 cm).

Eggs are laid on the leaves of privet, lilac, ash, elder or snowberry.

The chrysalis may spend two winters in a chamber several inches underground before emerging as an adult moth.

A grey moth marked with black. White dashes mark all the wing margins and there are partial white bands round the abdomen. The moth emerges from pine woods at dusk to feed, often probing flowers of honeysuckle (*Lonicera periclymenum*) with its long proboscis. Wingspan $2\frac{3}{4}$ in. (70 mm).

White dashes on wing margins

The large, dark-horned caterpillar feeds on the pine needles. At first it is bright green with white stripes, but as it grows a broad orange-brown band develops along the back.

The grey moth is well camouflaged on pine trees by day. In the evening it visits flowers and may be attracted to light.

Lozenge-shaped eggs are laid along pine needles, and hatch in early August.

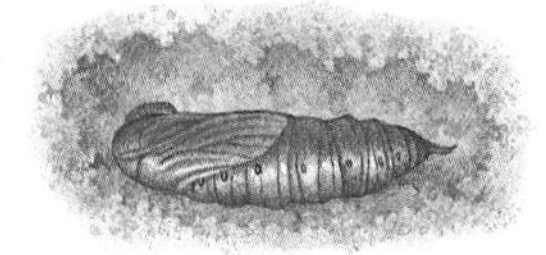

In October the caterpillar burrows into moss and pine needles and changes into a chrysalis and hibernates, usually until the following summer, but sometimes for a further year.

Pine hawk-moth *Hyloicus pinastri*

The 20th century has brought success to the pine hawk-moth in Britain. While many other moths and butterflies have decreased in numbers, the pine hawk-moth has extended its range considerably. In the 19th century it was rare, found only in Dorset and Suffolk. But after the First World War the newly formed Forestry Commission planted thousands of acres of land with Scots pine and Norway spruce (Christmas trees), and these are the food plants of pine hawk-moth caterpillars. The expansion of forestry has helped the moth to spread eastwards from Dorset and westwards from Suffolk, and it may now be found anywhere south-east of a line from the Wash to Plymouth. On the Continent the moth is so common that the caterpillars are destructive pests of conifer plantations.

Pine hawk-moths live for about a month and are on the wing in June, July and August, spending the day resting on the trunks of trees. At dusk they take wing to feed on flowers, such as honeysuckle and privet. Their quest may take them several miles from pine trees. The eggs laid by the female moths produce the colourful caterpillars that can be found eating pine needles in August and September.

This species, unlike other hawk-moths, turns into a chrysalis in a weak cocoon on or just under the soil surface. It hibernates from September until May.

Similar in shape and markings to the spurge and striped hawk-moths but distinguished by the much darker olive colouring of the wings. It is shown on lady's bedstraw (*Galium verum*) and broad-leaved willowherb (*Epilobium montanum*). Wingspan 3 in. (76 mm).

Eggs are laid in June or July on the upper side of the leaves of various bedstraw and willowherb species. They hatch in August.

Striped hawk-moth
Hyles lineata

Slightly larger than the bed-straw, with a continuous stripe down the fore-wings crossed by white veins. It is a regular but scarce migrant found all over Britain, but mostly in southern England, in May/June and in August. Wingspan 3¼ in. (83 mm).

Caterpillars vary in colour from olive-brown to reddish-brown to black. All are pink underneath.

The bedstraw hawk-moth is a moth of the meadows, but it may visit garden flowers to sip nectar in the evenings.

Bedstraw hawk-moth *Hyles galii*

A family of wild plants called bedstraws, that were once used to stuff mattresses, give this attractive moth its curious name. Bedstraws, which have small white or yellow flowers, grow all over Britain, and are one group of plants on which the moth lays its eggs. A former name, madder hawk-moth, comes from a second food plant, the madder, a species of which was used to obtain a red dye. The moth also has a third food plant for its caterpillars, the widespread willowherb.

The moths may be seen from May to July at dusk, or sometimes during the day, in flower-rich meadows where bedstraw or madder grow, or along tracks and in clearings where willowherb is found. However sightings are fairly rare as the bedstraw hawk-moth is an infrequent migrant from the Continent to Britain – mostly to England and Wales but occasionally to Scotland and Ireland, and even to Shetland and Orkney. The moths will breed in Britain for a few years immediately after summers in which large numbers have arrived. They took up residence in 1957 and 1958 following an invasion in 1956, and again in the three years following 1972 which saw the greatest influx ever recorded.

A beautiful pink hawk-moth which may be seen on June evenings. The one on the right is shown drinking bramble nectar. Wingspan 2¾ in. (70 mm).

The chrysalis is formed in a loose cocoon just below the surface of the soil, where it spends the winter.

The delicate pink wings, body and antennae of the elephant hawk-moth contrast strongly against its white legs.

Elephant hawk-moth *Deilephila elpenor*

The caterpillar, which is seen more often than the moth, can retract its head into its body when threatened, causing the front of the body to swell up like an elephant's head. The coloured false eyes on the head expand, completing a picture of menace to predators. But the caterpillars are quite harmless and have no form of active defence. They are found in July and August on willowherb or bedstraw. They feed mostly at night but may be found basking on the flowers during the day. Other food plants include enchanter's nightshade, fuchsia and balsam.

The moths are among the prettiest hawk-moths in Britain. They are found wherever willowherbs grow in profusion – in woodland clearings, along tracks, on waste ground in cities and along streams and river banks. They are on the wing in June and may be seen hovering in the evening feeding from the flowers of honeysuckle, valerian, soapwort and petunias.

The elephant hawk-moth is commonly found throughout southern and central England and the West Country, and is scattered in southern Scotland and Ireland. It will mate with its less common relative, the small elephant hawk-moth, and produce fertile hybrid moths.

Eggs are laid singly on leaves of willowherbs (*Epilobium* species). [× 2]

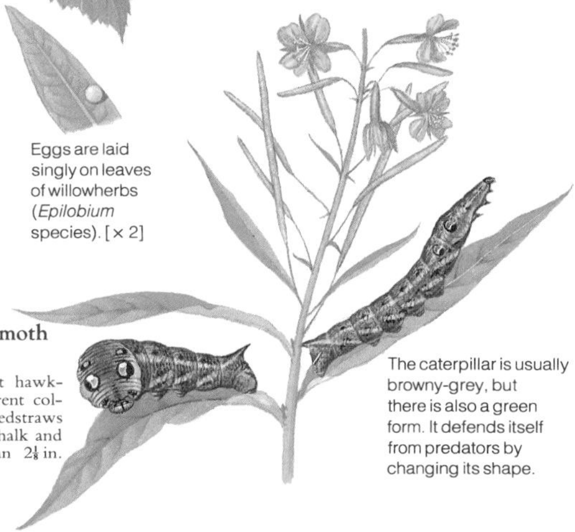

Small elephant hawk-moth
Deilephila porcellus

Smaller than the elephant hawk-moth, with slightly different colours. It lays its eggs on bedstraws (*Galium*) and is found in chalk and limestone areas. Wingspan 2⅛ in. (54 mm).

The caterpillar is usually browny-grey, but there is also a green form. It defends itself from predators by changing its shape.

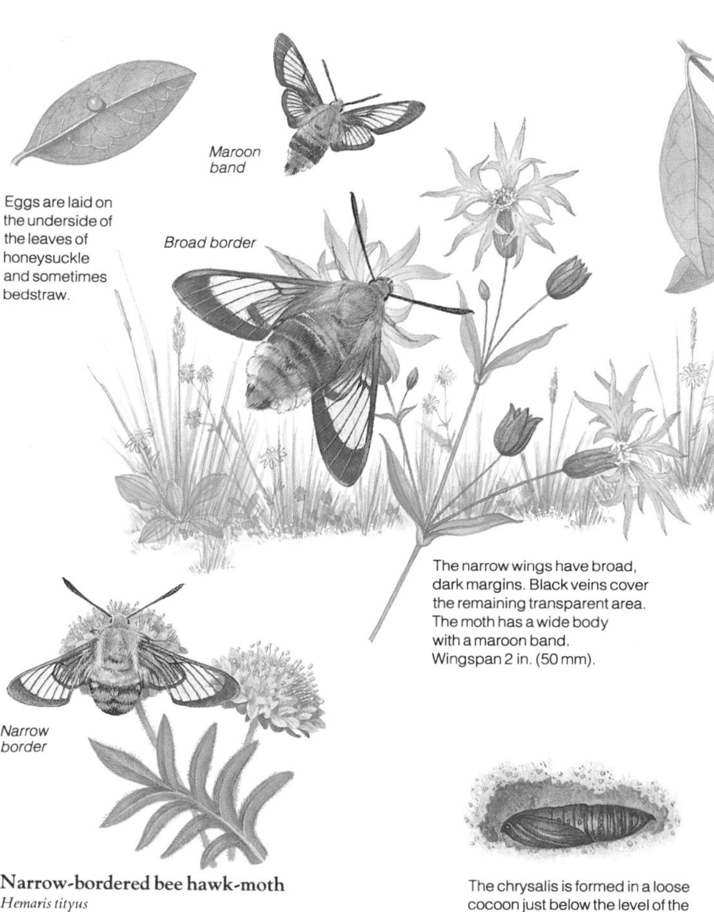

Eggs are laid on the underside of the leaves of honeysuckle and sometimes bedstraw.

The narrow wings have broad, dark margins. Black veins cover the remaining transparent area. The moth has a wide body with a maroon band. Wingspan 2 in. (50 mm).

The caterpillar – mainly green with reddish-brown beneath – feeds on the undersides of honeysuckle leaves.

The broad-bordered bee hawk-moth can be seen in May and June, feeding on flowers while in flight.

The chrysalis is formed in a loose cocoon just below the level of the soil, where it hibernates.

Narrow-bordered bee hawk-moth

Hemaris tityus

This species is the same size as the broad-bordered bee hawk-moth, but has narrower borders to the wings and no maroon band on the body. The caterpillar feeds on field scabious (*Knautia arvensis*) and devil's-bit scabious (*Succisa pratensis*).

Broad-bordered bee hawk-moth *Hemaris fuciformis*

Their similarity to the honey-bee, together with their transparent wings, gives the bee hawk-moths their name. In fact they are much larger than bees and are more likely to be confused with the humming-bird hawk-moth. The two types of moth share the same localities and feed from the same flowers while hovering, their wings beating so fast that they appear a blur. The bee hawk-moth, however, has a much shorter proboscis than the humming-bird hawk-moth.

Both species of bee hawk-moth, the broad-bordered and the narrow-bordered, are severely endangered in Britain and their populations have dwindled rapidly since the 1950s. The broad-bordered moth is now found mainly in a few very scattered localities in south and eastern England. The decline may be due to depredations by ichneumon parasites on the caterpillars. The narrow bordered is found in scattered localities in England, Scotland, Wales and Ireland. Both are seen in May and June.

Both moths fly by day and are found in woodland clearings, bogs, moorland, railway embankments, hedgerows and meadows near woods where wild flowers grow in profusion. The moths will also visit garden marigolds and rhododendrons.

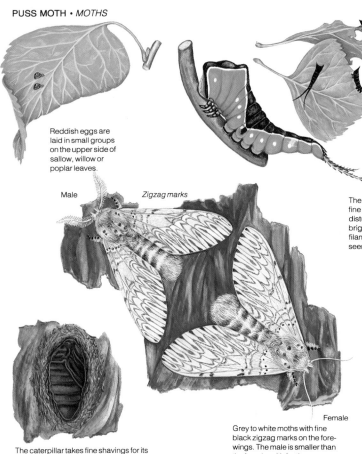

Reddish eggs are laid in small groups on the upper side of sallow, willow or poplar leaves.

Male

Zigzag marks

The young caterpillars are black with two fine 'tails' which they waggle about when disturbed. Older caterpillars are more brightly coloured and have red whip-like filaments at the end of the body. They are seen in July and August.

The threatening head of the puss moth caterpillar rears up, its fore-legs in the air, in response to a predator.

Puss moth *Cerura vinula*

The cat-like fluffy hair covering the body of the puss moth is the source of its name. It is common throughout Britain, from urban areas to woodlands, between April and July, and is most likely to be found in damp areas where sallow, willow and poplar grow well. The young caterpillar is black but later develops a black-and-green pattern which helps to break up the outline of the body and blend it against its background. When disturbed by a predator it adopts an alarming attitude of menace. The head rears up and is drawn back into the thorax, causing it to swell and reveal a scarlet collar and two staring false eyes. At the same time the twin tails curl forward and two red, whip-like filaments called flagella emerge. The more the caterpillar is provoked the further the flagella protrude over its head. Its final defence is to spray formic acid over the predator from glands behind its head.

The cocoon is a remarkably hard case built into the bark of a tree. It is made of pieces of bark chewed up by the caterpillar and blended with silk. Before the moth hatches, the chrysalis uses a cutting device on its head to break through one end of the cocoon which was made especially thin.

Female

Grey to white moths with fine black zigzag marks on the fore-wings. The male is smaller than the female, with feathery antennae which are half as long as the fore-wings. Wingspan of female $3\frac{1}{8}$ in. (80 mm).

The caterpillar takes fine shavings for its tough cocoon which is formed on tree trunks or posts in August. The chrysalis spends the winter in the cocoon. The drawing shows the cocoon opened to reveal the chrysalis.

The eggs are laid in small groups on the upper surface of sallow and willow leaves.

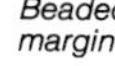

A hairy grey moth with a dark band across each fore-wing. The margins of each wing are beaded in black and the abdomen is banded in black and white. Wingspan 1¼ in. (32 mm).

The caterpillars are similar in colour and shape to the puss moth (opposite), but are smaller and thinner. They are found in May/June and again in August/ September in the south.

A pair of sallow kittens, with their hairy fore-legs and banded wings, rest on the bark of a tree during the day.

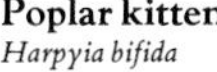

Poplar kitten
Harpyia bifida

Similarly patterned to the sallow kitten but larger and with darker markings. The poplar kitten is found from late May to July in Wales and England. Wingspan 1¾ in. (45 mm).

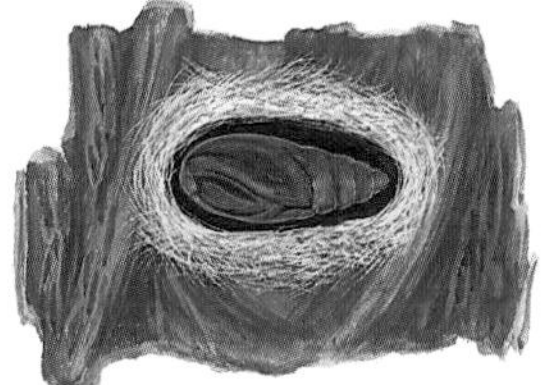

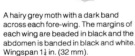

The chrysalis is formed in June and September, in a tough silk cocoon which is fixed to the trunk of a tree.

Sallow kitten *Harpyia furcula*

Sallow, or grey willow, is one of the willow species which produce pussy-willow flowers in spring. It is the main food plant for the caterpillars of several butterflies and at least ten moths. They include the sallow kitten, a grey moth with a hairy body that is particularly common in areas of scrub sallow on wastelands and heaths. It is found mostly in the English lowlands, but extends sporadically to the north of Scotland and into Wales. In Ireland it occurs in only a few places.

There are two generations each year in southern England, but only one further north. The moths are on the wing during May and June and again in August in the south. They are attracted to lighted windows and may be found resting during the day on the bark of sallow trees. The caterpillars, which will also eat the leaves of other willows, poplars and aspens, make an extremely tough cocoon when they are ready to turn into chrysalises. They gnaw chippings off the bark of the tree and mix them with silk.

The sallow kitten may be confused with the larger and widespread poplar kitten, which is found near poplar trees – the caterpillars' food plant – throughout England and Wales.

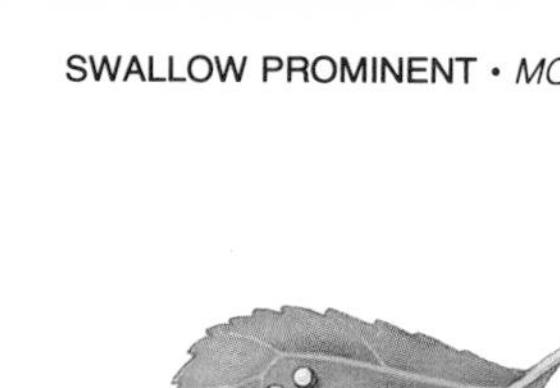

Creamy-white eggs are laid singly on the upper surface of poplar or willow leaves. [× 8]

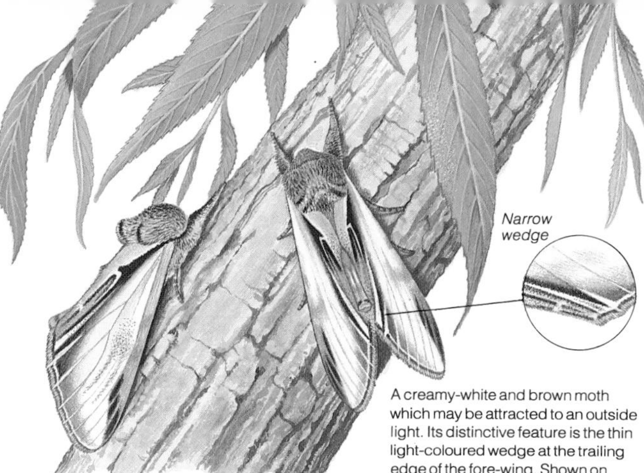

A creamy-white and brown moth which may be attracted to an outside light. Its distinctive feature is the thin light-coloured wedge at the trailing edge of the fore-wing. Shown on the trunk of a willow. Wingspan 2⅜ in. (60 mm).

When the swallow prominent moth rests on the bark of trees it can be extremely well camouflaged by its colour.

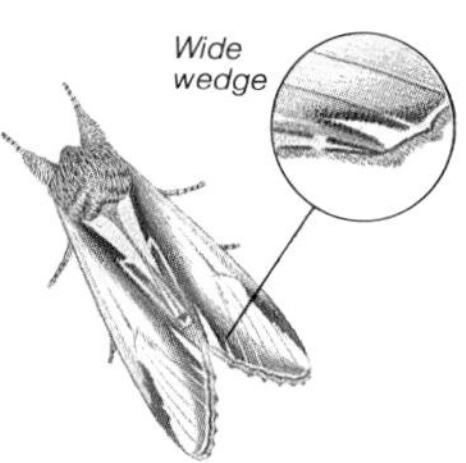

Lesser swallow prominent

Pheosia gnoma

Slightly smaller than the swallow prominent with a wider white wedge on the fore-wing. The caterpillar feeds on birch leaves. Wingspan 2⅛ in. (54 mm).

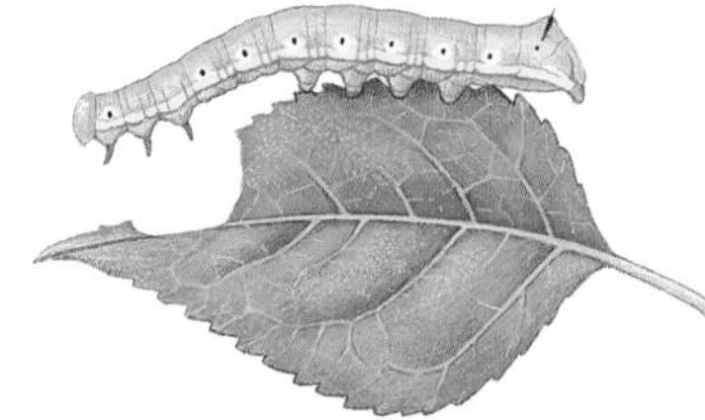

The pale green caterpillar has a yellow stripe along its side and a hump near the tail. There is also a brown form.

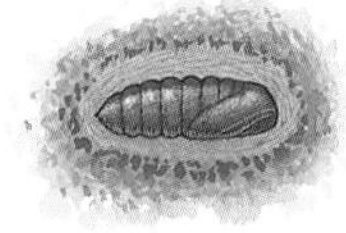

The first-generation caterpillars form a loose cocoon in leaf litter in July; those of the second generation overwinter as chrysalises in a silk cocoon just below the soil.

Swallow prominent *Pheosia tremula*

This common moth is frequently attracted to light at night and may fly into houses through open windows. It occurs in woody areas, especially near stands of silver birch trees, and in damp places where willows, aspens and poplars grow well. The moth may also be found in parks and gardens.

There are two generations a year in southern England and Wales, where the moth is on the wing in May and June and again in August. The caterpillars may be seen in June and July and in September and October. In Scotland and the north of England there is only one generation of moths each year, in May and June, and they tend to be paler with reduced markings. The moth is widely distributed in the British Isles and is especially common in the south of England. It is found throughout Wales and has a patchy distribution in Scotland. It occurs in a few localities in Ireland.

The swallow prominent is easily confused with the lesser swallow prominent which is on the wing at the same time. They can be distinguished by the white wedge on the fore-wing which is shorter and wider on the lesser swallow prominent. The lesser has a much wider distribution in the north.

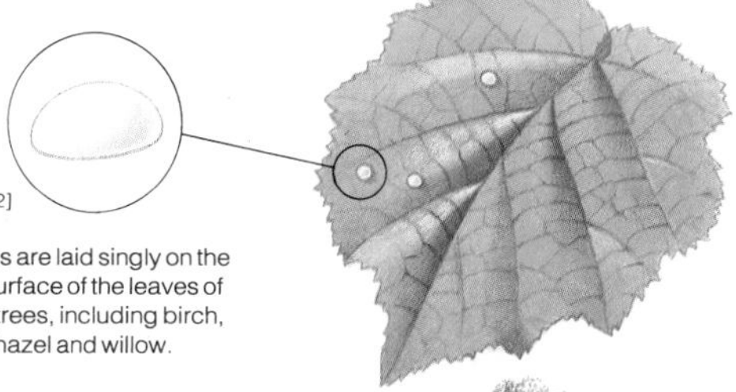

[× 12]

The eggs are laid singly on the upper surface of the leaves of various trees, including birch, poplar, hazel and willow.

When disturbed, the caterpillar assumes a characteristic position with its head and thorax reflexed upwards.

The chrysalis is formed underground, sometimes at the base of the tree on which the caterpillar has been feeding.

The coxcomb prominent occurs in various shades – from pale yellow-brown through red-brown to dark brown.

Coxcomb

A reddish moth with thin faint black lines along the wings. A tooth-shaped projection, or 'coxcomb', protrudes from the fore-wing over the hind-wing. It juts upwards when the wings are folded. Wingspan 2 in. (50 mm).

Coxcomb prominent *Ptilodon capucina*

This woodland moth has co-evolved with a wide variety of British native trees such as oak, alder, beech, birch, hazel, willow and sallow, as well as lime and white poplar which were introduced from abroad. The moth is common and widely distributed because of this great array of food plants for its caterpillars. It is found throughout England and Wales with rather scattered populations in Scotland and Ireland. Deciduous woodland, scrubby areas and town parks and gardens are all places where it can be seen. There are two generations a year in the south where moths are on the wing from May to September. In Scotland, there is only one generation, in May and June.

At rest the moth resembles a dead leaf because of the two humps along its 'back'. The hump on the thorax is typical of the prominent moths and gives them their name. The coxcomb prominent also has a protruding 'coxcomb' made by a tuft of hairs on the back edge of its fore-wing.

The caterpillars bend their heads over their bodies when a predator approaches, breaking up the obvious caterpillar outline and providing a form of camouflage. They vary considerably in colour, and may be pale yellow or darker green.

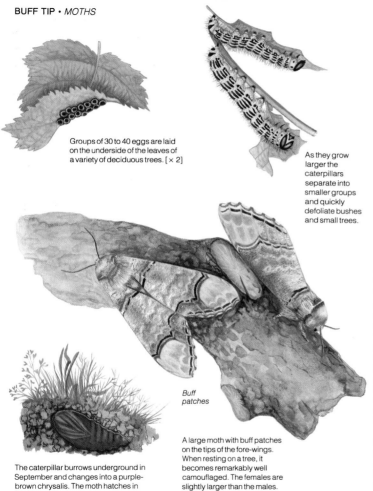

Groups of 30 to 40 eggs are laid on the underside of the leaves of a variety of deciduous trees. [× 2]

As they grow larger the caterpillars separate into smaller groups and quickly defoliate bushes and small trees.

In July, the newly hatched caterpillars remain together in close formation, eating only the underside of the leaf.

The buff tips on the fore-wings look like the broken end of a twig when they are folded together on bark.

Buff patches

The caterpillar burrows underground in September and changes into a purple-brown chrysalis. The moth hatches in late May or June.

A large moth with buff patches on the tips of the fore-wings. When resting on a tree, it becomes remarkably well camouflaged. The females are slightly larger than the males. Wingspan 2½ in. (64 mm).

Buff tip *Phalera bucephala*

The caterpillars of the buff tip moth eat a remarkably wide range of plants. In towns and cities, they are found in avenues of limes and poplars. In deciduous woodlands they eat the leaves of oak, sallow, aspen, whitebeam and hazel. On roadside verges they often defoliate small sapling trees. And in orchards they can strip the leaves from apple, cherry and cobnut trees. The caterpillars are gregarious when young, and have a disagreeable smell. They eat in groups and move off together to seek further green leaves when they have stripped a branch. Later they become solitary, and when they are fully fed they fall or crawl from the tree into leaf litter to make a chrysalis. The chrysalis spends the winter there, but may be found and eaten by foraging blackbirds and thrushes.

The moths, which are seen from May to July, are active at night and are attracted to light. They resemble twigs when resting, the buff tips on the fore-wings providing excellent camouflage when they are folded together. Buff tip moths are found throughout Britain, but are most common in central and south-east England. They also occur in scattered populations along the coast of Ireland.

The eggs are laid singly from May to July on the leaves of oak, beech, birch or hazel.

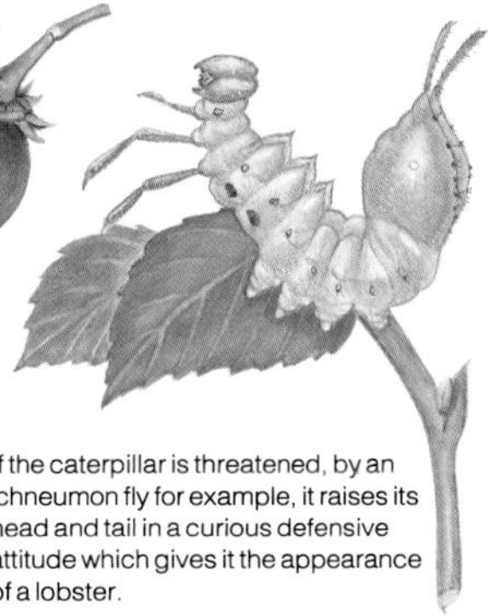

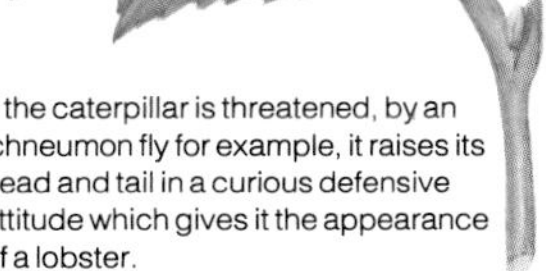

If the caterpillar is threatened, by an ichneumon fly for example, it raises its head and tail in a curious defensive attitude which gives it the appearance of a lobster.

A lobster moth, its head enveloped in hair, rests on the trunk of a tree with its front legs typically outstretched.

Feathery antennae on male

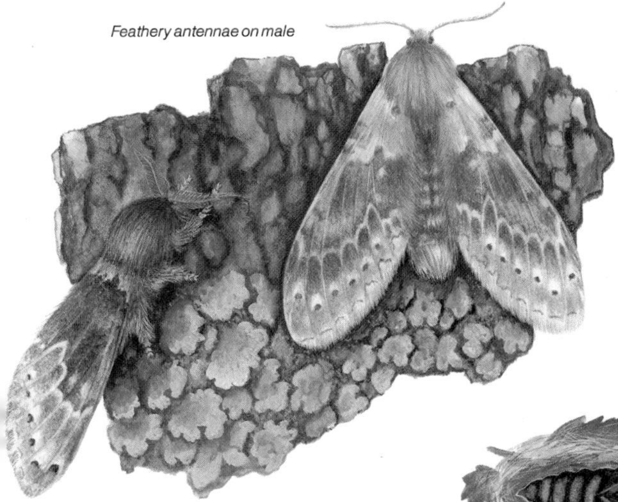

A brown-grey hairy moth which may be found resting on the trunks of small trees or bushes in beech woods during May and June. The fore-wings vary between light and dark. Males have feathery antennae. Wingspan 2¾ in. (70 mm).

In October, the chrysalis is formed in a silk chamber spun among leaf litter where it spends the winter.

Lobster moth *Stauropus fagi*

The extraordinary caterpillar of the lobster moth is unique in its appearance, and instantly identifiable. When disturbed by a predator it takes on a grotesque shape resembling a miniature lobster. To help it in this elaborate display, the head and 'tail' rear up over the body. A pair of filaments, called flagella, are waved in the air from the rear end of the abdomen. As a result of the change in shape, the predator might be uncertain that the caterpillar would make an appropriate prey, and might be deterred from attacking. Like the caterpillar of the puss moth (p. 156), the lobster caterpillar squirts formic acid over predators. The acid is emitted from glands below the thorax, and may deter predators such as tits, warblers, wrens and parasites such as ichneumon flies.

The moth itself occurs in two colour forms – one with light fore-wings, the other with dark fore-wings. Both may be seen in the same locality in May and June. The moth is found in deciduous woodland, heathland and scrubby areas near the caterpillars' food plants – oak, beech, birch and hazel. At rest it becomes perfectly camouflaged in leaves. It is unknown north of a line between North Wales and The Wash.

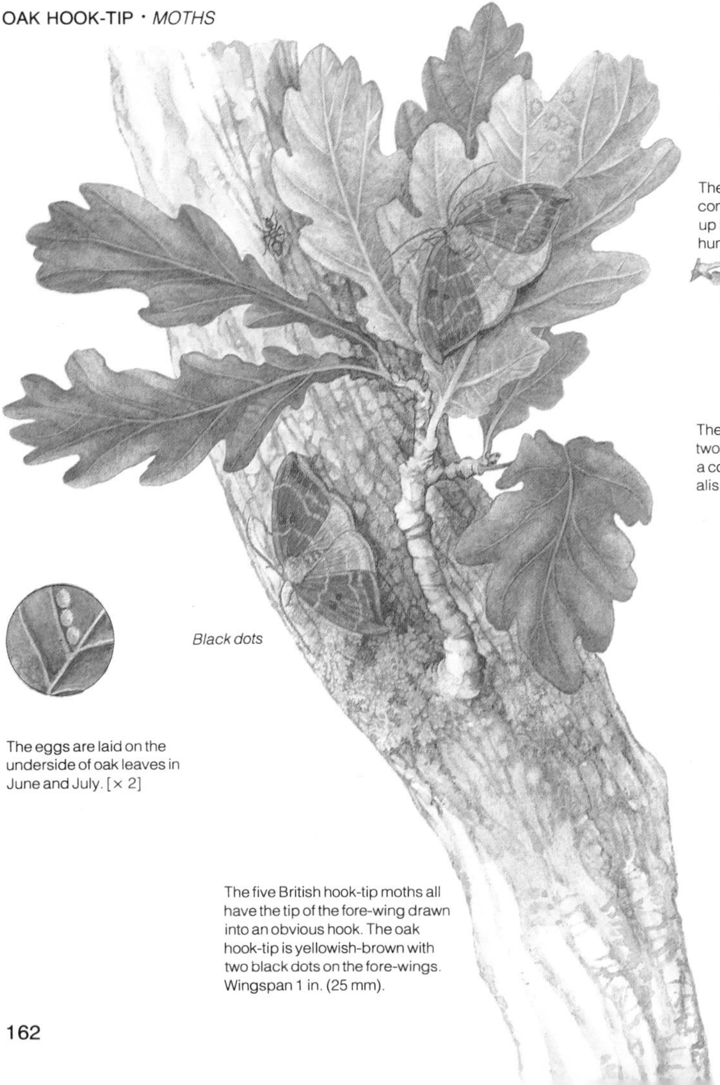

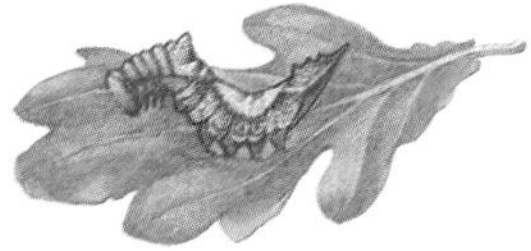

The caterpillar breaks up its outline – to conceal itself on oak leaves – by holding up both ends, emphasising its two small humps. It occurs in June and July.

The fully grown caterpillar draws together two oak leaves with silk thread, and forms a cocoon in which it changes into a chrysalis. It spends the winter in this stage.

The male oak hook-tip has antennae with comb-like 'teeth' with which it detects the scent of the female moth.

Black dots

The eggs are laid on the underside of oak leaves in June and July. [× 2]

The five British hook-tip moths all have the tip of the fore-wing drawn into an obvious hook. The oak hook-tip is yellowish-brown with two black dots on the fore-wings. Wingspan 1 in. (25 mm).

Oak hook-tip *Drepana binaria*

The caterpillar of the oak hook-tip moth has only seven pairs of legs instead of the usual eight pairs. Most caterpillars of moths and butterflies have three pairs of true (or jointed) legs on the segments behind the head, four pairs of prolegs (sucker-like false legs) in the centre of the body, and a pair of claspers on the rear segment. The true legs are used for walking and holding food, the prolegs are the main walking legs, and the claspers grip on to small twigs. Instead of gripping with its rear end, the oak hook-tip caterpillar holds it in the air to break up the typical caterpillar outline. This acts as a form of camouflage, making it less obvious to predators.

The moth is also unusual in not having a proper tongue for feeding. It may exist for its entire life of two or three weeks without taking in food – simply living on its fat reserves built up from the time it was a caterpillar. The hook-tip moths, of which the oak hook-tip is very typical, have co-evolved with a variety of native British trees, the leaves of which provide food for the caterpillars. The oak hook-tip feeds on oak, and the moth is seen in oak woods and along hedgerows from May to August throughout England and Wales.

The eggs are laid around the underside margin of bramble leaves. [× 2]

Pink markings

The fully grown caterpillar draws bramble leaves together with silk thread to form a protective cocoon in which it creates its chrysalis.

The peach blossom moth can be found in parks and large gardens in towns and cities, particularly in the south of England.

Peach blossom *Thyatira batis*

The peach blossom is one of the prettiest of British moths, with wing patterns as fresh and colourful as spring-time petals. It is also a common moth, found widely through England and Wales and in parts of Scotland and Ireland. There is always one generation each year and two in warm years in the south. Consequently the peach blossom is on the wing during blossom time in May and June and perhaps again in the autumn. The caterpillar is well camouflaged with its humps and projections at both ends of its body and a series of ridges in the middle. The chrysalises which are formed in September hibernate through the winter and hatch the following spring.

The moth's petal-like markings make ideal camouflage as it rests among the rose-coloured petals of brambles where it lays its eggs and where the caterpillars hatch to eat the bramble leaves. The caterpillars will also feed on the leaves of raspberry plants which grow wild in many parts of the countryside.

The peach blossom is attracted by lights, and can also be found at rest in mixed deciduous woodland, along rides in coniferous woodlands and along old hedgerows where well-established thickets of brambles occur.

The reddish-brown caterpillar has a thin brown line and five ridges along the upper surface, and a broader line along most of its side.

The moth gets its name from the delicate pink markings on the fore-wings, not for any fondness for peach blossom. It is well camouflaged for a life spent among foliage and flowers in spring and early summer. Wingspan $1\frac{1}{2}$ in. (38 mm).

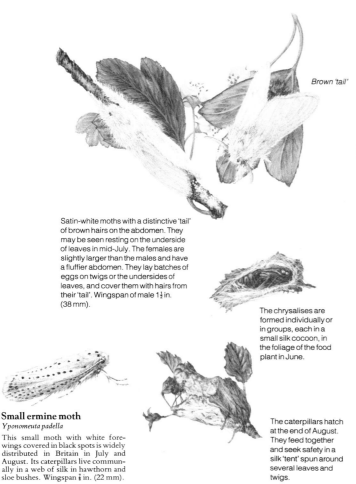

Brown 'tail'

Satin-white moths with a distinctive 'tail' of brown hairs on the abdomen. They may be seen resting on the underside of leaves in mid-July. The females are slightly larger than the males and have a fluffier abdomen. They lay batches of eggs on twigs or the undersides of leaves, and cover them with hairs from their 'tail'. Wingspan of male 1½ in. (38 mm).

In the spring the caterpillars venture outside their tent to feed side by side.

An infestation of brown-tail caterpillars in a hedgerow is evident from the tents of silk that the caterpillars spin.

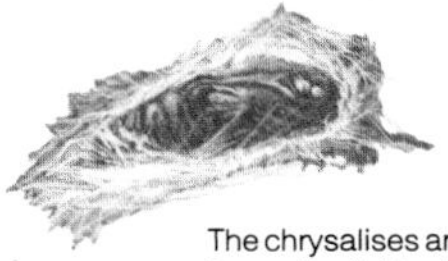

The chrysalises are formed individually or in groups, each in a small silk cocoon, in the foliage of the food plant in June.

The caterpillars hatch at the end of August. They feed together and seek safety in a silk 'tent' spun around several leaves and twigs.

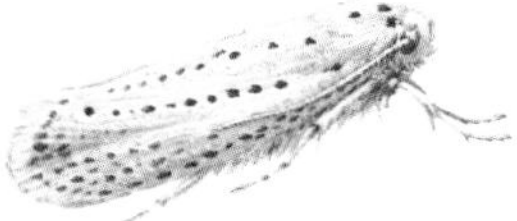

Small ermine moth
Yponomeuta padella

This small moth with white forewings covered in black spots is widely distributed in Britain in July and August. Its caterpillars live communally in a web of silk in hawthorn and sloe bushes. Wingspan ⅞ in. (22 mm).

Brown-tail tussock *Euproctis chrysorrhoea*

In the spring of 1782 a plague of brown-tail caterpillars struck the south-east of England. Hedges and fruit trees were laid bare, and the infestation was considered so serious that poor people in London were paid a shilling a bushel for the caterpillars' winter 'tents'. The tents were then burned by churchwardens, and special anti-moth prayers were said in churches. Today the caterpillars are controlled by chemical sprays, but they are still serious defoliators of hedgerows.

The success of the brown-tail tussock moth is due to the broad taste of the caterpillars. They eat the leaves of many trees, including oak, lime, poplar, plane, hawthorn, elm, sloe and sallow. They also feed on wayside bushes and flowers, including bramble, dog rose, sea buckthorn and wild strawberry. When they invade orchards they eat the leaves of apple, plum, pear and damson trees. The moths are found in coastal areas where the caterpillars thrive in the unrestricted growths of scrub. They are common in the south-east, Essex, Suffolk and Hampshire. The detachable hairs of both the caterpillar and the cocoon can cause 'caterpillar rash' of the skin, particularly in sensitive areas such as the face.

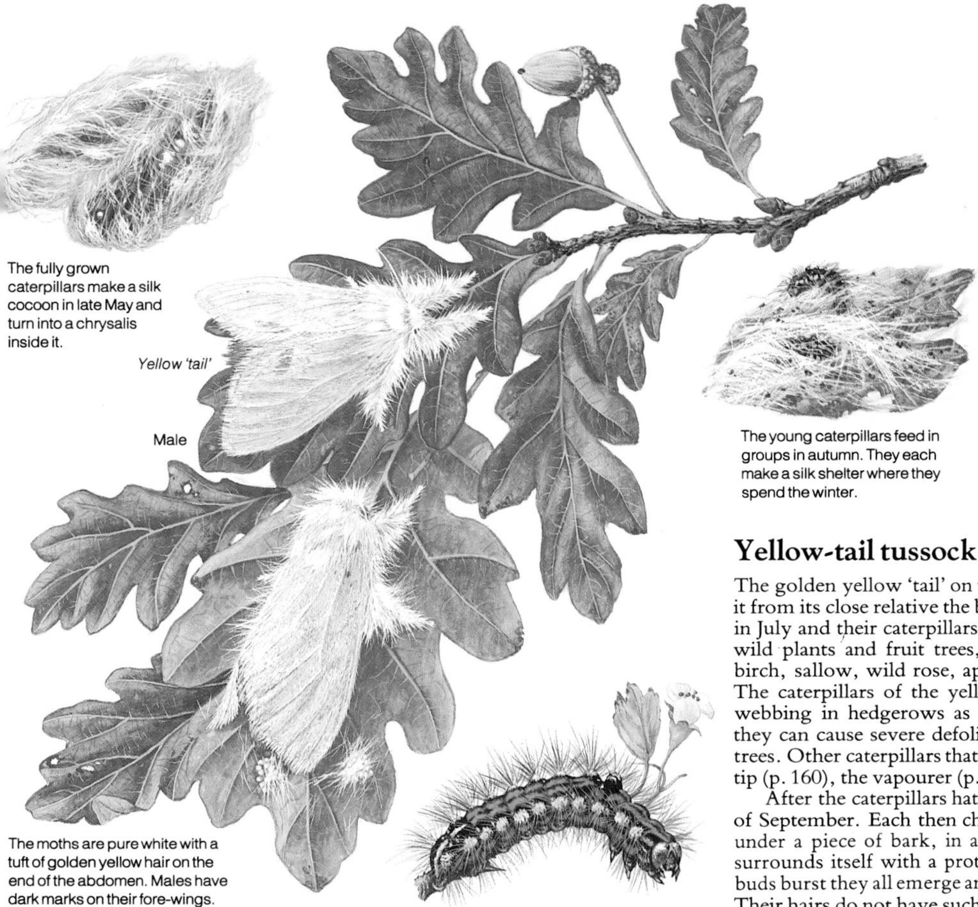

The fully grown caterpillars make a silk cocoon in late May and turn into a chrysalis inside it.

Yellow 'tail'

Male

Female

The moths are pure white with a tuft of golden yellow hair on the end of the abdomen. Males have dark marks on their fore-wings. The females lay their eggs in small groups on the twigs of several types of trees, covering them with protective hairs. Wingspan 1⅜ in. (35 mm).

When the caterpillars come out of hibernation in the spring, they are brightly coloured in black, white and red, and covered in long black hairs. At this stage they feed by themselves.

The young caterpillars feed in groups in autumn. They each make a silk shelter where they spend the winter.

A female yellow-tail moth lays a batch of eggs among grass in July. The young caterpillars will hatch in August.

Yellow-tail tussock *Euproctis similis*

The golden yellow 'tail' on this fluffy white moth distinguishes it from its close relative the brown-tail tussock. Both species fly in July and their caterpillars may be found on a wide variety of wild plants and fruit trees, including hawthorn, oak, beech, birch, sallow, wild rose, apple, plum, pear, cherry and hazel. The caterpillars of the yellow-tail do not make obvious silk webbing in hedgerows as the brown-tail caterpillars do, but they can cause severe defoliation of hedgerow plants and fruit trees. Other caterpillars that damage hedgerows include the buff tip (p. 160), the vapourer (p. 167) and the muslin (p. 185).

After the caterpillars hatch in August they feed until the end of September. Each then chooses a place to hibernate, perhaps under a piece of bark, in a crevice, or in moss or lichen, and surrounds itself with a protective silk cover. When the spring buds burst they all emerge and feed, fully exposed, on the leaves. Their hairs do not have such a bad effect on human skin as those of the brown-tail caterpillar. The yellow-tail moth is more widespread than the brown-tail, and is not restricted to the coast. It occurs mostly in southern England but is found as far north as southern Scotland and occasionally in Ireland.

The caterpillar may be either green or yellow, but both forms have four yellow tufts of hair along the back.

The male moth has feathery antennae which can detect the scent of a female at a distance of several hundred yards.

The chrysalis forms inside a silk cocoon among leaf litter, where it spends the winter.

A pale grey moth with hind-wings of a lighter colour than the fore-wings. The female's hind-wings are almost white. It is shown here on oak bark. Wingspan up to $2\frac{3}{4}$ in. (70 mm).

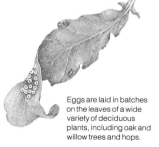

The moth, with its coating of white hair, may be seen on hop leaves in May and June.

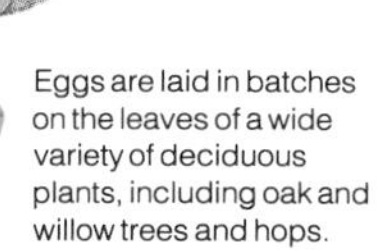

Eggs are laid in batches on the leaves of a wide variety of deciduous plants, including oak and willow trees and hops.

Pale tussock moth *Dasychira pudibunda*

Hop-pickers who used to come across the elaborately hairy caterpillars of the pale tussock moth called them hop-dogs. These curious creatures have now become far less common in England's hop fields since the introduction of insecticides. The more usual name tussock also refers to the caterpillars, with their tufts (or tussocks) of hair growing from the back and tail. The hairs, which are easily detachable, deter birds by giving them an unpleasant beakful if they should attempt to eat the caterpillar. And the bright colours provide a reminder not to attack similar prey again.

The moths, with a coating of white hairs over the head, thorax and legs, are seen in May and June. They are often found resting on trees in woods, parks and gardens with their hairy legs thrust forward in a characteristic way. They may also be attracted to light. The females lay their eggs on a wide range of deciduous trees and shrubs, including hops. The pale tussock is widespread in England and Wales, with a scattering in Ireland. It does not occur in Scotland. Black forms of the male moths are found in industrial areas where the lighter colour would make them more visible against dark backgrounds (see pp. 194–5).

The unusual caterpillar has four tufts of hair along its back and bunches of fine hairs at each end of the body.

Male

Batches of eggs are laid on the outside of the cocoon where they remain throughout the winter.

Female

White spots

Male

The male is chestnut coloured with white spots on the fore-wings. Wingspan 1⅜ in. (35 mm). The female's wings are almost non-existent, and she never leaves the cocoon from which she emerges.

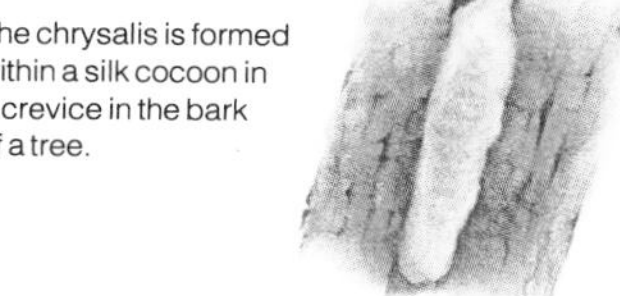

The chrysalis is formed within a silk cocoon in a crevice in the bark of a tree.

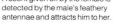

A scent given off by the female is detected by the male's feathery antennae and attracts him to her.

A female moth, with her under-developed and useless wings, sits among newly laid eggs on her old cocoon.

Vapourer moth *Orgyia antiqua*

This curiously named moth was discovered in Britain in 1782 when the word vapourer meant a braggart, or loud-mouthed talker. The moth may have received the name because of the frantic fluttering flight of the male which can be seen coursing down hedgerows during daylight between July and October.

The female vapourer is wingless, and spends her short life of about two weeks on the cocoon from which she hatched. She attracts males by giving off a volatile scent and, after mating, begins laying up to 300 eggs.

The vapourer moth is well distributed throughout Britain, including the London area, and in a few widely dispersed localities in Ireland. There are usually two generations a year, with only one in the north of Scotland. Infestations of the colourful caterpillars may occur between May and August on trees in urban areas and on heather moors. The caterpillar eats a wide range of plants, but mostly the leaves of fruit trees, sloe, heather, hawthorn, hazel and rose bushes. It is no longer a significant pest in orchards because of the use of insecticides. Young caterpillars can hang on silk threads when disturbed. They have tufts of hair which can cause a rash on human skins.

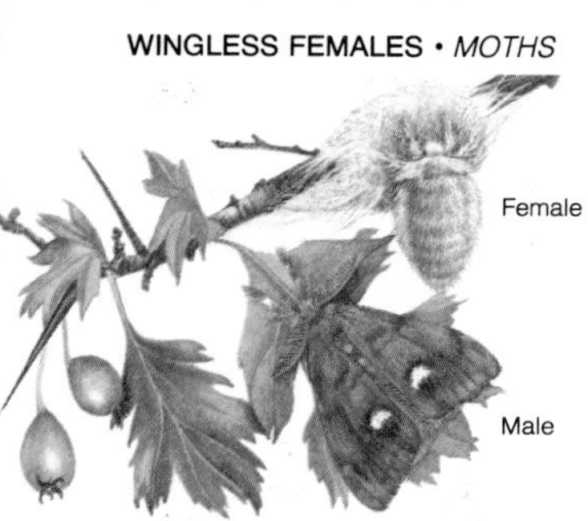

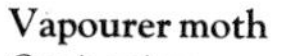

Scarce vapourer moth
Orgyia recens

Found mainly in south-west Yorkshire in woods and hedgerows. The hairy, wingless female never leaves the surface of her cocoon. There are two generations – in June/July and August/October.

Vapourer moth
Orgyia antiqua

A hairy moth common throughout Britain on trees and shrubs in woods and hedgerows. The male flies by day, but the wingless female always stays on her cocoon where she lays her eggs. There are two generations – in June/July and August/October. (See also p. 167.)

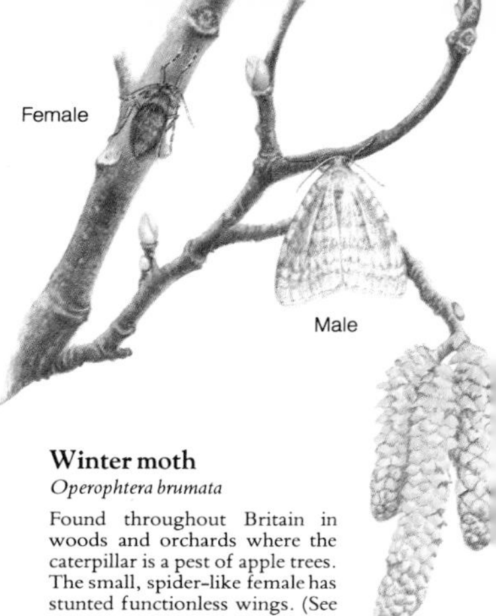

Winter moth
Operophtera brumata

Found throughout Britain in woods and orchards where the caterpillar is a pest of apple trees. The small, spider-like female has stunted functionless wings. (See also p. 189.)

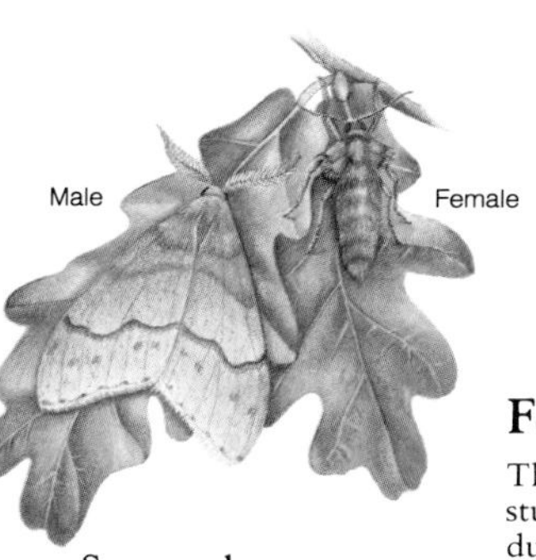

Scarce umber
Agriopis aurantiaria

Found in woods and hedgerows in October and November throughout Britain, though rare in Scotland. The spider-like female climbs to a resting place on twigs, usually of oak, birch or sloe (blackthorn), and the male joins her at night.

Mottled umber
Erannis defoliaria

A common moth in woods, hedgerows and orchards throughout Britain, from October to March. After hatching from her cocoon in the ground, the spider-like female crawls to a resting place on a branch or the trunk of a tree, where the male joins her to mate.

Female moths without wings

The females of some moth species have no wings, or wings so stunted as to be useless for flight. Most of these species hatch out during winter and early spring, and winglessness may have evolved to make a female less liable to be blown away in a gale. The species gains an advantage if the female lays her eggs on the same plant where she – as a caterpillar – originally fed, because it will be the correct food plant for her caterpillars. The wingless state also makes females less at risk from birds, as they would be more noticeable in flight.

Wingless females, all about $\frac{1}{2}$ in. (13 mm) long, attract the winged males by releasing volatile pheromones (insect hormones) soon after hatching. Males many yards downwind pick up the smell on their feathery antennae, and one newly hatched female may attract several males. There then follows a complex chemical battle among the sexes, involving aphrodisiac and deterrent pheromones, until one of the male moths finally mates with the female.

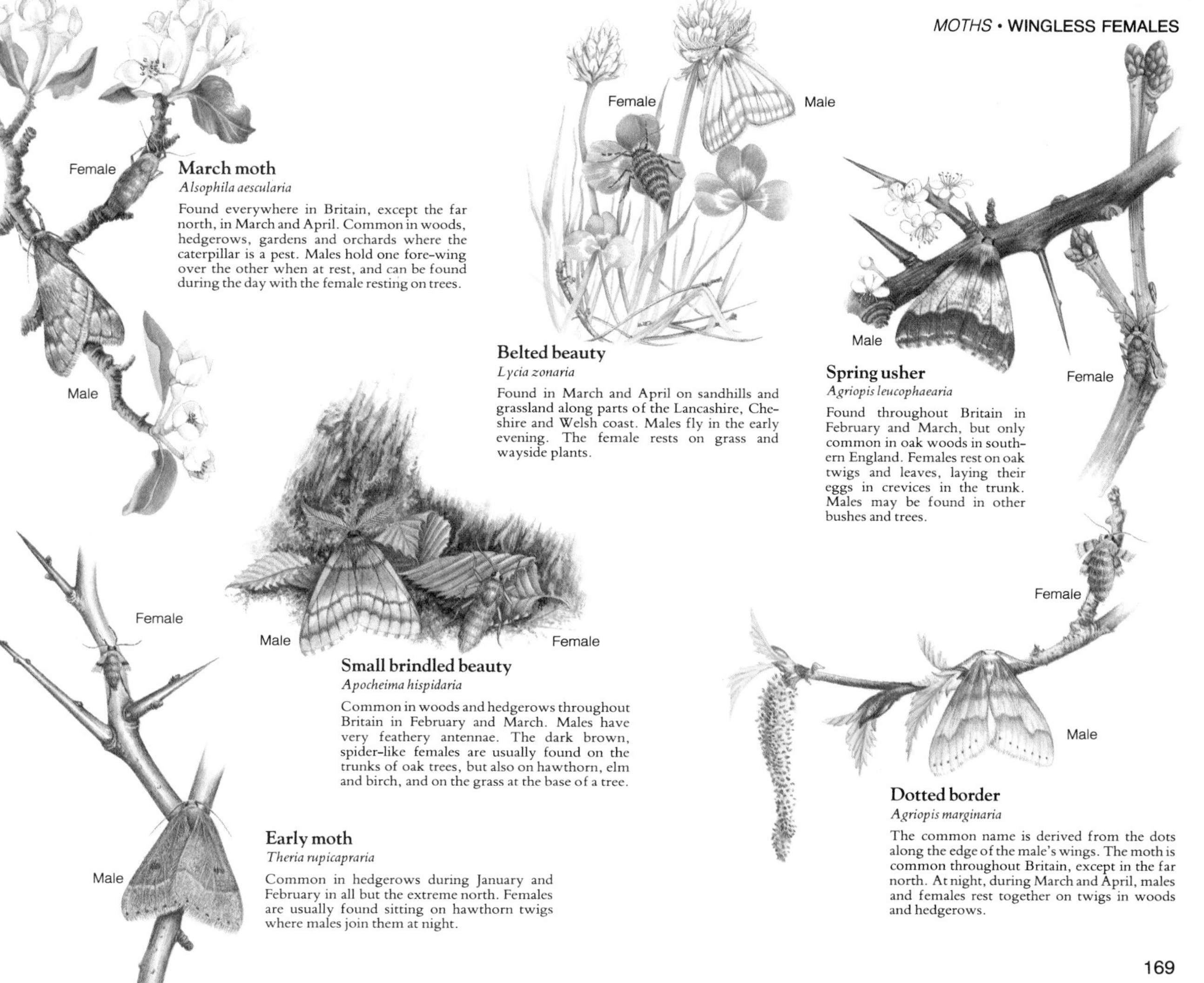

March moth

Alsophila aescularia

Found everywhere in Britain, except the far north, in March and April. Common in woods, hedgerows, gardens and orchards where the caterpillar is a pest. Males hold one fore-wing over the other when at rest, and can be found during the day with the female resting on trees.

Belted beauty

Lycia zonaria

Found in March and April on sandhills and grassland along parts of the Lancashire, Cheshire and Welsh coast. Males fly in the early evening. The female rests on grass and wayside plants.

Spring usher

Agriopis leucophaearia

Found throughout Britain in February and March, but only common in oak woods in southern England. Females rest on oak twigs and leaves, laying their eggs in crevices in the trunk. Males may be found in other bushes and trees.

Small brindled beauty

Apocheima hispidaria

Common in woods and hedgerows throughout Britain in February and March. Males have very feathery antennae. The dark brown, spider-like females are usually found on the trunks of oak trees, but also on hawthorn, elm and birch, and on the grass at the base of a tree.

Early moth

Theria rupicapraria

Common in hedgerows during January and February in all but the extreme north. Females are usually found sitting on hawthorn twigs where males join them at night.

Dotted border

Agriopis marginaria

The common name is derived from the dots along the edge of the male's wings. The moth is common throughout Britain, except in the far north. At night, during March and April, males and females rest together on twigs in woods and hedgerows.

The caterpillars, called cutworms, feed at night on a wide variety of low-growing plants. There is also a brown form. They spend cold periods of the winter resting in the soil.

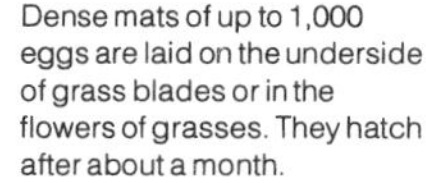

Dense mats of up to 1,000 eggs are laid on the underside of grass blades or in the flowers of grasses. They hatch after about a month.

Male

The fore-wings of the male are usually dark brown, and the female usually light brown. There is a black spot near the tip of each fore-wing. The hind-wings of both sexes are yellow with a black bar around the edge. The moths are most likely to be seen on an August evening. Wingspan $2\frac{3}{8}$ in. (60 mm).

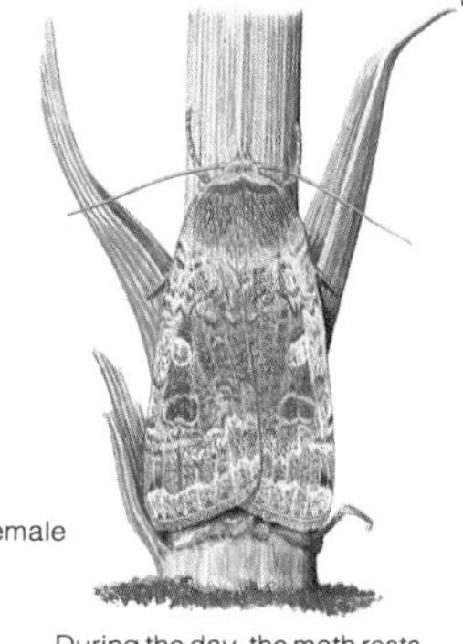

Female

During the day, the moth rests on the base of plants, particularly grasses, and may be disturbed by gardeners weeding an overgrown patch.

The large yellow underwing, identifiable by the black dots on its wingtips, feeds on flower nectar at night.

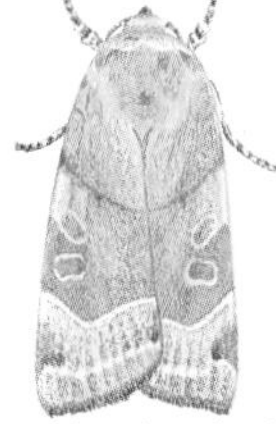

Broad-bordered yellow underwing
Noctua fimbriata

The fore-wings vary from pale to dark brown. The hind-wings are orange-yellow and the black border is wide. Wingspan $2\frac{1}{4}$ in. (57 mm).

A glossy chestnut-brown chrysalis is formed in a small cell underground in April.

Large yellow underwing *Noctua pronuba*

Several species of yellow underwing moth are found in Britain, but the large yellow underwing is the most common, occurring throughout the country. When the moth rests on vegetation during the day, the mottled colours of the fore-wings blend in with the background. However it is easily disturbed, and its yellow hind-wings flash brightly as it flies off at great speed. Some predatory birds may be deterred by the unexpected display, but many of the moths are caught and eaten. The colour of the fore-wings can vary greatly, from very pale to very dark in both sexes. The moths are seen – both in town and country – from June to October, with peak numbers in August. At night they feed on the nectar of flowers and will come to lights.

The caterpillars are known as cutworms, surface caterpillars, or brown grubs. They feed in gardens at night on low-growing plants, including strawberries and turnips, gnawing them through at ground level. In the day they often feed half buried in the stems of wild flowers such as violets and primroses.

The broad-bordered yellow underwing is a woodland species found throughout Britain, except in the far north of Scotland.

The grey caterpillar, with two little humps, feeds at night on willow and poplar leaves between April and July. During the day it rests on the bark and is hard to find.

Purplish-brown eggs are laid in crevices in the bark of willow or poplar trees.

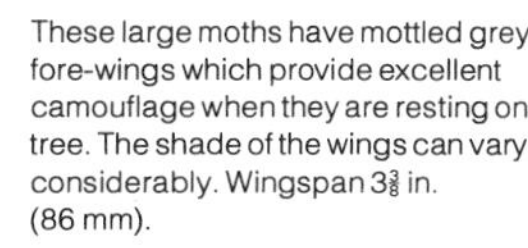

These large moths have mottled grey fore-wings which provide excellent camouflage when they are resting on a tree. The shade of the wings can vary considerably. Wingspan 3⅜ in. (86 mm).

Dark crimson underwing
Catocala sponsa

The fore-wings vary as much as the red underwing's. The hind-wings are crimson-purple. Wing-span 2¾ in. (70 mm).

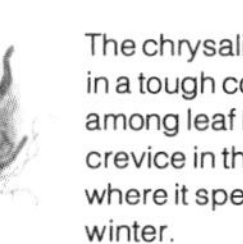

The chrysalis is formed in a tough cocoon among leaf litter or in a crevice in the bark where it spends the winter.

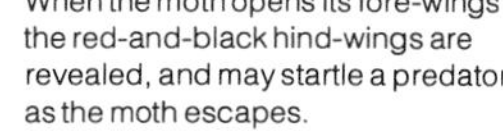

When the moth opens its fore-wings the red-and-black hind-wings are revealed, and may startle a predator as the moth escapes.

The red underwing moth flies at night, and may be seen on trees drinking sap that oozes from a wound in the bark.

Red underwing *Catocala nupta*

The colour scheme of this large moth is so effective that one moment it can be resting almost invisibly on the bark of a tree and the next it can produce a startling display of bright red. The flash of colour comes from the hind-wings which, in the resting position, are covered by the drab fore-wings. If a predatory bird comes too close, the moth opens its wings to fly away and the surprise of the unexpected colour may confuse the bird long enough for the moth to escape to another tree and vanish from sight under the camouflage of its fore-wings.

The red underwing is found in August and September, mostly in southern and eastern England, and not at all in the north of England, Scotland or Ireland. It is most likely to be seen in open woodland, parks or gardens where poplars and willows grow to provide food for its caterpillars. The moth has a set of brushes on its middle pair of legs which are thought to produce pheromones to attract females. The caterpillar has the shape and colour of a twig and when disturbed it clings closely to the tree.

The dark crimson underwing is a less-common relative of the red underwing. It is restricted mostly to southern England, especially Hampshire.

Eggs are laid on the tips of young scale-like leaves of the Monterey cypress or Lawson cypress, where they spend the winter.

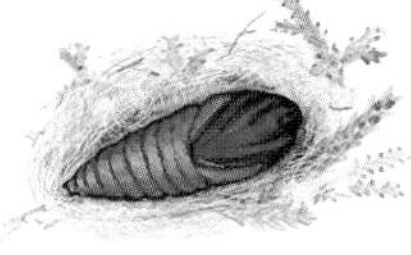

Fully fed caterpillars change into a chrysalis in leaf litter during August. They are enclosed in a cocoon of silk and hatch after about a month.

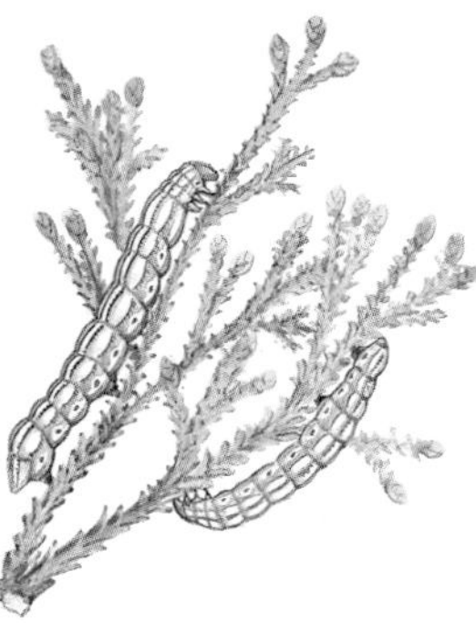

Dark to olive-green caterpillars hatch out in April or May. At first, they feed on the flower buds and tender leaf shoots, then move to older leaves. They are rarely seen, since they feed high up.

A Blair's shoulder knot moth rests on a fence, where its colour and markings provide an effective camouflage.

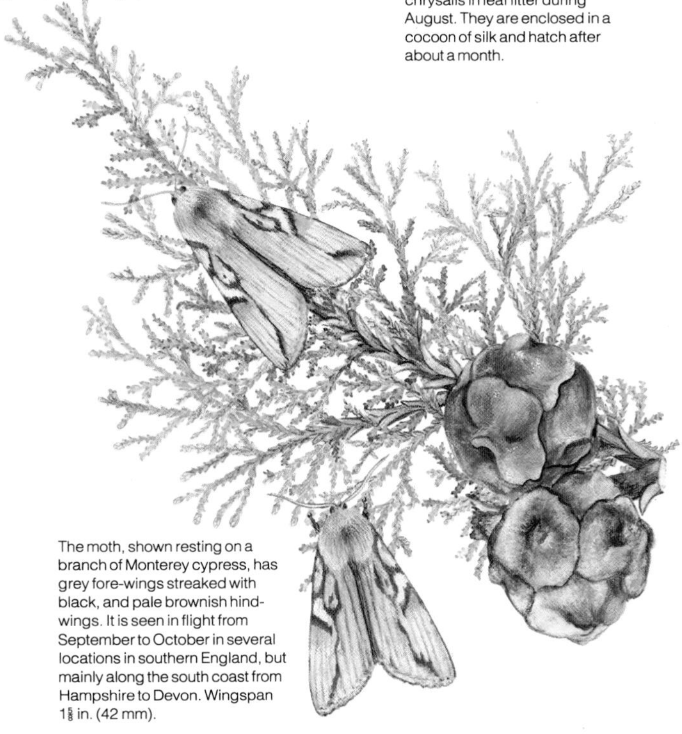

The moth, shown resting on a branch of Monterey cypress, has grey fore-wings streaked with black, and pale brownish hind-wings. It is seen in flight from September to October in several locations in southern England, but mainly along the south coast from Hampshire to Devon. Wingspan 1⅝ in. (42 mm).

Blair's shoulder knot *Lithophane leautieri*

Within the last century a number of moths, most of them from the Continent, have colonised Britain. Some have exploited newly introduced garden trees; others may have arrived because of subtle changes in climate. Blair's shoulder knot was first seen in the Isle of Wight in 1951. In the next ten years it spread along the south coast eastwards into Kent and westwards as far as Devon. By the early 1980s it was found throughout southern England, in Wales and East Anglia and as far north as Leicester.

Blair's shoulder knot is probably an immigrant from France, where the caterpillars feed on juniper and Italian cypress leaves. In Britain, it is an urban moth, and the caterpillars feed on the Monterey cypress, which was introduced into Britain from California in 1838. These enormous trees are now well established in parks and gardens. As the Monterey cypress grows abundantly in the Midlands and northern England, Blair's shoulder knot will probably continue to move northwards. The caterpillars also probably feed on Lawson cypress.

The moth's common name comes from the man who first saw it in Britain, the entomologist Dr K. G. Blair. The markings at the base of each fore-wing are known as 'shoulder knots'.

Other newcomers to Britain

Large thorn

Ennomos autumnaria

The colour of the moth varies from pale to deep golden-yellow, the female being larger than the male. It was first seen in Kent in 1855, but is now found in other parts of south-east England and in East Anglia. It flies in July. Brown twig-like caterpillars feed on the leaves of a variety of deciduous trees and shrubs. Wingspan of the male 1⅝ in. (42 mm), the female 2 in. (50 mm).

Cypress pug

Eupithecia phoeniceata

This native of the Mediterranean was first discovered by the British lepidopterist Baron de Worms in Cornwall in 1959. It feeds on cypress, with another species, also called the cypress pug (*E. intricata*). It has a remarkably long season – from the end of May to November – and is seen in southern England. Wingspan 1½ in. (38 mm).

Varied coronet

Hadena compta

A dark brown moth with attractive black and white markings, seen mainly in gardens in June. The earliest sightings were in Kent in 1948, but now it is also found in East Anglia. The yellow-brown caterpillar occasionally feeds on the seeds of bladder campion, but its usual food plant is sweet william. Wingspan 1⅛ in. (28 mm).

Wormwood shark

Cucullia absinthii

A moth with grey fore-wings and black markings found in July and August, mostly in England and Wales. It is most abundant in urban areas, especially London and the Midlands. In August and September the green caterpillar feeds on the flowers and seeds of mugwort (*Artemisia*). Wingspan 1½ in. (38 mm).

White speck or American wainscot

Mythimna unipuncta

Most common from late August to early October. The colouring varies from a pale yellow or red-brown to almost black. It was first recorded in the Scilly Isles in 1957 and has now spread along the south coast to Dorset. Caterpillars feed on grasses. Wingspan 1⅝ in. (42 mm).

L-album wainscot

Mythimna l-album

The ground colour of this moth varies from a pale grey-brown to a darker red-brown. First seen in Cornwall in 1933, it has moved east along the coast to Sussex. It flies in two generations, the first in July and the second in September and October. Caterpillars feed on tall fescue (*Festuca arundinacea*). Wingspan 1⅜ in. (35 mm).

Brighton wainscot

Oria musculosa

The first moth was found in Brighton in 1883. It has now spread through southern England, particularly Wiltshire, and its caterpillars live in the stems of wheat, oats and barley. It flies in July and August. Wingspan up to 1¼ in. (32 mm).

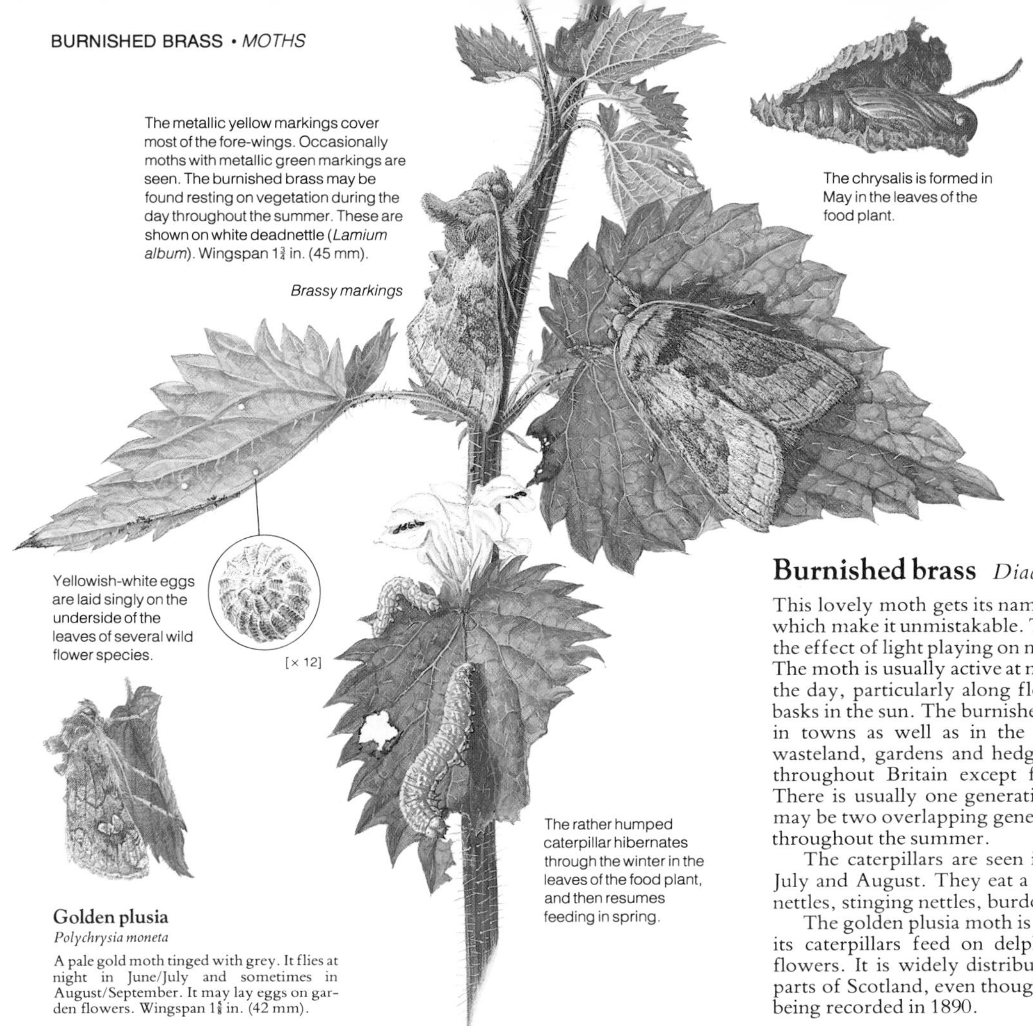

The metallic yellow markings cover most of the fore-wings. Occasionally moths with metallic green markings are seen. The burnished brass may be found resting on vegetation during the day throughout the summer. These are shown on white deadnettle (*Lamium album*). Wingspan 1¾ in. (45 mm).

Brassy markings

The chrysalis is formed in May in the leaves of the food plant.

Yellowish-white eggs are laid singly on the underside of the leaves of several wild flower species.

[× 12]

The rather humped caterpillar hibernates through the winter in the leaves of the food plant, and then resumes feeding in spring.

Golden plusia

Polychrysia moneta

A pale gold moth tinged with grey. It flies at night in June/July and sometimes in August/September. It may lay eggs on garden flowers. Wingspan 1⅝ in. (42 mm).

A burnished brass moth shows off the array of hairs on its legs and the spectacular crest on its thorax.

Burnished brass *Diachrysia chrysitis*

This lovely moth gets its name from the shiny brass-like wings which make it unmistakable. The metallic colour is produced by the effect of light playing on microscopic contours on the scales. The moth is usually active at night but may also be seen flying in the day, particularly along flowery ditches where it feeds and basks in the sun. The burnished brass is a common moth, found in towns as well as in the countryside. It frequents fields, wasteland, gardens and hedgerows, and is widely distributed throughout Britain except for the Orkneys and Shetlands. There is usually one generation a year, but in the south there may be two overlapping generations, and the moth may be seen throughout the summer.

The caterpillars are seen in March and April, and again in July and August. They eat a variety of plants, including deadnettles, stinging nettles, burdock and viper's bugloss.

The golden plusia moth is found in parks and gardens where its caterpillars feed on delphinium, monkshood and globeflowers. It is widely distributed in England and Wales and in parts of Scotland, even though it is a newcomer to Britain, first being recorded in 1890.

Y-shaped mark

The fore-wings contain a distinctive Y-shaped mark. The moths can be found – by day or night – feeding from flowers during the summer. When resting – often head downwards – the moth displays three elegant plumes of hair on the thorax. Wingspan $1\frac{5}{8}$ in. (42 mm).

Eggs are laid singly on the leaves of a variety of common plants. [× 12]

The caterpillars may be either green or dark green. They feed by night and rest up in dark crevices during the day.

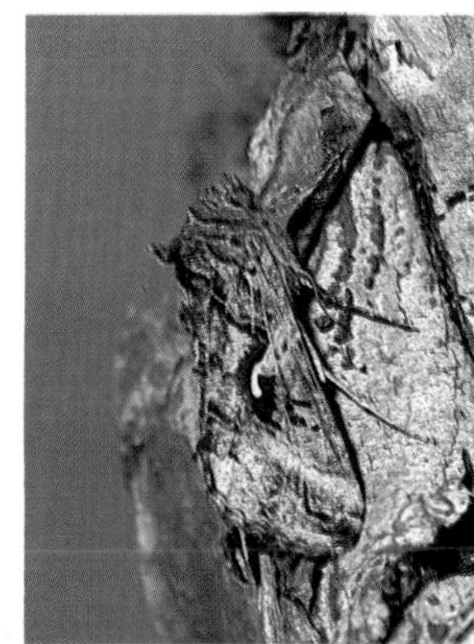

On the bark of a poplar tree, the silver Y is effectively camouflaged by its grey wings. But the tell-tale Y mark is visible.

Silver Y *Autographa gamma*

Both its English and scientific names describe this moth's characteristic feature – the white mark on each fore-wing that can be read either as a Y or as the symbol for the Greek letter gamma (γ). The silver Y is an extremely abundant moth which is most often seen during the day, either feeding on the nectar of garden flowers or flitting rapidly between flowers in meadows. It is a fast flyer and a regular migrant to Britain from the Continent. Great numbers of moths arrive between spring and late summer. One Essex entomologist has recorded 7,398 silver Ys attracted to his moth-light on one night. The silver Y is found throughout Britain, even up to the Shetlands and Orkneys. The early migrants give rise to a second generation in the autumn when the moth becomes most abundant. Neither the moths nor their caterpillars are believed to survive the British winter. The male moths have an unusual feature in the tufts of hair in the abdomen which protrude like a brush during courtship and release pheromones that attract females.

The beautiful golden Y is a species of moth which shares the same habitats and food plants as the silver Y, but its caterpillars survive the British winter.

Beautiful golden Y
Autographa pulchrina

The fore-wings are golden-orange, and the Y mark is broken up into a V and a dot. The moths are seen in June and July. Wingspan $1\frac{1}{2}$ in. (38 mm).

The fully grown caterpillar forms its chrysalis inside a cocoon spun among the foliage of its food plant or in leaf litter.

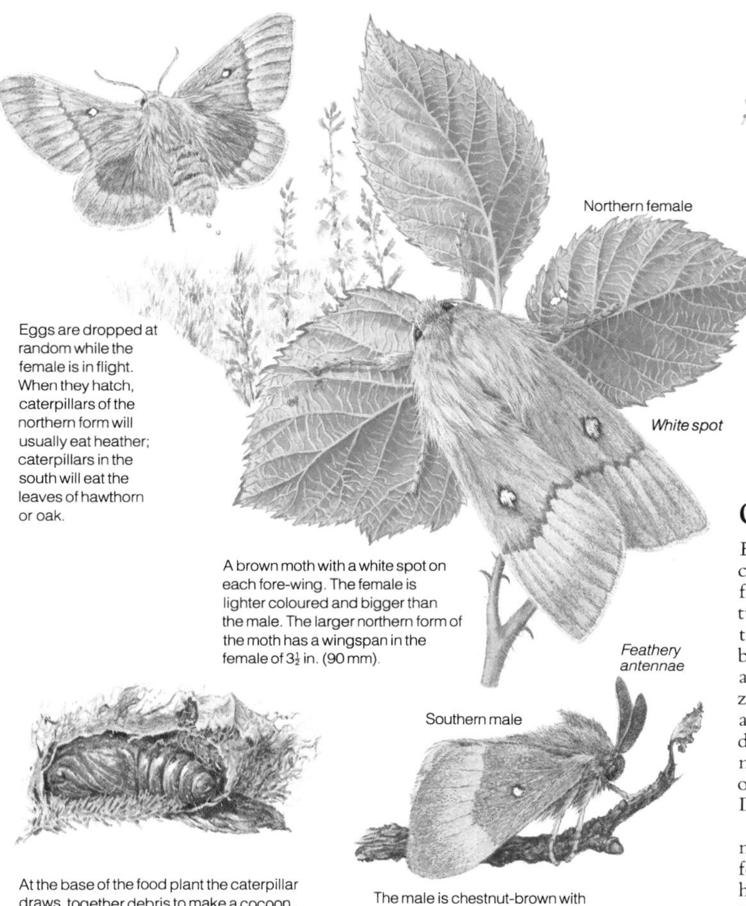

Eggs are dropped at random while the female is in flight. When they hatch, caterpillars of the northern form will usually eat heather; caterpillars in the south will eat the leaves of hawthorn or oak.

A brown moth with a white spot on each fore-wing. The female is lighter coloured and bigger than the male. The larger northern form of the moth has a wingspan in the female of $3\frac{1}{2}$ in. (90 mm).

At the base of the food plant the caterpillar draws together debris to make a cocoon, and the chrysalis is formed inside.

The male is chestnut-brown with feathery antennae, and is usually seen flying rapidly about during sunny weather.

Caterpillars are covered with orange hairs and are quite brightly coloured in white, black, brown and red. They are often found in a typical 'L' shape.

A male oak eggar moth rests between bursts of energetic flight, its antennae alert to volatile smells from the female.

Oak eggar *Lasiocampa quercus*

Eggar moths were probably named after the egg-shaped cocoons that the caterpillars spin low on the ground. Britain has four kinds of eggar, and the oak eggar is the largest, occurring as two different sub-species. The southern sub-species is found throughout the south of Britain in July and August. The dark brown males are very fast flyers and are often seen coursing along hedgerows and over waste ground in their characteristic zigzag manner. The females, which are much paler in colour, are less energetic, and attract males from as far as $1\frac{1}{2}$ miles downwind by releasing volatile scents called pheromones. The northern sub-species is darker in the female and larger. It occurs on moorland in Scotland and the north of England, and on Dartmoor and Exmoor. It is on the wing in May and June.

The caterpillars eat the leaves of various shrubs and trees. On moors they will eat heather, bramble or birch. Elsewhere they feed on hawthorn, sloe, oak or dogwood. In winter they hibernate and resume feeding in the spring. At the end of a good year the caterpillar will turn into a chrysalis before winter begins. However, after a bad year, the caterpillars may feed right through the following summer and hatch the year after.

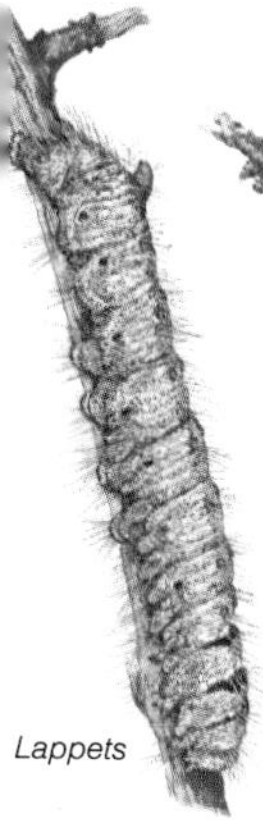

Wavy wing margins

Lappets

The caterpillars vary from grey, through bluish to reddish-brown. The skirt of lappets along the body hides the legs and blends well with the background. They hibernate in September.

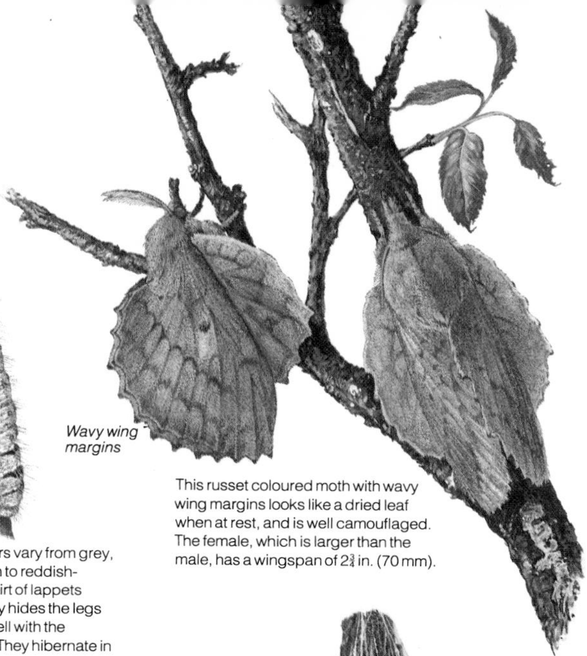

This russet coloured moth with wavy wing margins looks like a dried leaf when at rest, and is well camouflaged. The female, which is larger than the male, has a wingspan of 2¾ in. (70 mm).

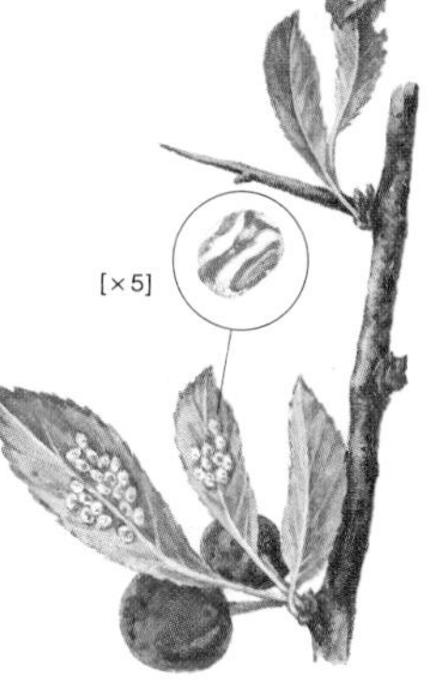

The large eggs are laid in small groups on the underside of the leaves of apple, hawthorn, sallow and sloe in July and August. They hatch after two weeks.

Lappet moths rest in a characteristic tent-like manner which enhances their wing shape and colour to mimic dried leaves.

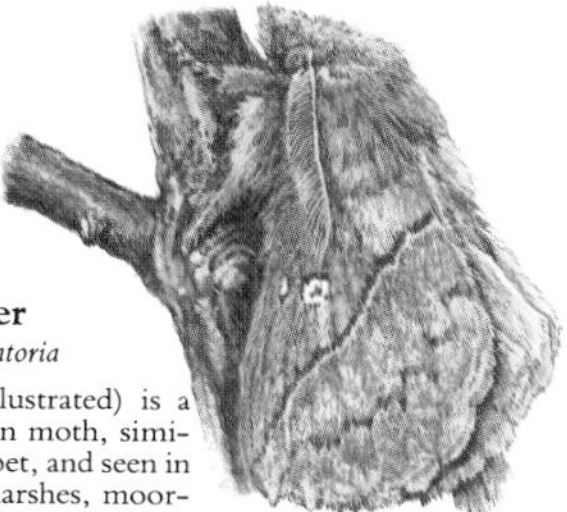

The drinker

Philudoria potatoria

The male (illustrated) is a reddish-brown moth, similar to the lappet, and seen in summer in marshes, moorland and along ditches. Females are larger and lighter in colour than males. Wingspan of male 2 in. (50 mm).

The chrysalis is formed in a cocoon made from the twigs of the food plant in May.

Lappet *Gastropacha quercifolia*

The lappet moth is named after its caterpillar which has a skirt of little flaps around its body. The term lappet referred to flaps and folds once common on women's hats and recalled in the words of the 18th-century poet William Cowper: 'Her head adorned with lappets, pinn'd aloft.' The caterpillar's lappets are more than an adornment: they combine with its flat underside to make it appear part of the twig on which it rests. If disturbed, it will show off two blue bands behind its head to scare off predators.

The moths, too, are good at concealment. At rest, their fore-wings are arched over the body while the hind-wings lie flatter, breaking up the moth-like outline. Their russet colours make them look like autumnal beech leaves, but they are seen in summer between May and August. There are normally two generations in southern England and Wales and one in the north; they are not found in Scotland or Ireland. Their haunts include hedgerows, woodlands, wet meadows and fenland.

The drinker is another moth of damp areas that also looks rather like a dead leaf. It is widespread throughout Britain and is on the wing between June and August. Its name comes from the caterpillar's habit of drinking dew drops.

Brightly coloured hind-wings

The distinctive brown-and-white markings break up the moth's outline when it rests on trees. The reddish-orange and black colours on the hind-wing and the abdomen – together with the red 'collar' – are used to startle predators such as sparrows. Wingspan 3 in. (76 mm).

[× 10]

Groups of glossy yellow-to-green eggs are laid on the underside of leaves of a large variety of common plants.

The front view of the male moth reveals the distinctive red patches on the legs and around the head.

The hairy caterpillars, called 'woolly bears', may be seen in parks, gardens and on roads. They hibernate when young and resume feeding in spring.

The fully grown caterpillars make a yellowish silk cocoon in leaf litter and then change into a glossy chrysalis.

Garden tiger *Arctia caja*

Most tiger moths are brightly coloured, attractive insects that might be mistaken for butterflies when their wings are opened wide. They are named after the tiger-like stripes on their fore-wings. The garden tiger occurs throughout Britain in July and August, but is not often seen, as it flies at night. No two garden tigers look exactly alike in size or colour. The dark marks on the fore-wings vary greatly in size and shape, and the colours of the hind-wing may be red, crimson, yellow or orange. The garden tiger has a battery of defensive weapons to use against predators, such as birds. It can produce a startling flash of colour by suddenly exposing its hind-wings, and it can rub its wings together to make a grating noise. If these effects fail to deter the predator, the moth can exude bright yellow blood from the front of its thorax. Young sparrows often try repeatedly to catch garden tigers that they have disturbed, but eventually leave them alone.

The caterpillars, which are frequently seen, are called 'woolly bears' as they are completely covered with long hair. They may be found in the garden in May and June, on dead-nettle, plantain, lettuce and strawberry plants, and can run quickly.

Cream spots on fore-wing

The fore-wings are black with contrasting cream blotches. When threatened by a predator the moths display the warning coloration on their hind-wings and abdomen, which are pinky-orange with black spots. Wingspan 2½ in. (64 mm).

Glossy white eggs are laid in neat groups on the leaves of a wide variety of common plants.

The chrysalis is formed in a weak cocoon in leaf litter in May. The moth hatches after a month.

The underside of a cream-spot tiger reveals a medley of colours, warning that its body is poisonous to predators.

Ruby tiger
Phragmatobia fuliginosa

A less-colourful tiger moth, common throughout mainland Britain in late May and June. Its caterpillars feed on a variety of wayside plants, including docks and dandelions. Wingspan 1½ in. (38 mm).

The caterpillar has reddish-brown hairs and a pink or red head, legs and claspers. It hatches in July, hibernates through winter and resumes feeding in February.

Cream-spot tiger *Arctia villica*

The cream spots on the fore-wings, which give the moth its name, vary enormously in size. On some moths they may be larger and fused together so that the dominant colour is cream; on others they may not exist at all and the fore-wings are entirely black. The spots on the hind-wing also vary in size and shape. The cream-spot tiger is on the wing between late May and early July. It usually rests on vegetation during the day, but occasionally flies in daylight. If handled it does not try to escape, but relies for its defence on its bright colours which are a warning to predators that its body is poisonous.

The dark caterpillars can be found on all sorts of wayside or garden weeds including chickweed, dock, dandelion and plantain, as well as on gorse where it eats the young shoots. If hedgerows are examined on warm, sunny days in April and May the hairy caterpillars of both the garden tiger and the cream-spot tiger may be found together. The cream-spot tiger occurs along the Essex coast, the south coast from Kent to Cornwall, South Wales and the Channel Islands, and is most likely to be found in woodlands, on hedgerows and in grassy places. At night it may fly into houses, attracted to the light.

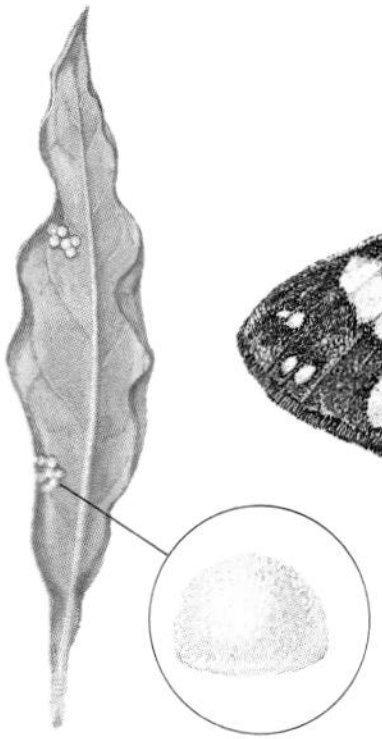

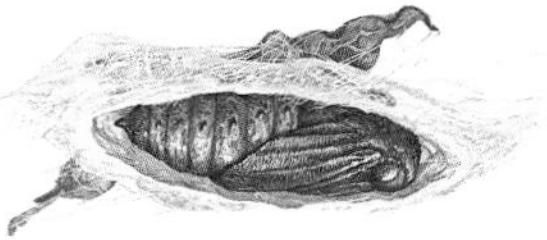

The chrysalis is formed in a weak cocoon in leaf litter in May.

The caterpillar has broken lines of yellow and black down the length of the body, with many white spots. The head is glossy black. It hibernates while still young.

The scarlet tiger flies throughout summer but is restricted to the southern half of England, and south Wales.

[× 12]

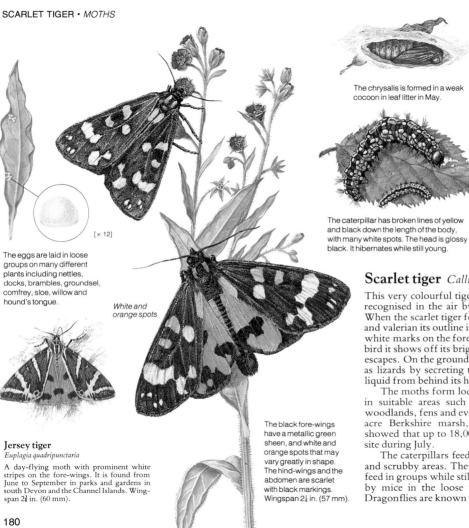

The eggs are laid in loose groups on many different plants including nettles, docks, brambles, groundsel, comfrey, sloe, willow and hound's tongue.

White and orange spots

The black fore-wings have a metallic green sheen, and white and orange spots that may vary greatly in shape. The hind-wings and the abdomen are scarlet with black markings. Wingspan $2\frac{1}{4}$ in. (57 mm).

Scarlet tiger *Callimorpha dominula*

This very colourful tiger moth flies during the day, and can be recognised in the air by its dipping and rising flight pattern. When the scarlet tiger feeds on flowers such as hemp agrimony and valerian its outline is broken up by the pattern of black-and-white marks on the fore-wings. If it is disturbed by a predatory bird it shows off its bright red hind-wings to startle the bird as it escapes. On the ground it can defend itself from predators such as lizards by secreting two blobs of poisonous, bright yellow liquid from behind its head.

The moths form localised and sometimes large populations in suitable areas such as damp meadows, clearings in wet woodlands, fens and even along coastal cliffs. One study in a 15 acre Berkshire marsh, conducted between 1939 and 1961, showed that up to 18,000 scarlet tigers could be present on the site during July.

The caterpillars feed on many plants that grow in meadows and scrubby areas. They emerge from hibernation in April and feed in groups while still young. The chrysalises are often eaten by mice in the loose vegetation where they form cocoons. Dragonflies are known to attack the moths.

Jersey tiger

Euplagia quadripunctaria

A day-flying moth with prominent white stripes on the fore-wings. It is found from June to September in parks and gardens in south Devon and the Channel Islands. Wingspan $2\frac{3}{8}$ in. (60 mm).

Cinnabar moths may be seen in the day flying slowly, which they can do safely as birds learn they are poisonous.

The dark brown chrysalis spends the winter in a weak cocoon in leaf litter or just below the surface of the soil.

The moths, which have glistening red-and-black colours, fly by day or night from May to mid-July. They may be seen weakly fluttering around meadows or at rest on plants. Wingspan $1\frac{3}{4}$ in. (45 mm).

The caterpillars, which are seen more often than the moths, are brightly coloured with orange-and-black bands. They may be found feeding in groups on summer days, and are fully grown in July and August.

Bright red markings

Batches of 30 to 40 yellow eggs are laid on the underside of ragwort or groundsel leaves in June and July. Coltsfoot is also recorded as a food plant.

Cinnabar moth *Tyria jacobaeae*

The red warning patches on the moth give it its name as they are the colour of the pigment mercuric sulphide, also known as vermilion or cinnabar. Both the moth and the caterpillar have striking colours, which serve as warnings to birds and other predators that they are inedible. The caterpillars' food plants, ragwort and groundsel, are rich in alkaloid poisons. These are stored in the caterpillars' bodies in a form that does not kill them but provides a chemical defence against birds, which find them nasty to eat. The poisons are passed on from the caterpillar, through the chrysalis to the moth, making it one of the most poisonous moths in Britain. It is inedible to most insect-eating lizards, birds and mammals.

The orange-and-black caterpillars feed together, and sometimes they are so numerous that they strip all the leaves from the plants in a particular area, and will wander about hopelessly looking for more food.

Cinnabar moths are common in Wales and southern England, but towards the north they become fairly local, and in Scotland and Ireland are restricted to central areas. They are on the wing in late spring and early summer.

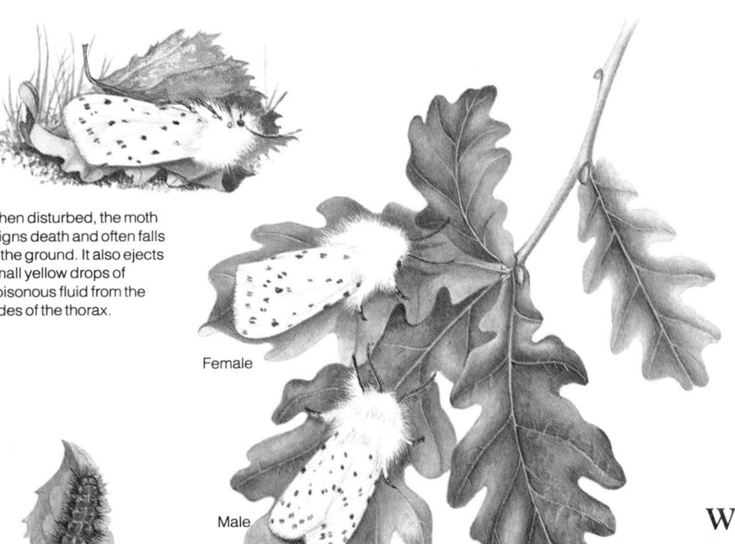

When disturbed, the moth feigns death and often falls to the ground. It also ejects small yellow drops of poisonous fluid from the sides of the thorax.

The wings are pure white with black spots, and the thorax has a furry covering of fine white hairs. The sexes are very similar, but the female has a broader abdomen and thinner antennae. Wingspan 1¾ in. (45 mm).

Glossy pale yellow eggs are laid in groups on the underside of the leaves of common plants such as dandelions and docks.

The magnificent antennae of a male white ermine stand out from the furry head. They detect the scent of females.

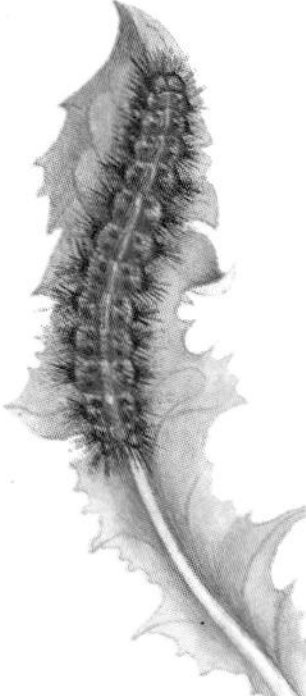

The caterpillars are dark brown and very hairy. They have a dark red line along the top, and may be found between July and September on a variety of plants. Occasionally there is a second generation of caterpillars in late autumn.

The chrysalis is formed in a substantial cocoon made partly of dead leaves on the ground, or in a crevice in bark. It spends the winter in this state, and the moth hatches the following June.

White ermine *Spilosoma lubricipeda*

The white winter fur of the stoat, known as ermine, is used to decorate the robes of peers and royalty. It has also given its name to this speckled white moth with its soft furry covering around the head and thorax. From late May to July the white ermine rests during the day on tree trunks or leaves, standing out brightly against the background. Its wings are folded tightly over its abdomen, and vary greatly in their pattern of spots. Some spots may be fused together and some may be absent. If the moth is disturbed it may fall to the ground and feign death. If provoked further it exudes a colourful and distasteful secretion containing large amounts of the chemical histamine which acts as a deterrent against birds.

The hairy caterpillars move quickly over the ground and give the moth its Latin name of *lubricipeda*, meaning fleet-footed. They are most undiscerning in their choice of food, eating all sorts of low-growing plants, including cultivated plants such as lettuces. When disturbed, they too curl up and feign death. The moth is widely distributed in Britain and is very common in the south of England. It is attracted to light and sometimes enters houses at night.

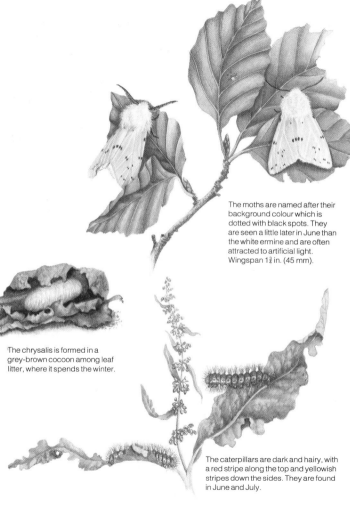

The moths are named after their background colour which is dotted with black spots. They are seen a little later in June than the white ermine and are often attracted to artificial light. Wingspan 1¾ in. (45 mm).

The males have more feathery antennae than the females and tend to be darker.

A male buff ermine rests on a leaf. The spots across its fore-wings are bigger than usual, and almost merge into lines.

The chrysalis is formed in a grey-brown cocoon among leaf litter, where it spends the winter.

The caterpillars are dark and hairy, with a red stripe along the top and yellowish stripes down the sides. They are found in June and July.

Buff ermine *Spilosoma lutea*

Studies of this moth, by the British naturalist Miriam Rothschild, have shown it is probably a mimic of the closely related white ermine, which is both poisonous and distasteful to predatory birds. Buff ermines have no deterrent poison, but fly a little later than the white ermine. By this time, birds will have learnt to avoid the white ermine, and consequently will avoid the buff ermine, which to them looks the same.

One generation of the buff ermine moth flies each year. It is most abundant in the south-east, but is seen in damp places in all parts of England and Wales, along the west coast of Scotland and in coastal areas of Ireland. It is extremely common on wasteland and in gardens in June and July and, because it is attracted to light, is sometimes found indoors. The caterpillars feed from late July to October on a variety of wayside plants, most commonly dandelions and docks.

Both the colouring and markings of this moth show considerable variation. Sometimes the spots on the fore-wings are absent, and occasionally they are fused into lines. There is even a black variety, on which the wings are a sooty black and the veins and spots are yellow.

Only one wing visible

The moths have long grey-blue wings with a yellow margin. One fore-wing is held over the other when the moth is resting. They are seen in deciduous woodland in July and August. Wingspan 1½ in. (38 mm).

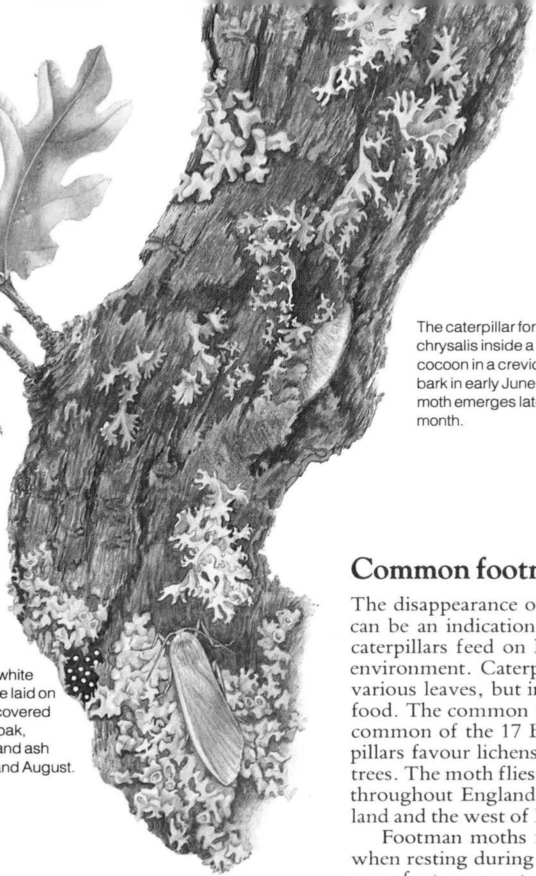

The caterpillar forms its chrysalis inside a weak cocoon in a crevice in the bark in early June. The moth emerges later that month.

A common footman moth rests on a blad of grass. The fore-wings are held flat ac ross its back, one overlapping the other.

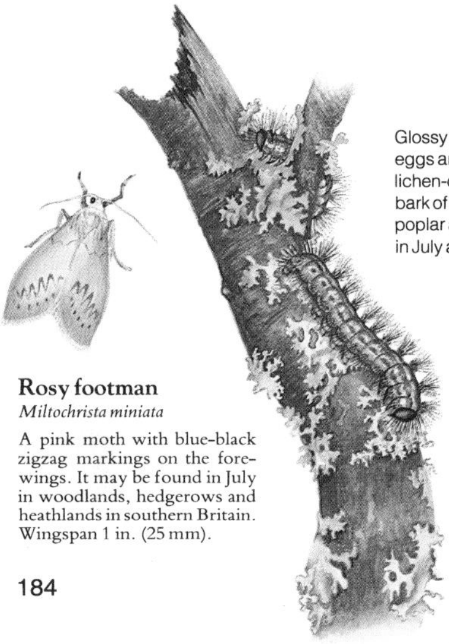

Glossy white eggs are laid on lichen-covered bark of oak, poplar and ash in July and August.

The caterpillars are grey with black-and-yellow hairs and a partial orange stripe along the side. They hibernate from September to the following spring.

Common footman *Eilema lurideola*

The disappearance of a species of footman moth from an are can be an indication of rising atmospheric pollution, as thei caterpillars feed on lichens which only grow in a fairly clear environment. Caterpillars in captivity have been known to ea various leaves, but in the wild lichens appear to be an essentia food. The common footman, as its name suggests, is the mos common of the 17 British species of footman moth. Its caterpillars favour lichens found on the bark of oak, poplar and ash trees. The moth flies in July and August in deciduous woodlanc throughout England and Wales and in a few localities in Scotland and the west of Ireland.

Footman moths fly at night and are therefore usually seer when resting during the day. Most species, including the common footman, rest with their long, thin wings wrapped fla over the abdomen, suggesting the stiff appearance of a footmar in livery – hence their common name.

Another footman moth that breeds in lichen on trees anc shrubs is the rosy footman. The dark, hairy caterpillar lives through winter, eating lichen during mild weather. The moth flies at dusk, so is usually seen at rest during the day.

Rosy footman

Miltochrista miniata

A pink moth with blue-black zigzag markings on the fore-wings. It may be found in July in woodlands, hedgerows and heathlands in southern Britain. Wingspan 1 in. (25 mm).

Veat rows of pale green ɘggs are laid on a wide ʻariety of common ɔlants such as ꞉hickweed, dandelion, ɩock and plantain.

Male

Female

Black specks

The caterpillar is easily disturbed and will drop to the ground and curl up, feigning death.

The male moth is smoky-grey with tufts of fine hair over the thorax. The female is pale creamy-white with a few small black spots. Wingspan $1\frac{5}{8}$ in. (42 mm).

Ꭿuslin footman

Vudaria mundana

ⱥ small moth that is found in ꞇony areas where its caterpil- ɩrs feed on lichen. It occurs in ɔuth-west and central Eng- ɩnd, southern Scotland and orth-west Ireland. The males ɾe attracted to light. Wing- ɔan $\frac{3}{4}$ in. (20 mm).

The caterpillar, which has purple warts and is covered in light brown-and-orange hairs, feeds on its food plant during July and August.

The brown chrysalis is formed in August in leaf litter where it overwinters.

A female muslin moth, with her white wings and furry 'ruff' around the head, rests conspicuously on leaves.

Muslin moth *Diaphora mendica*

The delicate white wings of the female moth give the impression of a fine muslin, lightly sprinkled with tiny black ink-spots. The female muslin moth is very similar to the white ermine, another moth which has wings of a startling whiteness (p. 182). However the female muslin has fewer black spots, and its wings are more transparent. Its abdomen is also white, whereas the ermine's abdomen is yellow. The male moth has dark grey or dark brown wings. The spots, which are almost hidden on the male by the darker colouring, vary from eight to ten on the fore-wings and from five to six on the hind-wings.

The moth is widespread in England and Wales, but is scarce in Scotland, and in Ireland is found in only a few places on the west coast. Suitable habitats include woodlands, hedgerows, parks, waste land and rough pastures. The muslin moth is found from April to July, and very occasionally there is a second generation in the autumn. It flies at night, and males are often attracted to lighted windows or outside lights. The females sometimes fly during the day in sunny weather.

The muslin footman is a much smaller moth with brown markings on its wings. It is found in late June and July.

Day-flying moths

Moths which fly in the daytime often have bright colours, like butterflies – the red and black of the burnet moths, or combinations of orange, white, red and brown of the garden tiger. Some of them are highly poisonous and use their colours as a warning to birds not to attack. Brightly coloured moths are not always fast flyers. Advertising that they have poisonous bodies is usually adequate protection, but if a bird does molest them, many have the additional defence of a poisonous spray or drop of deterrent liquid, emitted from the legs or thorax.

Other day-flying moths are quite dull in colour but are fast flyers. The silver Y and Mother Shipton flutter rapidly about flowery meadows visiting blossoms, and the humming-bird hawk-moth darts between flowers at great speed. The flight of the silver Y is so fast that birds would have great difficulty catching it.

Wayside flowers such as scabious, white campion and valerian are attractive lures to day-flying moths, which visit them for nectar. Brightly coloured moths, such as the cinnabar, the clouded buff and the burnets, can be confused with butterflies, as they often fly in the same habitats.

Clouded buff
Humming-bird hawk-moth
Mother Shipton
Cinnabar and caterpillars

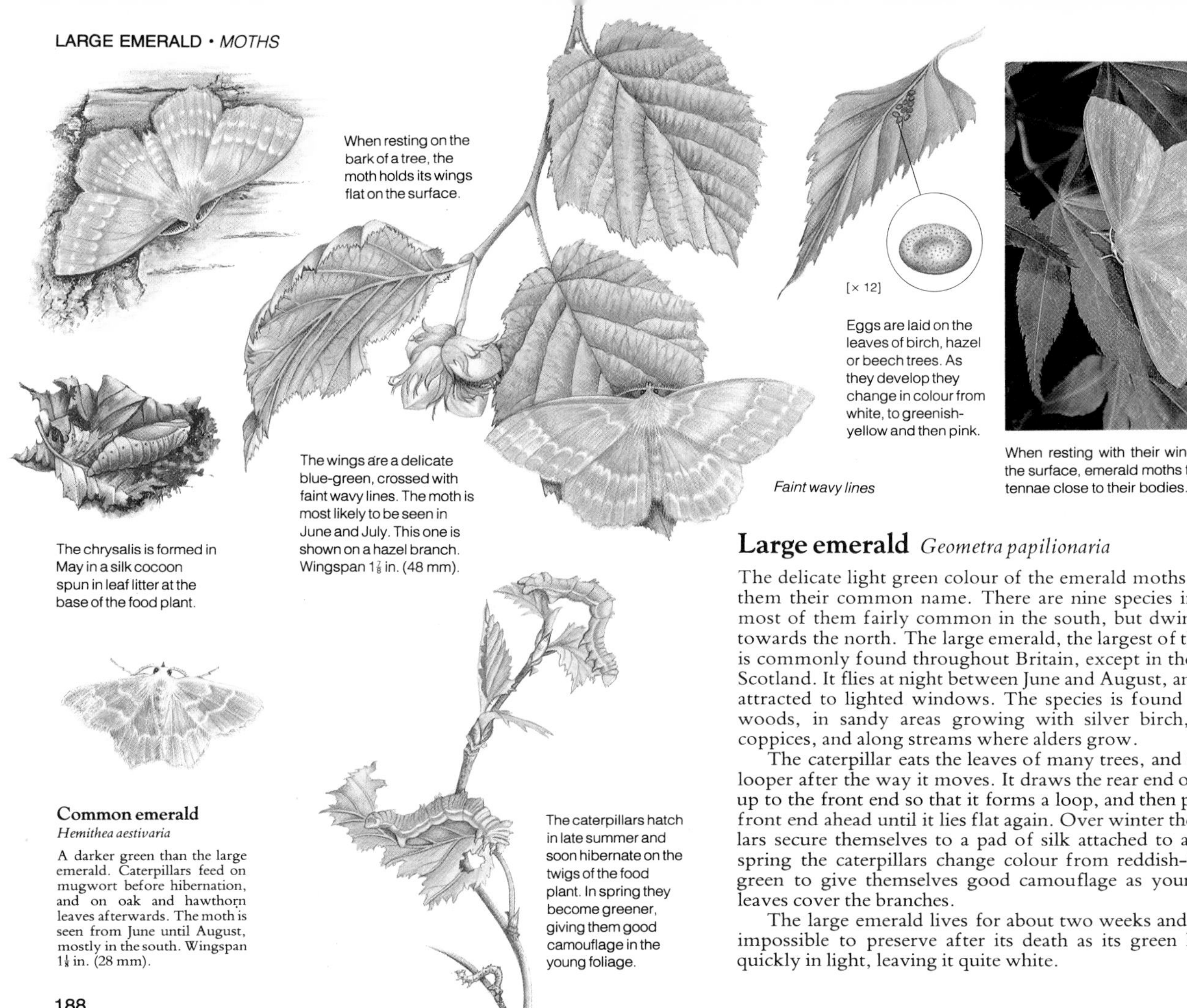

When resting on the bark of a tree, the moth holds its wings flat on the surface.

The chrysalis is formed in May in a silk cocoon spun in leaf litter at the base of the food plant.

The wings are a delicate blue-green, crossed with faint wavy lines. The moth is most likely to be seen in June and July. This one is shown on a hazel branch. Wingspan $1\frac{7}{8}$ in. (48 mm).

Eggs are laid on the leaves of birch, hazel or beech trees. As they develop they change in colour from white, to greenish-yellow and then pink.

When resting with their wings flush with the surface, emerald moths tuck their antennae close to their bodies.

The caterpillars hatch in late summer and soon hibernate on the twigs of the food plant. In spring they become greener, giving them good camouflage in the young foliage.

Common emerald
Hemithea aestivaria

A darker green than the large emerald. Caterpillars feed on mugwort before hibernation, and on oak and hawthorn leaves afterwards. The moth is seen from June until August, mostly in the south. Wingspan $1\frac{1}{8}$ in. (28 mm).

Large emerald *Geometra papilionaria*

The delicate light green colour of the emerald moths has given them their common name. There are nine species in Britain, most of them fairly common in the south, but dwindling off towards the north. The large emerald, the largest of the group, is commonly found throughout Britain, except in the north of Scotland. It flies at night between June and August, and is often attracted to lighted windows. The species is found in beechwoods, in sandy areas growing with silver birch, in hazel coppices, and along streams where alders grow.

The caterpillar eats the leaves of many trees, and is called a looper after the way it moves. It draws the rear end of its body up to the front end so that it forms a loop, and then pushes the front end ahead until it lies flat again. Over winter the caterpillars secure themselves to a pad of silk attached to a twig. In spring the caterpillars change colour from reddish-brown to green to give themselves good camouflage as young, green leaves cover the branches.

The large emerald lives for about two weeks and is almost impossible to preserve after its death as its green hues fade quickly in light, leaving it quite white.

The caterpillars hatch in spring and are dispersed by the wind from one tree to another. By mid-June they fall from the tree to form chrysalises on the ground. The moths emerge in October.

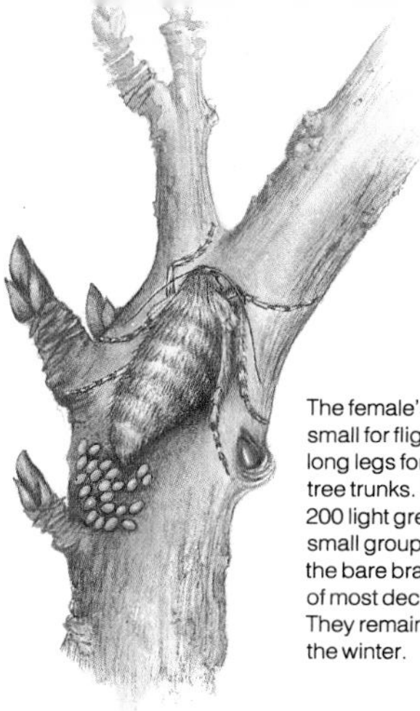

The female's wings are too small for flight, but she has long legs for climbing up tree trunks. She lays up to 200 light green eggs in small groups or singly on the bare branches or buds of most deciduous trees. They remain there through the winter.

A male winter moth approaches a wingless female on a tree. The female cannot fly, but is an energetic climber.

This familiar blemish on apples is caused by a caterpillar damaging the fruitlet soon after the blossom has set. The apple then develops with the scar. There is no caterpillar inside the apple.

This light brown moth is called the winter moth because it is seen between October and January. Only the male has functional wings, with a wingspan of 1 in. (25 mm).

Winter moth *Operophtera brumata*

The winter moth was such a serious pest during the last century that orchards in Kent and the Vale of Evesham were often completely stripped of leaves, giving the appearance of a winter scene in the midst of spring. Before the use of organic chemicals after the Second World War, a greasy band put on the trunk of a fruit tree would catch up to 100 of the wingless females as they climbed up the tree to mate and lay eggs. Nevertheless, other females would still manage to crawl up into the branches. Today attacks by winter moths on apple and pear trees are mostly controlled by chemical sprays.

The winter moth is found in gardens, orchards, hedgerows and scrubby areas throughout Britain between October and January. In oak woods winter moth caterpillars, like the caterpillars of the green oak tortrix moth (p. 207), feed on the leaves in great numbers in spring. They stop eating oak leaves in mid-June when the tannin content acts as a repellent, and move on to other deciduous trees.

The caterpillars of the mottled umber moth and the March moth (pp. 168–9) also eat the leaves and flower buds of fruit trees, and are loosely known as 'winter moth caterpillars'.

The caterpillars hibernate when young and resume feeding in May and June when they may strip soft-fruit bushes of their leaves.

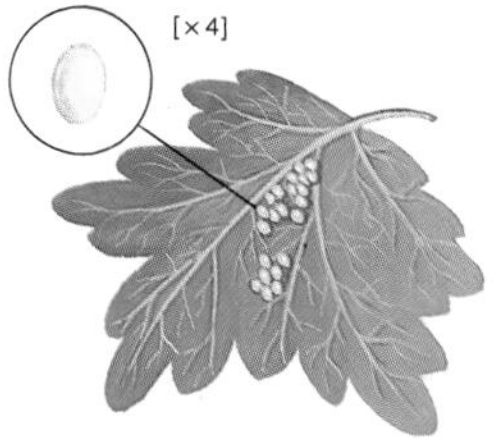

Eggs are laid on the underside of the leaves on currant, gooseberry and hawthorn bushes. They hatch after about ten days.

The moth is brightly coloured in black, white and orange, and may be seen flying during the day in July and August. The intensity of the markings and the background colour vary greatly, and there is a yellow variety called *lutea*. Wingspan $1\frac{3}{4}$ in. (45 mm).

The chrysalis of the magpie moth, with black and yellow bands, may be found on currant leaves in early July.

Clouded magpie
Abraxas sylvata

A woodland species of moth, found mostly in western England and Wales. Its wings carry a blurred version of the magpie moth's colouring. Wingspan $1\frac{1}{2}$ in. (38 mm).

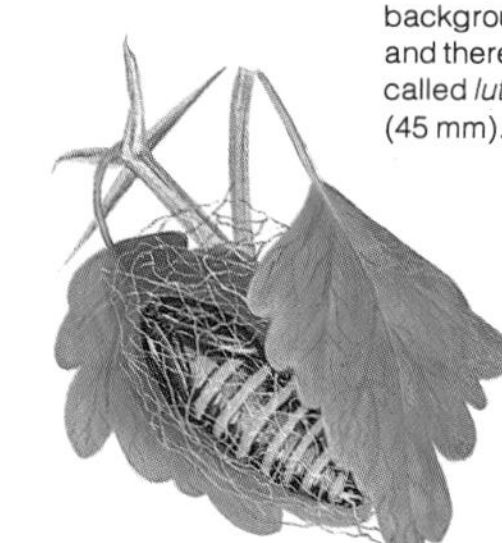

The chrysalis is glossy black with yellow bands, and is easily seen in its flimsy silk web on the food plant.

Magpie moth *Abraxas grossulariata*

This common black-and-white moth takes its name from the bird with similar colouring. It used to be called the currant moth, as the caterpillar can be a serious pest of currant bushes. An old German name of harlequin moth likens its spottedness to the costume of 'Harlequin' in early European comedy.

The magpie moth can be found throughout Britain, flying during the day and looking like a butterfly with its bright colours. Both the moth and the caterpillar have the same distinctive colouring and are often seen in gardens, hedgerows and wasteland. In the countryside the caterpillars live on hazel, hawthorn, sloe and field maple. In gardens they may defoliate currant and gooseberry bushes, and occasionally apricot and cobnut trees. They also attack flowering currants, orpines (*Sedum*), navelworts (*Umbilicus*) and spindles (*Euonymus*). They are typical 'loopers' or 'inch-measurers', as their lack of enough prolegs means that they must loop along when they walk. The moths vary greatly in their colours and patterns. Some have a white background, some yellow and others are almost completely black. The clouded magpie is a similar moth, but is slightly smaller and feeds on elm and beech leaves.

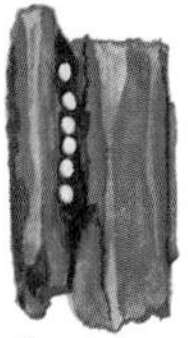

The female lays eggs on the bark of oak, birch and elm. The caterpillars hatch from early May.

Female

The caterpillars are grey and stick-like, and can be difficult to distinguish from twigs. They feed on oak, birch, elm, lime and sloe leaves in May and June.

Master of disguise: an oak beauty moth rests on the lichen-covered trunk of an oak tree, almost invisible to a predator.

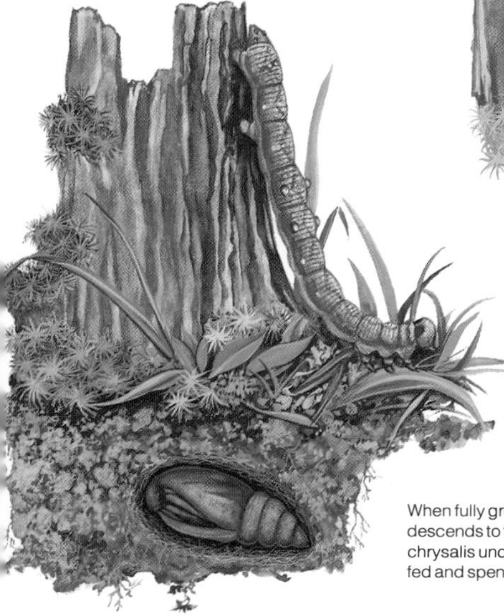

Male

The white speckled wings are covered with black-and-brown bands. The moth usually flies in March and April. Males are smaller than females with feathery antennae. Wingspan of female 2⅛ in. (54 mm).

When fully grown the caterpillar descends to the ground. It forms a chrysalis under the tree in which it fed and spends the winter there.

Oak beauty *Biston strataria*

The attractive colours and patterns on the wings of the oak beauty moth are best seen where it rests during the day on tree trunks, often near the ground, in spring. However it can be difficult to pick out as the speckling over the wings blends well with the irregularities and patterns of lichens and mosses which grow on bark. The dark bands and the speckling on the fore-wings can vary in shape from moth to moth. And a dark form, on which the fore-wings are black, is sometimes seen in industrial areas. The oak beauty is so closely related to the peppered moth (p. 192), that they have been known to mate and produce hybrids.

There is one generation of the oak beauty each year, and winter is spent in the chrysalis stage. The moths hatch between late February and early May, depending on the locality and the warmth of the season. Eggs which the females lay in spring become fully grown caterpillars by the middle of June when they form their chrysalises in readiness for the following winter. Consequently the species can spend up to ten months as a chrysalis. The moth is widely distributed in England, Wales and Scotland, but is found only locally in Ireland.

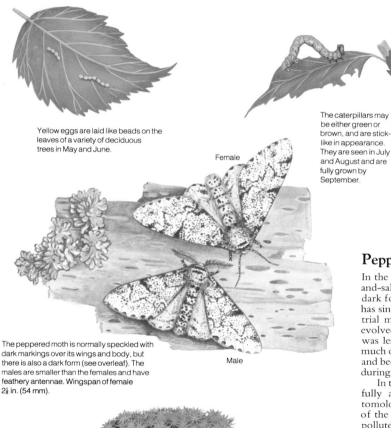

Yellow eggs are laid like beads on the leaves of a variety of deciduous trees in May and June.

The caterpillars may be either green or brown, and are stick-like in appearance. They are seen in July and August and are fully grown by September.

Two peppered moths rest on lichen-covered bark. The upper one is a melanic form, and stands out much more clearly.

Female

Male

The peppered moth is normally speckled with dark markings over its wings and body, but there is also a dark form (see overleaf). The males are smaller than the females and have feathery antennae. Wingspan of female $2\frac{1}{8}$ in. (54 mm).

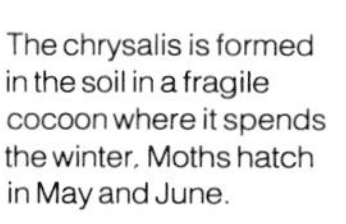

The chrysalis is formed in the soil in a fragile cocoon where it spends the winter. Moths hatch in May and June.

Peppered moth *Biston betularia*

In the 19th century the peppered moth was called the pepper-and-salt moth from the speckled pattern in its wings. In 1848 dark forms of the moth were discovered in Manchester, and it has since become famous as the best known example of industrial melanism (see overleaf). The dark form (*carbonaria*) had evolved in the polluted environment of industrial areas where it was less visible to predators. Now it is common throughout much of Britain. The normal form (*betularia*) is lightly speckled and becomes inconspicuous on bark and lichens on which it rests during the day.

In the 19th century the significance of the dark form was not fully appreciated. In the 1950s, however, the Oxford entomologist Bernard Kettlewell released normal and dark forms of the moth in the unpolluted Dorset countryside and in the polluted area around Birmingham. Comparisons of predation by birds confirmed that light-coloured moths were undetected in the countryside and dark moths survived in the city.

The moth is common throughout Britain in May and June. The caterpillars feed at night on the leaves of many trees, including oak, birch, elm, beech, sallow and plum.

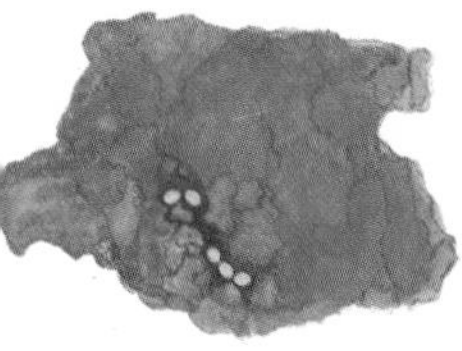

The eggs are laid on the bark of a wide variety of deciduous trees, including apples, pears, limes and willows.

Male

Female

The moths, which fly in April and May, have mottled brown wings with a hairy head and thorax. The male has feathery antennae and a smaller abdomen; the female has more transparent wings. Wingspan $1\frac{1}{2}$ in. (38 mm).

Pale brindled beauty
Apocheima pilosaria

A similar but lighter-coloured moth which is usually out during January, February and March in most parts of Britain. The female is wingless and lives in crevices in tree trunks; the male is attracted to light. Wingspan $1\frac{3}{4}$ in. (45 mm).

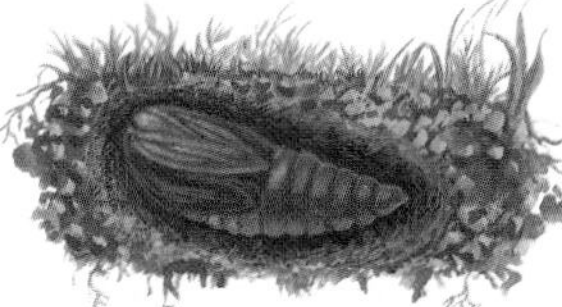

The fully grown caterpillar climbs down the tree in July and makes a chrysalis in a fragile earthen cocoon in the soil, where it spends the winter.

The young caterpillars are black with yellow bands. As they develop they become grey or reddish-brown. They feed by night during May, June and July.

A brindled beauty moth, resting on a tree trunk, is well camouflaged from predators against the lichen.

Brindled beauty *Lycia hirtaria*

During the last century the brindled beauty used to be a common sight in the streets of London and other cities in April and May. Suburban streets planted with forest trees such as oak, ash and elm supported large numbers of the caterpillars which used to defoliate branches in summer. Many of these forest trees eventually grew too big for the streets and were cut down, and many elms were destroyed by Dutch elm disease. However silver birch trees growing in parks, gardens and waste land still support plenty of the attractive brindled beauty moths in London. They may also be found on apple and pear trees. The males have large feathery antennae, and are smaller and darker than the females. The name of the moth refers to the attractive banded appearance of the wings.

The caterpillars look like twigs, holding themselves straight and rigid while resting. Their grey or reddish colouring camouflages them well on the leaves and stems of the trees, where they feed at night. The brindled beauty occurs throughout Britain as far north as Inverness. Its ground colour varies, producing light forms, yellow speckled forms and black forms.

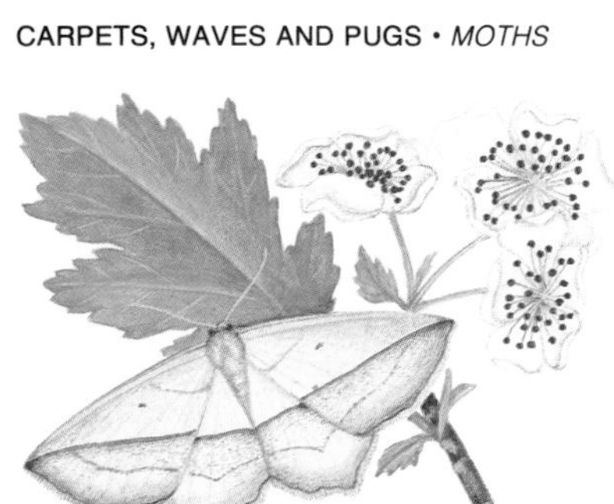

Blood vein

Timandra griseata

This pale grey-yellow moth, with its distinctive orange 'blood-vein' marking, is most common along waysides and woodland edges in southern England in June. The grey-brown caterpillar feeds on a variety of wayside plants. Wingspan $1\frac{1}{4}$ in. (32 mm).

Common pug

Eupithecia vulgata

This common moth can vary in colour from a pale grey-brown to almost black. It is found in a variety of habitats throughout Britain. Two generations fly each year, in May and June and in August. Pale red-brown caterpillars feed on hawthorn, sallow, bramble and other shrubs. Wingspan $\frac{3}{4}$ in. (20 mm).

Garden carpet

Xanthorhoe fluctuata

The wing pattern of this common moth varies greatly. It is found in gardens and waysides throughout Britain between April and September. The green caterpillars feed mainly on cabbage, wallflowers and currant bushes. Wingspan $\frac{7}{8}$ in. (22 mm).

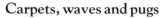

Yellow shell

Camptogramma bilineata

The colouring and the extent of black markings on the wings vary greatly. Four sub-species are known. It flies in June and July and is common in gardens and hedgerows throughout Britain. Wingspan $1\frac{1}{8}$ in. (28 mm).

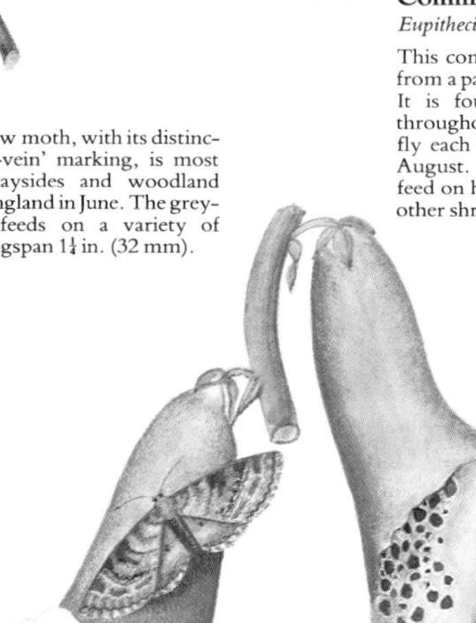

Foxglove pug

Eupithecia pulchellata

Attractively mottled in brown and orange, this moth is named after its food plant, the foxglove. In May and June, it can be seen in all parts of Britain where foxgloves grow. The green caterpillars feed from June to August on the stamens and unripe seeds inside the foxglove flowers. Wingspan $\frac{7}{8}$ in. (22 mm).

Carpets, waves and pugs

Three groups of small moths – loosely called carpets, waves and pugs – make up a large percentage of the 342 species of geometrid moths in Britain. A selection of medium-sized geometrids is shown on the preceding six pages (188–93). The carpets and pugs represent about a third of Britain's geometrids, and there are more than 25 species of waves. They all range in wingspan between $\frac{3}{4}$ in. and $1\frac{1}{2}$ in. (20–38 mm), and have relatively large wings to their small bodies – like the larger emeralds (p. 188) and magpie moths (p. 190).

Many carpets, waves and pugs can be recognised by the fine tracery of lines and patterns over their wings. In fact, some of the waves have names which describe fabrics, such as riband, satin and silky waves. Some rest with their wings flat on leaves showing off their patterns; others have their wings clapped together above their bodies like butterflies. Many are found in gardens, woodlands and along hedgerows. Most fly at night and are often attracted to lighted windows.

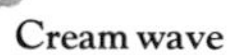

Cream wave

Scopula floslactata

This whitish moth, with faint wavy lines crossing its wings, is seen in woods in various parts of Britain from May to June. It is most common in southern England and rare in Scotland. From July to September, the grey-brown caterpillars feed on plants such as dock, bedstraw and woodruff. Wingspan ⅞ in. (22 mm).

Riband wave

Idaea aversata

A variable moth with a distinctive brown band across each wing. Common throughout Britain, it may be seen resting on palings, leaves or tree trunks from June to August. Caterpillars feed on a variety of wayside plants and hedgerow shrubs. Wingspan 1⅛ in. (28 mm).

Lime-speck pug

Eupithecia centaureata

The distinctive feature of this moth is the dark patch on the front of each forewing. It is found from May to September in gardens and wasteland throughout Britain, except in the far north. Caterpillars eat ragwort. Wingspan ⅞ in. (22 mm).

Scorched wing

Plagodis dolabraria

The scorch-like markings on the wings help to camouflage this moth. It flies in May and June in woodland rides and clearings in England, Wales and Ireland, but is local in Scotland. The brown caterpillar feeds on birch, oak, sallow and beech leaves. Wingspan 1⅜ in. (35 mm).

Grey pine carpet

Thera obeliscata

This grey-brown moth is found in May and June in coniferous woodland throughout Britain. The female is larger than the male. The bright green caterpillars feed mainly on the needles of Scots pine (*Pinus sylvestris*), but will eat fir and spruce needles. Wingspan up to 1¼ in. (32 mm).

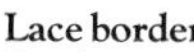

Lace border

Scopula ornata

A delicate white moth which gets its common name from the lace-like edge to its wings. It flies in two generations in May and June and again in August and September, in the chalky areas of southern England, where thyme and marjoram grow. Wingspan 1 in. (25 mm).

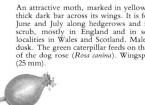

Barred yellow

Cidaria fulvata

An attractive moth, marked in yellow with a thick dark bar across its wings. It is found in June and July along hedgerows and in open scrub, mostly in England and in scattered localities in Wales and Scotland. Males fly at dusk. The green caterpillar feeds on the leaves of the dog rose (*Rosa canina*). Wingspan 1 in. (25 mm).

A large dark moth with dense grey scales over its head and thorax. The females are larger than the males, with fat abdomens. The moth may be seen resting on tree trunks or posts in June and July throughout Britain. Wingspan of female up to 3½ in. (90 mm).

Groups of 15–50 eggs are laid in crevices in the bark of several different trees. They hatch after ten days. Each female may lay up to 300 eggs.

The chrysalis is formed in a cell in earth and leaf litter in May. The moth hatches after four weeks.

The goat moth caterpillar is one of the largest wood-boring insects in Britain. It can be up to ½ in. (13 mm) wide.

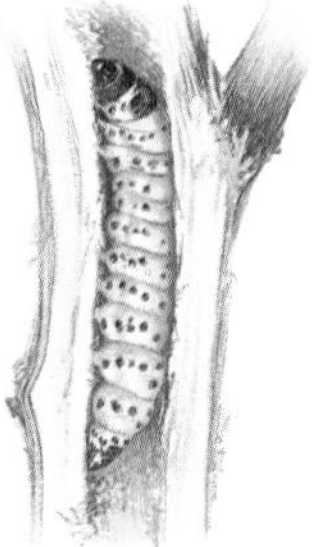

The caterpillar feeds in rotten wood for up to four years.

When fully grown the caterpillar may be 4 in. (10 cm) long. It then leaves the tree and may be seen wandering over the ground searching for a place to spin a cocoon.

Goat moth *Cossus cossus*

The caterpillar is more often seen than the moth, and its disagreeable smell has led to its association with goats. The caterpillars are also known as carpenterworms, and are related to the edible witchety-grubs of Australia. They burrow into the wood of ash, elm, lime, oak and poplar trees, and also into apple and pear trees. There may be 20 or 30 caterpillars living inside a woodland tree compared to two or three inside a fruit tree. Woodpeckers seek out and eat the caterpillars. Badly infected trees become disfigured and diseased with fungi, and fail to put on new growth each year. They eventually die.

The moths are rarely seen and are believed – probably falsely – to be eaten by 'goat suckers', an old English name for nightjars. The female has a distinctive horny egg-laying 'tail' for placing her eggs deep into bark crevices. As the major feeding stage is during the long life of the caterpillar, the moths live only for reproduction and dispersal. They have no tongues for feeding and live for about a month solely on the energy reserves that are passed on from the caterpillar.

Britain has two other goat moths, the leopard and the reed leopard, whose caterpillars also live inside plants.

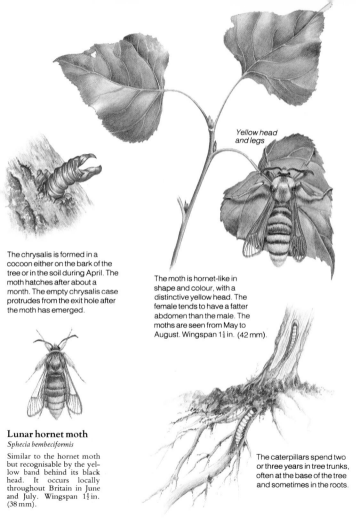

The chrysalis is formed in a cocoon either on the bark of the tree or in the soil during April. The moth hatches after about a month. The empty chrysalis case protrudes from the exit hole after the moth has emerged.

The moth is hornet-like in shape and colour, with a distinctive yellow head. The female tends to have a fatter abdomen than the male. The moths are seen from May to August. Wingspan 1⅝ in. (42 mm).

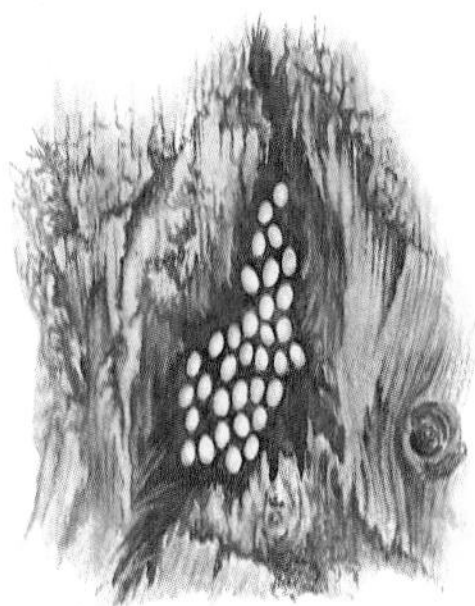

The eggs are laid in crevices on the bark of poplar, willows and occasionally aspen. [× 4]

The hornet moth may be seen during the day, perhaps resting on a tree, as its appearance makes it safe from birds.

Lunar hornet moth
Sphecia bembeciformis

Similar to the hornet moth but recognisable by the yellow band behind its black head. It occurs locally throughout Britain in June and July. Wingspan 1½ in. (38 mm).

The caterpillars spend two or three years in tree trunks, often at the base of the tree and sometimes in the roots.

Hornet moth *Sesia apiformis*

This alarming, brightly coloured moth looks remarkably like a hornet in both size and colour. It mimics the yellow-and-black warning colours and thick bodies of wasps and hornets, and also their transparent wings. It flies during the day and is easily seen by birds, but because of their unpleasant experiences with wasps they avoid it. Despite its fearsome appearance it is quite harmless, and has no sting. It is distinguished from the true hornet by the absence of maroon on the abdomen (see p. 243).

The caterpillar is a creamy-white colour as it spends most of its life inside wood and does not need protective colouring. It bores its way under the bark of poplars, willows and aspens, occasionally burrowing into deeper wood. Its pencil-thick tunnels can easily be distinguished from the tunnels of the goat moth which are the thickness of a finger. Several native British trees are susceptible to attack from the caterpillars, especially along edges of woodlands, in hedgerows and on scrub land. The hornet moth is locally distributed in England, particularly in the east, and also occurs in parts of Scotland and Ireland.

The lunar hornet moth is another species that resembles a hornet. Its black head distinguishes it from the hornet moth.

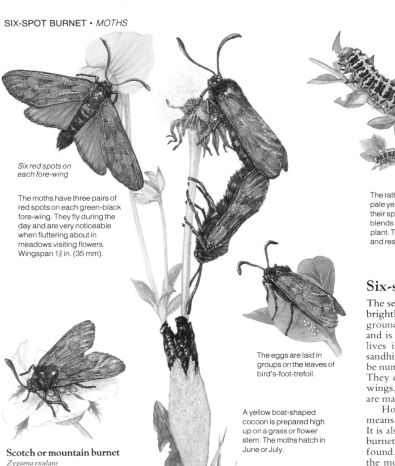

Six red spots on each fore-wing

The moths have three pairs of red spots on each green-black fore-wing. They fly during the day and are very noticeable when fluttering about in meadows visiting flowers. Wingspan 1⅜ in. (35 mm).

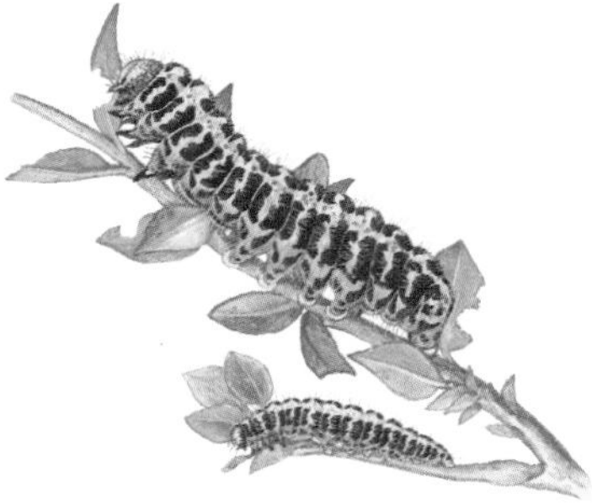

The rather dumpy caterpillars are pale yellow with black marks, and their speckled appearance blends them in with their food plant. They hibernate on the plant and resume feeding in spring.

Most burnets look alike from a distance. This species is identified by the number and arrangement of spots.

The eggs are laid in groups on the leaves of bird's-foot-trefoil.

A yellow boat-shaped cocoon is prepared high up on a grass or flower stem. The moths hatch in June or July.

Scotch or mountain burnet

Zygaena exulans

Can be recognised by the semi-transparent wings with five spots. The moth occurs only in the Aberdeen area of Scotland where it was discovered in 1871. It flies in July. Wingspan 1⅛ in. (28 mm).

Six-spot burnet *Zygaena filipendulae*

The seven species of burnet moth all fly during the day and are brightly coloured, with red spots on a greenish-black background. The six-spot burnet is Britain's most common burnet and is widespread throughout the country in June and July. It lives in downland meadows, open woodland glades and on sandhills along the coast. All the burnets live in colonies and may be numerous in places where clovers, trefoils and vetches grow. They can be distinguished from butterflies by their long, thin wings, metallic colours and slow flight. Their breeding places are marked by the yellowy cocoons attached to old plant stems.

How the moth got its name is uncertain. Burnet usually means dark brown, from the French words *burnette* and *brunette*. It is also used in the names of wild flowers, including the salad burnet which grows on chalky soils where burnet moths are found. However the name may come from the association of the moth's red spots with burning. The number and arrangement of the spots helps to identify each species, but the spots vary in size and some may be fused.

The Scotch or mountain burnet is found only in north-east Scotland where its caterpillars eat the leaves of crowberry.

Five red spots on each fore-wing distinguish this moth from the six-spot burnet. It flies over chalk grassland in early summer. Females attract males with scent as they leave the cocoon and often mate straight away. Wingspan 1⅜ in. (35 mm).

Five red spots on each fore-wing

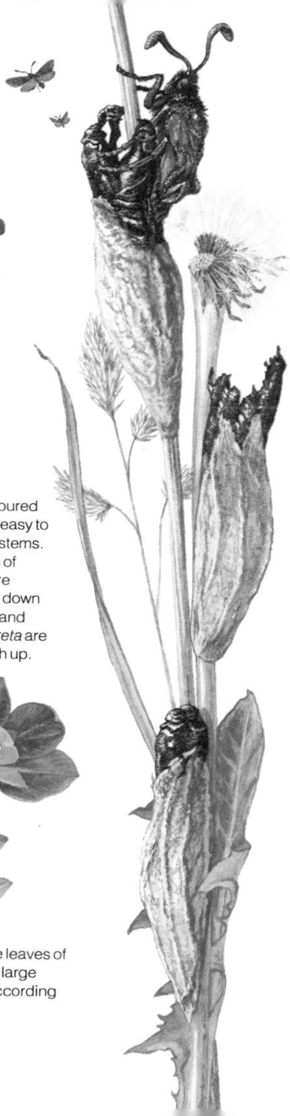

The light-coloured cocoons are easy to see on plant stems. The cocoons of *palustrella* are attached low down on the plant, and those of *decreta* are attached high up.

Caterpillars feed on trefoils and vetches. They hibernate in the autumn and resume feeding in the spring.

The five spots on the fore-wings sometimes join up, creating different patterns. These moths are known as aberrations.

Narrow-bordered five-spot burnet
Zygaena lonicerae

Similar in appearance to the five-spot burnet but with longer fore-wings and more pointed hind-wings. Wingspan 1⅜ in. (35 mm).

Eggs are laid on the leaves of bird's-foot-trefoil or large bird's-foot-trefoil according to the sub-species.

Five-spot burnet *Zygaena trifolii*

All the burnet moths are extremely poisonous. Their bodies contain cyanide derivatives which are formed by the caterpillar from its food plants, stored up and passed on to the moth. These deadly poisons act as a deterrent to birds which learn to reject the moths as sources of food.

The five-spot burnet is found mostly in southern England where it can be exceedingly common, even on motorway embankments. It also occurs in parts of Wales and on the Isle of Man, and may fly in the same places as the six-spot burnet. There are two sub-species of the moth, differing in size, behaviour, flight time and choice of food plant, but similar in appearance. In the west of England, Wales and the Isle of Man the larger sub-species, *decreta*, is found in marshy areas in late July and early August. Its cocoon is formed high up on plant stems and its caterpillar feeds on greater bird's-foot-trefoil. In the rest of England the smaller sub-species, *palustrella*, flies on downland in May and June. Its cocoon is formed low down on plants and its caterpillars feed on bird's-foot-trefoil.

The narrow-bordered five-spot burnet occurs throughout England in June and July in woods and plantations.

Swift moths hold their wings close together around their abdomens. The female common swift is much paler than the male and considerably larger, with similar white markings. Wingspan of female 1½ in. (38 mm).

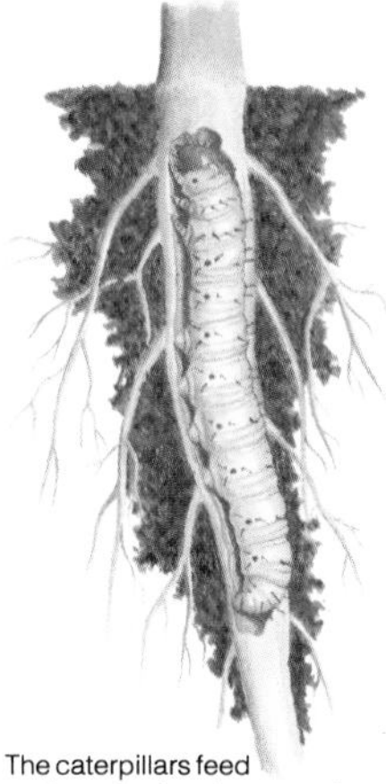

The caterpillars feed underground on the roots of a variety of plants. They feed through the winter if the weather is mild, and become increasingly active in February and March.

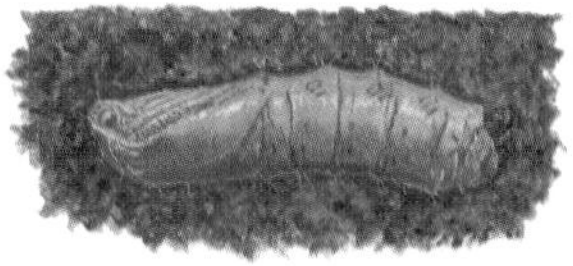

The chrysalis, formed underground, has a long abdomen and is covered in fine hairs. The moths hatch between mid-May and mid-July.

Male common swifts are often seen together flying low over meadows at dusk.

A variety of common swift with dark instead of white wing markings rests on bracken, where it hides during the day.

Common, or garden, swift *Hepialus lupulinus*

Their long wings and rapid flight have given the swift family of moths the same name as the species of bird renowned for its aerial powers. The moths also have a characteristic flap which holds the fore and hind-wings together in flight, providing a more efficient wing membrane. Male common swifts may be seen on an early summer evening flying over pastures in search of females. The common swift, also known as the garden swift, is smaller and more abundant than the ghost swift (opposite), and is found throughout Britain. It is on the wing from mid-May to mid-July.

Female swift moths lay their eggs while in flight, like the oak eggar moth and the marbled white and ringlet butterflies. The caterpillars are a serious pest, and bore into roots and stems of crops such as barley and wheat, and market-garden crops such as strawberries and lettuces. Hop roots are also attacked, as well as garden bulbs such as dahlias, gladioli, irises and lilies. In the wild the caterpillars feed on grasses, docks and dandelions. They hibernate through winter in the roots and finish feeding in the spring. In warm winters they can cause serious damage by continuing to feed rather than going into hibernation.

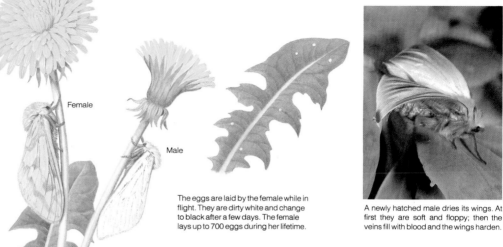

The long thin wings of the male are pale grey. The females are yellow with reddish markings. The moths are on the wing from June to August and males are often seen flying at dusk. Wingspan 2 in. (50 mm).

Female

Male

The eggs are laid by the female while in flight. They are dirty white and change to black after a few days. The female lays up to 700 eggs during her lifetime.

A newly hatched male dries its wings. At first they are soft and floppy; then the veins fill with blood and the wings harden.

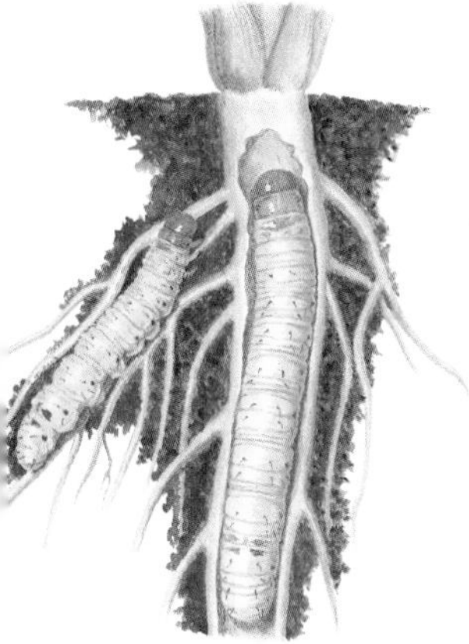

Ghost swift *Hepialus humuli*

The ghostly appearance of the males as they hover over damp meadows and churchyards at dusk has given this species of swift moth its name. The males fly erratically to and fro like pendulums in the half-light, probably seeking mates. Occasionally they disappear, only to reappear shortly afterwards. The white males are quite different in appearance from the females which are buff-yellow or brick red. In the courtship of moths it is usually the males which are attracted to the pheromones of the females, but with the ghost swift the females are attracted to the hovering males. The moths are out from June to the end of August, and are widely distributed.

The caterpillars of the ghost swift take two and occasionally three years to develop in the roots of plants. They feed on a very wide variety of grasses and crops, and as many as 50,000 caterpillars can occur in an acre of land. Bare patches in farm or market garden crops often indicate an infestation of ghost swift caterpillars – all possibly derived from a single female. The life-cycle of the ghost swift is much longer than that of the common swift. It may take three years to complete, compared to one year for the common swift.

In their first year the caterpillars feed on many sorts of grasses and leaves. In the summer of their second year the caterpillars tunnel into the roots of plants. When fully grown they may reach a length of $2\frac{1}{2}$ in. (64 mm).

When fully grown – either in the second or third year – the caterpillar changes into a brown and slightly hairy chrysalis in the soil in May.

A ring of eggs is laid around a stem of heather, purple loosestrife or brambles. Newly hatched caterpillars, in May and June, are black and hairy and may be seen eating in groups.

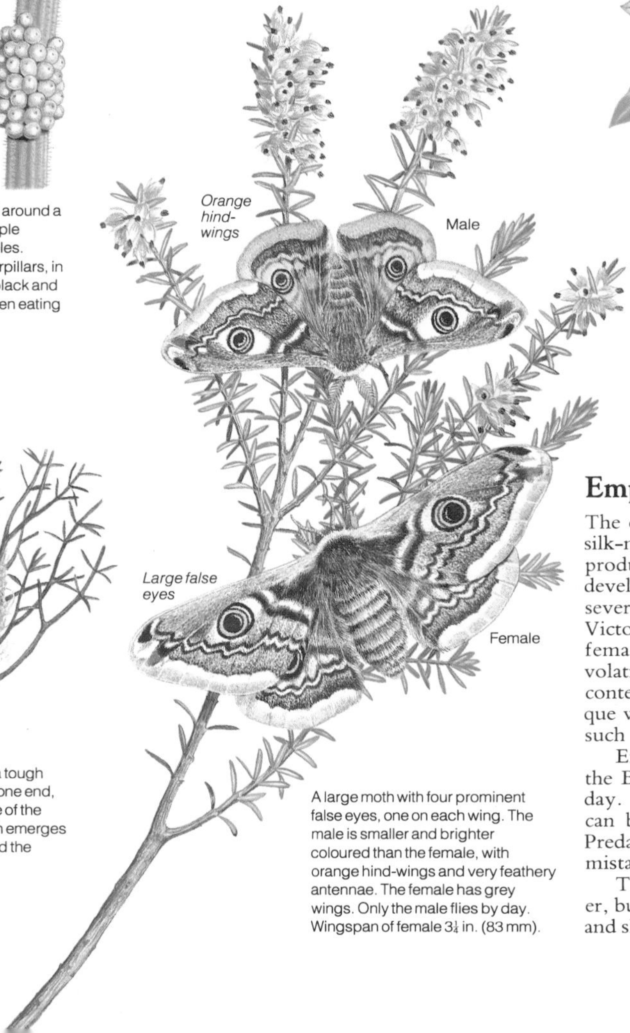

Orange hind-wings

Male

Large false eyes

Female

As they become older the colour of the caterpillar changes to green with yellow or orange warts sprouting black bristles.

A newly hatched male emperor moth dries its wings on a heather twig, showing off its colourful underside.

In July and August a tough cocoon, tapered at one end, is spun in the foliage of the food plant. The moth emerges from the tapered end the following May.

A large moth with four prominent false eyes, one on each wing. The male is smaller and brighter coloured than the female, with orange hind-wings and very feathery antennae. The female has grey wings. Only the male flies by day. Wingspan of female 3¼ in. (83 mm).

Emperor moth *Saturnia pavonia*

The emperor moth is the only native British member of the silk-moth family, however its cocoons are not suitable for silk production. The male, with its feathery antennae, has a highly developed sense of smell, and can detect females at a distance of several hundred yards. This fact was heavily exploited by Victorian lepidopterists who would lure male moths to captive females. Newly hatched females produce large amounts of volatile pheromones (insect hormones), and more than 100 contesting males might arrive at the 'calling' female. The technique was carried out on upland moors and southern heathlands such as Ashdown Forest and the New Forest.

Emperor moths can be found in April and May throughout the British Isles. The males fly fast over the heath during the day. The females are only active at night, but sometimes they can be seen sunning themselves on heather in the daytime. Predatory birds may be startled by the moth's large false eyes, mistaking them for the eyes of a mammal, such as a stoat.

The caterpillars of the emperor moth feed mostly on heather, but they will also eat the leaves of bramble, elder, loosestrife and sloe. Older caterpillars are superbly camouflaged.

The mature caterpillars are green with cream stripes along the sides and white spots. They feed on the leaves of silver-birch trees and may take four years to develop.

Female

A large brown moth with a hairy body. The female is larger than the male, with paler fore-wings. She flies at night. Wingspan up to $3\frac{1}{8}$ in. (80 mm).

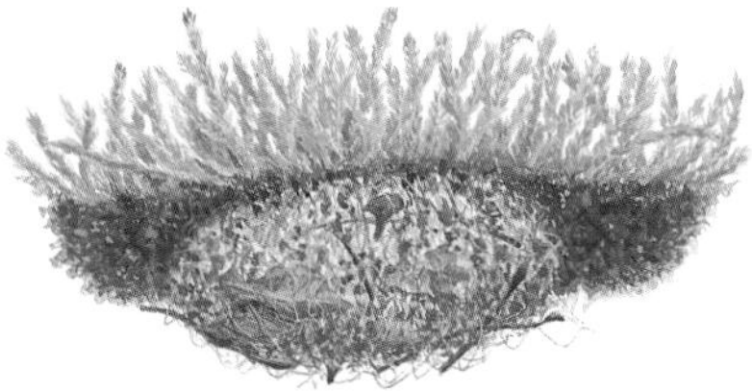

The chrysalis is formed in a cocoon under moss at the base of the tree in June. It may remain there for three years before hatching in late March or April.

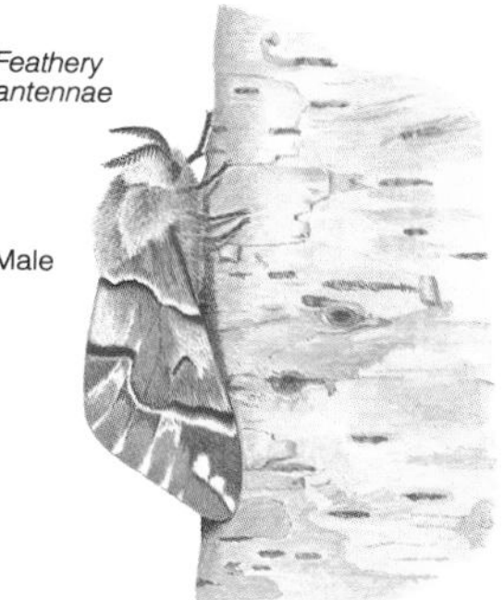

The male, with its darker fore-wings, flies during the day. It can be recognised by its feathery antennae.

A female Kentish glory clasps a birch twig while laying her eggs. The eggs stick to the bark until the caterpillars hatch.

Kentish glory *Endromis versicolora*

Earlier this century, the Kentish glory was found in considerable numbers in the southern counties of England, particularly in Kent. However, its numbers have rapidly declined, and it is now probably extinct in England. It survives in Britain only in Scotland – in Speyside, Deeside and along the Dee Valley. The weak power of the female to fly away from the area where she was born may be a major factor in its decline, but changes in climate and loss of suitable breeding areas are also to blame. The moth needs a young silver-birch heath, with many small trees and scrub bushes for its caterpillars to feed on. It probably did very well after the two world wars when trees were felled and scrub developed. Since then, however, many of these rough areas on sandy soils and heathlands have been ploughed up.

The Kentish glory is on the wing from March to May. The male can be seen during the day, flying rapidly around birch scrub. He has an excellent sense of smell and can detect a female several hundred yards away with his feathery antennae. Like the emperor moth, the Kentish glory suffered from the activities of Victorian collectors who used to attract dozens of male moths to a caged female and then kill them for their collections.

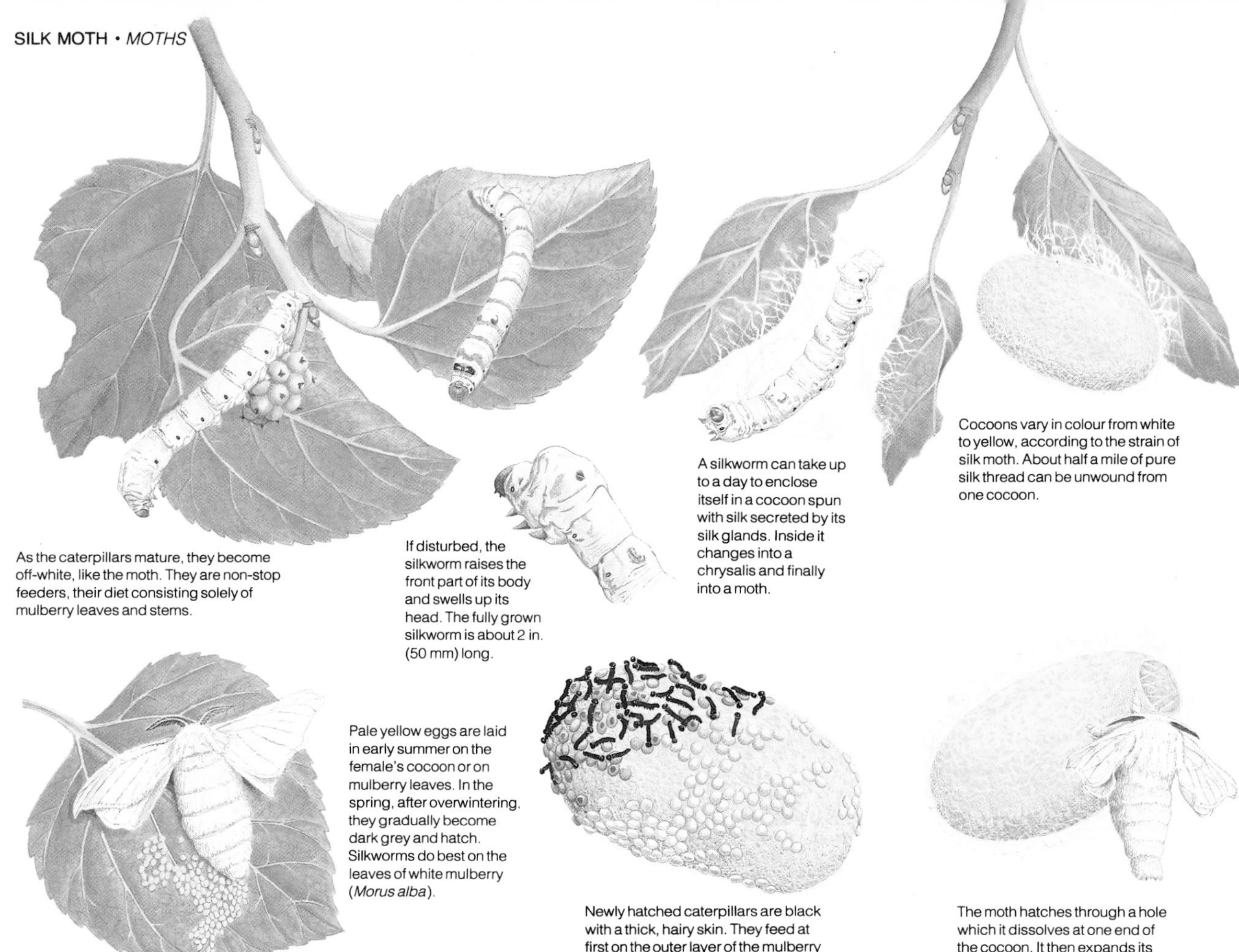

As the caterpillars mature, they become off-white, like the moth. They are non-stop feeders, their diet consisting solely of mulberry leaves and stems.

If disturbed, the silkworm raises the front part of its body and swells up its head. The fully grown silkworm is about 2 in. (50 mm) long.

A silkworm can take up to a day to enclose itself in a cocoon spun with silk secreted by its silk glands. Inside it changes into a chrysalis and finally into a moth.

Cocoons vary in colour from white to yellow, according to the strain of silk moth. About half a mile of pure silk thread can be unwound from one cocoon.

Pale yellow eggs are laid in early summer on the female's cocoon or on mulberry leaves. In the spring, after overwintering, they gradually become dark grey and hatch. Silkworms do best on the leaves of white mulberry (*Morus alba*).

Newly hatched caterpillars are black with a thick, hairy skin. They feed at first on the outer layer of the mulberry leaves.

The moth hatches through a hole which it dissolves at one end of the cocoon. It then expands its wings to dry them.

The short, whitish wings are about the same length as the body. Centuries of domestication have resulted in the loss of the ability to fly and the almost identical appearance of the male and the female. Females have swollen abdomens containing several hundred eggs. This species does not exist in the wild. Wingspan 1⅝ in. (42 mm).

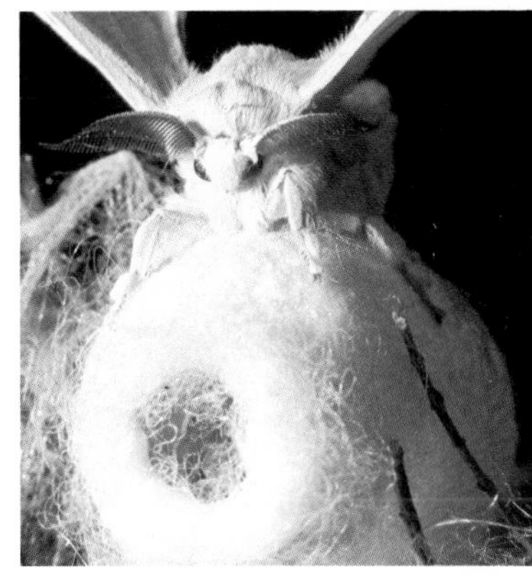

A newly hatched silk moth sits on its cocoon, drying its outstretched wings. The exit hole, through which it emerged, can be clearly seen.

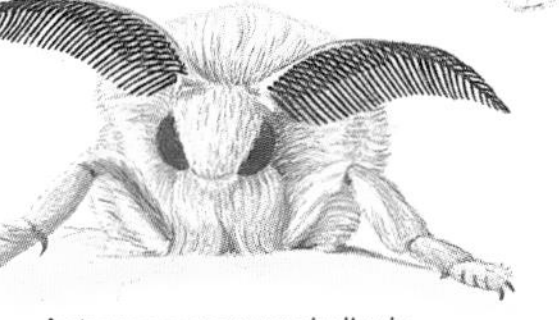

Antennae are very similar in both sexes. They are comb-like or pectinated, giving a greater surface area for receiving chemical signals.

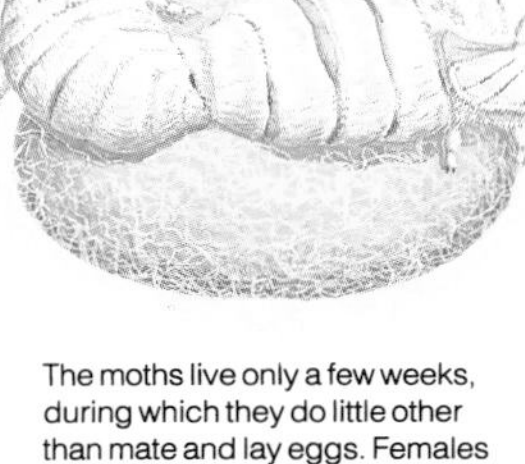

The moths live only a few weeks, during which they do little other than mate and lay eggs. Females attract nearby males by emitting a volatile scent from their abdomens.

Silk moth *Bombyx mori*

Silk is a natural product produced by spiders and caterpillars, particularly of the silk moth family. However the main silk used by man is produced by true silkworms, the caterpillars of *Bombyx mori*. This species is no longer found in the wild. Its domestication started in China about 5,000 years ago, when both caterpillars and moths began to be kept in enclosed boxes and bred solely for their silk. Centuries of living in captivity have resulted in a moth that cannot fly and a caterpillar that walks only short distances on its food plant.

The silk moth was introduced into Britain in the reign of James I (1603–1625), who hoped that silk production would boost the economy. Silkworms will eat only mulberry leaves, preferably those of the white mulberry. Yet most mulberry trees in Britain are of the black species. This is because James I was given the wrong advice when planting trees for the newly arrived silkworms. Many of these trees still survive.

Most silkworms in Britain today are reared in school laboratories, but there is still a small commercial interest. Lullingstone Silk Farm in Dorset thrives. In 1981 it produced the silk for the Princess of Wales's wedding dress.

Flat, translucent eggs are laid singly on the developing fruit or the leaves of apple trees, and hatch after 10–14 days.

Brown-gold patch

The moths are identified by the brownish-gold patch on the tips of the fore-wings. They normally rest on tree trunks or on vegetation during the day and fly at night. Wingspan ½ in. (13 mm).

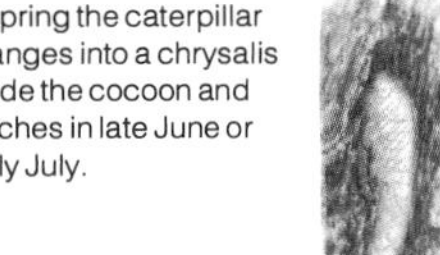

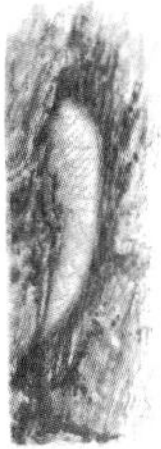

In spring the caterpillar changes into a chrysalis inside the cocoon and hatches in late June or early July.

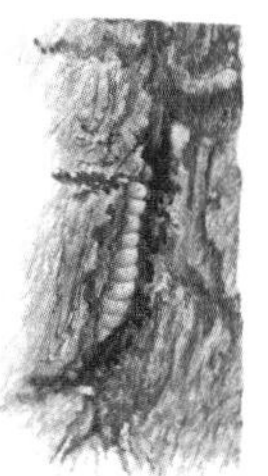

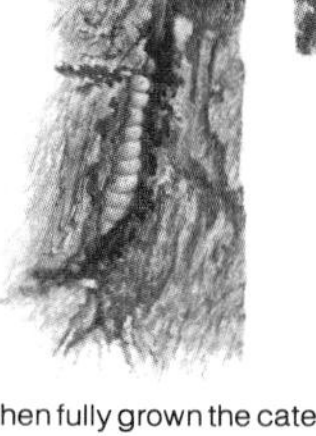

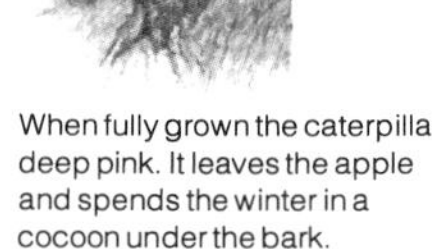

When fully grown the caterpillar is deep pink. It leaves the apple and spends the winter in a cocoon under the bark.

With its wings tightly folded, a codling moth rests on the twig of a tree, its brownish-gold wingtips clearly visible.

Codling moth *Cydia pomonella*

The codling or codlin was one of the old varieties of apple in Britain, and in ancient Saxon a cod-apple was a quince. The codling moth is a major pest of both apples and quinces and was probably known to the Roman statesman Marcus Cato in 200 BC when he wrote about 'wormy apples'. A maggot discovered in an apple – or a pear, quince or walnut – is probably that of the codling moth, although it could be the caterpillar of an apple sawfly (p. 241).

Just after blossom time the female codling moth flies among fruit trees at dusk laying her eggs, which look like shiny dew drops. When the caterpillars hatch they bore into the tiny apples where they grow as the apple swells. The tell-tale entry hole, stuffed with droppings, is the only clue that a caterpillar is inside the fruit, eating the flesh. When the caterpillars are fully grown they leave the apple and crawl onto the tree bark where they form a chrysalis in spring. They may be found and eaten by searching blue tits, great tits and treecreepers, but if they survive they hatch into moths in late June and early July. Codling moths are found throughout the south of England, particularly in Kent where apples are widely grown.

The caterpillars feed on the core of the developing apple. This is the stage of the codling moth which is most often discovered.

[Actual size]

Pea moth

Cydia nigricana

This relative of the codling moth is found mostly in the south-east and the Lincolnshire 'pea belt', where the caterpillars can be a serious pest of peas. Most common at the end of July. Wingspan ¾ in. (20 mm).

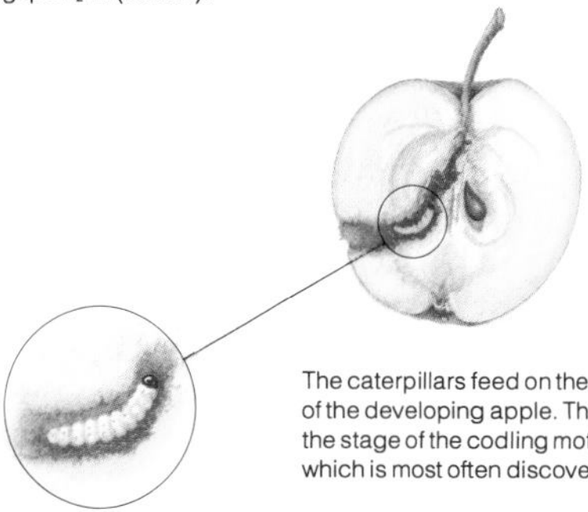

As the caterpillars develop they feed on oak leaves which they curl up with silk. If disturbed by wind or predators they hang from the tree on a silk thread. When fully grown they are ½ in. (13 mm) long and have four tiny spots on each segment.

The eggs are laid in small groups on the twigs of oak trees, where they spend the winter. In spring, the young caterpillars eat inside the buds.

A green oak tortrix moth rests during the day on the underside of an oak leaf. The moths take to the air when disturbed.

White fringe

The silvery-green fore-wings are held flat over the body when the moth is at rest. There is a distinctive white fringe just visible at the end of the fore-wings.

The moths can be seen as late as August. These arise from late-hatching caterpillars that find the older oak leaves less palatable and so take longer to develop.

Green oak tortrix moth *Tortrix viridana*

The old name oak leaf roller describes the shelter made by the caterpillars of the oak tortrix moth. They roll or fold together the sides of an oak leaf, using their own silk. Inside they feed on the leaf out of view of predators such as tits. If disturbed – by foraging wood ants, for example – they escape by dangling in mid-air on a silk thread. When danger has passed they climb back up the thread, gathering it in as they go.

Thousands of oak tortrix caterpillars live in the canopy of oak woods, together with other species of defoliating caterpillars. Winter moths and mottled umber caterpillars may be there too, sometimes completely eating away the first flush of oak leaves at the end of May. The incessant patter of the caterpillar droppings falling on the woodland floor sounds like rain falling through the trees. The oaks recover and produce a second set of leaves later, but they may look very bare in June. Other trees that are attacked include beech, sycamore, poplar and sallow.

There is one generation of the moths each year and they are very common throughout southern England from June to August. They rest by day and are often disturbed from low vegetation or branches by walkers in oak woodlands.

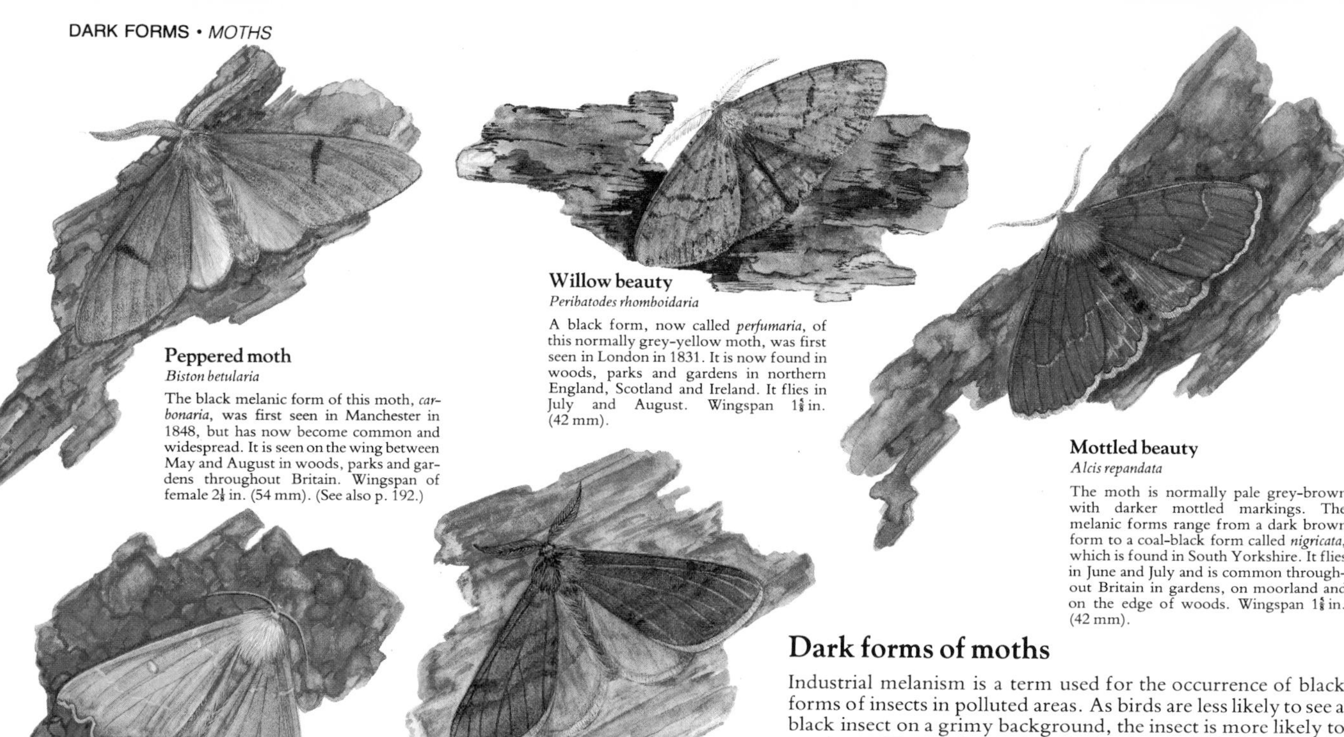

Peppered moth
Biston betularia

The black melanic form of this moth, *carbonaria*, was first seen in Manchester in 1848, but has now become common and widespread. It is seen on the wing between May and August in woods, parks and gardens throughout Britain. Wingspan of female 2⅛ in. (54 mm). (See also p. 192.)

Willow beauty
Peribatodes rhomboidaria

A black form, now called *perfumaria*, of this normally grey-yellow moth, was first seen in London in 1831. It is now found in woods, parks and gardens in northern England, Scotland and Ireland. It flies in July and August. Wingspan 1⅝ in. (42 mm).

Mottled beauty
Alcis repandata

The moth is normally pale grey-brown with darker mottled markings. The melanic forms range from a dark brown form to a coal-black form called *nigricata*, which is found in South Yorkshire. It flies in June and July and is common throughout Britain in gardens, on moorland and on the edge of woods. Wingspan 1⅝ in. (42 mm).

Scalloped hazel
Odontopera bidentata

In industrial areas, up to half of this common species, which is normally a pale greyish-yellow, may be the dark form. It is not an active flyer, but can be seen in May and June in woods and hedgerows all over Britain. Wingspan 1¾ in. (45 mm).

Pale brindled beauty
Apocheima pilosaria

The melanic form of this common moth, called *monacharia*, is smoky black and is seen mainly in South Yorkshire and around London. It usually flies from January to March and occasionally in November and December. The female is wingless. Wingspan 1⅝ in. (42 mm). (See also p. 193.)

Dark forms of moths

Industrial melanism is a term used for the occurrence of black forms of insects in polluted areas. As birds are less likely to see a black insect on a grimy background, the insect is more likely to survive and breed, increasing the incidence of blackness in the next generation. The peppered moth is the best known example, but 100 other species of British moth also have dark forms. A few are shown on these pages.

In the countryside, normal forms of some moths are found on trees covered in pale-coloured lichens. In industrial areas the lichens are killed by acid rain – rain which has combined with chemicals from chimneys to produce dilute sulphuric and nitric acid. Tree trunks are then blackened by particles of carbon from burnt coal and oil. Since the 1960s pollution in cities has decreased because of the Clean Air Acts and fewer dark peppered moths are now found. In Liverpool, for example, they have declined by 25 per cent.

Tawny-barred angle
Semiothisa liturata

The orange band along the fore-wings of the normal grey form is often still present in the melanic form, called *nigrofulvata*. It is found in June and July on the trunks and branches of fir trees in central and southern England. Wingspan 1⅛ in. (28 mm).

Waved umber
Menophra abruptaria

Several dark forms of this normally grey-brown moth are known. This one is called *fuscata*. It is most abundant in London, but can be seen as far north as Durham and in South Wales. It flies in April and May and is usually found resting on trees, fences and walls. Wingspan 1⅜ in. (35 mm).

Nut-tree tussock
Colocasia coryli

The melanic form of this moth, called *melanotica*, is usually only a slightly darker brown than the creamy coloured normal form. It is common in the Chilterns, but the species is found in woods and hedgerows in all parts of Britain. It flies in two generations, in May and June and again in August and September. Wingspan 1⅜ in. (35 mm).

Dark arches
Apamea monoglypha

Several melanic forms of this very common moth exist. A jet-black form is known in Yorkshire and another dark form, *monoglypha*, represents 30 per cent of the species found in the Scottish Highlands. It flies from July to September over open grassland and agricultural land throughout Britain. Wingspan 1⅞ in. (48 mm).

Small engrailed
Ectropis crepuscularia

This is a very common moth whose sooty melanic form is called *delamerensis*. It is well distributed in woods, parks, gardens and hedgerows throughout Britain. It flies in May and June. Wingspan 1½ in. (38 mm).

Green brindled crescent
Allophyes oxyacanthae

The normal form of this extremely attractive moth used to be known as Ealing's glory. The dark brown melanic form is called *capucina*. It is common in hedgerows and woods throughout Britain, except in the extreme north. Wingspan 1⅝ in. (42 mm).

Pale oak beauty
Serraca punctinalis

The black melanic form of this moth, called *humperti*, was originally sighted close to Sutton Coldfield, near Birmingham, but is now found all over southern England and in parts of Ireland. It can be seen on the trunks of oak and fir trees in June and July. Wingspan 1¾ in. (45 mm).

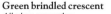

[×4]

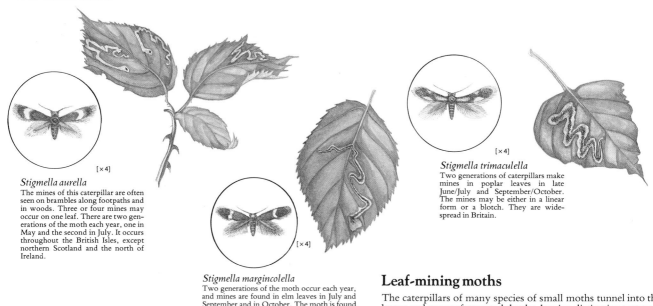

Stigmella aurella
The mines of this caterpillar are often seen on brambles along footpaths and in woods. Three or four mines may occur on one leaf. There are two generations of the moth each year, one in May and the second in July. It occurs throughout the British Isles, except northern Scotland and the north of Ireland.

[×4]

Stigmella trimaculella
Two generations of caterpillars make mines in poplar leaves in late June/July and September/October. The mines may be either in a linear form or a blotch. They are widespread in Britain.

[×4]

Stigmella marginicolella
Two generations of the moth occur each year, and mines are found in elm leaves in July and September and in October. The moth is found throughout Britain but is more abundant in the south.

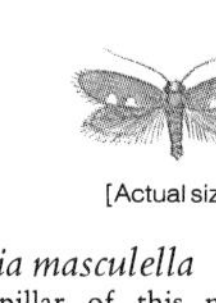

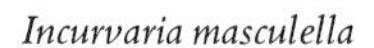

[Actual size]

Protective case

Incurvaria masculella
The caterpillar of this moth first makes a mine in a hawthorn leaf and then a protective case out of small pieces of leaf. It spends the winter as a chrysalis. The moths are seen in May throughout Britain, especially in England and Wales.

Leaf-mining moths

The caterpillars of many species of small moths tunnel into the leaves and stems of trees and shrubs, leaving distinctive patterns. These leaf mines are seen more often than the moths, but there is often no need to see either the moth or the caterpillar to identify the species, as the path eaten out follows a pattern which is unique to each species. Mines fall into two broad groups – linear tracks and blotches. If the mine is still occupied, the caterpillar can be seen against the light. The mine is caused by the caterpillar feeding mostly in the upper surface of the leaf. As it grows larger its track widens and the leaf discolours. If in the autumn the leaf falls, the caterpillar continues feeding in an area of leaf which remains green, and is called a 'green island'. How the leaf stays alive after leaf-fall is not yet known as the study of leaf mines is a new field.

When the caterpillar is fully grown it usually leaves the mine and forms a chrysalis on the soil. Some moths live in a mine at first, but later emerge and protect themselves with 'cases' made from pieces of leaf stuck around them with silk.

[×4]

Stigmella obliquella
The mines are found on willow leaves when the caterpillars are feeding in June and July and again in September and October. Two generations of moths hatch in May and August. They are found mostly in southern England and East Anglia.

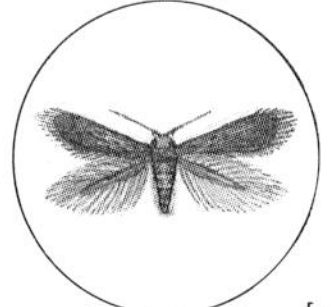

[×4]

Stigmella anomalella
Common and widespread mines on the leaves of wild or cultivated roses throughout Britain. Two generations of moths hatch in May and August.

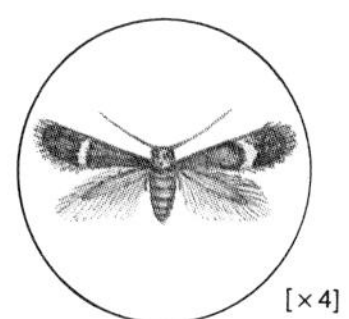

[×4]

Stigmella tityrella
The caterpillar makes distinctive 'S-bends' between the veins of beech leaves. The mines are seen from June to October. There are two generations of the moths, which are widespread in the British Isles.

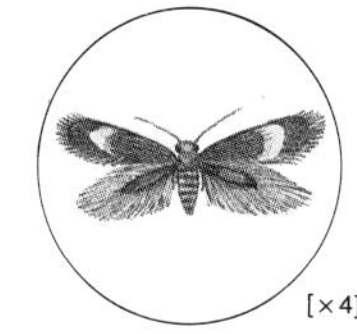

[×4]

Stigmella regiella
The mines are found in hawthorn leaves from August to November. The caterpillars spend the winter in the leaves and the moths hatch in late May and June. Widespread in England and North Wales.

A selection of other British moths

Britain has about 2,400 moth species, and some of the largest and most colourful have been illustrated in detail on pp. 144–207. The following six pages carry a selection of other interesting or common moths. Some are day-flying and are likely to be seen in the countryside. Most fly at night, and during the day they may be seen resting on tree trunks and vegetation.

The two largest moth families – the Noctuidae and the Geometridae – account for more than 750 British moths. Noctuids are thick-bodied and generally dull in colour, and their chrysalises are formed underground. Geometrids are frail compared to the noctuids and their caterpillars are the familiar 'loopers'.

Another 700 British moth species are collectively called micro-moths since their wingspan is less than ¾ in. (20 mm). Some of the micro-moths which cause galls and leaf mines on plants are illustrated on pp. 210–11.

Orange underwing

Archiearis parthenias

The males may be seen flying around silver birch trees on heathland in March and April. The species is found mostly in central and southern England. Wingspan 1¼ in. (32 mm).

Beautiful yellow underwing

Anarta myrtilli

The moth creates a mosaic of colours as it feeds on the nectar of wild flowers during the day from late April to August. It lays its eggs on heather and is restricted to Britain's declining heathlands. Wingspan 1⅛ in. (28 mm).

Male

Female

Common heath

Ematurga atomaria

The moth is named after the heathland and waste areas on which it is found in May and June. It occurs throughout England, Wales and Scotland, but mostly on the western coast of Ireland. The caterpillars feed on heather and clover. Wingspan 1⅛ in. (28 mm).

Female

Male

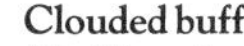

Clouded buff

Diacrisia sannio

A buff-coloured tiger moth with distinctive marks on the fore-wings. It may be seen in late June and July on heaths in Surrey and Dorset and moors in west Scotland, and occasionally on downs. The eggs are laid on bell heather. Wingspan 1⅝ in. (42 mm).

Frosted yellow
Isturgia limbaria

An orange-yellow moth with black borders to its wings. There are two generations, in May/June and July/August. It is rarely found now and may be extinct. Wingspan ⅞ in. (22 mm).

Speckled yellow
Pseudopanthera macularia

A familiar sight along woodland paths during June and July. It is found mostly in south-east and south-west England and north Wales. The eggs are laid on wood sage, dead-nettles and woundworts. Wingspan 1$\frac{3}{16}$ in. (30 mm).

Common crimson and gold
Pyrausta purpuralis

A widely distributed moth in Britain, found on rough hillsides and marshes among mint and thyme, the caterpillars' food plants. There are two generations each year, in May/June and July/August. Wingspan ⅞ in. (22 mm).

Chimney sweeper
Odezia atrata

A plain black moth with white wingtips that may be found in clearings and paths in woods and along hedgerows in June and July. It is found in central and northern England, Wales and Scotland, but infrequently in southern England. The caterpillars eat leaves of the pig-nut plant. Wingspan 1 in. (25 mm).

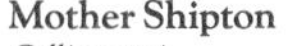

Burnet companion
Euclidia glyphica

A common day-flying moth found in May and June in flowery meadows where its caterpillars' food plants, clovers and trefoils, grow in large numbers. It is well distributed in England and Wales, and just reaches southern Scotland. It occurs in a few places in Ireland. Wingspan 1¼ in. (32 mm).

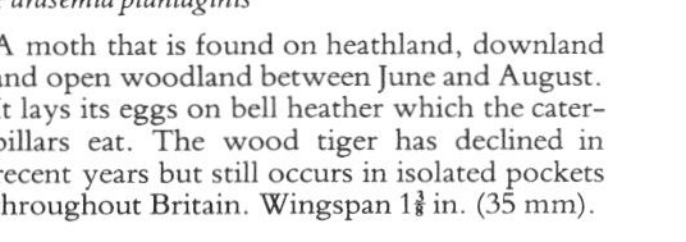

Wood tiger
Parasemia plantaginis

A moth that is found on heathland, downland and open woodland between June and August. It lays its eggs on bell heather which the caterpillars eat. The wood tiger has declined in recent years but still occurs in isolated pockets throughout Britain. Wingspan 1⅜ in. (35 mm).

Mother Shipton
Callistege mi

The moth gets its name from the pattern on the wings, which was said to resemble a Yorkshire witch, Mother Shipton. It visits wild flowers on sunny banks and railway cuttings in May and June throughout Britain. The caterpillars feed on clovers and melilots. Wingspan 1⅜ in. (35 mm).

Flame

Axylia putris

The flame moth can be identified by its reddish shoulders, pale fore-wings and its striking resemblance to a twig. It is widespread throughout Britain from May to July, beside woods and hedgerows and in gardens. It breeds on docks and nettles. Wingspan $1\frac{3}{8}$ in. (35 mm).

Flame shoulder

Ochropleura plecta

The flame shoulder can be distinguished from the flame moth by its pale flash of colour along the leading edge of the fore-wings. It is common and widespread throughout Britain, with two generations from May to September. It breeds on many garden weeds. Wingspan $1\frac{1}{4}$ in. (32 mm).

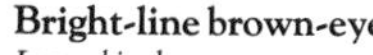

Bright-line brown-eye

Lacanobia oleracea

The moth's name describes the colouring on the fore-wing. Gardeners know it as the tomato moth, as the caterpillars will occasionally eat the leaves of tomato plants, as well as various common wild flowers. The moth may be seen over most of Britain from May to October. Wingspan $1\frac{1}{2}$ in. (38 mm).

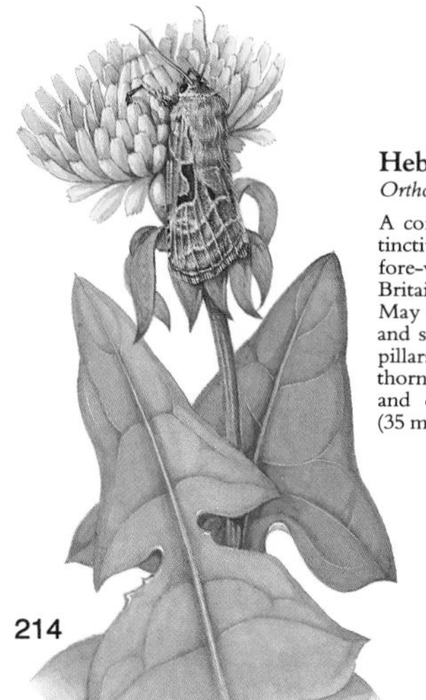

Hebrew character

Orthosia gothica

A common moth with a distinctive black mark on the fore-wing, found throughout Britain. It is on the wing in May and July near hedgerows and scrubby areas. The caterpillars eat sallow and hawthorn as well as dandelions and docks. Wingspan $1\frac{3}{8}$ in. (35 mm).

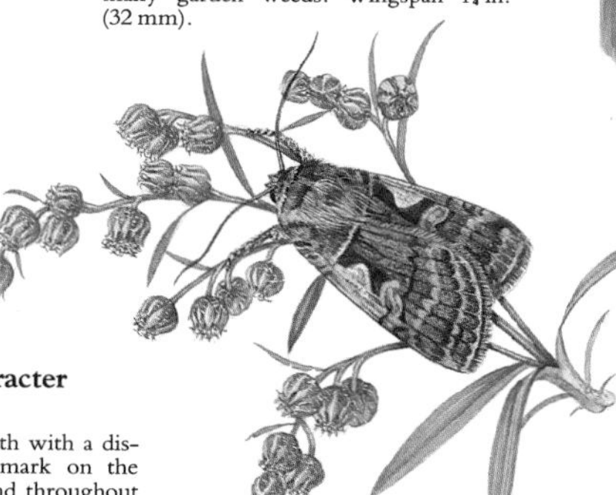

Setaceous Hebrew character

Xestia c-nigrum

A common moth throughout Britain, particularly in south-east England in May and June. The caterpillars eat a variety of common wayside weeds. Wingspan $1\frac{5}{8}$ in. (42 mm).

Shuttle-shaped dart

Agrotis puta

Common in the south of England and parts of Wales from May to September, but rare in Scotland and Ireland. The caterpillars feed on various common weeds. Wingspan $1\frac{3}{8}$ in. (35 mm).

Heart and dart

Agrotis exclamationis

A very common moth throughout Britain in May and June, particularly in the south. A second generation occurs in the south in July and August. The heart and dart is found in many habitats, including gardens, fields and waste areas. It breeds on a variety of wild flowers including chickweed and goosegrass. Wingspan $1\frac{1}{2}$ in. (38 mm).

Oak lutestring

Cymatophorima diluta

The moth gets its name from its caterpillar's food plant and the wavy lines across its fore-wings. It is seen in September, particularly in southern England, but also in north Wales and the Lake District. Wingspan $1\frac{3}{8}$ in. (35 mm).

Scalloped oak

Crocallis elinguaria

A pale buff moth with a dark band across the fore-wings and dots around the margins. It flies in July and August and is found throughout Britain. Eggs are laid on many trees, including oak and birch. Wingspan $1\frac{1}{2}$ in. (38 mm).

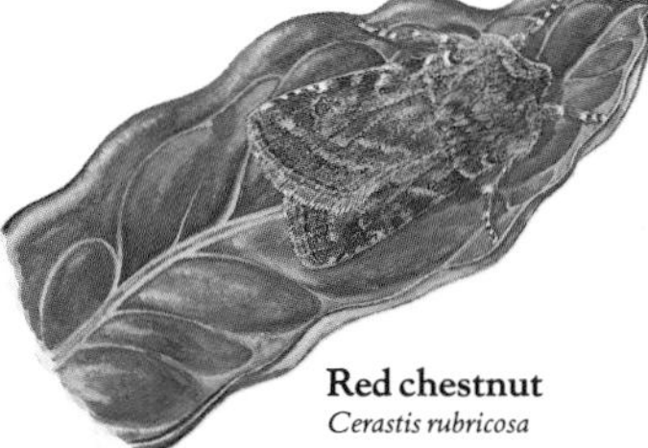

Red chestnut

Cerastis rubricosa

A very drab moth which is common and widely distributed in Britain in gardens, woods and fields in March and April. The caterpillars feed on chickweeds, docks and groundsel. Wingspan $1\frac{1}{2}$ in. (38 mm).

Broom moth

Ceramica pisi

The moth is named after one of the caterpillars' food plants, but they will also eat bracken, bramble and sallow. The broom moth is widespread in Britain in June and July. Wingspan $1\frac{1}{2}$ in (38 mm).

Figure of eight

Diloba caeruleocephala

The mark on its fore-wing gives the moth its name. It is found in the autumn in orchards and woods and along hedgerows, where it breeds on hawthorn and sloe (blackthorn). Common in southern and central England. Wingspan $1\frac{1}{2}$ in. (38 mm).

Black arches
Lymantria monarcha

A striking moth which occurs in England from Yorkshire southwards, particularly in the New Forest, and in Wales. It is scarce in Ireland. It is found near woods from July to September, and lays its eggs on oak. Wingspan $1\frac{5}{8}$ in. (42 mm).

Brimstone moth
Opisthograptis luteolata

A common moth which produces two generations each year and is often seen around lights between August and October throughout Britain. The caterpillars feed mainly on hawthorn. Wingspan $1\frac{3}{8}$ in. (35 mm).

Common wainscot
Mythimna pallens

The common wainscot is one of many wainscots, characterised by their plain streaky fore-wings. It is widespread throughout most of Britain from July to September in two generations. The caterpillars feed on grasses. Wingspan $1\frac{3}{8}$ in. (35 mm).

Feathered thorn
Colotois pennaria

The moth is named after the feathery antennae on the male. It is an autumn moth, on the wing from September to November, and is common in southern England. It is found near woods and hedgerows where its caterpillars feed on oak, silver birch and hawthorn. Wingspan $1\frac{7}{8}$ in. (48 mm).

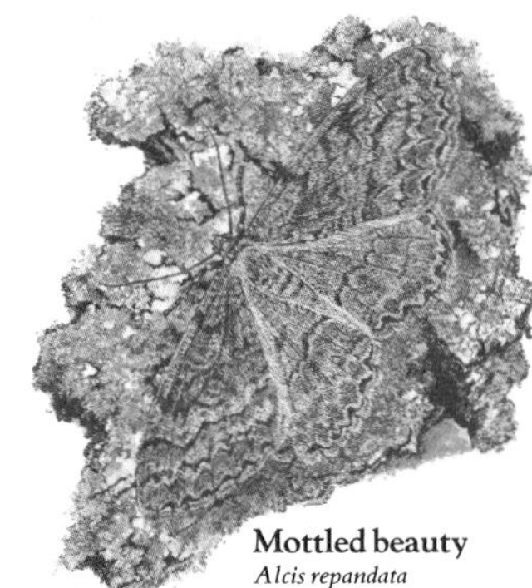

Mottled beauty
Alcis repandata

The zigzag lines across the fore-wings give good camouflage when the moth rests with its wings flat against a surface. It is widespread and common throughout Britain in woodlands and moorlands. Eggs are laid on hawthorn, silver birch and hazel leaves. Wingspan $1\frac{3}{4}$ in. (45 mm).

Dot moth
Melanchra persicariae

The white dots on the fore-wings make the dot moth easy to identify. It flies from June to August and is common in gardens in the south of England, where it feeds on common plants. Wingspan $1\frac{3}{4}$ in. (45 mm).

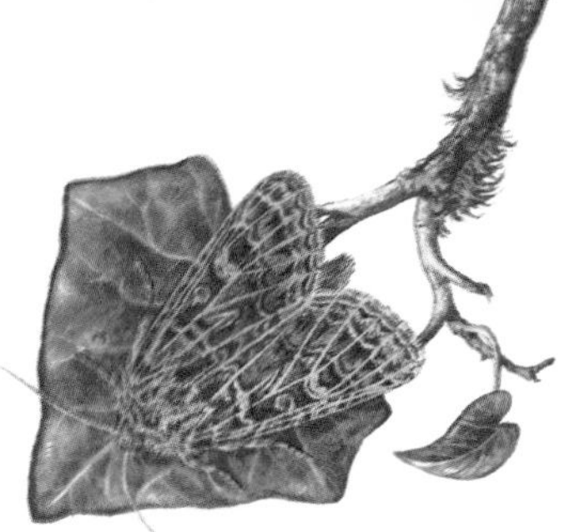

Gothic

Naenia typica

The pattern of white veins on the fore-wings, like tracery in gothic windows, gives the moth its name. The caterpillar feeds on many widespread weeds and hedgerow trees, and the moth is seen from June to August, throughout Britain. Wingspan $1\frac{3}{4}$ in. (45 mm).

Common quaker

Orthosia stablis

The beige fore-wings each have two brown patches and a pattern of white lines near the tips. The moths are abundant in England, Wales and southern Scotland from March to May. Wingspan $1\frac{3}{8}$ in. (35 mm).

Early thorn

Selenia dentaria

Two generations of the moth occur each year, the first in April and May and the second in July and August. The caterpillars feed on hawthorn and sloe. It is widely distributed in Britain. Wingspan $1\frac{1}{2}$ in. (38 mm).

Satellite

Eupsilia transversa

A woodland and hedgerow moth which is common in most parts of Britain from September to November. It is distinguished by the cream dot on each fore-wing. The caterpillars feed on oak, elm and beech. Wingspan $1\frac{3}{4}$ in. (45 mm).

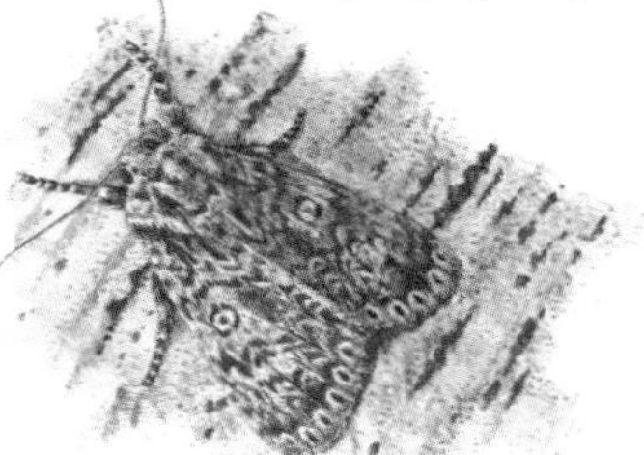

Poplar grey

Acronicta megacephala

Named after its caterpillar's food plant, the moth is ideally camouflaged for concealment on bark. It is most common in the south of England, and is seen between May and June. Wingspan $1\frac{1}{2}$ in. (38 mm).

Swallow-tailed moth

Ourapteryx sambucaria

A large moth with broad butterfly-like wings. The 'tail' on each hind-wing is normally obscured. The moth is often seen around lights in July and August, and is common in gardens throughout Britain, except northern Scotland. The eggs are laid on hawthorn and sloe. Wingspan $2\frac{3}{8}$ in. (60 mm).

Many moths, including the oak beauty and the brindled beauty, conceal themselves on bark during the day, their patterns and colours matching lichens that grow on the trees

In spring, many caterpillars can be found on oak branches, eating the young leaves. Green oak tortrix caterpillars hang in mid-air from long silk threads to escape predators. A woodland glade may be rich in butterflies and day-flying moths, such as the male oak eggar moth which flies at great speed in search of females.

Moths of the oak woods

More insects are dependent on oaks than on any other British trees. Oaks have one of the oldest evolutionary histories of any tree in Britain, and the longer a plant species has grown in a country the more time insects have had to get used to feeding on it. In mid-June each year the caterpillars of 110 species of moth and butterfly may be found on oaks. Caterpillars and the larvae of many other insects eat the tender young leaves, while others feed on the flowers, the developing acorns and roots. Trees can survive complete defoliation by caterpillars in May, when the sound of the droppings can be heard in woods like the patter of rain. But the trees put out new shoots and protect themselves by incorporating tannin into their leaves. By mid-August caterpillars find the leaves so unpalatable that only 65 species of butterfly and moth remain.

An oak wood is always a very open habitat. Shafts of sunlight stream down on to the woodland floor, stimulating wild flowers, bushes and saplings to grow. Here in the rich vegetation many moths spend their life-cycles.

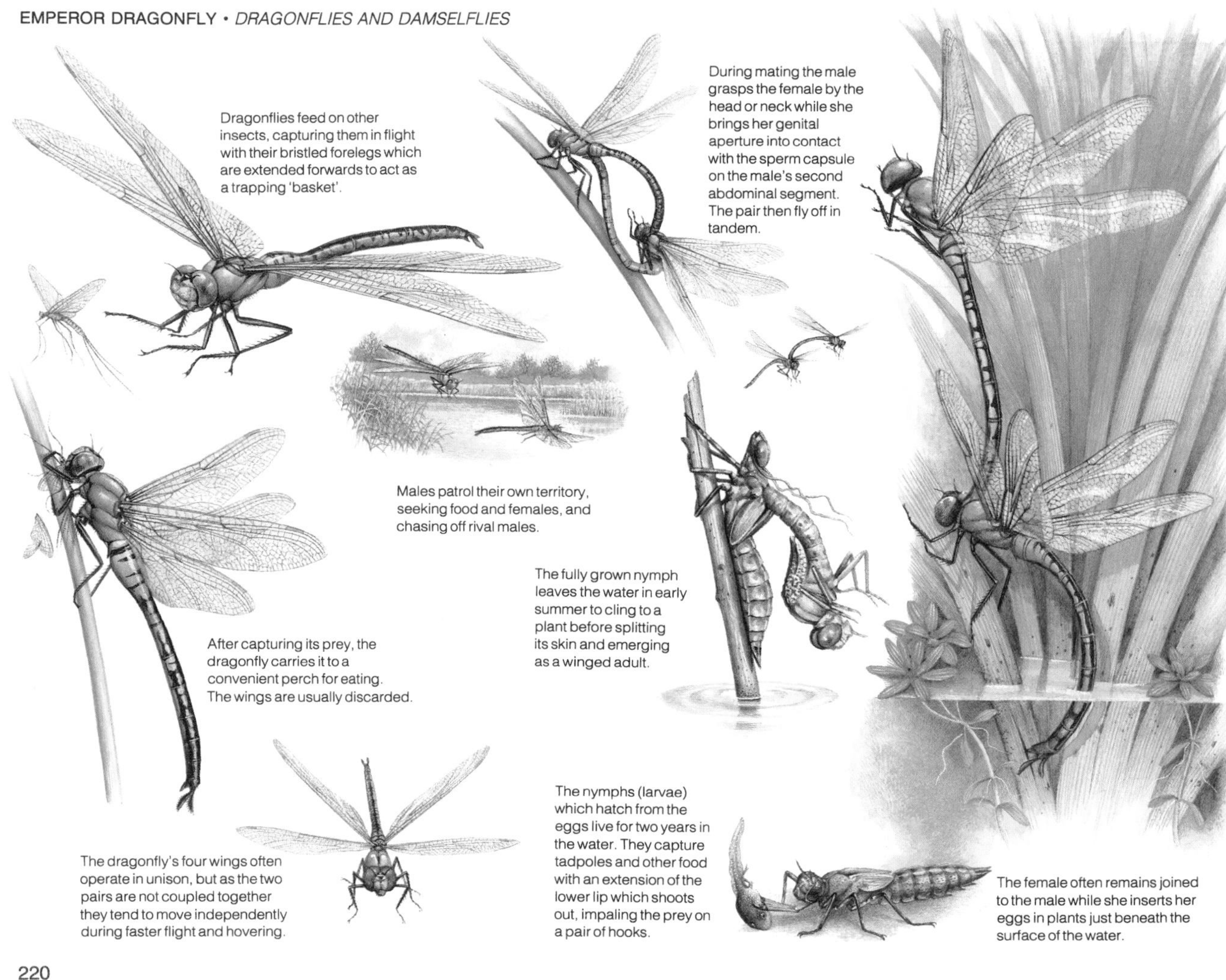

Dragonflies feed on other insects, capturing them in flight with their bristled forelegs which are extended forwards to act as a trapping 'basket'.

During mating the male grasps the female by the head or neck while she brings her genital aperture into contact with the sperm capsule on the male's second abdominal segment. The pair then fly off in tandem.

Males patrol their own territory, seeking food and females, and chasing off rival males.

The fully grown nymph leaves the water in early summer to cling to a plant before splitting its skin and emerging as a winged adult.

After capturing its prey, the dragonfly carries it to a convenient perch for eating. The wings are usually discarded.

The nymphs (larvae) which hatch from the eggs live for two years in the water. They capture tadpoles and other food with an extension of the lower lip which shoots out, impaling the prey on a pair of hooks.

The dragonfly's four wings often operate in unison, but as the two pairs are not coupled together they tend to move independently during faster flight and hovering.

The female often remains joined to the male while she inserts her eggs in plants just beneath the surface of the water.

Female emperors are usually shorter than males and the abdomen is greenish with a dark brown tip. Older females may become bluer.

The brilliant blue, green and silver colours of a male emperor dragonfly glisten in the sunlight as it settles on a waterside plant.

Emperor dragonfly *Anax imperator*

Four large wings and enormous eyes help to make dragonflies swift and efficient hunters. The emperor dragonfly can be found tirelessly patrolling up and down stretches of water at up to 18 mph (30 kph) in search of prey. Almost any flying insects, including smaller dragonflies, can fall victim to its strong legs and powerful jaws. Its habit of 'hawking' for food puts the emperor in the group of dragonflies known as hawkers to distinguish them from the fatter-bodied darters (see pp. 222–7).

The brilliant blue of the male and the black stripe on the bodies of both sexes make the emperor easy to distinguish from other large dragonflies, whose black markings are more broken up. It is found in southern England and Wales around lakes, large ponds and canals during June, July and August. It does not occur in Scotland or Ireland.

Like all dragonflies, the emperor has its own territory which it guards against intrusion by other male dragonflies. This often leads to aerial battles, and males are sometimes seen with pieces torn from their wings by their opponents. Adult emperors usually live for about a month, after a nymphal (larval) stage lasting for two years.

The largest wingspan of any British dragonfly. The abdomen of the male is a brilliant blue, with a black central band and thin black cross bands. Wingspan $4\frac{1}{8}$ in. (10.5 cm).

Other dragonflies: Hawkers

Their characteristic hawk-like habit of restlessly patrolling a territory gives hawker dragonflies their name. The hawker's territory is a stretch of river or lake, which the male defends against intruders, jostling with rival males and other species, and courting female hawkers which enter it.

Hawkers tend to have a larger wingspan and slimmer, longer body than darter dragonflies. Male hawkers are usually more brightly coloured than females – which, since dragonflies are keen-sighted and sensitive to colour, is valuable in sexual recognition. It is also useful for females to be less conspicuous to birds that prey on them, including flycatchers, bee-eaters and hobbies. Colour difference between the sexes is not universal, however, and scent and behaviour are probably sexual recognition factors used at close quarters. Some dragonfly colours are true pigments, others are the result of light diffraction in the body's cuticle, or outer layer.

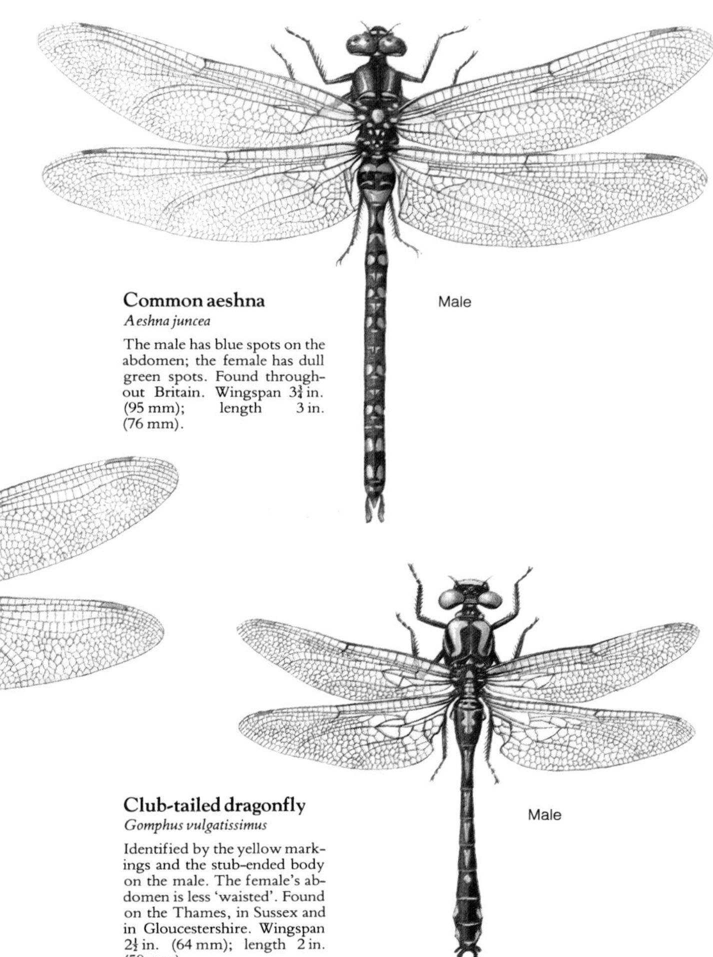

Common aeshna
Aeshna juncea

The male has blue spots on the abdomen; the female has dull green spots. Found throughout Britain. Wingspan 3¾ in. (95 mm); length 3 in. (76 mm).

Southern aeshna
Aeshna cyanea

Conspicuous green markings on the thorax and abdomen. Female does not have the blue tip. Most common in the south of England. Wingspan 4 in. (10 cm); length 2¾ in. (70 mm).

Club-tailed dragonfly
Gomphus vulgatissimus

Identified by the yellow markings and the stub-ended body on the male. The female's abdomen is less 'waisted'. Found on the Thames, in Sussex and in Gloucestershire. Wingspan 2½ in. (64 mm); length 2 in. (50 mm).

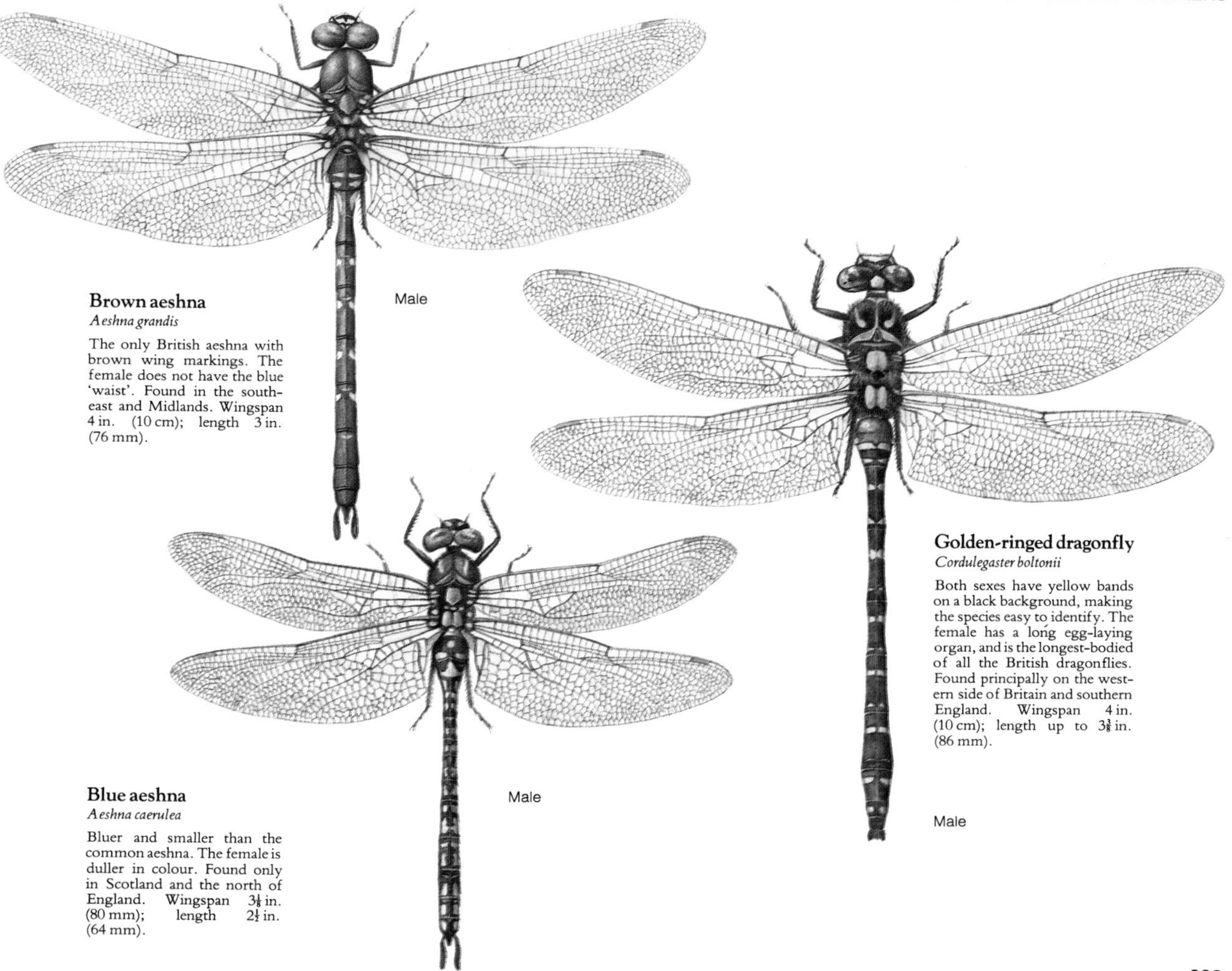

Brown aeshna

Aeshna grandis

The only British aeshna with brown wing markings. The female does not have the blue 'waist'. Found in the south-east and Midlands. Wingspan 4 in. (10 cm); length 3 in. (76 mm).

Blue aeshna

Aeshna caerulea

Bluer and smaller than the common aeshna. The female is duller in colour. Found only in Scotland and the north of England. Wingspan $3\frac{1}{8}$ in. (80 mm); length $2\frac{1}{2}$ in. (64 mm).

Golden-ringed dragonfly

Cordulegaster boltonii

Both sexes have yellow bands on a black background, making the species easy to identify. The female has a long egg-laying organ, and is the longest-bodied of all the British dragonflies. Found principally on the western side of Britain and southern England. Wingspan 4 in. (10 cm); length up to $3\frac{3}{8}$ in. (86 mm).

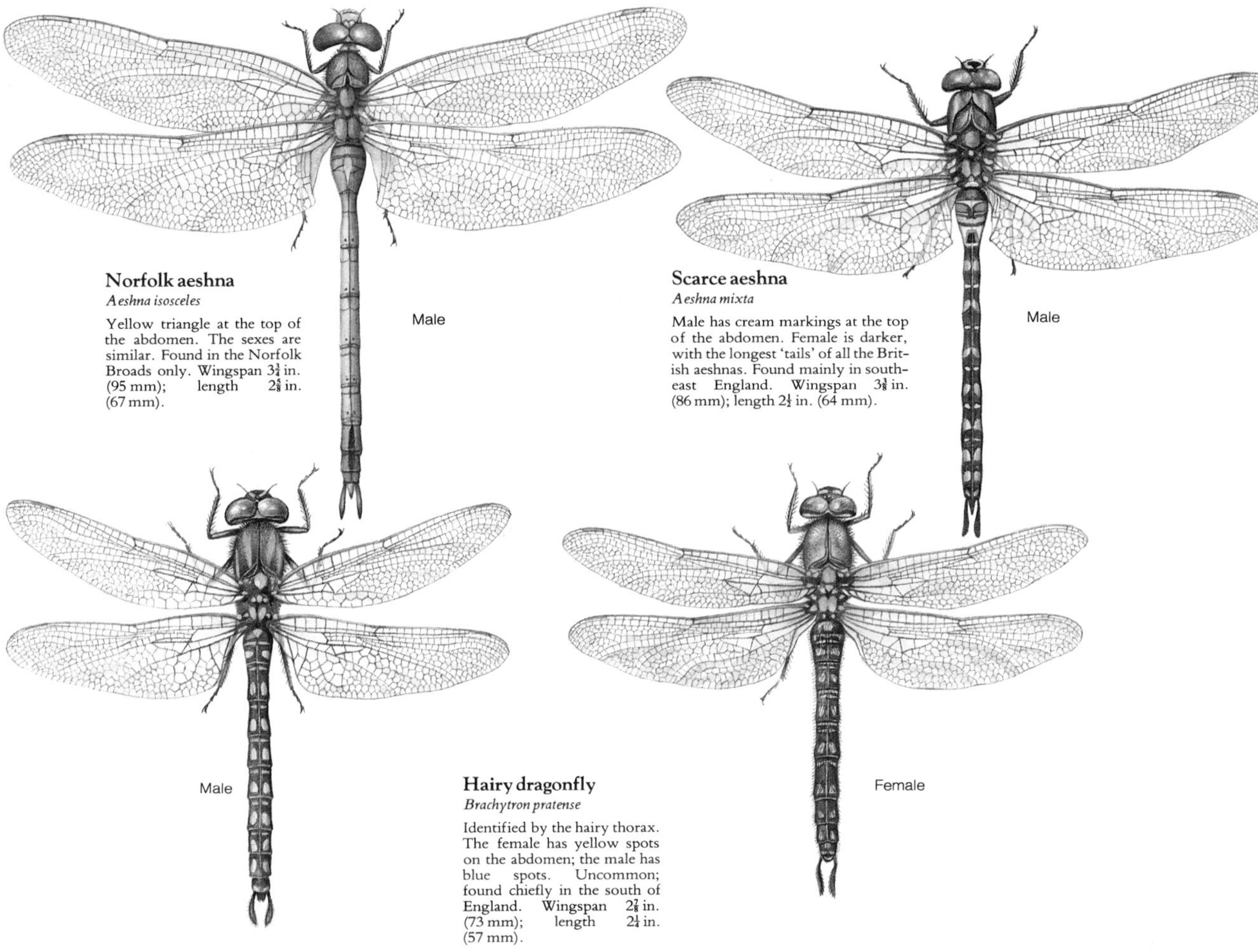

Norfolk aeshna

Aeshna isosceles

Yellow triangle at the top of the abdomen. The sexes are similar. Found in the Norfolk Broads only. Wingspan 3¾ in. (95 mm); length 2⅝ in. (67 mm).

Scarce aeshna

Aeshna mixta

Male has cream markings at the top of the abdomen. Female is darker, with the longest 'tails' of all the British aeshnas. Found mainly in south-east England. Wingspan 3⅜ in. (86 mm); length 2½ in. (64 mm).

Hairy dragonfly

Brachytron pratense

Identified by the hairy thorax. The female has yellow spots on the abdomen; the male has blue spots. Uncommon; found chiefly in the south of England. Wingspan 2⅞ in. (73 mm); length 2¼ in. (57 mm).

Other dragonflies: Darters

Sturdier-bodied than hawkers, the darter dragonflies are less restless movers and habitually spend time clinging to reeds and other waterside vegetation. They make occasional sallies and darts at prey or potential partners, and at intruders into their territory. The males of several darter species have a blue bloom on the abdomen; it comes from a coating of tiny granules that reflect only the blue part of the light spectrum.

Nymphs of both darters and hawkers are sluggish compared with the adults, but all have a quick-escape technique resulting from their method of respiration. They have gills right inside the abdomen and draw in oxygen-bearing water through the rectum to wash over these gills. When threatened, perhaps by fish, nymphs shoot out the water from the abdomen and the body thrusts forward rapidly in a form of jet propulsion.

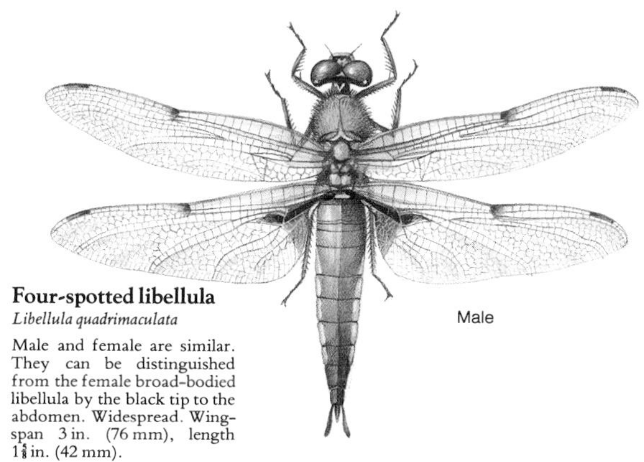

Four-spotted libellula
Libellula quadrimaculata

Male and female are similar. They can be distinguished from the female broad-bodied libellula by the black tip to the abdomen. Widespread. Wingspan 3 in. (76 mm), length 1$\frac{5}{8}$ in. (42 mm).

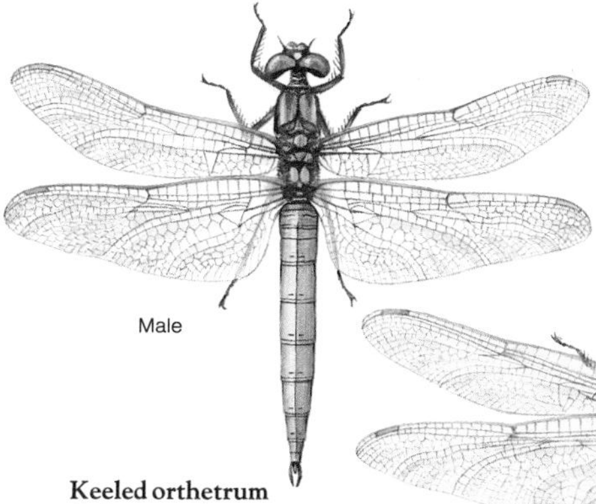

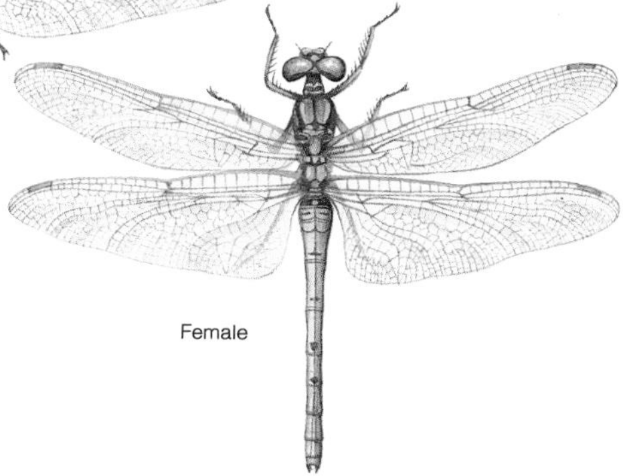

Male

Female

Keeled orthetrum
Orthetrum coerulescens

The male's entire abdomen is blue; the female is yellow-brown, with yellow-tinged wings. Found mainly in southern England. Wingspan 2$\frac{3}{8}$ in. (60 mm), length 1$\frac{5}{8}$ in. (42 mm).

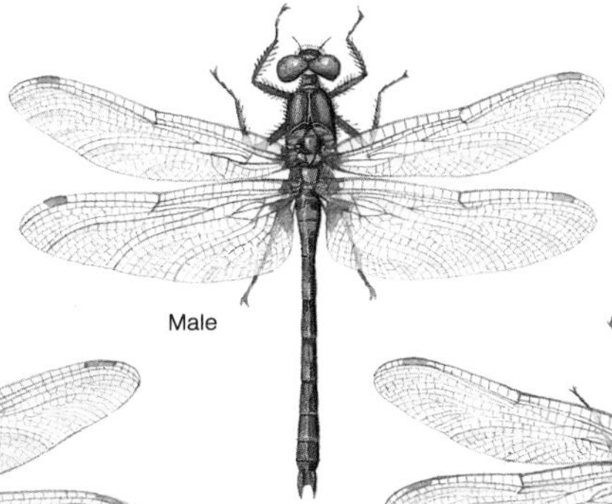

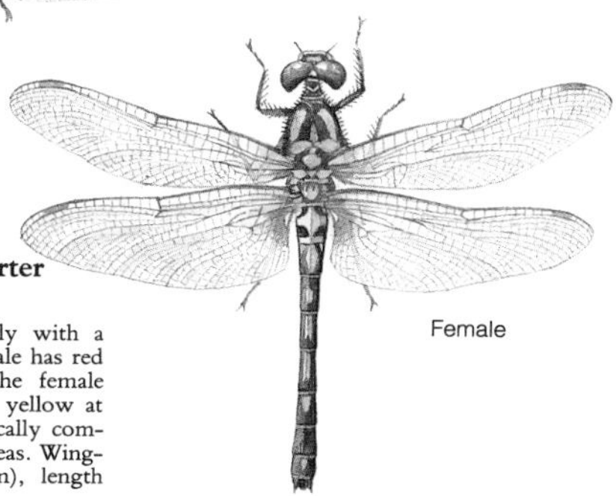

Male

Female

White-faced darter
Leucorrhinia dubia

The only dragonfly with a white face. The male has red body markings, the female yellow, with dark yellow at the wing base. Locally common in scattered areas. Wingspan 2$\frac{1}{8}$ in. (54 mm), length 1$\frac{1}{2}$ in. (38 mm).

Male

Female

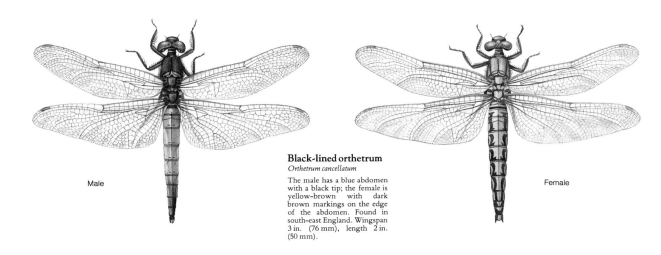

Black-lined orthetrum

Orthetrum cancellatum

The male has a blue abdomen with a black tip; the female is yellow-brown with dark brown markings on the edge of the abdomen. Found in south-east England. Wingspan 3 in. (76 mm), length 2 in. (50 mm).

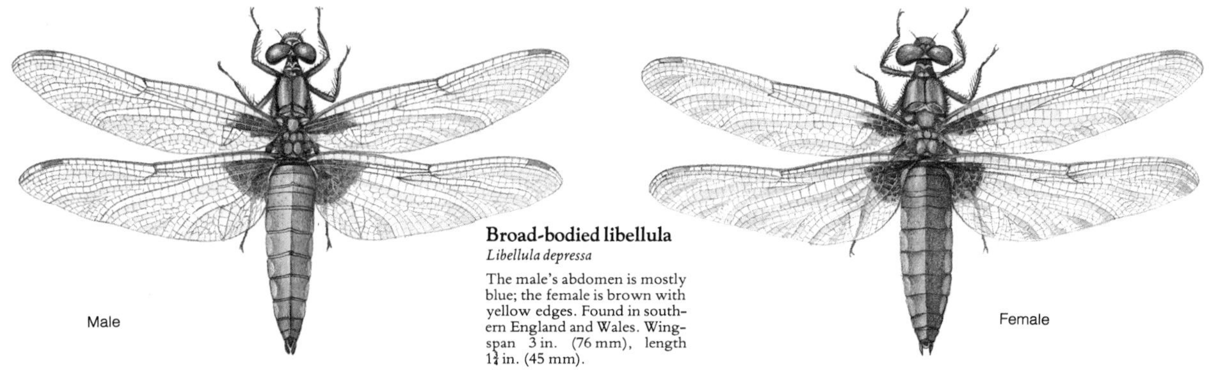

Broad-bodied libellula

Libellula depressa

The male's abdomen is mostly blue; the female is brown with yellow edges. Found in southern England and Wales. Wingspan 3 in. (76 mm), length 1¾ in. (45 mm).

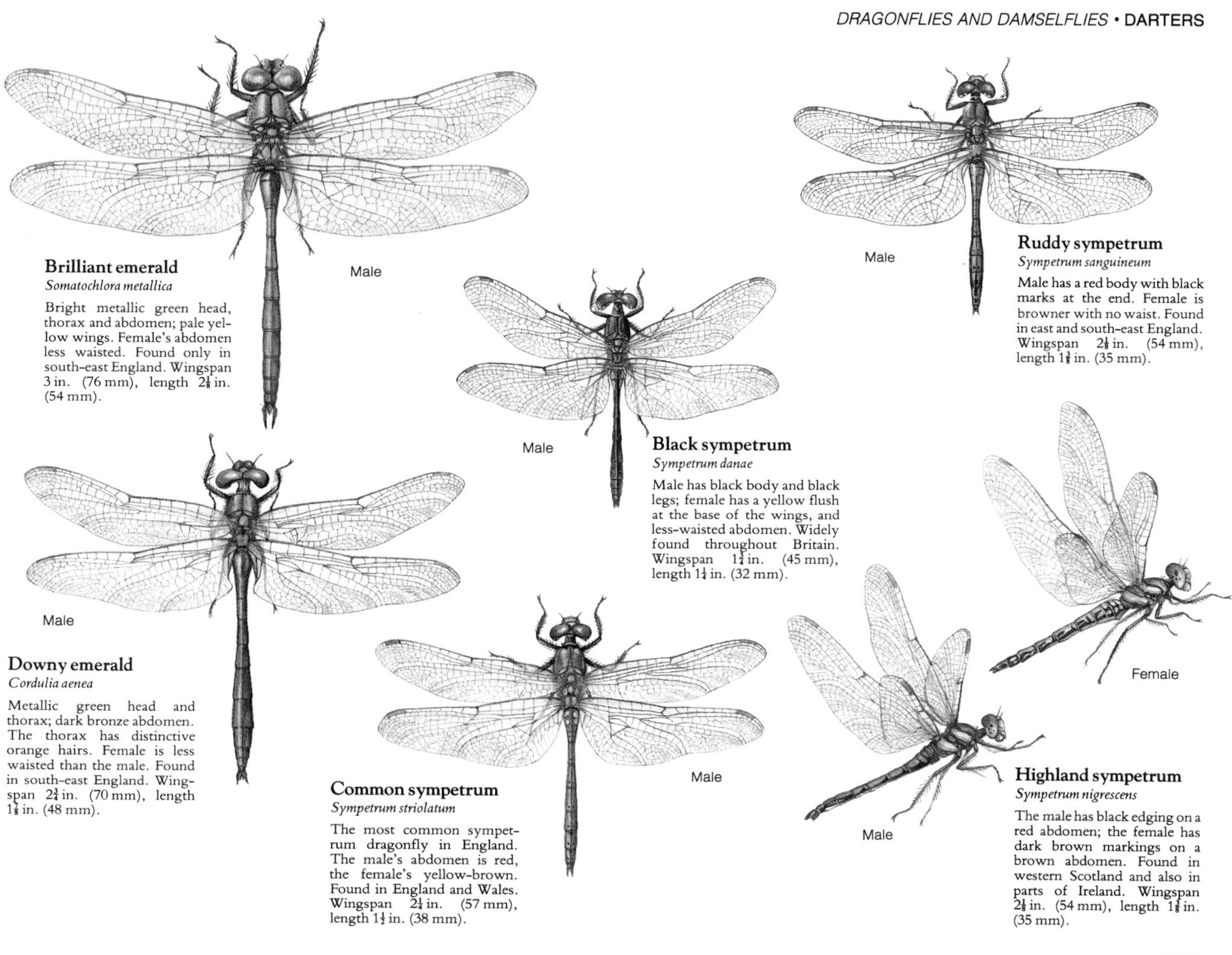

Brilliant emerald
Somatochlora metallica

Bright metallic green head, thorax and abdomen; pale yellow wings. Female's abdomen less waisted. Found only in south-east England. Wingspan 3 in. (76 mm), length 2⅛ in. (54 mm).

Downy emerald
Cordulia aenea

Metallic green head and thorax; dark bronze abdomen. The thorax has distinctive orange hairs. Female is less waisted than the male. Found in south-east England. Wingspan 2¾ in. (70 mm), length 1⅞ in. (48 mm).

Black sympetrum
Sympetrum danae

Male has black body and black legs; female has a yellow flush at the base of the wings, and less-waisted abdomen. Widely found throughout Britain. Wingspan 1¾ in. (45 mm), length 1¼ in. (32 mm).

Common sympetrum
Sympetrum striolatum

The most common sympetrum dragonfly in England. The male's abdomen is red, the female's yellow-brown. Found in England and Wales. Wingspan 2¼ in. (57 mm), length 1½ in. (38 mm).

Ruddy sympetrum
Sympetrum sanguineum

Male has a red body with black marks at the end. Female is browner with no waist. Found in east and south-east England. Wingspan 2⅛ in. (54 mm), length 1⅜ in. (35 mm).

Highland sympetrum
Sympetrum nigrescens

The male has black edging on a red abdomen; the female has dark brown markings on a brown abdomen. Found in western Scotland and also in parts of Ireland. Wingspan 2⅛ in. (54 mm), length 1⅜ in. (35 mm).

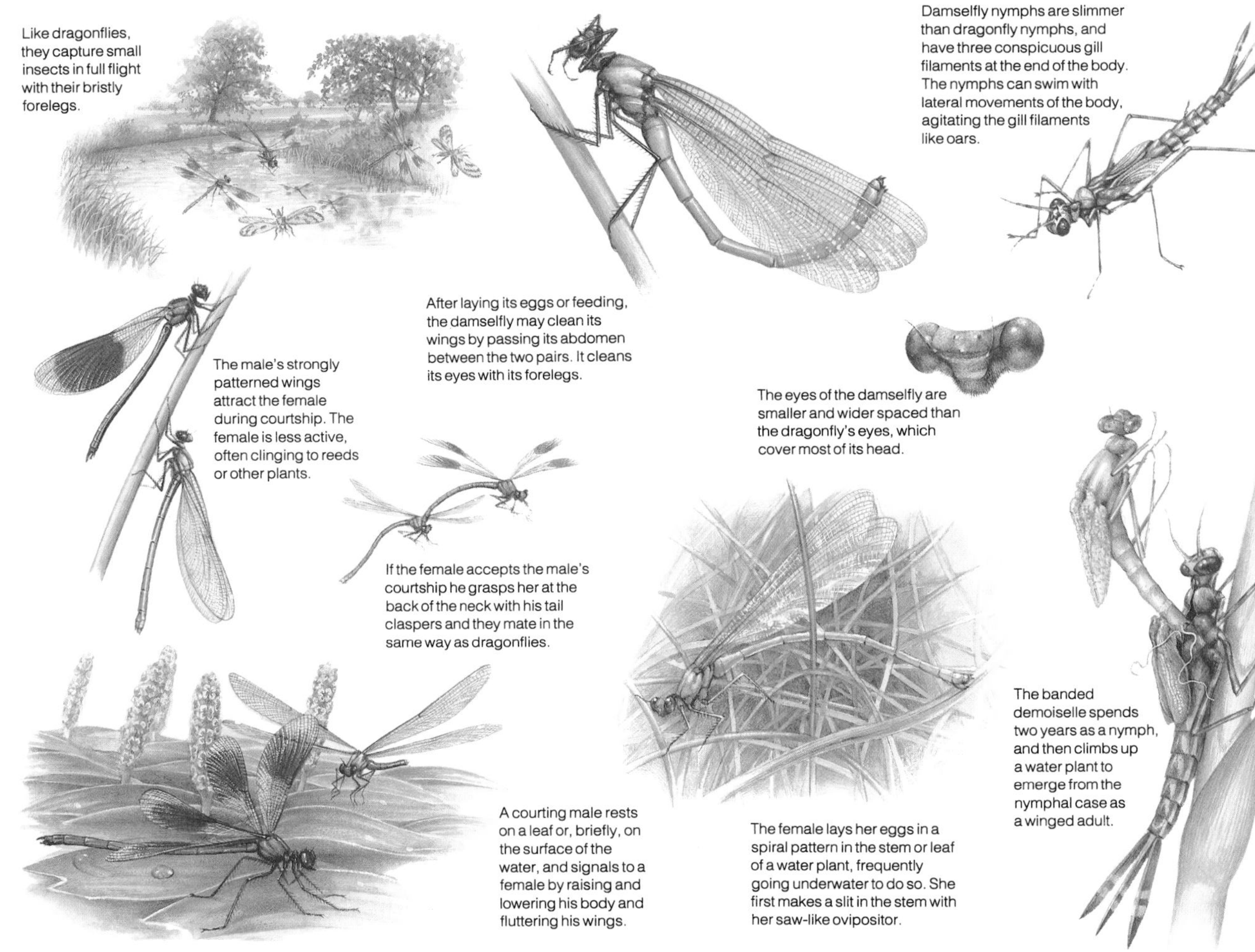

Like dragonflies, they capture small insects in full flight with their bristly forelegs.

Damselfly nymphs are slimmer than dragonfly nymphs, and have three conspicuous gill filaments at the end of the body. The nymphs can swim with lateral movements of the body, agitating the gill filaments like oars.

After laying its eggs or feeding, the damselfly may clean its wings by passing its abdomen between the two pairs. It cleans its eyes with its forelegs.

The male's strongly patterned wings attract the female during courtship. The female is less active, often clinging to reeds or other plants.

The eyes of the damselfly are smaller and wider spaced than the dragonfly's eyes, which cover most of its head.

If the female accepts the male's courtship he grasps her at the back of the neck with his tail claspers and they mate in the same way as dragonflies.

The banded demoiselle spends two years as a nymph, and then climbs up a water plant to emerge from the nymphal case as a winged adult.

A courting male rests on a leaf or, briefly, on the surface of the water, and signals to a female by raising and lowering his body and fluttering his wings.

The female lays her eggs in a spiral pattern in the stem or leaf of a water plant, frequently going underwater to do so. She first makes a slit in the stem with her saw-like ovipositor.

The needle-like body of a male banded demoiselle gleams like blue-green satin as it perches on tall blades of grass beside a stream.

One of Britain's biggest damselflies. The male has large blue patches on each of its four wings, and a polished-looking blue-green body. The female's wings are a metallic green. Wingspan 2⅜ in. (60 mm).

Banded demoiselle damselfly *Calopteryx splendens*

The weak, fluttering flight of damselflies helps to distinguish them from the larger, more powerful dragonflies. Damselflies also have a more delicate build. When resting they can hold their wings either vertically over the body like a butterfly or horizontally, while a dragonfly holds its wings horizontally. The eyes of the damselfly are more widely spaced than those of the dragonfly, giving its head a dumbbell-shaped appearance.

The banded demoiselle damselfly is found along fast-flowing streams, mostly in southern England but also in parts of northern England, Wales and Ireland. Like other damselflies it is on the wing from early summer.

Damselflies feed on other insects, such as caddisflies and alderflies, which they capture in flight or pick off riverside plants. Being relatively slow flyers, they themselves sometimes fall victim to the larger and faster dragonflies. The nymphs (larvae) of the damselfly are also carnivorous, and feed in the same way as dragonfly nymphs – by extending a barbed 'mask' from the lower jaw which impales the prey and draws it back to the mouth. In winter the nymphs hibernate in mud at the bottom of the stream. They have no pupa stage.

Other British damselflies

Smaller and more delicately built than dragonflies, damselflies have a much weaker, more fluttering, dancing flight. Their wings differ from those of dragonflies in being of more or less equal size and rounded at the tips. The two Calopteryx species, commonly called the beautiful demoiselle and the banded demoiselle (p. 229), are the largest of Britain's 17 damselfly species; others are considerably smaller, often with almost needle-thin abdomens.

Both damselflies and dragonflies have similar life histories, and are commonly found flying, feeding and mating over the same stretches of water. They are both predators and either capture insects with their legs while in full flight or snatch them off vegetation. So specialised have their legs become that they can only perch on or cling to vegetation; they are unable to walk on a horizontal surface. An additional handicap in walking is the length of body extending behind the legs.

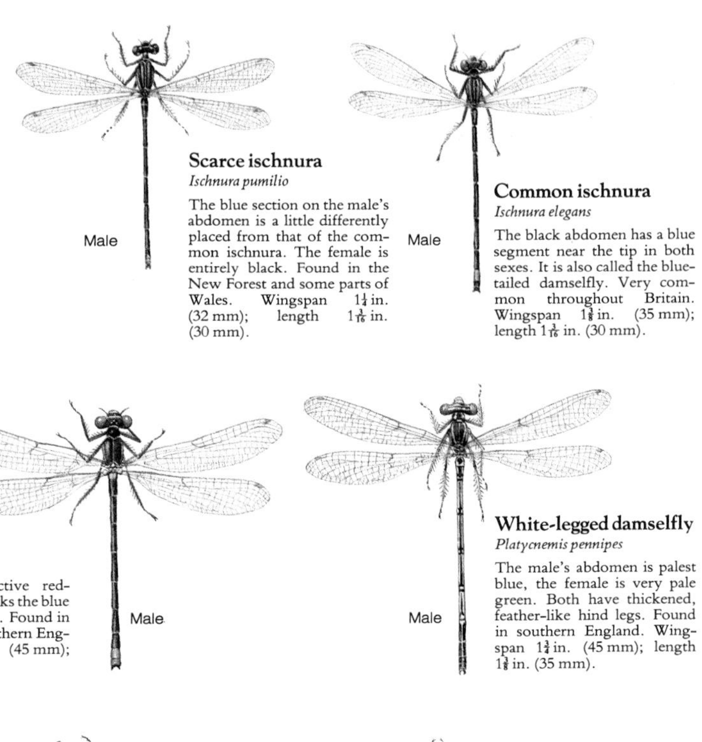

Scarce ischnura
Ischnura pumilio

The blue section on the male's abdomen is a little differently placed from that of the common ischnura. The female is entirely black. Found in the New Forest and some parts of Wales. Wingspan $1\frac{1}{4}$ in. (32 mm); length $1\frac{3}{16}$ in. (30 mm).

Common ischnura
Ischnura elegans

The black abdomen has a blue segment near the tip in both sexes. It is also called the blue-tailed damselfly. Very common throughout Britain. Wingspan $1\frac{3}{8}$ in. (35 mm); length $1\frac{3}{16}$ in. (30 mm).

Red-eyed damselfly
Erythromma najas

Both sexes have distinctive red-brown eyes. The female lacks the blue segments on the abdomen. Found in the Midlands, east and southern England. Wingspan $1\frac{3}{4}$ in. (45 mm); length $1\frac{3}{8}$ in. (35 mm).

White-legged damselfly
Platycnemis pennipes

The male's abdomen is palest blue, the female is very pale green. Both have thickened, feather-like hind legs. Found in southern England. Wingspan $1\frac{3}{4}$ in. (45 mm); length $1\frac{3}{8}$ in. (35 mm).

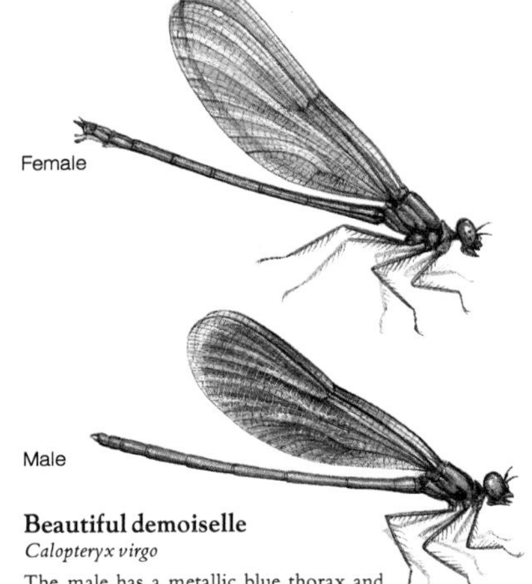

Beautiful demoiselle
Calopteryx virgo

The male has a metallic blue thorax and abdomen, and purple-brown wings. The female has a green thorax and brownish wings. Found mainly in southern England and South Wales. Wingspan $2\frac{1}{4}$ in. (57 mm); length $1\frac{3}{4}$ in. (45 mm).

Northern coenagrion
Coenagrion hastulatum

Male like other blue damselflies, but seen only in central Scotland. Female black. Wingspan $1\frac{5}{8}$ in. (42 mm); length $1\frac{3}{16}$ in. (30 mm).

Southern coenagrion
Coenagrion mercuriale

Smaller than common coenagrion, and found mainly in the New Forest and parts of Wales. Female blackish with white underside of head. Wingspan $1\frac{3}{8}$ in. (35 mm); length $1\frac{1}{8}$ in. (28 mm).

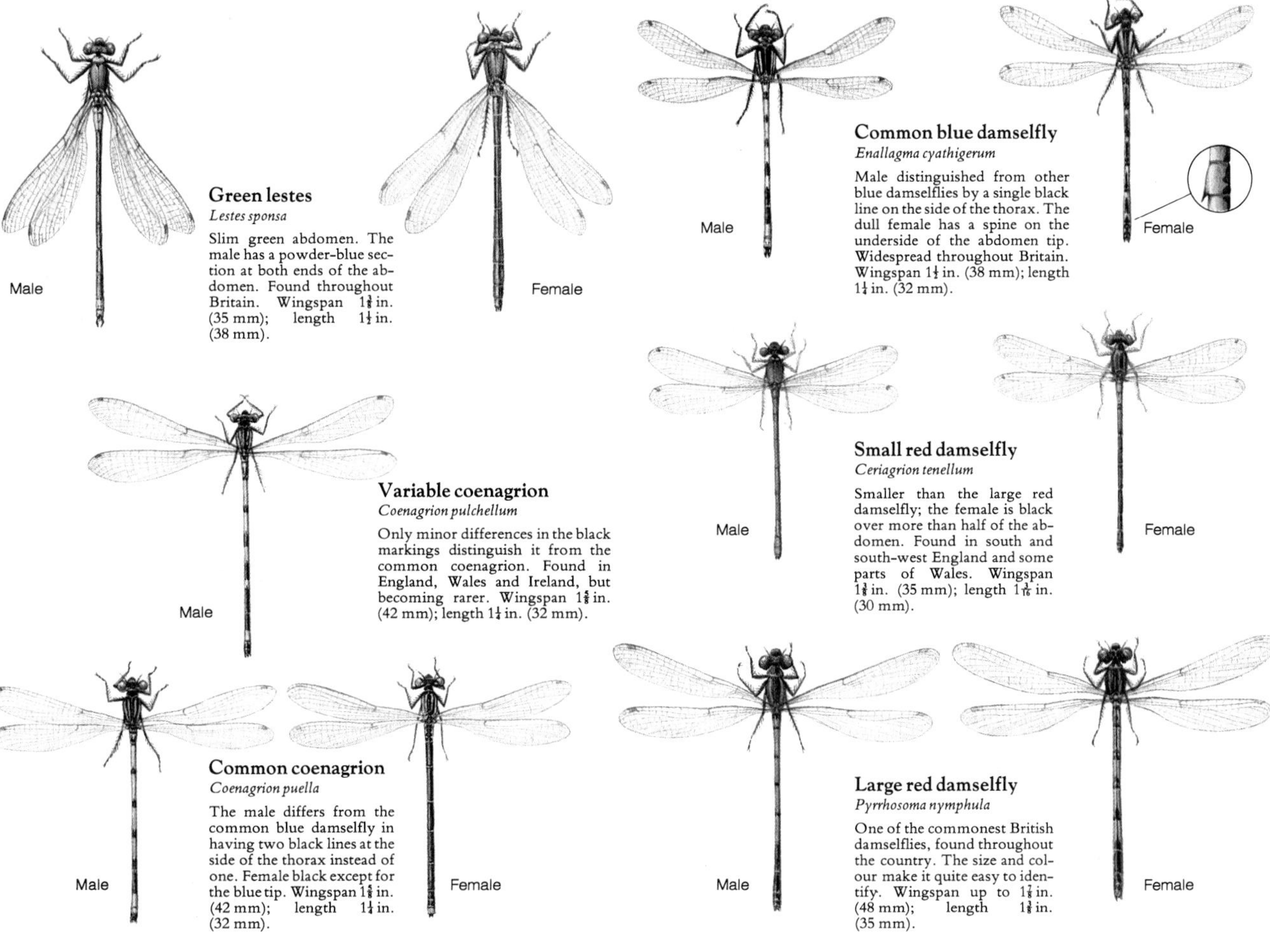

Green lestes

Lestes sponsa

Slim green abdomen. The male has a powder-blue section at both ends of the abdomen. Found throughout Britain. Wingspan 1⅜ in. (35 mm); length 1½ in. (38 mm).

Variable coenagrion

Coenagrion pulchellum

Only minor differences in the black markings distinguish it from the common coenagrion. Found in England, Wales and Ireland, but becoming rarer. Wingspan 1⅝ in. (42 mm); length 1¼ in. (32 mm).

Common coenagrion

Coenagrion puella

The male differs from the common blue damselfly in having two black lines at the side of the thorax instead of one. Female black except for the blue tip. Wingspan 1⅝ in. (42 mm); length 1¼ in. (32 mm).

Common blue damselfly

Enallagma cyathigerum

Male distinguished from other blue damselflies by a single black line on the side of the thorax. The dull female has a spine on the underside of the abdomen tip. Widespread throughout Britain. Wingspan 1½ in. (38 mm); length 1¼ in. (32 mm).

Small red damselfly

Ceriagrion tenellum

Smaller than the large red damselfly; the female is black over more than half of the abdomen. Found in south and south-west England and some parts of Wales. Wingspan 1⅜ in. (35 mm); length $1\frac{3}{16}$ in. (30 mm).

Large red damselfly

Pyrrhosoma nymphula

One of the commonest British damselflies, found throughout the country. The size and colour make it quite easy to identify. Wingspan up to 1⅞ in. (48 mm); length 1⅜ in. (35 mm).

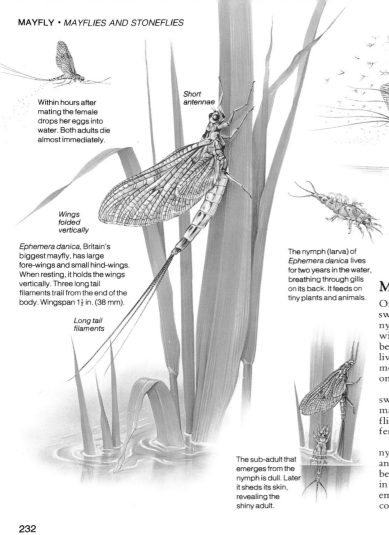

Within hours after mating the female drops her eggs into water. Both adults die almost immediately.

Short antennae

Wings folded vertically

Ephemera danica, Britain's biggest mayfly, has large fore-wings and small hind-wings. When resting, it holds the wings vertically. Three long tail filaments trail from the end of the body. Wingspan 1½ in. (38 mm).

Long tail filaments

In summer, male mayflies swarm over the water in the evening. When a female enters the swarm, mating takes place in mid-air.

The nymph (larva) of *Ephemera danica* lives for two years in the water, breathing through gills on its back. It feeds on tiny plants and animals.

An adult mayfly (top left) leaves its sub-adult skin below it, while another sub-adult (right) prepares to moult.

The sub-adult that emerges from the nymph is dull. Later it sheds its skin, revealing the shiny adult.

Mayfly *Ephemera danica*

On summer evenings the air around streams and lakes may swarm with mayflies. They emerge from their full-grown nymphs during the day, mate in the evening, and drop their eggs within hours. The following morning most will have died and been eaten by fish. Mayflies are unable to eat during their brief lives, as their mouthparts are almost useless. The female is little more than a sac of eggs, partly inflated with air so she can fly to one of the males who will make the eggs fertile.

The flight of the mayfly is weak, making it easy prey for swallows and martins as they swoop over the water. As trout eat mayflies in great numbers anglers imitate them with artificial flies – the 'green drake' for the sub-adult, 'grey drake' for the female and 'black drake' for the male.

The mayfly is unique among insects in emerging from the nymph as a sub-adult, equipped with wings but dull in colour and incapable of mating. Within a short time it sheds its skin to become the glistening adult. Forty-six species of mayfly occur in Britain, most of them widely distributed. They begin to emerge as adults in May – hence their name – but some species continue late into summer.

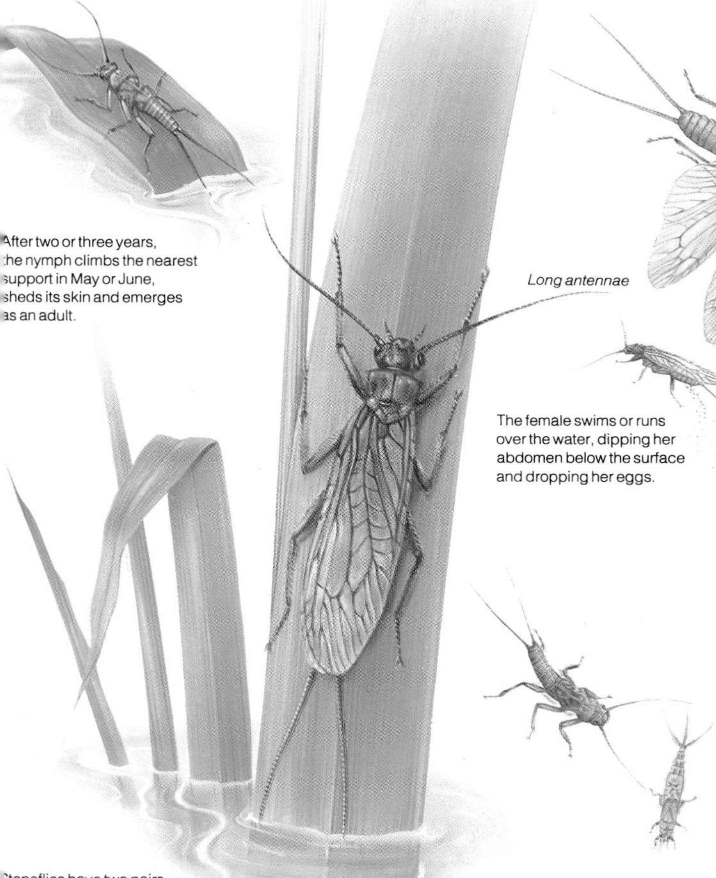

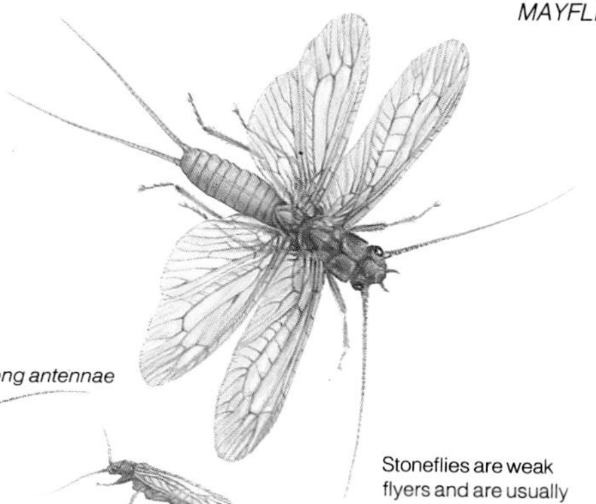

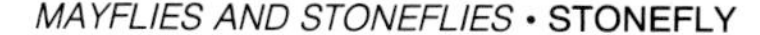

After two or three years, the nymph climbs the nearest support in May or June, sheds its skin and emerges as an adult.

Long antennae

The female swims or runs over the water, dipping her abdomen below the surface and dropping her eggs.

Stoneflies are weak flyers and are usually seen on the ground. *Perla bipunctata*, one of Britain's largest stoneflies, has a wingspan of about 2 in. (50 mm).

A stonefly discards its nymphal skin to start adult life. Most stoneflies are in the north and west of Britain.

Stoneflies have two pairs of wings which they fold flat along the body when resting. The antennae and tail filaments are almost as long as the body.

The nymph (larva) of the stonefly has a flat body and two tail filaments. The mayfly nymph, one of its prey, has three tail filaments.

Stonefly *Perla bipunctata*

Its habit of crawling over stony banks of rocky streams, especially in upland areas, gives the stonefly its name. Many of the 34 British species are widespread, but they are rarely found in still water and are very sensitive to water pollution. Most of the stonefly's life is spent in the water as a nymph (larva). The adults live for only two or three weeks. They are weak flyers and spend most of the time hiding among stones and vegetation beside the streams.

Adult stoneflies eat very little and live mainly on fats stored during the nymphal stage. They are preyed on by birds and fish, and anglers use them for bait. Even the two largest British stoneflies, *Perla bipunctata* and *Dinocras cephalotes*, are rarely seen because of their secretive habits. Other members of the group, such as the needlefly which looks like a tiny rolled umbrella, are about half their size and much thinner bodied.

The nymphs of the stonefly are preyed on by carnivorous insects such as water bugs, beetles and dragonfly nymphs. *Perla bipunctata*'s nymph is itself a predator of small water creatures, but other stonefly nymphs are vegetarian, feeding on simple plants such as algae.

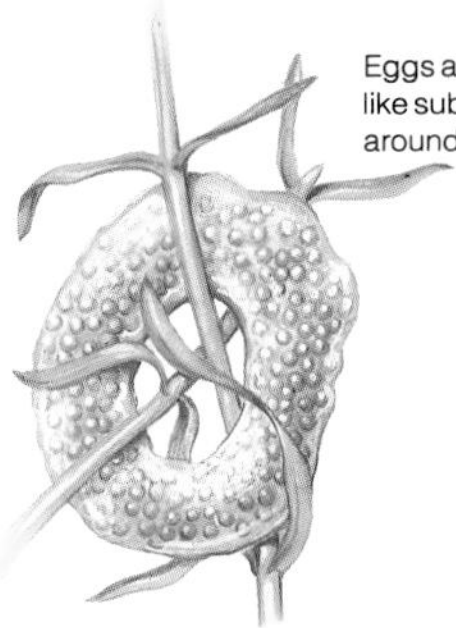

Eggs are laid in ropes of jelly-like substance entwined around submerged plants.

Caddisflies mostly fly at night, and are sometimes attracted to artificial light, like moths.

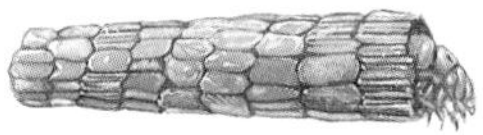

The larva of *Phryganea grandis* builds a protective case out of pieces of leaf. It feeds on algae and plant fragments as it drags the case over the lake bottom.

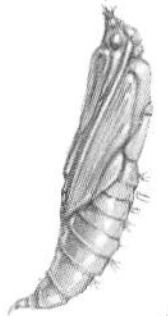

After a year, the larva changes into a pupa which emerges as the adult caddisfly in two or three weeks. Here the pupa is shown removed from its case.

Long antennae

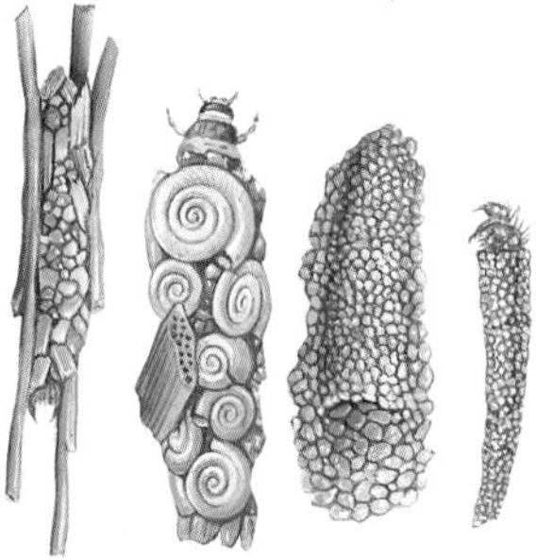

Other species of caddis make different types of cases out of pieces of stick, tiny shells or sand grains.

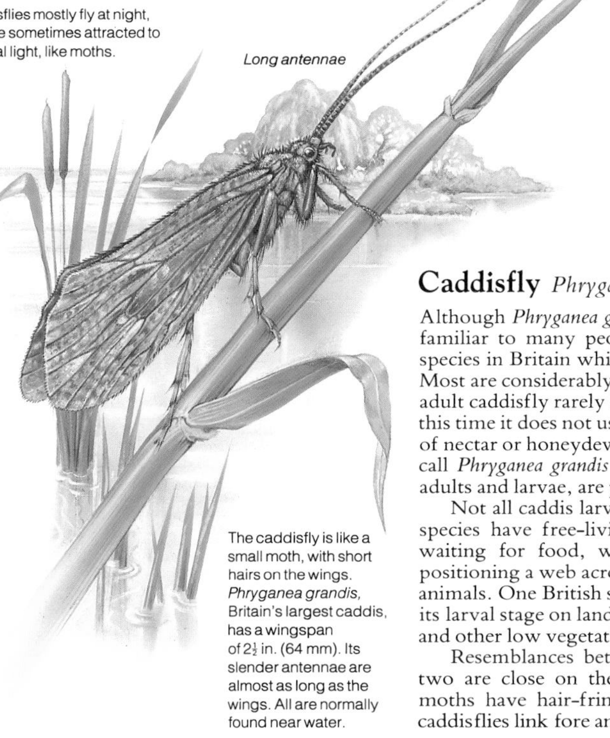

The caddisfly is like a small moth, with short hairs on the wings. *Phryganea grandis*, Britain's largest caddis, has a wingspan of 2½ in. (64 mm). Its slender antennae are almost as long as the wings. All are normally found near water.

In the daytime the caddisfly hides or waterside plants. Its wings are held ang-led like a roof over the body.

Caddisfly *Phryganea grandis*

Although *Phryganea grandis*, Britain's largest caddisfly, may b familiar to many people, there are 190 or so other caddisfly species in Britain which are less familiar and harder to identify Most are considerably smaller and brownish-grey in colour. Ar adult caddisfly rarely lives much longer than a week and during this time it does not usually feed, except perhaps for some drops of nectar or honeydew. Anglers know the adults as 'sedges' and call *Phryganea grandis* the large red sedge. Caddisflies, as both adults and larvae, are part of the diet of many fish.

Not all caddis larvae make a protective case to live in; some species have free-living larvae. Some lurk on the river bed waiting for food, while others spin webs between stones positioning a web across the current flow so that it captures tiny animals. One British species, *Enoicyla pusilla*, is unique in living its larval stage on land; it completes its life-cycle among mosses and other low vegetation near water.

Resemblances between caddisflies and moths suggest the two are close on the evolutionary tree. For example, some moths have hair-fringed wings as caddisflies do; and some caddisflies link fore and hind-wings in flight as moths do.

Vhile the female eats the saliva he has been offered, the male nates with her.

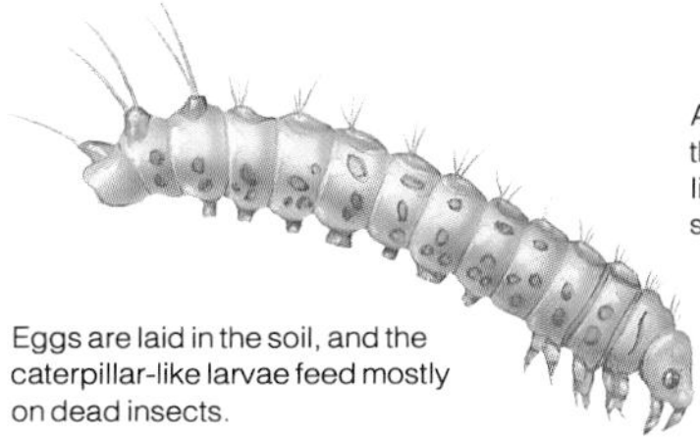

Eggs are laid in the soil, and the caterpillar-like larvae feed mostly on dead insects.

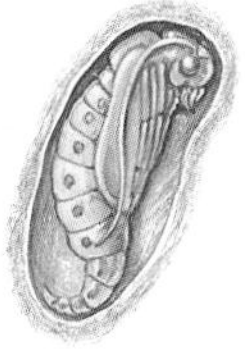

After hibernating through the winter, the larvae pupate in a small chamber lined with silk. The adults hatch in the summer.

The female's abdomen tapers to a point at the rear. As part of their courtship she is offered a drop of saliva which the male places on a leaf near her.

Scorpionflies are seen from May to July, often beneath hedgerows, feeding on dead insects or insect pupae.

Scorpion-like tip

Beak

The male's abdomen is shaped like a scorpion's tail. It is not a sting but a genital capsule tipped with a claw used to hold the female while mating. The beak-like head is used for feeding. Wingspan 1¼ in. (32 mm).

Scorpionfly *Panorpa communis*

Only the male scorpionfly has the distinctive reddish up-curved tip to the abdomen after which these insects are named. It is not a sting but the genital region. At the very tip is a claw which the male uses for grasping the female during mating. The exact shape of this genital capsule is the most reliable feature for distinguishing the three British species of scorpionfly from one another. The wing pattern is not a reliable distinguishing feature since it varies in individuals within one species. *Panorpa communis* and *Panorpa germanica* are the two largest and most common species, found throughout Britain. The third species, *Panorpa cognata*, is slightly smaller with a very square, broad segment at the base of the genital capsule. The species occurs mostly in chalky areas in southern England.

Scorpionflies seem to dislike direct sunshine and so are more often seen on the shady side of hedgerows. They also live near nettle beds and bramble thickets. They fly about the plants unhurriedly looking for dead insects and fruits to feed on, or for a mate. The male distracts the female with an offering of his saliva before he mates with her. Without this distraction she is likely to attack and kill him.

The female lays mats of eggs on reeds or other water plants in early summer. Each egg is like a tiny gas cylinder on end.

The larvae spend about two years on the bottom of a lake or river, moving with undulating motions of the body. They live on tiny insects.

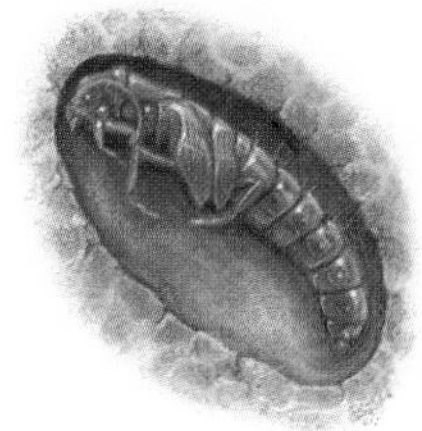

The larva crawls out of the water and turns into a pupa in an oval cell made in mud or debris. The adult emerges a few weeks later.

Alderflies are poor flyers, and when they do take off usually travel only a few yards. Wingspan about 1⅓ in. (35 mm).

The female alderfly lays the cylinder-shaped eggs on a stem and ranges them in compact rows to form an oval mass.

Alderfly *Sialis lutaria*

Despite their names, there is no direct connection between alderflies and alder trees, but both are typical of the lakeside, and the insects may well be found resting on the trees. The heavy-bodied alderfly rarely flies and is most often seen clinging motionless to a reed frond or stem. Such flights as it takes are usually at dusk. Of the two native species, *Sialis lutaria* is the commoner and appears in early summer. The very similar *Sialis fuliginosa* appears slightly later – in June or July – and likes faster-flowing waters.

Female alderflies are prolific egg-layers, often producing several batches of up to 2,000 eggs, characteristically arranged in neat mats. On hatching, the tiny larvae usually fall into the water, where they sink to the bottom and begin their two-year predatory life. By contrast, the adults, which live only a few days, eat very little except perhaps some petals of waterside flowers or pollen and nectar from them.

Anglers commonly use alderflies as bait, especially for trout. The adults are particularly convenient for this purpose because they are so slow-moving that they can easily be picked off vegetation between finger and thumb.

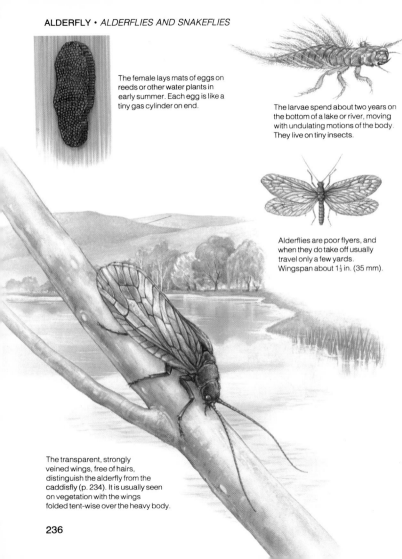

The transparent, strongly veined wings, free of hairs, distinguish the alderfly from the caddisfly (p. 234). It is usually seen on vegetation with the wings folded tent-wise over the heavy body.

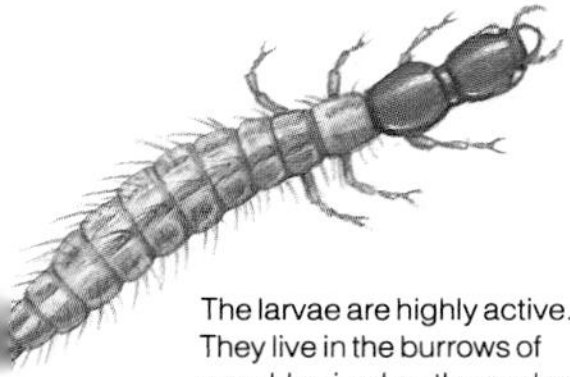

The larvae are highly active. They live in the burrows of wood-boring beetles and eat the beetle larvae.

The pupa forms under the bark. Female pupae have a sheath containing the egg-laying tube doubled back over the body.

Adults are on the wing between May and July. Although uncommon, they are seen in glades of conifer or deciduous woods.

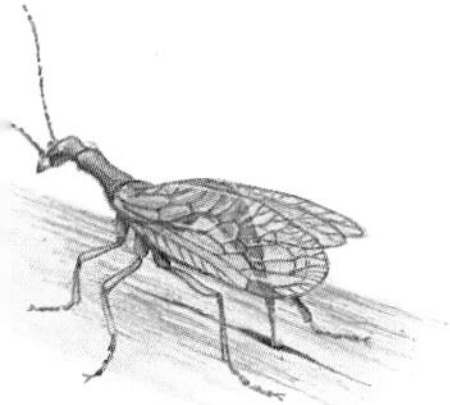

Females lay their eggs in cracks in tree bark, especially in diseased or dying trees. The eggs are often laid in the tunnels of bark-beetle larvae.

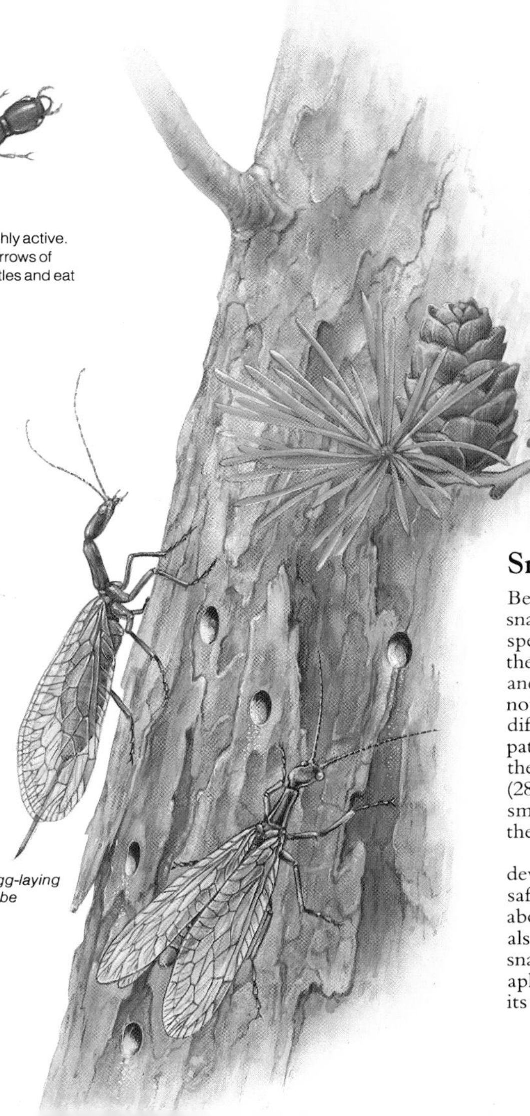

The triangular head can be bent at an angle to the neck-like extension of the thorax, giving the appearance of a threatening cobra – hence the name. The female has a long egg-laying tube that looks like a sting. Wingspan 1 in. (25 mm).

Egg-laying tube

Snakefly *Raphidia maculicollis*

Because of their distinctive shape and large, delicate wings, snakeflies are among the easiest insects to identify. Only four species occur in Britain, none of them very common. Mostly they occur among vegetation in light woodland or near rivers and streams. They do not fly very readily or far and so are rarely noticed. The four species are very similar to one another but differ slightly in the shape of the head and in the venation, or pattern of veins, in the wings. *Raphidia maculicollis* is probably the commonest. *Raphidia notata*, with a wingspan of about $1\frac{1}{8}$ in. (28 mm) and a tapering head, is the largest. *Raphidia cognata* is smaller and has a more triangular head. *Raphidia xanthostigma*, the smallest snakefly, is found mostly near willows.

Snakefly larvae are narrow-bodied with small but well-developed jaws. If startled they can easily run backwards to a safe place. The pupae are unusual in being fairly active; they run about freely, especially just before the adults emerge. They can also snap their jaws at tiny insects that disturb them. Adult snakeflies are predators, like the larvae, feeding mostly on aphids and scale-insects. When the adult emerges from its pupa, its wings are cloudy, but they soon become transparent.

The green lacewing has large eyes that glow like live coals when they catch the light.
Translucent lace-like wings
The larva forms a pupa in a cocoon of whitish silk attached to dead leaves or beneath bark or logs.

The larvae have huge jaws with which they suck the tissues of other insects, such as aphids. They are 5/16 in. (8 mm) in length.

The females of *Chrysopa carnea* lay their eggs at the end of long stalks of hardened mucus, helping to protect them from predators.

Chrysopa carnea, with its delicately patterned wings and green body, is one of the commonest green lacewings.

Brown lacewing
Kimminsia subnebulosa

Smaller than the green lacewing, with dusky grey-brown wings and body. It is widely distributed in Britain on low vegetation and shrubs. Wingspan 3/4 in. (20 mm).

Slender green insects with long antennae and large wings covered by a lacework of veins. They are seen in late spring and summer, but rarely fly during the day unless they are disturbed from low vegetation. They may be attracted to artificial light on summer evenings. Wingspan 1 3/16 in. (30 mm).

Green lacewing *Chrysopa carnea*

These delicate insects with their translucent, lace-like wings are most often seen perching low down on plants, frequently in gardens. There are two generations each year. The species *Chrysopa carnea* spends the winter as an adult, often in houses where its pale green colour changes to a drab pinkish-brown. In spring the green colouring returns as it becomes active again. These spring lacewings give rise to a summer generation which produces the next generation that hibernates through winter. Most other species of green lacewing hibernate as larvae.

Both adult lacewings and larvae eat soft-bodied insects, especially aphids. The larvae are completely carnivorous, and eat by piercing the aphids and sucking out their body liquids. The adults chew up their prey whole and may also drink the nectar of flowers. Many lacewing larvae avoid detection by birds by decorating themselves with debris and the skins of aphids, as well as their own cast-off skins. The adults can defend themselves by exuding an unpleasant-smelling fluid.

There are 14 species of green lacewings and 29 species of smaller brown lacewings in Britain. Both types are widely distributed, although they are most common in the south.

After dark, the giant lacewing flies along woodland streams, especially in the south of England.

The larvae live in moss near water where they feed on small, soft-bodied insects such as the larvae of midges (bloodworms).

The large size of the wings in relation to the body make the flight of the giant lacewing cumbersome and slow.

Britain's largest species of lacewing, with a reddish-brown head and lacy, mottled wings. They may be found on the foliage of waterside trees, or the undersides of bridges and the brickwork of culverts. Wingspan about 2 in. (50 mm).

Sponge fly
Sisyra fuscata

Closely related to the giant lacewing, but with duskier, more rounded wings. Found in similar situations between May and September. Wingspan ½ in. (13 mm).

Giant lacewing *Osmylus fulvicephalus*

The large size and the distinctively spotted wings of the giant lacewing make it an easy insect to identify. It is Britain's largest lacewing, found from May to July in many parts of England, Wales and Ireland, although it is rare in Scotland. Giant lacewings are sluggish flyers and during the day they usually rest on plants beside clear, unpolluted rivers and streams, frequently in colonies. They emerge at night, safe from the danger of birds, and fly along the river banks in search of mates and egg-laying sites, as well as small insects for food.

Their larvae are semi-aquatic, living in water or wet moss. They breathe air through openings, known as spiracles, in the abdomen and thorax. They hatch from eggs during July and feed on the larvae of other insects, particularly those of small flies. In winter they hibernate in wet moss, and the following spring they form pupae.

Another type of lacewing, the sponge fly, is found right through summer all over the British Isles, except in Scotland. It is similar to the brown lacewing (opposite page) but smaller, and has larvae that live in the water, eating freshwater sponges and microscopic animals.

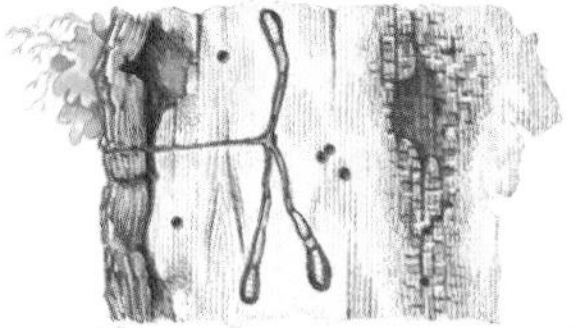

Female

The young larvae bore at right-angles to the tunnel in the outer sapwood, and later move closer to the surface.

Each larva forms its pupation chamber about ½ in. (13 mm) below the surface.

The giant wood wasp makes a distinctive buzzing sound in flight, and is a fearsome looking insect, although harmless.

Male

The female lays between three and seven eggs in each tunnel that she bores in unhealthy pine trees. She has up to 400 eggs, which hatch in three or four weeks.

A large black-and-yellow wasp with no 'waist' between the thorax and abdomen. The female has a formidable egg-laying organ which may be mistaken for a sting, but which is used to bore into trees to lay eggs. The male is smaller. The wasps range in size from ¾ in. to 1½ in. (20–38 mm).

Giant wood wasp *Urocerus gigas*

Horntail was the name once given to the giant wood wasp because of the impressive 'tail' on the female. These large wasps are found in pine woods and plantations in England, Wales and Scotland from June to October. They breed in rotten timbers of Scots pine, silver birch, larch and spruce. When laying eggs the female inspects the bark of the tree with her antennae and may make several exploratory bores with her ovipositor (egg-laying 'tail'). Finally, she repeatedly pushes her ovipositor into the wood. Occasionally she may become fatally trapped in the wood with her ovipositor stuck fast. The larvae spend up to three years in the tree, eating the wood, and the adults may not emerge until the tree has been cut down and used for timber.

Wood wasps and sawflies belong to the order Hymenoptera which includes ants, bees and wasps. They can be distinguished from bees and wasps by their lack of a conspicuous 'waist' on the abdomen. The giant wood wasp is the largest of the British wood wasps. Sawflies are named after the sawing action of the female's ovipositor as she lays her eggs in plants. The larvae of the sawfly look like caterpillars of butterflies and moths, and eat the leaves and flowers of plants, shrubs and trees.

Other British wood wasps and sawflies

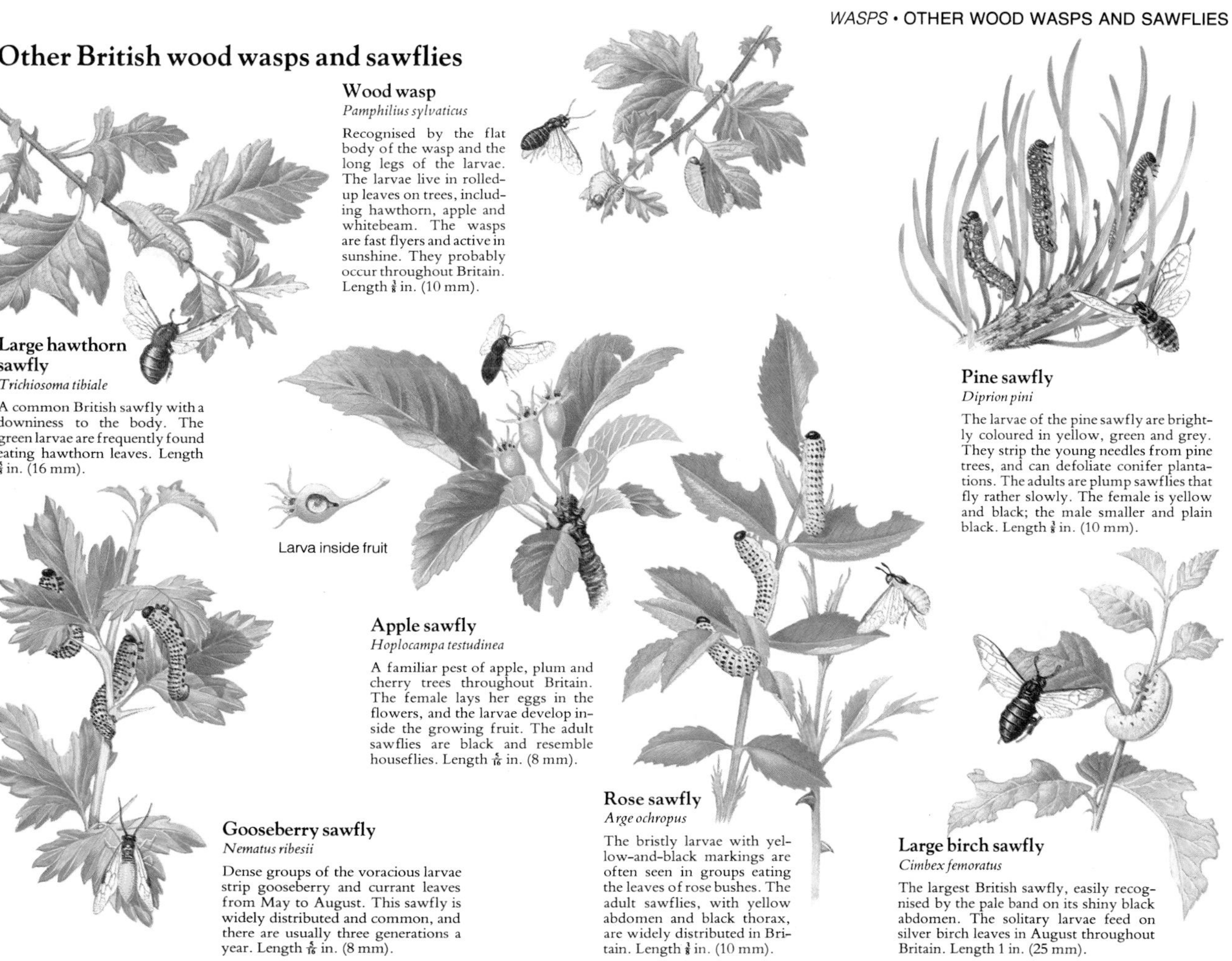

Wood wasp

Pamphilius sylvaticus

Recognised by the flat body of the wasp and the long legs of the larvae. The larvae live in rolled-up leaves on trees, including hawthorn, apple and whitebeam. The wasps are fast flyers and active in sunshine. They probably occur throughout Britain. Length ⅜ in. (10 mm).

Large hawthorn sawfly

Trichiosoma tibiale

A common British sawfly with a downiness to the body. The green larvae are frequently found eating hawthorn leaves. Length ⅝ in. (16 mm).

Pine sawfly

Diprion pini

The larvae of the pine sawfly are brightly coloured in yellow, green and grey. They strip the young needles from pine trees, and can defoliate conifer plantations. The adults are plump sawflies that fly rather slowly. The female is yellow and black; the male smaller and plain black. Length ⅜ in. (10 mm).

Apple sawfly

Hoplocampa testudinea

A familiar pest of apple, plum and cherry trees throughout Britain. The female lays her eggs in the flowers, and the larvae develop inside the growing fruit. The adult sawflies are black and resemble houseflies. Length 5/16 in. (8 mm).

Gooseberry sawfly

Nematus ribesii

Dense groups of the voracious larvae strip gooseberry and currant leaves from May to August. This sawfly is widely distributed and common, and there are usually three generations a year. Length 5/16 in. (8 mm).

Rose sawfly

Arge ochropus

The bristly larvae with yellow-and-black markings are often seen in groups eating the leaves of rose bushes. The adult sawflies, with yellow abdomen and black thorax, are widely distributed in Britain. Length ⅜ in. (10 mm).

Large birch sawfly

Cimbex femoratus

The largest British sawfly, easily recognised by the pale band on its shiny black abdomen. The solitary larvae feed on silver birch leaves in August throughout Britain. Length 1 in. (25 mm).

In late spring, queen wasps remove wood fibre from posts or logs and chew it into a paste to make their nests.

Common wasps usually build their nests underground, in burrows left by small animals such as mice or voles. The papery cells are built up in horizontal tiers rather than the vertical combs of a beehive.

In spring and early summer, worker wasps kill large numbers of small pests such as sawfly caterpillars, aphids and flies to feed their own larvae.

Queen wasps look for hibernation sites in October, and may come indoors and settle in curtains.

The black markings on the yellow face of the common wasp are used to distinguish it from other species.

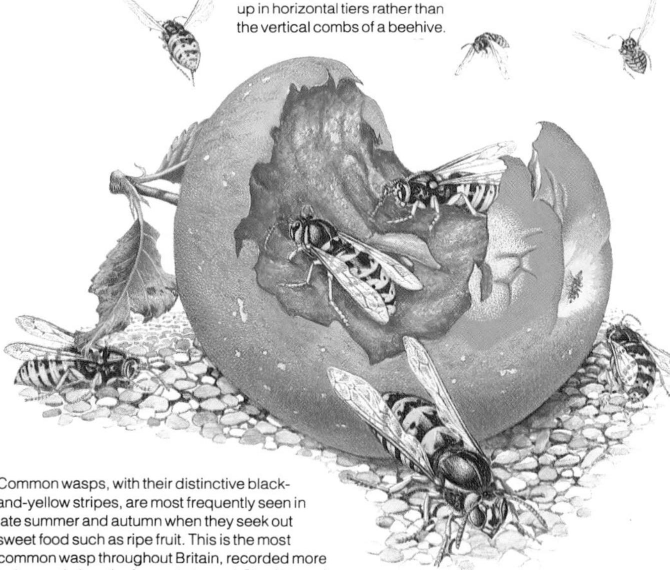

Common wasps, with their distinctive black-and-yellow stripes, are most frequently seen in late summer and autumn when they seek out sweet food such as ripe fruit. This is the most common wasp throughout Britain, recorded more in the south than the far north. Length $\frac{7}{8}$ in. (22 mm).

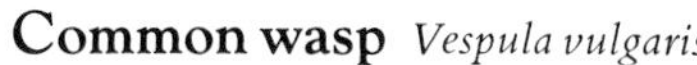

Common wasp *Vespula vulgaris*

There are seven species of social wasp in Britain, including the common wasp familiar in late-summer gardens. Unlike the honey-bee, the wasp has an unbarbed sting which can be used several times. It is a weapon to kill insects for food, and to provide a deterrent against lizards and birds. Like honey-bees, social wasps live in groups of queen, drones and workers – up to 2,000 common wasps in a colony compared to 50,000 bees.

Wasps, which include hornets, are not often seen early in the year as they spend their time killing insects such as aphids and caterpillars which they feed to their larvae. In return the wasps feed on a sweet saliva that the larvae produce. In late summer, the queen stops laying eggs, and there are no more larvae to provide saliva. The wasps then seek out other sources of sweet food such as jam and windfall fruit, and become scavengers in gardens and orchards. In the autumn the drones and the workers all die, leaving the fertilised queen to hibernate. W. H. Hudson wrote of hornets in *Hampshire Days* in 1903: 'These large-sized October hornets are all females, wanderers from ruined homes, in search of sheltered places, where, foodless and homeless . . . each may live through the four dreary months to come.'

Six more social wasps

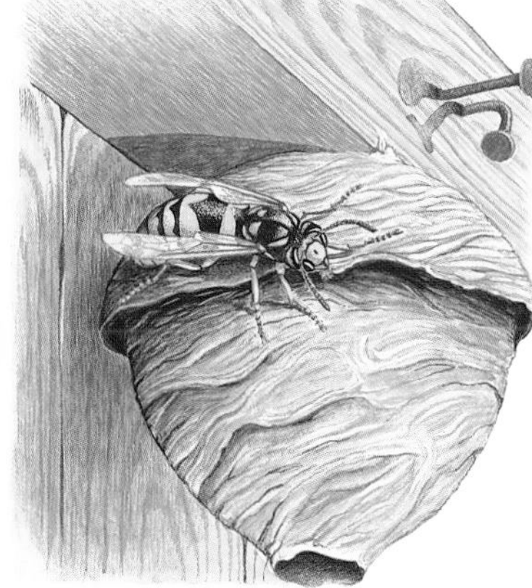

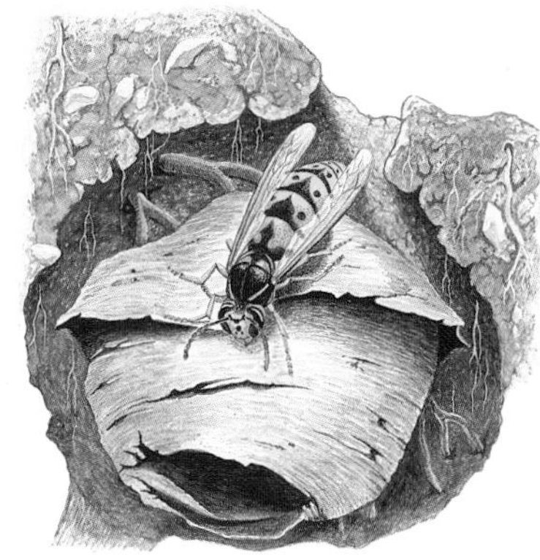

Hornet
Vespa crabro

The largest British wasp, but now rare. It has almost disappeared from south-east and central England, possibly because of persecution and the loss of old trees in which it nested. Length 1¼ in. (32 mm).

German wasp
Vespula germanica

A widespread species occurring mostly in England and Wales, decreasing northwards. It is identified by the three dots on its 'face'. It nests in the ground. Length ⅞ in. (22 mm).

Tree wasp
Dolichovespula sylvestris

This wasp makes its nest in enclosed places such as hollow trees, wall cavities and lofts, although some will live underground. It is found mostly in the south of England and patchily farther north, as far as the north of Scotland. Length ⅞ in. (22 mm).

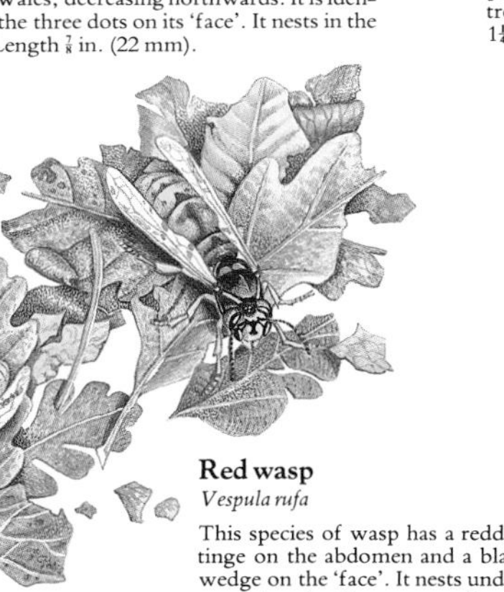

Cuckoo wasp
Vespula austriaca

The female wasp makes no nest but lays its eggs in the nest of the red wasp, which it closely resembles. The larvae are raised by the red wasp workers. The cuckoo wasp has a scattered distribution in the West Country, the north of England and Wales, Scotland and Ireland. Length ¾ in. (20 mm).

Red wasp
Vespula rufa

This species of wasp has a reddish tinge on the abdomen and a black wedge on the 'face'. It nests underground under litter, mats of grass and wood. It is common throughout the British Isles, excluding Orkney and the Shetlands. Length ⅞ in. (22 mm).

Norwegian wasp
Dolichovespula norvegica

More common in the north but has patchy distribution throughout England, Wales, Scotland and Ireland. Identified by the continuous black mark across its face. It nests on branches of trees and shrubs as well as under the eaves of houses. Length ⅞ in. (22 mm).

Solitary and parasitic wasps

The great majority of wasps in Britain do not live in colonies like the common wasp. They live alone, laying their eggs in solitary nests or in the bodies of living hosts. Many have the typical yellow-and-black markings of the social wasps; others have long, chestnut coloured bodies.

Female solitary wasps make burrows into which they deposit a single egg and a store of food – in many cases caterpillars, flies, spiders or aphids which are paralysed but alive, ready to be eaten by the wasp grubs when they hatch. Once the female wasp has laid her egg and provided the food store, she leaves and never sees the offspring.

Parasitic wasps build no nest for their offspring but inject their eggs into the bodies of caterpillars or the grubs of other wasps or bees. The egg hatches into a grub which eats the living host from within, leaving the vital organs until last.

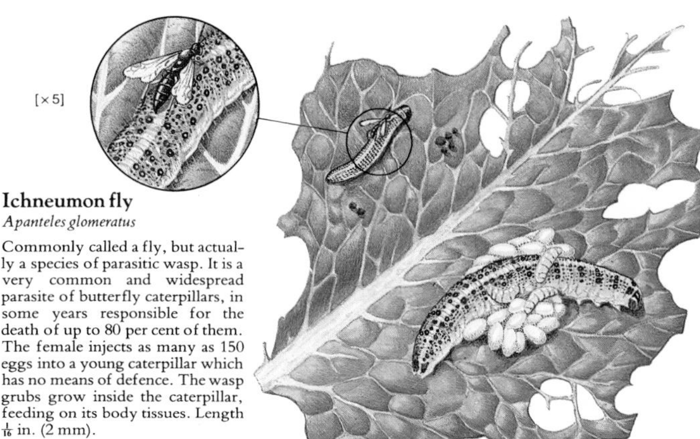

When fully grown, the parasites eat their way out of the host and make clusters of yellow cocoons. The host quickly dies.

Ichneumon fly

Apanteles glomeratus

Commonly called a fly, but actually a species of parasitic wasp. It is a very common and widespread parasite of butterfly caterpillars, in some years responsible for the death of up to 80 per cent of them. The female injects as many as 150 eggs into a young caterpillar which has no means of defence. The wasp grubs grow inside the caterpillar, feeding on its body tissues. Length $\frac{1}{16}$ in. (2 mm).

Sand digger wasp

Ammophila sabulosa

This is the largest species of wasp found in sandy and heathland areas from southern England to Cheshire, including Wales. It puts a paralysed caterpillar in a burrow, lays an egg on it and seals the burrow. The wasp larva develops in safety. Length $\frac{3}{4}$ in. (20 mm).

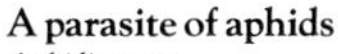

A chalcid parasite

Torymus auratus

The common spangle gall on oak leaves is caused by a small cynipid wasp that lives inside. This chalcid wasp injects its eggs into the galls and its larvae eat the larvae of the cynipid wasp. It is common in southern England.
Length $\frac{1}{8}$ in. (3 mm).

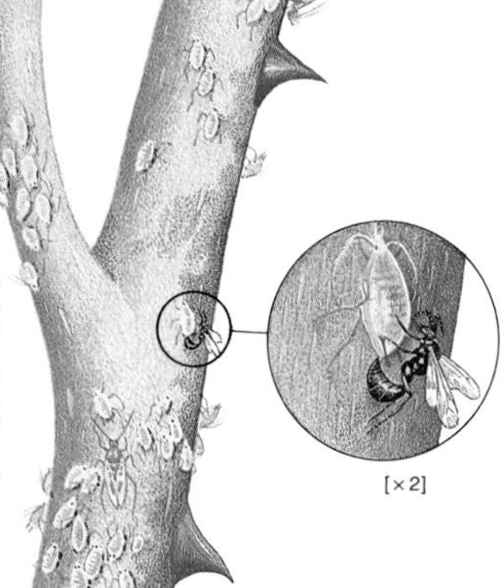

A parasite of aphids

Aphidius wasp

Aphids such as the rose aphid (greenfly) are parasitised by the *Aphidius* wasp. The female wasp identifies the aphid with her antennae and then curls up her body to inject an egg into it. The wasp larva feeds on the body tissue of the aphid and eventually emerges leaving the empty husk of the host on the plant.
Length $\frac{3}{16}$ in. (5 mm).

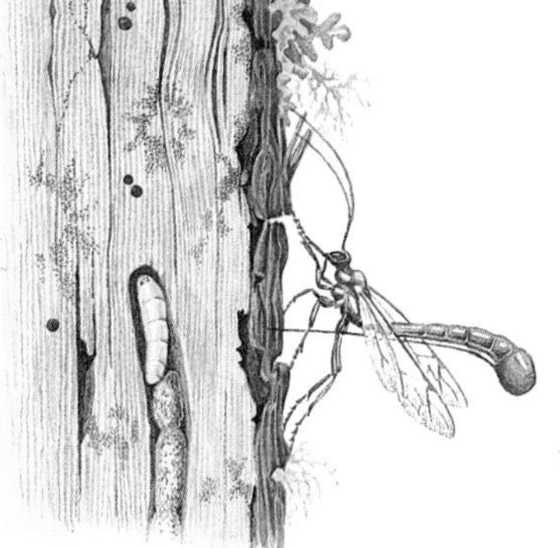

An ichneumonid parasite

Rhysella approximator

This parasitic wasp detects the tunnel of the alder wood wasp through the bark of a tree, bores a hole and lays an egg in the wood wasp's larva. However, when the *Rhysella* larva develops, it may in turn be parasitised by another parasitic wasp called *Pseudorhyssa* – a hyperparasite. Length $\frac{5}{8}$ in. (16 mm).

Spider-hunting pompilid

Anoplius viaticus

Another parasitic wasp which paralyses spiders with its venom. It constructs a burrow, pulls in its victim and lays an egg on its underside. The burrow is then sealed and the larva develops on the spider. The wasps are seen in early summer.
Length $\frac{1}{2}$ in. (13 mm).

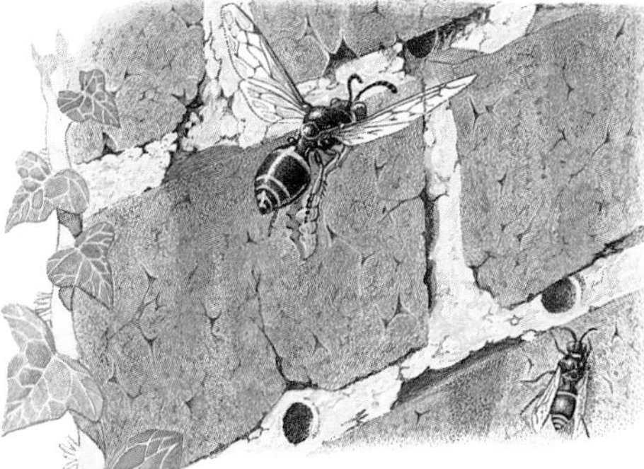

Mason wasp

Odyneurus spinipes

One of 19 species of vespid wasps found in Britain. Vespid wasps make a nest in loose mortar and furnish it with a paralysed caterpillar and an egg. The wasp larva develops on the caterpillar. This species is found as far north as Ayr in Strathclyde. Length $\frac{1}{2}$ in. (13 mm).

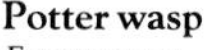

Potter wasp

Eumenes wasp

A solitary vespid wasp recognised by its curved abdomen. It occurs on sandy heathlands. The female makes a fragile pot on vegetation by mixing sand with her saliva. She stocks the pot with a paralysed caterpillar and an egg, and then seals it up for the larva to develop. Length $\frac{1}{2}$ in. (13 mm)

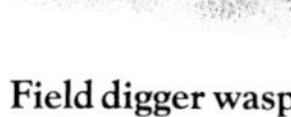

Field digger wasp

Mellinus arvensis

Occurs in sandy areas in the summer and autumn. The large female paralyses flies and puts them, together with her eggs, in cells prepared in the sand. The field digger wasp is widespread in Britain.
Length $\frac{1}{2}$ in. (13 mm).

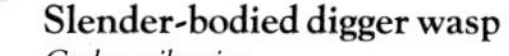

Slender-bodied digger wasp

Crabro cribrarius

This solitary wasp paralyses large flies, and places them, with an egg, inside a burrow. It occurs in sandy areas as far north as Nairn, Highland. Length $\frac{7}{16}$ in. (11 mm).

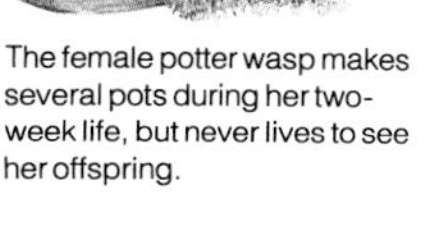

The female potter wasp makes several pots during her two-week life, but never lives to see her offspring.

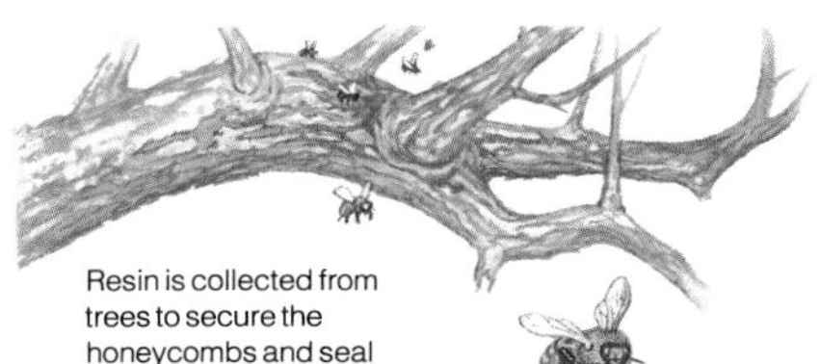

Resin is collected from trees to secure the honeycombs and seal gaps. Bees have collected warm tar in the absence of trees.

Cells where new queens will be hatched stand out from the ranks of worker cells. They are about $1\frac{3}{8}$ in. (35 mm) long.

Cells for new workers are the smallest of the breeding cells – only $\frac{3}{16}$ in. (5 mm) in diameter.

Cells for rearing new drones are $\frac{1}{4}$ in. (6 mm) in diameter.

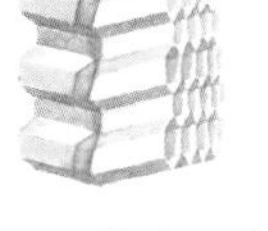

To prevent the honey from running out, cells are built sloping upwards at an angle of 13 degrees.

Water-carrying bees collect water from ponds and puddles each day in spring and summer so that wax can be made in the hive.

A bee presses the cell wall with her antennae to check that it is the correct thickness.

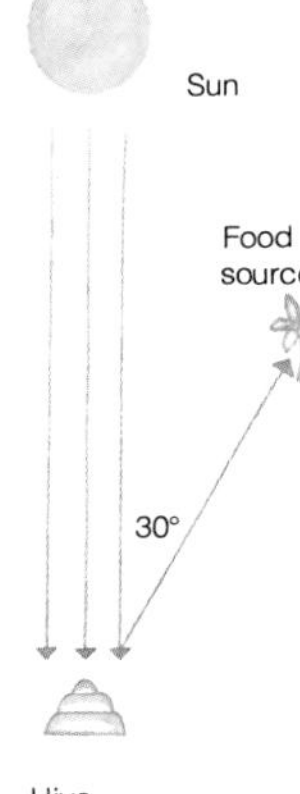

Other workers follow dancing bee

Bees inform others of a fresh source of food with a dance on the face of the honeycomb. A figure-of-eight dance, with the central path 30 degrees to the right, means that food is 30 degrees to the right of the sun.

Nectar – the sweet juice secreted by many plants – is stored in the bee's 'honey-stomach' to be regurgitated at the hive. Here it is being taken from the base of a bluebell.

Workers secrete scales of wax from glands on the undersides of their abdomen. They lift it on their legs and knead it into lumps with their jaws to make honeycomb.

A worker collects pollen from the ripe anthers of a flower. She carries it back to the hive in the pollen baskets on her back legs.

A worker regurgitates nectar from her honey-stomach into a cell of the honeycomb. The evaporated nectar becomes honey.

Drones are slightly larger than workers and have wider heads but no sting. They make a loud buzzing sound when flying and may be seen near a hive. Length $\frac{3}{4}$ in. (20 mm).

The queen is larger than the others, but she stays inside the colony for most of her life and is unlikely to be seen. Length $\frac{7}{8}$ in. (22 mm).

Honey-bees form colonies in hollow trees, or in cavity walls which they enter through air bricks.

After bees gather nectar and pollen from flowers, the nectar is evaporated into honey and mixed with the pollen to make food for the larvae.

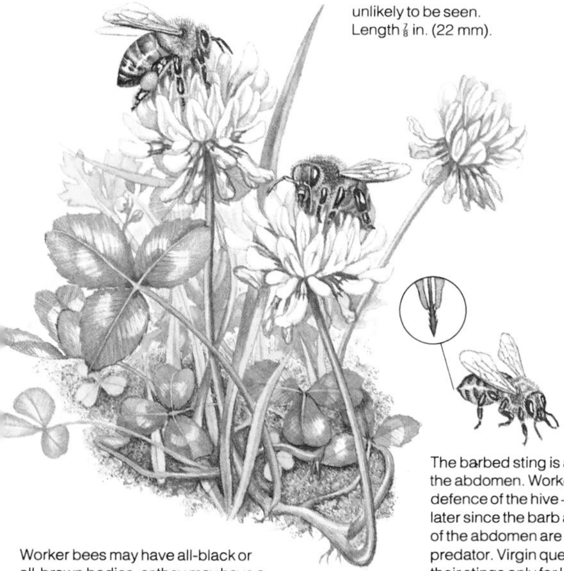

Worker bees may have all-black or all-brown bodies, or they may have a band of orange on the abdomen. Older bees lose some of the hairs on the thorax and have a bald appearance. Length $\frac{5}{8}$ in. (16 mm).

The barbed sting is at the end of the abdomen. Workers use it in defence of the hive – and die later since the barb and the tip of the abdomen are left in the predator. Virgin queens use their stings only for killing other queens. They survive, as their stings have no barbs.

Honey-bee *Apis mellifera*

The short life of the honey-bee, which in summer lasts for only three or four weeks, is filled with activity. Young bees start work in the colony's nursery repairing cells, cleaning out debris and feeding the growing larvae. Soon they make their first exploratory flights outside the hive to get to know their surroundings. Between flights they may guard the hive's entrance against intruders or help to ensure air circulation inside the hive by fanning the air with their wings, in company with other bees. Finally they join other mature bees in gathering water, nectar, pollen and resin to supply the hive's constant needs. They will fly as far as two miles from the colony and as they forage for pollen from plant to plant they pollinate wild flowers, farm crops and fruit trees. The bees that perform all these tasks are the workers, or sterile females. Unlike wasps which die off in the autumn, bees maintain a small part of their population through winter, in a state of semi-activity.

Honey is concentrated sugary nectar. It is used, together with protein-rich pollen, to feed the larvae and as winter food for the colony. A colony of 50,000 bees makes about 40 pounds of honey each summer.

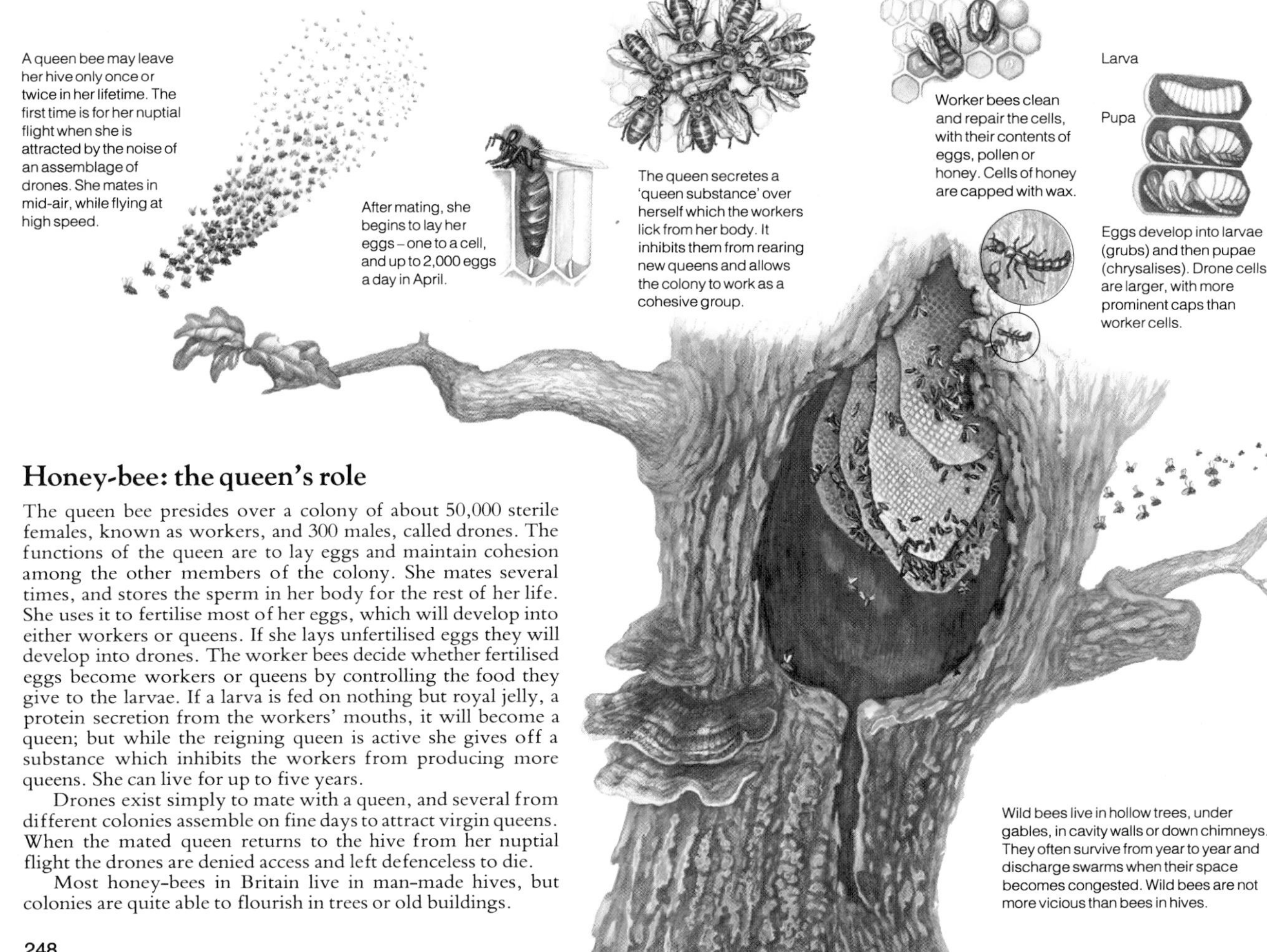

A queen bee may leave her hive only once or twice in her lifetime. The first time is for her nuptial flight when she is attracted by the noise of an assemblage of drones. She mates in mid-air, while flying at high speed.

After mating, she begins to lay her eggs – one to a cell, and up to 2,000 eggs a day in April.

The queen secretes a 'queen substance' over herself which the workers lick from her body. It inhibits them from rearing new queens and allows the colony to work as a cohesive group.

Worker bees clean and repair the cells, with their contents of eggs, pollen or honey. Cells of honey are capped with wax.

Eggs develop into larvae (grubs) and then pupae (chrysalises). Drone cells are larger, with more prominent caps than worker cells.

Wild bees live in hollow trees, under gables, in cavity walls or down chimneys. They often survive from year to year and discharge swarms when their space becomes congested. Wild bees are not more vicious than bees in hives.

Honey-bee: the queen's role

The queen bee presides over a colony of about 50,000 sterile females, known as workers, and 300 males, called drones. The functions of the queen are to lay eggs and maintain cohesion among the other members of the colony. She mates several times, and stores the sperm in her body for the rest of her life. She uses it to fertilise most of her eggs, which will develop into either workers or queens. If she lays unfertilised eggs they will develop into drones. The worker bees decide whether fertilised eggs become workers or queens by controlling the food they give to the larvae. If a larva is fed on nothing but royal jelly, a protein secretion from the workers' mouths, it will become a queen; but while the reigning queen is active she gives off a substance which inhibits the workers from producing more queens. She can live for up to five years.

Drones exist simply to mate with a queen, and several from different colonies assemble on fine days to attract virgin queens. When the mated queen returns to the hive from her nuptial flight the drones are denied access and left defenceless to die.

Most honey-bees in Britain live in man-made hives, but colonies are quite able to flourish in trees or old buildings.

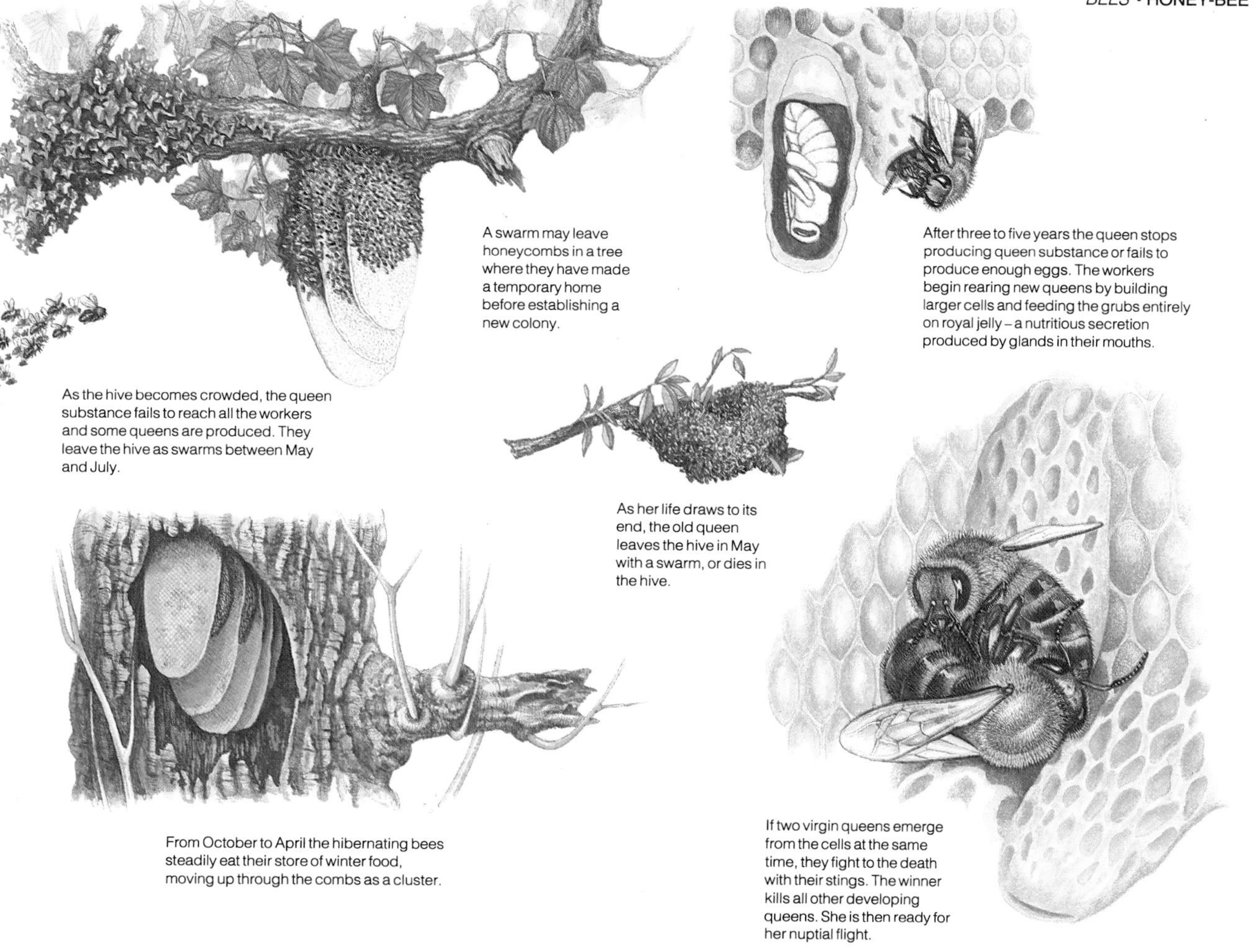

A swarm may leave honeycombs in a tree where they have made a temporary home before establishing a new colony.

After three to five years the queen stops producing queen substance or fails to produce enough eggs. The workers begin rearing new queens by building larger cells and feeding the grubs entirely on royal jelly – a nutritious secretion produced by glands in their mouths.

As the hive becomes crowded, the queen substance fails to reach all the workers and some queens are produced. They leave the hive as swarms between May and July.

As her life draws to its end, the old queen leaves the hive in May with a swarm, or dies in the hive.

From October to April the hibernating bees steadily eat their store of winter food, moving up through the combs as a cluster.

If two virgin queens emerge from the cells at the same time, they fight to the death with their stings. The winner kills all other developing queens. She is then ready for her nuptial flight.

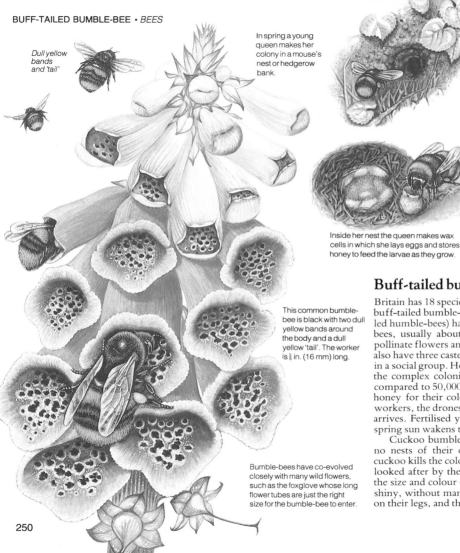

Dull yellow bands and 'tail'

In spring a young queen makes her colony in a mouse's nest or hedgerow bank.

Inside her nest the queen makes wax cells in which she lays eggs and stores honey to feed the larvae as they grow.

To attract females, male bumble-bees leave their scent along a circuit of 'buzzing-spots' which they patrol.

This common bumble-bee is black with two dull yellow bands around the body and a dull yellow 'tail'. The worker is $\frac{5}{8}$ in. (16 mm) long.

Bumble-bees have co-evolved closely with many wild flowers, such as the foxglove whose long flower tubes are just the right size for the bumble-bee to enter.

Buff-tailed bumble-bee *Bombus terrestris*

Britain has 18 species of bumble-bee, the largest of which is the buff-tailed bumble-bee *Bombus terrestris*. Bumble-bees (also called humble-bees) have much thicker, hairier bodies than honey-bees, usually about the same length. They forage for food, pollinate flowers and sting predators just like honey-bees. They also have three castes – workers, drones and a queen – which live in a social group. However, their colonies are much smaller than the complex colonies of honey-bees – up to 150 bumble-bees compared to 50,000 honey-bees. Bumbles do not make enough honey for their colonies to survive the winter. In autumn the workers, the drones and the old queen all die as the cold weather arrives. Fertilised young queens fly off and hibernate until the spring sun wakens them to found new colonies.

Cuckoo bumble-bees, of which there are six species, make no nests of their own, but enter bumble-bee colonies. The cuckoo kills the colony's queen and then lays its eggs, which are looked after by the host workers. The cuckoos usually mimic the size and colour of their hosts, but their bodies are relatively shiny, without many hairs. The females have no pollen baskets on their legs, and their buzz is less noisy.

Other British bumble-bees and cuckoo bees

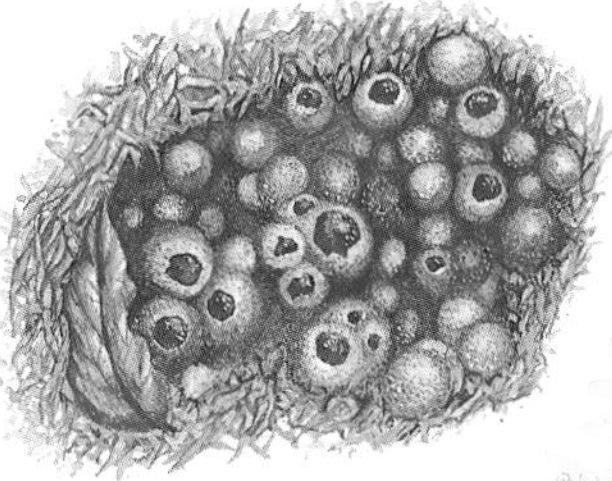

Bombus lucorum

The two yellow bands across the body make this species similar to *Bombus terrestris* (facing page), but *B. lucorum* has a distinctive white 'tail'. It is widely distributed in England, Wales and southern Scotland. Length of worker $\frac{5}{8}$ in. (16 mm).

Carder-bee

Bombus pascuorum

A relatively small bumble-bee, brown all over and without any distinctive coloured bands. The carder-bee is very common throughout Britain. Length of worker $\frac{1}{2}$ in. (13 mm). The carder-bee gets its name from the way it knits leaf litter together to make its nest on the ground.

Carder-bee's nest

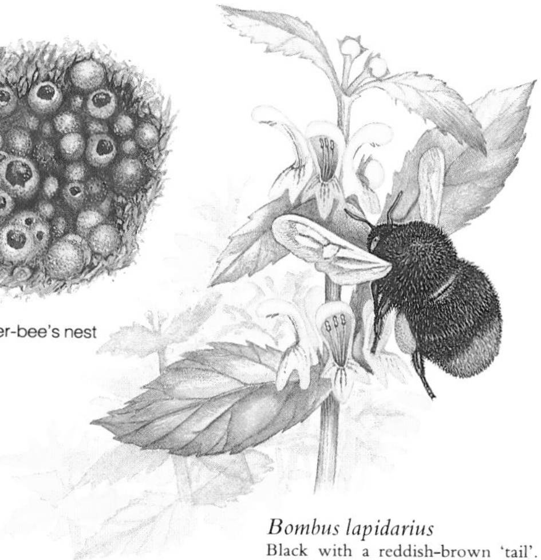

Bombus lapidarius

Black with a reddish-brown 'tail'. It is sometimes called the red-tailed bumble-bee and can be confused with its cuckoo mimic *Psithyrus rupestris*. It is mostly seen in southern England although it does occur elsewhere. It is shown on yellow arch-angel. Length of worker $\frac{1}{2}$ in. (13 mm).

Bombus pratorum

The two yellow bands make it similar to *Bombus terrestris* (facing page) and *B. lucorum*, but this species is smaller, with an orange 'tail'. It is widely distributed in England, Scotland and Wales. Length of worker $\frac{7}{16}$ in. (11 mm).

Bombus hortorum

This bumble-bee has three yellow bands (two of them sometimes merging) and a white 'tail'. It is widespread in Britain but decreases northwards. Length of worker $\frac{5}{8}$ in. (16 mm).

CUCKOO BEES

Psithyrus rupestris

A cuckoo mimic of *Bombus lapidarius*. It is not so hairy, so the segments on the abdomen are more visible. Sparse distribution in southern England and Ireland. Length of female $\frac{11}{16}$ in. (18 mm).

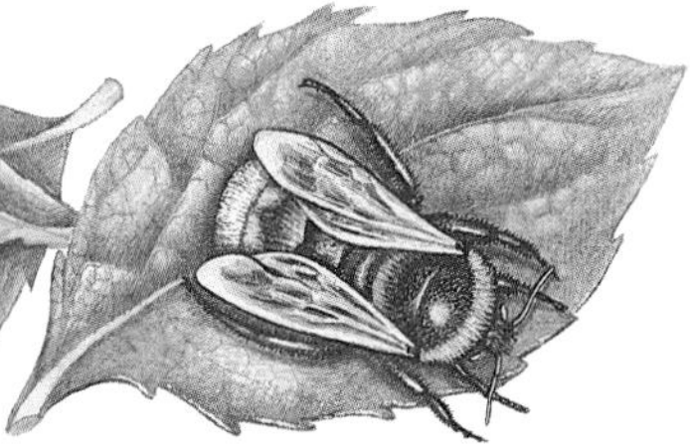

Psithyrus vestalis

The shiny body has white-and-yellow bands near the tip of the abdomen. The bee is a cuckoo mimic of *Bombus terrestris*, found only in England and Wales, and mostly in the south and east of England. Length of female $\frac{11}{16}$ in. (18 mm).

Solitary bees

The great majority of bees in Britain do not live in organised colonies like honey-bees and bumble-bees. They are solitary insects that make small nests in soil, hollow stems, decaying stumps or mortar. The female lays a few eggs in the hole and then moves on to build other nests. Once she has laid all her eggs she usually dies, leaving the nests stocked with food for the developing larvae to eat. Some species build their nests close together and then guard the entrances from predators, such as cuckoo bees which may try to take over the nests and lay their own eggs in them.

Britain has 227 species of solitary bee, compared to only one species of honey-bee. Many solitary bees look like honey-bees in shape and colour but are usually smaller. They do not have a worker caste – just males and females. They are dependent on flowers for food and are a major force in pollinating plants.

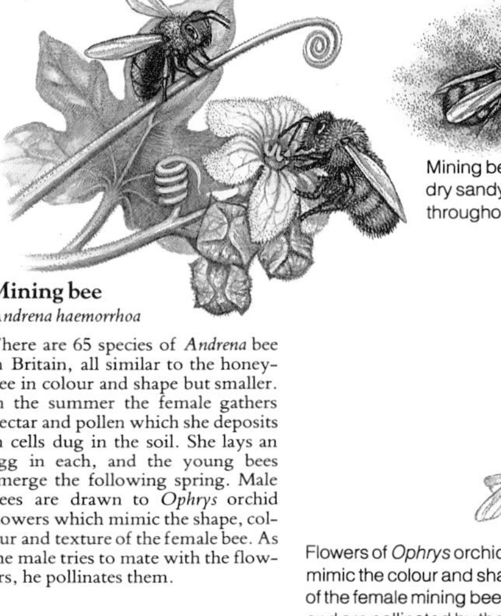

Mining bees dig nests in dry sandy banks throughout Britain.

Mining bee

Andrena haemorrhoa

There are 65 species of *Andrena* bee in Britain, all similar to the honey-bee in colour and shape but smaller. In the summer the female gathers nectar and pollen which she deposits in cells dug in the soil. She lays an egg in each, and the young bees emerge the following spring. Male bees are drawn to *Ophrys* orchid flowers which mimic the shape, colour and texture of the female bee. As the male tries to mate with the flowers, he pollinates them.

Flowers of *Ophrys* orchids mimic the colour and shape of the female mining bee and are pollinated by the male in his attempts to mate.

Wool carder bee

Anthidium manicatum

A black bee with yellow marks. It pulls white fluff off the stems and leaves of various plants, including mullein (*Verbascum*). It uses the fluff to line its nest in a wood tunnel and then lays an egg in a mixture of pollen and nectar. Found mostly in southern England.

Yellow-faced bee

Hylaeus signatus

There are 13 species of these bees with black-and-yellow faces. They make nests in hollow stems, and provide a store of regurgitated pollen and nectar, which also hardens to make partitions between the six or so cells. They are found in southern England but are not common.

Melitta haemorrhoidalis

This is a specialist feeder on the nectar of *Campanula* flowers and occasionally on meadow cranesbill. It is shown on harebell (*C. rotundifolia*). Widely distributed in England and Wales, but rather scarce in Scotland and absent from Ireland.

Macropis europaea

A bee with a shiny black body. It is a specialist feeder only on the nectar of yellow loosestrife (*Lysimachia vulgaris*). It is also the only member of its genus. Found in south-east England in wetland areas between Dorset and Norfolk.

Long-horned eucera

Eucera longicornis

An impressive bee with characteristic long antennae in the male only, and a light brown hairy thorax. The male's antennae are as long as its body. It makes colonies of nests between May and July but is susceptible to parasitic attack from cuckoo bees. It occurs in southern England.

Davies's colletes

Colletes daviesanus

There are eight British species of *Colletes* bee, distinguished by white bands on the abdomen. They nest 8–10 in. (20–25 cm) below ground in hard-packed sand or occasionally in loose mortar, and their larvae eat nectar. The commonest solitary bee in England and Wales; local in Ireland and Scotland. They may be seen on wild flowers such as cow parsley in July and August.

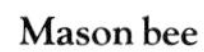

Mason bee

Osmia rufa

Like the honey-bee in shape but with red hair on the body. Females are larger than males and do not have white hairs on the face. The female stocks her cells with pollen and nectar, and then lays her egg. The bee hatches 14 weeks later but remains in its cocoon through the winter. Mason bees are common in Britain.

After laying an egg, the bee blocks the tunnel with mud. Each cell takes a day and she may make 20 in her month-long life.

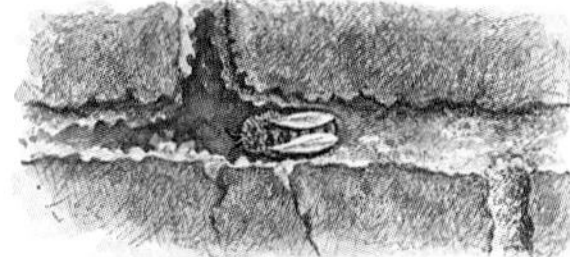

The bee cleans out holes in wall mortar or sandy banks. She will also use nail holes.

Patchwork leaf-cutter

Megachile centuncularis

Similar to the honey-bee but with orange hairs on the underside and powerful, shearing jaws for cutting leaves. In June and July the female cuts oval sections from the leaves of roses, lilacs, laburnums or willows. She rolls the leaf into a cylinder, seals it at one end, and provisions it with nectar and pollen. She adds an egg and seals the other end with a circular piece of cut leaf. Leaf-cutter bees are found mainly in southern England.

The leaf-cutter bee builds a row of egg capsules in a tunnel.

Humped sphecodes

Sphecodes gibbus

These are cuckoo bees which parasitise nests of *Halictus* bees where they kill the host female and lay their own eggs. They have few hairs on their bodies and no pollen-collecting apparatus. There are 16 species of *Sphecodes*, all of which appear very similar. Very common in England and Wales but not found in Scotland or Ireland.

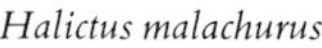

Halictus malachurus

Small hairy bees which could be confused with *Andrena* bees. The females hibernate and make burrows in the spring, guarding them from predators such as *Sphecodes* bees. They are found in southern England.

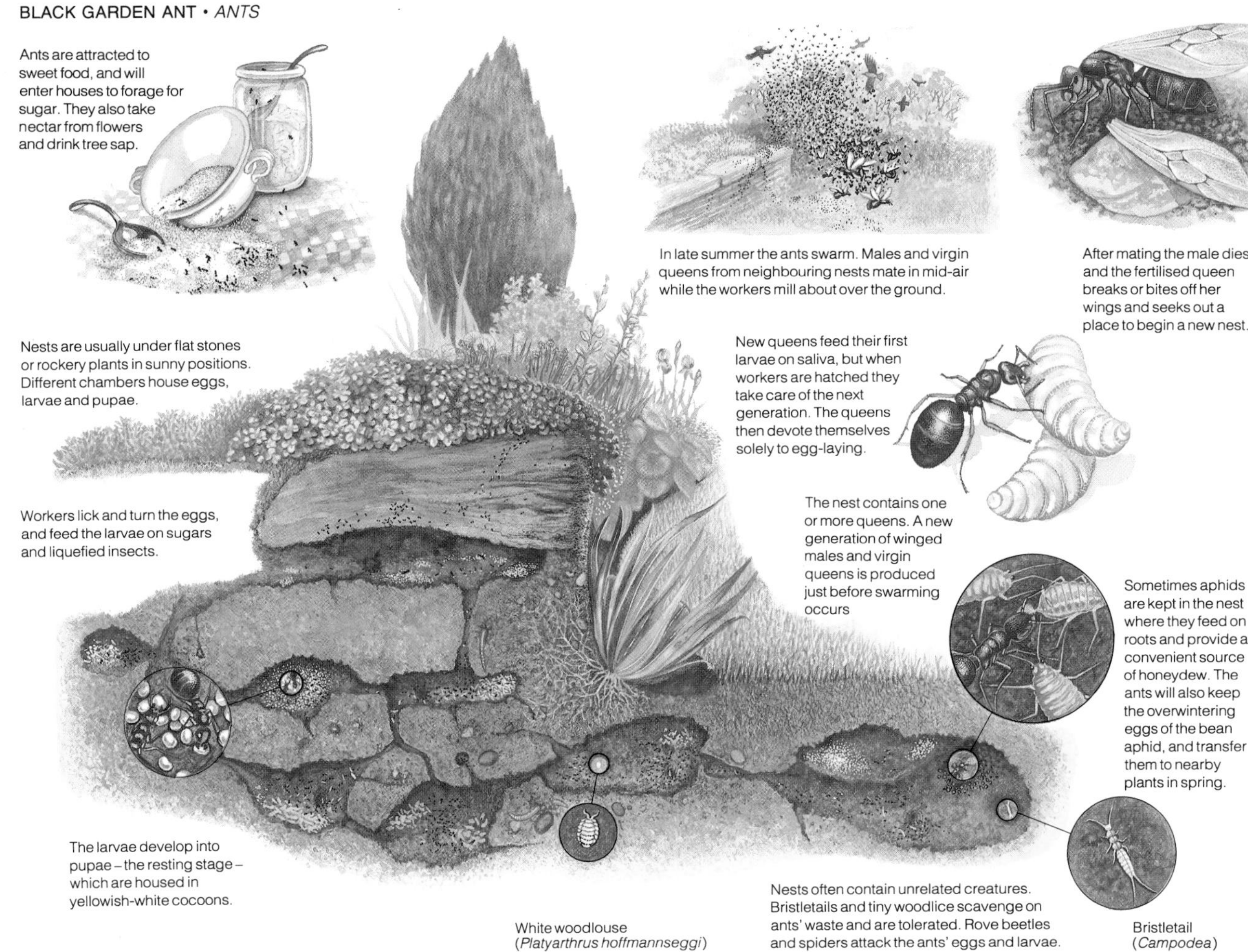

Ants are attracted to sweet food, and will enter houses to forage for sugar. They also take nectar from flowers and drink tree sap.

In late summer the ants swarm. Males and virgin queens from neighbouring nests mate in mid-air while the workers mill about over the ground.

After mating the male dies and the fertilised queen breaks or bites off her wings and seeks out a place to begin a new nest.

Nests are usually under flat stones or rockery plants in sunny positions. Different chambers house eggs, larvae and pupae.

New queens feed their first larvae on saliva, but when workers are hatched they take care of the next generation. The queens then devote themselves solely to egg-laying.

Workers lick and turn the eggs, and feed the larvae on sugars and liquefied insects.

The nest contains one or more queens. A new generation of winged males and virgin queens is produced just before swarming occurs

Sometimes aphids are kept in the nest where they feed on roots and provide a convenient source of honeydew. The ants will also keep the overwintering eggs of the bean aphid, and transfer them to nearby plants in spring.

The larvae develop into pupae – the resting stage – which are housed in yellowish-white cocoons.

White woodlouse
(*Platyarthrus hoffmannseggi*)

Nests often contain unrelated creatures. Bristletails and tiny woodlice scavenge on ants' waste and are tolerated. Rove beetles and spiders attack the ants' eggs and larvae.

Bristletail
(*Campodea*)

The ants may defend the aphid colony from enemies such as ladybirds and their larvae, and the larvae of lacewings and hoverflies. The ants can bite, and also exude drops of formic acid.

Black garden ants attend a 'herd' of aphids as they suck the sap of a young plant shoot and exude their sweet-tasting honeydew.

The black garden ant is the most common ant found in British gardens. The worker – the ant normally seen – is dull blackish-brown and up to $\frac{3}{16}$ in. (5 mm) long. They are often found feeding on the honeydew of aphids, particularly that of the black bean aphid which attacks broad beans.

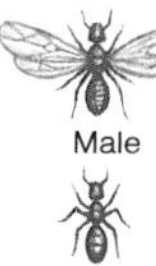

The queen, the male and the worker shown life-size. Worker ants are females that are unable to breed.

The aphids' excretory honeydew is rich in sugar. The ants may stimulate the aphids to produce more by stroking them with their antennae. The liquid is collected and taken to the nest for the larvae and queen.

Black garden ant *Lasius niger*

The black garden ant is the only native British ant which regularly enters houses, although it does not live there. The workers are foragers, and may invade kitchens seeking sugary foods. During late summer swarms of flying ants occur when queens and males from nearby nests rise into the air in dense clouds to mate. Swarming often takes place in hot, thundery weather – giving the black garden ant the reputation in folklore of being able to foretell the arrival of storms.

Black garden ants occur throughout the British Isles in gardens, grasslands, heaths and woods. They make their nests under plants, old logs and stones – sometimes under the flagstones of a garden path, with the stone forming the roof of the ants' tunnels. The tiny workers, rather than queens and males, are the type most often seen. They may be scurrying over the ground or foraging in plants for nectar or the honeydew exuded by aphids and scale insects. When workers meet they sometimes pass their antennae over each other to help in recognition, each colony having a distinctive scent. Nests of black garden ants are sometimes invaded by the queen of another species of ant, *Lasius umbratus*, which may take over the colony.

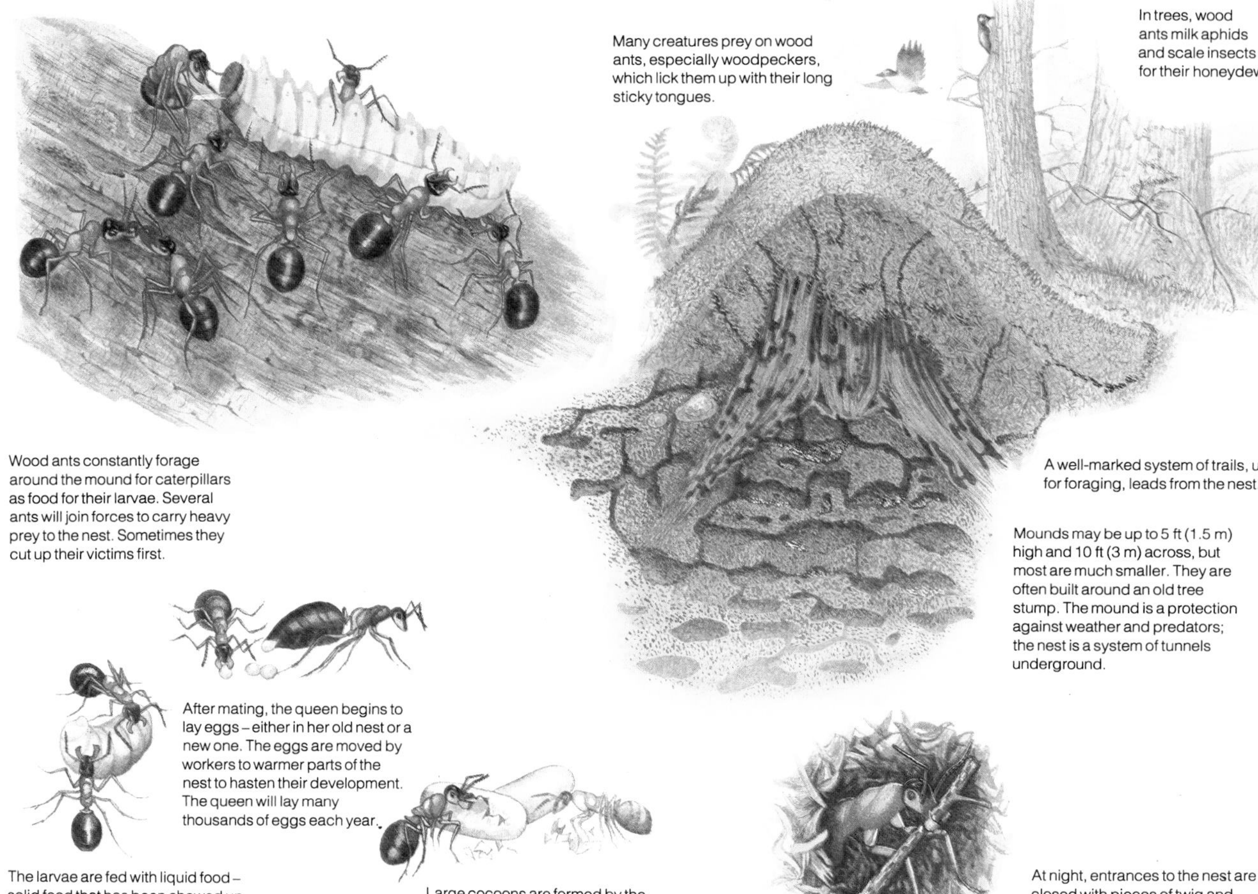

Many creatures prey on wood ants, especially woodpeckers, which lick them up with their long sticky tongues.

In trees, wood ants milk aphids and scale insects for their honeydew.

Wood ants constantly forage around the mound for caterpillars as food for their larvae. Several ants will join forces to carry heavy prey to the nest. Sometimes they cut up their victims first.

A well-marked system of trails, used for foraging, leads from the nest.

Mounds may be up to 5 ft (1.5 m) high and 10 ft (3 m) across, but most are much smaller. They are often built around an old tree stump. The mound is a protection against weather and predators; the nest is a system of tunnels underground.

After mating, the queen begins to lay eggs – either in her old nest or a new one. The eggs are moved by workers to warmer parts of the nest to hasten their development. The queen will lay many thousands of eggs each year.

The larvae are fed with liquid food – solid food that has been chewed up by workers and regurgitated.

Large cocoons are formed by the larvae; workers cut open the cocoons when the new ants are ready to emerge.

At night, entrances to the nest are closed with pieces of twig and guarded by workers.

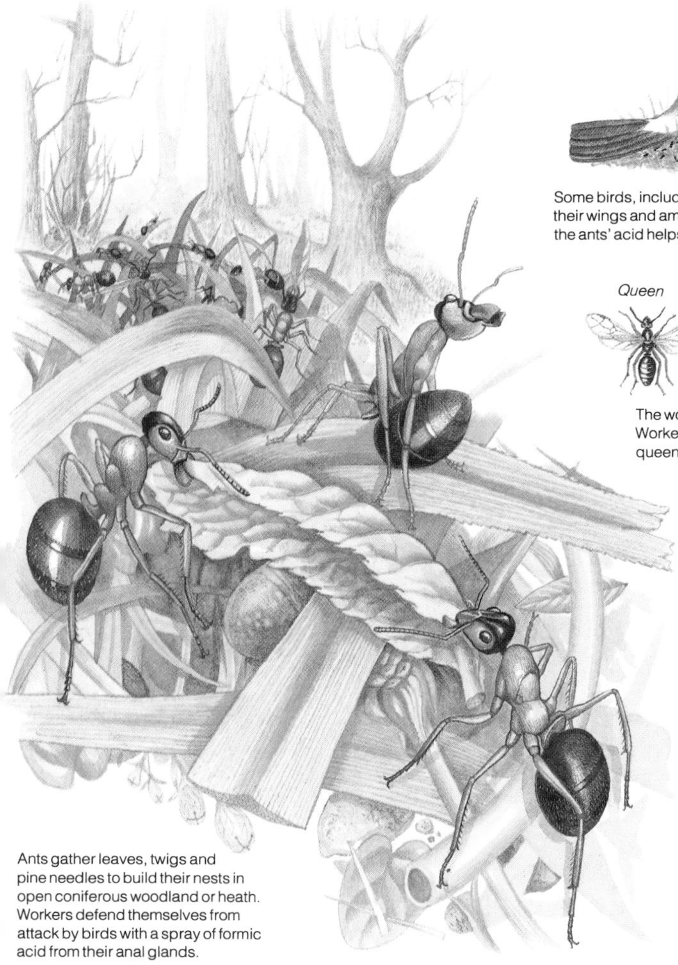

Some birds, including jays, thrust wood ants under their wings and among their feathers. Apparently the ants' acid helps to keep down mites.

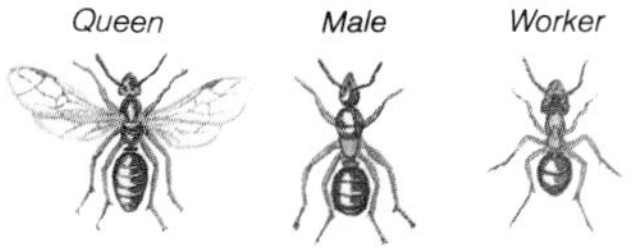

Queen *Male* *Worker*

The wood ant is Britain's largest ant. Workers are about ¼ in. (6 mm) long, queens and males about ⅜ in. (10 mm).

A group of wood ant workers drag a green caterpillar back to their nest where it will be eaten and perhaps fed to the growing ant larvae.

Wood ant *Formica rufa*

A large nest of wood ants has up to 300,000 workers, which spend much of their time supplying the enormous amount of food that the nest constantly needs. The nests are never far from trees where the ants hunt for insects, especially the caterpillars of moths and sawflies. They often kill their prey, and small enemies, by spraying them with formic acid from a gland at the rear of the abdomen, which they swing around to aim at the target. The acid travels a distance of several centimetres, and then penetrates the skin of the prey, paralysing it and destroying internal tissues. The prey is dragged back to the nest to be eaten, or fed in regurgitated form to the larvae (grubs). Wood ants also obtain food by 'milking' aphids and scale insects.

The wood ant *Formica rufa* is widespread in the southern half of England, and is found in parts of the Midlands and north. It does not occur in Scotland, where wood ant mounds are made by related species. In Ireland wood ants of any sort are rare.

Several wood ant nests may be found close together – most of them offshoots from a larger nest. The life-span of a worker is from one to two years, but queens can live as long as 15 years. There are often several queens in one nest.

Ants gather leaves, twigs and pine needles to build their nests in open coniferous woodland or heath. Workers defend themselves from attack by birds with a spray of formic acid from their anal glands.

Other ants commonly found in Britain

About 50 species of ant live in Britain. Some, including the Argentine and pharaoh's ants, have been accidently introduced from warmer countries and can survive only inside heated buildings. Ants, like most bees and wasps but unlike other insects, have a 'waist' (or petiole) consisting of one or two body segments between the thorax and the abdomen.

Different species may be carnivorous or vegetarian, or both, but all ants 'milk' aphids and scale insects of their sweet secretion, called honeydew, whenever they have the opportunity. Many species have powerful jaws and a sting, although only females (the queens and the workers) carry a sting as it is actually a modified egg-laying organ. Male and queen ants have wings which they use once only, during their courtship flight. After this airborne mating, the male dies and the queen rubs or pulls off her wings.

All the life-size illustrations on these two pages are of worker ants, the type most commonly seen.

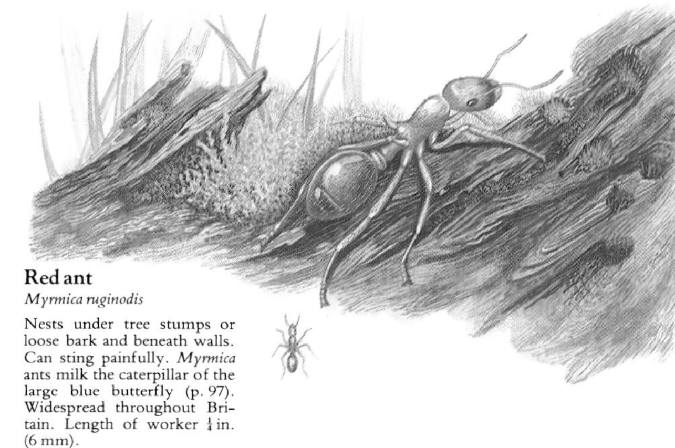

Red ant

Myrmica ruginodis

Nests under tree stumps or loose bark and beneath walls. Can sting painfully. *Myrmica* ants milk the caterpillar of the large blue butterfly (p. 97). Widespread throughout Britain. Length of worker ¼ in. (6 mm).

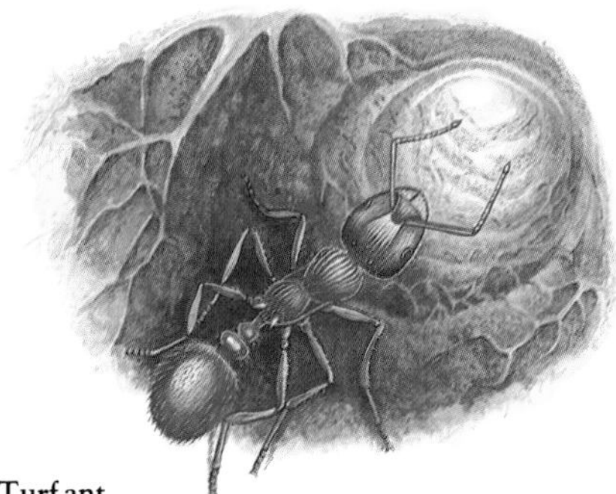

Turf ant

Tetramorium caespitum

Nests under stones and turf in heathland. Found mainly in south and east England. Length of worker ⅛ in. (3 mm).

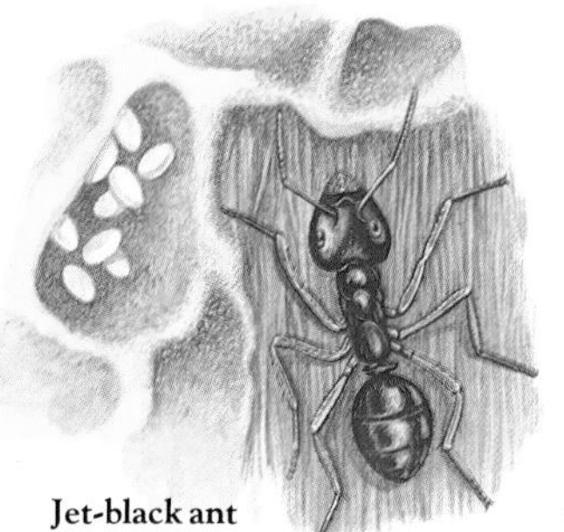

Jet-black ant

Lasius fuliginosus

Polished-black ant with large, heart-shaped head and yellow legs. Nests in stumps and beneath hedgerows. Climbs shrubs and trees to milk aphids. Mainly in south and south-east England. Length of worker $\frac{3}{16}$ in. (5 mm).

Argentine ant

Iridomyrmex humilis

Small, thin, blackish ant that can only survive in heated buildings in Britain. Introduced to Britain from the tropics about 1900. Length of worker $\frac{1}{16}$ in. (2 mm).

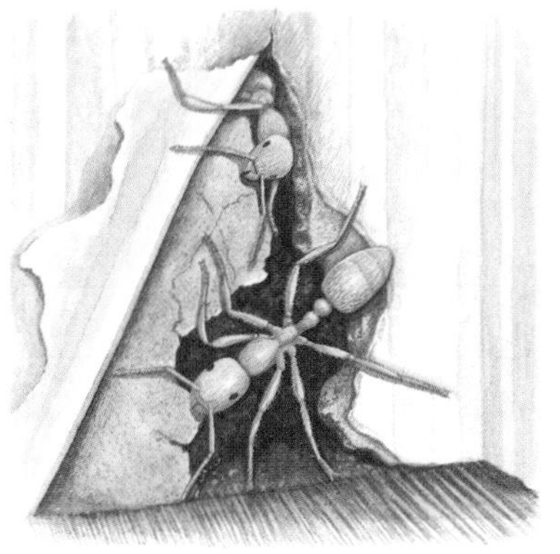

Pharaoh's ant
Monomorium pharaonis

Small yellow ant found throughout Britain only in heated buildings, especially in towns. Nests in crevices in walls. Introduced to Britain from the tropics. Length of worker $\frac{1}{16}$ in. (2 mm).

Yellow meadow ant
Lasius flavus

Pale yellow ant that causes mounds in meadowland. Farms aphids in nest. Widespread, especially in southern England. Length of worker $\frac{1}{8}$ in. (3 mm).

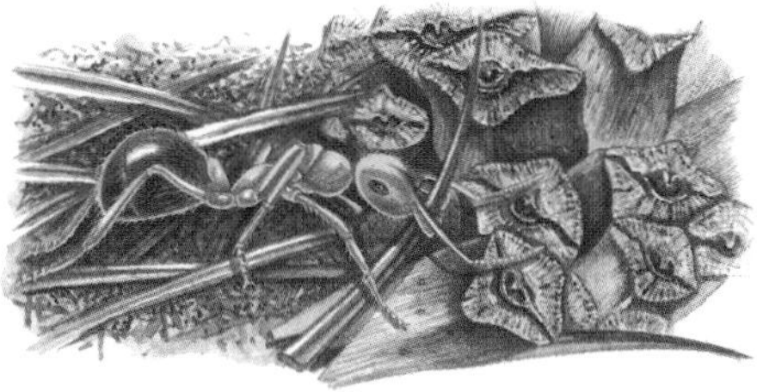

Formica lemani

Similar to the negro ant, but living further north and at higher altitudes. Length of worker $\frac{1}{4}$ in. (6 mm).

Negro ant
Formica fusca

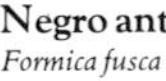

Nests under stones, walls and old stumps. Mainly in south and central England. Length of worker up to $\frac{1}{4}$ in. (6 mm).

Blood-red or slave-making ant
Formica sanguinea

Resembles the wood ant (p. 257), but does not make a mound. Removes pupae from nests of other *Formica* species and enslaves the emerging adults. Found only in small areas of south-east England and north-east Scotland. Length of worker $\frac{1}{4}$ in. (6 mm).

False ants

These two species of wingless female wasps may be mistaken for ants when seen on the ground or on plants.

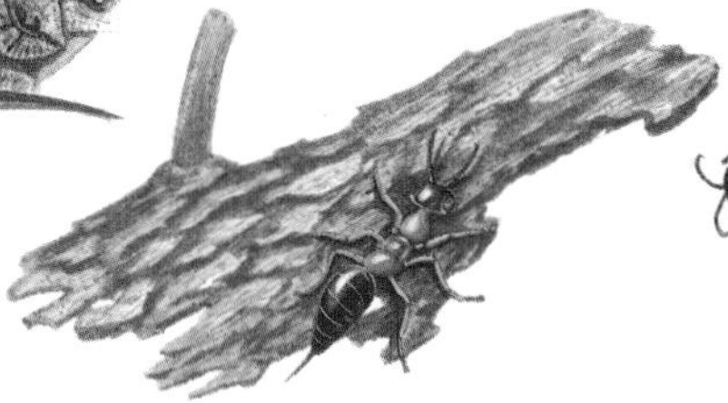

Male

Female

Tiphiid wasp
Methoca ichneumonides

Found on sandy heathland. It paralyses the larvae of tiger beetles and lays an egg on the body. Length $\frac{5}{16}$ in. (8 mm).

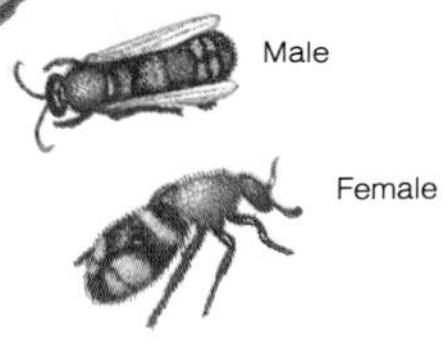

Velvet ant
Mutilla europaea

Wanders over the ground seeking the nests of bumble-bees where it lays its eggs on the bees' larvae. Can sting painfully. Length $\frac{1}{2}$ in. (13 mm).

True bugs: Heteroptera

All true bugs belong to the order Hemiptera, whose members are distinguished by having mouthparts in the form of a rostrum – a stabbing, sucking beak which is stuck into plants or prey. The rostrum is usually held under the body when not in use. The Hemiptera is divided into two sub-orders, the Heteroptera – from the Greek words for 'different' and 'wing' – and the Homoptera – from the Greek words for 'same' and 'wing'. All Heteroptera have fore-wings of two textures; they are hardened at the base but have transparent, membranous tips. The wings are folded flat on the body when the insect is at rest.

Many species of Heteroptera inject an enzyme into insects or other invertebrates to liquefy tissue for sucking through the rostrum. A few suck the blood of mammals and birds. Other species suck juices from berries and larger fruits. They are usually seen through the summer.

Assassin bugs

As the name implies, assassin bugs are hunters. They prey on other insects by seizing them with their specially adapted fore-legs and sucking their body tissues through a long, sharp beak. They range in length between about $\frac{1}{4}$–$\frac{3}{4}$ in. (6–20 mm).

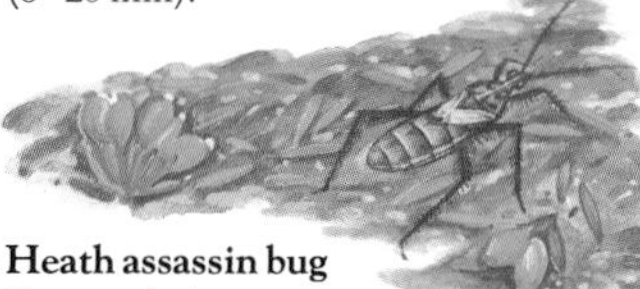

Heath assassin bug

Coranus subapterus

Hunts insects and spiders on the ground. Common on heaths and sand-dunes in England, Wales and Scotland.

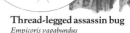

[× 2]

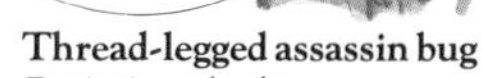

Thread-legged assassin bug

Empicoris vagabundus

Hunts its prey mostly on trees – both deciduous and coniferous – but also among marram grass in coastal sand-dunes. Found in England, Wales and Scotland.

Capsid bugs

More than 200 species of capsid bugs occur in the British Isles, varying widely in shape and diet. Most feed on plants and have fairly narrow bodies $\frac{1}{8}$–$\frac{1}{2}$ in. (3–13 mm) in length.

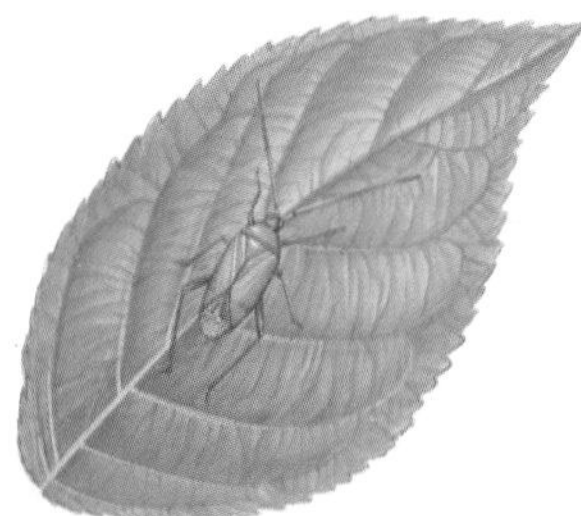

Common green capsid

Lygocoris pabulinus

Attacks a wide variety of plants, including potatoes, strawberries, apples, gooseberries, blackberries, pears, raspberries and roses. It is common throughout the British Isles.

Mirid bug

Miris striatus

Unlike most capsid bugs, the mirid bug is a part-predator, preying on aphids, caterpillars and the eggs of other bugs. Found throughout the British Isles.

Meadow plant bug

Leptopterna dolabrata

Found in damp meadows and other grassy areas feeding on a wide range of grasses. Occurs throughout the British Isles.

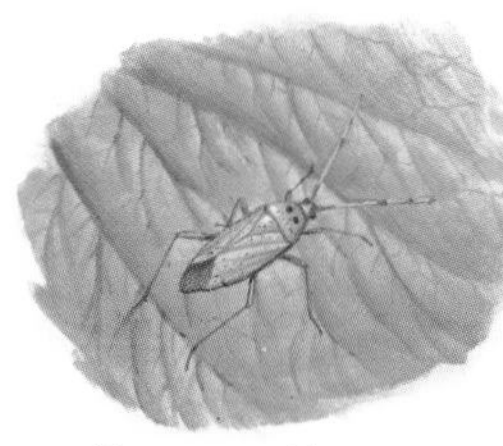

Potato capsid

Calocoris norvegicus

Feeds on a wide range of plants, including nettles, and can be a minor pest of potatoes, carrots and chrysanthemums. Found throughout the British Isles.

Flower bugs

This small group of predatory bugs occurs in flowers and vegetation. They are closely related to the blood-sucking bed-bugs which are parasites of mammals and birds. Length ranges up to $\frac{3}{16}$ in. (3–5 mm).

Common flower bug

Anthocoris nemorum

Preys on plant pests such as red-spider mites and greenfly, and sometimes sucks the sap of the plants. It is one of the most common bugs in the British Isles.

Damsel bugs

How they earned their name is a mystery, since damsel bugs are fierce predators, and help to keep down insect pests among cereal crops. They average about $\frac{5}{16}$ in. (8 mm) in length.

Field damsel bug

Nabis ferus

After hibernating through the winter the field damsel bug flies into cornfields and feeds on other bugs, caterpillars and aphids. Occurs throughout the British Isles.

Marsh damsel bug

Dolichonabis limbatus

The marsh damsel bug preys on other bugs, flies, moths and spiders that live among damp vegetation. Found throughout the British Isles.

Lacebugs

These small, flat bugs have transparent wings with a lace-like network of veins. The British Isles contain 23 species, the largest only $\frac{3}{16}$ in. (5 mm) in length. They all feed on plants.

Thistle lacebug (right)

Tingis cardui

Feeds on thistles, particularly the spear thistle, throughout the British Isles.

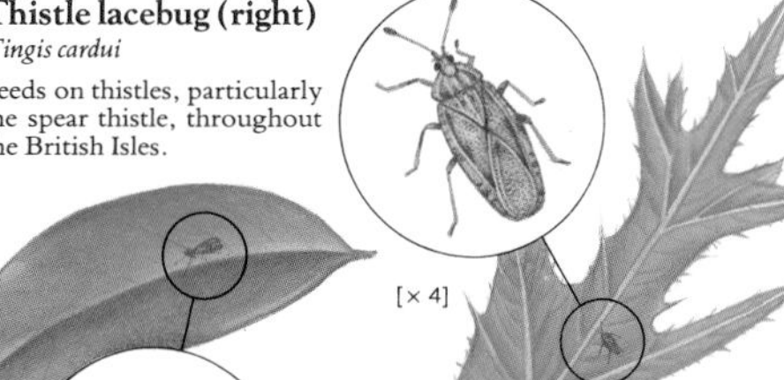

Rhododendron lacebug (left)

Stephanitis rhododendri

Feeds on rhododendrons, causing a white mottling, or sometimes brown spots, on the leaves. Found in England, south Wales and southern Scotland.

Shield bugs

The flat, broad bodies of these bugs, shaped like heraldic shields, give them their name. Most species are between $\frac{5}{16}$–$\frac{5}{8}$ in. (8–16 mm) in length. They feed mostly on the fruits and leaves of plants.

Green shield bug

Palomena prasina

Found on many plants, including hazel trees and beans, in England, Wales and Ireland.

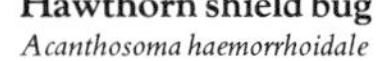

Hawthorn shield bug

Acanthosoma haemorrhoidale

Feeds on hawthorn berries or the leaves of hawthorn, oak and whitebeam. A common species, except in Scotland.

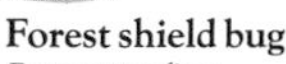

Forest shield bug

Pentatoma rufipes

Feeds mostly on oak and alder, but also on other deciduous trees. Common throughout the British Isles.

Pied shield bug

Sehirus bicolor

Feeds mainly on white deadnettle. Unlike most insects, the female looks after her eggs until they hatch. Common in southern England and Wales.

Parent bug

Elasmucha grisea

Feeds on birch leaves. Like the pied shield bug, the female cares for the eggs and also continues to look after the young when they have hatched. Found in most of the British Isles.

True bugs: Homoptera

The bugs in the sub-order Homoptera are distinguished from the Heteroptera by their fore-wings, which are always of one texture. They may be membranous or they may be hardened, but never a combination of the two as in the Heteroptera. When not in use, the wings make an angled roof shape over the body.

These bugs, like the Heteroptera, feed through a rostrum, or beak, but suck plant tissue, not animal matter. Their vegetarianism, however, is not always harmless. Indeed several species are serious pests of agriculture, taking sap, causing wilt and fruit failure, and passing on viruses. Except for their rostrum and wing structure, these insects are diverse – in size, form and habits. The scale insects also differ greatly in the sexes; only adult males have wings, females and nymphs living wingless and often legless beneath protective scales.

Black and red froghopper

Cercopis vulnerata

This strikingly coloured species is seen in early summer clinging to lush grass and low vegetation, especially in southern and central England. The nymphs live underground, feeding on roots. Length 3/8 in. (10 mm).

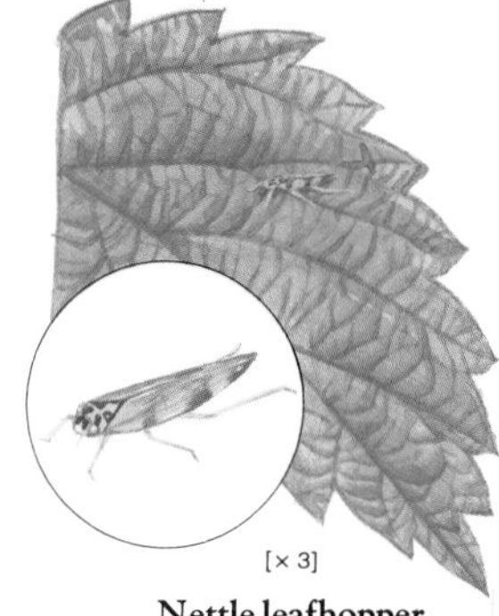

[× 3]

Nettle leafhopper

Eupteryx aurata

Common on nettles and other weeds in early summer. Small pale dots occur on the leaves where the bug has introduced its poisonous saliva during feeding. It feeds on potato leaves also, but not commonly enough to damage the plants, as happens in warmer countries. Length 3/16 in. (5 mm).

New Forest cicada

Cicadetta montana

Britain's only cicada, and apparently confined to the New Forest in Hampshire. Nymphs live underground and feed on roots. Adults like sunny open woodlands and clearings, and appear in May and June. Males have a sound-producing organ on the first abdominal segment and give out a continuous note all day long, but at such a high frequency that many people cannot hear it. Body length 3/4 in. (20 mm).

Larva
[× 2]

Common froghopper

Philaenus spumarius

The mottled adults can be seen all over Britain between May and September, leaping from stem to stem on grasses and other plants. Larvae exude the familiar frothy 'cuckoo-spit' to hide themselves from predators. Adult length about 5/16 in. (8 mm).

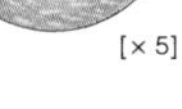

[× 5]

Citrus mealy bug

Planococcus citri

The females have legs and can move about a little, unlike most female scale insects which remain for life on the food plant where they hatch. They look like small white woodlice. This species has been introduced into Britain accidentally and has become a pest in greenhouses. Length 1/16 in. (2 mm).

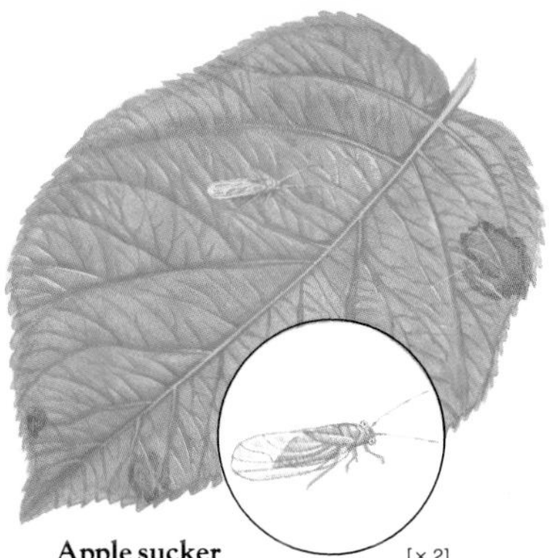

[× 2]

Apple sucker

Psyllus mali

These green pests are common on apple trees all over Britain from May to November, feeding on the flowers in spring – which ruins the crop – and later on the leaves. Their eggs are laid in the bark in late summer. Length about $\frac{1}{6}$ in. (4 mm).

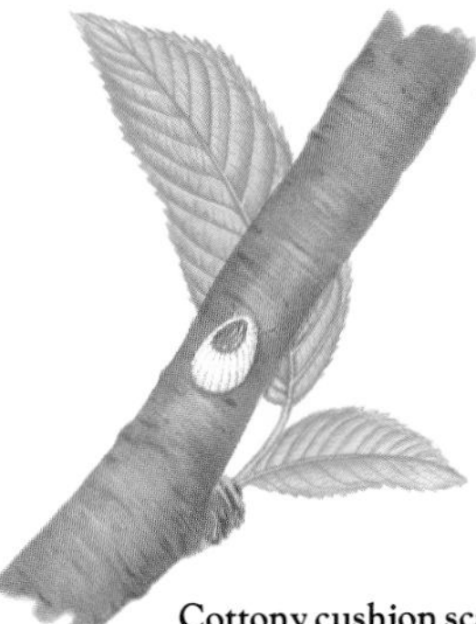

Cottony cushion scale

Icerya purchasi

Not a native species in Britain but accidentally introduced in imported fruit. The wingless and legless female is found on the shoots of fruit trees in summer. They also occur in greenhouses. Males are rarely seen. Length about $\frac{3}{16}$ in. (5 mm).

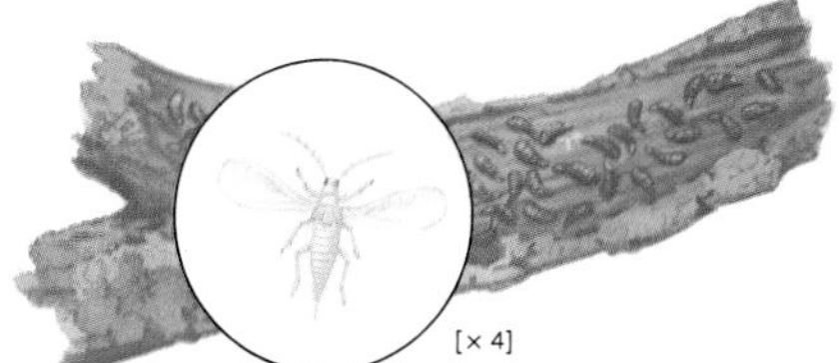

[× 4]

Mussel-scale

Lepidosaphes ulmi

The inconspicuous females of the species damage fruit trees and other deciduous trees; large numbers of them will cause considerable damage. The males have wings, and resemble midges. Length of female $\frac{1}{16}$ in. (2 mm), male slightly longer.

Horned treehopper

Centrotus cornutus

One of Britain's only two treehoppers, found from June to August, mainly in southern England. It lives in woodland on low trees or bracken. Its horns resemble sturdy thorns. Length about $\frac{1}{2}$ in. (13 mm).

Green leafhopper

Cicadella viridis

A common bug all over Britain, seen in early summer making jumps from plant to plant, but well camouflaged once it lands. The needle-like stylets of its mouthparts can penetrate plants deeply to suck out sap. Length about $\frac{5}{16}$ in. (6–8 mm).

[× 5]

Cabbage whitefly

Aleyrodes brassicae

A white, waxy coating covers this common bug, which sucks sap from the underside of cabbage leaves. It is seen all over Britain in summer. In large numbers, whiteflies can cause severe damage. Length $\frac{1}{16}$ in. (2 mm).

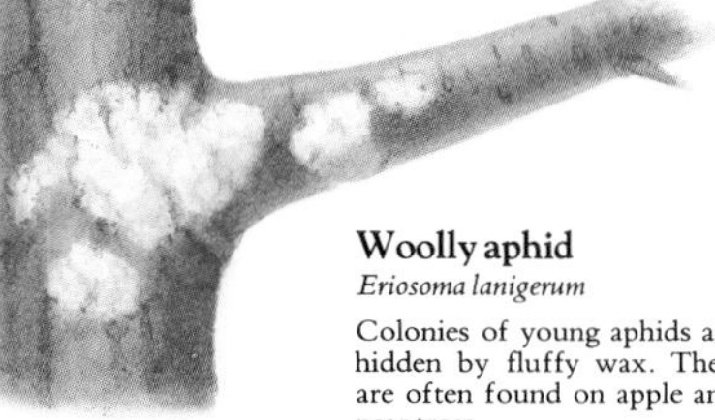

Woolly aphid

Eriosoma lanigerum

Colonies of young aphids are hidden by fluffy wax. They are often found on apple and pear trees.

Rose aphid (greenfly)

Macrosiphum rosae

These common green aphids infest rose bushes in spring. In summer, they migrate to other plants such as scabious and teasels.

Cabbage aphid

Brevicoryne brassicae

Spends its whole life on plants of the cabbage family, and can cause serious damage to brassica crops.

Currant blister aphid

Cryptomyzus ribis

The leaves of currant bushes form blisters and turn red when the aphids feed on the undersides in spring.

Other predators of aphids are tiny parasitic wasps which lay their eggs in the aphids' bodies. The wasp larvae feed on the aphids' tissues and leave through a hole in the dead aphid. Dead and hollow aphids are common among colonies.

Aphids can exude a waxy substance from the hind part of the abdomen which may deter some of their predators, such as a ladybird larva (shown here). Other enemies of aphids include adult ladybirds, lacewings and their larvae, the larvae of hoverflies, and birds.

In late summer, males and females – both with wings – are born and fly off to spindle trees where they mate.

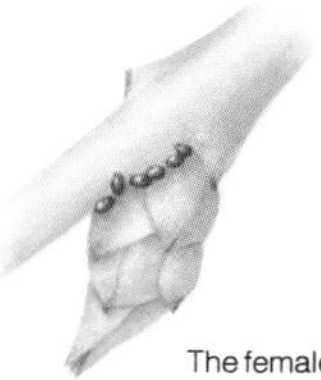

The females each lay four to six eggs on the stem or around the buds of the spindle tree. The eggs remain there until spring when females hatch and produce large colonies by parthenogenesis.

As the colonies become overcrowded, winged females are produced and fly to broad bean plants to begin the new year's cycle.

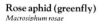

[× 2]
Wingless female

[× 2]
Winged female

[× 2]
Male

The black bean aphid, most abundant in early summer, is just one of 500 species of aphid which occur in Britain, feeding on a wide variety of plants.

The black bean aphid is dull black and up to ⅛ in. (3 mm) long. It is usually seen from late May in dense clusters on the upper stems, shoots and young leaves of broad bean plants. It may also occur on wild plants such as poppies, docks and thistles. In early summer the colony consists entirely of females, most of them wingless.

Summer aphids are reproduced by parthenogenesis – no males are involved. Each female produces a succession of fully formed females, which differ from the adults only through their smaller size.

Black bean aphid *Aphis fabae*

'Blackfly', 'greenfly', 'plant lice' and 'blight' are all names given to aphids, the sap-sucking bugs which smother young shoots of many plants in early summer. Aphids congregate on the new growth of plants where the sap is richest in nutrients. In early summer the flow of sap is often so powerful that the aphid does not need to suck but simply allows it to pour into its food canal. Plant sap is rich in sugar but low in protein, so the aphid must consume great amounts to satisfy its needs. It disposes of the excess sugar by excreting it as drops of sweet honey-dew. Ants then feed on the honey-dew by licking it from the aphids' bodies. Frequently the honey-dew drops on to the leaves below, causing the sticky deposit often found on lime, oak and other large trees. Later in the summer a mould may grow on the dried sugar, turning the leaves black. Aphids also spread virus diseases among plants, including raspberries, by sucking up the viruses in the sap and injecting them into another plant.

The black bean aphid (blackfly) and the rose aphid (greenfly) are two of the most widespread species, attacking broad beans, roses and other plants throughout Britain. Cabbage aphids and currant blister aphids are also common in gardens.

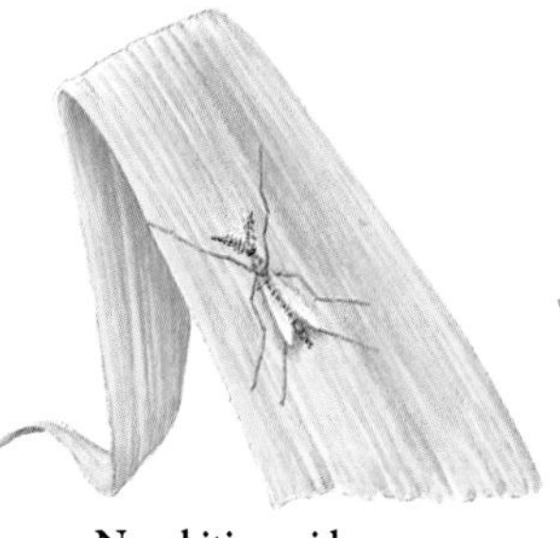

Non-biting midge
Chironomus annularis

This common midge looks like a mosquito (overleaf), but is more delicate in build and does not bite or feed on blood. It is common everywhere in Britain near water. Length $\frac{5}{16}$ in. (8 mm).

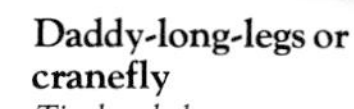

Daddy-long-legs or cranefly
Tipula paludosa

A grey-brown fly with a long thin body and narrow wings. It is the most common and widespread cranefly in Britain. Its legs break off easily if seized by a predator, and do not re-grow. Length $\frac{3}{4}$ in. (20 mm).

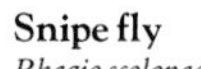

Snipe fly
Rhagio scolopacea

A yellow-bodied fly which is common all over Britain. The males sit alert on a bush or tree and dart out at other flies. Despite their wasp-like appearance they do not bite humans. Length $\frac{1}{2}$ in. (13 mm).

Black-and-yellow cranefly
Nephrotoma maculosa

This black-and-yellow striped cranefly is very common in fields and gardens throughout much of Britain. Length $\frac{11}{16}$ in. (18 mm).

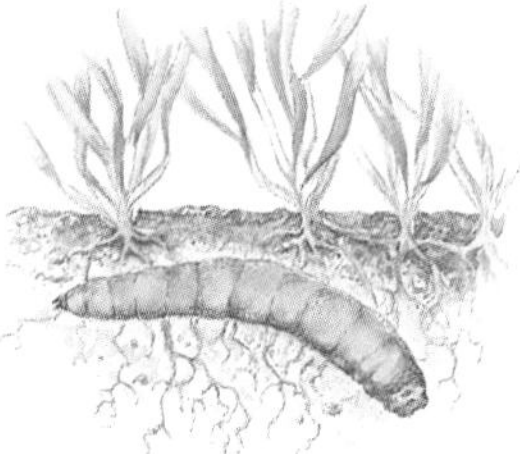

Leatherjacket

Most species of cranefly have distinctive maggot-like larvae known as leatherjackets which eat the roots of plants. Length 1 in. (25 mm).

Flies with long legs

The cranefly, or daddy-long-legs, with its large fragile legs is familiar on autumn evenings when it is attracted to electric lights, sometimes entering houses. Despite its long, pointed egg-laying organ it is harmless, like all the flies on these two pages. Winter gnats and non-biting midges are easily mistaken for the closely related mosquitoes and biting midges (overleaf). The words 'gnat' and 'midge' are commonly used to refer to small, long-legged flies that occur in swarms in the evening.

The other long-legged flies illustrated here are much stouter in build than craneflies and midges. The black St Mark's and fever flies are sluggish insects, conspicuous as they cling to hedgerow plants. In flight their long legs dangle beneath them. The snipe fly is commonly found in early summer sitting on plants. Occasionally groups of males are seen on a stretch of hedgerow or a bramble patch waiting for females. They set up small territories from which they dart out to drive off other males and pounce on passing females, attempting to mate.

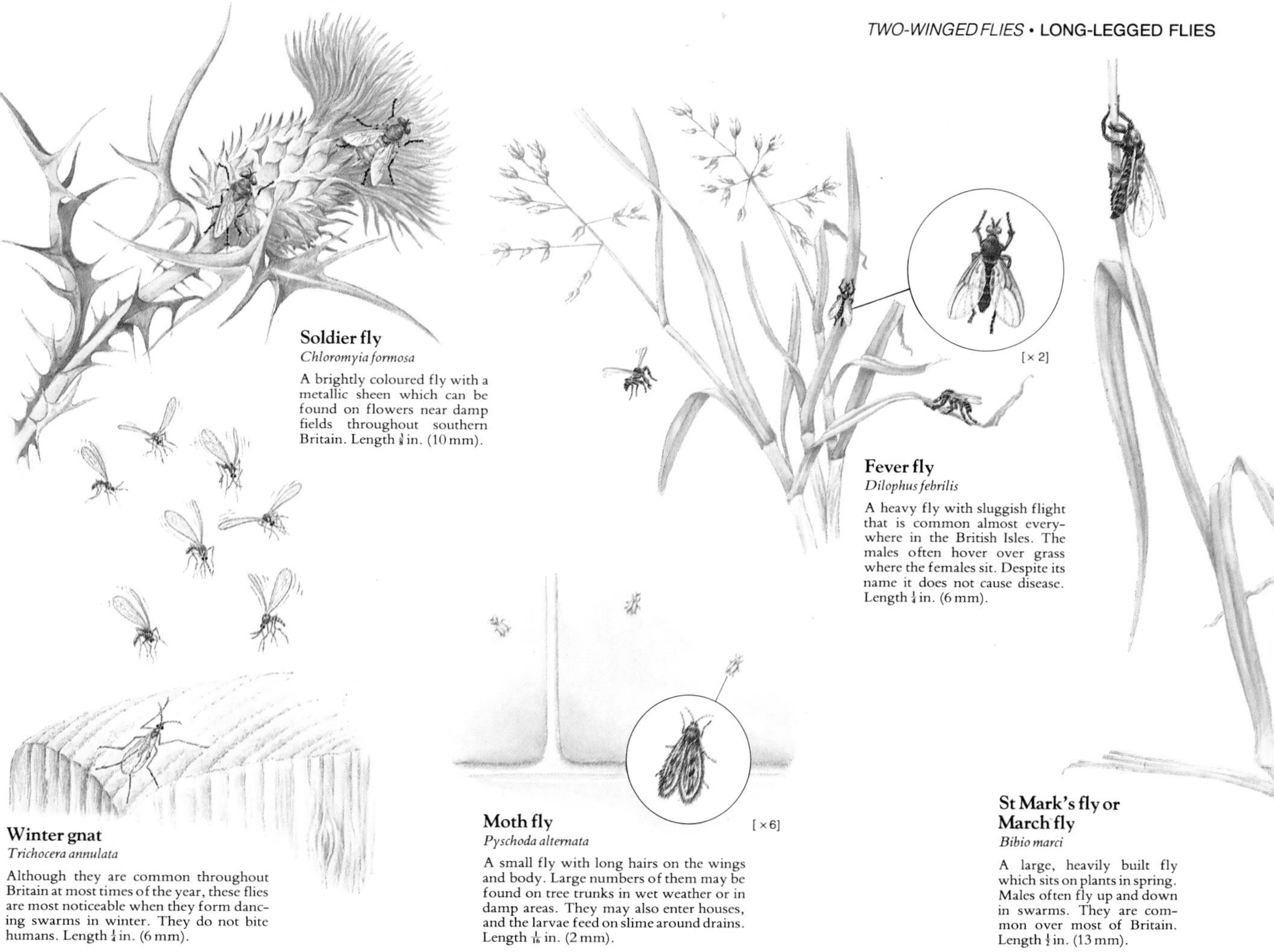

Soldier fly
Chloromyia formosa

A brightly coloured fly with a metallic sheen which can be found on flowers near damp fields throughout southern Britain. Length ⅜ in. (10 mm).

Fever fly
Dilophus febrilis

A heavy fly with sluggish flight that is common almost everywhere in the British Isles. The males often hover over grass where the females sit. Despite its name it does not cause disease. Length ¼ in. (6 mm).

Winter gnat
Trichocera annulata

Although they are common throughout Britain at most times of the year, these flies are most noticeable when they form dancing swarms in winter. They do not bite humans. Length ¼ in. (6 mm).

Moth fly
Pyschoda alternata

A small fly with long hairs on the wings and body. Large numbers of them may be found on tree trunks in wet weather or in damp areas. They may also enter houses, and the larvae feed on slime around drains. Length $\frac{1}{16}$ in. (2 mm).

St Mark's fly or March fly
Bibio marci

A large, heavily built fly which sits on plants in spring. Males often fly up and down in swarms. They are common over most of Britain. Length ½ in. (13 mm).

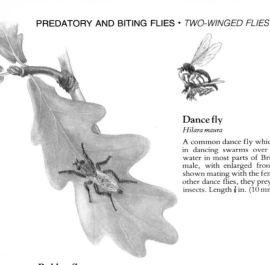

Dance fly
Hilara maura

A common dance fly which gathers in dancing swarms over pools of water in most parts of Britain. The male, with enlarged front legs, is shown mating with the female. Like other dance flies, they prey on other insects. Length $\frac{3}{8}$ in. (10 mm).

Robber fly
Asilus crabroniformis

A large fly with a bright yellow body that darts out from a perch on a plant to catch and eat other insects. It is found throughout southern England. Length $1\frac{1}{16}$ in. (27 mm).

Dance fly
Empis tesselata

A common species of fly which eats other insects, chiefly flies. It can be recognised by the prominent snout which is used for piercing its prey. Length $\frac{1}{2}$ in. (13 mm).

Robber fly
Machimus atricapillus

A common, dull grey robber fly found throughout Britain in woods. It darts out from its perch to kill and eat other insects. It may even perch on humans, but does not bite them. Length $\frac{9}{16}$ in. (15 mm).

Common yellow dung fly
Scatophaga stercoraria

A bristly yellow fly found wherever cows are kept. They feed on other flies and can be found perched on hedgerows surrounding cow pastures. They lay their eggs on dung. Length $\frac{3}{8}$ in. (10 mm).

Predatory and biting flies

Many flies are carnivorous, living on the blood or bodily juices of animals or insects. Robber flies, dance flies and dung flies are all predators of other insects. Both males and females will chase and capture prey, usually other flies, and suck out their juices. A male dance fly will wrap its prey in silk and present it to a female as part of their courtship. He then mates with her while she eats.

Mosquitoes, midges and horse flies all bite humans. The females need a meal of blood before they can develop their eggs, and often specialise on birds, small mammals, and even reptiles and amphibians. The males do not usually bite, but feed on the nectar of flowers. Female mosquitoes are potential carriers of blood parasites and the 'ague' of the Middle Ages was almost certainly a form of malaria. They have a pair of lancets which combine to form a hollow syringe through which blood is sucked. The largest of the biting flies – horse flies – include the cleg, which inflicts a severe bite without any warning noise.

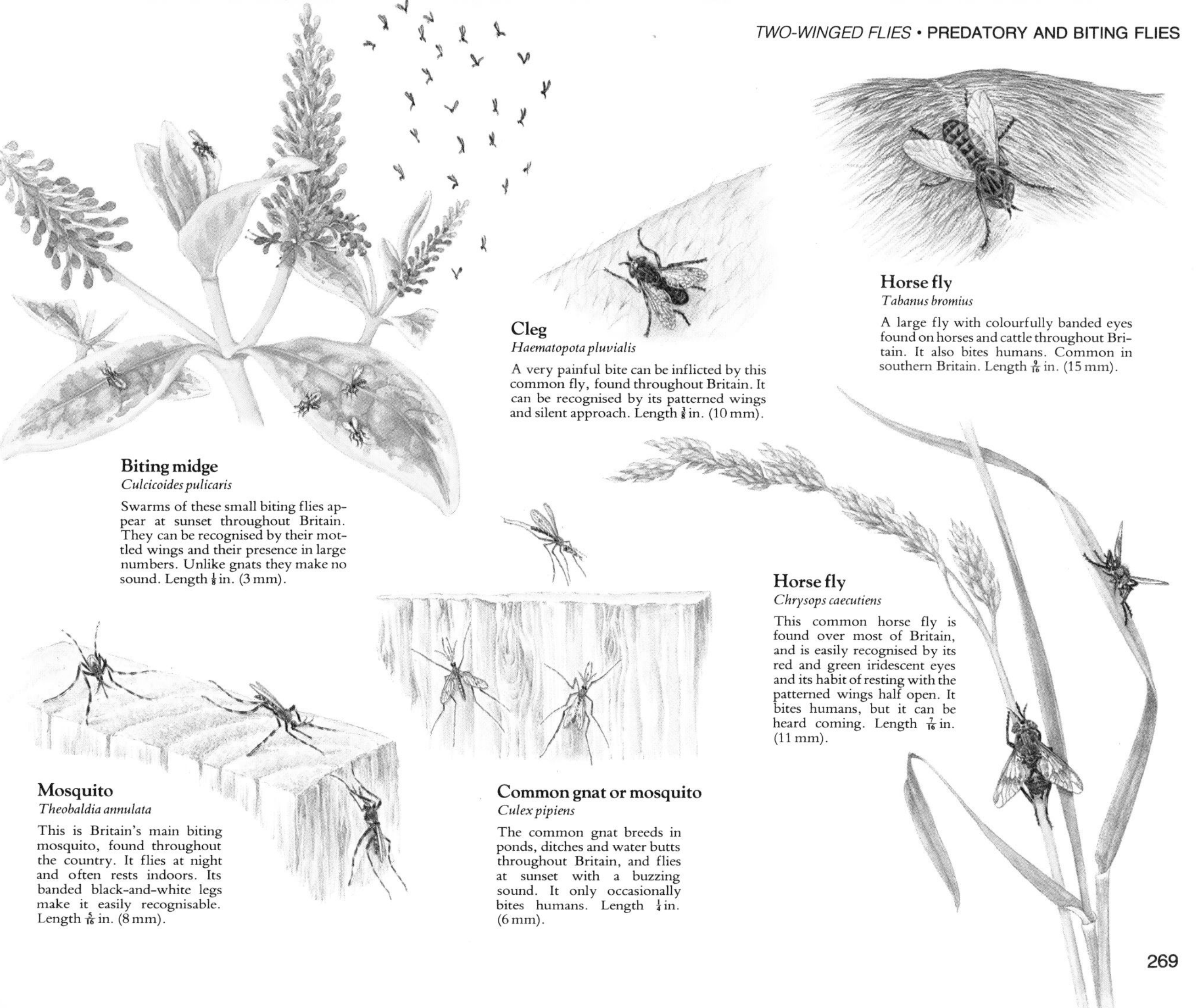

Horse fly
Tabanus bromius

A large fly with colourfully banded eyes found on horses and cattle throughout Britain. It also bites humans. Common in southern Britain. Length $\frac{9}{16}$ in. (15 mm).

Cleg
Haematopota pluvialis

A very painful bite can be inflicted by this common fly, found throughout Britain. It can be recognised by its patterned wings and silent approach. Length $\frac{3}{8}$ in. (10 mm).

Biting midge
Culcicoides pulicaris

Swarms of these small biting flies appear at sunset throughout Britain. They can be recognised by their mottled wings and their presence in large numbers. Unlike gnats they make no sound. Length $\frac{1}{8}$ in. (3 mm).

Horse fly
Chrysops caecutiens

This common horse fly is found over most of Britain, and is easily recognised by its red and green iridescent eyes and its habit of resting with the patterned wings half open. It bites humans, but it can be heard coming. Length $\frac{7}{16}$ in. (11 mm).

Mosquito
Theobaldia annulata

This is Britain's main biting mosquito, found throughout the country. It flies at night and often rests indoors. Its banded black-and-white legs make it easily recognisable. Length $\frac{5}{16}$ in. (8 mm).

Common gnat or mosquito
Culex pipiens

The common gnat breeds in ponds, ditches and water butts throughout Britain, and flies at sunset with a buzzing sound. It only occasionally bites humans. Length $\frac{1}{4}$ in. (6 mm).

Flies: bee and wasp mimics

When an otherwise defenceless insect such as a fly looks like an insect with powerful defences such as a wasp or bee, it is called a mimic. Mimicry occurs throughout nature, and it has produced a large group of flies that are difficult to distinguish from bees and wasps. The better a fly imitates a bee or wasp the better are its chances of surviving attack by birds or small mammals. Even a slight hesitation by a bird is enough to allow the fly to escape.

Honey-bees are accurately mimicked by the *Eristalis* hoverflies which feed alongside bees on flowers. Apart from their appearance they are completely defenceless and would easily fall prey to birds.

Many other species of hoverfly have bands of black and yellow, resembling the common wasp. These flies are uncommon at the time of year when young birds are learning the difference between good food and bad. When the flies become common the birds have learned that the black-and-yellow stripes of the wasp are a warning of danger.

Sunfly
Helophilus pendulus

A hoverfly common throughout most of Britain between April and October. It is seen near marshy ground or ditches, resting on waterside plants and hovering low over pools. Length $\frac{9}{16}$ in. (14 mm).

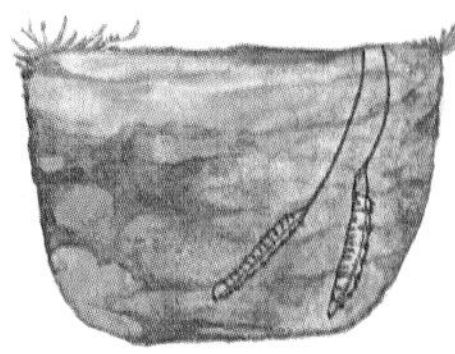

The rat-tailed maggot of the sunfly feeds on organic debris in mud, extending its 'tail' as a breathing siphon up to the surface.

Hoverfly
Syrphus ribesii

A small, active hoverfly common all over Britain and welcome in gardens because each of its larvae eats up to 800 aphids during its two-week larval stage. Seen from April to November. Length $\frac{1}{2}$ in. (13 mm).

The slug-like larva can detect light but not see clearly, so it finds its prey by scent.

Hoverfly
Episyrphus balteatus

A migrant species of hoverfly which is very common throughout Britain from April to November in years when there is a large influx from the Continent. Its larvae feed on aphids. Length $\frac{3}{8}$ in. (10 mm).

Hoverfly
Scaeva pyrastri

A conspicuous common hoverfly whose larvae consume huge numbers of aphids and will also attack nearby larvae of some flies and moths. Common all over Britain between May and November. Length $\frac{9}{16}$ in. (14 mm).

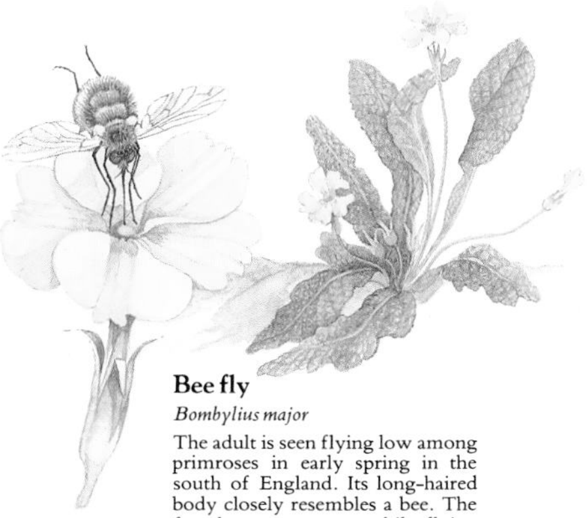

Bee fly

Bombylius major

The adult is seen flying low among primroses in early spring in the south of England. Its long-haired body closely resembles a bee. The female scatters eggs while flying and the hatched larvae find a mining bee's nest where they feed on the bee grub. Length $\frac{7}{16}$ in. (11 mm).

Drone fly

Eristalis tenax

A very common hoverfly in gardens throughout Britain in spring and autumn. It resembles the honey-bee and feeds alongside it. The larvae are rat-tailed maggots. Length $\frac{1}{2}$ in. (13 mm).

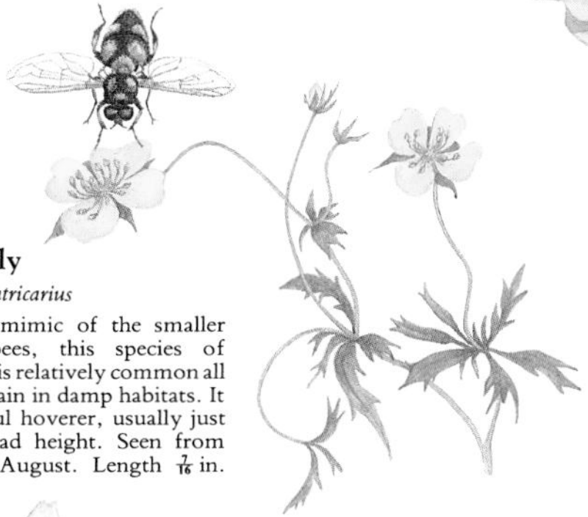

Hoverfly

Eristalis intricarius

A close mimic of the smaller bumble-bees, this species of hoverfly is relatively common all over Britain in damp habitats. It is a skilful hoverer, usually just above head height. Seen from June to August. Length $\frac{7}{16}$ in. (11 mm).

Hoverfly

Chrysotoxum bicinctum

The brilliant yellow-banded pattern makes this species a striking wasp mimic. Its larvae develop in ants' nests and the adults are on the wing between June and August. Found mainly in southern Britain. Length $\frac{7}{16}$ in. (11 mm).

Hoverfly

Volucella bombylans

This species, Britain's most deceptive bumble-bee mimic, exists in several colour forms that mimic different bee species. The larvae are scavengers in wasp nests. Found from May to August, mainly in southern Britain. Length $\frac{1}{2}$ in. (13 mm).

Bulb, or narcissus, fly

Merodon equestris

This bumble-bee mimic is a pest in gardens, where its larvae burrow into narcissus and lily bulbs to feed and spend the winter. Found in most parts of Britain from April to August. Length $\frac{1}{2}$ in. (13 mm).

Flies: plant-feeders and parasites

Many species of fly have larvae that feed on living or dead plant material. Some, like the thistle gall-fly, cause the living plant tissue to form a swelling in which the larvae can grow, securely protected and surrounded by food. Other types, such as the fruit fly, lay their eggs on fruit or seeds, and the larvae develop in the semi-liquid flesh of the fruit, breathing through tiny holes at the end of their bodies.

Parasitic flies can be divided into those that kill their hosts and those that do not. Tachinid and conopid flies lay their eggs on the bodies of caterpillars, bees and other insects. The growing larvae burrow into the host's body and feed on its internal organs, eventually killing it. Larger animals are able to support internal parasites without being killed. Sheep bot-flies and cattle warble flies develop inside the body of their host without causing serious harm.

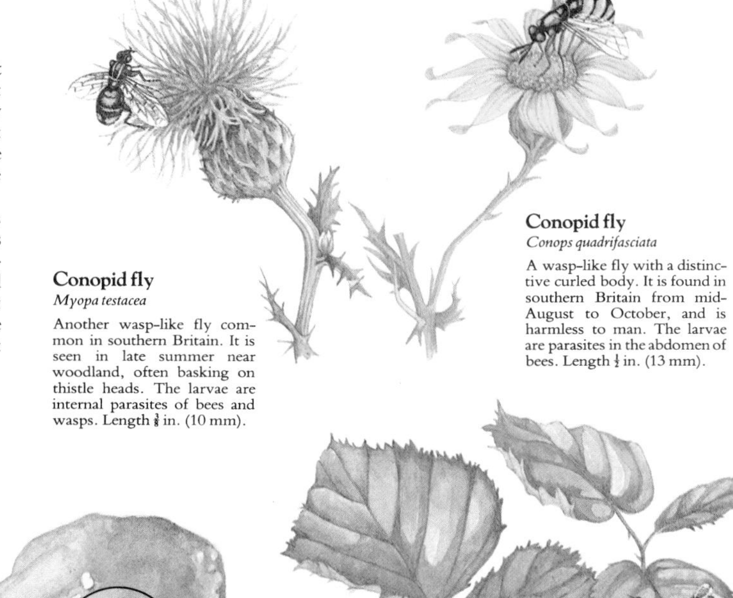

Conopid fly
Myopa testacea

Another wasp-like fly common in southern Britain. It is seen in late summer near woodland, often basking on thistle heads. The larvae are internal parasites of bees and wasps. Length ⅜ in. (10 mm).

Conopid fly
Conops quadrifasciata

A wasp-like fly with a distinctive curled body. It is found in southern Britain from mid-August to October, and is harmless to man. The larvae are parasites in the abdomen of bees. Length ½ in. (13 mm).

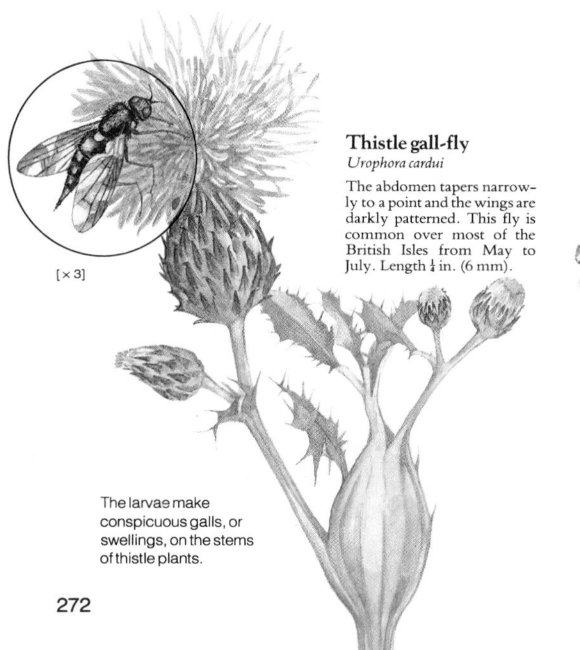

[× 3]

Thistle gall-fly
Urophora cardui

The abdomen tapers narrowly to a point and the wings are darkly patterned. This fly is common over most of the British Isles from May to July. Length ¼ in. (6 mm).

The larvae make conspicuous galls, or swellings, on the stems of thistle plants.

[× 3]

Fruit, or vinegar, fly
Drosophila funebris

A tiny fly found all over Britain and often seen in early autumn flying round rotting fruits such as apples; the larvae feed on rotting fruits. There are several similar species. Length ⅛ in. (3 mm).

Sepsis punctum

Shiny black ant-like flies which flick their wings up and down all the time. They are common all over Britain from June to September, and are often seen scurrying over plants in a dense swarm. Length ¼ in. (6 mm).

[× 2]

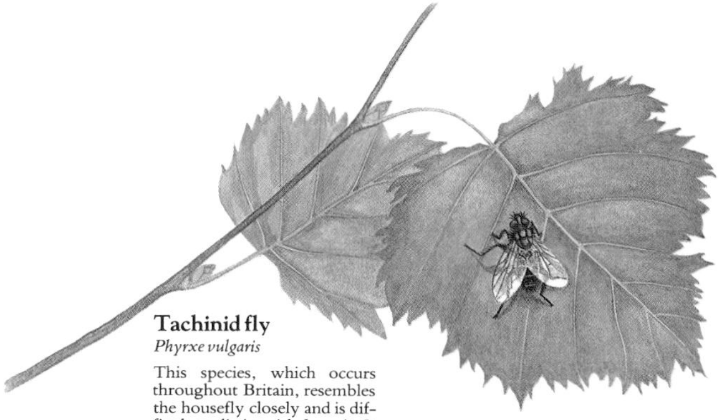

Tachinid fly

Phyrxe vulgaris

This species, which occurs throughout Britain, resembles the housefly closely and is difficult to distinguish from it. It is likely to be seen near trees from May to late September. Its larvae are internal parasites of caterpillars. Length $\frac{3}{8}$ in. (10 mm).

Sheep bot-fly

Oestrus ovis

A large, broad fly found over most of Britain, often resting in shady places near flocks of sheep. It lays its eggs on the sheep's head and the larvae work their way into the nostrils and sinuses of the animal, causing irritation and pain. Length $\frac{1}{2}$ in. (13 mm).

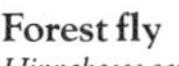

Forest fly

Hippobosca equina

Found only in the New Forest (Hampshire) and the surrounding area from May to October. Claws at the tips of the legs are used for clinging to ponies, cattle, dogs, and other animals, which they bite to feed on the blood. They can cling to humans but rarely bite. Length $\frac{5}{16}$ in. (8 mm).

Cattle warble fly

Hypoderma bovis

A large, hairy fly found as far north as Inverness. It lays its eggs on the legs of cattle and the larvae bore under the skin, working their way to the animal's back where they cause irritating swellings. Mature larvae emerge from the skin and pupate on the ground. The fly is seen in June and July. Length $\frac{5}{8}$ in. (16 mm).

Tachinid fly

Echinomyia fera

A common fly seen all over Britain and recognisable by its body colour. It is often found on flowers near ponds and streams from mid-August to October. Its larvae are parasites of caterpillars. Length $\frac{5}{8}$ in. (16 mm).

Cluster fly
Pollenia rudis

The flies' name comes from their habit of collecting in small groups on the outside walls of houses, from where they may enter lofts or rooms to hibernate. The larvae are parasites of earthworms. Length ⅜ in. (10 mm).

Autumn fly
Musca autumnalis

Very similar to the housefly, but on the wing only from February to October. It breeds in cow-pats, and enters houses in autumn to hibernate through the winter. Length $\frac{5}{16}$ in. (8 mm).

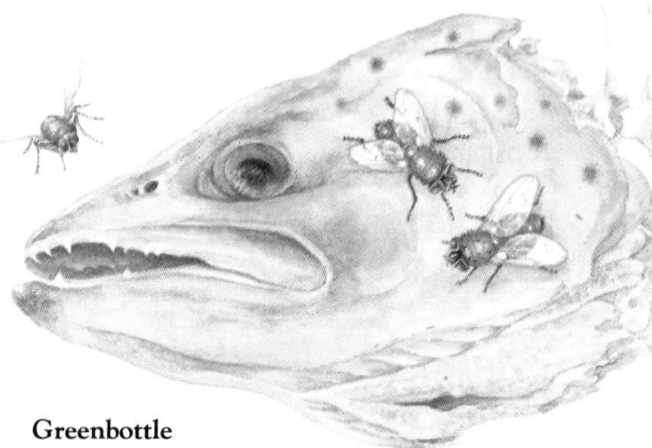

Greenbottle
Lucilia caesar

One of the most common of a large group of 'greenbottles'. At least five other unrelated flies are similar. The female lays her eggs on the bodies of dead animals or exposed meat. Length ⅜ in. (10 mm).

Stable fly
Stomoxys calcitrans

Very similar to the housefly but with a prominent proboscis. It breeds in manure and the adult fly bites animals – even occasionally humans. Length $\frac{5}{16}$ in. (8 mm).

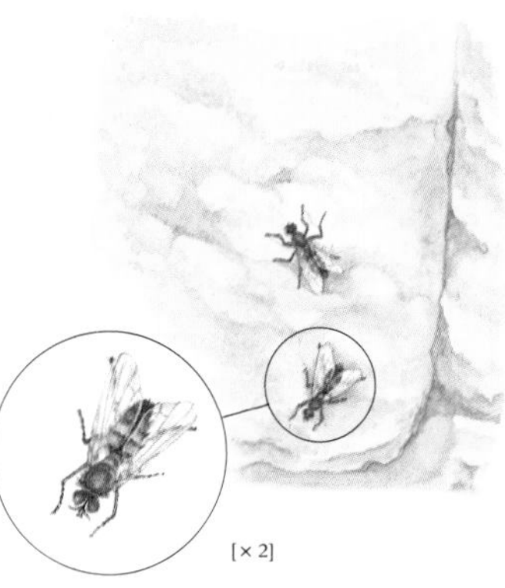

[× 2]

Lesser housefly
Fannia canicularis

Smaller than the housefly but no less common. They may breed in damp sludge around drains, and can be recognised by their incessant circling flight around pendant lamps. Length ¼ in. (6 mm).

Flies: houseflies and other pests

Housefly is the common name for the species *Musca domestica*, but it is often used for any medium-size fly found inside houses. Some species, including the cluster and autumn flies, enter houses in autumn to hibernate. Others are attracted by the smell of food. Any fly inside a house is a potential hazard as it constantly combs its hairy body to remove dirt, including any disease organisms it has picked up when feeding on carrion or animal droppings. The germs may then be deposited on work surfaces or exposed food. In addition, bluebottles, greenbottles, flesh flies and houseflies feed by regurgitating a liquid on to food and sucking it back after some of the food has dissolved. This can distribute a rich soup of disease organisms. Bluebottles, greenbottles and flesh flies are also the sources of the white maggots which ruin meat. As with most insects associated with man all these flies are widely distributed.

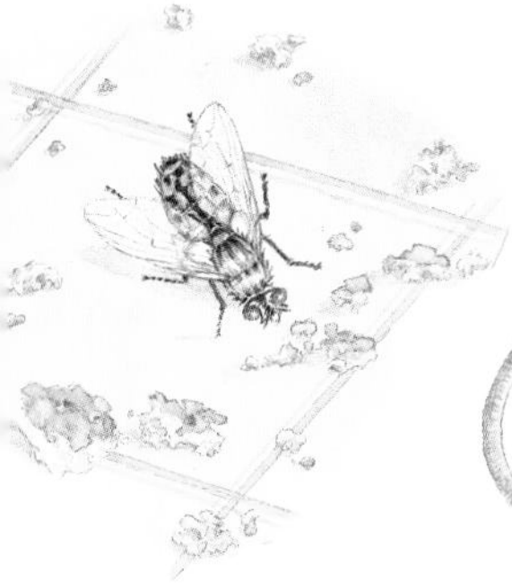

Flesh fly

Sarcophaga carnaria

A large fly with a chequered body that occasionally comes indoors when food is left uncovered. Length $\frac{5}{8}$ in. (16 mm).

The larvae of the flesh fly are typical of the maggots found in fly-blown meat.

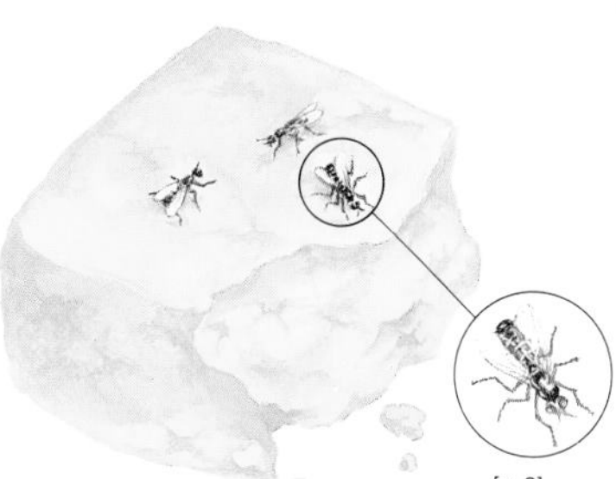

Cheese fly (cheese skipper)

Piophila casei

A small, shiny black fly whose larvae feed on cheese and meat products. It was once a common pest in cheese shops, but is now rare because of better hygiene. Length $\frac{1}{8}$ in. (3 mm).

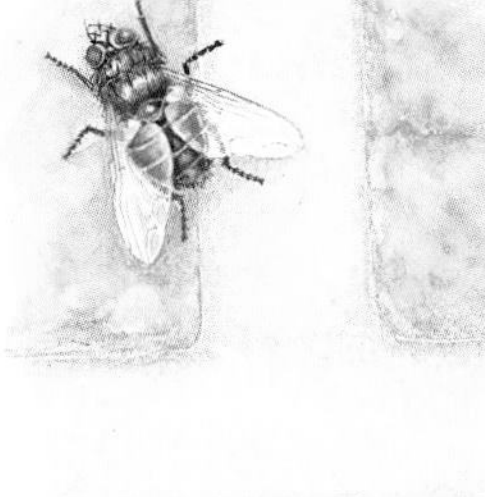

Common bluebottle (blowfly)

Calliphora vomitoria

These are the large metallic-blue flies that buzz loudly on the window pane. There are at least two species of bluebottle, but they are very difficult to tell apart. They lay eggs on exposed meat, which the larvae (maggots) then eat. Length $\frac{7}{16}$ in. (11 mm).

Housefly

Musca domestica

By far the most common fly in houses. The larvae normally live in manure but can exist in kitchen rubbish. It looks very much like the autumn fly but occurs all year round. Length $\frac{5}{16}$ in. (8 mm).

Greenbottle

Dasyphora cyanella

A metallic-green fly, unrelated to the *Lucilia* greenbottle but similar. It may be found in houses where the larvae feed on rotting food. Length $\frac{5}{16}$ in. (8 mm).

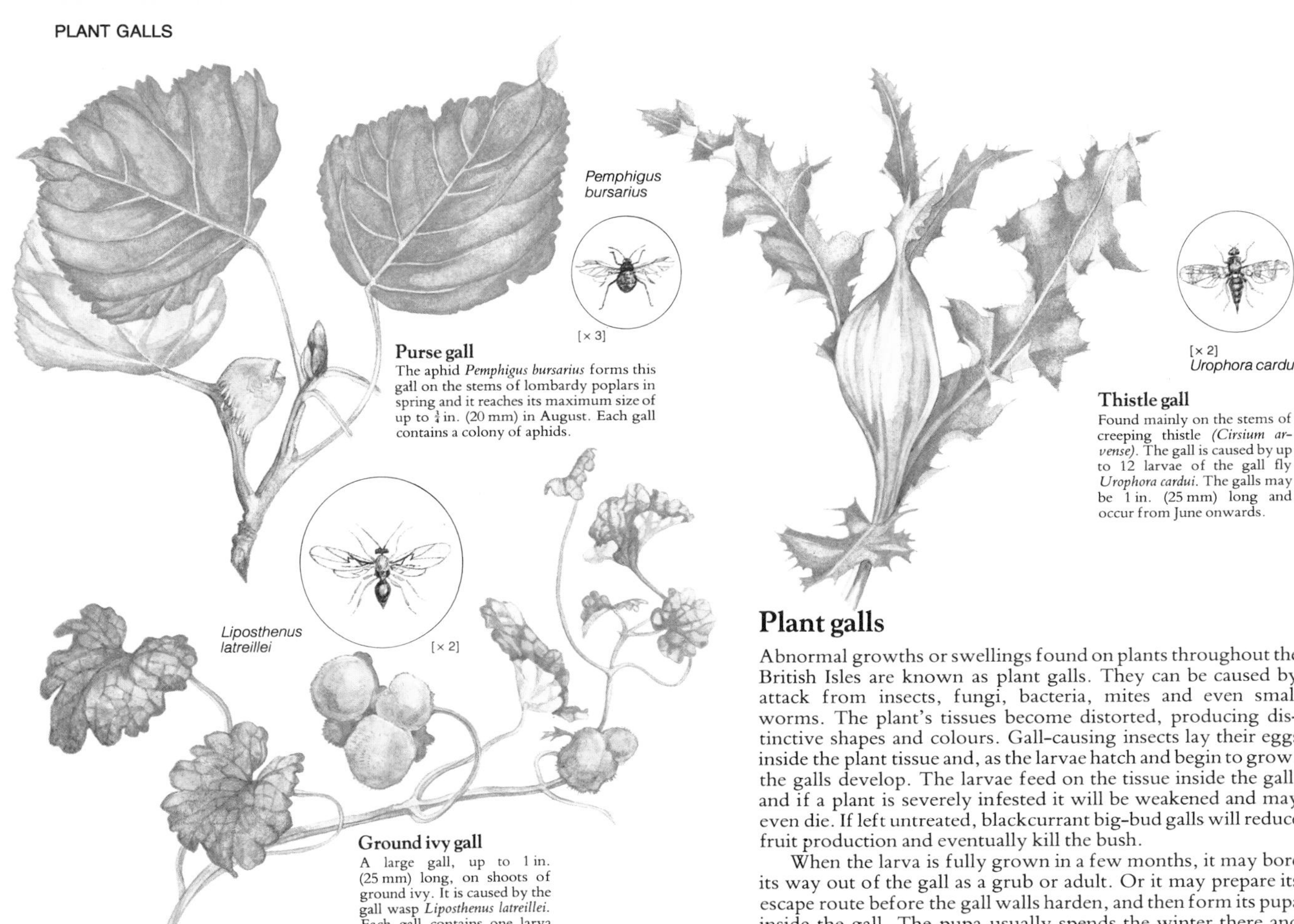

Purse gall
The aphid *Pemphigus bursarius* forms this gall on the stems of lombardy poplars in spring and it reaches its maximum size of up to ¾ in. (20 mm) in August. Each gall contains a colony of aphids.

Thistle gall
Found mainly on the stems of creeping thistle *(Cirsium arvense)*. The gall is caused by up to 12 larvae of the gall fly *Urophora cardui*. The galls may be 1 in. (25 mm) long and occur from June onwards.

Ground ivy gall
A large gall, up to 1 in. (25 mm) long, on shoots of ground ivy. It is caused by the gall wasp *Liposthenus latreillei*. Each gall contains one larva which forms a pupa in late summer and hatches as a gall wasp the following May.

Plant galls

Abnormal growths or swellings found on plants throughout the British Isles are known as plant galls. They can be caused by attack from insects, fungi, bacteria, mites and even small worms. The plant's tissues become distorted, producing distinctive shapes and colours. Gall-causing insects lay their eggs inside the plant tissue and, as the larvae hatch and begin to grow, the galls develop. The larvae feed on the tissue inside the gall, and if a plant is severely infested it will be weakened and may even die. If left untreated, blackcurrant big-bud galls will reduce fruit production and eventually kill the bush.

When the larva is fully grown in a few months, it may bore its way out of the gall as a grub or adult. Or it may prepare its escape route before the gall walls harden, and then form its pupa inside the gall. The pupa usually spends the winter there and hatches into an adult in spring.

The galls are all shown life-size, except where stated.

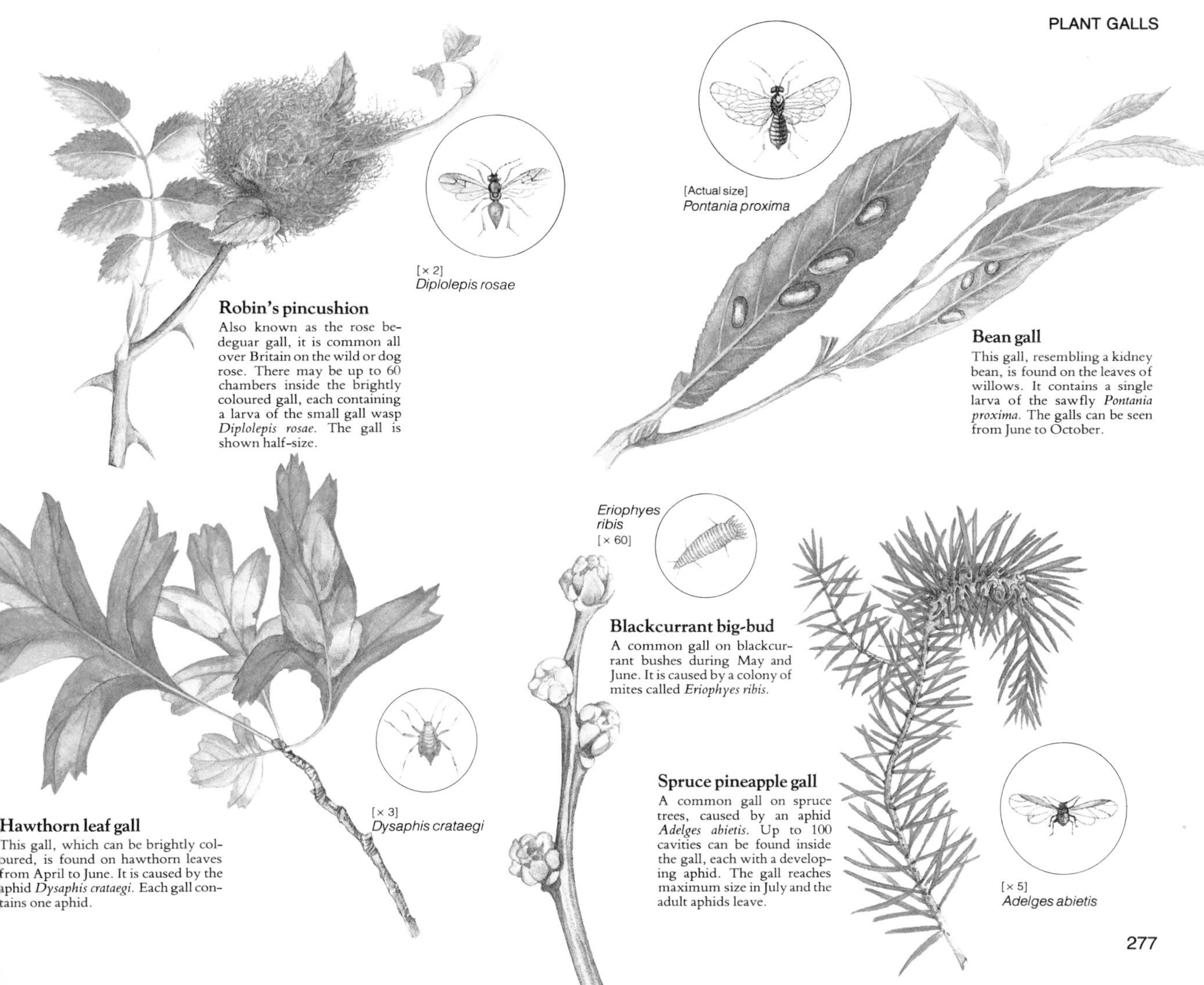

Robin's pincushion

Also known as the rose bedeguar gall, it is common all over Britain on the wild or dog rose. There may be up to 60 chambers inside the brightly coloured gall, each containing a larva of the small gall wasp *Diplolepis rosae*. The gall is shown half-size.

Bean gall

This gall, resembling a kidney bean, is found on the leaves of willows. It contains a single larva of the sawfly *Pontania proxima*. The galls can be seen from June to October.

Hawthorn leaf gall

This gall, which can be brightly coloured, is found on hawthorn leaves from April to June. It is caused by the aphid *Dysaphis crataegi*. Each gall contains one aphid.

Blackcurrant big-bud

A common gall on blackcurrant bushes during May and June. It is caused by a colony of mites called *Eriophyes ribis*.

Spruce pineapple gall

A common gall on spruce trees, caused by an aphid *Adelges abietis*. Up to 100 cavities can be found inside the gall, each with a developing aphid. The gall reaches maximum size in July and the adult aphids leave.

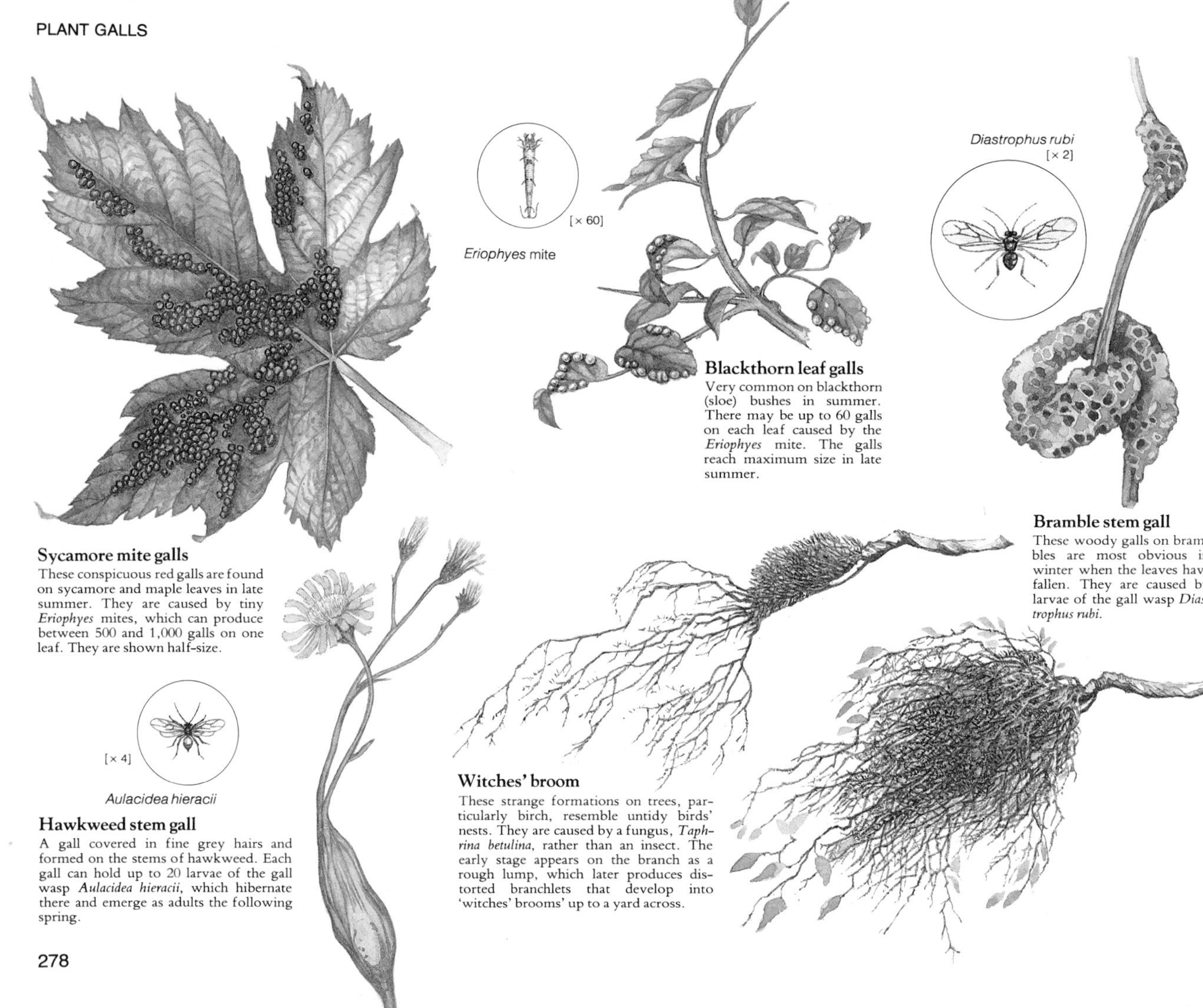

Sycamore mite galls

These conspicuous red galls are found on sycamore and maple leaves in late summer. They are caused by tiny *Eriophyes* mites, which can produce between 500 and 1,000 galls on one leaf. They are shown half-size.

Hawkweed stem gall

A gall covered in fine grey hairs and formed on the stems of hawkweed. Each gall can hold up to 20 larvae of the gall wasp *Aulacidea hieracii*, which hibernate there and emerge as adults the following spring.

Blackthorn leaf galls

Very common on blackthorn (sloe) bushes in summer. There may be up to 60 galls on each leaf caused by the *Eriophyes* mite. The galls reach maximum size in late summer.

Witches' broom

These strange formations on trees, particularly birch, resemble untidy birds' nests. They are caused by a fungus, *Taphrina betulina*, rather than an insect. The early stage appears on the branch as a rough lump, which later produces distorted branchlets that develop into 'witches' brooms' up to a yard across.

Bramble stem gall

These woody galls on brambles are most obvious in winter when the leaves have fallen. They are caused by larvae of the gall wasp *Diastrophus rubi*.

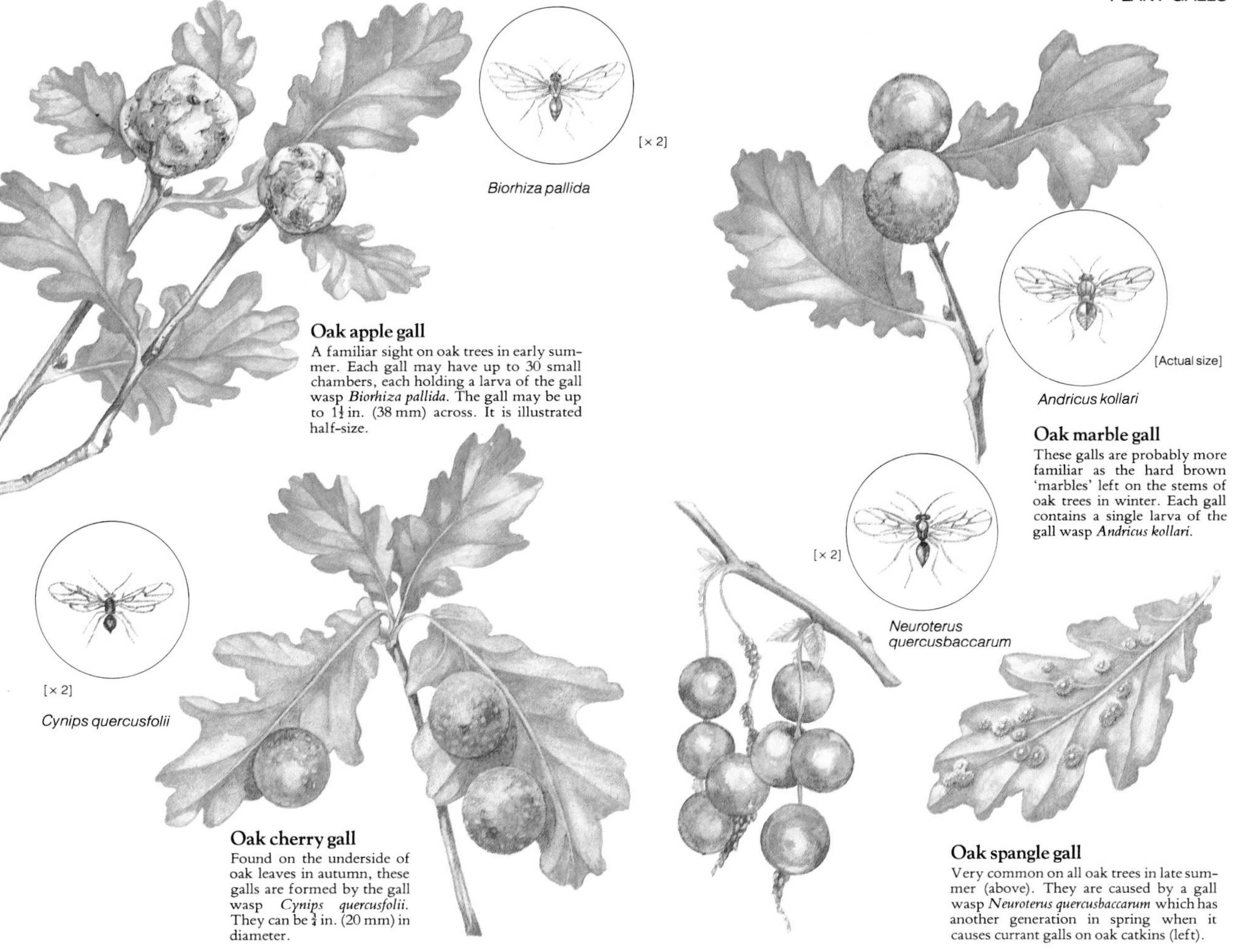

Oak apple gall

A familiar sight on oak trees in early summer. Each gall may have up to 30 small chambers, each holding a larva of the gall wasp *Biorhiza pallida*. The gall may be up to $1\frac{1}{2}$ in. (38 mm) across. It is illustrated half-size.

Oak marble gall

These galls are probably more familiar as the hard brown 'marbles' left on the stems of oak trees in winter. Each gall contains a single larva of the gall wasp *Andricus kollari*.

Oak cherry gall

Found on the underside of oak leaves in autumn, these galls are formed by the gall wasp *Cynips quercusfolii*. They can be $\frac{3}{4}$ in. (20 mm) in diameter.

Oak spangle gall

Very common on all oak trees in late summer (above). They are caused by a gall wasp *Neuroterus quercusbaccarum* which has another generation in spring when it causes currant galls on oak catkins (left).

The green tiger beetle often flies short distances, making a buzzing sound. [Actual size]

The beetle's large compound eyes and the wide gape of its serrated mandibles (jaws) make it a ferocious predator.

The larva digs a deep shaft in the sandy soil, where it lies in wait for ants or other small insects that pass near by.

A green tiger beetle seizes a caterpilla with its formidable jaws. It will eat severa creatures each day.

Green tiger beetle *Cicindela campestris*

This colourful beetle is one of the fastest running of British insects. When chasing other insects for food, it can cover the ground at a speed of up to 24 in. (60 cm) a second. It is most obvious on hot, sunny days in early summer as it scurries across sandy heaths or coastal dunes, often making short, rapid flight over low vegetation. The green tiger beetle, which is found almost everywhere in Britain, is the most common of five species of British tiger beetle. The other four are much rarer. They get their name from the large, powerful jaws which overlap when not being used.

The jaws of the adult beetle are matched by those of the larva which are used like gin-traps. The larva lives in a vertical shaft about 12 in. (30 cm) deep. It wedges itself in the entrance and holds its jaws level with the surface of the ground. When an insect – usually an ant – walks over or near the hole the jaws snap shut around it and it is taken to the bottom of the shaft to be eaten. After living for 16–18 months the larva changes into a pupa in the shaft. The beetle hatches in autumn but remains underground until it emerges the following spring to spend the summer in the open.

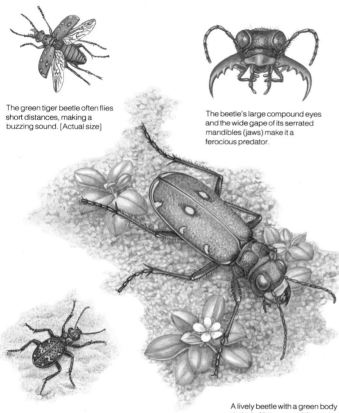

A lively beetle with a green body dotted with creamy-white spots. It can run rapidly in pursuit of small insects, and is fiercely carnivorous. Length $\frac{5}{8}$ in. (16 mm).

Wood tiger beetle
Cicindela sylvatica

A brown tiger beetle about the same size as the green tiger. It occurs in heathlands and woods in Surrey, Hampshire and Dorset during July and August. Length $\frac{9}{16}$ in. (15 mm).

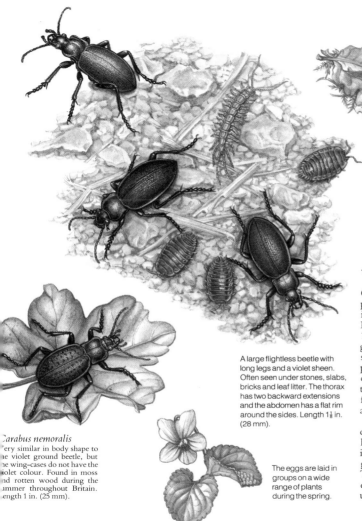

The larvae spend their lives in the darkness of leaf litter, and are carnivores like the adults.

The long-legged violet ground beetle is found almost everywhere in Britain, particularly from June to August.

A large flightless beetle with long legs and a violet sheen. Often seen under stones, slabs, bricks and leaf litter. The thorax has two backward extensions and the abdomen has a flat rim around the sides. Length $1\frac{1}{8}$ in. (28 mm).

Carabus nemoralis
Very similar in body shape to the violet ground beetle, but the wing-cases do not have the violet colour. Found in moss and rotten wood during the summer throughout Britain. Length 1 in. (25 mm).

The eggs are laid in groups on a wide range of plants during the spring.

Violet ground beetle *Carabus violaceus*

Ground beetles are fast-moving hunters of the night, using their powerful, sharp jaws to grasp and crush small creatures including many types of insects. By day they rest in dark places. In Britain there are 352 species of ground beetle, ranging up to $1\frac{3}{8}$ in. (35 mm) in length. Most species, including the violet ground beetle, have adaptations to a life on the ground, and some have their wing-cases fused together, making flight impossible. The violet ground beetle, named after the violet sheen on its black wing-cases, is one of the largest species. It is useful to farmers and gardeners as it eats large numbers of plant-feeding insects. It is particularly common in fields where cereals are grown, and in gardens throughout Britain.

Different sorts of ground beetle are found in every type of countryside, from dry sand-dunes to the wettest bogs. Their larvae are also predators, catching and eating other soft-bodied insects. The larvae take up to ten months to become fully grown. They then form a pupa in the soil or inside rotten wood. The adults of some species, including the violet ground beetle, emerge from their pupae in autumn but do not become active until spring. Their adult lives last about nine months.

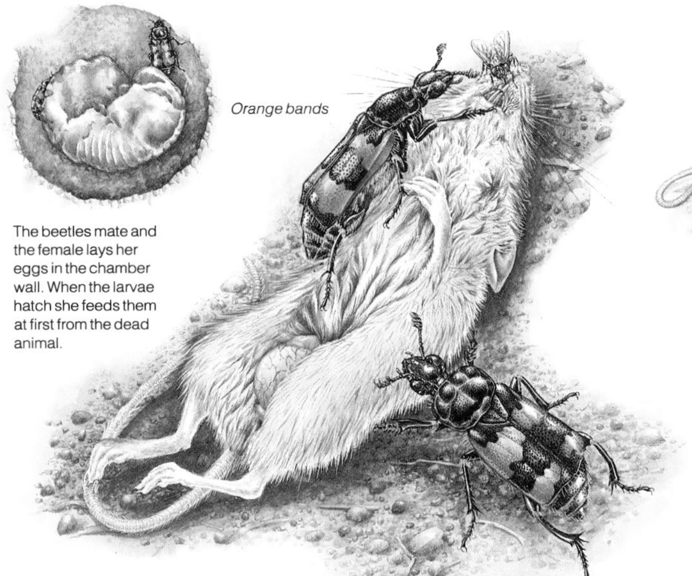

The beetles mate and the female lays her eggs in the chamber wall. When the larvae hatch she feeds them at first from the dead animal.

Orange bands

Beetles with bright orange bands across a black body. Usually found around the corpse of a small animal, such as a mouse or a bird. Length $\frac{5}{8}$ in. (16 mm).

A pair of beetles dig a shaft below the dead animal and drag it down. The skin is rolled off the body as it is pulled down.

The activities of sexton beetles help to dispose of the corpses of dead birds and small mammals.

Black burying beetle
Nicrophorus humator

Black, with orange-tipped antennae. Found all over Britain. Length $1\frac{1}{8}$ in. (28 mm).

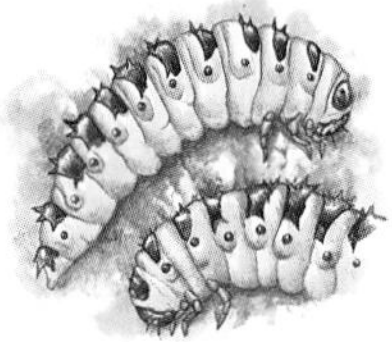

The developed larvae are helped into the carcass by the female which bites an entry hole. She leaves them when they can cope independently.

Sexton beetle *Nicrophorus vespilloides*

The black and orange sexton beetles are also known as burying or grave-digging, beetles because of their habit of burying dead animals as food for their offspring. The carcass is usually buried where it lies, but if it is on stony ground they may drag it to a softer area a yard or more away, or even bite off portions to bury elsewhere. The beetles are good flyers and can smell a decaying carcass up to two miles away downwind. They may be seen from early spring until late summer throughout Britain.

After a pair of beetles have buried a carcass the female lays her eggs near it and protects them from predators and parasites until they hatch. Any maggots that were already on the animal's body are eaten by the beetles before the maggots can eat the carcass. When the eggs hatch the female beetle at first feeds the larvae with partially digested pieces of food. As they develop they begin to eat the carcass.

All six British species of burying beetle are stoutly built insects with powerful legs and jaws. The black burying beetle *Nicrophorus humator*, is much larger than *N. vespilloides* and is often attracted to lights at night. In captivity, *Nicrophorus* beetles have lived almost 300 days.

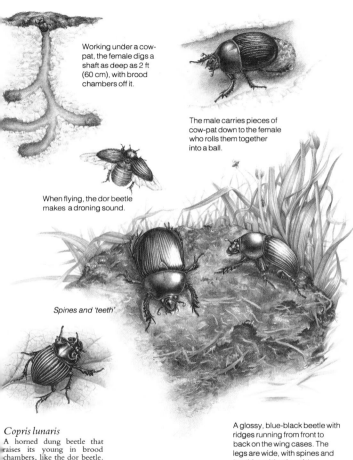

Working under a cow-pat, the female digs a shaft as deep as 2 ft (60 cm), with brood chambers off it.

The male carries pieces of cow-pat down to the female who rolls them together into a ball.

When flying, the dor beetle makes a droning sound.

The female lays a single egg in a depression in the top of the dung ball. She then encloses it, except for an air hole, by raising the sides of the depression. [× 3]

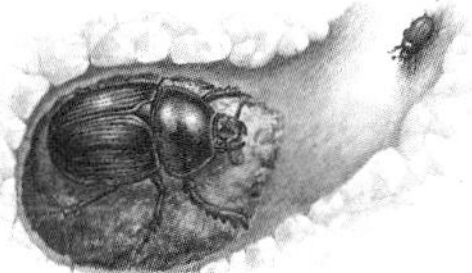

The female waits by the egg, defending it from predators, until the larva hatches.

The strong, spiny legs and jaws of the dor beetle are ideally suited for its life of burrowing in the soil and moving dung.

Spines and 'teeth'

A glossy, blue-black beetle with ridges running from front to back on the wing cases. The legs are wide, with spines and 'teeth', and the tips of the antennae are club-like. Length 1 in. (25 mm).

Copris lunaris

A horned dung beetle that raises its young in brood chambers, like the dor beetle. But both parents stay with the larvae until they leave the burrow. Length ⅝ in. (16 mm).

Dor beetle *Geotrupes stercorarius*

The dor beetle is one of a group called dung beetles, which get their name from their appetite for animal dung. Without them the countryside would be a less pleasant place, as they help to recycle the dropping of animals ranging from rabbits to horses. Different species specialise in different types of droppings. Dor beetles, which are common throughout Britain, concentrate on horse and cow dung. They bury dung balls in burrows as deep as 2 ft (60 cm) for their larvae to eat.

The name 'dor' comes from an old word meaning drone. The beetles fly with a droning sound in the evening as they seek out mates or fresh cow-pats, or are attracted to lights. Their hard, black outer skeleton is ideal for smoothing dung balls and for protection from enemies. However they fall prey to foxes, and the fox droppings are often rich in dor-beetle remains. The beetles may also become victims of blood-sucking mites.

Another dung beetle, *Copris lunaris*, is related to the sacred scarab beetle which was worshipped in ancient Egypt. It is now rare, found only in the south-east of England, especially Surrey. Like the minotaur beetle (p. 287), it is armed with a horn which it uses for courtship and for moving balls of dung.

Beetles of the woodland floor

The flight of the large and cumbersome stag beetle can disturb the quiet of a woodland glade on a summer's afternoon. Among the undergrowth, other beetles lurk in rotting wood, among moss or in the leaf litter. Dense woods, with dead trees decaying on the ground, are the main habitats of Britain's 4,000 species of beetle. The familiar ladybird can be seen on foliage or flying from plant to plant in search of aphids to eat and places to lay its eggs. And many types of small weevil beetles can be found on overhanging branches. Tortoise beetles sun themselves in damp patches, and bloody-nosed beetles plod over the ground, or on vegetation, on their long, wide legs.

If a rotten log is turned over, ground beetles are likely to be disturbed in their daytime resting places. In the crevices of the log other beetles may be living with woodlice, centipedes, tiny worms, snails and slugs. All these woodland creatures are eagerly eaten by birds and lizards, and even by weasels, foxes and badgers as they rummage through the undergrowth.

In a wood, an encounter with a beetle is always likely. A tiger beetle may scurry across the path after prey, or a wood-boring beetle may fly along a bridleway.

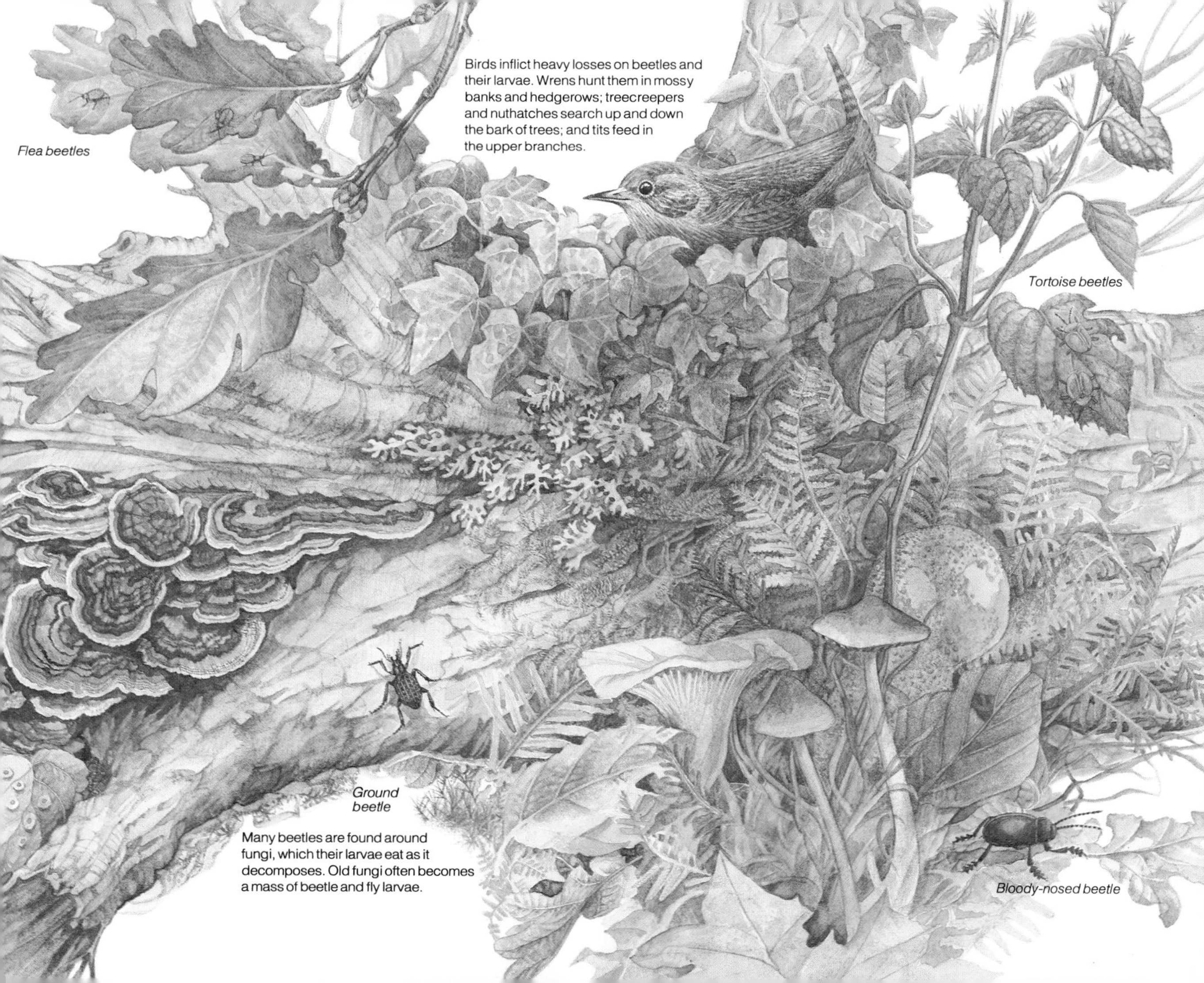

Birds inflict heavy losses on beetles and their larvae. Wrens hunt them in mossy banks and hedgerows; treecreepers and nuthatches search up and down the bark of trees; and tits feed in the upper branches.
Flea beetles
Tortoise beetles
Ground beetle
Many beetles are found around fungi, which their larvae eat as it decomposes. Old fungi often becomes a mass of beetle and fly larvae.
Bloody-nosed beetle

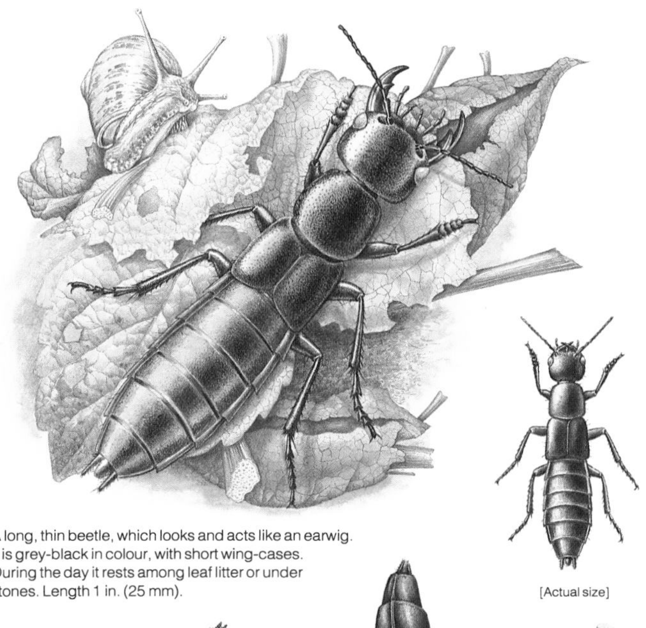

A long, thin beetle, which looks and acts like an earwig. It is grey-black in colour, with short wing-cases. During the day it rests among leaf litter or under stones. Length 1 in. (25 mm).

[Actual size]

The Devil's coach horse is a predatory beetle with a powerful pair of mandibles (jaws) for eating small creatures such as spiders, caterpillars and earwigs.

When threatened, it curls the abdomen over the body, and emits a deterrent smell.

The eggs are laid in the soil and hatch into larvae in a few days. [× 6]

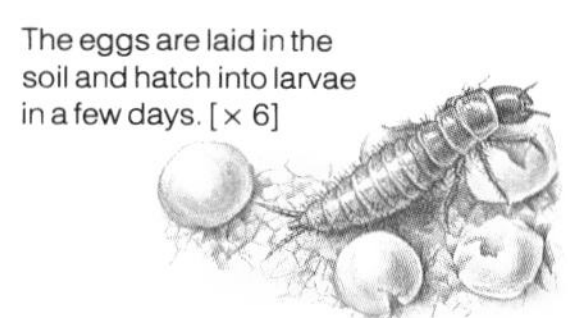

The larva is as carnivorous as the adult which it resembles. It forms a pupa (below) in leaf litter or moss where it spends the winter, and hatches the following spring.

The Devil's coach horse beetle reacts to a predator by curling its tail into a scorpion-like posture.

Devil's coach horse *Staphylinus olens*

In Irish mythology this beetle is a symbol of corruption, able to kill simply on sight. It is said that the Devil's coach horse will appear after dealing with the Devil and that it will eat sinners. On raising its 'tail' it casts a curse.

It is the largest of the British staphilinids, or rove beetles, of which there are nearly 1,000 species in Britain. They all have small wing-cases and antennae without club-shaped ends, and most of them are good flyers. Many rove beetles are found near dung or in ant hills.

The Devil's coach horse is a common species which often ventures into damp houses and gardens. Its threatening posture, which gave rise to its old English name of cock-tail, looks menacing but is harmless to humans. It is a carnivore and scavenger, eating spiders and smaller beetles as well as dead animals. It hunts mostly by night but may also be seen in the day. Birds such as robins, blackbirds and thrushes eat the beetle if they discover it hiding under litter or under logs by day. It defends itself by raising its tail and squirting two nauseous-smelling organic chemicals from glands near the anus into the face of the attacker, while snapping its jaws vigorously.

The male takes rabbit droppings or pieces of sheep droppings into the shaft, and the female packs them into the chambers.

'Horns'

Male

Black, shiny beetles with spiny legs and ridges along the wing-cases. The male has horn-like projections on the thorax. They are shown on the leaves of ragwort (*Senecio jacobaea*). Length $\frac{5}{8}$ in. (16 mm).

Female

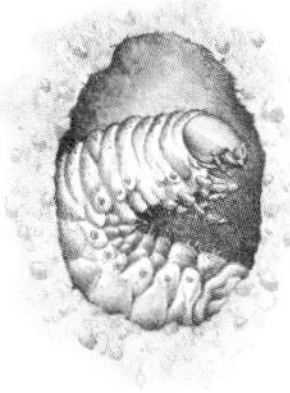

Eggs are laid in the dung, which the white larvae later use for food.

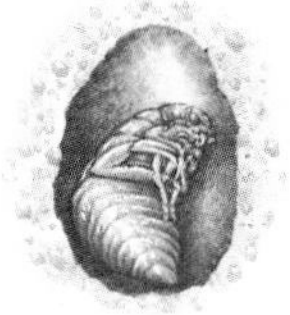

After three months, the larva forms into a pupa.

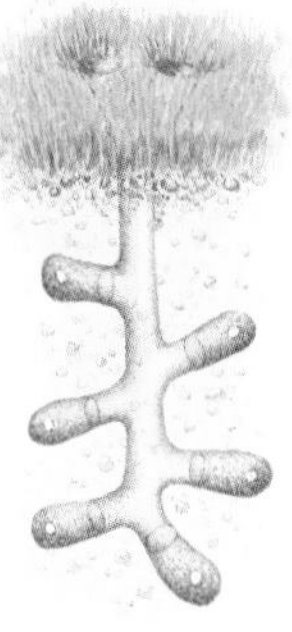

The female digs a shaft up to 24 in. (60 cm) deep in light, well-drained soil, with several brood chambers leading off it.

A male minotaur beetle collects rabbit droppings. He leaves the work of digging the burrow entirely to the female.

Minotaur beetle *Typhaeus typhoeus*

The three forward-pointing 'horns' on the male minotaur beetle are used in the same way as a stag's antlers – to engage in a contest with another male to win a female. The female minotaur has much shorter spikes and may be confused with the female dor beetle (p. 283), however she has no metallic colouring. Minotaur beetles can be common in sandy places as far north as southern Scotland in spring and early summer. The male beetle searches out the droppings of rabbits or sheep and rolls them with his horns into deep burrows which have been excavated in light soil by the female, using her powerful jaws and legs. She then lays an egg on each piece of dung, and when the larva hatches it uses the dung as a food store. After about three months the larva is fully grown and creates a space inside the old feeding chamber where it changes into a pupa. The adult beetle emerges after three or four weeks and may appear above ground for a short while in autumn before returning to the burrow to spend the winter.

The large size and hard cuticle (outer layer) of minotaur beetles protect them from all but the largest predators, such as hedgehogs and foxes.

This grey-black beetle is more common than the stag beetle but much less impressive in appearance. It can be confused with the female stag beetle but is slightly smaller and lacks the violet colouring on the wing-cases. Length 1¼ in. (32 mm).

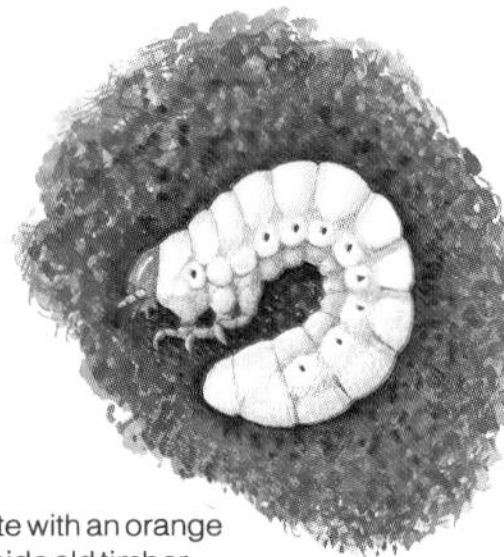

The larva is white with an orange head. It lives inside old timber, such as rotting tree stumps, eating the wood. It may take three years to become fully grown.

The pupa is formed in a small chamber in the wood. The adult hatches in late autumn but remains inside the chamber until spring.

Lesser stags occur on rotting wood. If an old tree is felled in winter, beetles may be found in their pupal chambers.

Lesser stag beetle *Dorcus parallelipipedus*

This large black beetle was given its name because of its resemblance to the female stag beetle. However it is completely black, and the male lesser stag is similar to the female, with normal sized jaws. Lesser stag beetles are more common than stag beetles but they are less often seen as they are active mainly at night, do not often emerge into the open, and fly only rarely. The beetles are most likely to be found in or on rotting timbers and stumps, especially beech, elm and ash, where they lay eggs.

After the larva hatches from the egg it spends three to four years eating the rotting wood. Trees infested with the lesser stag beetle are often visited by woodpeckers which feed on the large pale grubs. When it reaches full size, the larva creates a cell in the wood in late summer and changes into a pupa. The adult emerges from the pupa in late autumn, but stays inside the enclosed cell through the winter. It pushes or chews its way out the following spring. The beetles are likely to be seen any time between April and September. They live for about a month. Lesser stag beetles are found over most of the Midlands and southern England. They spend their adult lives without feeding on solids, surviving only on water and plant juices.

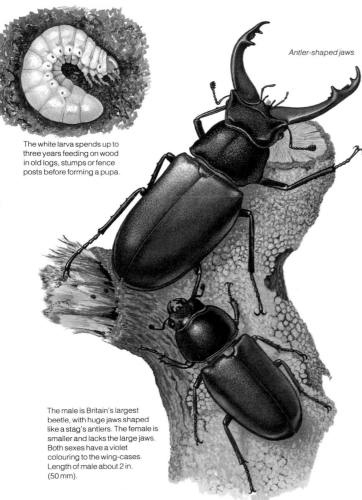

The white larva spends up to three years feeding on wood in old logs, stumps or fence posts before forming a pupa.

Antler-shaped jaws

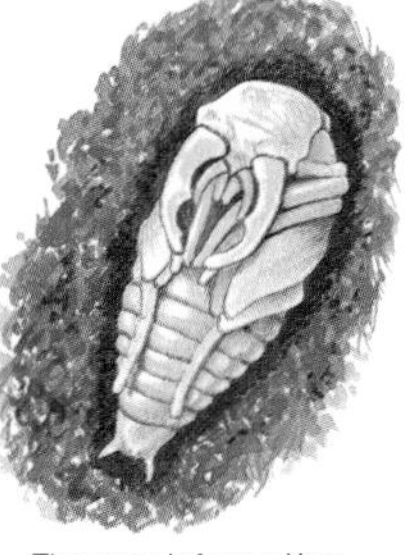

The pupa is formed in a small chamber in the wood, where it spends the winter before hatching the following spring.

In the Middle Ages, people believed the male stag beetle could fly with a live coal in its jaws and set house roofs alight.

The male is Britain's largest beetle, with huge jaws shaped like a stag's antlers. The female is smaller and lacks the large jaws. Both sexes have a violet colouring to the wing-cases. Length of male about 2 in. (50 mm).

Stag beetle *Lucanus cervus*

The male stag beetle with its ferocious-looking jaws is Britain's biggest beetle, but despite its appearance it is quite harmless. The female can give a sharp nip if handled, but the gigantic jaws of the male are ornamental; the muscles that move them are too weak to exert the leverage necessary to inflict a bite. The purpose of the jaws lies in courtship when rival males try to intimidate each other. Occasionally two males will engage in combat, rather like rutting stags, but no harm is done to either. After mating, the female will fly off in search of rotting tree stumps or logs to lay her eggs. Oak is a favourite wood but eggs are also laid in fruit trees, which may explain the large number of stag beetles in the south-east of England.

Both sexes fly quite often on warm summer evenings between June and August. They are sometimes seen in the southern suburbs of London as the coming of daylight leaves them exposed on lamp-posts and pavements. The beetles eat no solid food during their short adult lives but rely on fat reserves built up during the long larval stage which lasts up to three years. The female dies shortly after laying her eggs – only about a month after she herself emerged from her pupa.

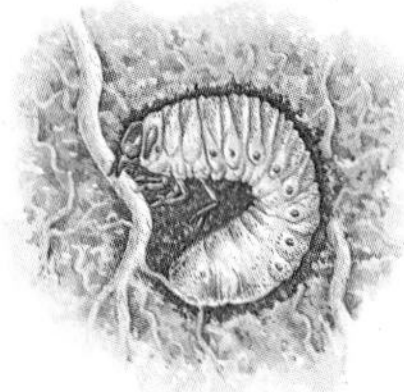

The larva is easily recognised from its white body and chestnut-coloured head. It has powerful jaws and eats the roots of a wide variety of grasses, including cereals. It always holds itself in this bent shape, and is 2 in. (50 mm) long.

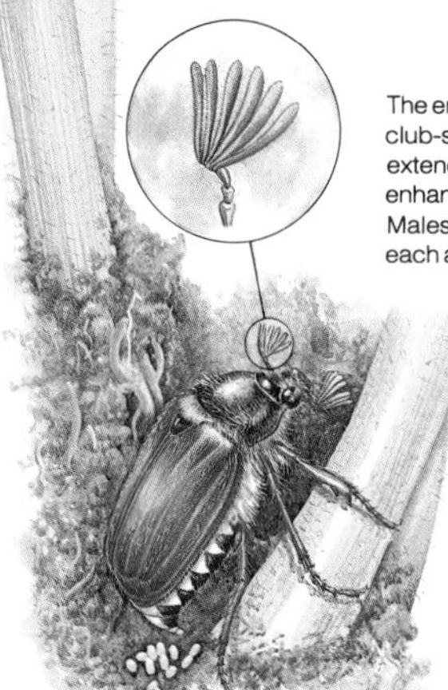

The ends of the antennae are club-shaped, but they can be extended into a wide fan, enhancing their sense of smell. Males have seven 'vanes' on each antenna, females only six.

Batches of 12–30 eggs are laid in the soil at the base of grasses, including cereals. They hatch into larvae after five to six weeks.

Rooks, magpies and black-headed gulls regularly search fields for the larvae which are sometimes called 'rookworms' or 'whitegrubs'.

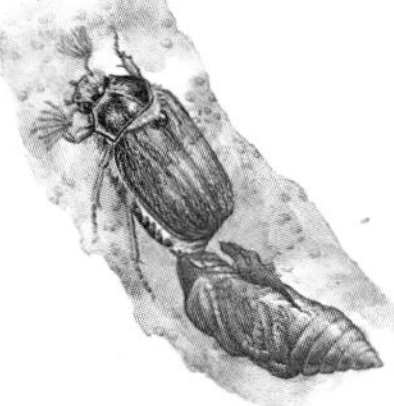

The adult hatches out of the pupa in the autumn and remains in its cell throughout the winter. It crawls out of the soil in May or June, hence the name May bug.

Garden chafer

Phyllopertha horticola

Also known as the field chafer or June bug, the garden chafer is similar in colour and shape to the cockchafer, but smaller. The wing-cases are brown, and the other parts are dark brown or dark green. Length ⅜ in. (10 mm).

After two to three years in the soil, the larva changes into a pupa in an earthen cell about 24 in. (60 cm) below the surface of the soil.

Adult beetles eat the foliage of deciduous trees, but they are not a serious pest like the larvae.

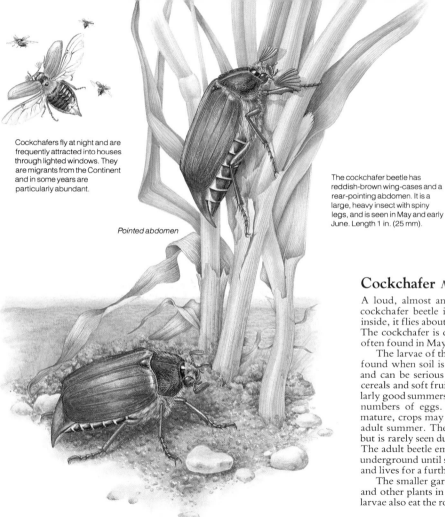

Cockchafers fly at night and are frequently attracted into houses through lighted windows. They are migrants from the Continent and in some years are particularly abundant.

The cockchafer beetle has reddish-brown wing-cases and a rear-pointing abdomen. It is a large, heavy insect with spiny legs, and is seen in May and early June. Length 1 in. (25 mm).

Pointed abdomen

Before taking to the air, cockchafers warm up their flight muscles by exercising their wings, producing a steadily increasing hum.

Cockchafer *Melolontha melolontha*

A loud, almost angry buzzing sound signals the arrival of a cockchafer beetle in a lighted room in early summer. Once inside, it flies about clumsily, colliding with things in the room. The cockchafer is commonly called the May bug as it is most often found in May or early June.

The larvae of the cockchafer are the white grubs sometimes found when soil is ploughed or dug. They feed on plant roots and can be serious pests of farm and garden crops, especially cereals and soft fruit. Great damage can be caused after particularly good summers when the female cockchafers have laid large numbers of eggs. As the larvae need two or three years to mature, crops may suffer for two or three seasons after a good adult summer. The cockchafer is found over most of Britain, but is rarely seen during the day because of its nocturnal habits. The adult beetle emerges from its pupa in October but remains underground until spring, when it pushes its way to the surface and lives for a further three or four months.

The smaller garden chafer may be found feeding on bushes and other plants in woods and gardens from May to July. The larvae also eat the roots of garden and field crops.

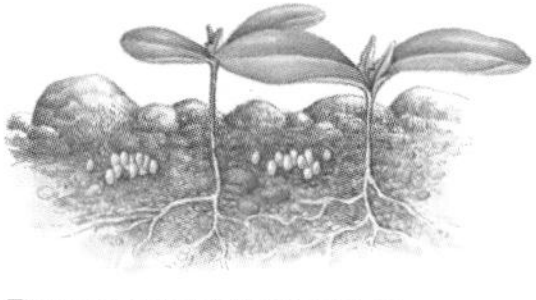

The eggs are laid in groups in the soil in May and June. The larvae hatch after about a month.

The shiny orange larvae, called wireworms, are a serious pest of root vegetables and the seedlings of farm crops. They live about a foot below the soil. When young they will eat dead or living plant matter.

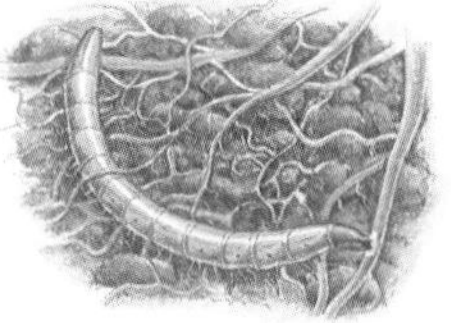

Wireworms live in the soil up to five years. Older wireworms eat only the roots of living plants, and grow to 1 in. (25 mm) long.

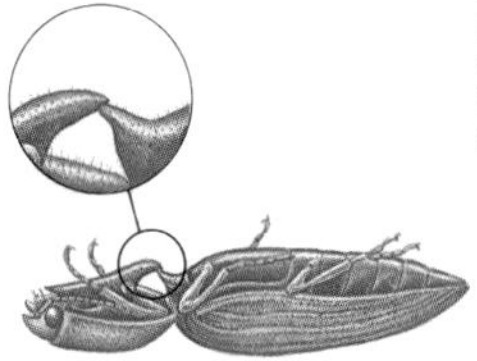

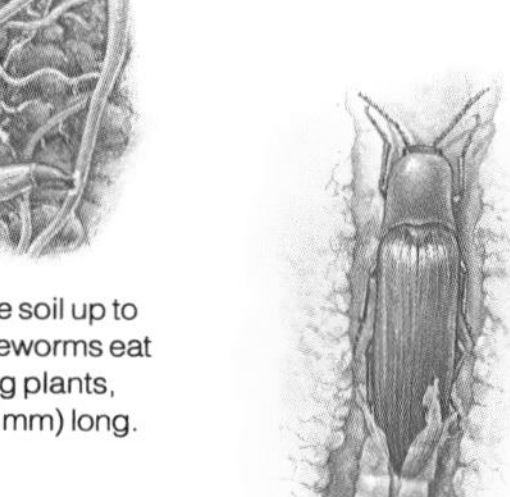

The pupa is formed in a cell about 9 in. (23 cm) below the soil in summer. The beetle hatches in October and hibernates in the cell until spring.

This brown-bodied beetle occurs on grass and shrubs and in leaf litter in spring and early summer.

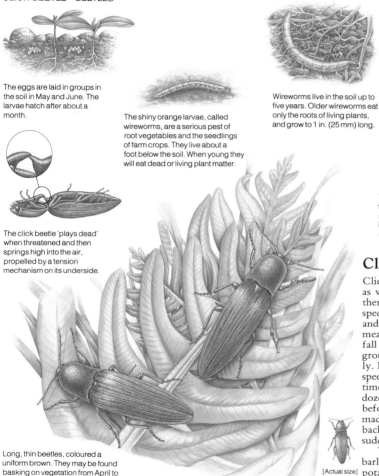

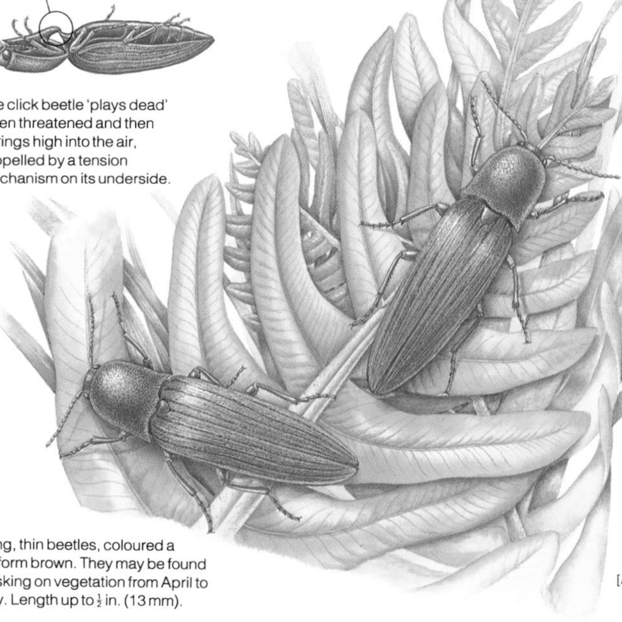

The click beetle 'plays dead' when threatened and then springs high into the air, propelled by a tension mechanism on its underside.

Long, thin beetles, coloured a uniform brown. They may be found basking on vegetation from April to July. Length up to ½ in. (13 mm).

[Actual size]

Click beetle *Agriotes lineatus*

Click beetles are also called skipjacks and their larvae are known as wireworms. The beetles are named after the way they flip themselves out of danger with an audible click. There are 65 species of click beetle in Britain, all with long bodies, small legs and toothed antennae. They are found in long grass, gardens, meadows and lawns deep in the turf or leaf litter where they may fall prey to searching birds. When disturbed they drop to the ground and feign death – a common reaction in beetles generally. However click beetles can jump about a foot into the air at a speed measured at 8 ft (2·5 m) per second, accelerating to 700 times the force of gravity. They sometimes somersault half a dozen times while in the air. Several jumps may be needed before they land the right way up. Such a powerful jump is made possible by the beetle's hinged thorax. While lying on its back the beetle arches its body under great tension which is suddenly released, flicking it into the air.

Wireworms are serious pests of cereals, including wheat, barley and oats; and of root crops, including beet, mangolds and potatoes. The adult beetles are also vegetarian, eating nectar, pollen, leaves and flowers.

Both the larva and the adult female produce a yellowish glow from the last three segments of the abdomen's underside. The female climbs to a vantage point and turns her abdomen upwards to attract males.

The larva eats small snails. It first immobilises the snail by pouring a digestive enzyme into the shell. This converts the body tissue into a liquid which it drinks.

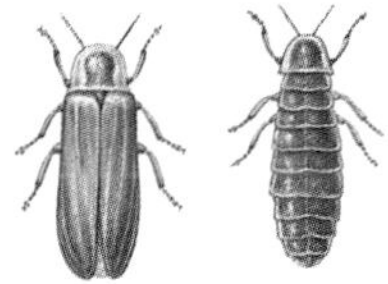

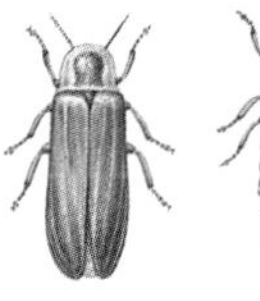

Male Female

[Actual size]

Glow-worms are most common in the south of England, but even there the distribution is very local.

Eggs are laid in June and July on vegetation close to the ground. They hatch after a month.

The male has a pair of wing-cases over the abdomen. The female is wingless with a segmented abdomen. Both occur from May to August. Length $\frac{5}{8}$ in. (16 mm).

Glow-worm *Lampyris noctiluca*

Fifty years ago glow-worms were common in the British countryside, so common in some localities that people could read by their light. Now they are very rare, probably because of loss of meadows and grassland. Glow-worms, relatives of the tropical fireflies, take their name from the female which emits the light. During the day the wingless females hide from predators, but at night they crawl on to vegetation so that they can display their light most effectively to attract males. The glow-worm's light is produced by cells that use oxygen, water and an enzyme to form the light-emitting substance oxyluciferin. The light is enhanced by a layer of reflector cells. In the early evening the glow is yellowy-green but changes to a brighter yellow after dark.

A female emits light at will when she wants to attract males. The light is surprisingly intense for such a small source. The male has excellent sight to spot the female at up to 10 yds, and wings to reach her. Each compound eye in the male is eight times more powerful than the female's, with 2,500 facets compared with 300. The male pinpoints the female accurately, and when directly above closes his wings and drops on to her.

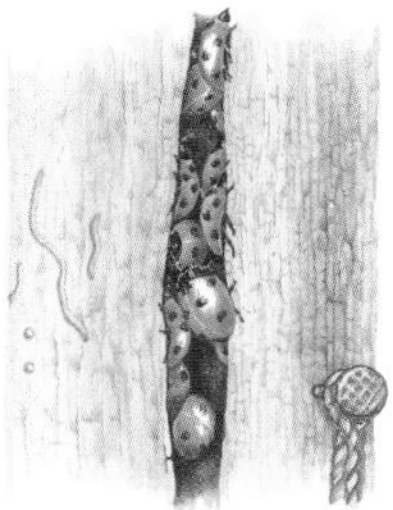

The adult ladybirds hibernate over winter and may even enter houses looking for suitable places. Many become infected with fungi and die.

Each female lays about 200 eggs, often on the underside of leaves close to colonies of aphids.

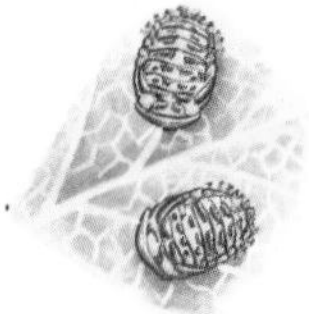

After three weeks, the larva turns into a pupa, strongly attached to a leaf or stem in an exposed position.

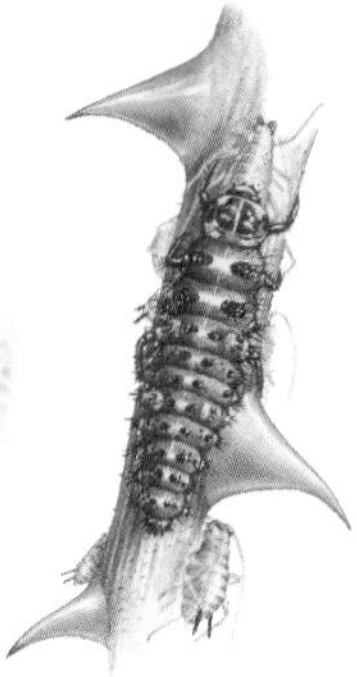

The slate-blue larva with yellow blotches is ½ in. (13 mm) long, much longer than the adult ladybird.

Clusters of hibernating ladybirds may be found crammed together under bark or beneath window-sills.

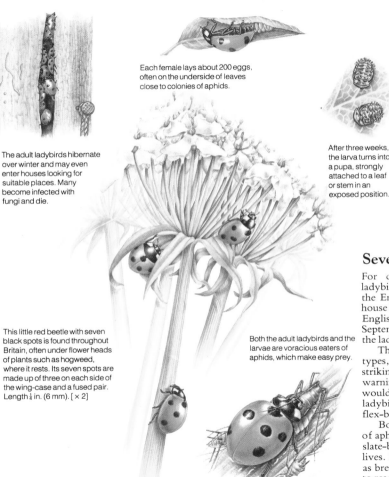

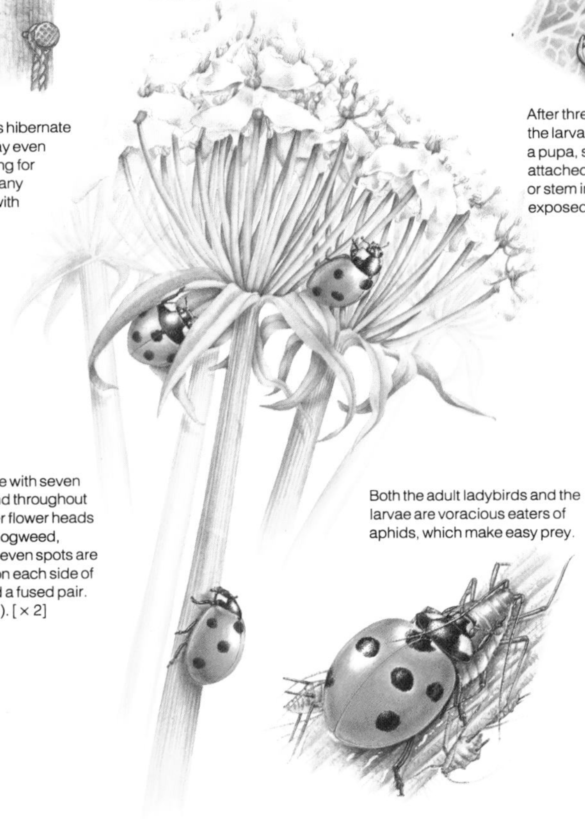

This little red beetle with seven black spots is found throughout Britain, often under flower heads of plants such as hogweed, where it rests. Its seven spots are made up of three on each side of the wing-case and a fused pair. Length ¼ in. (6 mm). [× 2]

Both the adult ladybirds and the larvae are voracious eaters of aphids, which make easy prey.

Seven-spot ladybird *Coccinella 7-punctata*

For centuries, children throughout Europe have placed ladybirds on their fingers and recited their national version of the English verse: 'Ladybird, ladybird, fly away home. Your house is on fire, your children will burn.' One explanation of the English rhyme is that it refers to the firing of the hop fields in September, after the harvest. However, French children warn the ladybird that the Turks are coming to kill their offspring.

The seven-spot ladybird is one of the most familiar British types, but there are also 40 other species in this country. The striking black, yellow and red colours of the ladybird are a warning to predatory birds that it contains alkaloid poisons, and would be distasteful and dangerous to eat. As an added defence, ladybirds can produce blobs of bright yellow blood from 're-flex-bleeding' points on their bodies.

Both the ladybirds and their larvae are voracious predators of aphids. Eggs are laid on plants infested with aphids, and the slate-blue larvae eat hundreds of aphids in their three-week lives. Ladybirds migrate to Britain from the Continent, as well as breeding here, and 'red tides' have occurred when they failed to reach land.

Six other species of ladybird

Eyed ladybird

Anatis ocellata

Britain's largest ladybird, with seven or eight spots on each of its pale red wing-cases. It is found on pine trees. Length $\frac{5}{16}$ in. (8 mm). [× $2\frac{1}{2}$]

Ten-spot ladybird

Adalia 10-punctata

A common woodland species which has several colour forms. It may have reddish-brown or black wing-cases and either yellow, black or orange spots. Its legs are yellow. Length $\frac{1}{6}$ in. (4 mm). [× 3]

Fourteen-spot ladybird

Propylea 14-punctata

A small but brightly coloured ladybird with black and yellow marks. It is often seen resting on vegetation. Found in the southern half of Britain. Length $\frac{1}{6}$ in. (4 mm). [× $3\frac{1}{2}$]

Two-spot ladybird

Adalia 2-punctata

Probably the most numerous of British ladybirds, usually with one large spot on each wing-case. However, variations occur with two or three spots on each wing-case. Length $\frac{1}{6}$ in. (4 mm). [× 3]

Twenty-four-spot ladybird

Subcoccinella 24-punctata

Unlike most ladybirds this species is a vegetarian, feeding on leguminous plants such as clover. The blotches on its wing-cases total between 16 and 20 rather than 24. Length $\frac{1}{8}$ in. (3 mm). [× 4]

Twenty-two-spot ladybird

Thea 22-punctata

A very small ladybird with 11 precise black spots on each wing-case. It occurs in limited areas throughout England, Wales and eastern Ireland. Length $\frac{1}{8}$ in. (3 mm). [× 4]

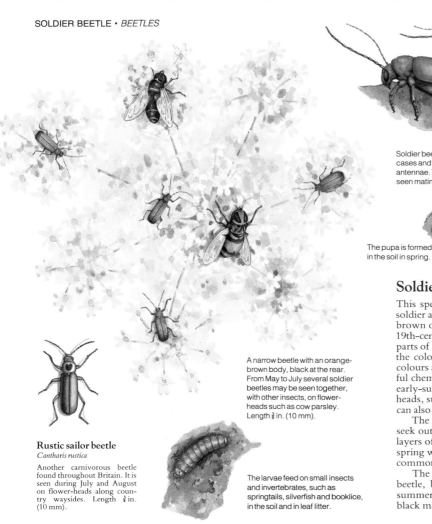

Soldier beetles have soft wing-cases and bodies, and long antennae. They are frequently seen mating on flower-heads.

A pair of soldier beetles, on the flower-head of a thistle, seek out small insects which they will kill and eat.

The pupa is formed in the soil in spring.

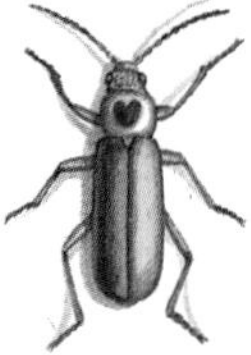

Soldier beetle *Rhagonycha fulva*

This species of beetle is just one of several that are known as soldier and sailor beetles, probably because of their colours. The brown or black wing-cases and red or black thoraxes resemble 19th-century military uniforms. *Rhagonycha fulva* is known in parts of Britain as the blood-sucker, also probably a reference to the colouring, as it does not suck blood. The soldier beetles' colours are actually a warning to birds that they contain distasteful chemicals and so are not edible. They are a familiar sight in early-summer meadows where they collect on large flower-heads, such as cow parsley, feeding on soft-bodied insects. They can also be found scavenging at the bodies of dead insects.

The flat, velvety larvae are armed with large jaws, and they seek out and eat small insects and other creatures in the surface layers of soil. They feed from early summer until the following spring when they form pupae in the soil. The adult beetle is very common from May to July all over the British Isles.

The rustic sailor beetle is less common than the soldier beetle, but may be seen on the same flower tops during the summer. It is about the same size but has black wing-cases and a black mark on the thorax.

A narrow beetle with an orange-brown body, black at the rear. From May to July several soldier beetles may be seen together, with other insects, on flower-heads such as cow parsley. Length ⅜ in. (10 mm).

Rustic sailor beetle

Cantharis rustica

Another carnivorous beetle found throughout Britain. It is seen during July and August on flower-heads along country waysides. Length ⅜ in. (10 mm).

The larvae feed on small insects and invertebrates, such as springtails, silverfish and booklice, in the soil and in leaf litter.

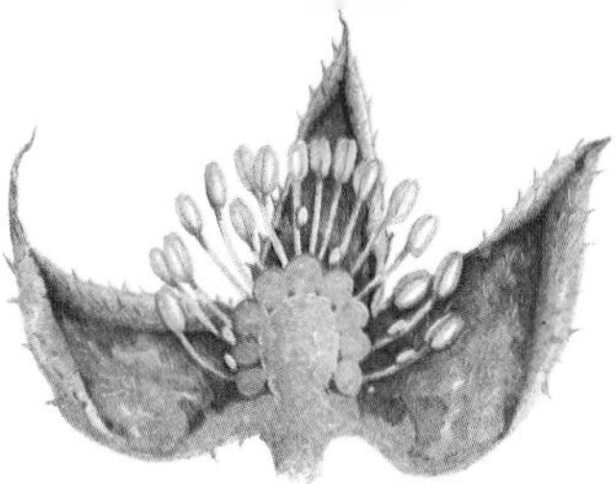

The beetles mate in June and lay eggs on raspberry flowers as they begin to set fruit. The eggs hatch in 10–12 days.

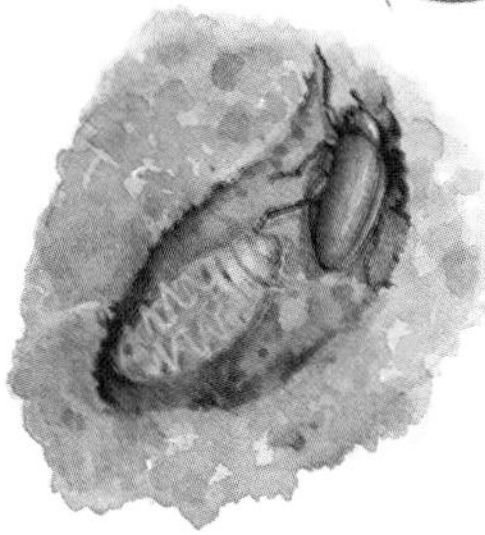

The pupa is formed in a cell beneath the soil, and the adult hatches in early autumn. It remains in the cell through the winter.

The larvae feed in the centre of the raspberries until they are about $\frac{5}{16}$ in. (8 mm) long.

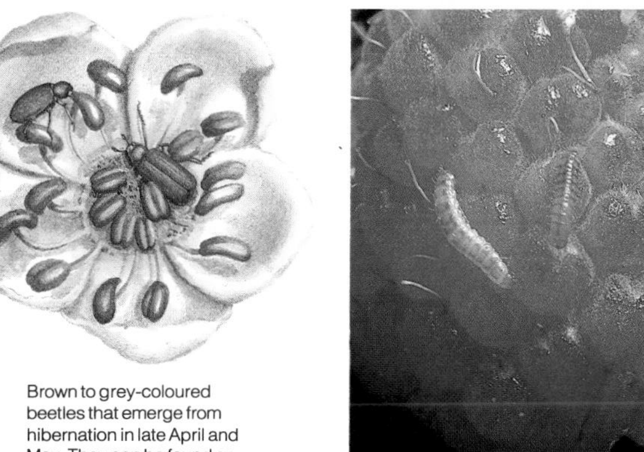

Brown to grey-coloured beetles that emerge from hibernation in late April and May. They can be found on the blossoms of spring-flowering plants such as hawthorn. Length $\frac{1}{8}$ in. (4 mm).

The semi-transparent 'raspberry fruit worms' become pink as they gorge themselves on the ripening red fruit.

Raspberry beetle *Byturus tomentosus*

In gardens and fruit farms throughout Britain this small, inconspicuous beetle is a common pest of raspberries. It is a rich golden-yellow colour when it hatches from its pupa, but the colour soon changes to a greenish-grey, making it very difficult to find on raspberry canes. The adult raspberry beetle is not a leaf-eater like many other beetles. It eats the nectar and pollen of garden and hedgerow flowers. However it lays its eggs in the flowers of raspberries, blackberries and loganberries. As the flowers lose their petals and the fruit begins to develop, the tiny eggs hatch into grub-like larvae, known as raspberry fruit worms. The larvae feed inside the developing fruit until they are full grown, usually in July or August. They then bore out of the ruined berry and burrow into the soil to form cells in which they change into pupae.

The adult beetles hatch after about four weeks, but stay in their cells until the spring, when they emerge to live on the surface for another two or three months.

The closest relatives of the raspberry beetle are the skin beetles, including the fur and larder beetles, whose larvae feed on preserved skins, furs and other animal products.

Long antennae

Yellow bands

Groups of eggs are laid in the dry, dead wood of many trees and shrubs, including oak, willow, chestnut, hawthorn, beech, laurel and wisteria.

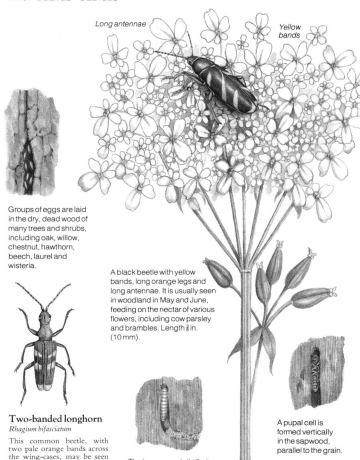

A black beetle with yellow bands, long orange legs and long antennae. It is usually seen in woodland in May and June, feeding on the nectar of various flowers, including cow parsley and brambles. Length ⅜ in. (10 mm).

The beetle mimics wasps in colour and shape, and also in behaviour. It runs quickly with jerky movements, and is wasp-like in flight.

The yellow band around the 'shoulders' of the beetle helps in its mimicry of wasps when seen by a potential predator.

Wasp beetle *Clytus arietis*

The strikingly marked wasp beetle belongs to the family called longhorns because of their long antennae. The wasp beetle is the most colourful of the group with wasp-like black and yellow marks. It feeds on the nectar and pollen of flowers with quick, jerky movements, and flies from flower to flower. The advantage of resembling a wasp is that birds avoid eating it, or at least hesitate long enough to allow it to escape. Wasp beetles are found all over Britain and may be common in or around woodland. Females search out dead or decaying timber, where they lay their eggs. The larvae take two years to develop fully, because of the poor value of dead wood as food. Pupae are then formed in a cell inside the wood, and after three or four weeks the adult beetles emerge. They remain inside the cell until the spring when they emerge to live for a further two to four months. Enemies of the beetle include birds which dig out the larvae and pupae, and parasitic wasps which bore into the wood and lay their eggs inside the beetle larvae.

A common longhorn beetle in coniferous forests is the two-banded longhorn which has increased in recent years as Forestry Commission plantations have spread.

Two-banded longhorn

Rhagium bifasciatum

This common beetle, with two pale orange bands across the wing-cases, may be seen on pine stumps all over Britain in coniferous plantations. Length ¾ in. (20 mm).

The larva spends its first year under the bark and its second in the sapwood.

A pupal cell is formed vertically in the sapwood, parallel to the grain.

The beetles also rest under bark, out of the sight of predators.

A grey-black beetle covered in fine hairs, and with whitish markings on the wing-cases. It can be seen from July to September, but is quite rare. Length ¾ in. (20 mm).

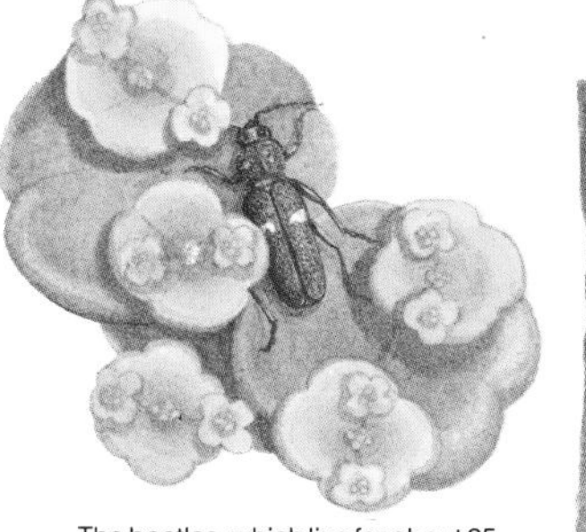

The beetles, which live for about 25 days, can sometimes be found sunning themselves on the flower-heads of plants.

Batches of 140–400 eggs are laid in cracks in pine wood. They hatch in about 14 days.

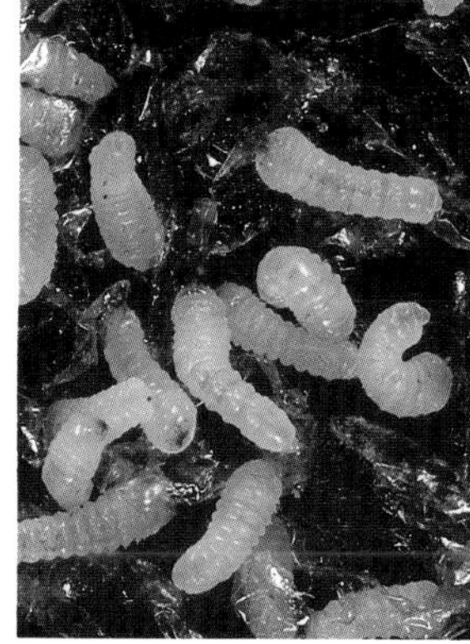

The white segmented bodies of the house longhorn larvae have distinctive orange heads with chewing mouthparts.

Variable longhorn

Stenocorus meridianus

This orangy beetle can be seen in many parts of Britain from May to July. It breeds in rotting stumps of sour cherry, ash and sallow. Length ¾ in. (20 mm).

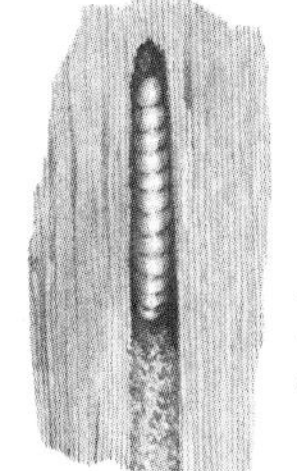

The larva lives for 2 to 10 years, at first in the outer sapwood and later in the heartwood.

The pupa is formed in a chamber as deep as 5 in. (12·5 cm) inside the wood. It usually hatches after two or three weeks.

House longhorn *Hylotrupes bajulus*

Exceptionally long antennae are the most distinctive feature of longhorn beetles and the reason for their common name. The antennae of house longhorns are shorter than average, but are still long enough to become entangled and even broken off during mating.

House longhorn beetles can be a serious pest. Adults need a temperature of at least 25°C before they can breed, and so have largely abandoned their original homes in pine forests for the warmer and more constant temperatures found in houses. The larvae, like those of all longhorn beetles, feed inside dead wood. An infestation of larvae can completely hollow-out the pine timbers in a building. Detection of the pest is difficult, as the only signs of its presence are the exit holes left by the newly emerged adults after the damage is done. Fortunately house longhorns are rare; they are mainly restricted to Surrey. However, they are starting to spread because of the importation of larvae-infested timber.

The variable longhorn is noted for the variety of its size and colouring – from orange to almost black. It lives and breeds in woodland, mainly in southern England.

When the beetle is threatened it ejects a bright liquid from its mouth or occasionally from a leg joint.

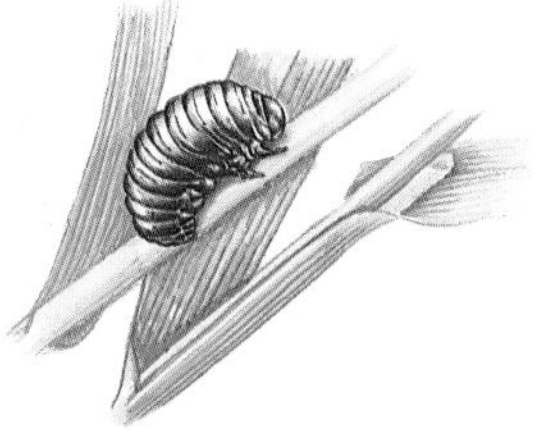

The larva is black and segmented, and may be found on grass through the summer.

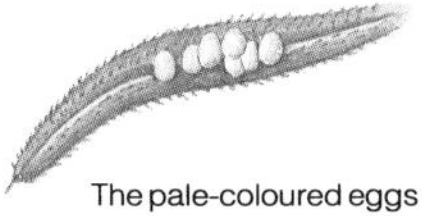

The pale-coloured eggs are laid in small groups on the underside of leaves in spring.

The stout black larva of the bloody-nosed beetle feeds openly on plants from spring until autumn.

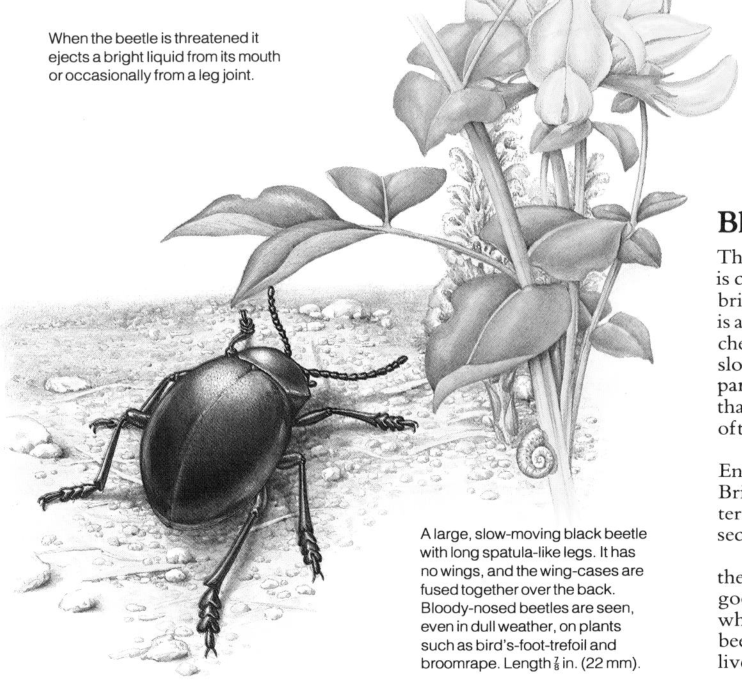

A large, slow-moving black beetle with long spatula-like legs. It has no wings, and the wing-cases are fused together over the back. Bloody-nosed beetles are seen, even in dull weather, on plants such as bird's-foot-trefoil and broomrape. Length ⅞ in. (22 mm).

Bloody-nosed beetle *Timarcha tenebricosa*

The curious method of defence used by the bloody-nosed beetle is called 'reflex bleeding'. If it is molested it will exude a drop of bright red fluid from its mouth and from a body joint. The fluid is a mixture of blood and a bitter-tasting secretion which acts as a chemical deterrent. The beetle's prominent black colour, its slow and ungainly walk, and the colourful defensive fluid are all part of a warning to predators such as lizards, mice and birds, that they should avoid it. If attacked by predators, beetles will often feign death.

The bloody-nosed beetle is found over most of southern England, especially in the south-west. It is the largest of the British leaf-eating beetles, and its conspicuous legs are characteristic of the group. They are long, with relatively wide sections and strong claws to gain a hold on leaves.

The beetles appear in early spring to mate, and the females then lay small batches of eggs on bedstraw plants, especially goosegrass. The larvae feed on plants from April to September when the pupae are formed, usually at the base of the plants. The beetles emerge the following spring. In captivity, they have lived for up to 182 days.

The beetles hibernate under bark or in leaf litter, and resume feeding in spring, especially on turnips, radishes and cabbages.

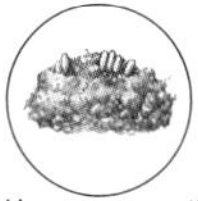

Eggs are laid in groups on the soil and hatch after six to ten days. [× 3]

The larvae feed on the roots of the cabbage family. They are fully grown in 18–30 days.

The pupa is formed in a small chamber in the soil, and the beetle hatches two or three weeks later.

A larva eats the inside of a cabbage stem. Larvae of several species feed on stems and roots, as well as leaves.

Small striped flea beetle *Phyllotreta undulata*

Farmers and vegetable growers throughout Britain fight a constant war against flea beetles. They are a common pest on a number of major food crops, and ragged leaves covered with tiny holes indicate their presence. Members of the cabbage family, on which the small striped flea beetle feeds, suffer most damage. There are 130 British species of flea beetle, many of them found in flower gardens and along waysides as well as among food crops. They have enlarged, very muscular hind legs, which give them the ability to jump two or three inches away, like fleas, when disturbed by predators.

Flea beetles prefer to eat the juicy leaves of seedlings, which appear in spring when the hungry adults emerge from hibernation. The worst damage to crops occurs in a dry spring when the seedlings develop slowly. The larvae feed on the same plants in May. Then in July a new generation of adults hatches and feeds through to August, so that crops are vulnerable to attack by flea beetles from spring to early autumn.

The shiny green colour of *Phyllotreta nigripes* makes it easy to see as it jumps about in the vegetation. It feeds mainly on the leaves of cabbages, turnips and swedes.

Flea beetle
Phyllotreta nigripes

This small metallic-green beetle is not so common as *Phyllotreta undulata*. It is a pest in gardens, where it feeds on docks and members of the cabbage family. Length $\frac{1}{8}$ in. (3 mm).

[Actual size]

Small brown beetles with yellow stripes, found in gardens from spring to autumn. The hind legs are larger than the other two pairs, allowing them to jump like fleas. Length $\frac{1}{8}$ in. (3 mm).

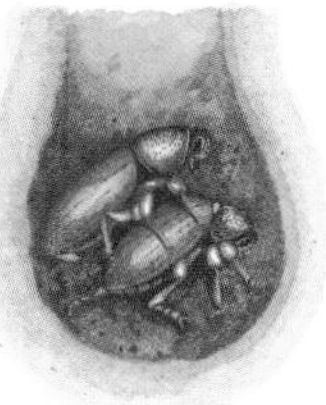

Male and female beetles excavate a nuptial chamber beneath the bark, where they mate.

When fully grown, the larvae pupate at the end of their tunnels.

Flight holes

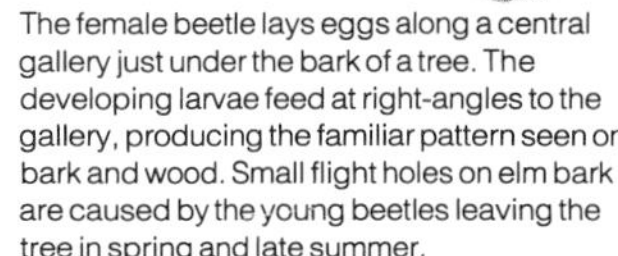

The female beetle lays eggs along a central gallery just under the bark of a tree. The developing larvae feed at right-angles to the gallery, producing the familiar pattern seen on bark and wood. Small flight holes on elm bark are caused by the young beetles leaving the tree in spring and late summer.

Small beetles with brown wing-cases and a black head and thorax. The beetles themselves are less often seen than the tunnels they cause under the bark of elm trees. Length $\frac{1}{8}$ in. (4 mm).

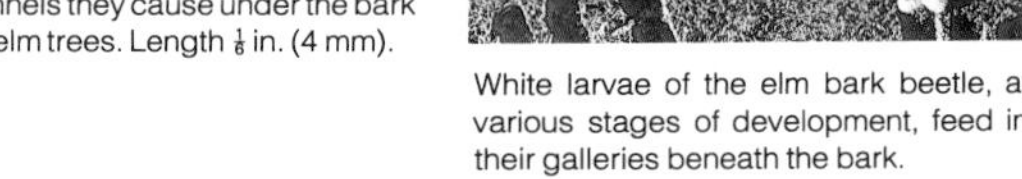

White larvae of the elm bark beetle, at various stages of development, feed in their galleries beneath the bark.

Small elm bark beetle
Scolytus multistriatus

This tiny beetle is similar in appearance to its larger relative, but is much smaller and often reddish-brown in colour. It also feeds in elm bark. Length $\frac{1}{16}$ in. (2 mm).

Elm bark beetle *Scolytus scolytus*

In 1970 a virulent form of Dutch elm disease arrived in Britain from North America. Within ten years over 25 million elms were lost, leaving the countryside, especially in the south, dotted with gaunt, bare skeletons that were once elm trees. The disease, which was first described in Holland, is caused by a fungus, *Ceratocystis ulmi*, spores of which are carried from tree to tree by the elm bark beetle.

Adult bark beetles feed on tree sap, mating and laying their eggs in galleries, which they tunnel beneath tree bark. The larvae live in these galleries, feeding on bark. Elm bark beetles, as their name implies, prefer to feed on elm trees. They are a major pest because the Dutch elm disease fungus thrives in their droppings and spreads rapidly through the bark in the galleries the beetles make. Two new generations of beetles a year, one in April and May and the other in July and August, fly off to colonise uninfected trees, carrying the disease with them. Preventing the spread of Dutch elm disease is very difficult.

The small elm bark beetle, *Scolytus multistriatus*, is less common than its larger relation, but is partially responsible for the spread of Dutch elm disease.

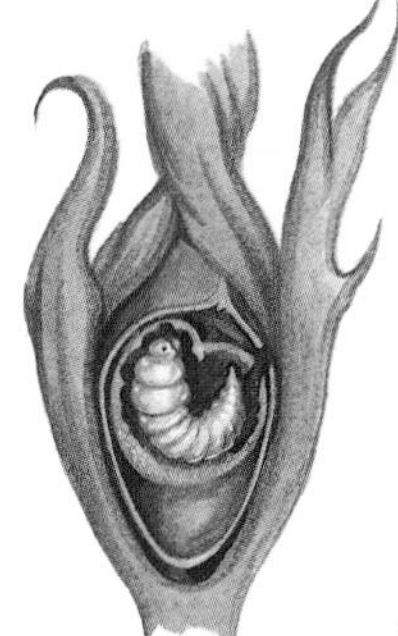

The larvae feed on the flowers and the developing seeds of clover (*Trifolium* species), and become fully grown after about 18 days.

The pupa is formed inside the clover seed pod, and the adult hatches out about six days later, in June. A second generation occurs in September, going into hibernation through winter.

Small beetles with long snouts and legs, and conspicuous antennae. They hibernate through winter in sheltered places, such as hedges and corners of fields, and emerge in May to feed on clover flowers and leaves. Length $\frac{1}{8}$ in. (4 mm).

Eggs are laid in small groups in developing clover flowers in the middle of May.

Clover seed weevils feed on leaves, leaving them pitted with holes. Weevils also bite notches around the leaf edge.

Clover seed weevil *Apion africans*

This tiny beetle, as its name implies, feeds on plants belonging to the clover family, frequently sown by farmers as a food crop for sheep and cattle. Adult beetles eat the leaves, but it is the grub-like larvae that do most damage – by boring into the growing seed pod of the clover flower and feeding on the small, succulent seeds inside. Larvae live and finally pupate inside the seed pod, thus remaining well hidden. Two generations of clover seed weevil larvae develop in this way each year.

All weevils are plant eaters and many are considered to be serious pests. They chew leaves using tiny serrated jaws at the end of their long snouts. Because they are small and active at night, they are difficult to detect. They are also abundant. Five hundred species of weevil are found in Britain. The clover seed weevil belongs to a group of particularly small weevils, known as apion beetles, all of which have larvae that live and feed inside the developing seed of various plants.

As a concealed larva, the clover seed weevil may be protected from detection by man, but not against attacks by parasitic wasps, which lay their eggs in the helpless larvae through the seed pod wall.

Other beetles commonly found in Britain

Beetles are the biggest group of insects in Britain, with more than 4,000 species. They make up a very diverse group, occurring both on land and in water. Many eat crops and are serious pests. Other are ferocious carnivores, eating other insects. All beetles have tough bodies with the first pair of wings modified into a pair of hard wing-cases, called elytra, but some have reduced wings, giving them a long, thin shape. Like many insects they have a larval and chrysalis stage, with some larvae living as wood-borers for up to four years. Some adult beetles have a life-span of almost three years.

The following four pages illustrate some of the common beetles that may be found in Britain in addition to those shown in more detail on pages 280–303.

Ground beetle

Pterostichus madidus

A common species of black beetle found throughout the British Isles, particularly in the north of England. It lives on the ground among surface debris, feeding on other insects. There are more than 20 species of *Pterostichus* beetles in Britain. Length $\frac{5}{8}$ in. (16 mm).

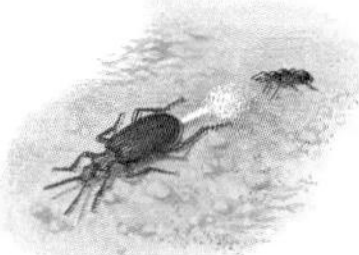

Bombardier

Brachinus crepitans

When threatened, it bombards its attacker with a poisonous spray which has the appearance of a puff of smoke coming from the abdomen. Found along the River Severn, the Thames estuary, the Essex coast and a few localities on the south coast. Length $\frac{5}{16}$ in. (8 mm).

Large striped flea beetle

Phyllotreta nemorum

Tiny black and yellow beetles which infest crops such as turnips and oil seed rape, eating the leaves. Widely distributed in Britain. They jump like fleas when disturbed. Length $\frac{1}{8}$ in. (3 mm).

Oil beetle

Meloe proscarabaeus

A black beetle with short wing-cases found in parts of England. It is named after the oily secretion it exudes over itself when disturbed. It is a parasite on the eggs and larvae of solitary bees. Length $\frac{3}{4}$ in. (20 mm).

Furniture beetle/Woodworm

Anobium punctatum

A small beetle whose larvae, known as woodworm, attack softwood timbers such as beams and furniture. It is widespread in houses throughout Britain. Length $\frac{1}{6}$ in. (4 mm).

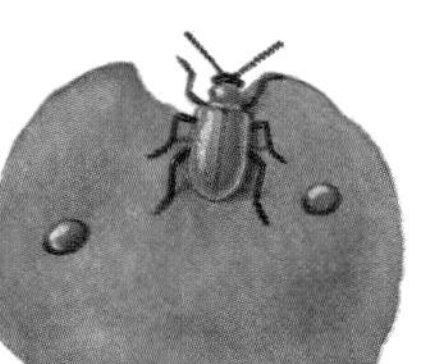

Lily beetle

Lilioceris lilii

Small red beetles which may be found in gardens where lilies are grown, particularly in the south of England. The larvae eat the leaves of the lily plants. Length $\frac{3}{8}$ in. (10 mm).

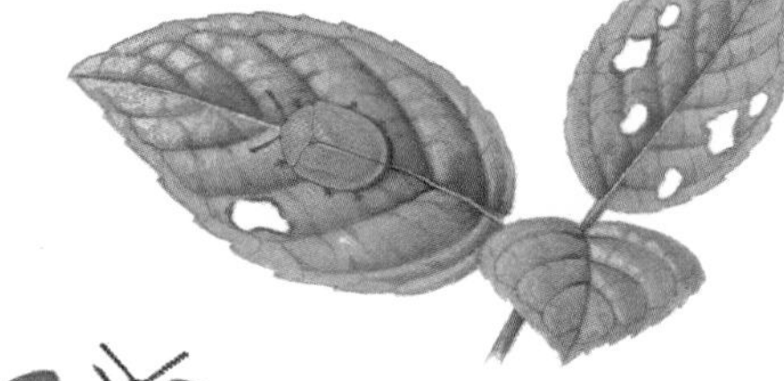

Green tortoise beetle

Cassida viridis

The flattened wing-cases and thorax completely cover the head and most of the legs. The beetle may be found on leaves in damp places or on flowers such as thistles in summer. Seen in July and August throughout Britain. Length $\frac{3}{8}$ in. (10 mm).

Great diving beetle

Dytiscus marginalis

The most common of the British diving beetles. The males have disc-like suckers on the front legs which they use to hold the female while mating. The long hind legs are used for swimming. The beetles can live for more than two years, eating aquatic insects, tadpoles and small fish. Length $1\frac{3}{8}$ in. (35 mm).

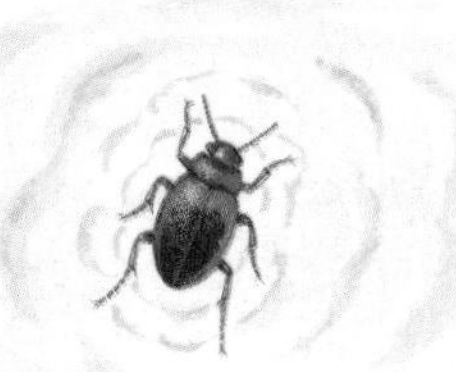

Screech beetle

Hygrobia herrmanni

Its name comes from the screeching sound it makes when seized by a predator. The noise is made by the abdomen being rubbed against the wing-cases. The screech beetle is found in muddy pools in England and South Wales. It feeds on insect larvae. Length $\frac{3}{8}$ in. (10 mm).

Death watch beetle

Xestobium rufovillosum

The tapping noise that this beetle makes as it bangs its head against wood is an eerie sound in the stillness of the night. In fact, the sound is probably the beetle's mating call. Like the larvae, the beetle feeds on damp rotting wood. As it rarely flies it is normally seen near the timber it infests. Length $\frac{1}{4}$ in. (6 mm).

Colorado beetle

Leptinotarsa decemlineata

The striped wing-cases make the beetle very distinctive. It is a serious pest of potatoes on the Continent, and occasional specimens are found in south-east England. The larvae are orange. Length $\frac{7}{16}$ in. (11 mm).

Great silver water beetle

Hydrophilus piceus

Britain's largest water beetle, found only in southern England. It lives in stagnant ponds where it eats water plants. A fine covering of hair over the body traps air which the beetle breathes when it is under water. The air gives it a silvery appearance as it dives. Length $1\frac{5}{8}$ in. (42 mm).

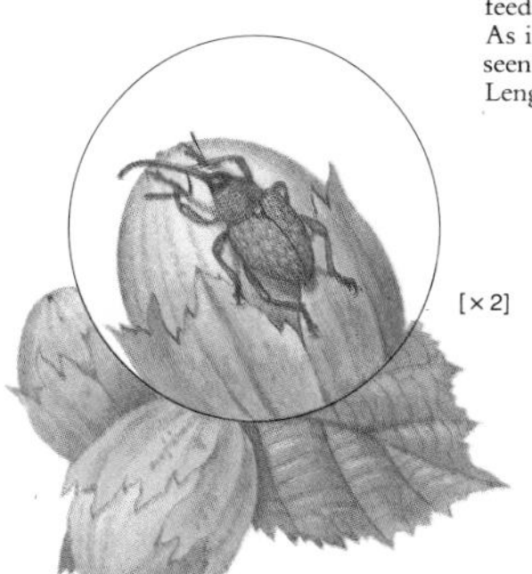

Nut weevil

Curculio nucum

The female uses her long snout to drill holes in hazel nuts where she places her eggs. Her jaws are situated at the tip of her snout and her antennae towards the base. The larvae develop inside the nuts. A widespread pest. Length $\frac{3}{16}$ in. (5 mm).

Blister beetle

Lytta vesicatoria

Metallic green beetles often seen on flower heads where they lay their eggs. The larvae ride on solitary bees to their nests where they feed on the bees' eggs, larvae, pollen and honey. Length $\frac{9}{16}$ in. (15 mm).

Whirligig beetle

Gyrinus natator

Groups of these small black beetles swim rapidly in circles on the surface of still water at a speed of 40 in. per second. They are scavengers, eating other insects that fall into the water. During autumn they can be numerous throughout Britain. Length $\frac{1}{4}$ in. (6 mm).

Fur beetle

Attagenus pellio

A small beetle with white spots on its back. The hairy larvae eat furs, wool and flour. It can be found throughout Britain. Length $\frac{1}{6}$ in. (4 mm).

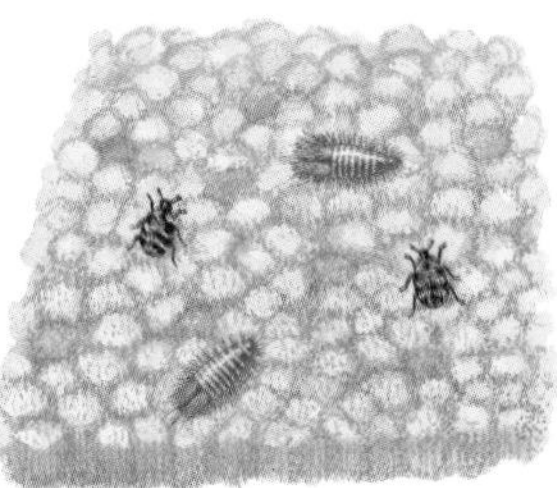

Carpet beetle

Anthrenus verbasci

A light brown beetle with white blotches over its back. It is normally found in houses where its furry larvae, called woolly bears, eat the woollen fibres of carpets and rugs. It is widely distributed in Britain. Length $\frac{1}{6}$ in. (4 mm).

Black weevil

Liparus coronatus

A widespread beetle with a distinctive long snout and glossy black body. Both the beetle and the larva eat carrot leaves. Length $\frac{3}{8}$ in. (10 mm).

Mealworm

Tenebrio molitor

The squirming orange larvae are sold in pet shops as food for birds and reptiles. In the wild they are found in birds' nests but they may be a pest in stored cereals. The beetle is attracted to lights in July and August. Length $\frac{5}{8}$ in. (16 mm).

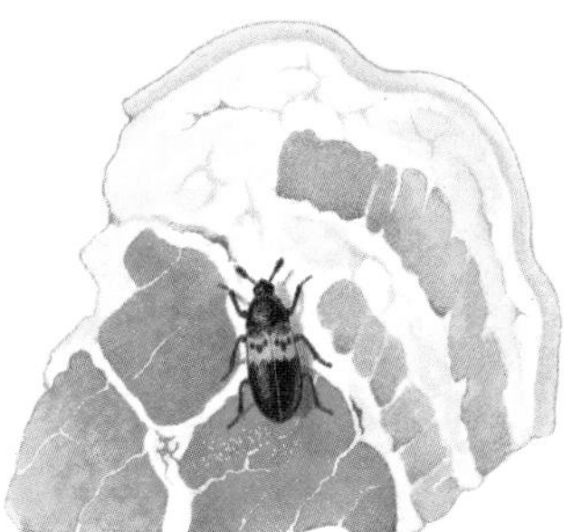

Larder or bacon beetle

Dermestes lardarius

A beetle that is normally found indoors. In spring the female lays about 200 eggs on anything of animal origin such as dried meats and skins which the larvae eat. The adult beetle has a band of light hair on the back. Length $\frac{3}{8}$ in. (10 mm).

Churchyard beetle

Blaps mucronata

A widespread beetle found in dark places, such as basements, cellars, crypts and farmyard sheds. It is also known as the cellar beetle. The pointed abdomen, long legs and slow movement are distinguishing features. Length 1 in. (25 mm).

Rose chafer
Cetonia aurata

An attractive green beetle which flies from May to August. They may be found on the petals of large flowers, particularly roses, on which they feed. Length $\frac{3}{4}$ in. (20 mm).

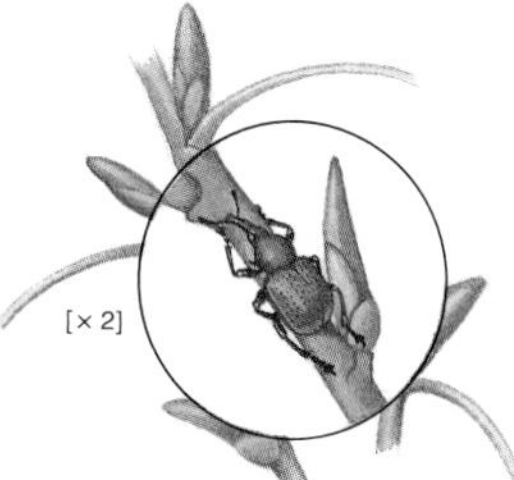

Byctiscus populi

This weevil-like beetle with its long snout is found on aspen trees where the female lays her eggs inside a curled-up leaf. They are locally distributed in England only. Length $\frac{3}{16}$ in. (5 mm).

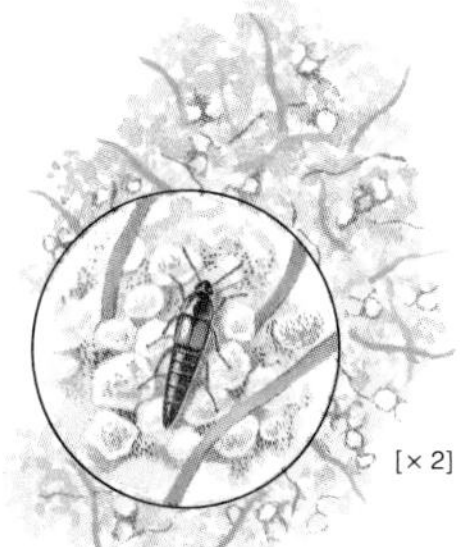

Tachyporus hypnorum

A small black beetle with a distinctive orange band on its thorax and a tapering abdomen. It is found in litter, moss, fungi and organic matter. Length $\frac{3}{16}$ in. (5 mm).

Black burying beetle
Necrodes littoralis

A widespread scavenging beetle which eats decaying plant and animal matter. It looks like other burying beetles such as the sexton (p. 282). Found near farmyards, river banks and on the coast. Length 1 in. (25 mm).

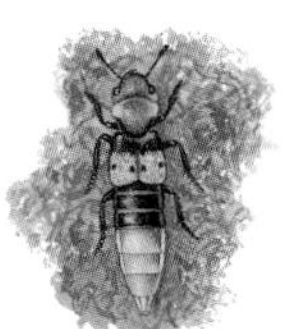

Rove beetle
Emus hirtus

A beetle with short wing-cases that lives among dung and decaying plant matter, especially on farms. It has a hairy body and moves quickly. Found in southern England. Length $\frac{9}{16}$ in. (15 mm).

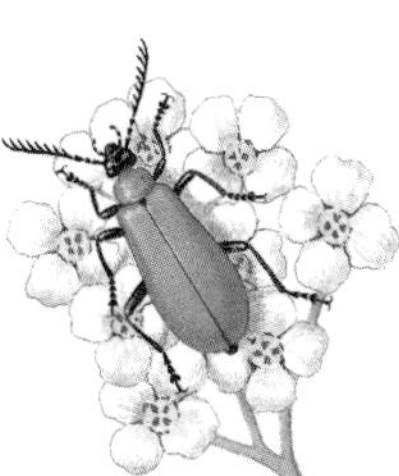

Cardinal beetle
Pyrochroa coccinea

This brightly coloured beetle may be found on vegetation and flowers along waysides and in woodlands in May and June in southern and central England. It has distinctive toothed antennae. Length $\frac{9}{16}$ in. (15 mm).

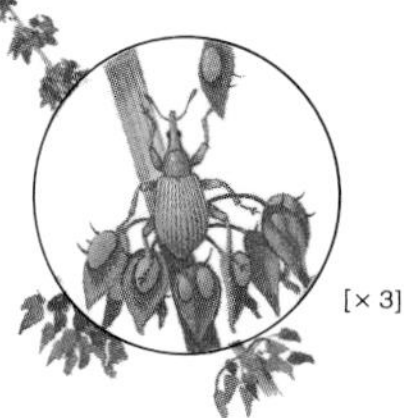

Apion miniatum

Apion beetles, with their long snouts, can be found throughout Britain on vegetation at the side of roads. They feed on the leaves and fruits of many wild flowers. Length $\frac{1}{8}$ in. (3 mm).

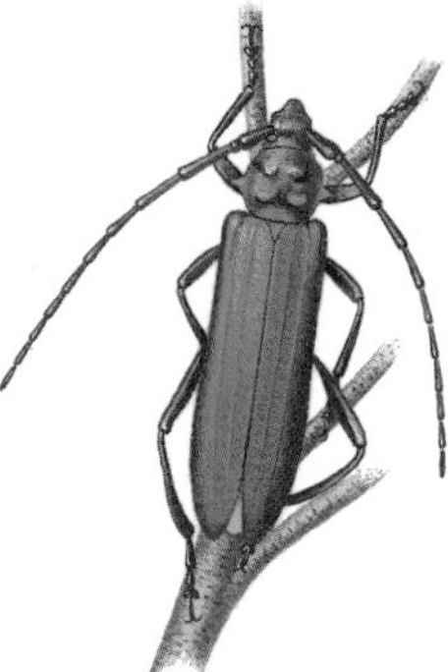

Musk beetle
Aromia moschata

A bright green long-horned beetle which is occasionally found on willow trees where its larvae feed. It is named after the musky smell that it produces. Length $1\frac{3}{16}$ in. (30 mm).

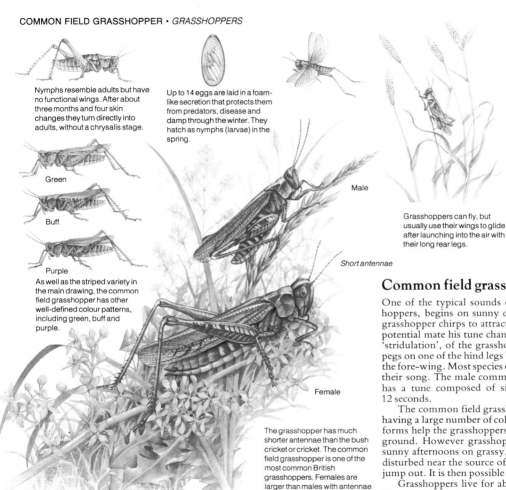

Nymphs resemble adults but have no functional wings. After about three months and four skin changes they turn directly into adults, without a chrysalis stage.

Up to 14 eggs are laid in a foam-like secretion that protects them from predators, disease and damp through the winter. They hatch as nymphs (larvae) in the spring.

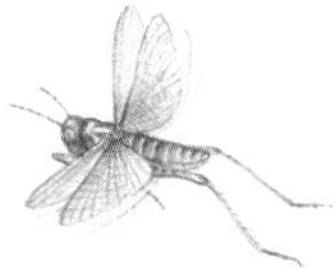

Green

Buff

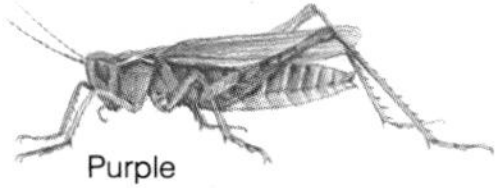

Purple

As well as the striped variety in the main drawing, the common field grasshopper has other well-defined colour patterns, including green, buff and purple.

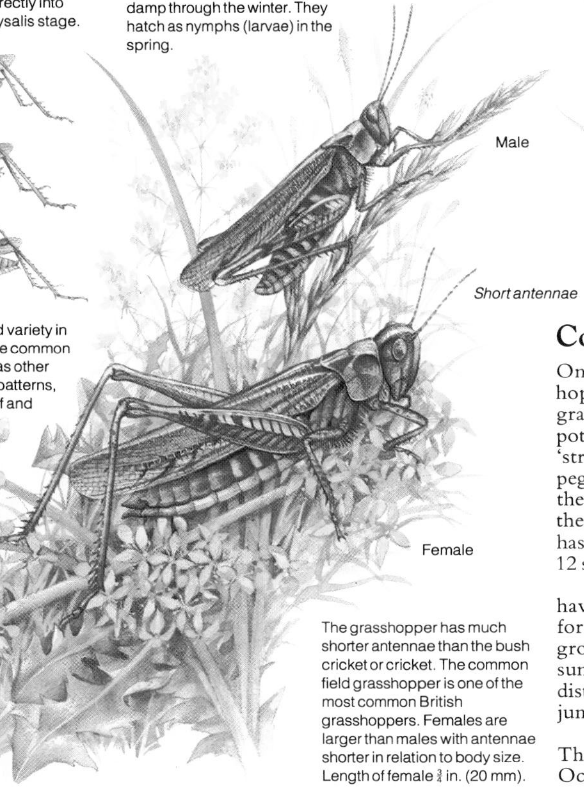

Male

Short antennae

Female

The grasshopper has much shorter antennae than the bush cricket or cricket. The common field grasshopper is one of the most common British grasshoppers. Females are larger than males with antennae shorter in relation to body size. Length of female ¾ in. (20 mm).

Grasshoppers can fly, but usually use their wings to glide after launching into the air with their long rear legs.

Grasshoppers do not become active until they have warmed their blood by basking in sunshine.

Common field grasshopper *Chorthippus brunneus*

One of the typical sounds of summer, the chirping of grasshoppers, begins on sunny days in late June or July. The male grasshopper chirps to attract females, and when he has found a potential mate his tune changes to a mating song. The song, or 'stridulation', of the grasshopper is produced by a row of tiny pegs on one of the hind legs being rubbed against stout veins on the fore-wing. Most species of grasshopper can be recognised by their song. The male common field grasshopper, for example, has a tune composed of six to ten chirps lasting for about 12 seconds.

The common field grasshopper is typical of many species in having a large number of colour variations. The different colour forms help the grasshoppers to blend in with almost any background. However grasshoppers can be found fairly easily on sunny afternoons on grassy, south-facing slopes. If the grass is disturbed near the source of a chirp, a grasshopper will usually jump out. It is then possible to follow and watch it.

Grasshoppers live for about five months on a diet of grass. They hatch in May and die as the cold weather arrives in October, leaving egg pods in the soil to survive the winter.

Eight more British grasshoppers

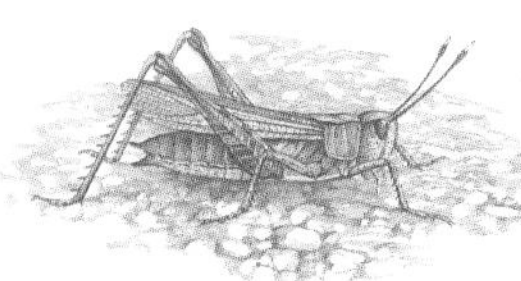

Rufous grasshopper
Gomphocerippus rufus

Usually brown, with thickened white-tipped antennae. Found on limestone and chalk grassland in southern England. Length of female 11/16 in. (18 mm).

Mottled grasshopper
Myrmeleotettix maculatus

The colour varies greatly, but all forms are mottled. Found throughout the British Isles on grassy heaths, downland and sand-dunes. Length of female 9/16 in. (15 mm).

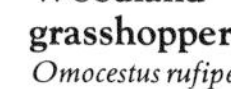

Woodland grasshopper
Omocestus rufipes

Similar to the common green grasshopper but with an orange or red underside. Found in woodland clearings in southern England. Length of female ¾ in. (20 mm).

Stripe-winged grasshopper
Stenobothrus lineatus

The name comes from a white stripe on the forewing. Found on chalk and limestone grassland in southern England only. Length of female ¾ in. (20 mm).

Meadow grasshopper
Chorthippus parallelus

The wings are insufficiently developed for the grasshopper to fly, but it is common on all types of grassland in the British Isles, except Ireland. Length of female ¾ in. (20 mm).

Common green grasshopper
Omocestus viridulus

Smaller and greener than the common field grasshopper. Found in grassy areas throughout the British Isles. Length of female ¾ in. (20 mm).

Lesser marsh grasshopper
Chorthippus albomarginatus

Commonly flies in damp grassland near the coast of England, Wales and parts of Ireland. Length of female 11/16 in. (18 mm).

Large marsh grasshopper
Stethophyma grossum

The largest species of grasshopper in the British Isles. It is restricted to marshland in southern England and western Ireland, particularly where bog asphodel and bog myrtle are growing. Length of female 1¼ in. (32 mm).

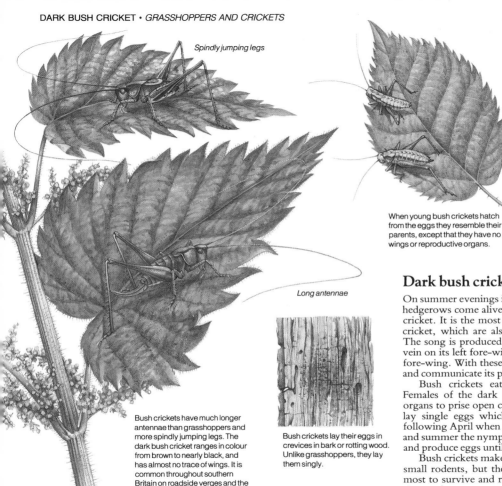

Spindly jumping legs

Long antennae

Bush crickets have much longer antennae than grasshoppers and more spindly jumping legs. The dark bush cricket ranges in colour from brown to nearly black, and has almost no trace of wings. It is common throughout southern Britain on roadside verges and the edges of woods. Length up to $\frac{3}{4}$ in. (20 mm).

When young bush crickets hatch from the eggs they resemble their parents, except that they have no wings or reproductive organs.

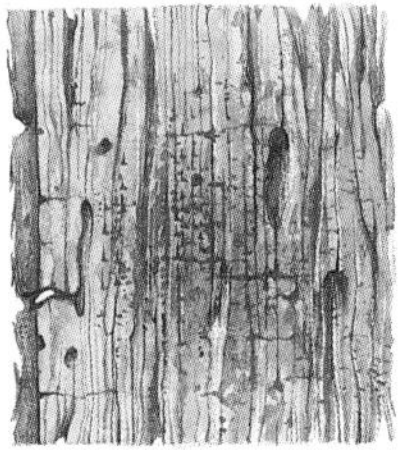

Bush crickets lay their eggs in crevices in bark or rotting wood. Unlike grasshoppers, they lay them singly.

The female dark bush cricket is instantly recognisable by her large egg-laying organ, shaped like a scimitar.

Dark bush cricket *Pholidoptera griseoaptera*

On summer evenings in the Midlands and southern England the hedgerows come alive with the chirring sound of the dark bush cricket. It is the most common of Britain's ten species of bush cricket, which are also known as long-horned grasshoppers. The song is produced only by the male as it scrapes a toothed vein on its left fore-wing across the thickened edge of the right fore-wing. With these bursts of song it seeks to attract females and communicate its presence to rival males.

Bush crickets eat both plants and soft-bodied insects. Females of the dark bush cricket use their long egg-laying organs to prise open cracks in rotting logs or under bark. They lay single eggs which remain there from autumn until the following April when the nymphs (larvae) hatch. During spring and summer the nymphs grow into adulthood, when they mate and produce eggs until they are killed by the autumn frosts.

Bush crickets make good food for ground-feeding birds and small rodents, but their camouflage and secretive habits help most to survive and reproduce. All are found in thick vegetation, and most are green to match their surroundings. They can escape danger by leaping a few feet at a time.

Five other British bush crickets

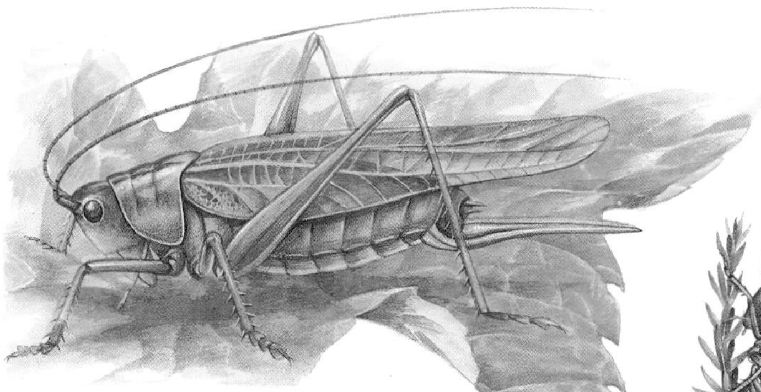

Great green bush cricket

Tettigonia viridissima

Britain's largest bush cricket, with unusually long wings. It is restricted to warm, sunny parts of the south, and is fairly common along the south coast of England, in dense patches of bramble or gorse. Body length up to 1⅝ in. (42 mm).

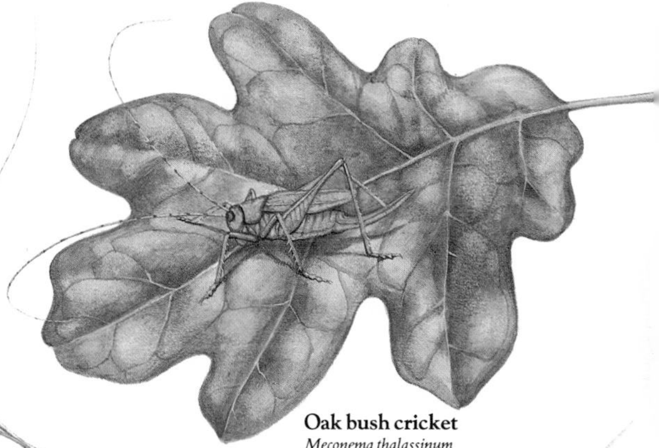

Oak bush cricket

Meconema thalassinum

A small bush cricket with yellow and brown marks on its upper side. It is found over much of England and Wales, mainly on oaks. Length up to ⅝ in. (16 mm).

Bog bush cricket

Metrioptera brachyptera

A mainly brown bush cricket with a bright green underside to the abdomen. It occurs in moist places on heathland and moors over much of England and Wales. Length ¾ in. (20 mm).

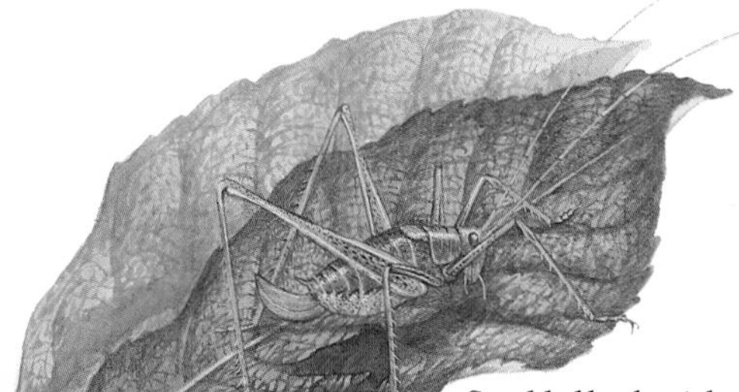

Speckled bush cricket

Leptophyes punctatissima

A bright green bush cricket covered in a speckled pattern of tiny dark brown spots. It is found on trees and bushes over most of England and Wales south of Yorkshire. Length up to ⅝ in. (16 mm).

Short-winged cone-head

Conocephalus dorsalis

A green bush cricket with a brown stripe down the back and a pale brown underside to the abdomen. It is found only in the southern and eastern counties of England, often on coastal salt-marshes. Length up to 11/16 in. (18 mm).

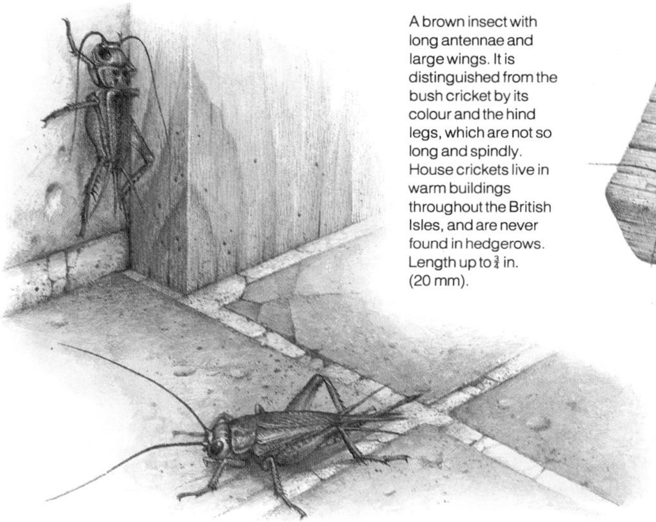

A brown insect with long antennae and large wings. It is distinguished from the bush cricket by its colour and the hind legs, which are not so long and spindly. House crickets live in warm buildings throughout the British Isles, and are never found in hedgerows. Length up to $\frac{3}{4}$ in. (20 mm).

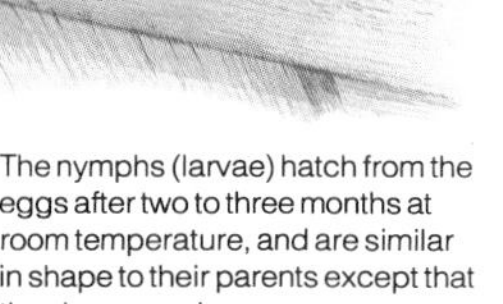

The nymphs (larvae) hatch from the eggs after two to three months at room temperature, and are similar in shape to their parents except that they have no wings.

As well as living in buildings, house crickets occur in rubbish heaps where fermentation provides warmth.

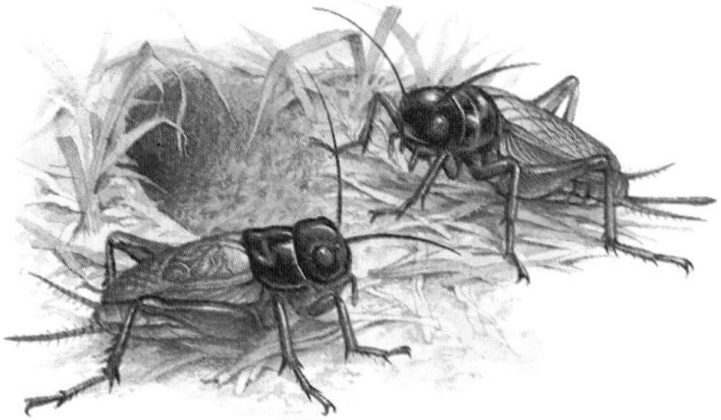

Field cricket
Gryllus campestris

A shiny black-and-yellow cricket with a large head. Field crickets are very rare. They live in burrows and are only rarely seen above ground. Length $\frac{7}{8}$ in. (22 mm).

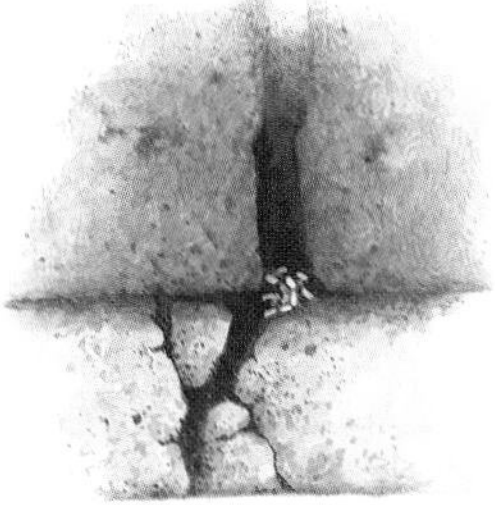

The female house cricket lays her eggs in cracks in tiles or planks, usually in late summer.

House cricket *Acheta domesticus*

Charles Dickens's novel *The cricket on the hearth* featured a house cricket that chirped when all was well, and became silent when unhappiness descended on the house. Like many British insects that live indoors, the house cricket is a native of North Africa, and was brought here probably sometime in the 17th century. As it comes from a warm climate it cannot survive a British winter outdoors. During the daytime it stays in warm crevices, but as night falls it emerges to feed and mate. The first sign of its presence is normally the drawn-out chirp of the male cricket as he advertises his presence to females. After mating, the female may lay up to 1,000 eggs during her six to nine months of life. The eggs hatch between a week and four months later, depending on temperature, and the nymphs (larvae) take between one and eight months to develop into adults. Both nymphs and adults will eat most scraps of animal or plant material. Despite a slight risk that they may carry disease, they are regarded almost as pets in most houses where they appear.

The field cricket, with its large black head, is an endangered species in Britain and is found in only a few places in the south of England. It emits a clear musical chirping in spring.

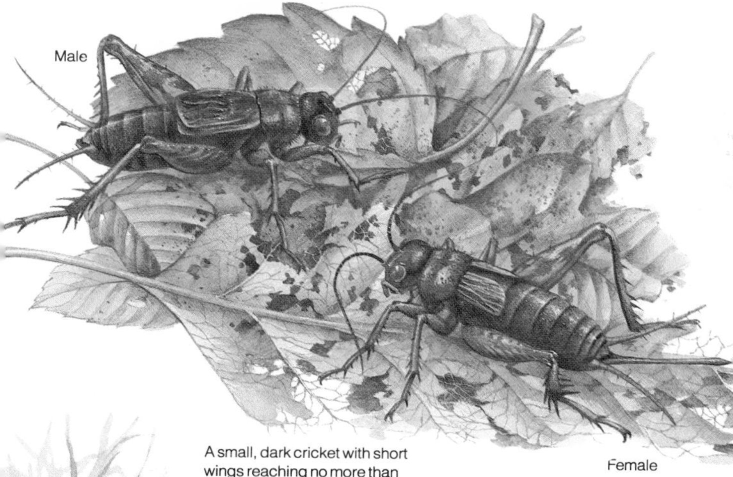

Male

Female

A small, dark cricket with short wings reaching no more than half-way down the abdomen. It is found only in the south of England, almost entirely restricted to the New Forest. The female can be distinguished from the male by her long egg-laying organ. Length $\frac{3}{8}$ in. (10 mm).

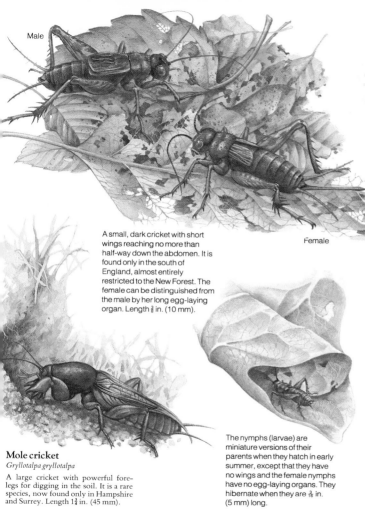

The female wood cricket lays eggs singly, below the soil. She may lay up to 200 eggs during her lifetime of three to six months.

The short wings of the wood cricket are useless for flight. It travels in a series of jumps – up to 2 ft (60 cm) at a time.

Mole cricket
Gryllotalpa gryllotalpa

A large cricket with powerful forelegs for digging in the soil. It is a rare species, now found only in Hampshire and Surrey. Length $1\frac{3}{4}$ in. (45 mm).

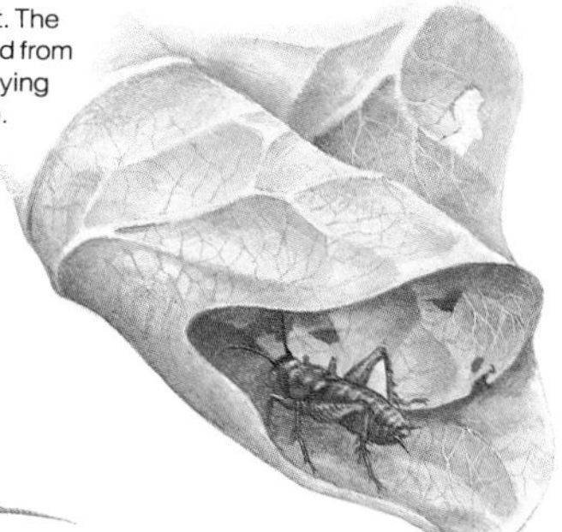

The nymphs (larvae) are miniature versions of their parents when they hatch in early summer, except that they have no wings and the female nymphs have no egg-laying organs. They hibernate when they are $\frac{3}{16}$ in. (5 mm) long.

Wood cricket *Nemobius sylvestris*

Unlike the house cricket, the wood cricket is a native of Britain. It lives among debris on the woodland floor in southern England. Despite being active during the day it is easily overlooked as its song is quieter than that of some of its relatives. The wood cricket resembles a small cockroach with its spiny legs and short wings, but unlike the cockroach it has powerful back legs which are used for jumping.

The life-cycle of the wood cricket spans at least two years. Eggs laid in late summer hatch the following May or June. The nymphs (larvae) reach adulthood the following summer. Most adults mate and die in their first autumn or winter but some survive to breed in the next spring or summer. Both adults and nymphs eat vegetable and animal matter, including other soft-bodied insects and the bodies of dead animals.

The mole cricket, a rare species found only in parts of Hampshire and Surrey, is now almost extinct in the British Isles. Its decline is possibly due to a slight climatic change, as Britain is on the edge of the mole cricket's European distribution. The female spends most of her time underground where she may raise several broods during her life of six to nine months.

Egg case

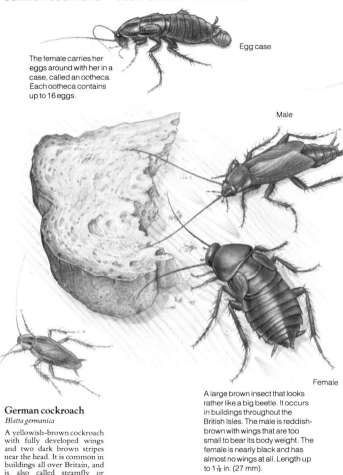

The female carries her eggs around with her in a case, called an ootheca. Each ootheca contains up to 16 eggs.

Male

The nymphs hatch in two to three months under warm conditions. They are small versions of the adults, except that they have no wings.

The long legs of the cockroach are well adapted for running so that it can scuttle back to its hiding place when disturbed.

Female

A large brown insect that looks rather like a big beetle. It occurs in buildings throughout the British Isles. The male is reddish-brown with wings that are too small to bear its body weight. The female is nearly black and has almost no wings at all. Length up to $1\frac{1}{16}$ in. (27 mm).

German cockroach
Blatta germanica

A yellowish-brown cockroach with fully developed wings and two dark brown stripes near the head. It is common in buildings all over Britain, and is also called steamfly or shiner. Length $\frac{1}{2}$ in. (13 mm).

Common cockroach *Blatta orientalis*

That widespread household pest, the common cockroach, has been in this country only for the past 400 years or so. The first probably arrived in Britain in the 16th century among a ship's cargo from either North Africa or southern Asia. As they came from a warmer climate they could only live here in the warm surroundings of heated buildings or in refuse tips among fermenting food. Although unable to fly, they have since spread throughout the British Isles. The common cockroach is one of six species of cockroach found in Britain, three of which have arrived from abroad. The three native species are restricted to southern England in woods and heaths, and are rarely seen.

Common cockroaches are pests of kitchens and bakeries, but modern insecticides and better hygiene are slowly making them rarer. They spend the daytime behind ovens or cupboards, and come out at night to feed on food scraps. They can spread disease after feeding on contaminated food or dead animals, but defend themselves against disease bacteria with an oily film containing a germicide that covers their bodies.

The German cockroach, which can fly, arrived in Britain from North Africa later than the common cockroach.

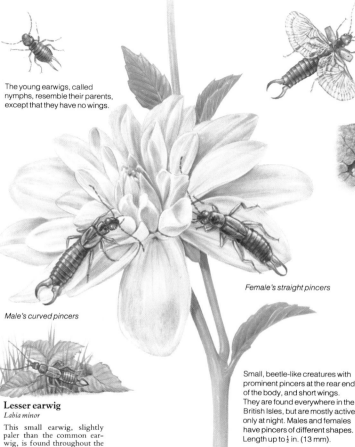

The young earwigs, called nymphs, resemble their parents, except that they have no wings.

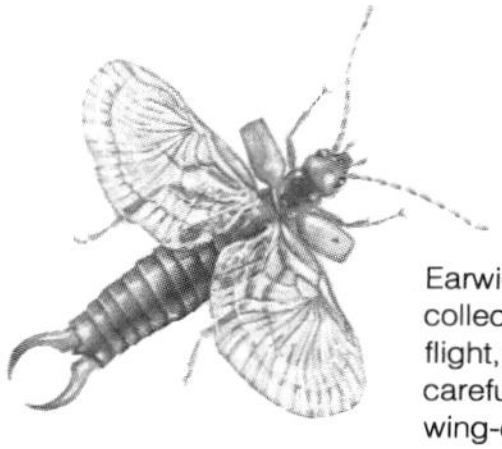

Earwigs are good flyers and often collect around lights at night. After flight, their wings have to be carefully folded to fit back into the wing-cases.

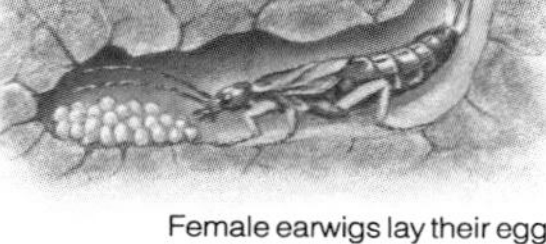

Female earwigs lay their eggs in batches of up to 50 in an underground cell, and then guard them until they hatch three or four weeks later.

A female earwig keeps guard over her batch of eggs which she licks regularly to protect them from moulds and bacteria.

Female's straight pincers

Male's curved pincers

Lesser earwig

Labia minor

This small earwig, slightly paler than the common earwig, is found throughout the British Isles but is often overlooked. It is a good flyer and may be attracted to lights on warm summer nights. Length $\frac{3}{16}$ in. (5 mm).

Small, beetle-like creatures with prominent pincers at the rear end of the body, and short wings. They are found everywhere in the British Isles, but are mostly active only at night. Males and females have pincers of different shapes. Length up to $\frac{1}{2}$ in. (13 mm).

Earwig *Forficula auricularia*

The female earwig is one of the few insects to show maternal care for its offspring. In the autumn, male and female earwigs retire together for the winter into a cavity in the soil at the base of a plant. In spring, the female lays a batch of yellowish eggs. The male leaves the 'nest', but the mother stays on to tend the eggs, carefully cleaning each egg to prevent the growth of moulds. When the young earwigs hatch after three or four weeks, the female guards them and brings them food for their first few days of life.

The earwig's name may originate in its custom of hiding in crevices and dark places, leading to a fear that it would crawl into the ear of a sleeping person. In reality it is a harmless vegetarian with a liking for dahlia and chrysanthemum petals. The most likely place to find one is inside a curled petal of a late-summer flower. Under the earwig's tiny wing-cases are two lace-like wings which it uses for its rare flights. Afterwards it refolds them with the pincers on the end of its body, and packs them away again like a tiny parachute.

The lesser earwig is normally seen flying on summer evenings, but can also be seen on compost heaps.

The world of 'minibeasts'

The thousands of species of tiny creatures that live in the leaf litter and soil of the woodland floor can be conveniently grouped under the term 'minibeasts'. They include small insects and spiders, as well as larger creatures such as woodlice, centipedes and earwigs. In addition, there are thousands of species too small to be seen with the naked eye. All the inhabitants of this dark, bustling world spend much of their lives hunting for food, in many cases preying on each other.

One way to see minibeasts at close quarters is to take a couple of handfuls of leaf litter, put it in a large paper funnel and shine a light on it from above. Trying to escape the light, and warmth, the tiny creatures burrow downwards and fall on to a tray placed underneath. With the exception of fleas and biting lice – which are only likely to be found on mammals and birds – minibeasts are quite harmless to humans.

Book louse/Bark louse

Order Psocoptera (68 species)

Soft-bodied insects with long antennae and biting mouthparts. Some, usually the outdoor species which are also called bark lice, have wings. Indoor species are usually wingless. They feed on pollen, algae and minute fungi, found on bark, dried vegetation and old birds' nests. Some live among old books, eating traces of mould on the paper. They are found throughout the year in all parts of Britain. Length $\frac{3}{16}$ in. (5 mm).

[× 2½]

Biting and sucking lice

Orders Mallophaga (250 species) and Anoplura (36 species)

Lice are active throughout the year and vary enormously in shape. They are parasites, rarely leaving their host. They are wingless and flattened from top to bottom so that they can lie flush to the skin or feathers. Some feed on the blood of mammals and have sucking mouthparts; others feed on the blood of birds and have biting mouthparts. Length $\frac{1}{8}$ in. (3 mm).

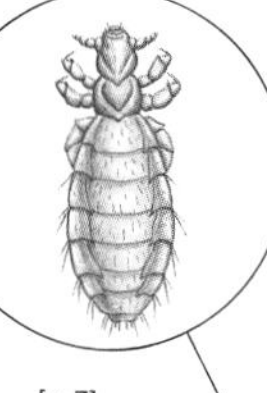

[× 7]

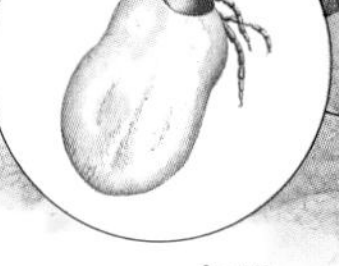

[× 1½]

Tick

Class Arachnida

Ticks are blood-sucking members of the spider class. They are active in spring and summer in woodland clearings and grassy places throughout Britain. They have a strong beak-like mouth with which they cling tenaciously to small animals. Their bodies swell up to hold the blood they feed on. Length $\frac{3}{8}$ in. (10 mm).

[× 6]

Fleas

Order Siphonaptera (47 species)

These dark brown, parasitic insects are wingless. Their mouths are adapted for sucking blood, and they are flattened from side to side so that they move easily through fur and feathers. Most are parasites of mammals, but a few prefer birds. They are active all year and are powerful jumpers. Length $\frac{1}{8}$ in. (3 mm).

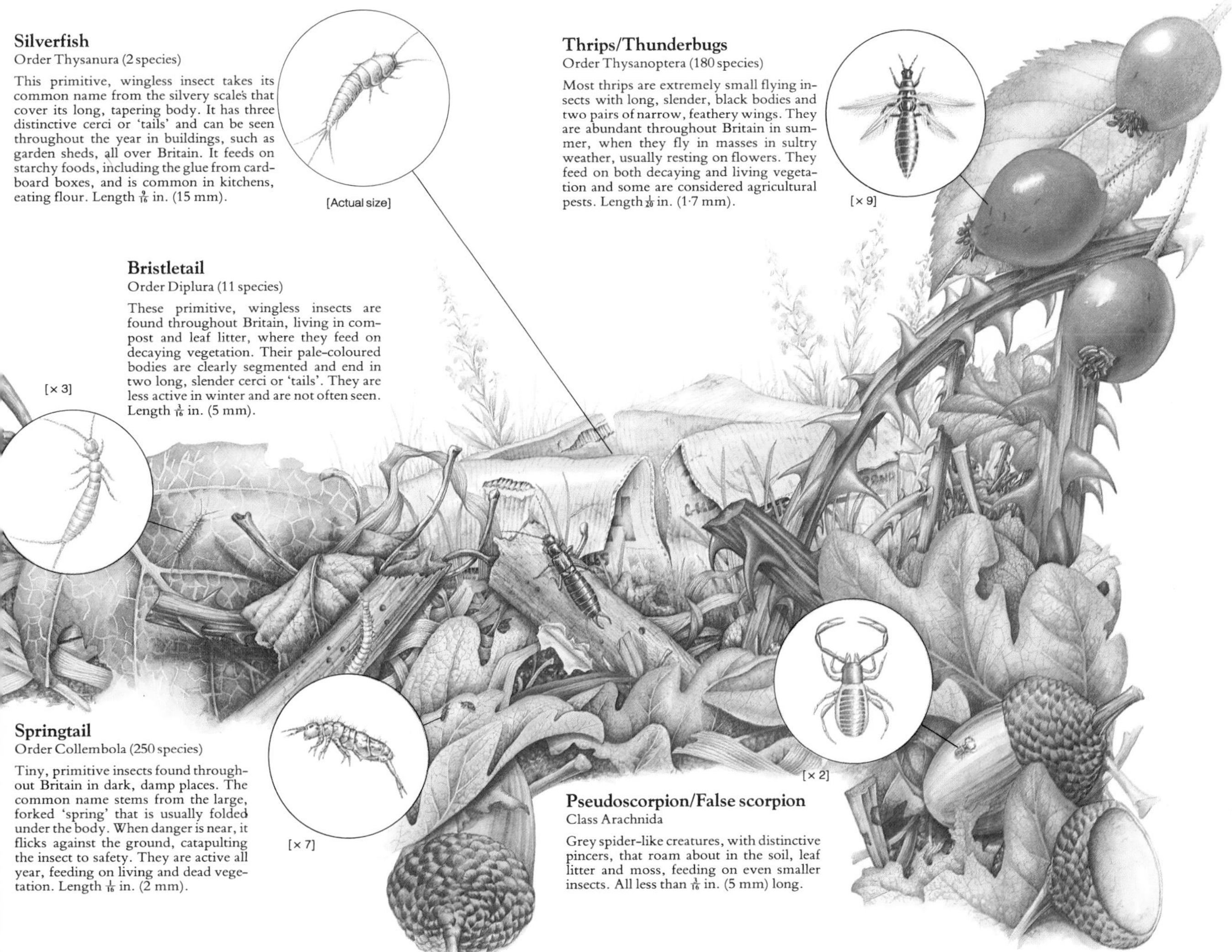

Silverfish
Order Thysanura (2 species)

This primitive, wingless insect takes its common name from the silvery scales that cover its long, tapering body. It has three distinctive cerci or 'tails' and can be seen throughout the year in buildings, such as garden sheds, all over Britain. It feeds on starchy foods, including the glue from cardboard boxes, and is common in kitchens, eating flour. Length $\frac{9}{16}$ in. (15 mm).

Thrips/Thunderbugs
Order Thysanoptera (180 species)

Most thrips are extremely small flying insects with long, slender, black bodies and two pairs of narrow, feathery wings. They are abundant throughout Britain in summer, when they fly in masses in sultry weather, usually resting on flowers. They feed on both decaying and living vegetation and some are considered agricultural pests. Length $\frac{1}{20}$ in. (1·7 mm).

Bristletail
Order Diplura (11 species)

These primitive, wingless insects are found throughout Britain, living in compost and leaf litter, where they feed on decaying vegetation. Their pale-coloured bodies are clearly segmented and end in two long, slender cerci or 'tails'. They are less active in winter and are not often seen. Length $\frac{3}{16}$ in. (5 mm).

Springtail
Order Collembola (250 species)

Tiny, primitive insects found throughout Britain in dark, damp places. The common name stems from the large, forked 'spring' that is usually folded under the body. When danger is near, it flicks against the ground, catapulting the insect to safety. They are active all year, feeding on living and dead vegetation. Length $\frac{1}{16}$ in. (2 mm).

Pseudoscorpion/False scorpion
Class Arachnida

Grey spider-like creatures, with distinctive pincers, that roam about in the soil, leaf litter and moss, feeding on even smaller insects. All less than $\frac{3}{16}$ in. (5 mm) long.

The female, with a white cross on her back, waits at the centre of the web for an insect to be trapped. Length of body ½ in. (13 mm).

The male – only about a quarter the female's size – does not share her web, but scavenges off it.

A spider waits at the centre of her web which, when the dew vanishes with the sun, becomes an almost invisible trap.

In autumn, up to 800 eggs may be laid in a single mass, protected by a layer of yellow silk.

The young spiderlings hatch in spring and at first cluster together in a ball. If disturbed, the ball disintegrates as they scatter.

When an insect becomes caught in the web, the spider bites and paralyses it. She then bundles it in silk and injects it with enzymes to turn its body tissues into liquid for eating.

Garden spider *Araneus diadematus*

A hedgerow in the early morning of late summer or autumn can sparkle with dew-laden webs. The largest will belong to one of Britain's 40 species of orb-web spiders which spin the disc-shaped webs traditionally associated with spiders. One species is the garden spider, found all over Britain and known by many other names, including garden-cross and diadem spider because of the white cross on its back.

The complex web is actually constructed twice before it is ready to trap insects. First it is spun with non-sticky silk produced from a gland at the tip of the female spider's body. The spider attaches tension lines to nearby plants, then spins a small inner spiral – where she will rest while waiting for her prey – followed by an outer spiral which traps the prey. She then goes back over the outer spiral eating the non-sticky silk and replacing it with gummed silk. She avoids sticking to her own web by coating her feet with oil. Once the web is too torn to work efficiently she will eat it and use the material again.

Some web spiders produce less elaborate webs, and the spitting spider has no permanent web at all. It traps its prey by squirting it with a mesh of silk.

Other web-making spiders found in Britain

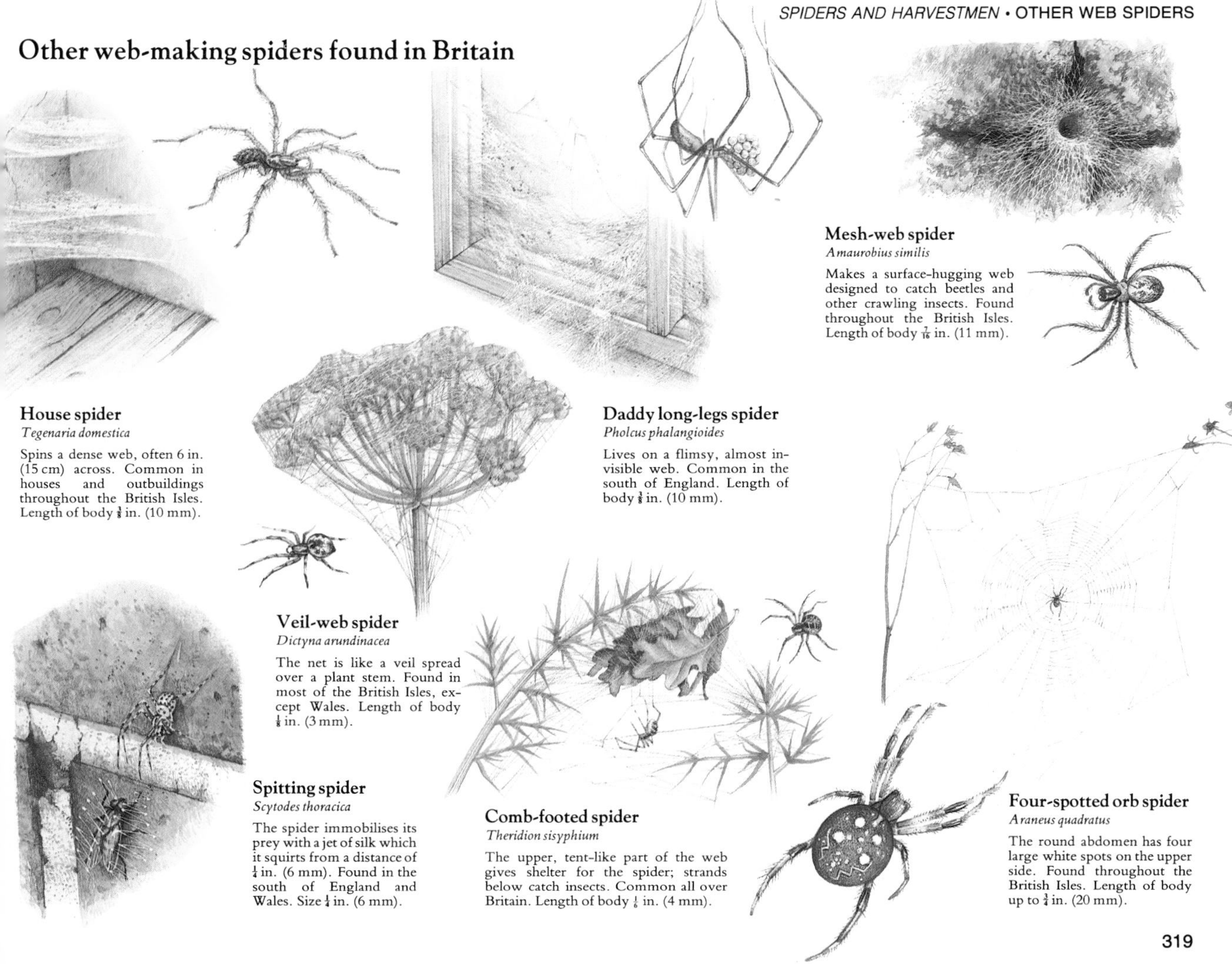

Mesh-web spider

Amaurobius similis

Makes a surface-hugging web designed to catch beetles and other crawling insects. Found throughout the British Isles. Length of body $\frac{7}{16}$ in. (11 mm).

House spider

Tegenaria domestica

Spins a dense web, often 6 in. (15 cm) across. Common in houses and outbuildings throughout the British Isles. Length of body $\frac{3}{8}$ in. (10 mm).

Daddy long-legs spider

Pholcus phalangioides

Lives on a flimsy, almost invisible web. Common in the south of England. Length of body $\frac{3}{8}$ in. (10 mm).

Veil-web spider

Dictyna arundinacea

The net is like a veil spread over a plant stem. Found in most of the British Isles, except Wales. Length of body $\frac{1}{8}$ in. (3 mm).

Spitting spider

Scytodes thoracica

The spider immobilises its prey with a jet of silk which it squirts from a distance of $\frac{1}{4}$ in. (6 mm). Found in the south of England and Wales. Size $\frac{1}{4}$ in. (6 mm).

Comb-footed spider

Theridion sisyphium

The upper, tent-like part of the web gives shelter for the spider; strands below catch insects. Common all over Britain. Length of body $\frac{1}{6}$ in. (4 mm).

Four-spotted orb spider

Araneus quadratus

The round abdomen has four large white spots on the upper side. Found throughout the British Isles. Length of body up to $\frac{3}{4}$ in. (20 mm).

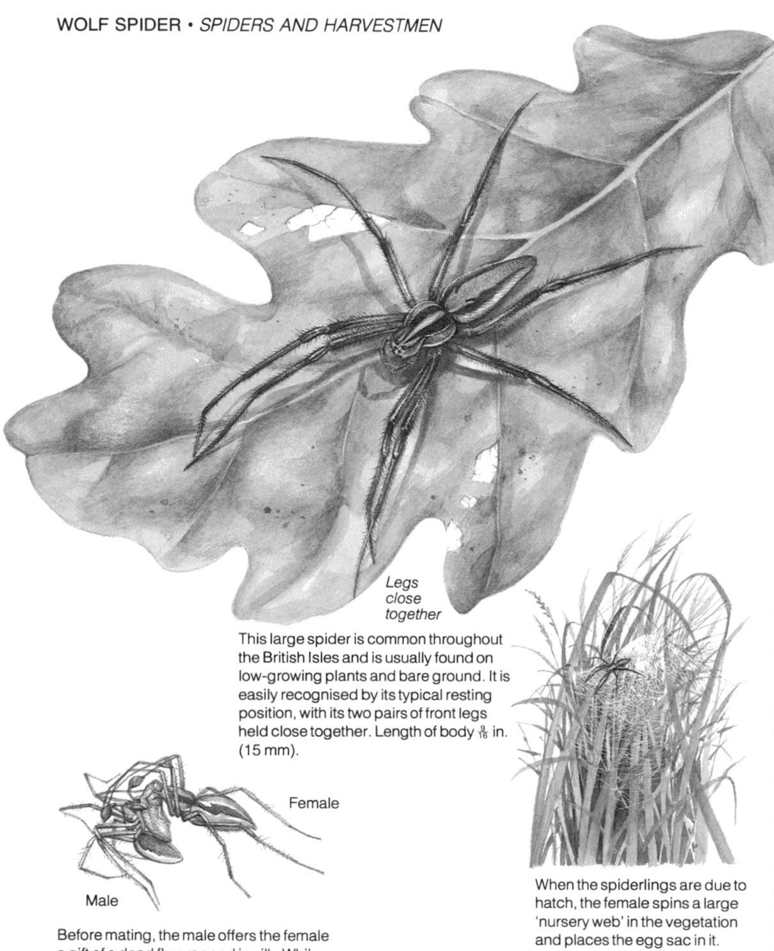

This large spider is common throughout the British Isles and is usually found on low-growing plants and bare ground. It is easily recognised by its typical resting position, with its two pairs of front legs held close together. Length of body $\frac{9}{16}$ in. (15 mm).

Before mating, the male offers the female a gift of a dead fly wrapped in silk. While she eats the fly, he mates with her. Without the gift she is likely to eat him.

When the spiderlings are due to hatch, the female spins a large 'nursery web' in the vegetation and places the egg sac in it.

The female lays her eggs in a silk ball and carries them around with her under her body for a week or so. The silk ball makes the female wolf spider easily recognisable.

A male wolf spider courts the larger female with a dead fly. He then transfers his sperm to her in syringe-like feelers.

Wolf spider *Pisaura mirabilis*

The familiar wolf spider is one of many British spiders that do not make webs to catch prey. Wolf spiders are often seen basking or scurrying over low vegetation and bare earth. They are hunters, well adapted to running down their prey in the same way as their namesake. Victims are quickly killed, or at least paralysed, by a venom which the wolf spider injects through its powerful fangs. The prey is then sucked dry of all its juices and left as a husk.

Because of their nomadic lives, webless spiders have to carry their egg-sacs around with them until the offspring are ready to hatch. Some wolf spiders – there are several species – even carry the young spiderlings on their backs for a week or more. All webless spiders use either speed or camouflage to catch their prey. One of the best camouflaged of all webless spiders is the crab spider, which seems to select flowers matching its body colour. It blends with the petals and waits for an unsuspecting insect to land. One of the most unusual British spiders is the water spider which can swim beneath water for up to 30 minutes, enveloped in a silver film of air. It eats small aquatic insects, and sometimes small fish fry and tadpoles.

Other British spiders that have no webs

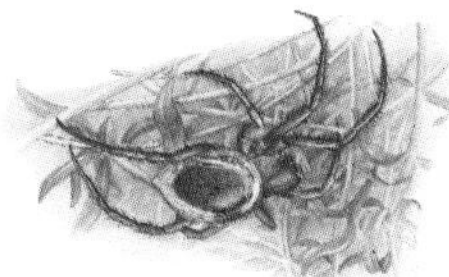

Water spider

Argyroneta aquatica

Britain's only spider that lives under water. It is found in many parts of the British Isles in slow-moving streams or ponds. It spins a silken dome for use as a 'diving bell', filled with air. Length of body up to ½ in. (13 mm).

A night-hunting spider

Clubiona terrestris

A reddish-brown spider with a dark head. It is common throughout Britain, and can be found at most times of the year on low plants or under stones. Length of body ¼ in. (6 mm).

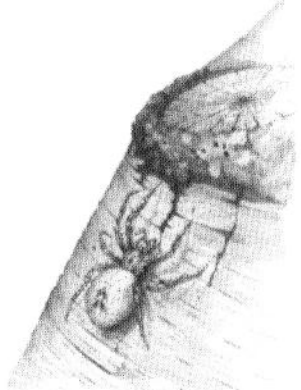

Buzzing spider

Anyphaena accentuata

A very common spider on trees and bushes throughout the British Isles, and recognisable from the black arrowhead markings on the body. The male makes a buzzing sound as he courts the female. Length of body ¼ in. (6 mm).

Small wolf spider

Lycosa pullata

One of the most abundant spiders in Britain, found everywhere in grassy places. It is most easily recognised by the blue egg sac carried by the female. Length of body up to ¼ in. (6 mm).

Zebra spider

Salticus scenicus

This distinctive black-and-white jumping spider is common throughout Britain. It can be found on brick walls, window sills and garden paths. Despite its small size it is a hunter of other small insects, and can jump a distance of up to 4 in. (10 cm). Length of body ¼ in. (6 mm).

Common crab spider

Misumena vatia

There are two common colour forms which are illustrated above. The spiders are easily recognised by their fat bodies, and are common in the south of England. Length of body up to ⅜ in. (10 mm).

Female

Male

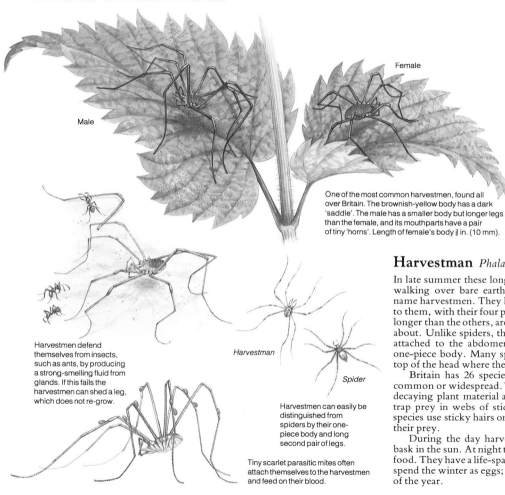

One of the most common harvestmen, found all over Britain. The brownish-yellow body has a dark 'saddle'. The male has a smaller body but longer legs than the female, and its mouthparts have a pair of tiny 'horns'. Length of female's body ⅜ in. (10 mm).

A harvestman crouches on a flowering heather plant, with its long second pair of legs stretched out in front.

Harvestmen defend themselves from insects, such as ants, by producing a strong-smelling fluid from glands. If this fails the harvestmen can shed a leg, which does not re-grow.

Harvestman

Spider

Harvestmen can easily be distinguished from spiders by their one-piece body and long second pair of legs.

Tiny scarlet parasitic mites often attach themselves to the harvestmen and feed on their blood.

Harvestman *Phalangium opilio*

In late summer these long-legged creatures are sometimes seen walking over bare earth in harvested fields, giving them the name harvestmen. They look like spiders and are closely related to them, with their four pairs of legs. The second pair, which are longer than the others, are used by the harvestman to feel its way about. Unlike spiders, the harvestman has the head and thorax attached to the abdomen without a dividing waist, giving a one-piece body. Many species have a prominent bump on the top of the head where the eyes are situated.

Britain has 26 species of harvestmen, but only a few are common or widespread. Their food ranges from small insects to decaying plant material and even bird droppings. They do not trap prey in webs of sticky silk, like some spiders, but a few species use sticky hairs on their mouthparts to ensnare and hold their prey.

During the day harvestmen avoid activity, but will often bask in the sun. At night they scurry over vegetation in search of food. They have a life-span of four to nine months. Some species spend the winter as eggs; other species exist as adults at any time of the year.

Four more harvestmen found in Britain

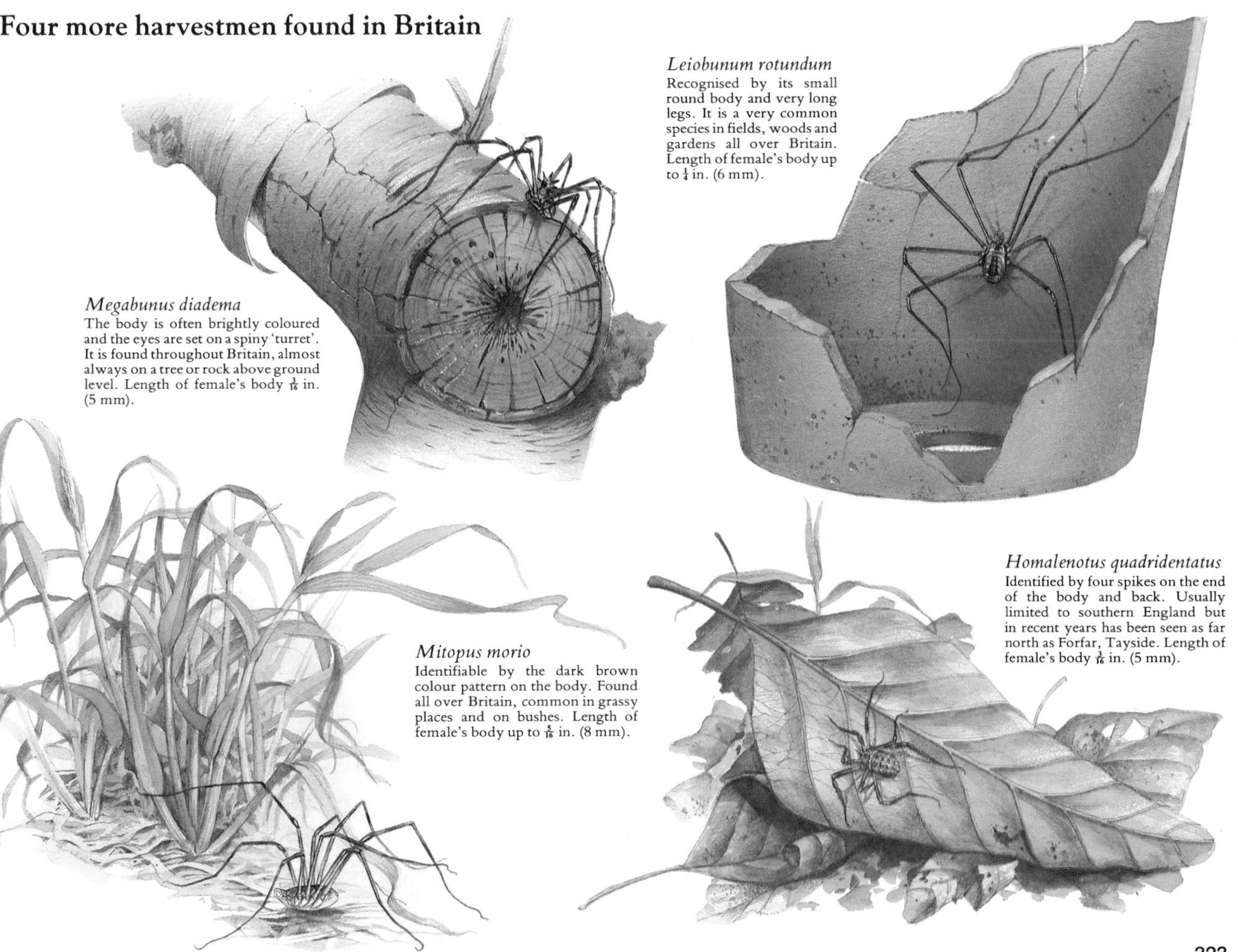

Leiobunum rotundum
Recognised by its small round body and very long legs. It is a very common species in fields, woods and gardens all over Britain. Length of female's body up to $\frac{1}{4}$ in. (6 mm).

Megabunus diadema
The body is often brightly coloured and the eyes are set on a spiny 'turret'. It is found throughout Britain, almost always on a tree or rock above ground level. Length of female's body $\frac{3}{16}$ in. (5 mm).

Homalenotus quadridentatus
Identified by four spikes on the end of the body and back. Usually limited to southern England but in recent years has been seen as far north as Forfar, Tayside. Length of female's body $\frac{3}{16}$ in. (5 mm).

Mitopus morio
Identifiable by the dark brown colour pattern on the body. Found all over Britain, common in grassy places and on bushes. Length of female's body up to $\frac{5}{16}$ in. (8 mm).

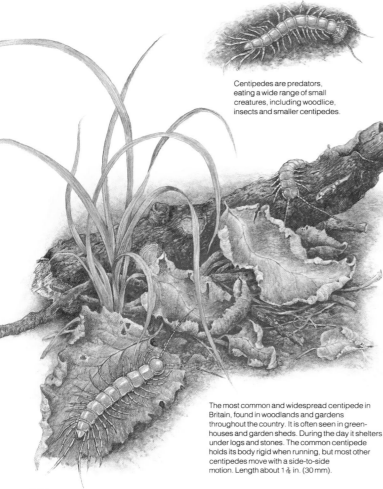

Centipedes are predators, eating a wide range of small creatures, including woodlice, insects and smaller centipedes.

Young centipedes hatch from eggs. They look like adults except that they are much smaller and usually have fewer pairs of legs.

Like insects, centipedes have a hard outer skeleton that has to be shed up to ten times so that they can grow.

The most common and widespread centipede in Britain, found in woodlands and gardens throughout the country. It is often seen in greenhouses and garden sheds. During the day it shelters under logs and stones. The common centipede holds its body rigid when running, but most other centipedes move with a side-to-side motion. Length about $1\frac{3}{16}$ in. (30 mm).

Common centipede *Lithobius forficatus*

Centipedes emerge into the open only at night. In the daytime they shelter in dark places under stones, beneath bark and in leaf litter. Although they are related to insects, their hard outer skin, or cuticle, does not have the waxy waterproof layer that insects possess to preserve their body moisture. If a centipede is exposed to dry, sunny conditions it will die in a few hours. This explains the absence of centipedes from all but the dampest houses. They live in almost total darkness, and none of Britain's 44 species of centipede has eyes of any sort. To catch the small creatures that make up their diet, they rely on vibration and touch, and the speed with which they can pursue fleeing prey. Once caught, the prey dies quickly from an injection of poison delivered by the centipede's front legs, which have been modified into sharp-pointed fangs.

Some British centipedes were brought to this country as unwanted passengers among cargoes of timber and plants. None is really dangerous, although some can give a painful bite if handled. The word centipede means one hundred feet, but the actual number of legs varies from 34 to 354, depending on the species. Each of the body segments carries one pair of legs.

Other British centipedes

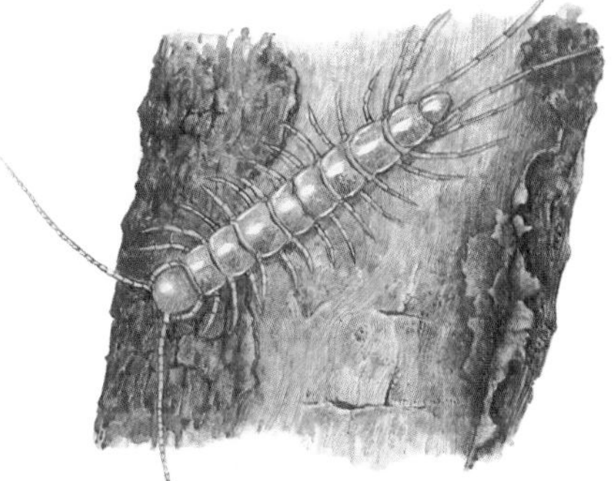

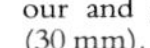

Lithobius variegatus
A species of centipede found only in Britain, usually in woodland. It is mottled in colour and grows up to $1\frac{3}{16}$ in. (30 mm).

Necrophloeophagus longicornis
Found in the soil of gardens and fields throughout Britain. Recognisable by its dark head and first few segments. Length up to $1\frac{3}{8}$ in. (35 mm).

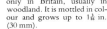

Scutigera coleoptrata
A long-legged centipede found only occasionally in Britain, usually inside buildings in the south of England. It has a bite as painful as a wasp sting. Length up to $1\frac{3}{16}$ in. (30 mm).

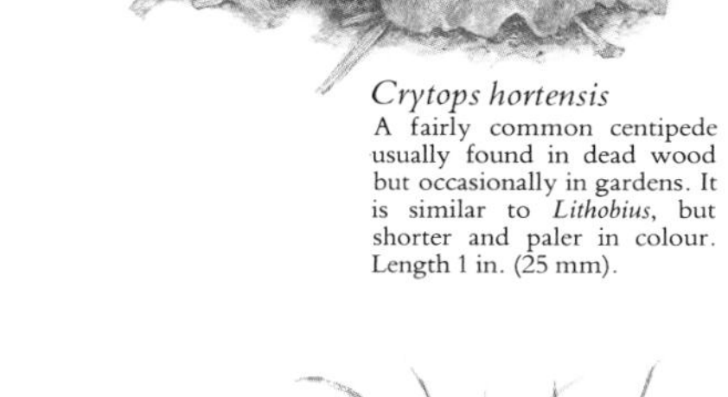

Crytops hortensis
A fairly common centipede usually found in dead wood but occasionally in gardens. It is similar to *Lithobius*, but shorter and paler in colour. Length 1 in. (25 mm).

Halophilus subterraneus
This long, thin centipede is common in soil all over Britain. It can be recognised by the 80 or more pairs of legs. Length up to $2\frac{3}{4}$ in. (70 mm).

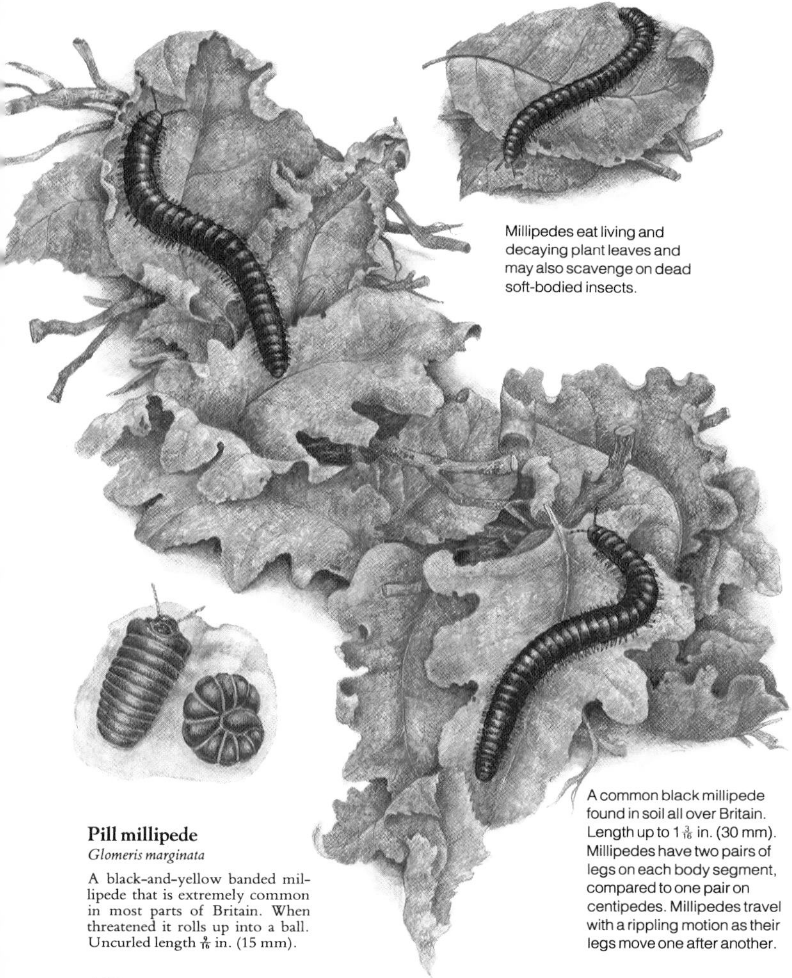

Millipedes eat living and decaying plant leaves and may also scavenge on dead soft-bodied insects.

If a millipede is attacked it curls up to protect its soft underparts. At the same time it can produce a repellent fluid from glands along its flanks.

The black snake millipede moves with a wave-like motion on its 96 pairs of legs. It spends winter under bark or in the soil.

A common black millipede found in soil all over Britain. Length up to $1\frac{3}{16}$ in. (30 mm). Millipedes have two pairs of legs on each body segment, compared to one pair on centipedes. Millipedes travel with a rippling motion as their legs move one after another.

Black snake millipede *Tachypodoiulus niger*

Like centipedes, millipedes dwell in the moist, dark world of leaf litter and soil. The two are often confused, but there is a clear point of distinction – millipedes have two pairs of legs on each body segment; centipedes have only one pair. Britain has 50 species of millipede, of which the black snake millipede is one of the most common. All species consist of many segments protected by a hard plate that forms their outer skeleton. The skeleton gives protection from predators, particularly when the millipede curls up into a flat ball to conceal its soft underparts. As it rolls up it can produce a foul-smelling liquid or vapour from glands along its sides.

Millipedes feed mainly on soft plant tissue, either living or dead. In attacking root crops and young plants they are agricultural pests, but they are beneficial to soil fertility by recycling dead and decaying leaves. Young millipedes, which hatch from eggs, are tiny copies of their parents, and take three to six months to mature. An adult millipede may live for several years.

The pill millipede is a squat, shiny species which can roll up into a complete ball when threatened, leaving no chinks in its armour. It is similar to the pill bug woodlouse (opposite page).

Pill millipede

Glomeris marginata

A black-and-yellow banded millipede that is extremely common in most parts of Britain. When threatened it rolls up into a ball. Uncurled length $\frac{9}{16}$ in. (15 mm).

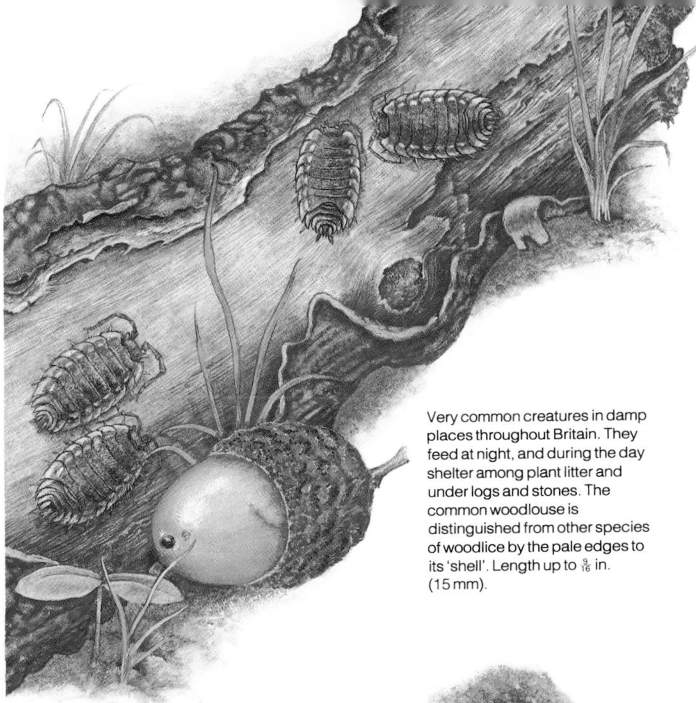

Very common creatures in damp places throughout Britain. They feed at night, and during the day shelter among plant litter and under logs and stones. The common woodlouse is distinguished from other species of woodlice by the pale edges to its 'shell'. Length up to $\frac{9}{16}$ in. (15 mm).

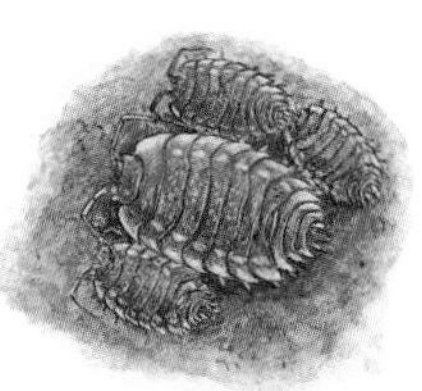

Female woodlice do not actually lay their eggs. They keep them inside pockets underneath the body, where the young woodlice hatch.

Woodlice belong to a group of animals called decomposers as they recycle dead plant matter back into the soil.

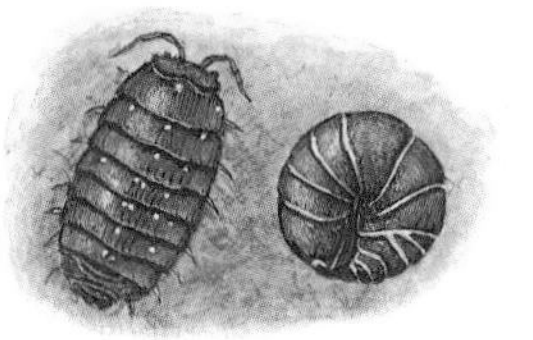

Pill bug
Armadillidium vulgare

Widespread in Britain, especially on chalky soils. The pill bug can tolerate dry conditions, and is often found inside houses. When alarmed it can roll itself into a complete ball. Length $\frac{11}{16}$ in. (18 mm).

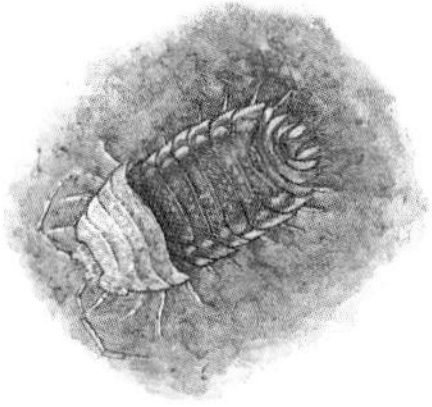

Like all arthropods (creatures with external skeletons), woodlice can grow only after shedding their old skins. But unlike other arthropods they shed their skins in two parts over several days.

Common woodlouse *Oniscus asellus*

The woodlouse is one of the few land-living relatives of the crab and lobster of the seashore. Its ancestors crawled from the sea and made their homes in dark, damp places on land. As they have not developed waterproof body coverings, they would dry out in sunshine. There are 46 species of woodlice in Britain, living mostly under logs or stones and along damp walls. They are active at night when darkness protects them from hungry birds and moist air prevents dessication.

Woodlice eat soft plant leaves, decaying plant matter including wood, and fungi. Like rabbits, they eat their own droppings to obtain maximum nourishment from their food. Bacteria in the droppings break down any undigested particles, which are absorbed on the second consumption. The female woodlouse deposits her eggs into a fluid-filled 'pouch' on the underside of her body. They hatch after 3–5 weeks, producing tiny replicas of the parents. A young woodlouse takes up to two years to mature and may live two to four years depending on species.

The pill bug, another species of woodlouse, rolls up into an armour-plated ball when threatened. It closely resembles the pill millipede (opposite page).

Earthworms mate when they come to the surface of the soil at night. Each earthworm has both male and female reproductive organs.

An earthworm has a good chance of escaping from a small bird by pushing against the sides of its hole with stiff bristles. If only a small part of its body is torn off, the worm can live and regrow it. However, if it is cut in half it will not grow into two worms; it dies.

Earthworms can swell parts of their bodies to anchor them in the soil, while thinning other parts to pull them forwards.

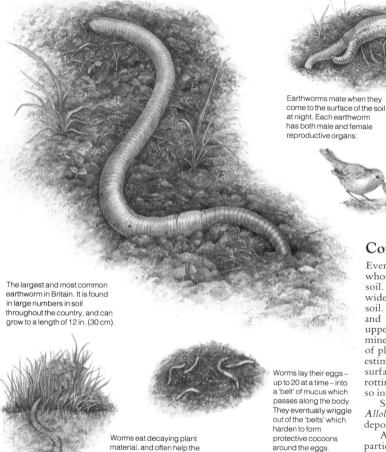

The largest and most common earthworm in Britain. It is found in large numbers in soil throughout the country, and can grow to a length of 12 in. (30 cm).

Worms eat decaying plant material, and often help the decomposition by dragging leaves down into the soil.

Worms lay their eggs – up to 20 at a time – into a 'belt' of mucus which passes along the body. They eventually wriggle out of the 'belts' which harden to form protective cocoons around the eggs.

Common earthworm *Lumbricus terrestris*

Every acre of grassland contains up to 3 million earthworms whose activities constantly help to maintain the fertility of the soil. The common earthworm, one of the most abundant and widespread species, lives in tunnels as deep as 6 ft (1.8 m) in the soil. The worms eat large amounts of soil, digesting the bacteria and organic matter and then excreting the remainder in the upper part of the tunnel. This action returns to the surface minerals which have been washed down by rain out of the reach of plant roots. Charles Darwin, author of *The Origin of Species*, estimated that earthworms bring eight to ten tons of soil to the surface of an acre of land each year. Earthworms also pull down rotting leaves into the soil to eat them out of danger from birds, so increasing the humus content of the soil.

Soil casts found on lawns are usually caused by the species *Allolobophora longa*. The common earthworm and other species deposit their casts in their tunnels.

A worm burrows by forcing its pointed 'head' between particles of soil, and then contracting strong muscles along its full length, which push against bristles growing on the body to push the worm forward. Worms can live up to two years.

Six other British earthworms

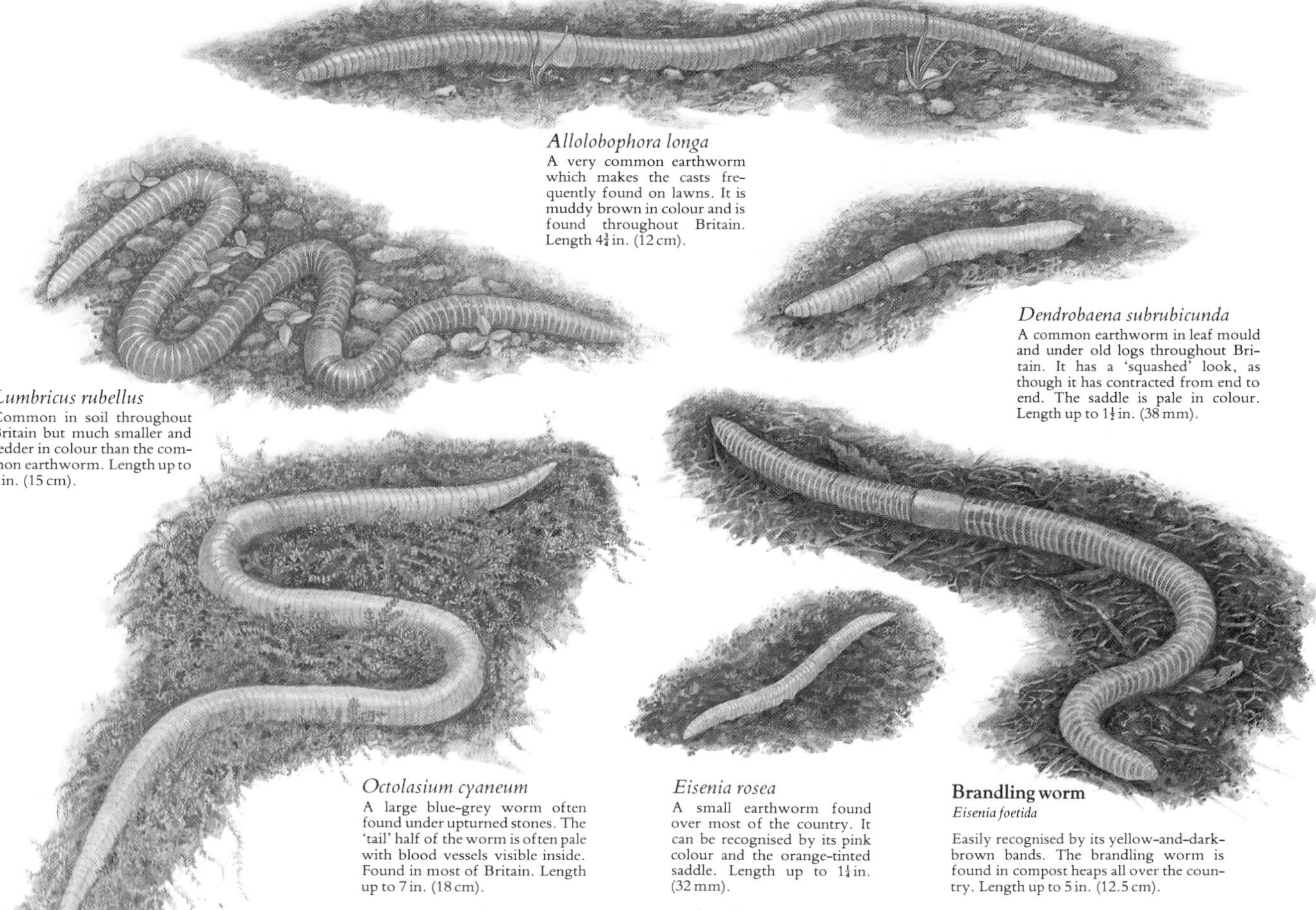

Allolobophora longa
A very common earthworm which makes the casts frequently found on lawns. It is muddy brown in colour and is found throughout Britain. Length 4¾ in. (12 cm).

Lumbricus rubellus
Common in soil throughout Britain but much smaller and redder in colour than the common earthworm. Length up to 6 in. (15 cm).

Dendrobaena subrubicunda
A common earthworm in leaf mould and under old logs throughout Britain. It has a 'squashed' look, as though it has contracted from end to end. The saddle is pale in colour. Length up to 1½ in. (38 mm).

Octolasium cyaneum
A large blue-grey worm often found under upturned stones. The 'tail' half of the worm is often pale with blood vessels visible inside. Found in most of Britain. Length up to 7 in. (18 cm).

Eisenia rosea
A small earthworm found over most of the country. It can be recognised by its pink colour and the orange-tinted saddle. Length up to 1¼ in. (32 mm).

Brandling worm
Eisenia foetida

Easily recognised by its yellow-and-dark-brown bands. The brandling worm is found in compost heaps all over the country. Length up to 5 in. (12.5 cm).

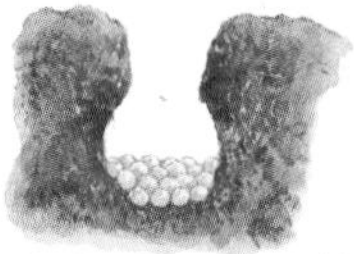

Chalky white eggs are laid in shallow depressions in the earth. Up to 40 eggs may be laid in one hole. Within a month small replicas of the adult hatch from them.

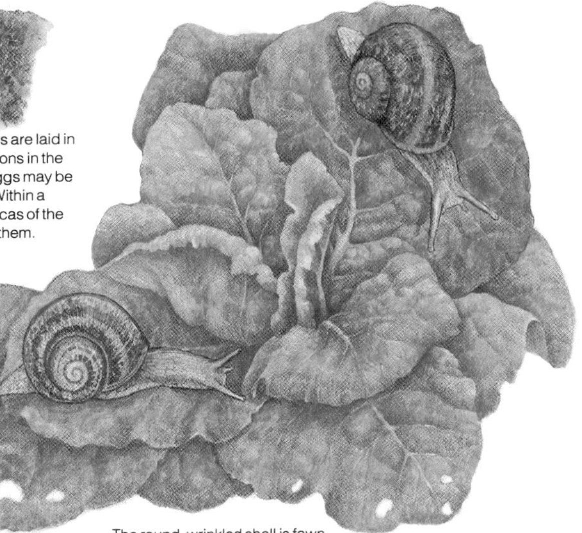

The round, wrinkled shell is fawn, usually patterned with up to five darker, flecked bands, but the patterning is very variable. Shell size up to $1\frac{1}{2}$ in. (38 mm) wide, $1\frac{3}{8}$ in. (35 mm) high.

In winter and during long dry spells, snails congregate in dry, sheltered places to hibernate. They seal up the shell opening with mucus to prevent loss of moisture.

Mating occurs on warm, wet nights in summer after a short courtship. Sperm is passed from each snail to the other, and both snails lay eggs.

Song thrushes eat huge numbers of snails, breaking open the shells on an 'anvil' – a stone. The lip of the shell usually remains intact.

Snails inhabit hedges, banks, gardens, walls and rocks throughout Britain, but in Scotland are mainly coastal.

Garden snail *Helix aspersa*

Snails are creatures of the night. During the daytime they rest in damp cracks and crevices to avoid predators and the heat of the sun. Their shells, which are made from a lime-rich substance, prevent the snail's soft body from drying out. During hot, dry spells in summer, and through the cold of winter, the shell can be sealed off with hardened mucus. The need for lime in the shells restricts snails to areas with alkaline soil. Few species are found on acidic moorland and heathland.

Britain has 80 species of land snail. Most eat plants, either living or dead, but a few species are carnivorous and prey upon other snails or small creatures in the soil. Each snail possesses both male and female sex organs and mating involves the exchange of sperm which is released after a harpoon-like dart is shot from each snail to the other. Both snails can lay their own eggs in batches of up to 40, and after about a month the eggs hatch into tiny copies of the parents. The shell of the young snail gets bigger as the snail grows. New material is added to the lip of the shell, gradually enlarging the spiral shape. Species with large shells may take up to two years to reach sexual maturity, and a few species may live up to ten years.

Six other British land snails

White-lipped banded snail

Cepaea hortensis

The thin, glossy, rather flattened shell is yellow, often with five dark bands, but the colour, number, and spacing of the bands is very variable and some shells are unbanded. The shell lip is white. The body is dark greenish-grey. The species is found throughout Britain among thick, wet vegetation, on trees and on sand-dunes. Shell size up to $\frac{5}{8}$ in. (16 mm) wide and $\frac{3}{4}$ in. (20 mm) high.

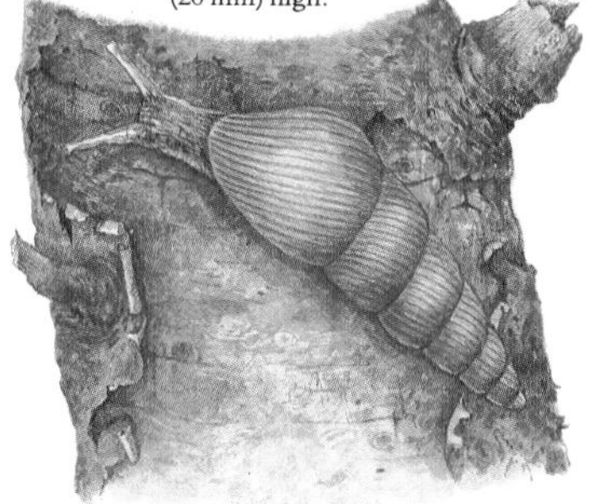

Tree snail

Balea perversa

The narrow cone-shaped shell is pale brown or greenish. The snail lives in dry rock crevices and on tree trunks. Locally common throughout Britain. Shell size up to $\frac{3}{8}$ in. (10 mm) long and $\frac{1}{10}$ in. (2·5 mm) across.

Dark-lipped banded snail

Cepaea nemoralis

The thick, globular shell is slightly shiny and often yellow but sometimes brown. Five dark bands are common but not always present. The number and spacing of bands varies. The lip is usually brown and the body yellow-grey. The snail is common in hedges and grassy places throughout Britain. Shell size up to $\frac{7}{8}$ in. (22 mm) wide and 1 in. (25 mm) high.

Garlic glass snail

Oxychilus alliarius

The narrow, wheel-shaped shell is shiny, translucent and pale yellow-brown or green. The body is blue-black. The snail lives on banks, walls, rocks, and in fields and woods all over Britain. It smells strongly of garlic if it is handled or disturbed. Shell size up to $\frac{3}{16}$ in. (5 mm) wide and $\frac{1}{4}$ in. (6 mm) high.

Roman or edible snail

Helix pomatia

A rare but unmistakable large snail with a thick, round, cream-coloured shell and pale yellow-grey ridged body. It is found locally in the chalk and limestone areas of southern England. The snails probably got their name because the Romans ate them while in Britain. Shell size up to 2 in. (50 mm) in width and height.

Moss snail

Cochlicopa lubrica

The blunt-ended, conical shell is glossy, translucent, and pale to dark brown. The snail is common everywhere in Britain in damp places including dead leaves, grass and under fallen branches, as well as among mosses. The body is pale brown. Shell size up to $\frac{1}{4}$ in. (6 mm) long and $\frac{1}{8}$ in. (3 mm) across.

When resting or threatened by a bird, the slug contracts to a semicircular hump, presenting a tough exterior.

During the day slugs shelter in dark, moist places to avoid the drying effects of the sun. They emerge at night to eat.

There are black, brown, brick-red, orange, and grey forms of this slug; juveniles have a dark band along each side. The thick body, up to 6 in. (15 cm) long when extended, is rounded at the tail and patterned with long tubercles, or lumps. The hole in the mantle (the saddle-like area on the 'back') is for breathing.

A pair of courting slugs circle each other as a preliminary to curling around one another and entwining their sexual organs for sperm transfer.

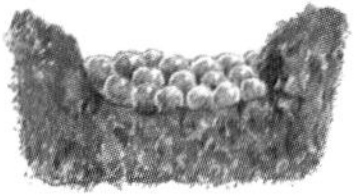

Eggs like translucent pearls are laid in small batches in loose soil or compost.

Great black slug *Arion ater*

Britain has 23 species of slug, and the great black slug is one of the largest and most common. Having no shell, slugs need a means of keeping their soft bodies from drying out. This is provided by a layer of sticky mucus over the body, giving slugs their characteristic sliminess. The mucus also provides protection by making the slugs difficult for birds to grip. And it helps them to move over sharp objects by acting as a lubricant, and to crawl up smooth surfaces because of its sticky nature. Wherever the slug goes it leaves behind a silvery trail of dried mucus.

The diet of slugs includes living and decaying plants, occasionally mixed with pieces of dead insects or animals. Slugs feed by scraping away the surface of a leaf or stem with their rasp-like mouthparts. Most garden slugs, including the great black slug, will eat seedlings of plants and soft fruits such as strawberries.

All slugs are hermaphrodites – that is, they have both male and female sex organs. After a complex mating ritual both partners lay eggs that live through winter and produce a new generation of tiny slugs in spring. An individual slug may live for three years.

Other common slugs

Netted slug (Field slug)

Deroceras reticulatum

This most common slug of gardens all over Britain is a pest on crops such as lettuces. The body varies from pale yellow to brown and grey, with many dark marks especially in the grooves between tubercles. The mantle's concentric grooves are centred over the breathing hole. Extended length up to 2 in. (50 mm).

Keeled slug

Milax sowerbyi

The narrow body, varying from pale to dark grey-brown, is speckled black and orange. The prominent 'keel' along the centre of the 'back' is lighter. The sticky mucus is yellow. The slugs are locally common in most of Britain, usually living underground, feeding on potatoes and other rootcrops. Extended length up to 3 in. (76 mm).

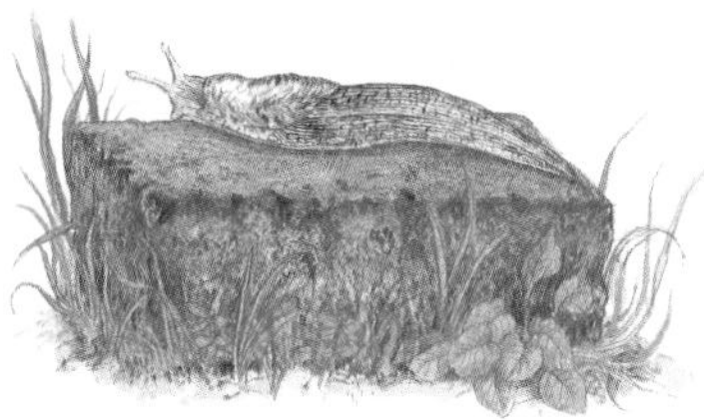

Great grey slug

Limax maximus

Two or three dark bands, sometimes broken, run along the pale brown or greyish body. The mantle, with 'fingerprint' grooves, is spotted or mottled and the tentacles red-brown. This slug is common in western parts of the British Isles. Extended length up to 8 in. (20 cm).

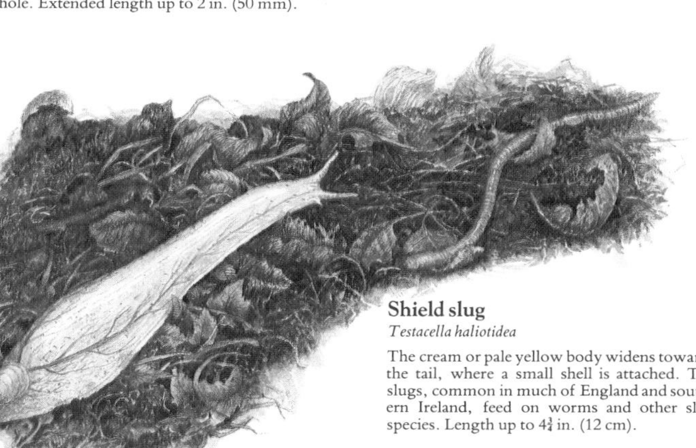

Shield slug

Testacella haliotidea

The cream or pale yellow body widens towards the tail, where a small shell is attached. The slugs, common in much of England and southern Ireland, feed on worms and other slug species. Length up to 4¾ in. (12 cm).

Garden slug

Arion hortensis

A widespread pest of farmland and gardens. A dark band runs along each side of the grey or blue-black body. The sole is orange, tentacles bluish. Some forms have an orange tail-tip. Extended length up to 1¼ in. (30 mm).

BUTTERFLY WATCHING AS A HOBBY

Getting to know butterflies and other insects

Sitting quietly on a downland slope or a grassy moor on a summer's day is a delightful introduction to the subject of butterflies and other insects. As butterflies in their myriad colours flutter over the grass and bumble-bees buzz from flower to flower, you will begin to see the close association between insects and the plants on which they all depend for food and shelter.

Every small area of Britain has a different population of insects, depending on its soil, its rainfall, the plants that grow there and the amount of sunshine it receives. And a fascinating hobby can grow out of identifying as many of the insects as possible, together with the plants they feed and breed on.

There are so many different types of insects in the countryside that it is impossible to remember all those that you might see on a day's outing. So keep a notebook to record the date, place, habitat and species seen on each outing. It can be added to each time you go out, and will serve as a reference from year to year.

Maps of insect distribution which appear in natural history books such as this all start at a local level. They are built up from information submitted by field naturalists – both amateurs and professionals – to the Institute of Terrestrial Ecology, at Monks Wood Experimental Station, Abbots Ripton, Huntingdon PE17 2LS.

The Institute enters the records in its computer and regularly issues up-dated maps. Comparing current and old maps can reveal whether a species is contracting or expanding its range. The Institute issues record cards giving a check list of insects such as butterflies, moths, bumble-bees and beetles which are likely to be seen throughout Britain. Anyone who is seriously interested in recording insects may apply to the Institute. The cards are filled in and returned at the end of the year for the records to be up-dated.

A butterfly monitoring scheme is also organised from the Institute. A selection of amateur naturalists send in weekly counts of butterflies seen along a regularly walked path in their localities each year. The reports help to keep an accurate assessment of what is happening to butterfly population nationally. It provides information about the spread of migrants, such as the red admiral and painted lady, across the country each year, and it records the fluctuations in the numbers of native species in a locality.

Techniques and equipment

One of the most important pieces of equipment to carry in the field is a hand lens. Lenses are available in different magnifications and can be bought from good photography shops. A lens which magnifies the image seven times is suitable for most purposes, and can be tied on a ribbon around the neck for easy access.

It is used by placing it against the eye – rather than against the insect – then bringing eye and insect together. Hand lenses are used for studying small creatures such as beetles, spiders, springtails, flies and ants.

If you begin to specialise in a particular group of insects, you will probably need one of the detailed handbooks for the identification of British insects published by the Royal Entomological Society of London, 41 Queen's Gate, London SW7 5HU.

Most larger insects, such as butterflies, can be identified in the field, and there is no need to catch them. However smaller flies and beetles are more difficult. It may be necessary to capture a small insect for a short time while you examine it, and then you will need a net. Butterfly nets, sweep nets and beating trays are all used to collect insects.

A butterfly net is for flying insects. To avoid injuring a butterfly after catching it, you should flip the bag of the net over the hard edge. The butterfly can then be studied through the net, or taken out carefully and examined. A sweep net, which has a straight, heavy side for dragging through long grass, collects caterpillars, spiders and beetles. A beating tray is held under hedgerows and overhanging branches while you give the plant a single hard blow with a stick. It catches caterpillars and other insects as they fall.

All this equipment can be obtained from Watkins and Doncaster, Conghurst Lane,

Four Throws, Hawkhurst, Kent TN18 5ED, or Worldwide Butterflies Ltd, Compton House, near Sherborne, Dorset.

Traps and lures

Pitfall traps can be prepared easily in woods, gardens or under hedgerows to catch small beetles, earwigs and woodlice which roam about after dark. Old yoghurt pots can be sunk in the leaf litter so that the rim is flush with soil level. First punch a hole in the bottom so that water will not collect and drown the insects. Insects that are in the trap the following morning can be studied, identified and then freed.

Smaller creatures, such as springtails and pseudoscorpions, can be obtained from leaf litter by putting some litter in a plastic funnel and shining a desk lamp on it from above. The insects will fall down the stem of the funnel and into a collecting jar. To prevent the leaf litter falling through the funnel, place some small twigs across the opening.

Treacling is a traditional method of attracting moths. A stiff mixture of black treacle, old jam, sugar and beer is boiled up and painted on tree trunks after dark. Regular inspection every few hours can reveal many types of moths, as well as ants, attracted to the sugary mixture.

Some moths, however, are not attracted to sugar, so moth lights which emit ultra-violet are used instead. Moths, unlike man, can see ultra-violet and are drawn towards it. Large numbers may arrive on a hot, sultry evening in summer, and will settle in the box beneath the lamp. In the morning they can be identified and freed. Alternatively, you can stand by the light and watch them arrive.

Fewer moths are attracted to ordinary light bulbs as they do not produce ultra-violet, but it is still worth inspecting an outside light for moths on a summer's night.

Photographing insects

Most insects do not wait to be photographed. The picture must be taken as soon as possible before they move out of range. Knowledge of the insect's behaviour will help you to decide how close you can approach without disturbing it. Stealth and patience are also needed. You may, for example, have to focus on a flower, and then sit and wait for the moment when you can capture the momentary visit of a butterfly.

Fixed-lens or non-reflex cameras can be used to take pictures of larger insects, and some models have a close-up lens that can be fitted. If you become seriously interested in photographing insects, however, you will need a single-lens reflex camera. With this type of camera, the scene that you see through the viewfinder is exactly what you photograph. It can be fitted with different sizes of lens for different types of work. Bayonet fittings are best for quick action.

For close-ups the best lens is a 'macro' of about 90–100 mm. This is adequate to take the type of photographs used in this book. An alternative lens system is an 80–200 mm zoom. To obtain greater magnification for smaller butterflies, such as blues and skippers, these lenses can be used with a set of three automatic extension tubes, fitted between the lens and the camera body. A 135 mm telephoto lens can also be used with extension tubes, allowing the photographer to take a picture from a greater distance, not to alarm the insect.

To obtain a 'sharp' picture, insects should ideally be photographed in direct sunlight, but many live in the shade of woodland or undergrowth, and need to be photographed with electronic flash. Two small flash guns mounted on either side of the camera, or a more expensive ring flash, will give even dispersal of light.

To photograph tiny insects such as ladybirds, ants or aphids you will need a bellows. This is an extendable box which is fitted like extension tubes, but must be mounted on a tripod. It gives extremely large magnification but is probably best used indoors with electronic flash.

Safeguarding insects

Codes of practice have been drawn up to safeguard insects in various habitats. For example, you are not permitted to collect or kill insects in nature reserves. The *Visiting Nature Reserves Code* can be obtained from the Royal Society for Nature Conservation, The Green, Nettleham, Lincoln LN2 2NR.

The Code for Insect Collecting, published by the Joint Commission for the Conservation of British Insects, governs the numbers of insects that can be taken, the use of light traps, and ways in which the environment should be respected. It can be obtained from the Royal Entomological Society of London, 41 Queen's Gate, London SW7 5HU.

A garden for butterflies, moths and bees

A typical suburban garden can attract more than 20 species of butterflies over a few seasons. Many moths are also likely to visit, and a garden full of flowers becomes a haven for honey-bees and bumble-bees.

Flowers with a rich store of nectar are a magnet to butterflies. As a butterfly's natural food source is found in the wild, it helps to interplant British wild flowers among more traditional garden plants. Packets of wild flower seeds are widely available from seed-merchants and garden centres.

If you wish to attract insects and other wildlife to the garden, avoid using insecticides, weedkillers and slug pellets as far as possible. They kill not only pests but beneficial insects such as bees and butterflies. And the poisons may be passed on to beetles and birds which eat the dead creatures.

In a flower garden, the predators of plant-eating insects will usually keep them under control. Ladybirds, ground beetles and lacewings, for example, will prey on aphids and plant-eating beetles.

Insects are attracted to different parts of each garden. Mixed borders, rough areas of lawn, rock gardens, ponds, kitchen gardens and trees all offer rich habitats.

Mixed border

Banked-up flowers in a mixed border facing the sun will attract butterflies, honey-bees and bumble-bees. A brick wall behind the border will heat up in the sun, and many butterflies – including peacocks, speckled woods and walls – will settle there to bask in the warmth.

Cotoneaster horizontalis fanned out against the wall will attract so many honey-bees to its tiny flowers that sometimes it seems that a swarm has arrived.

Roses are not particularly attractive to butterflies, but they can be interplanted with clematises, loganberries, raspberries and cultivated blackberries, which are.

Spaces between larger plants can be filled with azaleas, rhododendrons and foxgloves which attract bumble-bees in spring and early summer. In high summer, lavender and eryngiums produce blue flowers that become covered in insects, especially bumble-bees.

Aristocrat butterflies will feed on asters, daisies and chrysanthemums in summer, and skippers are attracted to red zinnias.

The buddleia is also known as the butterfly-bush because of its power to attract butterflies. In July and August the long flower-spikes provide nectar for white butterflies, aristocrats, some of the browns and occasionally a fritillary. Most of the buddleia species are acceptable to insects.

Ice plants, which flower late into the autumn, attract small tortoiseshells and painted ladies. There are several species, but *Sedum spectabile* is the best.

Michaelmas daisies also attract butterflies in late summer and autumn, but the old-fashioned, single-flowered varieties are more effective than the double-flowered forms.

At the end of a summer's day, moths will be attracted to the garden by the scent of tobacco plants and honeysuckle, and by night-scented stock whose powerful perfume wafts through the garden on the evening air.

Rough areas of lawn

If a part of the lawn is cut only twice each year – in early summer and autumn – various wild flowers will spring up. A flush of daisies will attract small heath butterflies, and the big flowers of dandelions are likely to bring peacocks and whites. Boggy areas may support cuckoo flower whose pale pink flowers attract the orange tip. Later in the summer ox-eye daisies may tower over the grasses, taking the place of the smaller daisies. Blue vetch may struggle up through the grass and lure passing butterflies, hoverflies and honey-bees.

Wild flowers can be introduced into a lawn by sowing packeted seed in an area that has been scarified with a rake.

Rock gardens

Many small plants, suitable for rock gardens, are attractive to butterflies. The annual cycle starts with primulas and crocuses to bring the spring insects, such as brimstone butterflies and honey-bees.

Later in spring come the mauve masses of aubretia, the white of perennial candytuft and the yellow of *Alyssum saxatile*. Decorative varieties of thyme flower in dense clusters of red, yellow and pink through the summer.

Old walls and rocks should be left with their lichens as food for the caterpillars of footman moths. Clumps of pellitory-of-the-wall, bittercress and purple dead-nettle, which grow on walls, provide food for noctuid moth caterpillars.

Ivy should be kept as food for caterpillars of the holly blue, and as hibernation sites for the brimstone. The brimstone will also visit the purple flowers of periwinkle which scrambles over stones.

Garden pond

The introduction of a pond into the garden will attract many insects whose life-cycles are partly spent in water. Dragonflies, damselflies, caddisflies and mayflies all have aquatic larvae. Rushes and bur-reeds around the edge will give resting places for the adult insects. Stands of willowherb, particularly great willowherb, will provide food for the caterpillars of the elephant hawk-moth.

Silver birch, alder, sallow and willow grow well around ponds, and their leaves will support noctuid moth caterpillars in spring and summer. Marsh marigolds, hemp agrimony and valerian can be planted around the edges. Yellow irises, white water-lilies and watercress grow in shallow water and will be used as resting places by damselflies.

Kitchen garden

Cabbages, cauliflowers, brussels sprouts and broccoli bring cabbage white butterflies to lay their eggs on the leaves. However, if you plant tomatoes or wormwood near by, the strong smell will deter the butterflies. Excess leaves pruned off tomato plants can be laid on the growing cabbages.

One way of controlling cabbage white caterpillars once the eggs have been laid is to inspect the cabbage leaves every three days and crush any groups of yellow eggs between finger and thumb.

Vegetable gardens will also attract many insects more desirable than cabbage whites. Blue butterflies will feed on the nectar of pea and bean flowers. Raspberry flowers also provide nectar for blue butterflies, as well as bumble-bees and honey-bees. If radishes are allowed to run to seed, the white flowers are likely to be visited by butterflies.

The edges of a kitchen garden can be planted with marjoram, chives, lavender and basil which will act as a lure to bees.

Trees and hedges

The leaves of willows, particularly the great sallow (*Salix caprea*) and grey sallow (*S. cinerea*), are food for many moth caterpillars. And the catkins are sources of pollen for honey-bees in spring.

Hedges are a constant source of flowers for butterflies. In February and March, sloe (blackthorn) flowers come out before the leaves, supplying nectar to butterflies waking from winter hibernation. In May and early June, hawthorn hedges can be covered in cascades of white or pink blossom. Hedges of viburnum, privet and choisya are all sources of nectar for butterflies during the summer.

The wild garden

If a sunny area of the garden is left to grow wild, it will become an insect haven. Clumps of nettles should be left to encourage peacocks and small tortoiseshells to lay their eggs. The purple flowers of thistles are also attractive to aristocrat butterflies, as well as whites and brimstones.

Ragwort, with its attractive yellow flowers, is a food plant for the caterpillars of the cinnabar moth. And, occasionally, the red-and-black moth itself may be seen during the day flapping through the garden.

Scabious and knapweeds attract blue, copper and brown butterflies to their nectar. Vetches which scramble up through the grass also attract blue butterflies, and cowslips and primroses may – with luck – attract the Duke of Burgundy fritillary. Dead-nettles, mints and mallow are all good nectar sources for butterflies and honey-bees.

During the winter, stacks of wood or old rotten timbers, can be left in the garden for hibernating butterflies and queen bumble-bees. And if it is not too damp, hibernating ladybirds may pack together in small crevices awaiting the arrival of spring.

How to breed butterflies

Butterflies can be bred at home all year round, and far greater success can be achieved than if they were breeding in the wild where eggs, caterpillars and chrysalises are eaten by predators.

The simplest way is to buy mail-order chrysalises from Worldwide Butterflies, Compton House, near Sherborne, Dorset DT 4QN; or Entomological Livestock Supplies, Fairmile Road, Halesowen, West Midlands B63 3PZ; or The Living World, Seven Sisters Country Park, Exceat, Seaford, East Sussex BN25 4AD.

The same companies also supply eggs which you can rear through the caterpillar and chrysalis stages. But first ensure a supply of food plants, perhaps in the garden or in nearby woods. It may be necessary to grow potted plants from seed.

Small tortoiseshell and peacock butterflies are quite easy to breed, and the caterpillars eat stinging nettles which can be dug up and replanted in pots. Small copper caterpillars can be reared on potted sorrels, and common blues on bird's-foot-trefoil.

Remember that you may have to look after caterpillars for six weeks, and that this period should not clash with holidays.

Where to start

Breeding can begin with any of the four stages of the butterfly's life. You may come across a mass of eggs or some caterpillars in the garden, or dig up some chrysalises when turning the soil. But you must be prepared for disappointing results. You may spend weeks, for example, caring for caterpillars which eventually grow into sawflies.

Alternatively, a pair of adult butterflies may be captured and temporarily put into a cage to breed. A plant that the caterpillars will eat when they hatch should be placed in the cage to encourage the female to lay her eggs on the leaves. A captured female will often have mated already, in which case there is no need for the male.

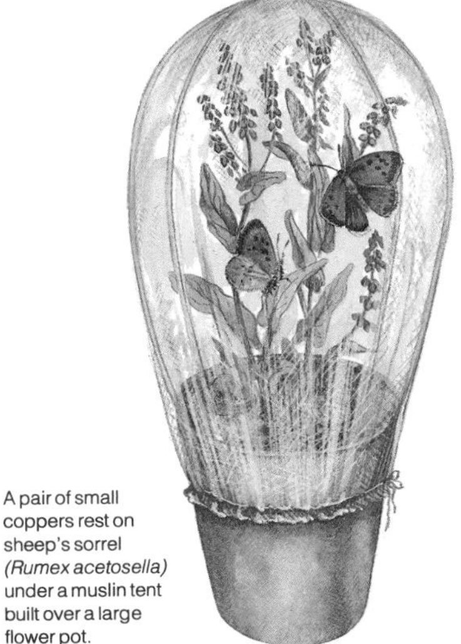

A pair of small coppers rest on sheep's sorrel *(Rumex acetosella)* under a muslin tent built over a large flower pot.

Make the cage by putting the plant into a 12 or 15 in. flower pot filled with potting compost. Make a framework of two or three wire hoops pushed down inside the pot, and cover it with muslin.

The butterflies themselves must also be given food. Dip pink or blue cotton wool into a solution of honey and water (a teaspoon of honey in half a cup of water) and place it in a small dish on the compost.

Put the cage in direct sunshine. Once the eggs have been laid, the butterflies can be liberated into the garden. The eggs will develop on the food plant.

Caring for the caterpillars

When the caterpillars hatch from their eggs, transfer them to a clean plastic sandwich box. Lift them with a soft paint brush and put them in the box with a supply of tender young leaves from their food plant. Put the lid back on the box to prevent their escape and place it out of direct sunlight. There will be sufficient air in the box for them to breathe between daily feeds. Do not allow condensation to build up on the inside of the box as tiny caterpillars drown easily.

Change the leaves every day, and also remove the droppings when they build up.

As the caterpillars grow bigger – after about a week – move them into a larger breeding cage or divide them into several boxes. Breeding cages can be bought from Watkins and Doncaster, Conghurst Lane, Four Throws, Hawkhurst, Kent, or Worldwide Butterflies. Alternatively, a cage can be made by covering a wooden frame, about 2 ft × 2 ft × 2 ft, with muslin.

When the chrysalis is formed

Many chrysalises have to be kept over winter, their normal hibernation period. Keep them on damp potting compost, blotting paper or moss. Check the cage every week or so, and when the compost begins to dry out spray it with water. Keep the cage outdoors in the shade, perhaps in a shed.

When it emerges, the butterfly will need something to crawl up and expand its wings while they dry. So put some twigs inside the cage, standing up against the side. If no support is provided, the butterfly's wings are likely to dry in a crippled state.

Freeing the butterflies

Release butterflies during sunny weather, preferably near flowers to provide nectar and food plants on which the females will lay eggs. Choose a time when there are no birds near by. Moths should be released at night.

Releasing butterflies is helpful to butterfly conservation, but should not be done without notifying the local conservation trust (p. 342). They need to know if insects are released in a different region from where they were obtained, so that their studies of insect distribution are not confused.

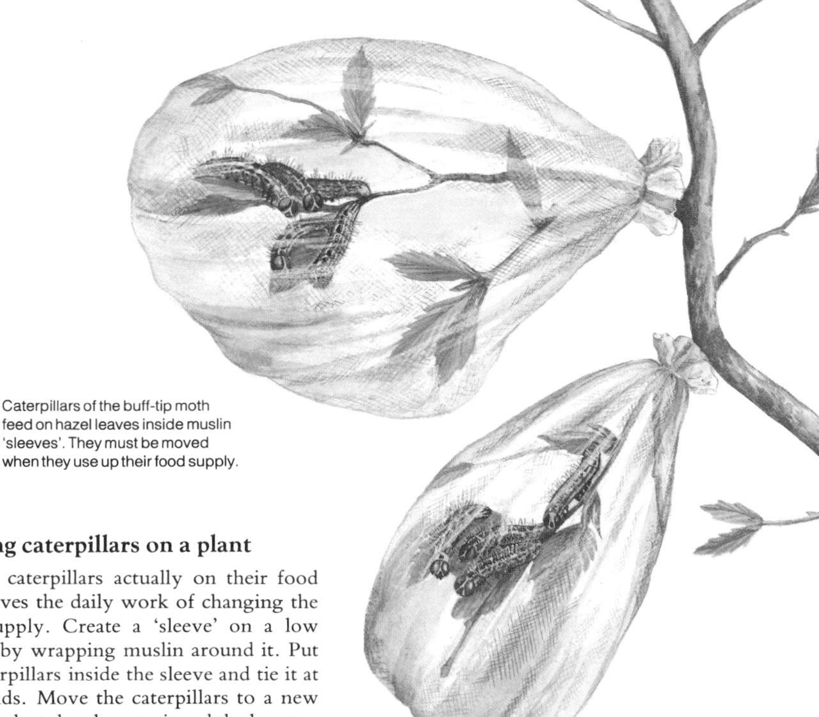

Caterpillars of the buff-tip moth feed on hazel leaves inside muslin 'sleeves'. They must be moved when they use up their food supply.

Rearing caterpillars on a plant

Raising caterpillars actually on their food plant saves the daily work of changing the food supply. Create a 'sleeve' on a low branch by wrapping muslin around it. Put the caterpillars inside the sleeve and tie it at both ends. Move the caterpillars to a new branch when they have stripped the leaves.

Some caterpillars will form a chrysalis in summer. Others will spend winter as caterpillars and form chrysalises in the spring.

Many moth caterpillars will want to leave the branch and pupate in the soil. When they need to find a pupation site they roam around restlessly and often their colours fade. It may be possible to bend down a low branch and sleeve the tip around a pot full of soil and leaf litter. Seal the drainage hole by laying a piece of tin over it.

Skin rashes

Remember that the caterpillars of some moths, particularly the brown tail, drinker and the garden tiger, can cause skin rashes, as some people are allergic to their hairs.

It is probably safest to avoid touching any hairy caterpillars with your bare hands, or if you do touch them to wash your hands immediately afterwards.

Where to see insects

Britain has 1,385 nature reserves run by 46 county trusts for nature conservation. By becoming a member of your local trust you will obtain details of all its nature reserves, covering many different types of habitat. Addresses of all the county trusts can be obtained from The Royal Society for Nature Conservation, The Green, Nettleham, Lincoln LN2 2NR.

In addition, there are many nature reserves managed by other conservation bodies. The Nature Conservancy Council, Attingham Park, Shrewsbury, SY4 4TW, administers National Nature Reserves. The Forestry Commission, 231 Corstorphine Road, Edinburgh EH12 7AT, administers Forest Nature Reserves. The Woodland Trust, Westgate, Grantham, Lincolnshire NG31 6LL, administers private woodlands. The Royal Society for the Protection of Birds, The Lodge, Sandy, Bedfordshire SG19 2DL, administers bird reserves, which are also rich in insect life.

The following is a highly selective list of sites that are renowned for the richness of their insect life.

Bernwood Forest Oxon and Bucks.

Mixed wood, coppice and forestry plantation of 1,000 acres, supporting the largest number of butterfly species recorded from one area in Britain – 42 species between 1975 and 1983. Managed by Forestry Commission and Nature Conservancy Council.

Blean Woods near Canterbury, Kent

Extensive coppice woodland of chestnut, oak, beech and hornbeam. Britain's best locality for the heath fritillary butterfly, which is protected under the Wildlife and Countryside Act of 1981. Many rare invertebrates, including beetles, millipedes and true bugs. Managed by the Kent Trust for Nature Conservation and the RSPB.

Clare Castle Country Park Clare, Suffolk

British native butterflies living in unrestricted countryside which is managed to encourage the butterflies and their food plants.

Dungeness Kent

Nature reserve on coastal gravel deposits. Migratory insects, such as hawk-moths, noctuid moths and hoverflies, can be seen, as well as birds and local flora. The bird observatory frequently operates a moth light at night, and visitors can watch the arrival of migrants. Managed by the RSPB.

New Forest Hants.

Heathland managed by the Forestry Commission. Excellent for butterflies and moths and aquatic insects, especially dragonflies and damselflies around watery areas. Also the home of the New Forest cicada.

Woods Mill Henfield, West Sussex

Headquarters of the Sussex Trust for Nature Conservation set around a nature trail through mixed woods, lake and ponds. A converted 18th-century mill has permanent ecological displays, including aquatic insects. Excellent place for field studies.

Sandwich Bay Kent

Coastal sand-dunes jointly owned by the RSPB, Kent Trust for Nature Conservation and the National Trust. In spring and summer it is an excellent vantage point for observing the arrival of migrant butterflies.

Wicken Fen Cambridgeshire

Typical fenland conserved 10 ft above the surrounding agricultural land. Site of the unsuccessful re-introduction of the swallowtail butterfly between 1955 and 1969.

Woodwalton Fen Woodwalton, Cambs.

A fen habitat conserved by the Nature Conservancy Council as a National Nature Reserve. It is one of the earliest nature reserves, acquired in 1919.

Butterfly farms

A wide range of tropical and British butterflies can be seen in close proximity at butterfly farms. The butterflies are kept in large, heated greenhouses, and visitors can walk among them and take photographs.

Brambles Wealden Forest Park Kent (on A291 between Canterbury and Herne Bay)

Brambles Butterfly World has butterflies living free in a large greenhouse. Also a pinned collection of all British butterflies.

Cotswold Wild Life Park Burford, Oxon

Butterfly house with a flight cage for tropical butterflies; 120 acres of parkland and gardens.

Eastbourne Butterfly Centre East Sussex
Large purpose-built greenhouse on the sea front at Eastbourne. Stream, waterfall, banana trees, hibiscus and willows support free-flying and breeding butterflies.

Guernsey Butterfly Farm Bordeaux, Guernsey
First of a chain of butterfly farms opened since 1973. The large greenhouse contains temperate and tropical plants and butterflies.

Jersey Butterfly Farm Haute Tombette, Jersey
Large greenhouse with tropical and British butterflies.

London Butterfly House Brentford, Hounslow, Gtr London
Greenhouse in the grounds of Syon House, with free-flying butterflies. Open all year, but butterflies restricted to a central greenhouse between December 1 and February 15. Butterfly garden outside.

Living World Seaford, East Sussex
Living insects, spiders, honey-bees, snails and marine life in two converted Sussex barns at the Park Centre of Seven Sisters Country Park and Forestry Commission conservation area.

New Forest Butterfly Farm Ashurst, near Lyndhurst, Hants.
Indoor tropical garden with butterflies, spiders, scorpions, honey-bees, ants and dragonfly ponds.

Worldwide Butterflies Compton House, near Sherborne, Dorset
Living collection of butterflies and moths in the breeding hall of Compton House. Temperate species bred outside in the butterfly garden during spring and summer. At Lullingstone Silk Farm, you can see silkworms feeding on mulberry leaves, and the reeling of silk threads from cocoons.

Museums with insect collections

County museums often have good collections of insects and can give details of local areas where butterflies and other insects can be seen. There are two main collections of insects in Britain.

British Museum (Natural History)
Cromwell Road, London SW7
National collection of British insects. Reference collections of butterflies and moths on permanent or temporary display. Greater part of the collection not on public display. Comprehensive bookshop covering popular and specialist fields of entomology.

Tring Zoological Museum Tring, Herts.
A selection of specimens representing the main orders of insect on permanent display. Spiders and scorpions are also represented. The collection is part of 2,250,000 butterflies and moths amassed by the second Baron Rothschild at the beginning of the century.

Societies for entomologists

Field studies for both adults and children are conducted by the Field Studies Council at residential centres throughout Britain. Information can be obtained from the Education Officer, Field Studies Council, Preston Montford, Montford Bridge, Shrewsbury SY4 1HW.

Young naturalists can become involved in projects such as butterfly surveys, pond studies and habitat preservation by becoming members of conservation bodies.

Youth membership of the National Trust, 36 Queen Anne's Gate, London SW1H 9AS, is open to anyone under 23. It had 24,000 members in 1984. Watch clubs are junior wings of the county trusts for nature conservation (15,000 members). The Panda Club, 11–13 Ockford Road, Godalming, Surrey GU7 1QU, is the junior branch of the World Wildlife Fund (6,000 members).

Amateur entomologists can pursue their interests further through three societies:

Amateur Entomologists' Society
355 Hounslow Road, Hanworth, Feltham, Middlesex
Caters for younger and less experienced entomologists. Publishes a quarterly bulletin and has an extensive range of leaflets and books. An advisory panel of experts covers all major insect orders, conservation, behaviour and foreign insects.

British Butterfly Conservation Society
Tudor House, Quorn, near Loughborough, Leicestershire LE12 8AD.
Dedicated to the conservation of endangered British butterflies. Fourteen regional branches. Publishes half-yearly bulletin.

British Entomological and Natural History Society 74 South Audley Street, London W1
Organises regional field meetings and indoor lectures in London. Interest covers all insect orders. Publishes *Proceedings and Transactions* three times a year and a few guide books on identification of caterpillars and smaller moths. Comprehensive museum collection open to members.

Insect habitats that are vanishing – and expanding

The traditional landscape of Britain has changed greatly in recent decades, as modern agriculture has brought greater efficiency to farming. Weed killers have destroyed native plants that once abounded in meadows and among crops. Chemicals have seeped into ponds and waterways, killing water plants. Broad-leaved woodlands have been felled and ploughed up to make way for cereals, and new forests of pine and fir trees have been planted on moors and heaths.

In the wake of this continuing revolution in the countryside, many insects are declining sharply in numbers, while a few species are thriving in new habitats.

Heathlands

Heaths are tracts of land, often on sandy soil, which are covered in heather, bracken, gorse, silver birch and Scots pine. They are the most threatened habitats in Britain, as thousands of acres have been ploughed up or 'improved' for agriculture in the 1970s and 1980s.

Britain has three main areas of heathland – the New Forest and Dorset heathland, the sandy areas on the Hampshire-Surrey border, and the Brecklands of Norfolk.

Butterflies and beetles are frequently found on heaths, but with the alteration of the land and the destruction of its plants the insects are vanishing.

Heather supports the emperor moth and the northern eggar moth, and the silver birch scrub of the Scottish uplands is the food plant of the Kentish glory moth caterpillar, now extinct in England.

Heathland streams and ponds provide a reservoir for aquatic insects, especially dragonflies and damselflies. The dung from grazing animals provides food for many beetles and flies, and the herb-rich forest clearings provide tender roots for the nymphs of the New Forest cicada.

Downland

The high chalk grasslands of the Downs and the Chilterns, rich in vetches, thyme and other wild herbs, are havens for blue butterflies, ants and bumble-bees. But downland is a fast-disappearing habitat. Wiltshire once contained 70 per cent of Britain's downland, but between 1937 and 1971 nearly half of the Wiltshire downland was ploughed up and turned over to food production. The remaining chalk downs, with their plants and animal life, are now threatened.

Many downland butterflies are dependent, as caterpillars, on chalk-loving plants – the common blue and dingy skipper on bird's-foot-trefoil, the green hairstreak on rock rose, the grizzled skipper on wild and barren strawberry and creeping cinquefoil. The long grasses are food plants for the caterpillars of the marbled white, the burnet moths and the meadow brown.

Scabiouses, knapweeds and thistles, which grow among the grass, provide nectar for brown butterflies. White and aristocrat butterflies, migrating to Britain from the Continent, also drink the nectar of the Downs on their journey north. A red admiral is just as likely to be seen on the top of downland as in a lowland garden.

Sheltered hollows facing south-west are favourite places for butterflies. The warmth of these sunny sanctuaries gives them longer hours to be active, to court, and to feed on flowers. The downland is also the home of the Roman snail and the glow-worm – both now extremely local. Ant hills may be common on the steeper slopes, with hills a foot high.

Farm ponds

Ponds were once far more numerous than they are today because agricultural land was not systematically drained, and grazing animals needed water in each of the many small fields. But ponds are now being filled in at the rate of one in ten every year in some counties. Some have been lost through the natural accumulation of debris, others through drainage.

Shallow water is vital for dragonflies, damselflies, diving beetles and mayflies which all have larval stages under water. Dragonflies, in particular, have suffered enormously, reflecting both the loss of ponds and canals and the pollution which occurs there. When herbicides and insecticides used on the land drain into the water, aquatic plants die off, leaving water insects exposed to predators.

A healthy pond is one where the aquatic plants emit bubbles of oxygen through the action of photosynthesis, the process by which plants use sunlight, water and carbon dioxide to grow. The oxygen they give off into a pond supports all its animal life – the fish, the insects and other invertebrates.

Deciduous woodland

Thirty-five per cent of deciduous woodland, the home of Britain's broad-leaved trees, has been destroyed since 1945. Most has been felled to make way for agriculture or conifer plantations, and many fine butterfly haunts have been lost.

Some of Britain's most beautiful butterflies are associated with oak woods, which also support more than 100 species of moth caterpillars in spring and early summer. The caterpillars of the purple hairstreak butterfly feed on the oak leaves and the butterflies themselves fly high in the canopy out of sight, often feeding on the honeydew left on the leaves by aphids.

Purple emperor caterpillars feed on sallow, and the butterflies establish territories around large oaks along forest rides. White admirals are dependent on the honeysuckle which climbs up trees or creeps over the woodland floor. Orange-speckled fritillary butterflies search in sunny glades for violets, the vital food plants of their caterpillars.

Where elm trees survive the ravages of Dutch elm disease, the white-letter hairstreak and large tortoiseshells continue to lay their eggs on the leaves.

Old rotting tree trunks provide homes for wood-boring beetles, and the stag beetle flies along rides in summer.

Conifer plantations

Coniferous woodland has expanded at a rapid rate since the Second World War due to planting by the Forestry Commission. The most insect-rich areas of conifer plantations are along the fire-breaks and rides and around the margins where many broad-leaved trees survive.

Orange tip butterflies seek out plants suitable for egg-laying, and some of the skippers play among the long grass with marbled whites. Fritillary butterflies may colonise glades and rides where violets have become established.

One of the successes of conifer plantations is the increase in the wood white butterfly, formerly a much rarer species. The sheltered forestry rides provide a favourable habitat where the butterflies lay their eggs on wild members of the pea family.

In the spring and autumn peacock butterflies sun themselves along rides and fire breaks. Brimstones may be seen where buckthorn provides food for the caterpillars and primroses give nectar for the butterflies themselves.

Stacks of poles – rich in bark and fibre – provide hibernation sites for aristocrats and small tortoiseshells. Ladybirds and other beetles abound in the timber stacks and on the cut bark; moths are attracted to the sugary sap; and wood ants – notorious in some forestry plantations – build enormous mounds out of the needles on which they rest in the sun. On these mounds the green woodpecker rids itself of irritating parasites by spreading its wings to be sprayed with formic acid by the disturbed ants.

Meadowland

Ancient hay meadows and water meadows are usually damp areas which support a rich collection of wild flowers. The rarer flowers include orchids, fritillaries, pasque flower, yellow rattle and ragged robin. Butterflies delight in colourful meadows, imbibing the nectar of the flowers and laying their eggs on the plants; however 95 per cent of British meadows have disappeared since 1949 because of agricultural development.

The long grasses of the surviving meadows support skippers and brown butterflies, especially the meadow brown. Whites and aristocrats seek nectar from the wild flowers. Ants collect wild-flower seeds and 'milk' aphids. Fritillary butterflies, gatekeepers and speckled woods patrol the hedgerows and shady areas. Grasshoppers and crickets, froghoppers, ladybirds, spiders and snails are all part of meadow wildlife.

On sunny days the top of the meadow can be alive with butterflies chasing flies or each other, bees chasing dragonflies, hoverflies hanging motionless over the flowers, and bumble-bees visiting flower after flower for their nectar.

INDEX

Acknowledgments

Artwork in *Butterflies and other Insects of Britain* was supplied by the following artists:

3, 8–13 Leonora Box · 14–17 Barbara Walker · 18–25 Jeane Colville · 26–27 Jim Russell · 28–37 Leonora Box · 38–39 Pat Flavel · 40–53 Leonora Box · 54–55 Pat Flavel · 56–71 Colin Emberson · 72–73 Richard Lewington · 74–83 Colin Emberson · 84–85 Kevin Dean · 86–107 Helen Senior · 108–9 Richard Lewington · 110–11 Barbara Walker · 111–13 Leonora Box · 114–17 Barbara Walker · 118–21 Liz Pepperell · 122–3 Kevin Dean · 124–7 Liz Pepperell · 128–43 David Baird · 144–55 Rachel Birkett · 156–7, 160–1, 172–3, 190–5, 208–9 Line Mailhe · 158–9 Richard Lewington · 162–3, 210–11 Barbara Walker · 164–5, 174–81, 198–9 Guy Michel · 166–7 Pat Flavel · 168–9, 182–9, 196–7, 206–7, 212–13 Brenda Katte · 170–1, 200–5 Josiane Campan · 214–17 Guy Michel/Colin Emberson · 218–19 Colin Emberson · 220–31 Dick Bonson · 232–9 Norman Lacey · 240–5 David Baird · 246–59 Ann Savage · 260–3 Stephen Adams · 264–5 Jeane Colville · 266–7, 274–5 Sally Smith · 270–3, 276–9, 284–5 Barbara Walker · 280–1 Elizabeth Rice · 282–3, 286–7, 290–1, 292–5, 300–1 Sandra Pond · 288–9, 304–7 Richard Lewington · 296–9, 302–3 Adrian Williams · 308–13 Dick Bonson · 314–15 Norman Lacey · 316–17 Sandra Pond · 318–23 Dick Bonson · 324–33 Tricia Newell · 334–5 Jim Russell · 340–1 Wendy Bramall.

The publishers wish to thank Brian Baker and Colin Sizer of Reading Museum for their help in providing art reference.

Photographs in *Butterflies and other Insects of Britain* were supplied by the following photographers and agencies. Names of agencies are in capital letters. The following abbreviations are used:
KRD – King, Read and Doré.
NHPA – Natural History Photographic Agency.
NSP – Natural Science Photos.
OSF – Oxford Scientific Films.

30–31 Richard Revels · 32 I. Beames/ARDEA, LONDON · 33 Richard Revels · 34 NSP/R. Revels · 35 Richard Revels · 36 NHPA/E. A. Janes · 37 WILDLIFE MATTERS/J. Feltwell · 39 NHPA/H. Metcalf · 43 NSP/R. Revels · 44 SEAPHOT/N. Downer · 46 Frank Blackburn · 47 NSP/R. Revels · 49 WILDLIFE MATTERS/J. Feltwell · 51 NHPA/E. A. Janes · 52 WILDLIFE MATTERS/J. Feltwell · 53 Brian Hawkes · 55 I. Beames/ARDEA, LONDON · 58 AQUILA/M. C. Wilkes · 59 J. S. & E. J. Woolmer/OSF · 63 Richard Revels · 64 K. G. Preston-Mafham/PREMAPHOTOS, WILDLIFE · 65 Richard Revels · 66 NSP/P. H. Ward · 67–69 BRUCE COLEMAN/J. Burton · 71 Richard Revels · 74 E. J. & J. S. Woolmer/OSF · 75 Richard Revels · 76 N. Fox-Davies · 77 NHPA/S. Dalton · 78 FRANK LANE/C. Newton · 79 NHPA/S. Dalton · 80 Richard Revels · 81 NHPA/B. Angel · 82 NSP/P. H. Ward · 83 NHPA/E. A. Janes · 90 NATURE PHOTOGRAPHERS/D. L. Sewell · 91 Richard Revels · 92 BRUCE COLEMAN/G. Doré · 93 Frank Blackburn · 94 Richard Revels · 95 NHPA/S. Dalton · 96 Richard Revels · 97 J. Thomas/BIOFOTOS · 98 Frank Blackburn · 99–100 Richard Revels · 101 J. L. Mason/ARDEA, LONDON · 102 J. S. & E. J. Woolmer/OSF · 103 WILDLIFE MATTERS/J. Feltwell · 104 BRUCE COLEMAN/D. Green · 105 E. & D. HOSKING/S. Beafroy · 106 Sdeuard Bisserot · 111 I. Beames/ARDEA, LONDON · 115 NSP/P. H. Ward · 116 R. Gibbons/ARDEA, LONDON · 117 NSP/P. H. Ward · 118 BRUCE COLEMAN/N. Fox-Davies · 119 BRUCE COLEMAN/H. Reinhard · 120 Sdeuard Bisserot · 121 Richard Revels · 125 BRUCE COLEMAN/N. Fox-Davies · 126 BRUCE COLEMAN/J. Burton · 127 AQUILA/J. Mills · 144 BRUCE COLEMAN/A. J. Deane · 145 Michael Tweedie · 146 J. L. Mason/ARDEA, LONDON · 147 AQUILA/T. Leach · 148 AQUILA/N. W. Harwood · 149 Heather Angel · 150 J. L. Mason/ARDEA, LONDON · 151 Heather Angel · 152 NATURE PHOTOGRAPHERS/A. Wharton · 153 Sdeuard Bisserot · 154 AQUILA/N. W. Harwood · 155 Michael Tweedie · 156 K. G. Preston-Mafham/PREMAPHOTOS, WILDLIFE · 157 AQUILA/N. W. Harwood · 158 Michael Tweedie · 159 Heather Angel · 160 NSP/P. H. Ward · 161 G. Doré/KRD · 162 NHPA/M. F. Tweedie · 163 NHPA/W. Murray · 164 WILDLIFE MATTERS/J. Feltwell · 165 Sdeuard Bisserot · 166 AQUILA/Sawford/Castle · 167 NATURE PHOTOGRAPHERS/S. C. Bisserot · 170 BRUCE COLEMAN/N. Fox-Davies · 171 J. A. Bailey/ARDEA, LONDON · 172–4 Michael Tweedie · 175 B. Rogers/BIOFOTOS · 176 BRUCE COLEMAN/F. Sauer · 177 NATURE PHOTOGRAPHERS/R. Tidman · 178 B. Rogers/BIOFOTOS · 179 AQUILA/N. W. Harwood · 180 Richard Revels · 181 Heather Angel · 182 E. & D. Hosking · 183 Richard Revels · 184 G. Doré/KRD · 185 Michael Tweedie · 188 NHPA/S. Dalton · 189 BRUCE COLEMAN/P. H. Ward · 190 J. A. L. Cooke/OSF · 191 NHPA/M. F. Tweedie · 192 Heather Angel · 193 Michael Tweedie · 196 NSP/J. D. Bradley · 197 J. L. Mason/ARDEA, LONDON · 198–200 Michael Tweedie · 201 SEAPHOT/N. Downer · 202 NHPA/G. J. Cambridge · 203 NATURE PHOTOGRAPHERS/A. Wharton · 205 BRUCE COLEMAN/Prato · 206 Michael Tweedie · 207 BRUCE COLEMAN/K. Taylor · 221 J. A. Bailey/ARDEA, LONDON · 229 NATURE PHOTOGRAPHERS/D. L. Sewell · 232 G. Thompson/OSF · 233 BRUCE COLEMAN/J. Burton · 234 Michael Tweedie · 235 NSP/P. H. Ward · 236 G. I. Bernard/OSF · 237 BRUCE COLEMAN/M. Dakin · 238 BRUCE COLEMAN/N. Fox-Davies · 239 R. Gibbons/ARDEA, LONDON · 240 BRUCE COLEMAN/M. Dakin · 242 NSP/P. H. Ward · 247 I. Beames/ARDEA, LONDON · 250 AQUILA/M. A. Bushby · 252 R. A. Preston-Mafham/PREMAPHOTOS, WILDLIFE · 255 K. G. Preston-Mafham/PREMAPHOTOS, WILDLIFE · 257 Brian Hawkes · 265 AQUILA/Sawford/Castle · 280 NHPA/S. Dalton · 281 Sdeuard Bisserot · 282 NATURE PHOTOGRAPHERS/P. R. Sterry · 283 NSP/J. A. Grant · 286 D. W. Greenslade/ARDEA, LONDON · 287–8 Heather Angel · 289 NATURE PHOTOGRAPHERS/S. C. Bisserot · 291 BRUCE COLEMAN/J. Burton · 292 R. Gibbons/ARDEA, LONDON · 293 AQUILA/T. & G. Coleman · 295 P. & W. Ward/OSF · 296 NHPA/S. Dalton · 297 Heather Angel · 298 BRUCE COLEMAN/J. Burton · 299 Rentokil Ltd · 300 BRUCE COLEMAN/G. Doré · 302 Heather Angel · 303 A Shell Photograph · 308 NSP/P. H. Ward · 310 Richard Revels · 312 I. Beames/ARDEA, LONDON · 313 Sdeuard Bisserot · 314 BRUCE COLEMAN/A. Davies · 315 Michael Tweedie · 318 Sdeuard Bisserot · 320 Keith Porter · 322–4 BRUCE COLEMAN/J. Burton · 326 NATURE PHOTOGRAPHERS/P. R. Sterry · 327 E. & D. Hosking · 328 Sdeuard Bisserot · 330 Heather Angel · 332 AQUILA/R. T. Mills.

The publishers also acknowledge their indebtedness to the following books and journals that were consulted for reference:

South's British butterflies by T. G. Howarth (Frederick Warne) · *A complete guide to British butterflies* by Margaret Brooks and Charles Knight (Jonathan Cape) · *The Mitchell Beazley pocket guide to butterflies* by Paul Whalley (Mitchell Beazley) · *Butterflies and moths in Britain and Europe* by David Carter (Pan Books) · *The moths and butterflies of Great Britain and Ireland* by John Heath (Blackwell) · *The moths of the British Isles* by Richard South (Frederick Warne) · *Moths* by E. B. Ford (Collins) · *The observer's book of caterpillars* by David Carter (Frederick Warne) · *The dragonflies of Great Britain and Ireland* by Cyril O. Hammond (Harley Books) · *Plant galls* by Arnold Darlington (Blandford Press) · *Bees, wasps, ants and allied insects of the British Isles* by Edward Step (Frederick Warne) · *Land and water bugs of the British Isles* by Southwood and Leston (Frederick Warne) · *Flies of the British Isles* by Colyer and Hammond (Frederick Warne) · *Beetles of the British Isles* by E. F. Linssen (Frederick Warne) · *Grasshoppers, crickets and cockroaches of the British Isles* by David R. Ragge (Frederick Warne) · *The Country Life book of spiders* by Dick Jones (Country Life Books) · *The Oxford book of insects* by John Burton (Oxford University Press) · *A field guide to the insects of Britain and northern Europe* by Michael Chinery (Collins) · *Encyclopaedia of insects and arachnids* by Maurice and Robert Burton (Octopus) · *The wonderful world of butterflies and moths* by Robert Goodden (Hamlyn) · *Insect life* by T. Rowland-Entwistle (Hamlyn) · *The living countryside* (Orbis Publishing Ltd) · *The dancing bees* by Karl von Frisch (Methuen).

Typesetting: VANTAGE PHOTOSETTING CO. LTD, EASTLEIGH · Separations: MULLIS MORGAN LTD, LONDON
Paper: KONINKLIJKE NEDERLANDSE PAPIERFABRIEKEN NV, MAASTRICHT · Printer/Binder: HAZELL WATSON & VINEY LTD, AYLESBURY
Cloth: REDBRIDGE BOOK CLOTH CO. LTD, BOLTON

40/130/1